We want to hear from you

Your comments, suggestions and corrections are invited. Please let us know if you find any significant errors in this publication. Also let us know what you would like to find in future editions of the Waggoner Cruising Guide. We want to expand our dining and activities information, and we seek your experiences.

You can contact us by telephone, mail, or e-mail. Don't hold back. We want to hear from you.

WAGGONER
CRUISING GUIDE

Editor/Publisher Robert Hale

Managing Editor
Stacia A.M. Green

Production Manager
Sheri Berkman

Contributing Editor
Tom Kincaid

Contributors Hiltje Binner, Norm Culver, Rich Hazelton, Kay Spence

Correspondents Bruce Evertz, Joe Forest, Mike Guns, Bill Hales, Ray & Nika Hansen, Heather & Matt Squires

Cover photo by Neil Rabinowitz

Cover design by Elizabeth Watson

Reference maps by Sheri Berkman & Daniel Hale

Staff photos by Robert Hale & Stacia A.M. Green

Caution

THIS BOOK was designed to provide experienced skippers with cruising information about the waters covered. While great effort was taken to make the Waggoner Cruising Guide complete and accurate, it is possible that oversights, differences of interpretation, and factual errors will be found. Thus none of the information contained in the book is warranted to be accurate or appropriate for any specific need. Furthermore, variations in weather and sea conditions, a mariner's skills and experience, and the presence of luck (good or bad) can dictate a mariner's proper course of action. The Waggoner Cruising Guide should be viewed as a guide only, and not a substitute for official government charts, tide and current tables, coast pilots, sailing directions, and local notices to mariners. The Waggoner Cruising Guide assumes the user to be law-abiding and of good will. The suggestions offered are not all-inclusive, but are meant to help avoid unpleasantness or needless delay.

The publisher, editors, and authors assume no liability for errors or omissions, or for any loss or damages incurred from using this publication.

Printed in the United States of America

Published by Weatherly Press Division
Robert Hale & Co. Inc.
1803 132nd Ave. NE, Suite 4
Bellevue, WA 98005-2261
USA

ISSN 1076-1578
ISBN 0-935727-17-5

Advertising
Advertising inquiries should be directed to:

Waggoner Cruising Guide
Robert Hale & Co. Inc.
1803 132nd Ave. NE, Suite 4
Bellevue, WA 98005-2261
USA

Toll-Free Phone (800)733-5330
Local Phone (425)881-5212
Fax (425)881-0731
E-mail:
waggtalk@waggonerguide.com

Web Site
www.waggonerguide.com

WAGGONER CRUISING GUIDE
2000

Cover: Neil Rabinowitz took this photo of two boats anchored and at play at the foot of Cassel Falls in Teakerne Arm, Desolation Sound.

Waterways, Bays and Marinas

Visit Our Web Site
★
www.waggonerguide.com
e-mail waggtalk@waggonerguide.com

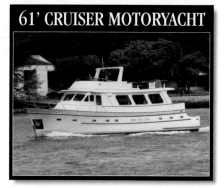

Welcome to
Alert Bay, British Columbia

Come visit us and share our rich culture and history

- ✔ U'mista Cultural Centre
- ✔ Alert Bay Ecological Park
- ✔ World's Tallest Totem Pole
- ✔ 'Namgis Burial Grounds
  (easily viewed from the roadside)
- ✔ Alert Bay InfoCentre - Art Gallery
- ✔ Big House

We have the following amenities to offer:

Fine Dining • Liquor Store • ATM • Infocentre
Moorage Facilities • Campgrounds • Showers
Grocery Stores • Marine Fuel Services • Shipyard
Restaurants • Pubs • Tennis Courts • Post Office
Pharmacy • Hospital • Churches • Electronic Repairs
Video Rental • Nature Trails

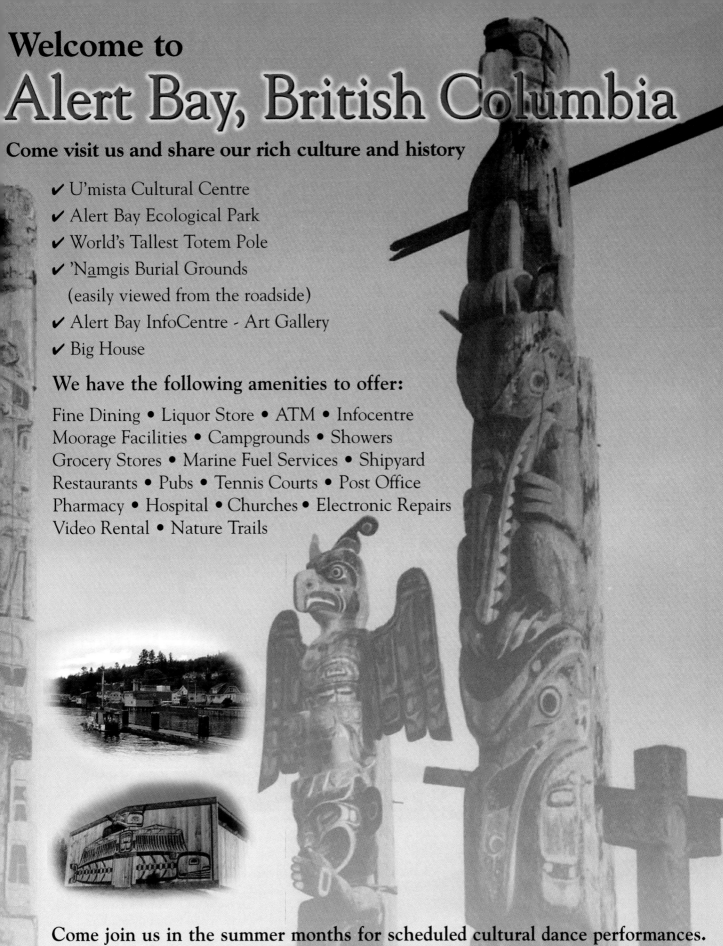

**Come join us in the summer months for scheduled cultural dance performances.
All within easy walking distance.**

Contact us for more information by
phone: (250) 974 - 5403, fax (250) 974 - 5499 or email: umista@island.net

PUBLISHER'S COLUMN

ONE OF THE GREAT pleasures of our long research cruises is coming upon the unexpected. The snapshot of Billy Proctor and me (I'm the ugly one, on the right) illustrates my point. Billy Proctor lives with his wife on a big piece of land at Shoal Harbour, on the other side of the peninsula from Echo Bay, north of Desolation Sound. Billy has lived and fished in that area all his life, and over the years has amassed a sizeable collection of artifacts, enough to fill a museum. So he built a museum, shown behind us in the picture. Billy gave us a tour, and shyly stood still for this picture.

Eleven weeks of cruising. In 1999 I spent 11 weeks on the boat (Marilynn spent eight), covering the waters from Olympia, at the bottom of Puget Sound, to Prince Rupert, at the top of British Columbia's saltwater, and down the West Coast of Vancouver Island. From cities to wilderness we were there, in the spring, summer and fall. The book you are holding is richer for it.

Highlights. The highlights were our brief trip out to the Spider Island area north of Hakai Pass, and the three-week trip down the West Coast of Vancouver Island. The West Coast of Vancouver Island is the finest cruising in the Northwest—the best of the best.

Waggoner is Number 1. Nearly every retailer confirms that the Waggoner is their best-selling Northwest boating guide, often by a wide margin. When we are cruising, most of the boats we see have the Waggoner on board. We were pleased when Northwest Yachting magazine's "Best-of" boating survey results, published in November 1999, listed the Waggoner as the most popular guide with their readers. Thank you!

Tell them you read about them in the Waggoner. Without advertising there would be no Waggoner. Don't be shy about telling the facilities and services along the way that you read about them in the Waggoner, or that you use the Waggoner. Your comments make a huge difference.

We're pleased to meet you. Each year quite a number of readers row over or stop on the dock to say hello. If you see us and care to visit, please don't hesitate. Marilynn and I look forward to meeting you.

Bob Hale

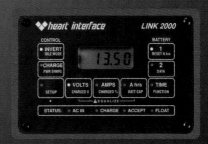

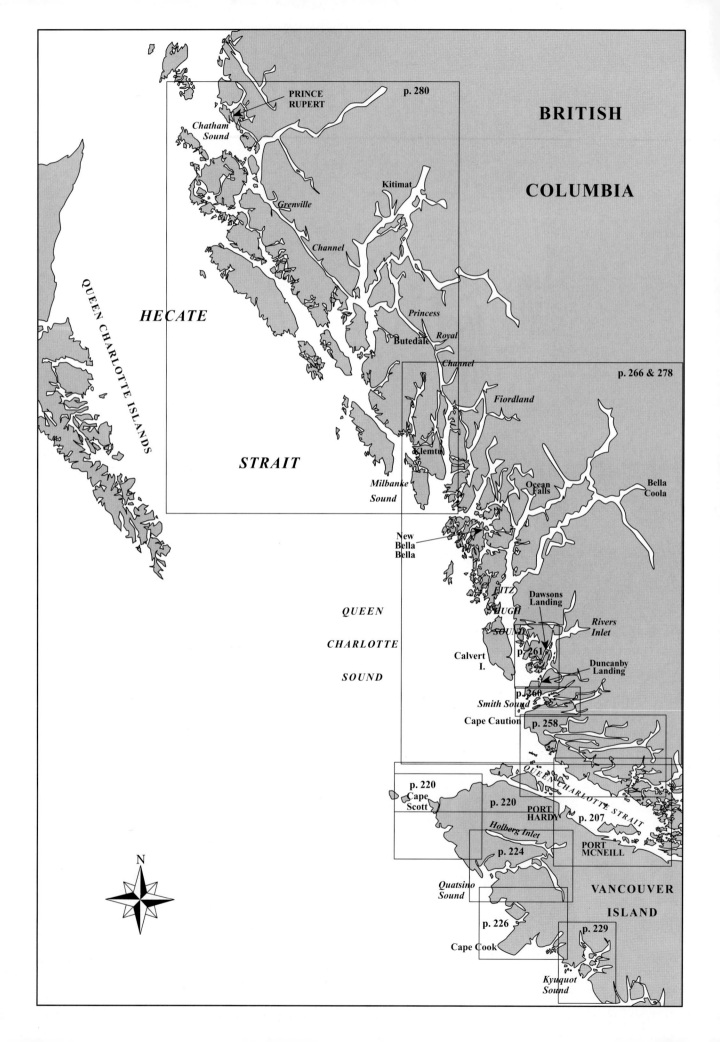

BRITISH

COLUMBIA

PRINCE
RUPERT

*Chatham
Sound*

Kitimat

Grenville

Channel

QUEEN CHARLOTTE ISLANDS

HECATE

Princess

Royal

Butedale

Channel

p. 280

Fiordland

Klemtu

Bella
Coola

Ocean
Falls

STRAIT

*Milbanke
Sound*

p. 266 & 278

New
Bella
Bella

QUEEN

CHARLOTTE

SOUND

FITZ

HUGH

SOUND

Dawsons
Landing

*Rivers
Inlet*

Calvert
I.

p. 261

Duncanby
Landing

Smith Sound

p. 260

Cape Caution

p. 258

QUEEN CHARLOTTE STRAIT

p. 220
Cape
Scott

p. 220

PORT
HARDY

p. 207

Holberg Inlet

PORT
MCNEILL

p. 224

*Quatsino
Sound*

VANCOUVER

ISLAND

p. 226

p. 229

Cape Cook

*Kyuquot
Sound*

N

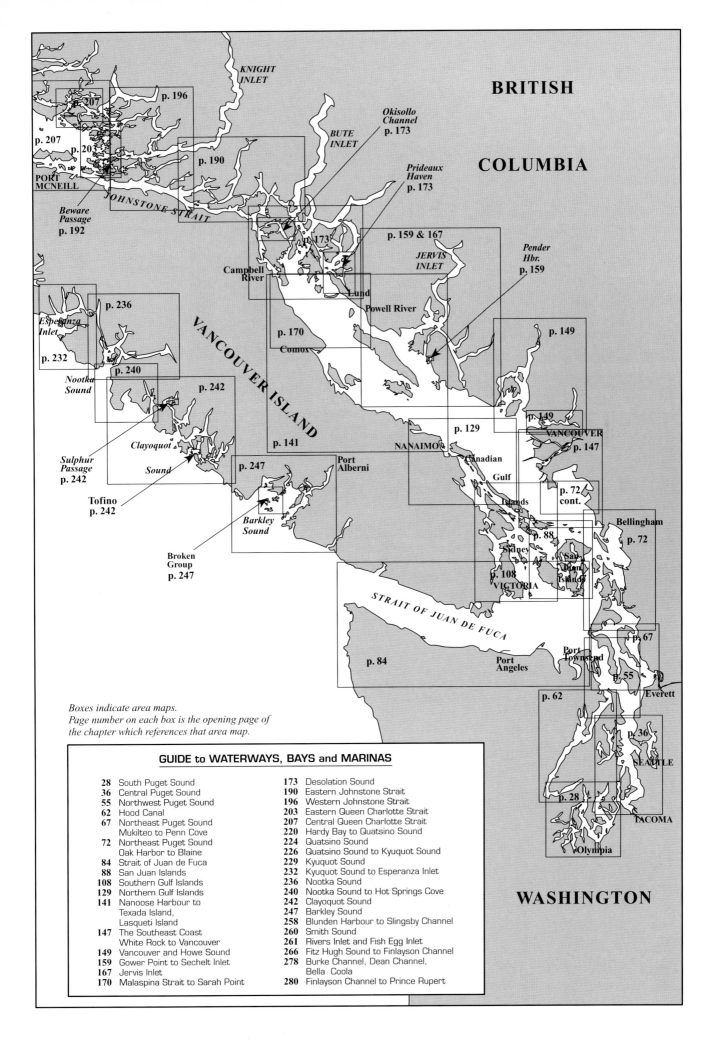

BRITISH

COLUMBIA

KNIGHT INLET

p. 196

Okisollo Channel p. 173

BUTE INLET

Prideaux Haven p. 173

p. 207

p. 20

p. 207

PORT McNEILL

Beware Passage p. 192

JOHNSTONE STRAIT

p. 190

p. 159 & 167

JERVIS INLET

Pender Hbr. p. 159

Campbell River

173

Lund

Powell River

p. 236

Esperanza Inlet

p. 232

p. 170

Comox

p. 149

Nootka Sound

p. 240

VANCOUVER ISLAND

p. 242

Clayoquot Sound

p. 141

p. 129

p. 149

VANCOUVER

p. 147

Sulphur Passage p. 242

Tofino p. 242

NANAIMO

Canadian

Gulf

p. 72 cont.

Bellingham

p. 72

p. 247

Port Alberni

Islands

p. 88

Barkley Sound

Sydney

San Juan Islands

Broken Group p. 247

p. 108

VICTORIA

STRAIT OF JUAN DE FUCA

p. 84

Port Angeles

Port Townsend

p. 67

p. 55

Everett

p. 62

p. 36

SEATTLE

Boxes indicate area maps.
Page number on each box is the opening page of
the chapter which references that area map.

p. 28

Olympia

TACOMA

WASHINGTON

Waves of Fresh Water

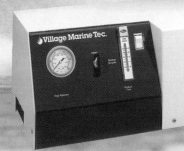

The Little Wonder™

The original 12 volt marine R/O watermaker. This is the ultimate system when you need pure, fresh, clean drinking water from a simple 12 volt system.

Available in a completely framed unit or modular design, you can choose from 200 or 250 GPD systems to meet your water consumption requirements.

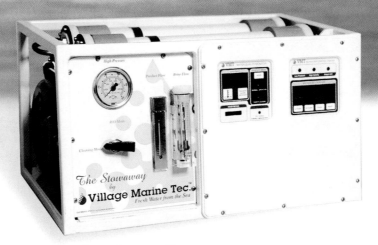

The Squirt™

Our most popular unit "The Squirt", a 110/220 powerhouse that meets the needs of the most demanding captain. Capacities from 200 to 600 gallons per day.

Our exclusive digital master control center monitors your watermaker and keeps you informed of maintenance needs and system functions. It thinks for you so you can spend your time enjoying your cruise rather than worrying about your equipment.

The Stowaway™

Normally a "Stowaway" is not something you like, but in this case it's something you will love. Using our Village Marine exclusive, 3 plunger titanium pump and our special Hi-Flow membrane, we are able to give you up to 800 gallons of fresh clean water a day from a compact unit that you can fit almost anywhere. (Available in 200, 400 and 800 GPD sizes) At a compact 22 inches wide by 11 inches tall including the membranes, you can almost put this in your duffel bag and not even know it is there. Another first from Village Marine Tec. the worlds marine R/O innovator.

 Village Marine Tec.™

Corporate Office & Manufacturing Facility ♦ 2000 W. 135th St., Gardena, CA 90249 ♦ 310-516-9911 ♦ 800-421-4503 ♦ FAX 310-538-3048
Factory Showroom & Service Facility
802/804 S.E. 17th St. Causeway, Ft. Lauderdale, FL 33316 ♦ 954-523-4900 ♦ 800-625-8802 ♦ FAX 954-523-2920
Shelter Island Drive, Suite B, San Diego, CA 92106 ♦ 619-226-4195 ♦ 800-774-9292 ♦ FAX 619-226-4199
www.villagemarine.com

 **Fisheries Supply**
Marine Supplies Since 1928

(206) 632-4462   (800) 426-6930   Fax: (206) 634-4600
mail@fisheriessupply.com   www.fisheriessupply.com

Western Marine
COMPANY

1494 Powell Street, Vancouver, B.C. V5L 5B5
(604) 253-7721   (800) 663-0600
sales@westernmarine.com

How to Cruise the Pacific Northwest

by Robert Hale

I HAVE CRUISED THE WATERS of the Pacific Northwest for 30 years now, the first 20 or so as a sailboater, the last several as a powerboater. Fortunately, Marilynn Hale shares this love of boating. I have often pondered, though, what it is that keeps us excited—what makes us go beyond the next point, beyond the next cape, beyond the next open water crossing.

I came upon a quote from Edwin Monk, Sr., the famous naval architect. Monk said it

Active Cove at Patos Island is one of the San Juan Islands' prettiest little coves.

is the *spirit of adventure*, still alive in most of us, that draws us to our boats. What an itch this spirit of adventure is, and what amazing waters the Pacific Northwest possesses to scratch this itch.

Marilynn and I have cruised among raw mountain ranges. We have seen and heard wolves, and watched bears on the beach overturn large rocks with one paw. We have watched eagles hunt, and listened to the loon's call. Killer whales have jumped beside the boat. Once, a quarter-mile from the Seattle shoreline, a gray whale passed only a few feet away.

Even around the cities, the Northwest retains the feeling of wilderness. Remarkably, however, it is a wilderness with a safety net. Wherever we cruised, we have found that moorage, fuel, supplies—even good restaurants—seldom are far away. The charts are complete and accurate, and the cities have cell phone coverage. The Coast Guard monitors the radio. The people speak English.

Protected inlets, bays and coves exist all along the way. The entire coast is served by marinas. If finer cruising grounds exist anywhere, I don't know of them.

FROM OLYMPIA NORTH, you needn't go far to have an outstanding cruise. Don't try to pack too much into a limited holiday afloat. Cruising takes time. On any given morning you can be up and out at first light, but over the course of a week most people are lucky to be out by noon (well, maybe 10:30). Two or three hours later, it's time to stop. If you've met some interesting people, or it's foggy or the wind is up, perhaps you won't move at all.

The farther north you go, the more spectacular the scenery gets. Puget Sound is perfect, except that the San Juan Islands are better. As good as the San Juans are, the Canadian Gulf Islands have a special appeal. Desolation Sound, 200 miles north of Seattle, is outstanding. And so on, around Vancouver Island and all the way to Alaska.

Wherever you are in these waters, you can have a memorable cruise. Speed is not important, nor is the distance you cover. The farther you go, the more time it takes and the more it costs. If you have the time and the money (and the boat and the experience), go the distance. If you don't have the time and/or the money, enjoy the waters close aboard.

CHARTERING, FLYING AND TRAILERING

Chartering. While most charter agencies are located in Puget Sound and the southern part of B.C., charter boats are available in Desolation Sound and north. You may not have as wide a choice in the more distant areas, but boats are there.

Flying. Many people cruise the more distant waters via the magic of float planes. It is not uncommon for one party to take the boat north

to Desolation Sound (about a week for most boats), and enjoy a week or two there. A second party flies in to Refuge Cove in Desolation Sound, and the first party flies home. Successive parties swap by float plane until it's time to move the boat back south. The final party delivers the boat home. Everybody has a fabulous time in the northland, but nobody takes the boat both ways. It works.

Trailering. A large number of people trailer a boat to popular cruising grounds all along the coast. It's faster than going by boat, it's affordable, and it avoids difficult passages across rough waters. Trailer boats can launch to see Puget Sound, the San Juan Islands, the Gulf Islands, Princess Louisa Inlet, Desolation Sound, Blackfish Sound, and even the sounds on the west coast of Vancouver Island. Some people have launched at Port Hardy, and—watching the weather *very* carefully—gone north around Cape Caution to Rivers Inlet and beyond.

Many boats trailer from the B.C. interior and launch at either Bella Coola or Prince Rupert. It's a long drive, but the waters they get to are some of the finest in the world.

HERE IS A BRIEF LOOK at what to expect in what we call "Waggoner waters."

South Puget Sound. For beauty, cruising in South Puget Sound is similar to cruising the San Juan Islands, except the crowds aren't there. Neither are the restaurants. South Sound has a number of excellent marine parks and several marinas, such as Jarrell's Cove, Longbranch and Boston Harbor. Plan to enjoy the scenery, swing on the anchor, catch some fish and swim a little. But except for Olympia and Gig Harbor, don't plan to go to town.

Central and North Puget Sound. Anchor out, dine out, enjoy the scenery, and have a jolly old time in these waters. The towns and cities of Gig Harbor, Tacoma, Des Moines, Winslow, Bremerton, Port Orchard, Poulsbo, Seattle, Edmonds, Kingston, Port Ludlow,

Skip and Bev Houser, from Grass Valley, Calif., spend three months each summer cruising their 21-foot Sea Ray. Shown here at Winter Harbour, on the West Coast of Vancouver Island.

Everett, Langley, Coupeville, Oak Harbor, LaConner, Anacortes, and Port Townsend offer a world of interesting stops. Anchorages abound in this area. Wintertime cruising is mother's milk for the locals. In the summer they all go north for vacation.

One new marina must be singled out—the Bell Harbor Marina on the Seattle waterfront. Close to shopping, dining, and the excitement of downtown Seattle, the Bell Harbor Marina is destined to be a legend. For a cosmopolitan experience, it can't be beat.

San Juan Islands. With their mountainous terrain, protected waterways, quiet anchorages and busy marinas, the San Juans are a paradise. We have spent weeks enjoying the San Juans, and each year we go back for more.

Gulf Islands. Read the San Juan Islands paragraph above and make it Canadian, only with more dining, more anchorages, and more marinas to spend time at. Each September we like to spend a week in the Gulf Islands. In fact, we think September is the best cruising month of all.

Vancouver. Vancouver is the most worldly city on the west coast of North America. Not the biggest or the most glittery, but the best. See it from False Creek, or from the new Coal Harbour Marina in Vancouver Harbour, or by bus from the elegant Union Steamship Marina on Bowen Island in Howe Sound.

Princess Louisa Inlet. It takes effort to get there, but the reputation is earned. Princess Louisa Inlet is majestic.

Desolation Sound. Books have been written about Desolation Sound. It's beautiful, rugged and remote, yet with pockets of civilization. A week is good, but not enough. Two or three weeks are more like it. You'll bore your friends with your tales when you get back home, and you won't care.

North to Sullivan Bay. To expand your cruising grounds north from Desolation Sound to Sullivan Bay we're talking about four-week cruises in well-equipped boats. Amazingly, the scenery only gets better. High mountains, anchorages in bowls carved into the rock, dangerous tidal rapids (except at slack water), and a small number of gourmet dining spots that will please you. Best for the more experienced boaters.

West Coast of Vancouver Island. Rugged and dangerous. Likelihood of high winds and steep seas. Rocks. Little contact with the outside world. Fog. Two to four weeks required. No finer cruising anywhere. When you've circumnavigated Vancouver Island, you've accomplished something.

Beyond Cape Caution. It's hard to believe that anything could improve on the waters south of Cape Caution, but somehow the central and northern B.C. coast manages to do it.

We're talking about time, now. Four weeks for part way, six weeks to hurry through and back again, eight weeks to do it right. Thousands of miles of shoreline, deserted anchorages, abandoned camps and villages, even an abandoned city. Abundant fishing. High mountains, eagles, raven, mink, cougar, wolves, bear, deer—all kinds of wildlife. Few people. You're on your own.

Carry ample fuel, water and food. Mostly protected waters, but a few areas where the seas can sink a boat. Typical anchorages 10-15 fathoms deep. Paradise for those lucky enough and skilled enough to make the trip.

Best months. The prime cruising months begin in April and end by October, with July-August being the most popular. People use their boats year-round in Puget Sound. On winter weekends the popular ports can be surprisingly busy. Cabin heat is a must in the winter and almost a must the rest of the year. Even for summer-only cruising, we would want cabin heat on our boat.

North of Puget Sound, pleasure boating is best done between early May and late September. Really dependable weather normally doesn't arrive until July. We usually take our long summer cruise beginning in early June and ending in early August. As we work north we see fewer and fewer boats. On the return trip in late July the situation is different. Boats everywhere.

Be careful with winter cruising north of Puget Sound. (Be careful in Puget Sound, too.) In the winter, storms lash the British Columbia coast. When you see what winter storms do to trees on exposed parts of the B.C. coast, you'll be happy to wait for summer.

About charts and other publications. To keep this book informative and up-to-date, we have stuck our nose into nearly every port, bay, cove, and notch along the coast. In the process, we have become staunch advocates of nautical charts and navigation publications. We now own more than 200 charts, and use them constantly. A good selection of charts not only will keep a boat out of trouble, but will let you enter places you wouldn't want to try without the chart.

Annual tide and current tables are essential. The U.S. Coast Pilot and the Canadian Sailing Directions should be considered essential. U.S. and Canadian light lists will be useful. We subscribe to the U.S. Notices to Mariners and the Canadian Notice to Shipping and Notices to Mariners, and find them extremely helpful. No charge for either one. Contact the respective Coast Guard offices.

An astonishing amount of information exists about this coast and safe navigation around it. I have trouble understanding the mentality that will invest great sums on the boat and its fuel, then scrimp on charts and other navigation publications. Actually, the money has nothing to do with it. The rocks, tides and weather are indifferent to the amount spent on any boat. They treat all boats equally.

Necessary equipment. The marine supply industry can provide useful boat equipment for as long as you care to pay for it. I happen to be a boat equipment junkie. Each year, our sturdy little research boat *Surprise* settles deeper on her marks as yet more gear is brought aboard.

I feel that the *minimum* navigation equipment for safe cruising could be reduced to just five items: a high-quality compass, adjusted by a professional compass adjuster; a quality hand bearing compass; a depth sounder or fish finder; a VHF radio with a good antenna; and a radar reflector. Of course, complete Coast Guard safety equipment is a must.

But I know a couple who cruised around Vancouver Island on their 26-foot Folkboat equipped only with a bulkhead compass, a hand bearing compass, complete charts, a radar reflector and a large Bruce anchor. Nothing else, not even a depth sounder. For depths they use a leadline.

Surprise has a few extra pieces of equipment: GPS, Loran, radar, autopilot, two VHF radios, handheld VHF radio, Steiner binoculars, two cabin heaters, inverter, microwave oven, survival suits…the list is embarrassingly long.

Clothing. Except for Desolation Sound in the summer, the waters in this area are cold. Even during warm weather you may welcome a sweatshirt or jacket. Layering works well. While rain gear is essential on sailboats, it can be useful on an enclosed powerboat. Shoreside attire can be as nice as you want, but most people do fine with comfortable sports clothes.

Law of the Boat

Wherever one of us is, that's where the other wants to be.—LAW OF THE BOAT

OF COURSE THE 26-foot Thunderbird sailboat was cramped, with no galley, no head and no headroom either. When Marilynn and I moved around, it was like a dance. One of us would slip aside just as the other went by. We couldn't get away from each other, so the Law of the Boat really didn't apply.

Then came the Tollycraft 26 powerboat, with what seemed like acres of room. Separation at last, we thought. But no. When I wanted to go forward, Marilynn was in the way. When Marilynn wanted to go out to the back deck, I was blocking the door. One of us couldn't move without the other being affected. Thus was born the Law of the Boat.

The larger Tolly 37 should have put to rest the Law of the Boat. But it hasn't. One of us is still standing exactly where the other wants to be. "Law of the Boat," we'll say, and we'll make room to get by. At least we realize it's the boat's fault, not ours. Or maybe we're just clumsy.

—Robert Hale

Cruising Tips From Our Experiences

At anchor two weeks into our cruise, we thought about all the little things that make a difference when we are out on the boat. Some of these points are mentioned elsewhere in the Waggoner, but listing them again does no harm.

Kill the wake. Sailboats don't make much wake, but powerboats do. Even when a powerboat slows down, its following wake will accompany it to a dock. We don't understand why this works, but we've found that if the boat is brought to a full stop and then shifted to reverse for a moment, it seems to kill the following wake. We learned this lesson when our Tollycraft 37's wake followed us into the Big Bay Marina and bounced all the moored boats around something awful. We caught hell for it, and deserved it.

Slow down when passing, either direction. Shortly after going from sail to power, I came to understand what I call the First Rule of Powerboating: *Never look back.*

Because if we powerboat skippers *would* look back, we would be appalled at what we do to other boats. Even knowing this, I'm sometimes guilty of not slowing down enough. But I'm trying, and I'm getting better.

Slow down when being passed, same direction. If a faster boat wants to pass, slow down for a moment and wave it by. If the slow boat is going 6 knots, the faster boat will have to speed up to 8 or 9 knots minimum, which will put out a sizeable wake. Better to idle back, let the big fuel-burner past, and then resume cruise speed.

Have flexible expectations. Marina facilities run the range from elegant to, shall we say, primitive. Managements span the same range. A person who expects perfect facilities and professional hospitality-industry service at every stop will spend a certain amount of time being disappointed. Especially in the remote areas, the docks and other facilities can be rather on the rough side. Service at the Indian

villages up the coast, for example, is provided on the Indians' terms, in the Indians' way, and that's different from the city approach most Waggoner readers are accustomed to. When we're out cruising we have found it helpful to relax and take things as they come. We appreciate the places that do things our way, but we get along with the places that don't. We are determined to have a good time, and we don't let rigid expectations interfere.

The one area we have less patience with is cleanliness. We think public washrooms, showers and laundry areas should be clean and in good condition, always. If we could have one message for marina operators, it would be, *keep those areas sparkling.*

Be self-reliant. Don't venture out with the idea that if things go wrong, you can always call the Coast Guard. An important part of good seamanship is being able to handle whatever's thrown at you.

Turn everything off. When you

leave the boat or turn in for the night, be sure that appliances, stoves and heaters are turned off.

Keep pets on leash, and clean up after them. Marina owners would prefer that pets didn't exist, but since so many people do cruise with pets the marinas accommodate them. Use the designated pet-walking areas. Don't let the dog lift his leg against the water faucet or power box. Carry little plastic bags and clean up if the pet doesn't make it to the potty area.

Help arriving boats land. Even if supper must be interrupted.

When helping arriving boats, follow the skipper's instructions. When we take a line we hold it loosely, awaiting instructions. Most skippers have a plan that will stop the boat and lay it alongside the dock. A bow line pulled tight at the wrong time can ruin the plan and cause all kinds of problems. The bow swings toward the dock and the stern swings away. Obviously, if the landing plan already

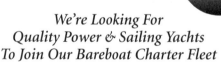

has failed and the boat is being swept off, the dock crew goes into action. Even then it's a good idea to confirm with the skipper rather than acting on one's own.

Carry and use all appropriate publications. Charts, charts, charts, *charts!* Tide and current tables. Local cruising guides.

Carry tools and spares. Our tool box lives in the main cabin, available for immediate access. It seems that we are in that box at least once a day, usually for something minor, but it has to be fixed. Carry all owner's manuals. Carry extra engine oil, transmission fluid, hydraulic fluid, coolant, and distilled water (for the batteries). Carry spare V-belts, ignition parts, impellers and filters. The list of tools and spares has no end. You can't prepare for everything, but you can prepare for likely problems.

Carry self-amalgamating tape. This is stretchy tape that sticks to itself but not to what it's wrapped around. Usually it is avail-able in black or white. The black is stronger. In 1998 we used self-amalgamating tape to repair a leaking high pressure fuel line, and to repair a broken oven door handle. The stuff is magic. We wouldn't be without it.

Carry shore power adapters for every electrical combination. If your boat has 30 amp shore power, you will need adapters for 15 amp, 20 amp and 50 amp outlets.

Turn off shore power before plugging in or unplugging. Since not all docks have breakers to turn off individual outlets, we always turn the boat's 110-volt switch to OFF before we hook up or unplug shore power. If the dock power has its own breaker, we turn it to OFF, too. When everything is hooked up, we turn the dock switch on, and then the boat switch.

First aid is important. Nobody knows when an accident might occur (that's what makes it an accident). In 1998, we witnessed a woman suffer a badly cut finger during a routine landing at Port McNeill. We got the message. The next season our own boat had a much more complete medical kit.

Use Scoot-gard. This is the bumpy, rubbery material carried on big rolls at the marine store. It keeps things from sliding around. We use it for drawer and shelf liners. The microwave oven sits on it. Whenever we want something to stay where we put it, but don't want to bolt or tie it into place, we use Scoot-gard. It's inexpensive and it works.

Don't be cheap. It's bad form to use a private marina's facilities and not pay for the privilege. Even if a direct charge is not made, usually *something* can be purchased. When we overnight at a marina, we pay the moorage, just as our readers do. We're glad the marina is there, and we want it to be there for the future. We are pleased to do our part.

U.S. and Canadian Customs Information

CUSTOMS MUST BE CLEARED whenever the U.S.-Canada border is crossed, either direction. Generally the process is quick and straightforward, but if the skipper isn't prepared with the proper information, it can be time-consuming. It is extremely important to follow all the rules, and be polite. While Customs officers are trained in courtesy and usually are cordial, they have at their disposal regulations that can ruin your day.

U.S. CUSTOMS

U.S. residents out of the U.S. less than 48 hours can import merchandise up to $200 in value per person without duty. If more than 48 hours the limit is $400 per person. For ease and simplicity, try to restrict what you bring back home to products made or grown in Canada.

Canadian citizens and U.S. citizens do not need passports but do require identification. The skipper should know the nationality of all persons on board.

Processing fee. Pleasure vessels 30 feet in length or more must pay an annual processing (user) fee of $25 to to enter or re-enter the United States. This applies to U.S. and non-U.S. vessels. Vessels less than 30 feet are not subject to the fee, provided they have nothing to declare. Payment is required at or before the vessel's first arrival each calendar year. If you report by telephone, they charge your credit card. A non-transferable decal will be issued upon payment. Renewal notices for the next year's decal are mailed in the autumn.

Reporting to U.S. Customs. Customs *must* be cleared at a designated point of entry or by telephone (800)562-5943. We clear customs by cellular telephone while underway, with excellent results. To avoid delays, have the following information available at the time you report your arrival:

- VESSEL REGISTRATION NUMBER.
- VESSEL NAME AND LENGTH.
- USER FEE DECAL NUMBER if applicable.
- CANADIAN CLEARANCE number. *Required* for U.S. moored boats, but you might not be asked for it.
- ESTIMATED DATE OF DEPARTURE. *Required* for Canadian moored vessels.

Release Number. You will receive a release number when you complete your arrival report to customs. Log this number with the date, time and place where the vessel reported. Keep the number for at least one year.

PIN Small Boat Clearance. Most pleasure vessel operators who have entered the U.S. in the Puget Sound area have already been assigned Personal Identification Numbers (PINs). With the PIN, the vessel operator can call (800)562-5943 to clear U.S. Customs easily. Vessel operators who do not have a PIN will be assigned one at their first customs clearance. With a PIN, you can report your arrival any time from one hour before departing Canada to the time when you land in the U.S., or while underway.

I-68 Program. The U.S. Immigration and Naturalization Service's I-68 "Canadian Border Boat Landing Permit" program has caused a great deal of confusion, uncertainty, and ill-will in B.C. and Washington State.

Fortunately, the program is not being enforced in the Northwest, nor is it likely to be enforced. In our opinion you can ignore it.

Designated U.S. Ports of Entry

To clear customs by telephone, call (800)562-5949. Local Port of Entry telephone numbers, listed below, are for information only. In all likelihood you will never have occasion to use them.

Aberdeen	(360)532-2030
Anacortes	(360)293-2331
Bellingham	(360)734-5463
Blaine	(360)332-5771
Everett	(425)259-0246
Friday/Roche Hbr.	(360)378-2080
Neah Bay/	
Port Angeles	(360)457-4311
Point Roberts	(360)945-2314
Port Townsend	(360)385-3777
Seattle	(206)553-4678
Tacoma/Olympia	(253)593-6338

Above numbers for weekdays only. Nights, weekends, holidays call (800)562-5943.

CANADA CUSTOMS

Except for vessels clearing by CANPASS-Private Boats (see below), all vessels arriving in Canada from a foreign country must clear customs immediately after the vessel comes to rest. The master or the master's designated representative must report to customs in person or by telephone by calling (888)226-7277 or from a customs direct line phone. No one else may leave the vessel, and no baggage or merchandise may be removed from the vessel.

U.S. citizens do not need passports, but do need to carry identification. Citizens of other countries need passports, and some need visas. *Carry birth certificates for all minors aboard*—you may be asked for them. If you are bringing a child other than your own into Canada, have a notorized statement authorizing you to take the child into Canada, and proof that the person signing the statement does have custody of the child.

You *must* report at a designated port of entry. At some locations customs officers will be present; at many others you will report by telephone. Even if you report by telephone, your boat may be subject to inspection.

To avoid delays, have the following:
- VESSEL REGISTRATION NUMBER.
- VESSEL NAME AND LENGTH.
- NAMES, ADDRESSES, CITIZENSHIP AND BIRTHDATES of all passengers.
- ESTIMATED DEPARTURE DATE (U.S. boats).

Canada Customs will give you a clearance number and instructions for where to post it on your boat (usually a side window). Log this number, with the date, time, and place of clearance. Vessels are subject to reinspection while in Canadian waters, usually by RCMP officers when their patrol boat reaches a marina. The officers are well trained and very polite, but be sure you don't have anything aboard you shouldn't have.

CANPASS-Private Boats. In August 1995 Revenue Canada introduced CANPASS-Private Boats, a pre-clearance program for Canadian and U.S. residents entering Canada from the U.S. by boat. With a CANPASS permit, a vessel clears Canadian Customs and Immigration by calling, toll-free, (888)226-7277 up to 4 hours before departing U.S. waters, and may proceed directly to its destination unless directed by an officer to go to a designated site. Each new CANPASS permit holder will have to report the first time to a designated site in order to have paperwork verified.

The CANPASS application comes with four pages of instructions. Briefly, however, the program is limited to citizens or permanent residents of Canada or the U.S. with no criminal activities, no customs or immigration violations. The approval process takes several weeks. Each person aboard must be approved for CANPASS or the vessel must clear customs at a designated reporting station. One application can cover the applicant, spouse, and any dependent children residing with the applicant. The cost is $25 (Cdn.), and they can charge your Visa or Mastercard account. Renewal forms are sent yearly.

To get more information and an application, call (888)226-7277, or write: CANPASS-Private Boats, #28-176th St., Surrey, BC V4P 1M7, Canada.

Firearms restrictions. You may not bring handguns, automatic weapons, pepper spray or mace into Canada. Under certain circumstances some long guns are allowed. Contact Canada Customs for instructions, (800)461-9999.

Food restrictions. Other than restricted foods, you can carry quantities of food appropriate to your anticipated stay. However, no apples, no pitted fruit (such as apricots, plums, quince,

peaches, nectarines). Cherries are okay. No potatoes, no fresh corn. House plants are okay if carried aboard.

Pets. Owners of dogs and cats must bring a certificate issued by a licensed American or Canadian veterinarian clearly identifying the pet and certifying that it has been vaccinated against rabies during the previous 36 months.

Liquor & tobacco restrictions. Not more than 1.14 liters (38.5 oz.) of hard liquor, or 1.5 liters of wine, or 24 12-ounce bottles of beer or ale per person of legal drinking age. Legal drinking age in B.C. is 19 years old. Not more than 1 carton of cigarettes and 2 cans of tobacco and 50 cigars per person 19 or older.

Designated B.C. Points of Entry for Pleasure Craft Reporting
All locations contact Canada Customs toll-free (888)226-7277

Bamfield:	Customs Dock (May 15 - Sept. 30)	Sidney:	Angler's Anchorage Marina Canoe Cove Marina Port Sidney Marina Royal Victoria YC Out Station Van Isle Marina
Bedwell Hrbr.:	May 1 - Sept. 30 only 0800-2000 daily Standby: 2000-2400 2400-0800 ($54.00 fee)		
Campbell River:	Coast Marina Discovery Harbour Marina	Vancouver:	False Creek Government Dock Steveston Gas Dock Burrard Inlet All marinas until further notice
Nanaimo:	Nanaimo Port Authority Basin Brechin Point Marina		

Port Alberni:	Government Dock	Victoria:	Oak Bay Marina,
			Royal Victoria YC
			    (Cadboro Bay)
			Victoria Inner Harbour
			    Customs Dock

Port Hardy	Government Dock (May 15 - Sept. 30)		
Powell River:	Government Dock		
Prince Rupert:	Fairview Government Dock Yacht Club Rushbrook Govt. Dock	White Rock:	White Rock Government Dock Crescent Beach Marina

---

Pleasure Craft Operator Proficiency (Licensing)

ON APRIL 1, 1999, Canadian Operator Proficiency and age and horsepower restrictions for pleasure craft went into effect. The age and horsepower restrictions are as follows:

Persons under 12 and unaccompanied or unsupervised by a person 16 years of age or older are not allowed to operate a boat with an engine more powerful that 7.5 kw (10 hp).

Persons at least 12 years of age but not yet 16 years of age and unaccompanied or unsupervised by a person 16 years of age or older are not allowed to operate a boat with an engine more powerful than 30 kw (40 hp).

Persons under the age of 16 are not allowed to operate personal watercraft.

Operator proficiency

Effective September 15, 1999, persons under age 16 are required to meet proficiency standards (proof of passing an approved training course) to operate a power-driven vessel. Visitors from foreign countries are waived for 45 continuous days, subject only to licensing requirements from their home jurisdictions.

Other requirements go into effect in 2002 and 2009, and are of no concern to boaters in 2000.

Pumpout Stations and No Discharge Zones in B.C.

About pumpouts. Holding tank pumpout stations are becoming more common in British Columbia, but all boats with holding tanks should be equipped to pump overboard as well. Most of the B.C. saltwater areas do not have cities or large towns, which means they have no sewage treatment facilities and no pumpouts.

No Discharge Zones. Nine saltwater bays, harbors and areas with poor water circulation in British Columbia appear to be headed for designation as No Discharge Zones for solid waste (sewage). Approved holding tanks will be required in these areas. Macerator treatment systems, even if approved in the U.S., will not qualify.

It will still be legal to pump holding tanks overboard in B.C., but not in no discharge zones. Once in deep, cold water, the relatively minute amount of waste from a boat, or even a fleet of boats, is insignificant.

"Gray water" is not included in the no-discharge regulations. It's okay to take a shower and wash dishes.

These proposed no discharge zones probably will not be written into law until autumn 2000 at the earliest.

Carrington Bay	Pilot Bay
Cortes Bay	Prideaux Haven
Mansons Landing	Roscoe Bay
& Gorge Harbour	Smuggler Cove
Montague Harbour	Squirrel Cove

How to Cross the Strait of Juan de Fuca

To the San Juan Islands, Haro Strait, Victoria

Important: Courselines suggested below are approximate and for reference only. They assume good conditions and the absence of current. Since current always is present, appropriate course adjustments will be called for.

THE STRAIT OF JUAN DE FUCA has a well-earned reputation for being rough at times. It's true that a boat crossing the strait can take a beating its crew will not want to repeat, but often the crossing can be almost flat. And if conditions truly are foul, alternate routes exist. The secret to an easy crossing lies in picking your times and not being foolhardy.

Summer weather pattern
During the high summer cruising season, the "typical" weather pattern calls for near-calm conditions in the early morning, when the air over the entire region is cool. As the summer sun heats the land, the air over the land rises, and colder ocean air funnels down the Strait of Juan de Fuca to replace the rising land air. This is called a sea breeze, and usually it develops in the late morning or early afternoon. By late afternoon the sea breeze can be quite strong, creating short, high seas that can really work you over. After sundown, as the interior air cools and drops, the wind dies away.

The general plan, therefore, calls for an early morning departure. Listen carefully to the VHF marine radio's official weather reports and forecast. If the report says the wind already is blowing 15-20 knots, with more wind expected, don't cross. Wait until the wind

subsides or take an alternate route.

The most popular alternate route is around the south end of Whidbey Island, north through Saratoga Passage, and through LaConner. Continue out Guemes Channel and across Rosario Strait to Thatcher Pass. Thatcher Pass will take you into the San Juan Islands, where you can work your way to your destination in protected waters. Rosario Strait can be rough, too, but usually not as rough as the eastern Strait of Juan de Fuca. And Rosario Strait is only four miles wide between the Guemes Channel and Thatcher Pass, so even if the water is rough you won't be in it for long.

Point Wilson to Middle Channel (Friday Harbor)
Let's say you want to cross from Point Wilson, at the mouth of Puget Sound, to Middle Channel, known locally as Cattle Pass, at the southern tip of San Juan Island. That's the direct route to Friday Harbor. Crossing the Strait of Juan de Fuca to Cattle Pass, the ideal plan is to time your arrival at Cattle Pass for shortly after the current turns to a flood. Use the San Juan Channel current predictions.

If you do it right, you'll carry the last of a dying ebb out Admiralty Inlet, past Point Wilson, and well across the strait.

Just before reaching Cattle Pass, the current will turn to flood, flushing you nicely through the pass and into San Juan Channel. Since you can have 2-4 knots of current in Admiralty Inlet, and a couple knots of current in the strait, riding the ebb can save considerable time,

even in a fast boat. The less time you're exposed, the less time you have to meet trouble.

The current can run hard through Cattle Pass, so it's best not to fight it. In a slow boat, you can just sit there making little headway.

If you draw a straight line between Point Wilson and Cattle Pass (use chart 18465, Strait of Juan de Fuca—Eastern Part), the line would go approximately through Smith Island. Smith Island lies about half-way across the strait. It is a low, lonely pile of brown sand with a big lighthouse on it. Shoals, covered with dense kelp, extend westward from the island for nearly two miles.

So you can't go straight to Cattle Pass; you have to run west of Smith Island, then make a turn to starboard. At Point Wilson you'll set a course of 301 degrees magnetic until you're abeam the Smith Island light, where you'll turn to a course of 330 degrees magnetic to fetch Cattle Pass. (From Cattle Pass to Point Wilson, reverse the process: run 150 degrees magnetic until the Smith Island light bears abeam to port, then turn to 121 magnetic to fetch Point Wilson.)

You may find that once you've raised it, Smith Island won't let you go. It takes forever to put Smith Island astern.

Partridge Bank, between Point Wilson and Smith Island, should be avoided. Heavy kelp is an obstacle, and if the wind is up seas will be worse in the shallow water over the bank.

To Rosario Strait or Deception Pass
From the mouth of Admiralty Inlet, plot a course that leaves the Point Partridge bell buoy off Whidbey Island to starboard. From the Point Partridge bell buoy, plot a course to take you *east* of Lawson Reef, which lies about 1¾ miles off the entrance to Deception Pass. A bell buoy marks the reef. Once past Lawson Reef, turn to port to run into Rosario Strait. (The straightest course from the Point Partridge bell buoy to Rosario Strait would take you inside and parallel to the commercial traffic lane. Pleasure craft are restricted from running in the commercial lanes in that way.)

To Haro Strait (Roche Harbor)
Leaving Point Wilson, run 301 degrees magnetic until the Smith Island light is abeam to starboard. Then turn to starboard just enough to run toward the west side of San Juan Island, but east of the commercial traffic lane. The course should be about 310 degrees magnetic. Once near San Juan Island, turn to port and follow the island coastline north.

If you're returning from Roche Harbor, follow the San Juan Island coastline until you're off False Bay, then turn to 130 degrees magnetic until the Smith Island light is abeam to port. Turn to 121 degrees magnetic to fetch Point Wilson.

Both the flood and ebb currents run strongly along the west side of San Juan Island. Even in a fast boat it is best to make this passage with favorable current. The Canadian Hydrographic Service's book *Current Atlas: Juan de Fuca Strait to Georgia Strait* illustrates these current flows in convincing diagram form, and is highly recommended. Our Weatherly Press publication *Washburne's Tables* makes using the *Current Atlas* much easier.

To Victoria
From Point Wilson, a course of approximately 275 degrees magnetic will get you to Victoria. Settle down for a 30-mile trip, and watch for floating kelp and other drift. Returning from Victoria, a course of about 95 degrees magnetic should raise Point Wilson in time to make late-run corrections for the effects of current. In slow boats, the trip between Victoria and Point Wilson usually can be made on a single favorable tide. In all boats, significant time will be saved by using the current.

Even the best plan can go awry. While over the years the editors have made many easy crossings of the strait (only a few have been "memorable"), it's important to understand that conditions can change with little warning. When you're several miles offshore and the wind decides to make up, you can't pull over until things improve. You have no business in the strait unless you're in a seaworthy, well-equipped boat.

The Point Wilson Rip

ONE OF THE MOST FRUSTRATING PIECES OF WATER we face in the Northwest is the infamous Point Wilson tide rip just off Port Townsend. The rip usually (but not always) forms on a fairly strong ebb tide, and may or may not be accompanied by westerly wind. The patch of rough water can extend for several miles north and west of Point Wilson.

I have learned three ways to avoid being bounced around by the Point Wilson rip.

The first is to round Point Wilson at or near slack water. Usually, the rip doesn't form until well into a strong ebb cycle, so timing your arrival to coincide with slack water should get the job done.

If, however, you must go that way while the rip is tearing the Strait of Juan de Fuca to shreds, you can pick one of two routes around it.

The first is to hug the Point Wilson shore as closely as you dare, keeping close to shore until you pass Middle Point, before heading across to the San Juan Islands or heading west to Victoria. The fact that the current runs more slowly close to shore prevents the rip tide from having the same wild effect as farther out.

The other route is to stay close to the Whidbey Island shore (avoiding the shoal water off Partridge Point and staying east of Partridge Bank) until past Smith Island before turning toward your destination.

We were making a night crossing of the Strait one year, on our way to Victoria for the Swiftsure sailboat race. It had been a warm, calm evening, so the forward hatch was propped open. One of the forward vee-berths was occupied by our friend Ned Brown, and the other was Ole Hansen's. Ole was at the helm when we pumped head-on into the Point Wilson rip. We buried the bow, hurling water over the deck and back into the cockpit, where Ole struggled to keep the boat on course.

Ned woke up when he was slammed against the overhead, but noted sleepily that all the water cascading down through the open hatch was landing on Ole's bunk, not his, so he rolled over and went back to sleep.

Ole hasn't entirely forgiven Ned to this day, and I started to develop my theories about how to avoid that nasty rip, which hasn't caught me since.

—Tom Kincaid

Fog

Fog can develop unexpectedly on the strait. Sometimes it is only a thin mist, other times it can be pea-soup thick. While you're in good visibility, keep regular plots of your progress. *Always know exactly where you are.* This way, when fog hits you'll be able to plot courses that will keep you safe. In fog, put up a radar reflector so large vessels can see you on their radar in time to steer clear of you. Slow to 5 or 6 knots to dodge drift and avoid other boats that appear close aboard. Speeds of 5 or 6 knots are easy to use for time-speed-distance calculations. At 5 knots, a mile takes 12 minutes. At 6 knots, a mile takes 10 minutes.

Regardless of the size of your boat, it is in fog that you and your crew will be grateful for your relatively modest investment in a large, high-quality compass, and the compass adjuster's time to adapt the compass to your boat. *Trust that compass.* Fog disorients even the most experienced mariners. If you run a compass course you know to be good, at a speed you can depend on, for a time you calculate based on speed and distance, you should arrive surprisingly close to your destination.

The Strait of Juan de Fuca is not to be feared, but it is to be respected. The strait will punish lack of respect. Be sure your boat is seaworthy, well-equipped, and in excellent condition. Carry plenty of fuel. Let the weather set your plans. Don't be afraid to wait. Know where you are always, and watch for changes.

About Anchoring

IN ADDITION TO BEING THE EDITOR OF THE WAGGONER, since 1984 I have been the Pacific Northwest sales representative for Bruce anchors. I have specified anchors, compared anchors, argued anchors, studied anchors, taught anchors, and written about anchors. Most importantly, I have gone out and used anchors. Gathering information for the Waggoner has meant that more time is spent at docks, but given the choice, the little ship *Surprise* prefers to anchor.

Many people do not share this enthusiasm for anchoring. Watching how some of them go about it, their fears are understandable. But there are a few general principles that will help even a novice to anchor successfully.

Use good gear. Big, strong anchors work; small, cheap anchors don't. The most experienced cruisers seem to carry the biggest anchors. For obvious reasons I like Bruce anchors. But the other popular designs are good, too. Well-equipped, wide-ranging boats are found carrying all of the common designs: Bruce, CQR (plow), Danforth and Northill.

Make sure your anchor is made of high-quality steel. If it's wedged in a rock, you don't want it to bend. While Danforth style anchors are easiest to bend, within the limits of their design they can be made strong and expensive, or weak and cheap. There are no strong, cheap Danforth style anchors.

Read the sizing charts carefully, and *size your anchor for storm conditions.* Some sizing charts are written for 20-knot winds. Others are written for 30 knots. The Bruce chart is written for 42 knots. When the wind comes on to blow *hard* at 0300, you don't want a 20-knot anchor out there.

Carry ample rode. For an anchor to bury and hold properly, you should pay out anchor rode at least *five times* the water depth. In 20 feet of water you would want 100 feet of rode out. In 60 feet of water you would want 300 feet out. Often, especially in crowded anchorages during high summer season, it will not be possible to anchor on 5:1 scope (five times the depth of the water). That is understood. But I've watched people put out 30 feet of rode in 20 feet of water, and wonder why the anchor wouldn't bite. For the deep waters of the Pacific Northwest, carry at least 300 feet of anchor rode, whether all-chain or combination chain and rope. Opinions vary about how much chain a combination rode should include, but no one would criticize you for having about a foot of chain for every foot of boat length.

Read the tide tables. If the overnight low tide isn't very low, a shallow anchorage can be just right. On the other hand, if the moon is either new or full (the two times during the month when the tidal range is the greatest) the shallow anchorage might go dry at low tide. You also want to know the maximum height of the tide during your stay. Set your scope for five times the water depth at high tide, or if you can't get five times, as much as you can get away with.

Set the anchor well. To get the best bury in the bottom, you want the angle between the anchor and the boat to be as flat as possible. After lowering the anchor, back well down before you set the hook. After the anchor is set, you can shorten up to avoid swinging into other boats or onto a sand bar.

You'll know, by the way, when the anchor is set. The anchor rode pulls straight. The boat *stops.* If you have any doubt as to whether the anchor is set, then probably it isn't. Weed can foul an anchor, especially a Danforth style anchor, and many bottoms have weed. I've heard of anchors grabbing a sunken tire and dragging it across the bottom. Contributing Editor Tom Kincaid recalls an anchor caught in a mess of old electrical wire.

Once the anchor is set, you don't have to pour on all 600 horsepower to prove your point. Anchors gain holding power through pulling and relaxing over time, a process called *soaking.* An anchor put down for lunch might be recovered with little effort. Left overnight it might feel as if it had headed for China.

Look at your chart. For happy anchoring you want a good holding bottom, appropriate depths, and protection. The nautical chart can help you with all these needs. If the chart says *Foul,* don't anchor there. If the chart shows submerged pilings at the head of the bay, avoid the head of the bay. If the chart shows 200-foot depths right up to the shoreline, that's a bad spot. If the chart shows the bay open to the full sweep of the prevailing wind and seas, find another bay or you'll be in for a rough night.

I find the easiest anchorages to be in 20-50 feet of water, with a decided preference for the 20-30 foot depths. Approach slowly, take a turn around the entire area to check the depths, and decide where you want the boat to lie after the anchor is set. Then go out to a spot that will give you a 5:1 scope, and lower the anchor. Back way down, set the hook, and shorten up to the desired location.

Carry a shore-tie. In many locations you will set the anchor offshore, back in toward shore to set, and take the dinghy in with a rope from a stern cleat to tie around a rock or tree. Boats line Tod Inlet tied this way. In many deep bays it's the only way you can anchor. And sometimes you'll find a little niche that will hold just your boat, if the stern is tied to shore. Carry at least 600 feet of inexpensive polypropylene rope for shore ties. Often you will be able to pass the line around a tree and bring it back to the boat. When you depart, you can recover the shore tie without leaving the boat.

Secure the anchor rode to the boat. I talked with a man with a 32-foot boat, a brand-new Bruce anchor, and several hundred feet of expensive chain anchor rode, which he had not made fast to the boat. He laid the anchor down in deep water and backed away. The anchor rode snaked out faster and faster, until to his horror the man saw the chain's end shoot across the foredeck and vanish overboard.

Cruising from dock to dock is fun, and no one can fault the conveniences. But a world of possibilities opens to those who have good anchoring gear and know how to use it. These guidelines cover most anchoring situations. Practice in good anchorages, where it's safe. Watch how other boats anchor. The skills are easy to learn.

Big Anchors

WOLFERSTAN SAYS that the geography of Kanish Bay (and, we assume, Small Inlet) often allows them to escape strong westerly winds from Johnstone Strait and Discovery Passage. We can report that this isn't *always* the case.

On a recent visit we anchored behind the nob of land near the southeast corner of Small Inlet, and sailed wildly back and forth on the anchor in 35-40 knot winds. We paid out extra rode, and as the wind increased we paid it out again. The anchor rode required chafing gear at the bow roller. Gusts picked cells of spray off the flat surface of the water and carried them a hundred yards at a time. By morning the wind had died away. It takes only one such experience to convince a skipper that he wants a big, strong anchor— a *big,* strong anchor—and ample anchor rode.

–Robert Hale

Buoys, Beacons and Ranges

Red, Right, Returning means leave **Red** navigation aids off your **Right** hand when you're **Returning** from seaward. If the navigation mark is *not* red, leave it off your *left* hand when you're returning from seaward.

This is the general rule in U.S. and Canadian waters, with two subtle refinements:

- A red and white aid marks mid-channel. Both inward bound and outward bound, leave the red and white buoy off your left hand.
- A red and green aid marks an obstruction, or marks the meeting of two or more channels, but the aid can be passed on either side safely.

Nuns

All red buoys marking channels are shaped as cones, and are called NUNS. Most nun buoys are painted solid red. If the nun buoy has a green horizontal band painted on it, the buoy marks the meeting of two channels, with the left channel being the preferred, or main, channel. (If you leave the buoy off your right hand, you will be in the left channel.) Nuns can be lighted or unlighted. If lighted, the light will be red.

Cans

All green buoys marking channels are called CANS. They are shaped like, well, *cans*. Most can buoys are painted solid green. If the can buoy has a horizontal red band painted on it, the buoy marks the meeting of two channels, with the right channel the preferred, or main, channel. Cans may be lighted or unlighted. If lighted, the light will be green.

Buoys float, and are held in place by heavy anchoring systems. The chain between the buoy and the anchor must be long enough to let the buoy float in the highest tides and largest seas possible. As a result, at low tide the buoy can swing in a large circle. Winds and tidal currents move the buoys. They don't stay in exactly the same place.

Beacons

BEACONS are permanent navigation aids attached to the earth. They can be located on land, installed on docks or breakwaters, or mounted on pilings. A lighthouse is a beacon. A beacon not on land will be placed in shallow water *outside* a channel. Leave a beacon considerable room. Do not pass a beacon close aboard.

An unlighted beacon is called a DAYBEACON. A lighted beacon is called a MINOR LIGHT. A minor light marking the right side of a channel will carry a red light (red, right, returning). A minor light marking the left side of a channel will carry a green light. If a minor light marks the meeting of two channels, the light will be red if the left channel is preferred (red, right, returning); green if the right channel is preferred.

DAYMARKS are the colored panels mounted on beacons. Red panels are triangle shaped; green panels are square. A triangle shaped red panel with a green horizontal stripe indicates the meeting of two channels, with the left channel the preferred, or main channel. A square panel painted green with a red horizontal stripe indicates the meeting of two channels, with the right channel the preferred, or main channel.

Whenever a navigation aid is marked with a horizontal stripe of contrasting color, the color at the top of the aid indicates the preferred, or main, channel.

Approaching a channel from seaward, buoys and beacons are numbered, beginning with the marks to seaward. Red buoys, beacons, and minor lights carry even numbers, such as 2, 4, 6, and so on. Green buoys, beacons, and minor lights carry odd numbers, such as 1, 3, 5, and so on. Depending on the channel, it might be appropriate to skip some numbers, so that buoy 6 is roughly opposite buoy 5, even if no buoy 4 exists.

Ranges

RANGES are used to help a boat stay in the middle of a narrow channel.

Ranges are rectangular panels, stood vertically, each with a wide stripe running from top to bottom down the middle of the panel. Ranges don't float. They are attached to the earth and are arranged in pairs, one behind the other. The rearmost range board stands taller than the front board. To use a range, steer until the rear range board appears to be on top of the front board. You can steer toward a range, looking ahead, or away from a range, sighting astern.

Buoys and beacons are not selected and placed at random. They follow a plan, although to a newcomer the plan may at times seem obscure. In the San Juan Islands, for instance, the navigation aids in Lopez Sound and Harney Channel assume that entry from the sea is from the east, from Rosario Strait. Coming from the east, such as from Lopez Pass or Thatcher Pass, you would leave the red navigation aids off your right hand.

However, the situation changes at the ferry dock located at Upright Head, at the north tip of Lopez Island. There, the assumption is that one is returning from the sea via Upright Channel, and the light on the dock is red. If you were coming from Lopez Sound or Thatcher Pass, this light would be on your left hand—the opposite of what you might expect.

Despite the complexity of the buoyage and light system, you will find that as you understand it better your enjoyment afloat will increase. At some point you will want a thorough explanation of the entire system. For U.S. waters it will be found in the introduction to the Coast Guard *Light List*. For Canadian waters it will be found partly in the introduction to the Canadian Coast Guard *List of Lights, Buoys and Fog Signals*, and completely in the Canadian Coast Guard publication, *The Canadian Aids to Navigation System*. Latest editions of these publications should be aboard every boat. Available at chart agencies.

INNER LIGHT 8, a minor light marking the Shilshole Bay entrance channel, illustrates many facts about navigation aids. First, it is a beacon, attached to the earth. Second, it is attached to the earth outside the navigable channel. This is why it is good practice to give beacons a generous berth, even when they are surrounded by water—the tide might be in. Third, the red-painted triangular dayboard shows that this beacon marks the right side of the channel, and should be off the right hand when returning from the sea (Red, Right, Returning). Because all right-side channel markers carry even numbers, the number 8 in the middle of the dayboard confirms that the beacon is on the right. Last, the white board with the red circle means "restricted operations." In this case the restriction is the 7-knot speed limit.

THE SHILSHOLE BAY ENTRANCE RANGE. To use a range, align the boards one above the other, as these boards are, and follow that course. The boards have lights for night approaches. The first (lower) board's light is shown on the chart as *Qk Fl R 20ft.*—Quick Flashing Red, 20 feet above Mean High Water. The upper board's light is shown on the chart as *E Int R 6sec 81ft. E Int* means Isophase. With an Isophase light, the duration of light and darkness are equal. The red light shows for three seconds and is dark for three seconds.

Can Buoy

Nun Buoy

FOR A VESSEL RETURNING FROM THE SEA, the green painted can buoy marks the left side of the channel, and the red painted nun buoy marks the right side. The left-side mark has an odd number, and the right side mark has an even number. Either or both buoys could be lighted or unlighted.

Differences Between U.S. and Canadian Charts

CANADA AND THE UNITED STATES are two separate nations, and their charts, while similar in many ways, have a number of important differences.

U.S. charts are in fathoms and feet; most Canadian charts are metric. *With all charts, read the chart title and margin information to see if the chart is metric, fathoms and feet, or feet.* The U.S. has announced its intention to convert its charts to metric, but at the moment only one U.S. chart in the Pacific Northwest has metric measurement. That chart is *18460, Strait of Juan de Fuca Entrance.* One side of the sheet is in fathoms and feet; the other side is metric. A few Canadian charts haven't been updated to metric and remain in fathoms and feet.

Metric charts show soundings and heights in meters. A meter (spelled *metre* in Canada) equals 39.37 inches, or 3.28 feet. Two meters equals 6 feet 7 inches, or just over one fathom. The difference is significant. Don't confuse fathoms with meters.

Waters appear to be deeper on U.S. charts. This difference is important wherever the water is shallow, and is the result of the two countries using different CHART DATUMS.

Depths on a chart are measured from the

chart datum, also called the REFERENCE PLANE or TIDAL DATUM. On Canadian charts, the chart datum is either Lowest Normal Tides, or Lower Low Water, Large Tide. For that reason, you don't find many "minus tides" in Canadian tide tables.

On U.S. charts, however, the chart datum is Mean Lower Low Water. Mean Lower Low Water is the mean level of the lower of the two low tides each day. Since the U.S. chart datum has half the lower waters above it and half below it, U.S. tide books show minus tides.

It's not a question of whether the tide drops lower in Canada or the U.S. It's a question of where the depth is measured from. U.S. charts start their measurements from a point higher than Canadian charts. The difference can be as much as 1.5 meters, or almost 5 feet.

Example: Assume that you are in the U.S., skippering a sailboat. The sailboat's keel draws 5 feet, and you want to anchor overnight in a bay with a charted depth of one fathom (6 feet). According to the tide table, low tide will be minus 1.5 feet at 0700. Knowing that your boat, with its 5 feet of draft, would be aground in 4.5 feet of water, you would look for a more suitable anchorage.

If this bay were in Canada, the Canadian chart would show a depth of perhaps just 1 meter (assuming a Lowest Normal Tide lower

than the tide at 0700). The tide table would show a low tide at 0700 of perhaps .4 meters. You would add the 1 meter depth from the chart to the .4 meter low tide from the tide table, and get 1.4 meters of water at 0700. Since you draw more than 1.4 meters (55 inches), you would not anchor in the bay that night.

Important exception: Both Canadian and U.S. charts show soundings in the other country's system when the charts cover both sides of the border. The U.S. chart would convert Canadian meters to U.S. fathoms, but would adopt the Canadian chart datum in Canadian waters. The Canadian metric chart would convert U.S. fathoms to meters, but would adopt the U.S. chart datum in U.S. waters. This is explained in the chart legends.

Clearances appear to be greater on U.S. charts. U.S. charts measure clearances from Mean High Water. One-half the high waters are above the mean. Canadian charts measure clearances from Higher High Water, Large Tides. The same bridge, over the same waterway, would show less vertical clearance on a Canadian chart than on a U.S. chart. Metric Canadian charts show heights and depths in metres, while charts in fathoms and feet show

(Continued page 22)

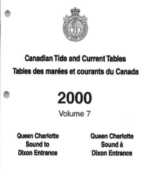

(Continued from page 20)

heights in feet and depths in fathoms. A Canadian metric chart might show a bridge clearance as "3", meaning 3 meters above Higher High Water, Large Tides. A U.S. chart would show a similar bridge clearance as "12" or more, meaning 12 feet or more above Mean High Water.

Canadian charts use more symbols to show buoys and tide rips. Canadian charts use symbols that approximate the shapes of buoys, with descriptive letters to indicate the buoy's characteristics. U.S. charts use a single diamond-shaped symbol for nearly all navigation buoys, with descriptive letters to indicate the buoy's characteristics. On U.S. chart 18421, Strait of Juan de Fuca to Strait of Georgia (1:80,000), for example, the bell buoy marking Buckeye Shoal, north of Cypress Island, is shown as

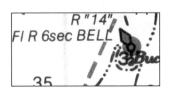

But on Canadian chart 3462, Juan de Fuca Strait to Strait of Georgia (1:80,000), the buoy is shown as

Canadian charts may use arrows to show the location of the buoy or beacon. If other detail on the chart makes precise location difficult, the Canadian chart will offset the symbol slightly, in the direction of the preferred navigable water. The offset is indicated by an arrow pointing to the actual location of the buoy or beacon. Sometimes the arrow is not easily noticed at a quick glance, so be aware.

Chart No. 1 cracks the code. Nautical charts are filled to overflowing with important navigation information. Unfortunately, so much of the information is in the form of symbols, abbreviations, and undefined terms that it can be offputting to the inexperienced. Each country publishes a book that shows each symbol, explains each abbreviation, and defines each term used on its charts. The U.S. book is titled *Chart No. 1,* and the Canadian book is titled *Chart 1.* They are available at their respective chart agencies, and the prices are modest.

The Canadian Coast Guard publication *The Canadian Aids to Navigation System* explains the Canadian buoyage and light system, and is highly recommended. The cost is $7.50 (Canadian) from Canadian Hydrographic chart agents.

Don't overlook the introductions to these books. The introductions are full of essential information.

VHF Radio Procedures

THE VHF RADIO IS AN IMPORTANT PIECE of safety equipment, and should be monitored when the boat is underway. While monitoring, you will hear weather and safety warnings, and be aware of much that is happening around you. A boat close by, for example, may be having problems and call for help. By monitoring your radio you can respond.

Station licenses

U.S. vessels. Until 1996, U.S. pleasure craft were required to have station licenses for their marine VHF radios. In 1996, however, the requirement was dropped for pleasure craft under 65 feet, operating inside the U.S. only. U.S. vessels operating in foreign waters still needed a U.S. station license. With the 1999 dropping of station licenses in Canada (see below), it is expected that U.S. pleasure craft exempted from station licenses no longer will need a station license to travel in Canadian waters. As the Waggoner went to press, though, the implementing regulations had not wound their way through the U.S. bureaucracy. Technically, all U.S. vessels operating in foreign waters still are required to have station licenses. When the implementing regulations are adopted, we will report this information on our web site www.waggonerguide.com. (As a practical matter, Canadian authorities do not enforce U.S. radio license laws, and U.S. authorities are not going to follow a boat into Canada.)

Even if your otherwise exempt vessel has a station license, do not use your call sign. When using your radio identify yourself by your vessel name. (The Waggoner boat *Surprise* has a station license, but we no longer use our call sign. We simply say, "This is *Surprise.*") If the vessel is unnamed or you wish to absolutely, positively identify yourself, use the state registration number or, if the vessel is documented, the vessel's official number. U.S. pleasure craft longer than 65 feet, and all U.S. commercial vessels, still must have station licenses. The cost is $115 for 10 years, and covers VHF radios, radar, EPIRBs, and a number of other radio products. Applications are available wherever VHF radios or other electronic equipment are sold, or from the Federal Communications Commission at (888)225-5322.

A station license serves the entire vessel, regardless of the number of radios the vessel has. The station license also covers the use of a tender's VHF radio (such as a handheld model) as long as the radio is used in tender service, and as long as it is not used on land. It's all right for two or more radios from the same vessel with the same call sign to talk to each other.

Canadian vessels. Beginning in March 1999, station licenses no longer were issued to Canadian vessels so long as 1) the vessel is not operated in the sovereign waters of a country other than Canada or the USA; 2) the radio equipment on board the vessel is capable of operating only on frequencies that are allocated for maritime mobile communications or marine radio navigation. Vessels not meeting those two requirements must have station licenses.

Operator's Permit

Canada requires each person operating a VHF radio to have a Restricted Operator's Certificate. For Canadian residents a test must be passed, but the certificate is free and issued for life.

The U.S. does not require operator's permits for VHF radio use within the U.S. For foreign travel, however, a Restricted Radio Operator's permit is required. The U.S. individual permit is issued for life, and costs $45. If you are from the U.S. and you take a boat to Canada, you will need Restricted Radio Operator permits (we have ours).

Cellular telephones

No license is required for marine use of a cellular telephone. Cellular telephone coverage is excellent throughout Puget Sound, the San Juan Islands, and the entire Strait of Georgia area. For AT&T Wireless and CanTel subscribers, coverage ceases at the north end of the Strait of Georgia. For AirTouch Cellular and B.C. Cellular subscribers, coverage extends, with a few "holes," to Port Hardy. B.C. Cellular/AirTouch also serves Prince Rupert, and the West Coast of Vancouver Island at least to Tofino. For a fee, AT&T Wireless and CanTel subscribers can arrange for temporary service from B.C. Cellular by calling (800)661-2355.

Short term and monthly programs are available.

For emergency, distress, and rescue operations, *cellular telephones are not substitutes for VHF radios.* If you have a problem and need help, get on Channel 16 and start calling. The Coast Guard and neighboring vessels will hear you. You will be impressed with the Coast Guard's efficiency and professionalism.

Satellite telephones

Satellite telephones are now a practical reality for many cruising boats. While equipment and air time are still on the expensive side, they do provide complete telephone service without concern about cellular coverage. Boats cruising Puget Sound and the Strait of Georgia up to Desolation Sound can use cellular telephones quite reliably. But from Desolation Sound north, cellular service is spotty. We think the satellite systems will gain popularity.

How to use the VHF radio

The easiest way to get a general sense of radio use is to monitor channel 16, channel 22A, and the working channels. You'll hear experienced, and inexperienced, people in action. The difference will be obvious. To use the radio, call on the *calling channel,* channel 16. Pleasure craft in the U.S. are encouraged to use the alternative calling channel 09. This works only when the station you are calling also is monitoring channel 09. When communication is established, switch to a *working channel* for your conversation. Except for distress, you may not have a conversation on channel 16. Channel 09 may be used for conversations, but because it is an alternate calling channel in the U.S., they should be brief.

The low power switch

VHF radios can transmit at 25 watts, their highest power rating, or at 1 watt, the low power mode. Handheld VHF radios usually have a maximum power of 4.5 to 5 watts and low power of 1 watt. Whenever practical use the low-power mode. Other vessels a few miles away then can use the same channel without interference from you. The difference between high power and low power affects transmission distance only. Reception ability is unaffected.

Handheld radios should use low power whenever possible. The battery lasts longer.

DSC. DSC stands for Distress Safety and Calling, part of the Global Maritime Distress and Safety System (GMDSS). Basically, if you have a DSC radio and push the red button, the radio sends out an automatic distress message on channel 70, with your vessel's name and location. DSC radios are complicated and very expensive. For pleasure craft purposes, many problems must be overcome before DSC will be in wide use. A target date of 2005 is mentioned for full implementation, but it is unlikely that pleasure craft will be included then or for the forseeable future. For now at least, DSC is not an issue for pleasure craft.

Mayday hoaxes. Each year, false Mayday calls cost the U.S. and Canadian Coast Guards millions of dollars ($2 million in Seattle alone) and in some cases put lives at risk. Sometimes the hoax is Junior playing with Grandpa's radio, some-

Marine Operator Channels Washington Waters

Bellingham 26/85
Everett 24
Olympia 85
Port Angeles 25
Seattle 25/26
Tacoma 28
Whidbey Is. 87

Marine Operator Channels B.C. Waters

Alert Bay 26/86
Bamfield 27
Bella Bella 25
Big Bay 25
Brooks Peninsula 87
Campbell River 27
Campbell River (Elk Falls) 64
Cape Caution 02
Courtenay 23
East Thurlow 24
Estevan Point 23
Ganges 27/64
Grenville Channel 24
Holberg 60
Jordan River 23
Kyuquot 01
Madeira Park 25
Nanaimo Harbour 87
Pachena Point 87
Parksville (Qualicum) 28
Patrick Point 24
Pender Harbour 25
Port Hardy 24
Powell River 85
Prince Rupert 25/26
Prince Rupert (Mt. Hays) 27
Rivers Inlet 03
Sarah Point 60
Sayward (Newcastle Ridge) 28
Sechelt 86
Stuart Island 25
Tofino 24
Vancouver 23/25/26
Vancouver (Bowen Island) 24
Vancouver (Fraser River) 86
Victoria 26/86
W. Vancouver (Hood Pt.) 85
Winter Harbour 27

For a complete list of VHF channels and their use, see the Green Pages special reference section.

The Waggoner Web Site carries changes and updates to this edition throughout the year.

www.waggonerguide.com

times it the result of things getting too festive, sometimes the caller has a mental problem. Within the past few years the Prince Rupert region installed Direction Finding equipment, which zeroed in on the location of the Mayday call. After a couple people were arrested and heavily penalized, false Mayday calls in the Prince Rupert region declined dramatically. *Direction Finding equipment is being installed in the Puget Sound and Port Angeles region.* Radios are not toys, and false Mayday calls are not jokes. Those who place such calls will be learning just how unfunny they are.

MAREP weather reporting

MAREP stands for *Mariner Reporting* program. MAREP was set up by the Canadian Atmospheric Environment Service with the cooperation of the Canadian Coast Guard. With MAREP, individual vessels can report, in plain language, actual weather conditions around them. The weather patterns throughout the region surrounding Vancouver Island are extremely difficult to predict. Often, large differences in weather—especially wind strengths—can be found across an area of only a few miles.

MAREP stations are established around the north end of Vancouver Island at Bonilla Island, Cape Scott, and Kyuquot. Even where no MAREP stations are located, the Canadian Coast Guard actively solicits reports from all vessels. If you find significant differences between the forecasted weather and your local weather, call the Canadian Coast Guard on channels 26, 84 or 22A. Your information will be relayed to the Atmospheric Environment Service, and quite possibly influence the next forecast.

Marine operator telephone communication

Boats that do not have cellular telephones, or boats outside the cellular telephone coverage area, will use their VHF radio and marine operators for telephone calls. The complete list of marine operators is included in this section. Calls can be made collect or billed to a calling card or credit card.

In 1996, Maritel, based in Gulfport, Mississippi, purchased the U.S. West marine operator operations in the Pacific Northwest. The marine operator channels were retained, but all services and billing now are through Maritel. Vessel owners can establish a Maritel account, which simplifies billing and provides extra security. Non-subscribers can call collect, bill to a calling card or credit card, or use third-party billing. Marine Identification Numbers (MINs) issued by U.S. West no longer are valid. For more information, contact Maritel at (888)627-4835.

Canadian vessels can establish a marine account and Marine Identification Number (MIN) for easier billing. For more information, contact B.C. Tel at (800)663-0640 (inside B.C.), or (604)432-2574 (outside B.C.). As of December, 1999, telephone calls *no longer can be made through the Canadian Coast Guard.*

Ship to Shore Public Correspondence

Do not call the marine operator on channel 16. Marine operators do not monitor 16.

Washington waters: To place a call in Washington waters, select the telephone channel with the transmitter closest to your vessel location. If the channel is clear of traffic, press the transmit button for six seconds. If connection is made, you will hear a recorded message with instructions from Maritel. If not, change to another nearby marine operator channel or wait until your vessel is in another location.

B.C. waters: In Canada, call the B.C. Tel marine operator on the channel closest to your vessel location.

Shore to Ship Public Correspondence

Washington waters: To place a call to any vessel cruising in U.S. waters, contact Maritel at (800)955-9025 or (888)627-4632. The Maritel operator will call the vessel on channel 16.

B.C. waters: To place a call to a vessel cruising in British Columbia waters, contact the marine operator in Vancouver, B.C. and ask the operator to call the vessel via the appropriate Canadian Coast Guard station. The Coast Guard station will call the vessel on channel 16. If the vessel does not respond promptly, the call may be put on a wait list and the vessel will be notified at each Coast Guard information broadcast on the continuous marine broadcast channel.

Weather Broadcasts

WX1 CONTINUOUS BROADCAST, Seattle, Neah Bay, Cape Lazo, Alert Bay, Eliza Dome, Klemtu

WX2 CONTINUOUS BROADCAST, Saltspring Island, Nootka, Calvert Island, Mt. Gil, Dundas Island

WX3 CONTINUOUS BROADCAST, Olympia, Mt. Helmcken, Bowen Island

WX4 CONTINUOUS BROADCAST, Puget Sound, San Juan Islands

21B/161.65 MHz CONTINUOUS BROADCAST, Mt. Park, Discovery Mtn., Holberg, Mt. Ozzard, Mt. Hays, Kitimat

West Coast Marine Weather

Observation Sites

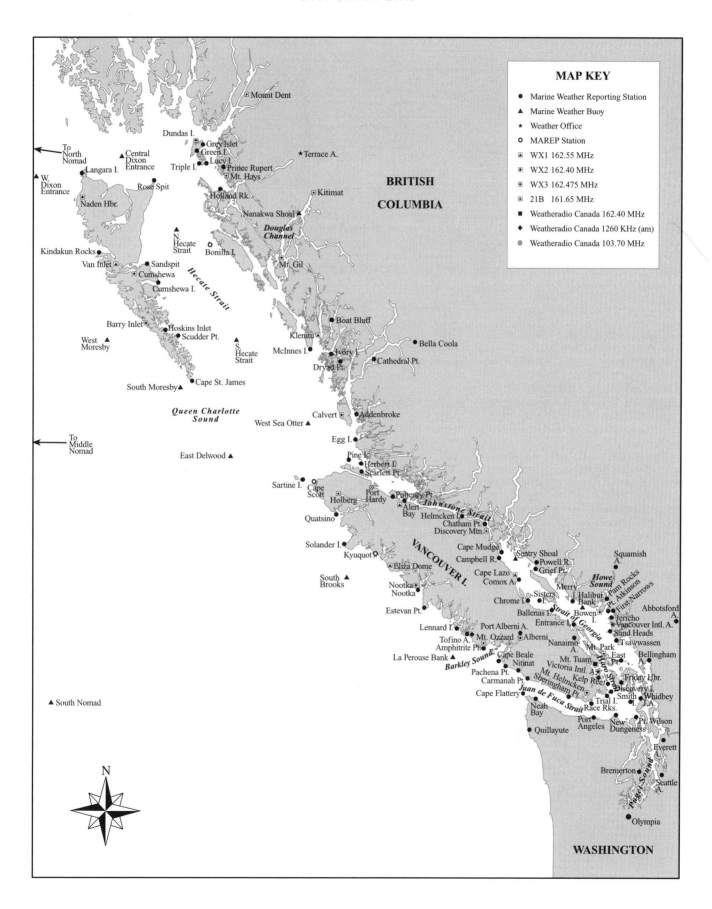

MAP KEY

- ●   Marine Weather Reporting Station
- ▲   Marine Weather Buoy
- ★   Weather Office
- ○   MAREP Station
- ⊡   WX1 162.55 MHz
- ⊡   WX2 162.40 MHz
- ⊡   WX3 162.475 MHz
- ⊞   21B   161.65 MHz
- ■   Weatheradio Canada 162.40 MHz
- ◆   Weatheradio Canada 1260 KHz (am)
- ⊗   Weatheradio Canada 103.70 MHz

BRITISH

COLUMBIA

VANCOUVER I.

WASHINGTON

N

State and Provincial Parks and Public Wharves

This beautiful swimming and sunbathing beach is at Montague Harbour Marine Park in the Gulf Islands.

THE WATERS FROM PUGET SOUND north into B.C. are dotted with more than 200 state and provincial parks, and in B.C., more than 220 public wharves. The properties range from primitive, with no amenities, to fully developed, with well-tended trails, ample parking, docks and mooring buoys, running water and hot showers, campsites, interpretive centers and park rangers.

Washington Parks
At the state level, parks are administered by the Washington State Parks Department and by the Department of Natural Resources (DNR). Usually, DNR sites are on the primitive side. State Parks, which tend to be more developed, often charge for overnight moorage at buoys and docks. For docks and floats, expect to pay $8 per night for boats under 26 feet, $11 per night for boats 26 feet and over. For mooring buoys expect to pay $5 per night. No fee is charged for anchoring. Day use is free.

Most state parks charge moorage fees from May 1 through September 30, except year-round at Blake Island, Jarrell Cove, Fort Worden, Cornet Bay (Deception Pass), and Mystery Bay.

Annual moorage permits are valid from January 1 through December 31. Permits cost $50 for boats under 26 feet, and $80 for boats 26 feet and over. You can get a permit through any park that charges moorage fees, or through the Washington State Parks Moorage Permit Program, (360)902-8608.

Campsite fees must be paid in addition to dock or mooring buoy fees. The annual moorage permit does not apply to campsite fees.

Self-register ashore for moorage or campsites. If a ranger must come out to your boat, you may be charged an additional $5 (even if you have an annual permit displayed). Moorage is limited to 72 hours at any park.

Boat launch sites
State parks with boat launches charge fees of $3 or $4, depending on the park. Boat launching is without charge if a campsite fee has been paid. An additional $1 fee is charged at "Popular Destination" parks: Birch Bay, Deception Pass, Fort Canby, Fort Casey, Fort Ebey, Fort Worden, and Larrabee.

Annual launch permits cost $40. If you buy before April 30, the cost is $30. Contact Washington State Parks HQ, (360)902-8608.

Reservations
Washington state parks moorage is unreserved. Leaving a dinghy or other personal property at a buoy or dock does not reserve moorage. Rafting is permitted but not mandatory. Rafting is allowed on buoys, within safe limits.

Reservations (for campsites only) in all state parks are now accepted. For more information, call toll-free at (800)452-5687.

Department of Natural Resources parks generally are primitive or have few facilities, and most do not charge fees.

B.C. Parks
British Columbia has an extensive marine parks system. Most parks have floats or mooring buoys, and most have safe, all-weather anchorages. Marine parks are open year-round. Some have no on-shore facilities, others have day-use facilities, picnic areas, and developed campsites. Parks with developed campsites will have toilet facilities. Most parks have drinking water, although you might see signs at the taps instructing that water be boiled before drinking. Some parks turn the water off in the winter.

Moorage fees are charged at only three B.C. Provincial marine parks: Sidney Spit, Newcastle Island, and Montague Harbour. Tent sites at these parks are extra.

No rafting is permitted on mooring buoys. One boat per buoy. For more information and maps of B.C. Parks, contact B.C. Parks General Information (250)387-5002.

Public Wharves
In British Columbia, public wharves provide moorage for commercial vessels (primarily the fishing fleet) and pleasure craft. Commercial fishing boats have priority at many public wharves. Especially in the off-season, public wharves are filled with fishing boats, leaving little or no moorage for pleasure boats. Facilities vary, from a dock only to fully-serviced marinas. Most of the fully-serviced marinas now are operated by local harbor authorities or their equivalents (see below). Public wharves are easily identified by their red-painted railings.

The Canadian government is in the process of divesting control of its wharves to local authorities. Locally run public wharves charge market rates, and may reserve space for pleasure craft. Moorage fees vary.

For more information on government wharves in B.C., call (604)666-6271.

Marine Parks Guide Supports B.C. Marine Parks

PROFITS FROM THE NEW *BC Marine Parks Guide* go to the B.C. Marine Parks Forever Society to help pay for more marine parks. The book contains complete descriptions and color photos of the 80+ marine parks now in the B.C. system. Each park gets a page with photo, map, and details of the park's history, facilities and character. The book is published by Pacific Yachting magazine. $16.95 in Canada, $12.95 in the U.S.

Another excellent guide to British Columbia's marine parks is *Anchorages and Marine Parks*, by longtime boating author and publisher Peter Vassilopoulos. This 298-page book describes B.C. and San Juan Islands marine parks, with photos, maps and piloting information. It also details anchorages throughout these waters. The book is aboard the Waggoner boat and we use it. $19.95 in Canada and the U.S.

Waterways, Bays, and Marinas

Olympia to Prince Rupert

Marinas • Fuel Docks • State Parks • Provincial Parks • Piloting • Anchoring

Alert Bay, B.C.

IN THE CHAPTERS that follow, the Waggoner Cruising Guide presents complete and up-to-date information about the waterways and facilities between Olympia and Prince Rupert, including the West Coast of Vancouver Island.

The data on marinas, fuel docks, and state and provincial parks was compiled by direct interview right up to press time. The descriptions of waterways and anchorages are from our own experience, and the experiences of people we trust.

South Puget Sound

Olympia • Case Inlet • Carr Inlet • Tacoma Narrows

SOUTH PUGET SOUND, GENERAL

SOUTH PUGET SOUND begins at Olympia and ends at the Tacoma Narrows. For scenic quality, easier seas and lack of crowding, it is an excellent region to explore. For some reason, Seattle boats that have no trouble voyaging hundreds of miles north have problems venturing just a few miles south. Yet South Sound is dotted with marine parks, and served by enough marinas to meet most needs. We like South Sound and recommend it.

The waters are generally flatter in South Sound. The channels are relatively narrow and have enough bends to prevent the wind from getting enough fetch to create large seas. Rips, of course, still form where channels meet, and the skipper must be aware of them.

With Olympia as South Sound's only city of any size, you can get away from civilization yet be only a short distance from it. First-time visitors usually are surprised at the beauty of South Sound. Mt. Rainier, a dormant volcano 14,410 feet high, dominates many vistas. The islands and peninsulas tend to be either tree-covered or pastoral, with pockets of homes or commercial enterprise. Most marine parks have docks, buoys and anchoring. The marinas are friendly and well-kept.

BUDD, ELD, TOTTEN INLETS

Budd Inlet Use chart 18456 (recommended) or 18448. The entrance to Budd Inlet is a mile wide between Dofflemyer Point and Cooper Point, and deep enough for all recreational boats. Approaching from the north, simply round Dofflemyer Point, where a lovely, white-painted light light blinks every 10 seconds, and head for the Capitol dome (unless the political fog rising from a convening Legislature obscures it). Continue past Olympia Shoal, which is marked by lighted beacons on the shoal's east and west sides. From Olympia Shoal pick up the 28-foot-deep dredged and buoyed channel that leads into the harbor. A spoils bank from channel dredging lies east of the channel. The spoils area is quite shoal. Parts of it dry, so stay in the channel.

South of the privately-owned West Bay Marina the channel branches at a piling intersection marker. The eastern leg leads to the Port of Olympia's Swantown Marina and boatyard; the western, or main, channel leads past the Port of Olympia large ship docks to Percival Landing and the Olympia Yacht Club

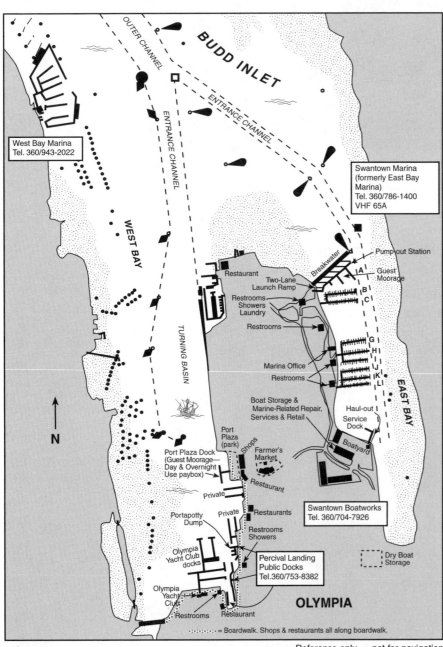

Olympia

Reference only — not for navigation

The Capitol Dome is open seven days a week.

The new Port Plaza dock offers free 4-hour moorage.

Percival Landing, looking north. Docks at right of photo have 30 amp power.

The Farmers' Market clown ties balloons into delightful shapes for this little girl.

at the head of the inlet. On both sides of the channel the water shoals rapidly to drying flats. Stay well within the channel. The Olympia harbor has a no-wake rule.

West Bay Marina no longer has guest moorage or a fuel dock, and the Olympia Yacht Club has guest moorage for members of reciprocal yacht clubs only. Percival Landing and Swantown Marina have moorage for all. A timbered walkway surrounds the Percival Landing area. It's a popular place for a strolling, with an excellent view of harbor activities. Some boaters find the number of walkers just above their boats to be disconcerting, although we found the nights to be quiet. Swantown Marina, in East Bay, does not have the crowds

looking at the boats.

All the moorages give access to Olympia, including the Capitol itself, which is just a few blocks uptown. Deschutes Basin, the southernmost tip of Puget Sound, and Capitol Lake are blocked by a dam and crossed by city streets. They are used by small boats launched from the city park just across the street from Percival Landing and the yacht club.

Anchorage in Budd Inlet is in 10 to 20 feet, mud bottom, along both shores, with Butler Cove and Tykle Cove preferred. Many waterfront homeowners have mooring buoys along the shores, so consider your swinging room when choosing an anchoring site. A launch ramp is located at the Thurston County

park just south of Boston Harbor, near Dofflemyer Point. Boston Harbor also has a launch ramp and parking for tow vehicles and trailers. The City of Olympia's Priest Point Park has one of the finest sand beaches in southern Puget Sound.

Olympia. Olympia is one of the most interesting and charming stops in Puget Sound, the more so because so few boats from central and northern Puget Sound ever visit. Northern boats should change their ways. Olympia is an undiscovered treat.

Capitol Campus. Olympia is the state capital, and we heartily urge a tour of the capitol campus and its buildings. The grounds are beautiful and the buildings magnificent. (If the lawmaking were as impressive as the buildings, we would have quite a government.) Informative tours are conducted on the hour, 10-3, seven days a week. The grounds tour is at 1pm. No charge for these tours.

It's an easy walk from the boat moorages to the capitol. If you skirt Capitol Lake to the east, you will find the footpath that leads up a steep hillside to the campus. To make the climb possible, the path switches back 11 times between the bottom and top. We're sure the path is wheelchair accessible, but a sturdy helper would be a good idea. Once at the top, head for the dome and the tours. Adult or child, you will not be disappointed.

Downtown Olympia. We're taken with downtown Olympia. Somehow, and we don't know how, parts of it got stuck in the '50s. If you've seen the film *Pleasantville*, you'll recongnize the storefronts. The State Theater's tall art deco sign is not a bit out of place in Olympia's downtown. Eating spots such as King Solomon's Reef and The Spar have employees who have been there 20-40 years, and

Tours of the Capitol Dome Legislative building begin hourly, 10-3.

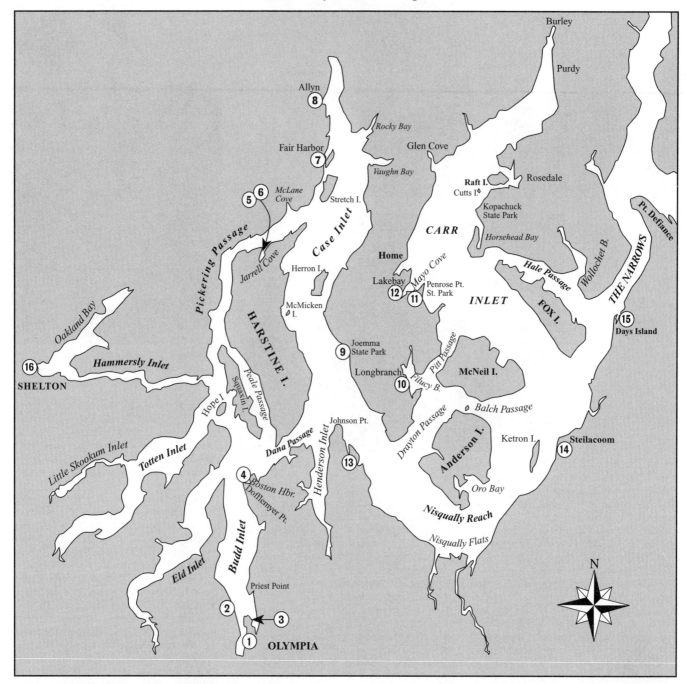

are open every day of the year so their regular customers have somewhere to go, even at Christmas.

Don't miss The Spar, with its tobacconist shop and walls decorated by ancient, mural-size Darius Kinsey logging photographs. We perched at the counter and shared a late-evening hard ice cream milkshake, then walked back through genuine swinging doors, through the High Climber Room (the bar), and inspected the cigar-smoking lounge in the very back. The next morning we returned to the Spar for omelettes that carried us clear through to suppertime. Toast from the special Spar bread is worth every penny of the 55-cent upcharge. Our waitress, Genia Sutter, had been there 17 years, and was appropriately engaging and irreverent. Good thing we got there early. When we left, customers were standing in line out-side.

Farmers' Market. The Farmers' Market, between Percival Landing and the Port of Olympia's Swantown Marina, is open 10-3 Thursday-Sunday, from April through October. Everything sold is grown or made locally, except for a few fruits which aren't available locally, and come from Yakima. Musicians perform on a covered stage, and a clown ties balloons into fantastic shapes to the delight of all. A worm garden has a plastic side so the creatures can be seen wriggling at their work. The market's roof is topped by a weathervane in the shape of a traditional flying pig.

① **Port Plaza Dock.** This is a new, all-concrete set of floats on the east side of the waterway that leads to Percival Landing and the

Olympia Yacht Club. Water, but no power. The docks are intended for day use, such as dining and shopping, 4 hours no charge, overnight moorage okay. Self-register at a kiosk at the head of the ramp.

① **Percival Landing Park,** 217 Thurston Ave., Olympia, WA 98501, (360)753-8382. Located at the southern tip of Budd Inlet, adjacent to downtown Olympia, near shopping, restaurants and other facilities. Guest moorage accommodates 50-70 boats in three sections: one with 30 amp power; the others with no power. The section with power is on the east side of the waterway at the very south end. Shore power receptacles are spaced approximately every 30 feet. The floats to the north have water but no power.

If you see a sign that says "No Moorage,"

Swantown Marina in Olympia is a complete, well-maintained facility.

it refers only to the float where the police boat is kept. The other floats are available. The float on the west side of the waterway (next to the Oyster House restaurant) has no power. All the floats have access to restrooms, showers, pumpout, portapotty dump. Self-register at kiosks. Cash or checks only, no credit cards. No manager is on site, so you may have to look around to find everything, including the registration kiosks. Good grocery shopping at Bayview Thriftway, west of the yacht club. Limited guest moorage during Wooden Boat Show, May 13-14, 2000; Olympia Lakefair, July 11-16, 2000; Harbor Days, with its tugboat races, September 1-3, 2000.

② **West Bay Marina,** 2100 West Bay Drive, Olympia, WA 98502. (360)943-2022. Located on west side of Budd Inlet. Permanent moorage only. The haulout and repair are closed, but they do have a pumpout.

③ **Swantown Marina** (Formerly East Bay Marina), 1022 Marine Drive NE, Olympia, WA 98501, (360)786-1400. Monitors VHF channel 65A. Open all year, guest moorage available. Restrooms, showers, laundry, pumpout, portapotty dump, 15, 20, 30 & 50 amp power. Two-lane launch ramp, dry boat storage and long-term parking. Register in the marina office. Groceries, restaurants, post office, doctor, liquor store. Downtown Olympia is within walking distance, as is the Farmers' Market.

Swantown Marina is quiet, spacious and well-maintained. In 1999 a boatyard opened at the south end of the marina, with 77-ton Travelift

haulout. Other boating related services are expected to be available.

Priest Point Park, at Priest Point, east side of Budd Inlet. Open summer and winter, day use only. Restrooms, no showers, no power. Anchor out only, well offshore due to shoaling. Park is 300 acres. Stretch of sandy beach, picnic tables and shelters, children's play equipment, trails. No camping.

Burfoot County Park, ½ mile south of Dofflemyer Point. This is a 60-acre county park, open all year, day use only. Restrooms, no showers, no power. Picnic tables and shelters, trails, play area. Anchoring or beaching only. Buoys mark an artificial reef for diving.

Boston Harbor. Use chart 18448. Boston Harbor is a halfmoon-shaped bay between Dofflemyer Point and Dover Point. Anchorage is possible, but much of the bay is taken up by the Boston Harbor Marina.

④ **Boston Harbor Marina,** 312 73rd Ave. NE, Olympia, WA 98506, (360)357-5670; fax (360)352-2816. Monitors VHF channel 16. Open all year, guest moorage, gasoline and diesel, CNG, 20 amp power, picnic area, restrooms, no showers. Easily seen from the mouth of Boston Harbor. The store has groceries and ice, beer and wine, fresh seafood, some marine supplies, boat rentals. *(Marina map page 32)*

Eld Inlet. Use chart 18448. Eld Inlet lies immediately west of Budd Inlet, and extends about 5 miles south from Cooper Point before it becomes Mud Bay (aptly named). Hold to a mid-channel course past

See area map page 30

The store at Boston Harbor Marina is to the right of this photo, but here are the launch ramp and the docks.

Reference only — not for navigation

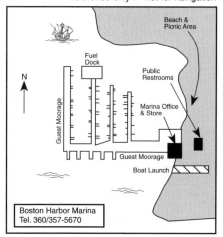

Boston Harbor Marina

Cooper Point, which has an extensive drying shoal northward from the point.

Eld Inlet has no marinas, but anchorage is good, mud bottom, along both shores. A shallow bay about a mile south of Flapjack Point includes Sam Devlin's boat building shop and an unused marine railway, as well as a launch ramp. Directly across the inlet is the waterfront activities center for The Evergreen State College. The center has a float, and buildings to store the canoes and other small craft used by the students. Despite considerable research, Contributing Editor Tom Kincaid reports that he is unable to confirm that swimsuit-optional bathing occurs at the site.

Frye Cove County Park, just north of Flapjack Point in Eld Inlet. Open all year for day use only, toilets, no other services. Anchoring or beaching only. The park has picnic shelters, barbecues, hiking trails.

Hope Island Marine State Park, junction of Totten Inlet and Pickering Passage. Use chart 18448. This is one of the newest parks in the state system, and is undeveloped. A resident caretaker lives on the island. The park has mooring buoys, and decent anchorage can be had in 5 fathoms or less on the east side. Good clamming on low tides. Other than trails through primeval woods, no facilities ashore. No fires permitted, pack out all garbage.

Totten Inlet. Use chart 18448. Enter Totten Inlet past Steamboat Island. Steamboat Island is connected to the mainland by a causeway from Carlyon Beach. Homes and a private marina are located on the island and mainland beach. The beach is marked by a quick flashing light. All of Totten Inlet is less than 10 fathoms deep. The inlet shoals to drying mud flats toward its south end, called Oyster Bay.

On the west side of Totten Inlet, about three miles southwest of Steamboat Island, is the entrance to **Skookum Inlet,** called by the locals "Little Skookum," to differentiate it from Hammersley Inlet, which they call "Big Skookum." Little Skookum is a pleasant exploration, but not navigable beyond Wildcat Harbor except by dinghy. Little Skookum is one of south Puget Sound's major oyster growing areas.

HAMMERSLY INLET AND SHELTON

Hammersley Inlet. Use chart 18457 (recommended); 18448. Hammersley Inlet extends westward about 6 miles to Oakland Bay and the city of **Shelton**. A shoal blocks the entire south side of the entrance to Hammersley Inlet. Enter past Point Hungerford, along the north shore. A beacon with a flashing red light marks Point Hungerford. The shoal has geoducks—Contributing Editor Tom Kincaid admits that he dug some there one day while he was aground. As chart 18457 shows, depths in Hammersley Inlet range from 10-30 feet. Currents flood in and ebb out. The strongest currents occur around Cape Horn, a sharp, constricted bend just inside the entrance.

Moorage is available at the Shelton Yacht Club, about a mile from town. Shelton is the site of major lumber and pulp mills, with acres of rafted logs in storage in front of the town. **Oakland Bay** becomes increasingly shallow north of Shelton, but is navigable at other than extreme low tide, and could offer anchorage on mud bottom.

⑯ **Port of Shelton,** West 410 Business Park Rd., Shelton, WA 98584, (360)426-1151. The marina is managed by the Shelton Yacht Club, (360)426-9476. Generally 15-20 slips are available for visiting boats of average size. No fuel. Least depth 10 feet, 30 amp power, portable toilet on the dock, pumpout, no showers. Groceries, restaurants, services are a mile away.

PEALE AND PICKERING PASSAGES AND CASE INLET

Pickering Passage. Use chart 18448. Pickering Passage extends northward from Totten Inlet past the west sides of Squaxin Island and Harstine Island. Mid-channel courses encounter no obstructions. **Peale Passage** extends along the east side of Squaxin Island, through shallow but passable depths. The **Squaxin Island State Park** is closed.

Harstine Island. Use chart 18448. Harstine Island is connected to the mainland at Graham Point by a bridge with a Mean High Water vertical clearance of 31 feet. Along the northwest shore of the island is **Jarrell Cove**, which contains both 43-acre Jarrell Cove State Marine Park and the Jarrell's Cove Marina.

The small marina between Jarrell Cove and Dougall Point is private, and serves Harstine Island residents.

⑤ **Jarrell's Cove Marina,** E. 220 Wilson Rd., Harstine Island, Shelton, WA 98584, (800)362-8823, (360)426-8823; fax (360) 432-8494. Use chart 18448. The fuel dock has diesel, gasoline and propane. Facilities include 30 amp power, restrooms, showers, laundry, pumpout, portapotty dump, 200 feet of guest moorage. Get a slip assignment from the fuel dock before landing, even for a short stay. This is a large, well-maintained marina with many facilities. The store has groceries, ice, some marine hardware, books, fishing licenses. Open 7 days a week Memorial Day to Labor Day, closed Monday through Thursday in winter. Owners: Gary and Lorna Hink.

⑥ **Jarrell Cove Marine State Park,** northwest end of Harstine Island. Open all year. This is a large, attractive park with 682 feet of dock space, 14 mooring buoys, restrooms, showers, pumpout, portapotty dump, picnic shelters, standard campsites. Mooring buoys have minimum 10 feet of water at all times, but the inner end dock can rest on mud bottom on minus tides. We are assured that the outer end has sufficient mooring depths on all tides. Fishing, clamming, hiking, birdwatching.

Caution. Favor the north shore when entering Jarrell Cove. A spit extends across the mouth from the point on the south side of the entrance. Boats go aground on low tides.

McLane Cove, located across Pickering Passage from Jarrell Cove, is protected, quiet, and lined with forest. Anchorage is in 10 to 20 feet. It is a peaceful alternative to the more popular Jarrell Cove.

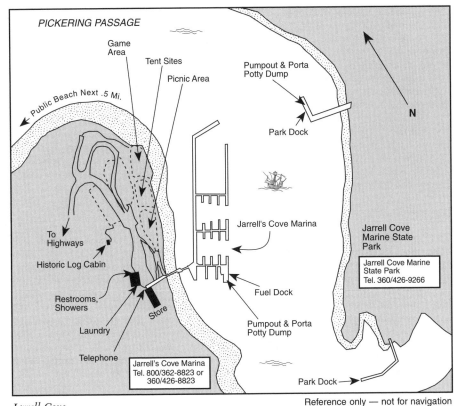

PICKERING PASSAGE

Game Area

Tent Sites

Picnic Area

Public Beach Next .5 Mi.

Pumpout & Porta Potty Dump

Park Dock

N

To Highways

Historic Log Cabin

Jarrell's Cove Marina

Jarrell Cove Marine State Park

Jarrell Cove Marine State Park Tel. 360/426-9266

Restrooms, Showers

Store

Fuel Dock

Laundry

Pumpout & Porta Potty Dump

Telephone

Jarrell's Cove Marina Tel. 800/362-8823 or 360/426-8823

Park Dock

Jarrell Cove

Reference only — not for navigation

Stretch Island. Use chart 18448. Stretch Island has good anchorage in the bay that lies south of the bridge to the mainland. The bridge has a 14-foot vertical clearance. The channel under the bridge dries at low tide.

Stretch Point Marine State Park, Stretch Island. Open all year, accessible only by boat. No power, water, restrooms or showers. Day use only, with 5 buoys for overnight mooring. Buoys are close to shore because of a steep dropoff. Swimming and diving, oysters and mussels, smooth sand beach. Rustic shelters have been built on shore, but no camping is allowed. Pack out all garbage.

Reach Island. Use chart 18448. The southern end of Reach Island is **Fair Harbor**, home of Fair Harbor Marina. The bay has limited anchorage. The channel north of the marina, under a bridge with a vertical clearance of 16 feet, goes dry on a minus tide.

⑦ **Fair Harbor Marina,** P.O. Box 160, E. 5050 Grapeview Loop Rd., Grapeview, WA 98546, (360)426-4028. Open 7 days a week in the summer, call for hours in the winter. Gasoline only at the fuel dock, 350 feet of guest moorage, 30 amp power. A comfortable marina in a lovely setting, owned and operated by Susan and Vern Nelson. Best to call ahead for moorage space. Minor repairs and haulout. Kerosene, alcohol, propane, charts, hardware, tackle & bait, groceries, picnic areas. Excellent gift shop—Susan really knows how to buy. If you wish to golf at Lakeland golf course or visit the Maritime Museum of Puget Sound, both nearby, you must call ahead to arrange transportation.

Allyn. Allyn, located near the head of Case Inlet, has a launch ramp and limited moorage on a float at the end of a long pier. Allyn is surrounded by shoal water, but can be approached by holding a midchannel course until opposite the pier, then turning in.

⑧ **Port of Allyn,** P.O. Box 1, Foot of Drum St., Allyn, WA, 98524, (360)275-2192. Open all year, launch ramp, 10 slips, 20 & 30 amp power, restrooms, no showers, no fuel. Shallow; no sailboats or large boats on low tides. Services and restaurants nearby.

Rocky Bay. Rocky Bay offers some protection for anchoring, particularly behind a small sandspit extending from Windy Bluff. Enter with caution, and round the little rocky islet off the end of the spit before circling in to anchor.

Vaughn Bay. Use chart 18448. Vaughn Bay can be entered at half tide or better. Take a mid-channel course past the end of the spit, then turn to parallel the spit until safe anchoring depths are found near the head of the bay. Water skiers and jet-ski enthusiasts can be disruptive during the day, but they quit at sundown and leave the bay peaceful at night. The small town of Vaughn on the north shore has a launch ramp and some supplies.

Herron Island. Herron Island is all privately owned, with a ferry to the mainland.

McMicken Island Marine State Park, on Case Inlet, off the east side of Harstine Island, (360)426-9226. Use chart 18448. Open all year, 5 mooring buoys, toilets, but no power,

water or showers. Mooring buoys lie on the north and south sides of McMicken Island. There's plenty of room to anchor on either side, although when we tried to anchor on the west side of the spit between McMicken Island and Harstine Island, the anchor seemed to bump along on rock and wouldn't bite. Be sure your anchor is well set. McMicken Island is accessible by boat only, except on low tides, when you can cross to Harstine Island by foot. You'll find primitive trails, but watch for poison oak. No overnight camping. An artificial reef is north of the island. Fishing, good clamming, camping, swimming. Do not pass east of McMicken Island because of a drying spit and an uncharted rock (we touched there once, in a boat that drew less than 3 feet).

Harstine Island State Park, east shore of Harstine Island. This park lies across the bay from McMicken Island. Open all year, day use only, no power, water or toilets. Hiking trail. At low tide you can cross to McMicken Island State Park. Anchoring only. Clamming and beachcombing.

⑨ **Joemma State Park,** formerly Robert F. Kennedy State Park, southeast Case Inlet, just north of Whiteman Cove. Summer only, closed October through April. The park has 500 feet of dock space, 5 mooring buoys, boat launch, new restrooms, picnic areas, primitive campsites, no power, no showers. This is the most recent addition to the state marine parks system, and includes a Cascadia Marine Trail campsite. The docks are excellent, with good camp and picnic sites (including a covered shelter) on shore. When we visited in mid-spring, Dungeness crabbing was exceptional, right at the dock. Rings only, no pots at that time. The docks are exposed to southeast storms.

DRAYTON PASSAGE, PITT PASSAGE, BALCH PASSAGE

Anderson Island. Use chart 18448. Taylor Bay offers limited anchorage near the entrance, but is exposed to southerlies. **Oro Bay** has a shallow entrance, but limited good anchorage is available once inside. Tacoma Yacht Club and Bremerton Yacht Club have outstations in Oro Bay. **Amsterdam Bay** is very shallow. Safe anchoring depths are right in the middle, when that spot is not already occupied by local residents' boats. The shores are rural and picturesque. If low tide isn't too low, it's a good place to spend the night. Observe a 5 mph or lower no-wake speed to prevent damage along the shoreline. **Eagle Island Marine State Park,** off the north shore of Anderson Island, has mooring buoys.

Eagle Island Marine State Park, Balch Passage, between Anderson Island and McNeil Island. Use chart 18448. Open all year, day use only, 3 mooring buoys, no toilets, power or water. Boat access only. Avoid the reef, marked by a buoy, off the west side of the island. Fishing and clamming. Watch for poi-

See area map page 30

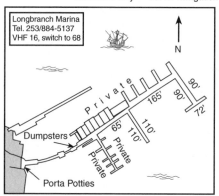

Reference only — not for navigation

Longbranch Marina
Tel. 253/884-5137
VHF 16, switch to 68

N

Private

90'
165'
90'
72'
65'
110'
110'
Dumpsters
Private
Private
Porta Potties

Longbranch Marina

son oak on the island. No camping or fires, no garbage collection.

Filucy Bay. Use chart 18448. Filucy Bay is a popular destination and a fine anchorage. You can anchor inside the spit to the south of the entrance. The north section of Filucy Bay is wooded, quiet, and protected, with good bottom. The Longbranch Marina welcomes visiting boaters. The store across the road from the docks remains open, but is actively for sale.

⑩ **Longbranch Improvement Club Marina,** P.O. Box 111, Longbranch, WA, 98349, (253)884-5137. Monitors VHF channel 16, switch to 68. A popular South Sound stopover. Open all year, but hours vary in winter. Has 45 slips plus 800 feet of side-tie dock space for guest moorage. First-come, first-served, no reservations taken. The marina has 30 amp power, portable toilets only, no showers.

Usually, there is no charge for 2-hour day moorage, but if day moorage boats are taking space from incoming overnight boats they may be asked to pay a fee or move along. Anchorage is available in the sheltered bay.

Mechanic and divers on call. Dances are held Memorial Day and Labor Day at the Longbranch Improvement Club; and usually are sold out. Great views of Mt. Rainier. *(Marina map left)*

Pitt Passage. Use chart 18445sc (highly recommended), or 18448. Pitt Passage is a winding, shallow passage between McNeil Island and the mainland. Because the passage is shoal, many skippers avoid it. Safe passages, however, can be made between tiny Pitt Island and McNeil Island. The water west of Pitt Island is shoal.

If you are coming from the south (such as from Longbranch), set a course to pass between the red nun buoy 6 and the beacon close to shore. Favoring the McNeil Island shore, run north until you are abeam the red daybeacon 4, off the north tip of Pitt Island. Then turn westward to leave Wyckoff Shoal buoy 3 and Wyckoff Shoal buoy 1 to starboard. We would give both Wyckoff Shoal buoys a good offing.

McNeil Island is a major state prison. Boaters are asked to maintain a 100-yard clearance from its shores. *Don't pick up hitchhikers.*

CARR INLET

Mayo Cove. Use chart 18448. Mayo Cove has Penrose Point State Park on its eastern shore, and the town of Lakebay, complete with a marina, at the head of the bay. The bay is shallow, and drying shoals on either side require a mid-channel approach, but Mayo Cove is very pretty and worth the visit. For exploring, take the dinghy up the inlet that leads to Bay Lake.

⑪ **Penrose Point Marine State Park,** west shore of Carr Inlet at Mayo Cove, (253)884-2514. Summers, open for mooring and camping 7 days; winters day use only, except overnight mooring weekends and holidays. Dock has 304 feet of side-tie space, 8 mooring buoys and a mooring float. The float grounds on lower tides. This is a large and popular park, and an excellent destination in South Sound. Facilities include picnic sites, restrooms, showers, pumpout, portapotty dump and showers. No power. Standard and primitive campsites, hiking trails, nature trail, clamming, swimming, fishing. At low tide enter the cove with care.

⑫ **Lakebay Marina,** 15 Lorenz Road K.P.S., Lakebay, WA 98349, (253)884-3350. Open all year, gasoline at fuel dock, 15 amp power, propane available, 10 slips guest moorage, asphalt launch ramp, long term parking, fishing supplies, restrooms, no showers. You may have to call ahead for services in the winter. Maximum boat length 50 feet, draft 6 feet. Groceries, ice, beer.

Von Geldern Cove. Use chart 18448. Von Geldern Cove is a shallow bay, but anchorage is possible near the entrance, although exposed to northerly winds. Most of the shoreline is residential. The town of Home, with a launch ramp, has some supplies. Take the dinghy under the bridge at the head of the bay and explore the creek until it's too shallow.

Glen Cove is protected by a spit, but is very shallow and not recommended for overnight anchorage.

Rosedale is a small community tucked in behind **Raft Island**. Use chart 18448. Good anchorage. Enter the bay to the north of Raft Island, since a causeway connects the island to the mainland across the very shoal south side.

Cutts Island Marine State Park. Open all year, day use only and overnight moorage, 9 mooring buoys. Accessible by boat only. Toilets, but no power or water. No camping or fires allowed. Underwater marine park. Easy row to Kopachuck Marine State Park. Cutts Island is connected to Raft Island by a drying shoal. Watch your depths if you try to

The new covered area (left side of photo) and excellent docks make Longbranch a popular stop.

cross between Cutts Island and Raft Island. We started, but the bottom got so close we could distinguish between boy clams and girl clams, and went back. We are told that in bygone days Cutts Island was an Indian burial ground, and its local name is Dead Man's Island.

Kopachuck Marine State Park, 2 miles north of Fox Island, just north of Horsehead Bay, (253)265-3606. Open all year for day use, overnight camping and mooring. Two mooring buoys, restrooms, showers. Good bottom for anchoring if buoys are occupied, but unprotected. Underwater park with artificial reef for scuba diving. Kitchen shelters, picnic sites. Standard and primitive campsites, including a Cascadia Marine Trail campsite. Playground, short trail. Clamming, fishing. Swimming in shallow water off the beach area.

Horsehead Bay. Use chart 18448. Horsehead Bay is an excellent anchorage, surrounded by fine homes. A launch ramp is near the harbor entrance. On one visit we tried several times to anchor just inside the gravel spit that separates Horsehead Bay from Carr Inlet, but couldn't get the anchor to bite. A short distance inside the bay brought excellent holding ground.

Fox Island. Use chart 18448. Fox Island is connected to the mainland by a bridge with a 31-foot vertical clearance across Hale Passage. Good anchorage can be found behind **Tanglewood Island**, which has a pavilion used by yacht clubs and other groups for special occasions. Residents of Fox Island are very protective of their privacy, so it would be a good idea to stay aboard until invited ashore.

Wollochet Bay. Use chart 18448. Wollochet Bay winds a couple of miles into the mainland off Hale Passage. The shores of the bay are lined with homes, many with mooring buoys out front, but good anchorage can be found. The mouth of the bay is open to southerly winds. Inside, the waters are protected. Tacoma Yacht Club has an outstation near the head of the bay.

Ketron Island is privately owned, and has a ferry service to Steilacoom.

HENDERSON INLET, NISQUALLY, STEILACOOM, TACOMA NARROWS

Henderson Inlet. Use chart 18448. Henderson Inlet extends about 5 miles south from Itsami Ledge. The inlet has been the site of major logging operations over the years, and log rafts are still stored along the west side. Anchorage is good along about half of the inlet before it becomes too shallow, near the entrance to Woodward Creek.

⑬ **Zittel's Marina, Inc.,** 9144 Gallea St. NE, Olympia, WA 98506, (360)459-1950. Open all year, hours may vary in the winter. Gasoline and diesel at fuel dock. Guest moorage in unoccupied slips when available (don't count on availability), 20 & 30 amp power, restrooms, no showers. Haulout and repairs available, store with limited marine supplies, groceries, stove alcohol, bait and tackle.

Johnson Point is a popular salmon fishing area. Two launch ramps are located at Johnson Point, but no facilities for visiting boaters.

Tolmie Marine State Park, 8 miles northeast of Olympia. Open all year for day use and overnight moorage, except closed Mondays and Tuesdays for day use in winter. Five mooring buoys, restrooms, showers, but no power. Buoys lie well offshore; beach and shallows extend out some distance. The underwater park for scuba diving includes sunken wooden barges. Hiking trails, picnic sites with kitchens. Nice sandy beach. The park includes a small saltwater lagoon marsh area with interesting wildlife. No camping.

Nisqually Reach. Use chart 18448. Nisqually Reach is the body of water south of Anderson Island to the mainland. It is a navigable channel marked by buoys and the extensive mudflats of the Nisqually River delta. The delta area is a wildlife refuge, and is accessible by boat only at half tide or better, by way of the Luhrs Beach launch ramp near Nisqually Head. Contributing Editor Tom Kincaid has entered the river itself by dinghy, but from the water side the entrance is hard to spot.

Steilacoom. Use chart 18448. Steilacoom Marina has very limited moorage. A picnic area is on a small pebble beach nearby. Steilacoom has a launch ramp, float and fishing pier. Steilacoom, incorporated in 1854, is the oldest incorporated town in Washington. If you'd like to experience a real, old-time soda fountain, Bair Drug and Hardware, a historical delight with its ancient fixtures, tables, chairs and stools, is a short distance away. Good for lunch, too. A museum, restaurant and other services are nearby.

⑭ **Steilacoom Marina,** P.O. Box 88876, 402 First Street, Steilacoom, WA 98388, (253)582-2600. Open all year, 100 feet of guest moorage, 20 amp power, restrooms, portapotty dump. Convenience store has a little bit of everything. Saltars Point Park, with its fine gravel beach, is right next door.

Tacoma Narrows. Use chart 18474; 18448. All of the water in southern Puget Sound flows through Tacoma Narrows, with 3-4 knot currents common. At the south end of the Narrows on the east side is Day Island, home to the Day Island Yacht Club, Narrows Marina, and Day Island Marina. The yacht club, which recently dredged its moorage, welcomes members of reciprocal yacht clubs. The Tacoma Narrows Bridge, more than a mile long and 180 feet above the water, is one of the world's longest suspension bridges.

   If you go through the Tacoma Narrows against the current, you can find opposite-flowing current along the sides.

⑮ **Narrows Marina Tackle & Marine,** 9007 S. 19th St., Tacoma, WA 98466, (253)564-4222. Open all year, gasoline and diesel fuel. No guest moorage. Has restrooms, no showers. Concrete launch ramp, long term parking, nautical charts, electronics, hardware, tackle and bait. This is a large, fishing and marine oriented stop.

Titlow Park, Tacoma Narrows Waterway. Located on the Tacoma side, about 1 mile south of the Tacoma Narrows Bridge. Open all year, mooring buoys, park with swimming pool, volleyball, and tennis courts. Titlow Park is a state-designated marine preserve, with excellent diving.

Penrose Point State Park has a good dock and excellent facilities ashore.

Central Puget Sound

Gig Harbor • Tacoma • Vashon Island • Bremerton • Poulsbo
Bainbridge Island • Seattle

Gig Harbor. These youngsters were enjoying ice cream in the shade one warm afternoon.

Charts

18441	Puget Sound – Northern Part (1:80,000)
18445sc	FOLIO SMALL-CRAFT Puget Sound-Possession Sound to Olympia including Hood Canal
18446	Puget Sound – Apple Cove Pt. to Keyport (1:25,000) & Agate Passage (1:10,000)
18447sc	FOLIO SMALL-CRAFT Lake Washington Ship Canal (1:10,000) & Lk. Washington (1:25,000)
18448	Puget Sound – Southern Portion (1:80,000)
18449	Puget Sound – Seattle to Bremerton (1:25,000)
18453	Tacoma Harbor (1:15,000)
18474	Puget Sound – Shilshole Bay to Commencement Bay (1:40,000)

GIG HARBOR

Gig Harbor. Use chart 18474; 18445sc; 18448. Gig Harbor is one of the most perfectly protected harbors in all of Puget Sound, and one of the most charming towns. The south shore is lined with moorages for substantial commercial fish boat and pleasure boat fleets. The entrance to Gig Harbor is narrow, especially at low tide. Maintain a mid-channel course around the end of the spit.

Gig Harbor offers all services to boaters, from overnight moorage to fuel to major repairs and haulouts. You can anchor in 5-7 fathoms throughout most of the bay, although it shoals close to both shores and toward the head of the bay. Weed on the bottom can foul some anchors.

The City of Gig Harbor maintains Jerisich Park with its long moorage float.

We enjoy walking up and down Gig Harbor's village-like commercial streets. The shops, galleries and antiquing are excellent, and the architecture turn-of-the-century. At least two shops serve enormous hard ice cream cones, and have chairs out front where you can enjoy your treat in the shade. You'll find several good restaurants, from casual to elegant. On the casual side, the Tides Tavern, a short distance inside the mouth of the bay, is a perennial favorite. If you are lucky, you'll find room to tie the boat at their private dock. More likely, you'll take the dinghy over or approach by land.

For a great view of Gig Harbor and Mt. Rainier, the local Lions Club built an observation area called the Finholm View Climb. The stairway is at the head of the bay, across

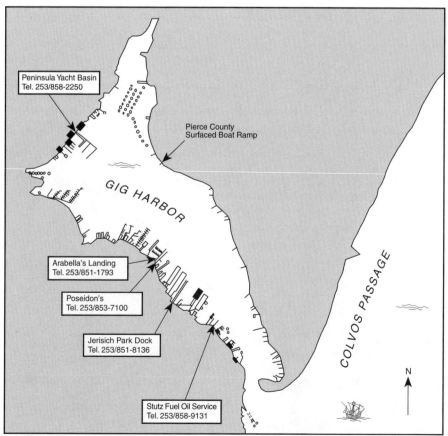

Gig Harbor

Peninsula Yacht Basin
Tel. 253/858-2250

Pierce County
Surfaced Boat Ramp

GIG HARBOR

COLVOS PASSAGE

Arabella's Landing
Tel. 253/851-1793

Poseidon's
Tel. 253/853-7100

Jerisich Park Dock
Tel. 253/851-8136

Stutz Fuel Oil Service
Tel. 253/858-9131

N

Reference only — not for navigation

At low tide the entry to Gig Harbor is narrow, but easily run.

the street from the Shorelines Restaurant.

Book lovers owe themselves a visit to Mostly Books in Gig Harbor, a delightful small town bookstore with an unusually complete nautical section. Jo Graffe is the owner.

Speed limit: A no-wake speed of 5 MPH or less is enforced within Gig Harbor and 200 feet outside the entrance.

① **Arabella's Landing,** 3323 Harbor View Dr., Gig Harbor, WA 98332, (253) 851-1793. Open all year, approximately 1000 feet of guest moorage and shared slips, 30 & 50 amp power, restrooms, showers, laundry, secured gate and pumpout. Stan and Judy Stearns developed this classy marina, located a short distance past the city dock. They have a well-trained crew to help with landings and make life pleasant.

The marina can accommodate boats larger than 100 feet. It has excellent concrete docks, impeccable lawns, lush flower gardens, brick walkways, complete wheelchair access, and a clubhouse and lounge for group gatherings. The moorage fee includes power and showers. Reservations recommended. The Bayview Marina, just east of Arabella's Landing, is under the same ownership.

① **Jerisich Park,** 3211 Harborview Dr., Gig Harbor, WA 98332, (253)851-8136, or view at www.ci.gig-harbor.wa.us. Open all year, 400 feet of dock space. This is a popular and attractive public dock and park, located just west of the Tides Tavern on the downtown side of Gig Harbor. All new docks, with a dinghy dock near shore on the west side. A pumpout is at the outer end of the dock. The pumpout is closed from Dec. 1 through April 1. Restaurants, services, groceries, restrooms,

portapotty dump all within walking distance. Check your tide table; close to shore you could be left dry at low tide.

① **Peninsula Yacht Basin,** 8913 N Harborview Drive, Gig Harbor 98335, (253)858-2250. Open all year, guest moorage in unoccupied slips as available. Maximum boat length 80 feet, 10 foot depth at zero tide, 30 amp power, restrooms, showers. Located on the north shore of Gig Harbor, next to Shoreline Restaurant. Reciprocal privileges with Gig Harbor Yacht Club.

① **Poseidon's,** 3313 Harborview Dr., Gig Harbor, WA 98332, (253)853-7100; fax (253)853-3313. Open all year with gasoline & diesel fuel, 250 feet side-tie moorage, 30 & 50 amp power, restrooms, bait, ice, tackle, casual restaurant, lounge with Internet access, portapotty dump, 3 no-charge pumpouts. The facility is fully wheelchair accessible.

Poseidon's is a brand-new development on the south shore of Gig Harbor, a short distance beyond the Jerisich Park dock. We toured the property in November, after the fuel dock was running but before other services were completed, and it's first-class in every way. They plan to have pizza, pasta and other casual foods in their deli/dining area, along with beer and wine. They also plan to make fresh cinnamon buns every morning. The back side of the float nearest shore is reserved for dinghies. The portapotty dump and pumpouts are on the fuel dock. No charge for their use. The lounge area is equipped with computer stations (bring your own laptop) and super-fast T-1 telephone lines for Internet access and e-mail.

① **Stutz Fuel Oil,** 3003 Harborview Dr., Gig Harbor, WA 98335, 253-858-9131. Open all

year with gasoline & diesel fuel, kerosene by the pail. Located next to the Tides Tavern. Closed Sundays. If the dock is unattended, walk up the ramp to the office. If the gate on the pier is locked, they're closed. The fuel pump on the pier is a dummy, simply to show that this is the fuel dock. But it doesn't pump a drop.

TACOMA AREA

Point Defiance. Use chart 18453; 18474; 18448. Point Defiance marks the northern end of Tacoma Narrows, and is noted for swirling currents and excellent salmon fishing. The entire point is a major Tacoma park, complete with trails, a zoo, aquarium, gardens, sports facilities and picnic areas. A number of mooring buoys are placed along the shore between the point and Ruston.

Ruston is about 2 miles east of Point Defiance. This is the Tacoma terminus of the ferry to Vashon Island. The smelter slag breakwater protects the Tacoma Yacht Club's docks (members of reciprocal yacht clubs welcome) and Breakwater Marina's moorage. The

Point Defiance Boathouse Marina and a new Anthony's Home Port restaurant are west of the ferry dock. A large launch ramp operated by the Park Department is east of the ferry dock. Long-term tow vehicle and trailer storage is available a couple of blocks up the hill from the launch ramp. Call (253)591-5325.

② **Breakwater Marina,** 5603 N. Waterfront Drive, Tacoma, WA 98407, (253)752-6663; fax (253)752-8291. Open all year, gasoline & diesel fuel, stove alcohol, propane, 15 & 30 amp power, restrooms, showers, laundry, pumpout station. Guest moorage is in unoccupied slips only, so call ahead for availability. Complete repairs available. They have a tidal grid that accommodates boats to 50 feet in length. *(Marina map page 39)*

② **Point Defiance Boathouse Marina,** 5912 N. Waterfront Drive, Tacoma, WA 98407, (253)591-5325. Open 7 days a week all year except Thanksgiving and Christmas. Gasoline and pre-mix available, mooring buoys nearby. Restrooms, pumpout, no

Reference only — not for navigation

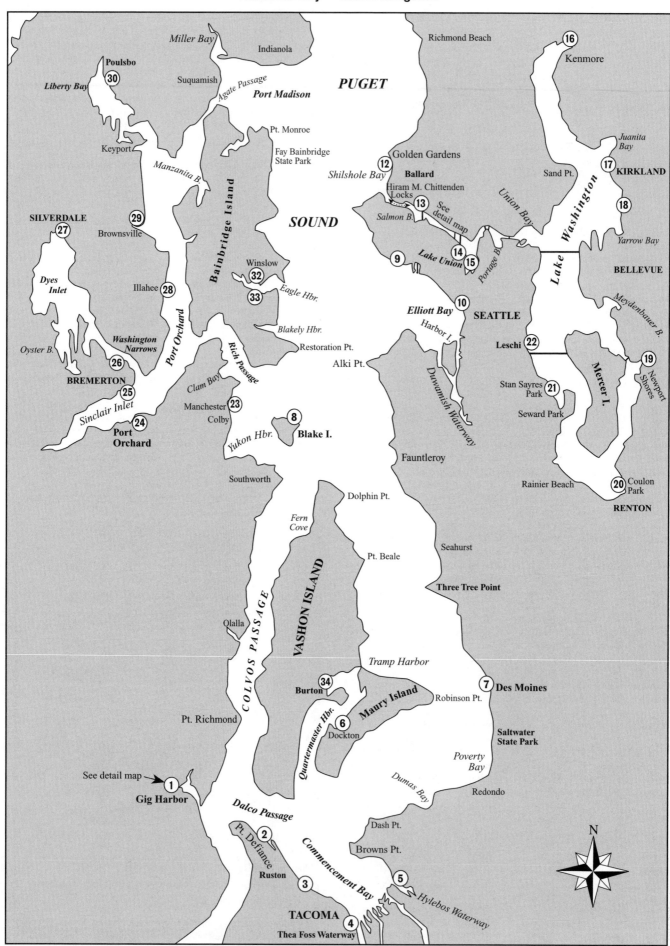

Miller Bay
Indianola
Richmond Beach
16 Kenmore
Poulsbo
30
Liberty Bay
Suquamish
Agate Passage
PUGET
Juanita Bay
Keyport
Port Madison
17 **KIRKLAND**
Manzanita B.
Pt. Monroe
Fay Bainbridge
State Park
Golden Gardens
12
Sand Pt.
18
29
Ballard
SILVERDALE
Shilshole Bay
Hiram M. Chittenden
Union Bay
27
Brownsville
Locks
13
See
Yarrow Bay
*Dyes
Inlet*
Illahee
28
Salmon B.
detail map
9
14
BELLEVUE
*Washington
Narrows*
Winslow
32
Lake Union
15
Portage B.
Oyster B.
33
Eagle Hbr.
Meydenbauer B.
26
BREMERTON
Blakely Hbr.
Elliott Bay
10
SEATTLE
25
Restoration Pt.
Harbor I.
Leschi
22
19
Sinclair Inlet
Alki Pt.
*Newport
Shores*
24
**Port
Orchard**
Clam Bay
Manchester
Colby
23
Stan Sayres
Park
21
Mercer I.
Rich Passage
Duwamish Waterway
Seward Park
Yukon Hbr.
8
Blake I.
Fauntleroy
Rainier Beach
20 Coulon
Park
Southworth
Dolphin Pt.
RENTON
*Fern
Cove*
Seahurst
Pt. Beale
Three Tree Point
VASHON ISLAND
Olalla
Tramp Harbor
34
Burton
7 **Des Moines**
Robinson Pt.
6
Maury Island
**Saltwater
State Park**
Pt. Richmond
Dockton
*Poverty
Bay*
See detail map
1
Dumas Bay
Redondo
Gig Harbor
Dalco Passage
Dash Pt.
2
Pt. Defiance
Commencement Bay
Browns Pt.
Ruston
5
3
Hylebos Waterway
TACOMA
4
Thea Foss Waterway

PUGET

SOUND

COLVOS PASSAGE

Quartermaster Hbr.

N

power or showers. Bait, tackle, snacks, souvenirs and gift items at Point Defiance Boathouse Tackle Shop. Public fishing pier. Within walking distance to the Point Defiance Zoo and Aquarium. Bus service to greater Tacoma. This is primarily a facility for launching and recovering small boats stored in their extensive boathouse.

THE SOUTHERN SHORELINE of Commencement Bay is mostly parks, interspersed with buildings, housing, restaurants and other facilities. Numerous mooring buoys, maintained by the Metropolitan Park District, are available for overnight stays. At least two restaurants provide moorage for their patrons, and moorage is available at Old Town dock. Following this shoreline southeastward leads into the **Thea Foss Waterway** (formerly City Waterway) which is lined with moorages and boating related businesses. Totem Marina has fuel and some moorage, and the public dock at 15th Street has 200 feet of visitor moorage, most of it reserved for seaplanes. Picks Cove, on the north side of the waterway next to the new bridge, has visitor moorage, haulout and repairs.

It's a bit of a walk, but we recommend a visit to downtown Tacoma. The magnificent Union Station on Pacific Avenue has been rebuilt as the Federal Courthouse, and has exquisite displays of Dale Chihuly glass sculpture. Next door, in a new building that shares Union Station's architecture, the Washington State History Museum, opened in 1997, is outstanding. Allow at least 2 hours to see the museum; 3 or 4 hours would be better. Excellent for families.

In 2000, construction of a new glass museum is scheduled to begin in the same Union Station complex, and later, the Tacoma Art Museum is to move to a new building at the north edge of that complex. Across Pacific Avenue, the University of Washington's Tacoma Campus is developing. Downtown Tacoma is very different from other Puget Sound cities. It's worth experiencing.

The Port of Tacoma occupies much of the delta land at the mouth of the Puyallup River, which is navigable by skiff as far as Sumner.

③ **Old Town Dock,** next to Commencement Park, Tacoma. Open all year, ample dock space, mooring buoys. Public parks-style restroom, no showers. No power on the dock. This is a high quality pier with mooring floats attached. The Old Town district of Tacoma, with its interesting shops and eateries, is just up the way. The Ocean Fish Co., a busy fish market with chowder and salads to go, is at head of the pier. The history of old Tacoma is displayed on panels. A short distance away a large sundial sculpture can be seen from the water.

④ **Totem Marina,** 821 Dock St., Tacoma, WA 98402, (253)272-4404. Unoccupied slips used for guest moorage when available. Gasoline and diesel fuel, restrooms, showers, laundry, pumpout, 20 & 30 amp power. Haulout and dry storage. Walk to downtown Tacoma and the Tacoma Dome.

④ **15th Street Dock,** City of Tacoma Public Works, 15th and Dock Street, Thea Foss Waterway,

Thea Foss Waterway, Tacoma. The Tacoma Dome is in the background.

Tacoma, WA 98409. Open all year, 200 feet of dock space, no power, water or restrooms. The dock is a designated float plane port. Boats can use it only as room is available. Float planes have priority. Tie up on the shorter part of float located south of gangway. Watch the depth at zero tide or lower.

④ **Picks Cove Marine Center,** 1940 East D St., Tacoma, WA 98421, (253)572-3625; (800) 663-3625; fax (253)572-0503, www.pickscove.com. Open all year,

guest moorage to 45 feet in unoccupied slips, call for availability. Restrooms & showers. All new docks, pumpout station, 35-ton Travelift, boatyard, marine supplies and parts. This is the closest marina to the Tacoma Dome (6 blocks). They have a well-stocked marine store, boat sales, and good-size yard for repairs.

Hylebos Waterway. The Hylebos Waterway follows the north shore of Commencement Bay, and includes a number of moorages, boat

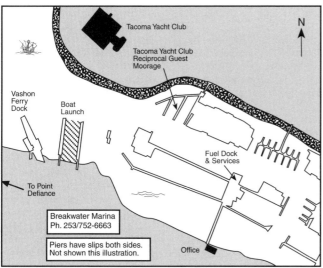

Breakwater Marina

Reference only — not for navigation

See area map page 38

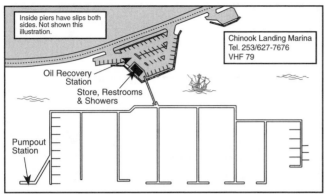

Inside piers have slips both sides. Not shown this illustration.

Chinook Landing Marina
Tel. 253/627-7676
VHF 79

Oil Recovery Station

Store, Restrooms & Showers

Pumpout Station

Chinook Landing Marina

Reference only — not for navigation

builders, and boat service businesses. Along the north shore, a mile or so in from Browns Point, the Tyee Marina (no facilities for visiting boats) is tucked in behind a breakwater made of derelict boats and concrete barges. Entry to the marina is at the east end between two of the derelicts, one named *Talitiga,* which is tied to a round red buoy, and a concrete barge tied to a white buoy. Guest moorage is available at the Chinook Landing Marina farther up the waterway.

Dockton has a large play and picnic area.

Lots of dock space at Dockton.

⑤ **Chinook Landing Marina**, 3702 Marine View Drive #100, Tacoma, WA 98422, (253)627-7676; fax (253) 383-2823. Monitors VHF channel 79. Open all year, guest moorage available. This is an excellent facility, with 8-foot depth at zero tide, 30 & 50 amp power, restrooms, showers, laundry, pumpout, 24-hour security, and a small convenience store. Larger boats should call ahead for availability. *(Marina map above)*

Browns Point Park, Use chart 18453; 18474; 18448. Browns Point, Tacoma, WA. Open all year, day use only and overnight mooring. Has 3 mooring buoys, picnic tables and a swimming beach. The lighthouse is the focal point.

VASHON ISLAND, COLVOS PASSAGE, EAST PASSAGE, DES MOINES, BLAKE ISLAND

Colvos Passage. Use chart 18474; 18448. The current always flows north in Colvos Passage, so if you are heading north in an flood tide it is a good choice. Colvos Passage offers little to entice a boater to stop, although Contributing Editor Tom Kincaid has anchored off Olalla and dinghied in to the little store for a snack.

Harper State Park, 1.5 miles west of the ferry landing at Southworth. Open all year, day use only. Anchoring only. The gravel launch ramp is usable at high tide only, but is the closest launch to Blake Island, 1 mile away.

Quartermaster Harbor. Use chart 18474; 18448. Quartermaster Harbor indents the south end of Vashon Island for about 4 miles. It is protected on the east by Maury Island, which connects to Vashon Island by a narrow spit of land. Dockton Park is a popular destination.

Anchorage is good throughout most of Quartermaster Harbor, including the village of Burton, beyond the Burton Peninsula. Anchorage at Burton is well-protected with excellent holding, on an unusually sticky mud bottom. Be prepared to spend extra time cleaning the anchor and chain. The Quartermaster Yacht Club (members of reciprocal clubs welcomed) is at Burton, as is the Quartermaster Marina, which now takes guest boats. The village of Burton has a well-stocked convenience store and several other small shops. The Back Bay Inn B&B is reported to have outstanding dining. A taxi is on Vashon Island, and buses go to Tacoma and Seattle.

㉞ **Quartermaster Marina,** PO Box 97, Burton, WA 98103, (206)463-3624. Open all year, 44-foot and 50-foot slips, plus side-tie moorage, 30 & 50 amp power, garbage drop and recycling, best to call for moorage reservations.

Least depth is 8 feet on a 3-foot minus tide. Haulout to 28 feet at the marina, to 45 feet next door. Hull & mechanical repairs are available. No fuel, but propane is available nearby.

⑥ **Dockton Park,** P.O. Box 11, Vashon, WA 98070, (206)463-2947. Open all year, concrete launch ramp, 58 guest slips, rafting OK, restrooms, showers, pumpout and portapotty dump (March through October only), no power, no garbage pick-up, no services within walking distance. Dockton is a popular 23-acre park on the west side of Maury Island, in Quartermaster Harbor. The park has a launch ramp, play equipment, trails, bandstand, firepits, picnic tables and a picnic shelter with barbecues inside. The picnic shelter can be reserved by calling (206)296-4287. Excellent destination.

Anchoring note: We have heard occasional reports of anchor dragging north of the Dockton Park docks, so we tested for ourselves. The reports have merit: We found only fair to poor holding. If you anchor there, be sure of your set. *(Marina map page 41)*

East Passage. Use chart 18474; 18448. East Passage lies between Vashon Island and the mainland. Most large ships bound to or from Tacoma or Olympia use this route. Tidal currents normally are a little stronger in East Passage than in Colvos Passage on the west side of Vashon Island, so boaters use East Passage when running with the current, and Colvos Passage when bucking the current.

Dash Point State Park, 5 miles northeast of Tacoma, (253) 593-2206. Use chart 18474; 18448. Open all year, mooring buoys, restrooms, showers, no power. Sandy beach, standard, utility and primitive campsites and swimming. Fishing from the public fishing pier.

Redondo has an excellent launch ramp, complete with a float.

Saltwater Marine State Park, 2 miles south of Des Moines, (206)764-4128. Open all year, 2 mooring buoys, overnight camping. Restrooms, showers, no power. This park emphasizes scuba diving, and has an outside shower for scuba rinse-off. Great sand bottom swimming beach. The mooring buoys are exposed to southerly

See area map page 38

winds. Vault toilets. Primitive campsites. Picnic tables and shelters, kitchen shelter, children's play equipment. Seasonal concession stand.

Point Robinson. Use chart 18474; 18448. Point Robinson is surrounded by a county park that can be approached by dinghy. The lighthouse is beautiful and the park has a nice beach, but no other facilities for boaters.

Tramp Harbor, where Vashon Island joins with Maury Island, offers convenient anchoring depths, but only minimal protection from winds, particularly from the north. It is seldom used for overnight anchorage.

⑦ **City of Des Moines Marina,** 22307 Dock St. S., Des Moines, WA 98188, (206)824-5700, or view at www.ci.des-moines.wa.us. Use chart 18474; 18448. Monitors VHF channel 16, switch to 68. Open all year. Gasoline, diesel fuel, propane. This 840-slip marina and public pier has 65 guest slips. Maximum boat length is 55 feet, channel depth 10 feet. Stop at the fuel dock for directions to an empty berth. The docks have 15, 20 & 30 amp power. You'll find restrooms, showers, pumpout, portapotty dump, and two 4-ton overhead sling launches. At the south end of the harbor the Des Moines Yacht Club has guest moorage

Reference only — not for navigation

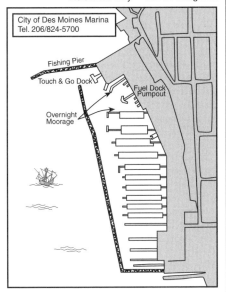

City of Des Moines Marina

Reference only — not for navigation

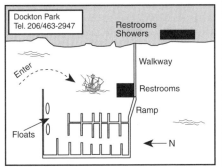

Dockton Park

See area map page 38

Blake Island. The longhouse and excellent grounds make this an outstanding marine park.

for visiting members of reciprocal clubs. Several marine supply stores are nearby. All services, including laundry, groceries, and several restaurants, are within walking distance. The 670-foot public fishing pier runs east-west. To enter the marina leave the fishing pier to port.

Yukon Harbor. Use chart 18449; 18474; 18448; 18441. Yukon Harbor offers good anchorage, well protected from the south but open to the northeast.

A linear mooring system has been installed on the west side of Blake Island.

⑧ **Blake Island Marine State Park.** Use chart 18449; 18474; 18448; 18441.Open all year, with 1744 feet of dock space in the breakwater-protected marina, and mooring buoys around the island. A linear mooring system is installed on the western (back) side of the island. Blake Island is located just a short hop from Elliott Bay or Shilshole. The park is accessible only by boat, and is one of the most popular stops on Puget Sound. Trails criss-cross the island. Wildlife is abundant.

Blake Island has primitive campsites, including a Cascadia Marine Trail campsite. Water

The protected marina at Blake Island has room for several boats, but always seems full. This photo was taken in April.

is available, but no garbage drop. There is an underwater reef for scuba diving. The park has picnic shelters, volleyball courts, nature trail, and approximately 12 miles of hiking trails through dense forest. The restaurant is a replica of an Indian longhouse and is open June through Labor Day.

The marina is on the northeast shore of the island. To enter, follow the dredged channel marked by red and green marked beacons. The water is shoal on both sides of the beacons, so stay in the marked channel. Immediately inside the breakwater, one float is for the boat that brings guests to the Indian longhouse restaurant, and another is for the State Parks boat. The rest are available on a first-come, first-served basis.

A gem of a park.

SEATTLE

Elliott Bay. Use chart 18449; 18474; 18448; 18441. Elliott Bay, the center of Seattle's shipping industry, is one of the busiest ocean ports in the world. Keep a sharp watch for ferries coming and going from Colman Dock, for tugs with tows, and for commercial vessels of all kinds. Large vessels are very slow to maneuver, and should always be given a wide berth. When there's any doubt at all, cross *behind* commercial vessels, not in front of them.

Piers 89, 90 and 91 in Smith Cove are heavily used by commercial ships. The Port of Seattle's grain terminal occupies part of the shoreline north of the regular commercial piers, and Myrtle Edwards Park, including a fishing pier, stretches along about a mile of the Elliott Bay waterfront. The piers on the central waterfront, now considered too small for modern maritime commerce, have been converted to many other uses, including a hotel, shops, museums, a wonderful aquarium, and places to sit and watch the harbor activity.

At Pier 36 south of the ferry dock, the U.S. Coast Guard has its Seattle headquarters, including the Coast Guard Museum and the Vessel Traffic System.

Downtown Seattle now is served by two excellent marinas: the Elliott Bay Marina on the north shore below Magnolia Bluff, and the Port of Seattle's new Bell Harbor Marina at Pier 66 on the Seattle waterfront. These two marinas make downtown Seattle easy and safe to visit. We like them both, and strongly recommend them to our readers.

⑨ **Elliott Bay Marina,** 2601 W. Marina Place, Seattle, WA 98199, (206)285-4817; fax (206)282-0626. Monitors VHF channel 78A. This is a beautiful marina, immaculately maintained, open all year. The fuel dock has gasoline and diesel (see Yacht Care, below). Guest boats use unoccupied slips when available. Make reservations by phone (preferred) or radio. The marina has 30 & 50 amp power, restrooms, showers, laundry, pumpout, portapotty dump. Excellent 24-hour security.

Enter through either end of the breakwater. The marina office is on the ground level of the main building, between Maggie Bluffs

Elliott Bay Marina docks are wide and well kept. Building at head of dock houses office, two restaurants.

Summer Nights at the Pier, next to Bell Harbor Marina. The crowd gathers. Downtown Seattle in the background.

cafe and Elliott Bay Yacht Sales. Restrooms, showers, 30 & 50 amp power. A concierge service can book reservations at other marinas, get float plane tickets, help with routes, set up repairs, and more. Dockside service. Free cable TV hook-up. Elegant dining at Palisades restaurant, casual dining at Maggie Bluffs, and sushi at Sanmi Sushi restaurant. The fuel dock has a mini-mart. It's 5 minutes by car to downtown Seattle.

A bike and walking path runs from the marina along scenic Myrtle Edwards waterfront park to the downtown waterfront. We took about an hour each way to walk between the marina and Pier 70. Seattle Yacht Club has an outstation (no reciprocal moorage) at the marina. Great views of downtown, Mt. Rainier, Olympics. *(Marina map page 44)*

Yacht Care, 2601 W. Marina Place, Seattle, WA 98199, (206)285-2600. Open 7 days, summer and winter. Gasoline and diesel fuel. Restrooms, pumpout, portapotty dump, no power, no showers. Customs clearance is available. Located in the Elliott Bay Marina at the end of "G" dock. Service department open weekdays for mechanical repairs. Mini-mart carries beer and wine, snacks, bait, fishing licenses.

⑩ **Bell Harbor Marina,** Pier 66, 2203 Alaskan Way, Seattle, WA 98121, (206)615-3952; fax (206)615-3965. Monitors VHF channel 66A. Open year-round. This new marina has 30 & 50 amp power, water, restrooms and showers, garbage/recycling pickup, pumpout, and 24-hour security.

The Port of Seattle's Bell Harbor Marina is part of Seattle's new Central Waterfront Development. The marina opened in 1996, and has made downtown Seattle an easy cruising destination. Depending on the mix, the docks will hold as many as 70 visitor boats. The waterfront, with its aquarium and variety of shops and eateries, is available. It's a safe, 2-block walk to the excitement of the Pike Place Market.

A quaint trolly runs the length of the waterfront, all the way to Pioneer Square. Visitors can leave the boat at Bell Harbor and take in a Kingdome event. Anthony's Pier 66 restaurant is excellent and popular. The Odyssey Maritime Discovery Center, opened in July, 1998, has outstanding interactive exhibits that explain the ecology, commerce and impact of Puget Sound. You can paddle a kayak, load a container ship, run radio-controlled tugboats in a small pond, and ride the train across the country in a boxcar. Odyssey is a treat for adults and children alike. We highly recommend a visit.

This marina has become extremely popular. With its views of Seattle's skyscrapers and the commercial bustle all around, the cosmopolitan atmosphere is the opposite of a snug little anchorage hidden up the coast. It's a chance to use the boat as a base for a holiday in the city, and heavy emphasis is placed on security. We spent a night at Bell Harbor in late summer, walked the waterfront, had an excellent supper and a perfect night's sleep.

See area map page 38

Next morning we shopped at the Pike Place Market.

Bell Harbor's facilities are top-notch, with excellent wheelchair access. The staff is professional and alert. Reservations are taken.

Because of rough water in Elliott Bay, the breakwater entry is narrow. Boats larger than 70 feet will find the entry and turning basin a little tight. Approximately 1900 feet of outside pier apron devoted to large vessels, including major cruise line ships. The Seattle waterfront has taken a major turn for the better.

Breakwater note: The breakwater's steel panels squeak and scrape as they move with the waves. The sounds are disconcerting at first, and some people are quite affected by them. They didn't bother us, but everybody is different.

Radio note: Contrary to information in many of their ads, the marina monitors VHF channel 66A, not 66. If you call on channel 66 they will hear you, but they reply on 66A and you will not hear them. Use channel 66A. *(Marina map below)*

Washington Street Moorage. The Washington Street Moorage, alongside the city's fire department, has dock space for a few boats. There is no protection from the wakes of passing ferries, and security can be a problem. The moorage is close to the Kingdome, and is sometimes used by people attending events there.

East Waterway. Both sides of East Waterway are lined with docks for commercial vessels, most of them loading or unloading containers. The waterway is navigable to Spokane Street, where a fixed bridge and foul ground block further navigation.

West Waterway. Use large-scale chart 18450. West Waterway and the connecting Duwamish River make a splendid sightseeing voyage.

You'll enter past the busy Todd Shipyard and the now-closed Lockheed Shipyard at the mouth, and along an incredible variety of docks, ships, barges, small pleasure boats, mega-yachts, and abandoned hulks. Commercial buildings are on both sides, and the modest homes of South Park.

You will go under the First Ave. S. Bridge, vertical clearance 39 feet, and past the "back door" of the Boeing Company's Plant 2 to the 16th Ave. S. Bridge, vertical clearance 34 feet. The First Ave. S. Bridge will open on signal, except during rush hour traffic. The 16th Ave. S. Bridge does not open. The famed Delta Marine facility, builder of commercial fish boats and now mega-yachts, is a short distance beyond the 16th Ave. S. Bridge.

Not far past Delta, a low bridge blocks progress to all but small, open boats. Contributing Editor Tom Kincaid has followed the river upstream as far as Kent in an outboard powered dinghy.

Don Armeni Park and Seacrest Park are located between Harbor Island and Duwamish Head. Don Armeni Park has a 4-lane launch ramp with floats. Seacrest Park has a fishing pier.

Shilshole Bay. Use charts 18446, 18447, 18441, 18473 (charts 18446 & 18447 show the best detail). Shilshole Bay indents the shoreline of Puget Sound north of West Point, and leads via a dredged channel to the Hiram M. Chittenden Locks and the Lake Washington Ship Canal. The Shilshole Bay Marina lies north of the dredged channel, with entrances from

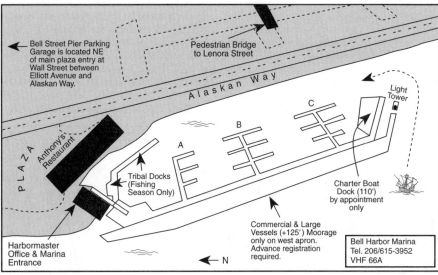

Bell Harbor Marina

Reference only — not for navigation

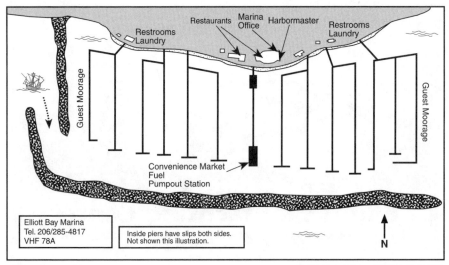

Elliott Bay Marina

Reference only — not for navigation

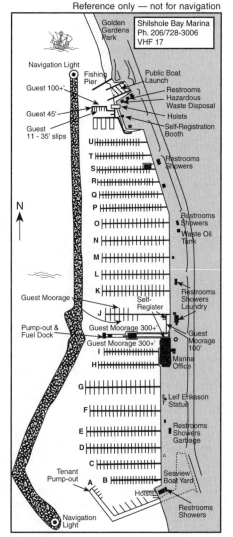

Shilshole Bay Marina

The guest moorage at Shilshole Bay Marina is spacious and well-maintained.

marina. The boatyard has propane and repair-yard supplies. A wide launch ramp is at the north end of the marina. Walking distance to several restaurants with lounges, two hamburger stands, a West Marine store, and Admiralty Marine (used equipment). Regular bus service to all of Seattle. Golden Gardens Park, with beach and picnic areas, is located a short walk north of the marina. *(Marina map page 44)*

⑫ **Shilshole Texaco Marine**, 7029 Seaview Ave. NW, Seattle, WA 98117, (206)783-7555. Open 7 days a week all year. Texaco fuel dock with gasoline, diesel, kerosene. The Port of Seattle operates a pumpout at the outer end of the dock. Convenience store carries ice, beverages, snacks, local guidebooks. Friendly people, clean, efficient operation.

Hiram M. Chittenden Locks. Use chart 18447. The dredged channel leading to the Hiram Chittenden Locks is well marked, and passes under the Burlington Northern bascule bridge, vertical clearance 43 feet. The bridge is kept open unless a train is due. The opening signal is one long and one short blast, the same signal as for the Ballard, Fremont, University, and Montlake bridges.

Depending on how your luck is that day, your wait at the locks, either direction, can be as short as zero or as long as several hours. Our attitude is that it takes as long as it takes, and that's how it is. We've seen people get very upset at the wait, but being upset doesn't

both the north and the south behind a long rock breakwater.

Lacking local knowledge, boats bound for the locks should pick up the Shilshole Bay Lighted Approach Buoy (locally called the Ballard Blinker) and follow the marked channel to the locks. *Caution:* The water between the channel and Magnolia Bluff shoals rapidly. Each year a number of boats go aground there.

⑫ **Shilshole Bay Marina**, 7001 Seaview Ave. NW, Seattle, WA 98117 (206)728-3006; fax (206)728-3391. Monitors VHF channel 17, 24 hrs. Open all year, office hours 0800-1630 Monday-Friday; 0800-1300 on Satur-day. This is a large, popular, well-equipped marina operated by Port of Seattle. Gasoline, diesel, kerosene and pre-mix are available at the Shilshole Texaco Marine fuel dock. The marina has 40 guest slips and 1900 feet of side-tie dock space for visiting boats. Minimum 15 foot depth at zero tide. Has 30, 50, & 100 amp power, restrooms, showers, laundry, pumpout, portapotty dump. Guest moorage is on a first-come, first-served basis, or by reservation 72 hours in advance. The reservation fee is $5. Waste oil disposal stations, recycling and trash receptacles are available.

A complete boatyard (Seaview West) with Travelift haulout is at the south end of the

speed things along.

Approaching from Puget Sound: If you are approaching from Puget Sound, you'll starboard-side tie to the wall on the south side of the channel under the railroad bridge. The current always flows from the lake into the sound. Approach carefully and be well-fendered. Wait your turn and do not crowd ahead. Government vessels and commercial vessels have priority over pleasure craft, and will be directed into the locks ahead of pleasure craft.

Red and green lights on the large and small locks indicate when you can enter. Red light means no; green light means yes. A loud hailer also tells you what to do.

Lock attendants do not respond to most radio calls from pleasure craft, but if you must communicate with them, call on VHF channel 13, using the 1-watt low-power mode.

There are two locks, a large lock 825 feet long and 80 feet wide, and a small lock 150 feet long and 30 feet wide. On a busy summer weekend, the large lock can take a half-hour or more to fill. Lock attendants will direct entering vessels to one lock or the other by light signals and loud hailer. Each vessel should have available bow and stern mooring lines at least 50 feet long with a 12-inch eye spliced in one end. Fenders should be deployed on both sides of the boat.

The lock attendants are conscientious, ex-

Outward bound in the large lock. Boats on the wall ease their lines as the water drops.

perienced and helpful. They make eye contact with the helmsman of each vessel as it enters the lock, and signal their intentions for each vessel. They are polite, but they give direct orders. Do exactly what they tell you to do. They have seen everything and know how to deal with problems.

If directed into the large lock, larger vessels will be brought in first and tied along the walls. Smaller vessels will raft off. Large vessel or small, be sure you have 50-foot mooring lines bow and stern in case you are put on the wall. If you are to lie along the wall the lock attendant will throw a line to you. Tie your mooring line to his line and he will take it to a cleat on top of the lock wall.

There is usually some current in the locks, flowing from the lakes toward the sound. Enter as slowly as you can without losing steerage way. Once your lines are made fast, prepare to assist boats directed to lie alongside you. When the lock is closed and the water begins to rise, the vessels along the wall must keep a half-turn on their cleats and continuously take in slack. When the water has stopped rising, make all lines fast until you are told to leave.

If directed into the small lock, you will lie alongside a floating wall equipped with yellow painted "buttons." Loop your line around the button and make the end fast to a cleat. The floating walls rise or fall with the water level, so you will not need to tend your lines during the transit. *Caution:* It is always possible that a floating wall could jam in its tracks. Stand by to slack your lines quickly if that should happen.

When directed to do so, move out of the locks slowly but with steerage way.

Approaching from the lakes: If you are westbound from the lakes to the sound, you still will need 50-foot mooring lines bow and stern in case you lie along the wall of the large lock. However, you will be able to hand your line to the attendant instead of tying it to a line

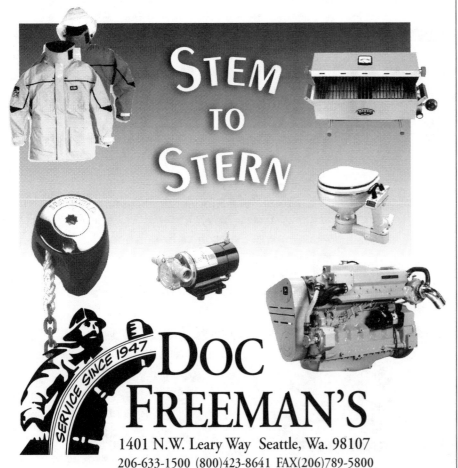

Marilynn Hale tends the bow line in the large lock.

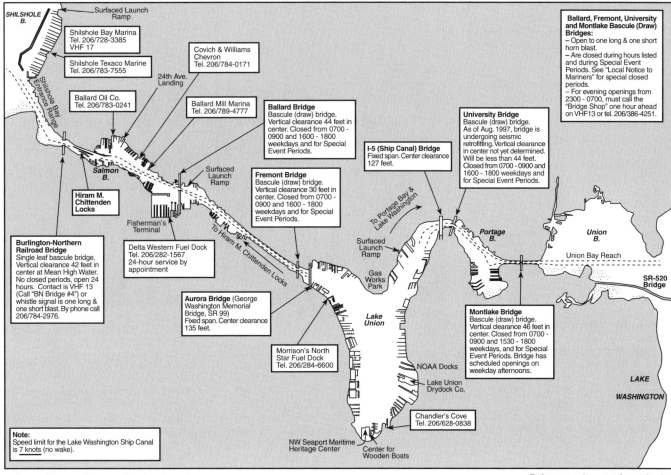

Lake Washington Ship Canal and Lake Union   Reference only — not for navigation

tossed to you. Boats along the large lock wall will slack their lines as the water drops.

LAKE WASHINGTON SHIP CANAL

Use chart 18447. The Lake Washington Ship Canal connects the Hiram Chittenden Locks with Lake Washington, a distance of approximately 5.5 miles. Except for a marked course in the middle of Lake Union, a 7-knot speed limit is enforced all the way to Webster Point, at the entrance to Lake Washington. Most boats travel about 6 knots. If no bridge openings are needed, allow about an hour to get between Lake Washington and the locks, about 30 minutes between Lake Union and the locks. The Lake Washington Ship Canal has major fuel depots, ship repair yards, and moorages.

⑬ **24th Avenue Landing,** foot of 24th Ave. NW on the north side of the Ship Canal, east of locks. Open 0700-0200 all year, no overnights. Dock has 300 feet of space, 40-foot maximum boat length. No

power, water or showers. Restrooms are next door at the Yankee Diner. Ballard business district within walking distance.

⑬ **Ballard Oil Co.,** 5300 26th Ave. NW, Seattle, WA 98107, (206)783-0241. Open 7 days in the summer. Just east of the locks, on the north side of the Ship Canal. Diesel only. Set up to handle larger and commercial vessels.

Covich & Williams Chevron, 5219 Shilshole Ave. NW, Seattle, WA 98107, (206)784-0171. On the north side of the Ship Canal. Open weekdays, Saturday hours only until noon; closed Sundays. Open all year, gasoline, diesel, kerosene. No power, restrooms or showers. Carries filters, absorbent products, anti-freeze, environmental products, fuel additives. Will honor permits.

Salmon Bay. Use chart 18447. The Port of Seattle's Fishermen's Terminal is located on the south side of the Lake Washington Ship Canal at Salmon Bay, a half-mile east of the locks. Fishermen's

Terminal caters primarily to the large Seattle based fishing fleet, although a guest float is located along the inner bulkhead at the head of the west wall. Fuel is available, as well as access to major repair facilities, and stores offering a great variety of marine services and supplies.

Dining: Chinook's is very good. The mooring float is in front of the restaurant.

Delta Western Fuel Dock, Pier 4, Fishermen's Terminal, Seattle, WA 98119, (206)282-1567. Open all year, with 24-hour service by appointment. Diesel only. Lube oil, filters, some parts and supplies are available.

⑬ **Ballard Mill Marina,** 4733 Shilshole Ave. NW, Seattle, WA 98107, (206)789-4777. Open all year, guest moorage limited to unoccupied slips as available. Restrooms, pumpout, 20 & 30 amp

power, showers. East of Covich & Williams Chevron fuel dock on the north side of the Ship Canal. Free pumpout on the east dock. Stores, restaurants, marine supplies, haulout and repairs nearby.

JUST EAST OF THE SALMON BAY terminal you will pass under the **Ballard Bridge**, vertical clearance 45 feet at the center. A launch ramp is east of the bridge on the north side of the canal. Working east, you will pass large ship building and ship repair facilities. Then you will pass park areas on both sides of the waterway as you approach the **Fremont Bridge**, vertical clearance 30 feet in the center. The Fremont Bridge is the lowest of the bridges that cross this waterway. Both the Ballard Bridge and the Fremont Bridge open to one long blast and one short. During weekdays, all the bridges that cross the Lake Washington Ship Canal remain closed from 0700-0900 and from 1600-1800, *except* the Montlake Bridge. Its afternoon closures are from 1530-1800.

Nighttime bridge openings. The bridges are unattended at night between 2300 and 0700. One crew, based at the Fremont Bridge shops, opens bridges for vessel traffic. To arrange openings during these nighttime hours you must call one hour ahead on VHF channel 13, or by telephone (206)386-4251.

Ewing Street Moorings, 624 W. Ewing St., Seattle, WA 98119, (206)283-1075. Open all year, 2 transient slips, call for availability. Has 20 & 30 amp power, restroom, no showers. This is a small, cozy and somewhat rustic moorage, almost hidden from the canal.

Lake Union. Use chart 18447. Lake Union is surrounded by ship and boat moorages, houseboat moorages, and boating related businesses. It's the center of Seattle's boat sales industry. In the middle of the lake a speed range, marked by four buoys, is for sea trials. Other than the speed range, the 7-knot speed limit is enforced. A launch ramp is on the north shore, east of Gas Works Park. Gas Works Park is easily identifiable by the painted remnants of an industrial coal gas plant. Tyee Yacht Club

Lake Union is the center for boat sales and repair in Seattle. Several waterfront restaurants are located along its shores.

and Puget Sound Yacht Club have moorages on Lake Union. The large Fisheries Supply marine store is located near Gas Works Park.

The south end of Lake Union is the home of Northwest Seaport, whose 4-masted schooner *Wawona* is open for tours. Next door are the Center for Wooden Boats and the Naval Reserve Center. A large West Marine store is within walking distance. Along the eastern shore you'll find a major ship repair yard (Lake Union Drydock) and the National Oceans and Atmospheric Administration (NOAA) fleet of survey vessels.

⑭ **Morrison's North Star Marina,** 2732 Westlake Ave. N., Seattle, WA 98109, (206)284-6600. Open all year, 7 days a week. Union Oil fuel dock with gasoline and diesel, no guest moorage. Restrooms, no showers. Handles oil changes; call for appointment. Carries kerosene, limited marine hardware, local charts, bait, groceries, ice. Pumpout available. Friendly and well-run.

⑮ **Chandler's Cove,** 901 Fairview Ave. N. #C170, Seattle, WA 98109, (206)628-0838. Call ahead for availability of guest moorage. Several restaurants, snacks, ice. Easy walk to the Center for Wooden Boats and Northwest Seaport.

⑮ **H.C. Henry Marina,** 809 Fairview Place N., Seattle, WA 98109. Open all year, 24 hours, 7 days a week, with 100 feet of guest space. Located at the south end of Lake Union. Has 220 volt power only and pumpout, but no restrooms or showers. Four full-service restaurants with lounges are within walking distance. Several small shops nearby.

⑮ **Marina Mart,** 1500 Westlake Ave. N., Seattle, WA 98109, (206)682-7733. No guest moorage, free pumpout only.

Portage Bay. East of the **University Bridge**, vertical clearance 44 feet in the center, Portage Bay is the home of Seattle Yacht Club and Queen City Yacht Club, as well as other moorages. The University of Washington has several facilities along the north shore. The bridge opens to one long blast and one short.

Montlake Cut. East of Portage Bay, the Montlake Cut connects to Union Bay and Lake Washington. The Cut is narrow, and during periods of heavy boat traffic wakes can be turbulent as they bounce off the concrete side walls. Slow, steady speeds are called for. The **Montlake Bridge,** which crosses the Cut, has a vertical clearance of 46 feet in the center. The bridge opens to one long blast and one short.

Union Bay. Use chart 18447. Union Bay lies just east of the Montlake Cut, and connects with Lake Washington. The dredged channel is well marked. The University of Washington's

The Center for Wooden Boats is an excellent place to visit at the south end of Lake Union.

waterfront activities center is on the north shore, and the arboretum is on the south shore. Except for the dredged channel, the bay is shoal.

LAKE WASHINGTON

Lake Washington. Use chart 18447. Lake Washington, 16 miles long, defines the eastern border of Seattle, and washes the edges of Kenmore, Bothell, Kirkland, Medina, Bellevue, Mercer Island and Renton. The SR-520 floating bridge has a vertical clearance of 45 feet at its west end and 54 feet at its east end. The I-90 floating bridge has a vertical clearance of 35 feet in the center of each end.

Sand Point. North from Webster Point, the first notable place for visiting boats is the former Naval Aviation base of Sand Point. Sand Point now includes Magnuson Park, which has a 2-lane launch ramp with floats. It is also the Northwest District headquarters for the National Oceans and Atmospheric Administration (NOAA), which has a long piling pier along its north shore. The small marina west of the NOAA pier belongs to the Navy.

Kenmore. The Harbor Village Marina at Kenmore provides access to a restaurant, and anchorage is possible anywhere in the area. Kenmore is home to Kenmore Air, a major seaplane operation. Stay well clear of seaplane operating areas. Kenmore is also the mouth of the Sammamish River. Shoal water abounds. Find the buoys and stay in the dredged channel. The river is navigable by small, low, shallow-draft boats all the way to Lake Sammamish.

⑯ **Harbor Village Marina,** 6155 NE 175th St., Seattle, WA 98155, (425)485-7557. Open all year, limited guest moorage. Unoccupied slips used when available. 30 & 50 amp power, restrooms, showers, laundry, pumpout. Also a 300-foot breakwall for guests to tie to during daylight hours; no fee, tie up at your own risk. Restaurant nearby. The marina has one of the few pumpout stations on Lake Washington.

⑯ **Cap Sante-Lake Washington,** (formerly Davidson's Marina) 6201 NE 175th St., Seattle, WA 98155, (425)482-9465, (800)455-5794. Open all year, except closed Sundays during the winter. Gasoline at the fuel dock. No guest moorage. Restrooms, no power, no showers. Store carries life jackets, parts, accessories, ice. Full service repairs available.

Logboom Park, north shore of Lake Washington, Kenmore. Open all year, day use only, moorage available. Restrooms, no power, no showers. Trails, fishing pier, children's play equipment, picnic areas, outdoor cooking facilities. The park is on the Burke-Gilman Trail, a walking and cycling trail that runs from from Lake Union to the Sammamish River Trail.

Saint Edward State Park, northeast shore of Lake Washington. Open all year, day use

only. Restrooms, showers, no power. Anchoring or beaching only. Picnicking, trails, fishing, indoor swimming pool. Tennis and handball courts, gymnasium. The 300+ acre park is at the top of a bluff; trails lead down to a sandy beach.

Juanita. Anchorage is possible in Juanita Bay, which shoals gradually toward all shores.

Kirkland. The City of Kirkland, in Moss Bay, operates the Marina Park docks for the use of visitors, and has a good launch ramp. It's a popular destination for Lake Washington cruising. Kirkland's downtown area, with excellent restaurants and a wide variety of shops and galleries, is just a few steps from the docks. A mile south of Marina Park is the privately owned Carillon Point Marina, with guest moorage and access to restaurants and other businesses. Several restaurants in the area have their own docks for patrons.

⑰ **Marina Park,** 123 Fifth Ave., Kirkland, WA 98032, (425)828-1218; fax (425)828-1220. Launch ramp adjacent; fee required. Open all year, 66 guest slips, restrooms, no power or showers. This is a large and popular Lake Washington destination. Excellent access to downtown Kirkland. Nearby groceries, ice, doctor, post office, liquor store.

⑱ **Carillon Point Marina,** 3240 Carillon Point, Kirkland, WA 98033, (425)822-1700;

fax (425)828-3094. Open all year, guest moorage in unoccupied slips used when available, 30 & 50 amp power, restrooms, showers, pumpout, portapotty dump. This is a nice marina adjacent to a high-quality hotel, with restaurants and shopping. They give 2-hour free moorage while dining or shopping. Downtown Kirkland is 1.5 miles away by road.

⑱ **Wilcox's Yarrow Bay Marina,** 5207 Lake Washington Blvd., Kirkland, WA 98033, (425)822-6066. Fuel dock with gasoline and diesel open all year. No guest moorage. Has restrooms, pumpout, no showers.

Cozy Cove and **Fairweather Bay** are entirely residential, but anchorage is possible.

Meydenbauer Bay. Meydenbauer Bay is the home of a marina that does not normally offer overnight moorage, and the Meydenbauer Bay Yacht Club, which has some moorage for members of reciprocal clubs. Downtown Bellevue, with excellent shopping, is nearby. Anchorage is possible in Meydenbauer Bay, although the water is deeper than most pleasure craft prefer. The marina off Beaux Arts Village, a short distance south of Meydenbauer Bay, is reserved for Beaux Arts residents.

Luther Burbank Park, Northeast end of Mercer Island, (206)296-2976. Open all year, day use only, dock space for 30 or more boats. Restrooms, no power, no showers. Park has

The Bremerton Marina is a popular place, even on a cloudy day.

Port Orchard Marina has excellent, well-maintained facilities.

picnic areas, swimming areas, tennis courts, amphitheater, art displays.

Newport Shores. Newport Shores has a large marina and launch ramp. The East Channel Bridge has a vertical clearance of 65 feet.

⑲ **Mercer Marine,** 3911 Lake Washington Blvd. SE, Bellevue, WA 98006, (425)641-2090. Open all year, except closed on Sundays during the winter. The fuel dock has gasoline. No guest moorage. Located at the Newport Yacht Basin. Complete repairs available. Also stove alcohol, propane, marine supplies and parts. Adjacent to a public launch ramp.

⑳ **Gene Coulon Memorial Beach Park,** 1201 Lake Washington Blvd., Renton, WA 98055, (425)235-2560; fax (425)277-5541. Open all year, day use and overnight moorage. The park has 13 guest slips available, restrooms, showers, no power. Pay at the drop box. Showers in summer only, at the swim center. Ivar's restaurant in the park. Eight lanes for boat launching, very well organized. This is a big, attractive and much-used park, with picnic shelters, playground equipment, tennis courts, horseshoe pits, volleyball courts, grassy areas and beaches. It has a fishing pier and a paved walkway along the water. Located on the southeast shore of Lake Washington, next to the Boeing complex.

Rainier Beach has a launch ramp and a private marina. It is the home of the Rainier Yacht Club. Limited guest moorage to visiting members of reciprocal clubs.

Seward Park occupies the Bailey Peninsula. Andrews Bay is a popular anchoring spot. The park includes a fish hatchery, hiking trails. A small private marina, with a small guest dock, is at Lakewood.

㉑ **Lakewood Moorage,** 4500 Lake Washington Blvd. S., Seattle, WA 98118, (206)722-3887. Open all year; closed Mondays in summer and Sundays in winter. Very limited guest moorage. Restrooms, no showers.

Stan Sayers Memorial Park, southwest edge of Lake Washington. Open all year. Temporary, day-use moorage only, not enough depth for larger boats. Restrooms, no power, no showers. Launch ramp with boarding floats. Tie up to the floats. Pit area for hydroplanes during Seafair.

㉒ **Leschi Yacht Basin**, 202 Lake Washington Blvd., at Leschi Marina, Seattle, WA 98122, (206)328-4456. Open all year. The fuel dock has closed. Limited guest moorage. Unoccupied slips used when available, 30 amp power, restrooms, showers. Look for the banner from water. Restrooms are in the restaurant. Adjacent restaurants have their own guest docks.

RICH PASSAGE, PORT ORCHARD, BREMERTON, SILVERDALE

Rich Passage. Use chart 18449; 18474; 18448. Rich Passage, winding but well buoyed, is the ferry route between Seattle and Bremerton. Keep a sharp lookout ahead and astern and give the ferries room to maneuver. Naval vessels of all kinds also use Rich Passage to and from the Bremerton Naval Shipyard. From the west entrance the city of Bremerton and the Naval Shipyard are clearly visible. The Navy asks that boats cruising past the shipyard maintain a 100-yard clearance from the ends of its piers.

Manchester State Park, Middle Point, Rich Passage. Open summers 7 days, day use and overnight camping; open only weekends and holidays in the winter for day use and overnight camping. Restrooms, showers, no power. Anchoring only; a bit rough because of boat traffic in Rich Passage. Park is located in a shallow cove; good for wading in summer; scuba diving offshore. Picnic tables and shelters with fireplaces. Standard and primitive

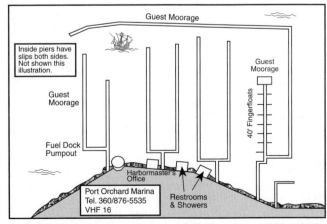

Port Orchard Marina   Reference only — not for navigation

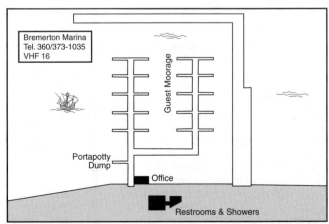

Bremerton Marina   Reference only — not for navigation

campsites. Nature and hiking trails, volleyball court and horseshoe pits. Old gun battery and emplacements to explore.

㉓ **Port of Manchester**, P.O. Box 304, Manchester, WA 98353. Open all year, 200 feet of guest dock space, day use only. Dock can be dry on low or minus tide. A launch ramp is adjacent to the dock. No power or other facilities at the dock, but restaurants, groceries, restrooms and drinking water are nearby.

Fort Ward Marine State Park, southwest of Winslow on Bainbridge Island. Open all year, overnight moorage at 2 buoys. The buoys are exposed to wind and wakes from passing boat traffic. Toilets, launch ramp, picnic tables and hiking trails. Underwater park is for expert scuba divers only, because of strong currents in Rich Passage. Clamming, crabbing, fishing. Birdwatching from two bird blinds. Remains of historic fort emplacements to explore. No camping.

Port Orchard. Use chart 18449; 18448. The city of Port Orchard has long been a popular destination for Puget Sound boaters. It has a number of marinas that welcome visiting boats, including one, the Port Orchard Marina, that is operated by the Port of Bremerton. The Port Orchard Yacht Club, which welcomes visiting reciprocal yachts, is west of the Port Orchard Marina. Several other marinas offer permanent moorage. Anchorage is in 5-10 fathoms, mud bottom. A passenger ferry runs between Port Orchard and Bremerton.

㉔ **Port Orchard Marina**, 8850 SW State Hwy 3, Port Orchard, WA 98366, (360) 876-5535, fax (360)895-0291. Monitors VHF channel 16. Open 7 days a week all year, except closed Thanksgiving and Christmas. Gasoline and diesel at the fuel dock, guest moorage in 44 slips (40-foot maximum), and side-tied along 1500 feet of inside dock space (another 1500 feet is on the outside of the long dock).

The marina has 30 & 50 amp power, restrooms, showers, laundry, pumpout and portapotty dump. This is one of Puget Sound's most popular destinations. They now take reservations. No charge for day use. It's one block to downtown Port Orchard, where you will find several antiques and collectibles shops, restaurants, and the other usual services: library, post office, doctor. Marine supplies and repairs are nearby. Close to Waterfront Park, and a boat launch. The launch does not have extended term parking for tow vehicles and trailers. Seasonal farmers' market. Enter the marina around the west end of the breakwater. The entrance is marked with navigation lights. *(Marina map page 50)*

Golf: McCormick Woods, one of the finest golf courses in the area, is 4 miles away. (360)895-0142. In all, 6 golf courses are within 11 miles.

㉕ **Bremerton Marina**, 8850 SW State Hwy 3, Port Orchard, WA 98366 (mailing address), (360)373-1035, fax (360)479-2928. Monitors VHF channel 16. Open all year, except closed Thanksgiving and Christmas. All guest moorage, 45 slips, 500 feet of side-tie dock space. The marina has 30 amp power, restrooms, showers, laundry, pumpout and portapotty dump. This is an excellent facility, located in next to the ferry dock in downtown Bremerton. It is operated by the Port of Bremerton. Downtown Bremerton, while a little thin on shopping, is within walking distance.

Points of interest include the Naval Museum and the historic destroyer USS *Turner Joy*, the adjacent waterfront park, and the attractive city boardwalk. Fuel is available across Sinclair Inlet at the Port Orchard Marina. Many boaters take the passenger ferry to Port Orchard, where the dining, antique shopping, and boutiques are popular. The Bremerton Marina is secured by a locked gate, as are the restrooms and laundry area. The lock combination is displayed on the inside of the gate, where visiting boaters can see it but outsiders can't. Kitsap County transit buses can take you anywhere you wish to go.

Construction activity at the Washington State Ferries teminal, next to the Bremerton Marina, should not affect water access. Upland parking, however, will be reduced during construction. *(Marina map page 50)*

See area map page 38

Washington Narrows. Use chart 18449. Washington Narrows connects Sinclair Inlet with Dyes Inlet. The Narrows is crossed by two bridges with a minimum vertical clearance of 80 feet. Tidal currents, averaging over 2 knots, flood west and ebb east. Signs ask boaters to maintain minimum speed to reduce wake damage to the shorelines and to boats moored at the marina in Anderson Cove. A launch ramp with float and fishing pier are on the north side of the Narrows about halfway along, part of the Lebo Street Recreation Area.

㉖ **Port Washington Marina**, 1805 Thompson Drive, Bremerton, WA 98337, (360)479-3037. Open all year, 5 days. Guest moorage in unoccupied slips, 100 feet of dock space, 6-foot least depth. The marina has 30 and limited 50 amp power, restrooms, showers, laundry, pumpout.

Phinney Bay. Phinney Bay is the home of the Bremerton Yacht Club, with guest moorage for visiting reciprocal yachts. Anchorage is good throughout the bay, which shoals toward each shore.

Ostrich Bay. Use chart 18449. Ostrich Bay offers good anchorage, mud bottom. The most popular anchorage is along the west side of the bay, facing dense forest. We have spent a number of pleasant nights at this spot. For some reason this entire area is overlooked. Even when the docks at Port Orchard and Bremerton are full on summer 3-day holiday weekends, Ostrich Bay has been almost empty.

Oyster Bay. A narrow but easily-run channel leads off Ostrich Bay into Oyster Bay, where perfectly protected anchorage is available toward the center of the bay. To enter, keep between the lines of mooring buoys and mooring floats on both sides of the channel. The channel shoals to about 1 fathom at zero tide. Deep draft vessels should use it only when there is enough water. Oyster Bay is surrounded by homes.

㉗ **Silverdale Marina (Port of Silverdale)**, P.O. Box 310, Silverdale, WA 98383, (360)698-4918. Use chart 18449. Open all year. Guest moorage along 1300 feet with a least depth of 10 feet at low tide. Restrooms, 115 volt power, pumpout, no showers, 2-lane launch ramp. No long term parking. The marina is adjacent to county-run Silverdale Waterfront Park. This park has picnic tables, fire pits, children's play area, and a pavilion. Restrooms are at the park. Services are available close by, including groceries. Security cameras and nighttime patrols have been added.

BROWNSVILLE, POULSBO, NORTHERN PORT ORCHARD

㉘ **Illahee Marine State Park.** Use chart 18449. Located on Port Orchard Bay, 3 miles northeast of Bremerton, (360)478-6460. Open all year, mooring and overnight camping. Guest moorage has 350 feet of side-tie dock space, 5 mooring buoys. Restrooms, portapotty dump, no power or showers. The dock is protected by a floating concrete breakwater. Park has 3 kitchen shelters, picnic tables, campsites, horseshoe pits, ball field, hiking trails. Popular for fishing and sunbathing. Most services are in the upland area, reached by a steep trail.

㉙ **Port of Brownsville**, 9790 Ogle Rd. NE, Bremerton, WA 98311, (360)692-5498; fax (360)698-8032; fuel dock (360)692-0687. Or view web site at www.portofbrownsville.org. Monitors VHF channel 16, switch to 68. Use chart 18446 or 18449. Open all year, 7 days. Fuel dock has gasoline, diesel, propane. Guest moorage in 25 24-foot slips and side-tie moorage along 1300 feet of dock, 20 & 30 amp power, restrooms, showers, laundry, free pumpout, portapotty dump. Paved 2-lane launch ramp and parking. A breakwater marks the entrance to the marina. As the marina map on page 53 shows, the north and east breakwaters have been extended and joined, greatly expanding guest moorage. The area around the fuel dock has been dredged, so you don't have to hug the south side of the dock, as in earlier years. The Brownsville Marine and Deli has groceries and deli items, limited marine supplies. A park is adjacent, with picnic tables and barbecue. The Keyport Naval Museum of Undersea Warfare (excellent, worth the visit) is nearby. This is a pleasant, friendly marina. *(Marina map page 53)*

Fletcher Bay. Use chart 18449. Fletcher Bay is very shallow. It is not a good anchorage.

Manzanita Bay. Use chart 18446. Manzanita Bay is a popular overnight sheltered anchorage for Seattle-area boats. The bay is all residential and has no public facilities ashore, but the holding ground is excellent. Although the bay is lined with lovely homes, the surrounding hills and forests give a feeling of seclusion. We like Manzanita Bay.

Poulsbo. Use chart 18446. Poulsbo, on **Liberty Bay**, is one of the most popular destinations on Puget Sound, partly because it is close to the major population centers, and partly because it is such a delightful place to visit. Settled originally by Scandinavians, the downtown business district still loudly (to say the least) maintains its Norwegian heritage. Everything most boaters need is available either near the water or at the malls located on the highway about a mile away.

The waterfront portions of Poulsbo make for a lovely walk. Victorian homes and gardens have been restored and preserved to perfection. The highway above may have the malls, but the town below has the charm.

The entrance to Liberty Bay is past the Keyport Naval torpedo research and testing facility, and around Lemolo Point. The Navy asks a no-wake speed past its facility. A sign on the beacon off Lemolo Point asks boaters

Poulsbo in early April. The docks are full.

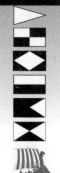

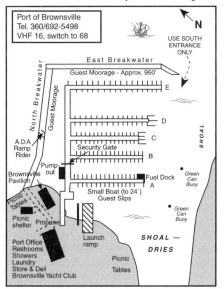

Reference only — not for navigation

Port of Brownsville
Tel. 360/692-5498
VHF 16, switch to 68

Port of Brownsville

to slow down in all of Liberty Bay. Buoys post the speed limit. Three major marinas are located along the north shore of Liberty Bay: a private marina; the Poulsbo Yacht Club; and the marina owned by the Port of Poulsbo.

The private marina has no guest moorage. At the Poulsbo Yacht Club, reciprocal moorage is along the northwest perimeter of the floating breakwater. Some reciprocal moorage is still available on the inside of the older breakwater.

③⓪ **Poulsbo Marina/Port of Poulsbo,** P.O. Box 732, 18721 Front St., Poulsbo, WA 98370. (360)779-9905 M-F 0800-1630; (360)779-3505 weekends; fax (360)779-8090. E-mail port@poulsbo.net. Open all year, 7 days. Register by 2000 hours to get the combination for the showers and restrooms. The fuel dock has gasoline & diesel. The marina has 130 guest slips, 12-foot depths at low tide, and— at last—30 amp power on all docks. Good restrooms and showers, laundry, pumpout, portapotty dump, launch ramp and picnic area. Reservations are accepted for E dock (40-foot slips). A meeting room now is available. Groceries, tackle and bait are nearby. Viking Marine Center, under new ownership since late 1998, has just about everything you might need for the boat, including charts and books.

Restaurants and many shops that specialize in gifts, collectibles, and home accessories are nearby in downtown Poulsbo. Dining and shopping are popular. The marina is close to doctors, a post office, and a liquor store. The Marine Science Center is worth a visit, especially with the kids. Shopping centers, with supermarkets and the usual stores, are a few blocks away.

Agate Passage. Use chart 18446. Agate Passage connects Port Orchard with Port Madison, and is crossed by a highway bridge with a vertical clearance of 75 feet. Currents in the pass can run as high as 6 knots at spring tides, flooding south and ebbing north. The channel through the pass is well marked, but in general, a mid-channel course will serve.

For some reason, many craft go through Agate Passage too fast, creating havoc for slower craft. Agate Pass isn't very long. Keep the speed down, look astern to judge the wake, and give fellow boats a break.

PORT MADISON AND BAINBRIDGE ISLAND

Miller Bay. Use chart 18446. Miller Bay indents the Northwest corner of Port Madison, and is very shallow, including the entrance. It should be entered only at half tide or better, or with local knowledge. Like many such bays on Puget Sound, Miller Bay has a drying shoal in the middle, so navigable water can be found only around the perimeter.

Bay Marine, Inc., P.O. Box 396, 20622 Miller Bay Road, Suquamish, WA 98392, (360)598-4900. Open Tuesday-Sunday, all year, 3 guest slips, 35-foot maximum length. No other facilities. Haulout to 34 feet, parts and complete repairs are available. Launch ramp. Most services are available in nearby Suquamish.

Suquamish. Suquamish has a pier but no float. Ashore is largely an Indian village, one highlight of which is Chief Seattle's grave on a hillside a block from the waterfront. The Suquamish Tribe also maintains an Indian museum along Agate Passage, south of Suquamish.

See area map page 38

The City Dock at Winslow usually is full, but there's room for the dinghy at the park. Restrooms are ashore.

Indianola. Indianola is distinguished by the long dock that used to serve passengers and freight during Mosquito Fleet days. Now a log float is installed during the summer to give access to the town, which has some supplies. Overnight moorage is not allowed.

Inner Port Madison. Use chart 18446. The inner, residential bay extends for about 1.5 miles into the north end of Bainbridge Island. This is where Port Madison Yacht Club is located, and a large outstation of Seattle Yacht Club (no reciprocity). Anchorage is good throughout, with a wide bight about 0.75 mile inside the entrance. Farther in, **Hidden Cove** is a lovely spot. For Seattle area boats, this is an often-overlooked area to have a picnic lunch or a quiet night at anchor. The shores are private, but the setting is idyllic.

Fay Bainbridge State Park, south of Point Monroe on Bainbridge Island. Open all year, 3 mooring buoys, exposed. Restrooms, showers, no power. The park has three kitchen shelters, fireplaces, fire rings, a beach area, launch ramp, and utility and primitive campsites. Also children's play equipment, horseshoe pits, fishing, clamming, concession stand in summer.

Murden Cove. Murden Cove has convenient anchoring depths, but little protection from winds. It's a long row to shore, partially over drying flats. The residential community of Rolling Bay is at the head of the bay.

Eagle Harbor. Use chart 18449. Eagle Harbor is the site of the town of Winslow, and is the western terminus of a ferry to downtown Seattle. The town has a lighted visitors' float off a fine waterfront park. Several of the marinas can provide guest moorage if a permanent tenant is away. Queen City Yacht Club, Meydenbauer Bay Yacht Club and Seattle Yacht Club have outstations in Eagle Harbor. We enjoy walking the streets of Winslow. Its shops offer art, crafts, books, and antiques. The grocery store has *everything*.

Enter Eagle Harbor by way of a marked channel past foul ground that extends south from Wing Point. Nun buoy 2 is at the end of this foul ground, and the Tyee Shoal Beacon

is a short distance south of buoy 2. The ferries round Tyee Shoal Beacon, but other craft can use buoy 2 safely, following the rule of Red, Right, Returning. Follow the markers all the way in. Shoal water extends out to the channel on both sides.

③② **Eagle Harbor Waterfront Park,** 692 HWY 305 NE, Bainbridge Island, WA 98110, (206)842-1212. Open all year, day use and overnight moorage at 100 feet of dock, use both sides. Launch ramp. Watch your depth at low tide. Restrooms, but no power, water or showers. Restrooms are open daylight hours only. New pumpout and portapotty dump. Good anchorage in the harbor, but it's very crowded. You might have better luck at the newly-installed linear moorage system. The park has a dinghy dock. A good spot, popular year-round. Playground, tennis courts, picnic sites. Retail shops and restaurants are within walking distance.

③② **Harbour Marina,** P.O. Box 11434, Eagle Harbor, at Harbour Pub, Bainbridge Island, WA 98110, (206)842-6502. Open all year, call ahead. Unoccupied slips used for guest boats when available. Has 30 amp power, restrooms, showers, laundry, pumpout. Located directly below Harbour Public House, an

English-style pub with beer, wine, and food. The pub is bright, clean, and pleasant, and the food is good. No kids allowed in pub. There is clearly-marked moorage for visiting the pub. It's a 5-10-minute walk to downtown or Waterfront Park.

③② **Winslow Wharf Marina,** P.O. Box 10297, Winslow, WA 98110, (206)842-4202. Monitors VHF channel 09. Open all year, 7 days in summer, 5 days in winter. Guest moorage in unoccupied slips when available. Maximum boat length 50 feet, 20 & 30 amp power, restrooms, showers, laundry, pumpout, portapotty dump. Look for the sign at the end of the registration dock. A deposit is required for a security gate and restroom card, and the gate is locked at 1700. The Chandlery, a well-stocked marine supply store, carries a little bit of everything. Two blocks to downtown; restaurants, many galleries, farmers' market. Seattle Yacht Club and Meydenbauer Bay Yacht Club each have some dock space reserved for their members. The spaces are clearly marked, and non-member boats may not use them.

③③ **Eagle Harbor Marina,** 5834 Ward Ave. NE, Bainbridge Island, WA 98110, (206)842-4003. Open all year, but limited guest moorage, call ahead. Marina has 20, 30 & 50 amp power, restrooms, showers, laundry, pumpout. Located on the south side of Eagle Harbor. A sauna and exercise room are available, and a B&B is adjacent to the marina. No restaurants or stores in the immediate area.

Blakely Harbor. Use chart 18449. In the early days Blakely Harbor was the site of major lumbering and shipbuilding activities, but now it is a quiet residential neighborhood. Some stub pilings remain from old docks. Anchorage should be chosen well away from the head of the bay. Good anchorage in 6-8 fathoms can be found far enough into the bay to be well protected, yet still have a view of the Seattle skyline. Sunset on a clear evening is beautiful. The entrance is unobstructed except by Blakely Rock, 0.5 mile off. Give Blakely Rock a good offing.

Eagle Harbor's new linear moorage has allowed more boats to visit without adding to the already-crowded anchoring conditions.

Northwest Puget Sound

Edmonds • Kingston • Admiralty Inlet • Port Townsend

Edmonds. Use chart 18473; 18446; 18441. Edmonds, a prosperous community with a small-town feel to it, is about 8 miles north of Shilshole Bay on the east side of Puget Sound. It has a major rock breakwater-protected marina (the Port of Edmonds Marina) with excellent facilities for visiting boats. Marine repair shops are located near the harbor. In the town, a short distance away, you'll find excellent restaurants, and interesting shops and galleries. The town "walks" well. You'll feel cozy and welcome.

① **Port of Edmonds,** 336 Admiral Way, Edmonds, WA 98020, (425)774-0549; fax (425)774-7837. Monitors VHF channel 69. Open 7 days a week all year. Fuel dock has gasoline & diesel. The marina has 1000 feet of guest side-tie dock space, plus unoccupied slips when available. They can accommodate boats to 60 feet. The docks are served by 30 amp power, restrooms, showers, laundry and pumpout.

Enter through the middle of the breakwater. Guest moorage and the fuel dock are immediately to the south. The marina has a large do-it-yourself boatyard, haulout and towing. Limited groceries, tackle and bait are available. Two excellent public beaches are nearby, and a public fishing pier. An artificial reef for scuba diving (the first such site in the state) is located next to the ferry dock. Fishing charters are available. It's a short walk to several nearby restaurants. Liquor store, post office, doctor, laundry, groceries and shops are in town, about 9 blocks away. The marina provides a van service for guests. The personnel are friendly and helpful. A good stop. *(Marina map this page)*

Kingston. Use chart 18446; 18473; 18441. Kingston, in Appletree Cove on the west side of Puget Sound, is the western terminus of the ferry run to Edmonds. A Port-owned marina lies behind a breakwater in Appletree Cove. A marine supply store is nearby, and shopping is a short distance up the road. Several eateries, from simple to deluxe, are located around the ferry parking area.

On the other side of the ferry vehicle holding lanes, two decks overlook Puget Sound. A path leads to a sand beach filled with driftwood. It's a pleasant walk, and great for families.

On Saturdays during the summer a farmers' market, quite popular, is held on park grounds next to the marina. When we visited, we found a wide variety of baked goods, organic small-farm produce, honeys, jams and balms, fabric crafts, woodcrafts, live plants, and artwork. We bought several things. Couldn't say no.

② **Port of Kingston,** P.O. Box 559, Kingston, WA 98346, (360)297-3545, fax (360)297-2945, or e-mail at ptkingston@aol.com. Open all year, 44 guest slips, 30 amp power, restrooms, showers, laundry, pumpout, portapotty dump. The fuel dock has gasoline, diesel & propane. The marina has an 8000-

Reference only — not for navigation

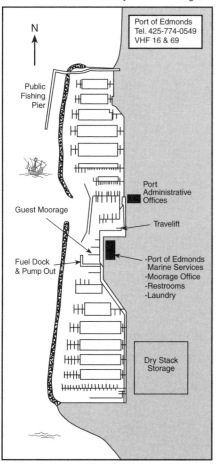

Port of Edmonds

Reference only — not for navigation

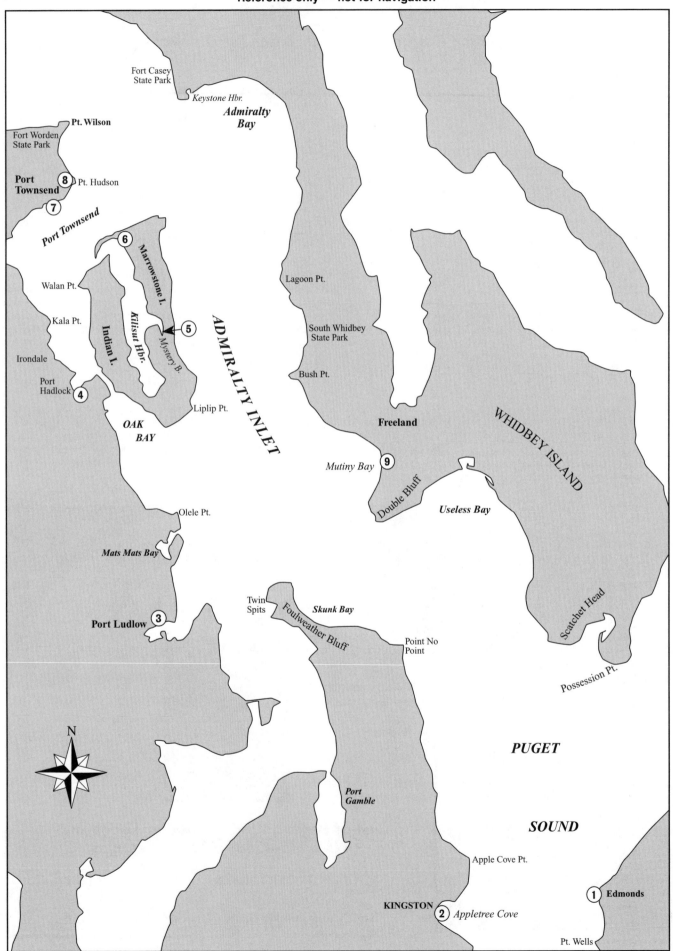

Fort Casey
State Park

Keystone Hbr.

*Admiralty
Bay*

Pt. Wilson

Fort Worden
State Park

**Port
Townsend** (8) Pt. Hudson

(7)

Port Townsend

(6)

Marrowstone I.

Walan Pt.

Lagoon Pt.

Kala Pt.

Kilisut Hbr.

(5)

Mystery B.

ADMIRALTY INLET

South Whidbey
State Park

Indian I.

Irondale

Bush Pt.

Port
Hadlock (4)

Liplip Pt.

*OAK
BAY*

Freeland

WHIDBEY ISLAND

Olele Pt.

Mutiny Bay (9)

Double Bluff

Useless Bay

Mats Mats Bay

Scatchet Head

Twin
Spits

Skunk Bay

Port Ludlow (3)

Foulweather Bluff

Point No
Point

Possession Pt.

N

PUGET

***Port
Gamble***

SOUND

Apple Cove Pt.

KINGSTON (2) *Appletree Cove*

(1) **Edmonds**

Pt. Wells

lb. capacity hoist for launching. A new dual-lane concrete launch ramp, with a float between the 2 lanes, is available. Parking is available for tow vehicles and trailers.

Enter the marina around the end of the rock breakwater, leaving two pilings that mark the edge of the dredged channel to port. Guest moorage is along a dock that runs parallel to the breakwater, with the fuel float at the shore end of the channel. The first 4 slips are reserved for Kingston Cove Yacht Club reciprocal moorage. Working toward the inner end of the dock, first are the 50-foot slips, then 40-foot, then 30-foot. Moorage is first-come, first-served. Moor in any unreserved space and walk up to the Port office to register. *(Marina map this page)*

ADMIRALTY INLET

Admiralty Inlet. Use chart 18441. Admiralty Inlet begins at Point No Point in the south, and ends at Point Wilson in the north. Admiralty Inlet is wide, deep and straight, with no reefs or shoals as hazards. It makes up for this good design by its infernal habit of being the only patch of rough water for miles. Flood current or ebb, it makes no difference, Admiralty Inlet waters swirl and lump up. If the wind is light, you'll see the swirls. If the wind is blowing, you'll be in the lump. Use the Bush Point current tables to predict the times of slack water, and the time and strength of maximum current.

If Admiralty Inlet is rough and you have to be there anyway, try to favor the eastern or western shores. We have had good luck on the western shore. We run along Marrowstone Island, far enough off to avoid the rocks shown on the chart. Usually we can sneak around Marrowstone Point inside the rough water just outside, and into Port Townsend Bay. The idea is, stay out of the middle.

If you are northbound past Point No Point

Guest moorage at Kingston is on this dock, protected by a high breakwater.

Shortly before opening, the canopies go up for the Saturday Farmers' Market at Kingston.

and you can see that Admiralty Inlet is rough (you can see it), head west, behind Marrowstone Island, and go through Port Townsend Canal into Port Townsend Bay. Port Townsend Canal currents are based on the Deception Pass current tables.

Point No Point. Use chart 18441. Point No Point, on the west side of Puget Sound, is a popular salmon-fishing spot, and a place where boats heading up-sound and down-sound tend to converge. Boat traffic can get heavy, especially if the salmon are running and the waters are covered—literally covered—with small sport fishing boats working along the tide-rip.

Watch out for this tide-rip. When a strong wind opposes a big tide, the waters off Point No Point can turn not just rough but dangerous, very dangerous. On Labor Day, 1999, a Sea Ray, about 27 feet long, was drying out in Kingston. The day before, a strong wind-against-current sea had set up off Point No Point, and the Sea Ray went through. It came off one wave and buried its nose in the next wave. The foredeck hatch was torn open and about 50 gallons (400 pounds) of green water poured below. When we met the owner the following day he still was visibly shaken. He'd had an uncomfortably close call.

About the time the Sea Ray had its adventure, a 40-footer had it worse. It too buried its bow in a wave and tore open the foredeck hatch, putting much water below. The next wave blew out the windshield. Water came

Reference only — not for navigation

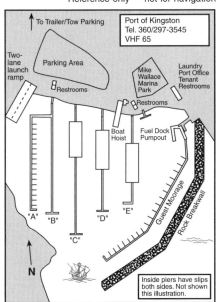

Port of Kingston

Port of Kingston
Tel. 360/297-3545
VHF 65

To Trailer/Tow Parking

Parking Area

Two-lane launch ramp

Restrooms

Mike Wallace Marina Park

Laundry
Port Office
Tenant Restrooms

Restrooms

Boat Hoist

Fuel Dock
Pumpout

Guest Moorage

Rock Breakwall

"A" "B" "C" "D" "E"

N

Inside piers have slips both sides. Not shown this illustration.

See area map page 56

aboard, and that boat went down. Fast. Other boats were in the area and everybody was saved, but they had to be pulled from the water.

These conditions are rare at Point No Point. We've rounded countless times without a problem. But in a way that makes Point No Point more dangerous. In Vancouver, locals know that Point Atkinson often is very rough, and always treat those waters with respect. Since Point No Point usually is fairly easy to get by, we assume it always will be easy, and that's when we can get in trouble.

Port Ludlow. Use chart 18477; 18473; 18441. Port Ludlow indents the western shore of the Olympic Peninsula. It was once the site of a major Pope & Talbot sawmill, and has now been turned into a fine residential area and destination resort. Anchorage is good south of the marina, and in the inner harbor.

The landlocked Port Ludlow inner harbor is reached by passing between two little islands near the head of the bay. Good anchorage, mud bottom, can be found in about 15 feet. Check your chart before entering the inner harbor, to assure that you are passing *between the two islets*. We know of one skipper who inadvertently passed between the westernmost islet and the mainland, and went aground. Deeper draft boats should watch the depth sounder closely when entering the inner harbor at low tide. The passage is more shallow than the bays it connects.

The inner harbor is a favorite destination in Puget Sound, protected from all winds. Until a few years ago it was surrounded by dense forest. Development has removed much of the forest and replaced it with private homes, but the bay retains at least some of its old charm. Meydenbauer Bay Yacht Club has an outstation on the peninsula that forms the inner harbor.

③ **Port Ludlow Marina,** 1 Gull Drive, Port Ludlow, WA 98365, (360)437-0513; (800)308-7991; fax (360)437-2428. Monitors VHF channel 16, switch to channel 68. Web site www.ptludlow.com; e-mail dkeeley@orminc.com. Open all year, 7 days. Gasoline, diesel, propane, CNG, stove alcohol. Guest moorage is in 50 slips

Private homes have replaced the dense forest that once surrounded the Port Ludlow inner harbor. Still, the bay remains popular.

and along 460 feet of dock, plus unoccupied slips when available, with 30 & 50 amp power, restrooms, showers, laundry, pumpout, portapotty dump. Reservations best by telephone, but okay by radio.

Two restaurants, both with lounges, are within walking distance. Free shuttle for marina guests to 27-hole golf course. The marina store carries groceries, beer, wine, ice, books, fishing tackle and bait, limited marine hardware and supplies. Nearby doctor, camping, post office. Marine mechanics are on call from Port Townsend. This is a well-protected harbor, but when entering, watch charts and depth sounder.

Mats Mats Bay. Use chart 18477; 18473; 18441. A course between Port Ludlow and Mats Mats Bay should be drawn to avoid Snake Rock, close to shore, and Colvos Rocks and Klas Rocks, farther offshore. Colvos Rocks are marked by a buoy at each end, and Klas Rock is marked. Snake Rock is not.

Mats Mats Bay has a dogleg entrance with a least depth of 5 feet. A lighted range shows the center of the narrow channel. Once in the bay, you'll find anchorage in 3 fathoms in the middle. Mats Mats Bay is well protected from almost any wind, and is a favored hidey-hole. A launch ramp is at the south end of the bay. A large rock used to almost block the entrance to the bay, but it was blasted out several years ago, and buoys now mark the channel. Pay attention to all buoys, and do not stray from the marked channel, especially at low water.

Oak Bay. Use chart 18477; 18473; 18441. Oak Bay, with convenient anchoring depths, is at the southern approach to the Port

Townsend Canal. Oak Bay County Park is on the west side of the channel, a mile or so south of the entrance to the canal.

Oak Bay County Park, northwest shore of Oak Bay. Open all year, restrooms, no power, water or showers. Anchoring or beaching only. Marked by a rock jetty. Launch ramp, campsites, picnic tables, swimming, scuba diving, clamming, crabbing.

Port Townsend Canal. Use chart 18464; 18441. The Port Townsend Canal (also known as the Hadlock Canal) runs from Oak Bay to Port Townsend Bay through a relatively narrow dredged channel. The canal is spanned by a bridge with a 58-foot vertical clearance. Currents run 2.5-3 knots. Port Townsend Canal is a secondary station under the Deception Pass reference station in the current tables.

Irondale and Port Hadlock. Use chart 18464; 18441. The towns of Irondale and Port Hadlock are west of the northern entrance to the Port Townsend Canal. An old alcohol plant has been converted into a resort at Hadlock, complete with a breakwater-protected marina. Anchorage in the area is good, sand bottom, but be careful to stay north of the little island between Irondale and Port Hadlock.

④ **Port Hadlock Bay Marina,** P.O. Box 1369, Port Hadlock, WA 98339, telephone (360)385-6368; (800)785-7030; fax (360)385-6955. Open all year, 30 & 50 amp power, reservations recommended. Restrooms and showers, pumpout. The marina has mostly permanent moorage. The adjacent Old Alcohol Plant Lodge has a restaurant and lounge. No

Reference only — not for navigation

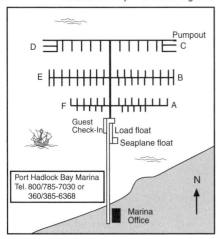

Port Hadlock Bay Marina

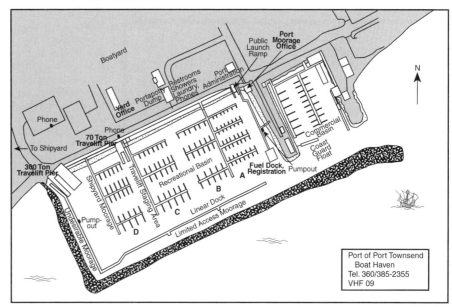

Port of Port Townsend Boat Haven

Reference only — not for navigation

groceries, repairs, or marine supplies at marina, but a general store and laundromat are close. *(Marina map above)*

Kilisut Harbor. Use chart 18464. Kilisut Harbor is entered through a channel between Walan Point and the spit that protects the harbor. The channel is well marked, though shallow, averaging about 11 feet. The channel swings past Fort Flagler State Park on the north shore, where there is a launch ramp. Picnicking and camping facilities are ashore.

Following the channel into Kilisut Harbor leads to Mystery Bay, where the village of Nordland has a float and a store. Mystery Bay State Park has a long mooring float parallel to the shore. Small boats can be launched over the beach. Anchorage is good, mud bottom, throughout the bay.

⑤ **Mystery Bay Marine State Park,** in Kilisut Harbor on Marrowstone Island. Use chart 18464. Open all year, 683 feet dock space with 4.5-foot depth at zero tide, 7 mooring buoys. Pumpout, portapotty dump, no power, no restrooms, no showers. The park is open for day use only, but overnight mooring is okay at the dock. The dock lies parallel to shore. Vault toilet on shore. One-lane launch ramp.

⑥ **Fort Flagler Marine State Park,** on Marrowstone Island. Use chart 18464 (preferred); 18441. Open all year, day use, overnight mooring and camping. Has 244 feet of dock space with 6-foot depth at zero tide, 7 mooring buoys (buoys removed in winter). Restrooms, showers, laundry, portapotty dump, no power. A popular park. Launch ramp, underwater park for divers. Snack and grocery concession. Boat rentals, fishing supplies. Standard, utility and primitive campsites. Campsite reservations are a good idea in summer. Call (800)452-5687 for reservations.

Port Townsend. Use chart 18464; 18441. Port Townsend has two marinas, the privately-operated Point Hudson Marina and the Port of Port Townsend's Boat Haven marina. Point Hudson is closer to downtown, but Boat Haven is closer to a supermarket.

Port Townsend is a major marine center, with craftsmen skilled in every nautical discipline available to service boats. It is the home of the annual Wooden Boat Festival, held each year the weekend after Labor Day.

This is one of our favorite towns. The commercial district is lined with imposing stone and brick buildings from before 1900, when the residents hoped that Port Townsend would become the principal city on Puget Sound. Victorian homes, most of them beautifully restored and cared for, are on the hill above the business district. Port Townsend's upper business district is located at the top of a long flight of stairs from the lower district. Port Townsend is a haven for writers, craftspeople and artists of all kinds. Tourists overwhelm the town during the summer, but that shouldn't keep anybody away.

The park float at Mystery Bay has room for many boats.

We arrived at the Nordland General Store too late to join the boys for morning coffee, but the stove and chairs were waiting.

⑦ **Port of Port Townsend Boat Haven,** P.O. Box 1180, 2601 Washington Street, Port Townsend, WA 98368, (360)385-2355. Or view at:www.portofporttownsend. dst.wa.us and e-mail at: Info@ portofporttownsend.dst.wa.us. Monitors VHF channel 09. Open all year. Gasoline and diesel fuel at The Fish'n' Hole. Guest moorage includes 900 feet of dock space and unoccupied slips as available, with 20, 30, & 50 amp power, restrooms, showers, laundry, pumpout, portapotty dump, moderate-risk waste facility. Customs clearance is available.

The marina is west of the ferry dock, and entered between a rock breakwater and a piling wavebreak. The first section is reserved for Coast Guard vessels and commercial fish boats. The fuel dock is to starboard after passing the Coast Guard pier. Arrangements for moorage should be made at the moorage office.

You can call ahead to check availability of slips. After hours, see a map outside the marina office, with empty slips marked. Do not moor at the fuel dock—temporary tie-up only while getting a slip. There is a new public launch ramp with paved access and parking. New Travelift haulout to 300 tons. Repairs for everything are available nearby. A large Safeway supermarket is across the highway.

Major boat building and repair facilities and a chandlery (Admiral Ship Supply) are adjacent to this marina. A West Marine store is nearby. *(Marina map page 59)*

The Fish'n' Hole, Port of Port Townsend, Port Townsend, WA 98368, (360)385-7031. Gasoline and diesel fuel, open all year. Fuel dock only. Located inside the breakwater of the Port of Port

Townsend Marina. Floating store carries snacks, bait, tackle.

⑧ **Point Hudson Resort & Marina,** Point Hudson, Port Townsend, WA 98368, (360)385-2828; (800)826-3854. Open 7 days a week all year, 60 slips and 800 feet of dock space, maximum boat length approximately 65 feet. Has launch ramp, 20 & 30 amp power, restrooms, showers, laundry. Reservations accepted. Customs clearance is available by phone. Ice, charts, event facility, RV park, motel, three restaurants on the property or nearby. Point Hudson is adjacent to downtown.

Enter Point Hudson between two piling breakwaters that force the channel into a distinct bend, directly into the prevailing north-westerly summer winds. This discourages sailing into the Point Hudson marina in anything larger than a dinghy. Inside are a number of finger floats on the east shore, a center float, and a long float along the west shore. The marina office is in a white building on the east side. Fleet Marine's haulout and repair facility, with chandlery, is located at the end of the dredged basin, with a work yard for maintenance. Other marine businesses in the area include Port Townsend Sails, Brion Toss's Center Harbor Rigging shop, and several wooden boat shops. *(Marina map page 61)*

Old Fort Townsend Marine State Park, between Glen Cove & Kala Point, Port Townsend, WA, (360)385-3595. Use chart 18464; 18441. Open summers only, 4 mooring buoys, restrooms, showers, no power. The park has swimming, playgrounds, hiking trails, picnic tables, fire rings, kitchen shelters, play equipment. Self-

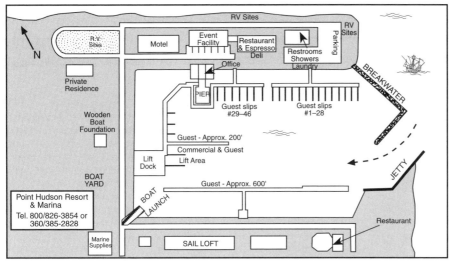

Point Hudson Resort & Marina

Reference only — not for navigation

Kayakers at the Point Hudson Marina enjoy a water-level view of classic wooden boats during the annual Wooden Boat Festival. The festival is held the weekend after Labor Day at Point Hudson in Port Townsend.

guided nature trail, clamming, fishing, scuba diving. Campsites.

Fort Worden Marine State Park, north of Port Townsend, (360)385-4730. Use chart 18464; 18441. Open all year, 128 feet of dock space, 8 mooring buoys. Restrooms, showers and laundry, no power. The dock is protected by a wharf. Use the dock or buoys; this is not a good anchorage. Underwater park for scuba diving. Launch with 2 ramps. Tennis courts, picnic areas, snack bar concession near moorage area. Hiking trails, swimming, fishing. Utility and primitive campsites. Campsite reservations taken year-round. Call (800)452-5687.

Upland, the old officers' quarters can be rented overnight. Fort buildings house the Centrum Foundation, which conducts workshops and seminars on the arts each summer, and the Marine Science Center, where visitors can view a variety of marine life.

Point Wilson. Use chart 18464 (large scale) or 18441. Point Wilson is the corner where Admiralty Inlet turns into the Strait of Juan de Fuca. On an ebb a nasty tide-rip can build immediately north of Point Wilson, and stretch well across the mouth of Admiralty Inlet. If it's a big ebb and opposed by strong westerly winds, the seas in this area are not merely nasty, they are dangerous. They become high, steep and close together. They break. They are not long rollers, they are pyramid-shaped, and have no consistent pattern except for being ugly.

Since boats bound for the San Juan Islands or out the Strait of Juan de Fuca often time their passages to take advantage of an ebb, skippers must be aware of what can happen at Point Wilson, especially if a westerly is blowing. In such conditions, the wise approach is to favor the Whidbey Island side. The even wiser choice is to wait until slack water or the beginning of the flood. Better yet, wait for the wind to drop and then go at slack water.

The bigger the ebb, the greater the chance for a tide-rip. A small ebb can produce no rip at all, particularly if the wind is light. Use the Bush Point current tables to

Hood Canal

predict the time of slack water and strength of maximum current. Those who think that a fast boat makes current tables unnecessary are wrong, and Point Wilson will prove them so.

ADMIRALTY INLET—
WHIDBEY ISLAND SIDE

⑨ **Mutiny Bay Resort,** P.O. Box 249, 5856 S. Mutiny Bay Rd., Freeland, WA 98249, (360)331-4500. Use chart 18477; 18473; 18441. Open all year, reservations recommended for guest moorage. Mooring buoys are for resort guests only. Restrooms, showers, no power. Resort sells charts, tackle and bait. Nearby doctor, post office, liquor store.

South Whidbey State Park, on Admiralty Inlet, 3 miles south of Greenbank, Whidbey Island, (360)331-4559. Use chart 18441. Open all year, day use and overnight camping. Overnight camping is restricted to weekends and holidays between November 15 and February 14. Restrooms, showers, no power. Anchoring in calm conditions or beaching only, underwater park for scuba diving. Picnic sites. Hiking trail. Standard and primitive campsites.

Fort Casey State Park, 3 miles south of Coupeville on Admiralty Inlet. Use chart 18441. Open all year, day use and overnight camping, restrooms, no power or showers. Anchoring or beaching only, 2-lane launch ramp with boarding floats. Underwater park with artificial reef for scuba divers. Picnic areas, standard and primitive campsites. Lighthouse and interpretive center. Historic displays, remains of the old fort to explore.

We Are Amazed
at the hundreds of changes, updates and additions we make to each new Waggoner Cruising Guide.

Stay Up to Date.
Make a current edition of the Waggoner Cruising Guide part of your boat's standard equipment.

Charts
18441	Puget Sound – Northern Part (1:80,000)
18445SC	FOLIO-SMALL CRAFT Puget Sound – Possession Sound to Olympia including Hood Canal
18448	Puget Sound – Southern Part (1:80,000)
18458	Hood Canal – South Point to Quatsop Point including Dabob Bay (1:25,000)
18473	Puget Sound – Oak Bay to Shilshole Bay (1:40,000)
18476	Hood Canal to Dabob Bay (1:40,000)
18477	Puget Sound – Entrance to Hood Canal (1:25,000)

Use charts 18476; 18445sc; 18477; 18458; 18441; 18448. Hood Canal is a 65-mile-long glacier-carved fjord. Because the shorelines are fairly straight with few protected anchorages, Hood Canal is less used by pleasure craft than many other waterways. Most boaters don't realize that shrimping, oyster gathering, clamming and fishing are outstanding. The shrimping season is short: 3 weeks in May, just two days each week. But on those days, the boats are thick. In clear weather the views of the Olympic Mountains are spectacular. Other than shrimpers and knowing fishermen, however, Hood Canal is largely undiscovered.

The best chart for Hood Canal is 18476, which shows the entire canal except for the very mouth. That area is shown well on charts 18473 and 18477. Small Craft chart 18445 shows the entire canal, but in less convenient format.

Several rivers flow from the Olympic Mountains into Hood Canal, and each has formed a mudflat off its mouth. Although the shoal off the Dosewallips River, a couple of miles south of Pulali Point, is marked, the shoals off the Duckabush, Fulton Creek, Hama Hama and Lilliwaup Rivers are not marked, nor is the extensive shoal off the Skokomish River at the Great Bend. Care must be taken to avoid running aground.

Pleasant Harbor and the Alderbrook Inn Resort can take larger boats, but many of the other marinas and parks on Hood Canal are aimed at trailerable boats. This has disappointed some people in larger boats, who had hoped for more facilities for boats their size.

Hood Head. Anchorage can be found behind Hood Head on the western shore of Hood Canal, but the water shoals rapidly to drying flats near the head of the bay.

Bywater Bay State Park, 1 mile north of the Hood Canal Bridge on the west shore of Hood Canal. Day use only, toilets, no power,

water or showers. Anchoring only, well offshore. Launch ramp, crabbing and clamming, hiking trails.

Port Gamble. Use chart 184473; 18477; 18476. Port Gamble is a fine anchorage, protected from wave action by a sandspit at the entrance. Anchorage in 3 to 5 fathoms is possible everywhere. Many people prefer the area just inside the spit. A range outside Port Gamble will keep you to a mid-channel course as you enter or depart. Sight astern to keep the range lined up while entering. Your course will lead you close to the ends of the old Pope & Talbott sawmill docks. A section of the old I-90 floating bridge from Lake Washington is moored in the bay, with some Indian-owned fishboats tied to it. Mooring to this bridge is discouraged.

Hood Canal Floating Bridge. Use chart 18473; 18477; 18476. The east end of the Hood Canal Floating Bridge has a vertical clearance of 55 feet. Clearance on the west end is 35 feet. While the bridge can be opened for larger vessels, it is not manned and you must call (360)779-3233 to arrange an opening. You will reach a State Dept. of Transportation office in Tacoma, and they will answer, "Olympic Radio." They will take your name, telephone number, name of your vessel, date and time of desired opening, and whether you are inbound or outbound. They also will ask what width opening you need (300 feet or 600 feet). One hour's notice is needed to get a crew to the bridge and prepare it for opening.

Caution: Sisters, two substantial rocks about 200 yards apart, lie 0.4 mile south of the Hood Canal bridge on the west side. The rocks dry at half tide. The southern rock is marked by a large lighted beacon, yet from time to time an unwary boat manages to go up on these rocks. For safety, if you have passed under the western end of the bridge, turn eastward at once and run to the middle of the bridge before turning south into Hood Canal.

Salsbury Point County Park, just off the northeast end of the Hood Canal Bridge. Day use only, restrooms, no power or showers. Anchoring only, 2 launch ramps. Picnic tables, fireplaces, children's play area. Nature trail. Sandy beach for experienced scuba divers, because of strong currents.

Squamish Harbor. Squamish Harbor has convenient anchoring depths, but the harbor is quite open, and has numerous rocks and reefs that must be avoided. It is seldom used for overnight anchorage.

Thorndyke Bay. Thorndyke Bay is too open to provide a snug anchorage.

Restricted Area. Use chart 18476. For about 4 miles south from Vinland, the eastern shore

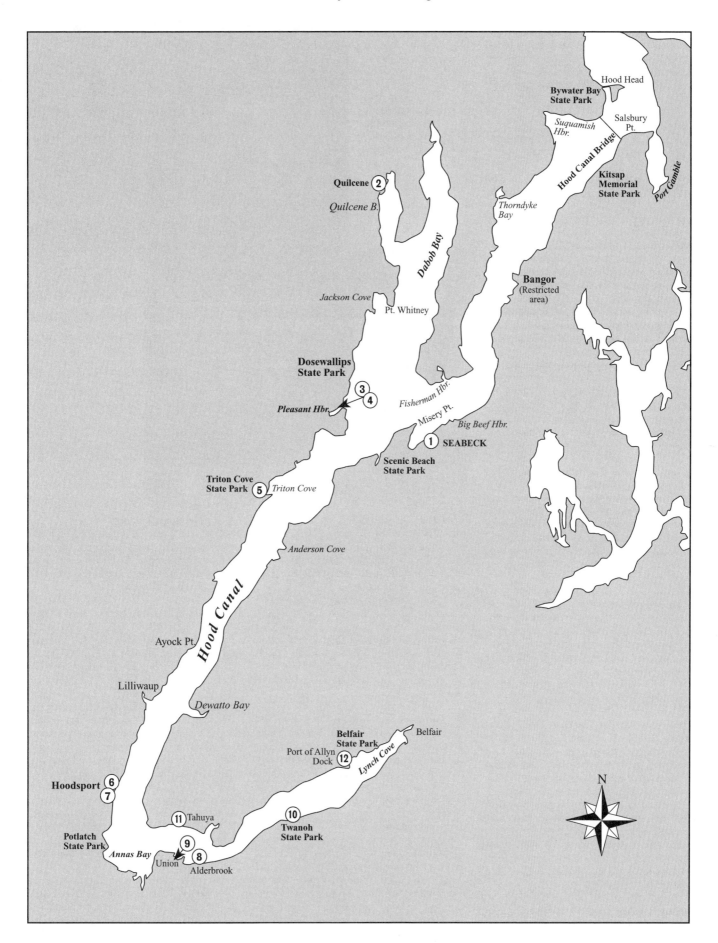

Hood Head
Bywater Bay State Park
Salsbury Pt.
Suquamish Hbr.
Hood Canal Bridge
Kitsap Memorial State Park
Port Gamble
Thorndyke Bay

Quilcene ②
Quilcene B.

Dabob Bay

Bangor (Restricted area)

Jackson Cove
Pt. Whitney

Dosewallips State Park

③
④
Pleasant Hbr.
Fisherman Hbr.
Misery Pt.
Big Beef Hbr.
① SEABECK
Scenic Beach State Park

Triton Cove State Park ⑤ Triton Cove

Anderson Cove

Hood Canal

Ayock Pt.

Lilliwaup

Dewatto Bay

Belfair State Park
Belfair
Port of Allyn Dock ⑫ Lynch Cove

Hoodsport ⑥
⑦

⑪ Tahuya
⑩
Twanoh State Park

Potlatch State Park
Annas Bay
⑨
Union
⑧
Alderbrook

N

See area map page 63

of Hood Canal is a Naval Restricted Area, and is patrolled constantly to keep passing vessels well offshore. This is the location of the Bangor Naval Station, home port for a fleet of nuclear submarines. Several of these awesome machines usually are visible to passing craft.

Seabeck Bay. Use chart 18476. Anchorage is possible behind Misery Point, with good protection from the south and west.

① **Seabeck Marina,** P.O. Box 177, 15376 Seabeck Hwy NW, Seabeck, WA 98380, (360)830-5179. Monitors CB channel 13. Open all year. Gasoline only. Guest moorage available, 2-fathom depth at zero tide, reservations needed May-August. The docks are pretty rough. Restrooms, portapotty dump, no power or showers. Groceries, water and ice. Take-out pizza (this is where Seabeck Pizza comes from), espresso, deli, general store. Sling for haulout, repairs available. Some marine supplies. Fishing tackle and bait. Camping at Scenic Beach State Park ½ mile away. Seabeck conference grounds nearby.

The marina once was protected by a clever floating breakwater made of large steel balls. One by one the balls have sunk, but there are no guarantees they are on the bottom. The safe entry is around the west side of the floating breakwater. A sign on a float marks the spot.

Kitsap Memorial Marine State Park, 4 miles south of Hood Canal Bridge, (360)779-3205. Use chart 18476. Open all year, day use and overnight camping, 2 mooring buoys. Restrooms, showers, no power. Picnic sites, kitchen shelters, fireplaces. Standard campsites. Swimming beach. Playground, horseshoe pits, volleyball courts, baseball field. Buoys are exposed to wind and tidal currents.

Scenic Beach State Park, south of Seabeck, (360)830-5079. Use chart 18476. Open for day use all year and overnight camping summer only. Restrooms, showers, no power. Anchoring only. Kitchen shelter, fireplaces, fire rings, horseshoe pits, volleyball areas. Standard and primitive campsites. Scuba diving, swimming, hiking, shellfishing.

Fisherman Harbor. Use chart 18476. Fisherman Harbor can be entered only on top of high water, but once inside offers protected anchorage in 5 to 15 feet. Follow the natural channel into the bay, then turn south and follow the spit until anchoring depths are found. All the land around the bay is privately owned. Years ago, we tiptoed into Fisherman Harbor in a sailboat at something less than high tide. It was careful going, with a close watch from the bow and a bit of luck, but the boat got in without touching. Less foolish souls should wait for higher water.

Dabob Bay. Use chart 18476. Most of Dabob Bay is a Naval Restricted Area, with lights on Point Syloplash, Point Whitney, and Point

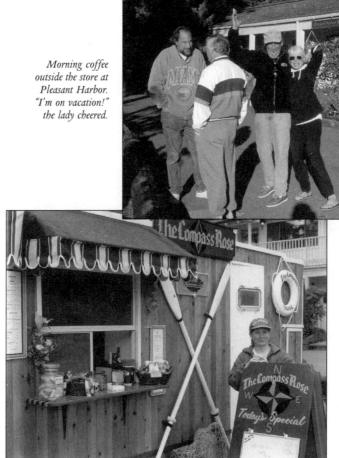

Morning coffee outside the store at Pleasant Harbor. "I'm on vacation!" the lady cheered.

She sells seashells down by the seashore. Robin Foss sells chowder, oysters, clams and shrimp at Pleasant Harbor Marina.

Zelatched that warn when caution must be used (flashing green) or when the area is closed (flashing red). South of Pulali Point, the western shore of Dabob Bay is not within this restricted area, and includes **Jackson Cove**, where good anchorage can be found.

A State Fisheries Department oyster research laboratory is at Whitney Point, with a good launch ramp alongside. A breakwater-protected marina is at the village of **Quilcene**. Caution should be exercised when transiting Dabob Bay and Quilcene Bay to avoid the large number of shrimp pots throughout the bays in season.

② **Quilcene Boathaven,** P.O. Box 98, Quilcene, WA 98376, (360)765-3131. Open 7 days in summer, as needed in winter. Gasoline and diesel at fuel dock. Some guest moorage available. Has 20 & 30 amp power, restrooms, showers, pumpout, portpotty dump, marine repairs and supplies, ice. This is a small, rustic marina away from the more heavily-used destination marinas nearby.

Pleasant Harbor. Use chart 18476. Pleasant Harbor is a major stopping point on Hood Canal, with a fine destination resort marina and a State Park float. There's room to anchor, 3-7 fathoms, mud bottom. The Pleasant Harbor Marina has excellent facilities for visiting boats. The Pleasant Harbor "Old" Ma-

rina has no guest moorage.

Pleasant Harbor is full of boats in May, when the annual 3-week-long shrimping season is running. Shrimping is allowed only on Saturdays and Wednesdays, and during those three weeks it's kind of crazy.

③ **Pleasant Harbor Marina,** 308913 Hwy 101, Brinnon, WA 98320, (360)796-4611, fax (360)796-4898. Monitors VHF channels 09 & 16. Open all year 0800-1900, except closed Thanksgiving and Christmas. Gasoline and diesel at the fuel dock. The marina has 40 plus guest slips and unoccupied slips as available, 30 & 50 amp power. Facilities include new and sparkling restrooms and showers, a laundry, pumpout, and portapotty dump.

This is a popular destination, with groceries, ice, bait, tackle, marine hardware, beer and wine, pizza parlor (Seabeck pizza—superb), gift shop, barbecue and picnic area, hot tub and swimming pool. When we visited in September, a second swimming pool was under construction at the north end of the property. A comfort station, with laundry, restrooms and showers, is planned for the northern dock but not yet built.

At the head of the main dock a delightful lady named Robin Foss runs Compass Rose, a chowder and espresso stand, housed in a trailer. The chowder is her mother's recipe, and her mother used to cook for the fisher-

men. We tried some of Robin's chowder and it's excellent. Robin also sells oysters and clams—fresh, right off the boat. Compass Rose is open six months a year, during the summer season.

Betty and Chuck Finnila, who bought the marina in 1994, have upgraded the grounds, replaced docks, added new docks, and greatly improved the facilities. The gift shop is outstanding and the convenience store well-stocked.

Large expansion plans are in the works. They have acquired the adjacent property and plan to develop a luxury hotel and restaurant. On the next hillside—read, mountaintop—construction has begun on a fabulous 18-hole golf course, with courseside building lots available. Chuck drove us to the sites of several of the holes and we were awed by the views. The property is a failed campground development; roads and utilities already are in. The golf course is scheduled to open in 2001.

If all these plans come to fruition, Pleasant Harbor Marina will become a remarkable destination marina. Based on what we've seen Chuck and Betty Finnila accomplish already, we have no reason to doubt the future. *(Marina map this page)*

④ **Pleasant Harbor Marine State Park,** (360)796-4415. Open all year for day use and overnight mooring. No camping. Dock has 218 feet of space. Vault toilet, portapotty dump, pumpout, no power.

Dosewallips State Park, 1 mile south of Brinnon. Open all year for day use and overnight camping. Restrooms, showers, no power. Anchorage only, outside the delta flats. Hiking trails, picnic areas, standard, utility, and primitive campsites.

Triton Head. Use chart 18476. A State Park launch ramp is at Triton Head, and anchorage is possible off this little bight.

⑤ **Triton Cove State Park,** west side of Hood Canal, south of the Dosewallips River.

Open all year, day use only, small dock with float. Restrooms, no power, no showers. Improved concrete launch ramp, picnic area.

⑥ **Hoodsport Marina & Cafe,** 24080 Hwy 101, Hoodsport, WA 98548, (360)877-9657. Open all year, guest moorage, call ahead for availability. Restrooms, no power or showers. Restaurant (free moorage while dining). Water, gasoline nearby. Groceries 1 block away.

⑦ **Sunrise Motel & Resort,** North Hwy 101, Hoodsport, WA 98548, (360)877-5301. Open all year, no power. Restrooms and showers in motel rooms. Stay on your boat or rent rooms. Popular spot for divers. Underwater park, scuba air station. Dive shop.

Potlatch Marine State Park, south of Hoodsport, (360)877-5361. Use chart 18476. Open all year, day use and overnight camping and mooring. Restrooms, showers, no power. Five mooring buoys are offshore in deep water. The park has a picnic area, an underwater park for scuba diving, short hiking trails, and standard, utility and primitive campsites. Good wildlife-watching.

⑧ **Alderbrook Inn Resort,** E. 7101 Hwy 106, Union, WA 98592, (360)898-2200; (800) 622-9370. Or view at www.alderbrook inn.com. Open all year, 1200 feet of dock space, 30 amp power, restrooms, showers, pumpout, portapotty dump. Reservations taken for large vessels. A fine resort, with an 18-hole golf course, tennis courts, indoor pool and Jacuzzi. Boat rentals and crab pot rentals are available. Swimming dock, playground, volleyball court, horseshoe pit, outdoor barbeques, restaurant (no alcohol served). Fuel, groceries, laundry, launch ramp nearby.

Alderbrook has been remodeled and is open to the public.

⑨ **Hood Canal Marina,** P.O. Box 86, E 5101 Hwy 106, Union, WA 98592, (360)898-2252. Open all year. Gasoline only. Guest moorage available, call ahead. 30 amp power,

restrooms. Full-time mechanic on-call. Grocery store nearby.

⑩ **Twanoh Marine State Park,** 8 miles west of Belfair, (360)275-2222. Use chart 18476. Open all year, day use and overnight camping & mooring, except no camping in winter. Has 192 feet of dock space, 7 mooring buoys. Restrooms, showers, pumpout, portapotty dump, no power. This is a large and popular park, with launch ramp, wading pool and playground, picnic areas, kitchen shelters, and fireplaces. Standard, utility and primitive campsites, tennis courts, hiking trails, seasonal concession stand.

⑪ **Summertide Resort & Marina,** NE 15781 Northshore Rd, Tahuya, WA 98588, (360)275-9313, (253)925-9277. Moorage available from May-September, 560 feet of dock space, 22-foot maximum boat length. Reservations necessary. Restrooms, showers, laundry, no power on docks. Launch ramp and RV spaces with full hook-ups. Small boat marina, most people rent cottages or camp. Small store carries ice, propane, groceries, bait, tackle, fishing licenses.

HOOD CANAL BECOMES SHALLOW toward its end near Belfair, with extensive drying flats in Lynch Cove, where the Union River enters Hood Canal. Convenient anchoring depths, mud bottom, can be found throughout this end of the Canal.

Belfair State Park, 3 miles west of Belfair on the north shore of Hood Canal. Open all year for day use and overnight camping. Restrooms, showers, no power. Anchor far offshore if at all. Drying mudflats restrict approach to small, shallow-draft boats only. Popular, well-equipped park, camping reservations required in summer. Call (800)452-5687.

⑫ **Port of Allyn,** North shore of Hood Canal, 3 miles south of Belfair, (360)275-2192. Open all year, 4 slips, watch depth at low tide. Has 20 & 30 amp power, restrooms, no water or showers. Launch ramp. Very limited space for visiting boats. Call ahead if you want to hook up to power.

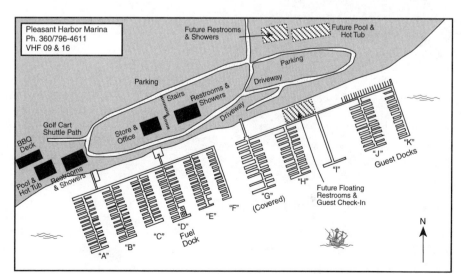

Pleasant Harbor Marina

Reference only — not for navigation

Tell Them You Read About Them In the Waggoner.

Northeast Puget Sound—
Mukilteo to Penn Cove

Everett • Langley • Port Susan • Saratoga Passage • Coupeville

Charts

18423sc FOLIO SMALL-CRAFT
Bellingham to Everett
including San Juan Islands
(1:80,000)
Blaine (1:30,000)

18441 Puget Sound – Northern
part (1:80,000)

18443 Approaches to Everett
(1:40,000)

18444 Everett Harbor
(1:10,000)

18445sc FOLIO SMALL-CRAFT Puget
Sound – Possession Sound
to Olympia including
Hood Canal

This float with wheelchair access was installed at the Port of Everett in 1998.

The 13-lane launch ramp at Everett gets plenty of use.

Mukilteo. Use chart 18443. The Mukilteo State Park has a 4-lane launch ramp with floats in season. It is exposed to ferry wakes and waves generated by winds on Possession Sound and Port Gardner. Adjacent to the ferry dock a small float, part of the state park, gives access to restaurants and other businesses ashore. The Mukilteo Lighthouse can be visited.

Everett. Use large-scale chart 18444 (preferred) or chart 18443. The Port of Everett Marina is the largest marina north of Marina del Rey, and is home to a substantial fishing fleet as well as private pleasure craft. Entry is about a mile upstream from the marked mouth of the Snohomish River. Information about moorage can be obtained from the fuel dock just inside the piling breakwater. *Caution:* River currents can be quite strong, particularly on an ebb tide. Allow for the current as you maneuver.

While you are in the river and approaching the marina entrance, watch for debris in the water and pay close attention to your navigation. Several buoys, including one buoy marking a sunken ship, can be confusing. While the channel can be entered between buoy 3 and buoy 5 off the south end of Jetty Island, for complete safety we recommend that you enter by leaving buoy 5 to port. The channel leads past the newly-constructed U.S. Navy homeport facilities. Large-scale chart 18444 is very helpful. We urge you to use it.

Caution: At night, lights ashore in the new Navy facilities make the entrance channel buoys very difficult to see and identify. Any vessel approaching at night should be extremely cautious.

Everett has all services, including fuel, water, electricity, pumpout, haulout and repair. Chandleries and a wide range of supply and repair shops are on port property or line Marine Drive. The marina is a good long hike from the central business district, but bus and taxi service are available.

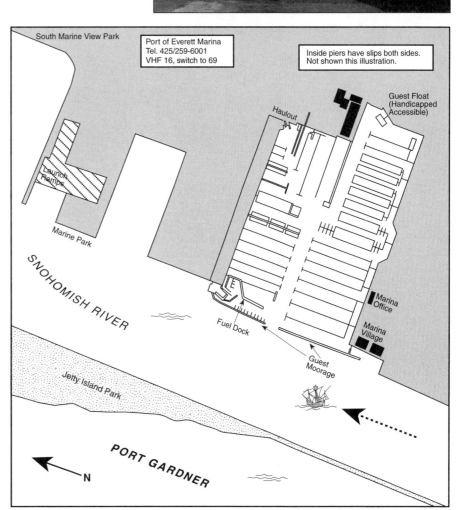

South Marine View Park

Port of Everett Marina
Tel. 425/259-6001
VHF 16, switch to 69

Inside piers have slips both sides.
Not shown this illustration.

Haulout

Guest Float
(Handicapped Accessible)

Launch Ramps

Marine Park

SNOHOMISH RIVER

Fuel Dock

Marina Office

Marina Village

Guest Moorage

Jetty Island Park

PORT GARDNER

N

Port of Everett Marina

Reference only — not for navigation

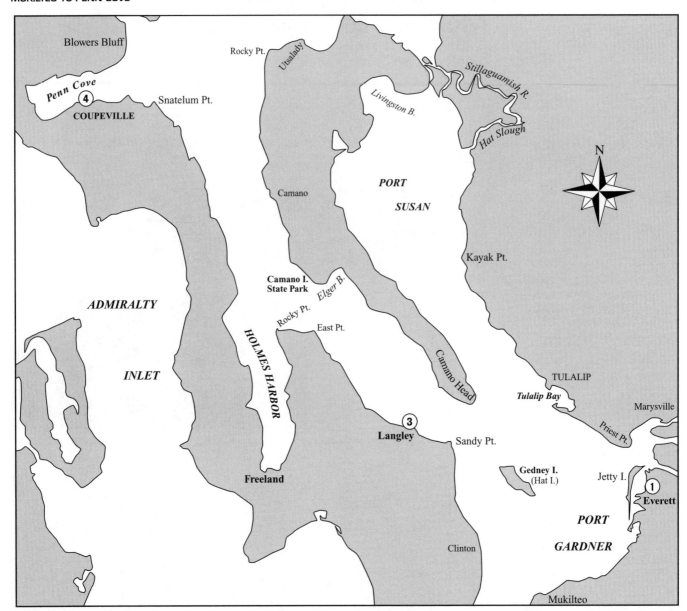

Across the river from the marina is a Port-owned float at Jetty Island, which has what is probably the largest pure sand beach on Puget Sound. The Langus Waterfront Park, with a fine launching facility, is on the north shore of the main river channel, a short distance upstream from the Port of Everett Marina.

Farther up the Snohomish River, Dagmar's Landing is a large dry-land storage facility with a huge fork lift truck and a long float. A detailed chart or local knowledge are required before attempting to go up the river beyond Dagmar's.

① **Port of Everett Marina,** P.O. Box 538, 1720 W. Marine View Drive, Everett, WA 98206, (425)259-6001; fax (425)259-0860; e-mail marina@portofeverett.com. Monitors VHF channel 16, switch to 69. Open all year, gasoline and diesel at fuel dock. Guest moorage along 1800 feet of dock with depths 11-20 feet, unoccupied slips used when available, 20 & 30 amp power, restrooms, showers (in 1999 the north marina basin got a new building

with new restrooms and showers), laundry, new vacuum pumpout, portapotty dump. New handicapped accessible guest moorage is available. Customs clearance is available. Watch for strong currents when landing at the guest dock. Haulout and yard storage are available for repairs and maintenance. The portapotty dump and pumpout are free of charge. The Everett Marine Park, a 13-lane launch ramp run by Port, is just north of marina.

The Port of Everett is a large, complete marina, with shops, full repairs and services nearby. An attractive marina village, with shops and good restaurants, has been built adjacent to the south mooring basin. This has changed the marina from a place to tie up to a destination worth visiting. The new wheelchair-accessible float is next to the street in the south basin. Harbor Marine and West Marine, both of them well-stocked marine chandleries, are on the property. *(Marina map page 67)*

Jetty Island. Jetty Island is a delightful low sand island located across the river from the

Everett Marina and Everett Marine Park. It is open all year for day use, with dock space for several boats. Boats can overnight at the dock. Jetty Island has toilets but no showers, no power, and no water for boats. The toilet is closed in the winter.

River currents can make landing at the docks interesting. Before approaching the dock, be sure your boat is well fendered, with dock lines ready and contigency plans agreed upon. Jetty Island is a wildlife preserve, with great birdwatching. The Parks Department offers nature programs during the summer, and runs boats from the Port of Everett to the island. For information call (425)259-6001.

① **Everett Marine Park** is on the the Snohomish River, north of the Port of Everett Marina. The park is open all year, with 700 feet of guest moorage, restrooms and pumpout, but no power, no showers. The park has a 13-lane launch ramp with boarding floats. An attendant is on duty summer and fall.

Run and jump among the logs on Jetty Park's beach. The docks have room for several boats.

Snohomish River Delta. The Snohomish River Delta has three main mouths—Steamboat Slough, Ebey Slough, and the main river—each of which is navigable for all or part of its length. Cautious boaters can cruise the delta country.

Contributing Editor Tom Kincaid has cruised all of this area, some of it several times, in a 30-foot sailboat, a 36-foot powerboat, and an outboard-powered dinghy. The waters are subject to tidal action. Drying flats are off the river mouths. Enter only during the hours of highest tides. The Snohomish River Delta is a fascinating place, with wildlife, calm anchorages, and quiet.

Langus Waterfront Park, north shore of the Snohomish River. The park is open all year and has restrooms, but no guest moorage, power or showers. This is a City of Everett park, with a 2-lane concrete launch ramp and boarding floats. It has a wide concrete float for fishing and launching rowing shells.

Grand in scale... friendly in spirit.

Gedney Island. Gedney Island, known locally as Hat Island, is privately owned. The marina on the north shore is for Gedney Island property owners, who are served by a private ferry from the Everett Marina.

Tulalip Bay. Anchorage is possible, but Tulalip Bay is very shallow, with a reef guarding the entrance and drying shoals inside. There are several private floats and mooring buoys owned by members of the Tulalip Indian tribe, which owns the surrounding land.

Port Susan. Use chart 18441. Kayak Point in Port Susan is a Snohomish County Park, with a launch ramp and load- and unload-only floats. Anchorage is good close to the beach. North of Kayak Point, Port Susan shoals to drying flats, through which meander the two mouths of the Stillaguamish River. At high tide it is possible to cross over these flats and enter South Pass to Stanwood, although the bridge just beyond Stanwood is very low. Contributing Editor Tom Kincaid has seen local fishboats use this channel, but neither he nor we have used it ourselves.

Kayak Point County Park. This park is open all year, has restrooms but no showers. Anchoring only, close to shore. The anchorage is exposed to southerly winds. The launch ramp has boarding floats and the park has a fishing pier. No overnight moorage at the pier.

Maneuvering room is tight, but the Langley Boat Harbor is "never full."

Saratoga Passage. Use chart 18441. Saratoga Passage separates Camano Island from Whidbey Island. The waters are better protected, and often smoother than Admiralty Inlet. Certainly the current is less. Boats running between Seattle and the San Juan Islands often choose this inside route via Deception Pass or LaConner when the wind and seas are up in Admiralty Inlet.

This is not to say the waters are always smooth. In July 1996 we encountered uncomfortable seas while southbound in Saratoga Passage during a 25-knot southerly storm, and were forced to run back to Oak Harbor for shelter. Over Labor Day weekend in 1998 a northerly, with winds stronger than expected, created uncomfortable conditions, especially off Strawberry Point.

Saratoga Passage is relatively free of all dangers, but it does have two tricks: Rocky Point(s) and Holmes Harbor. A study of the chart shows two Rocky Points in Saratoga Passage. One is on Whidbey Island at the entrance to Holmes Harbor; the other is at the north end of Camano Island.

Southbound boats may be tempted to go straight into Holmes Harbor instead of turning southeast past the Whidbey Island Rocky Point. If you're not watching your chart, the appeal is quite strong. Follow the Camano Island shoreline.

Camano Island State Park, 14 miles southwest of Stanwood, (360)387-3031. Open all year for day use and overnight camping. Restrooms, showers, no power. Anchoring only. Launch ramp. Underwater park for scuba diving. Standard and primitive campsites.

Langley. Use chart 18441. The Langley Boat Harbor serves the delightful village of Langley. If the boat harbor is full, as it usually is during the summer, anchorage is good south of the harbor, unless strong northerly winds make the area uncomfortable. Before giving up, however, you should know that Ben Reams, the harbormaster, is quite creative when it comes to getting another boat tied up. His motto is, "We're never full. We'll fit you in." To fit boats in, Ben is not shy about moving and re-tying boats already in the marina. When you come back you may find your boat moved. That's part of being at Langley. *Be sure you are well-fendered, both sides.* The fuel dock next door to

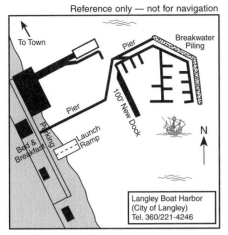

Reference only — not for navigation

Langley Boat Harbor
(City of Langley)
Tel. 360/221-4246

Langley Boat Harbor

the boat harbor is closed, although the store and service department remain open. The town of Langley itself certainly is worth a visit. The streets are lined with old buildings that house interesting shops, excellent galleries, and fine restaurants. The bakery has fresh hot buns and coffee in the morning.

③ **Langley Boat Harbor/City of Langley,** P.O. Box 366, Langley, WA 98260, (360)221-4246 or e-mail at langcity@whidbey.com. Guest moorage at 35 slips in the summer, 15 in the winter, follow harbormaster's directions. A new, 100-foot-long float provides side-tie moorage for larger vessels, or as many as eight smaller boats. They fit everyone in. The docks have 20 & 30 amp power, restrooms, showers, launch ramp (high tide only). In 1998 they acquired a waste pumpout barge. Nearby Langley has groceries, liquor store, post office, doctor. Watch early morning minus tides if anchoring. *(Marina map above)*

Elger Bay. Elger Bay is a good anchorage, mud bottom, with surprisingly good protection from northerly winds. Watch your depths close to the head of the bay.

Holmes Harbor. Use chart 18441. Holmes Harbor indents the eastern shore of Whidbey Island for about 5 miles in a southerly direction. It is deep and relatively unprotected from strong northerlies, but has a good launch ramp at the head and anchorage along either shore. Honeymoon Bay is a good spot to anchor. Holmes Harbor is subject to williwaws, the unusually strong gusts of wind that spill across the low portion of Whidbey Island. A friend of contributing editor Tom Kincaid's, in a heavy 36-foot sailboat, was knocked flat and all the battens torn out of his mainsail by one such williwaw while he was maneuvering to anchor with the main still set.

Honeymoon Bay. Honeymoon Bay is a favored anchorage on the west shore of Holmes Harbor. Private mooring buoys take up most of the good spots, but with a little diligence satisfactory anchoring depths with adequate swinging room can be found. Honeymoon Bay is exposed to northerly winds.

Penn Cove. Use chart 18441. Penn Cove lies about 10 miles north of Holmes Harbor. The cove extends about 4 miles west from Long Point, with the town of Coupeville on the southern shore. Anchorage is good along both shores and toward the head of the bay, but be aware that strong winds from the Strait of Juan de Fuca can blow across the low neck of Whidbey Island at the head of the cove. This is where the famous Penn Cove mussels come from. Watch for the mussel-growing pens, and give them room.

Coupeville. Use chart 18441. The town of Coupeville is served by the Coupeville Wharf, a 415-foot-long causeway on pilings that extends over the beach to deep water. You won't miss it. We like Coupeville. It's quaint and old and friendly, with a variety of shops, galleries and restaurants. A good display of Indian canoes is just up the road from the head of the Wharf. The town welcomes tourists.

④ **Coupeville Wharf, operated by Port of Coupeville,** P.O. Box 577, Coupeville, WA 98239-0577, (360)678-5020. Open all year, 350 feet of dock space, watch depths at low and minus tides. Gasoline and diesel at the fuel dock. Restrooms and showers are available, but no power. There is also room to anchor. At the outer end of the wharf, the Coupeville Harbor Store & Deli (great Thai food) has souvenirs, books, snacks, ice and limited groceries. Marine repairs are nearby. More groceries, restaurants, and antiques shopping are within 4 blocks.

Captain Coupe Park, 9th & Otis Streets, Coupeville, WA, (360)678-4461. Open all year with restrooms and nearby portapotty dump, no power, no showers. Anchoring only. A launch ramp with a float installed in the summer. The dump station is a short distance upland from beach. It is designed for RV use but portapotties are okay. The park is about ¼-mile by water from Coupeville Wharf. It's better to anchor closer the wharf. There are mud flats around the launch area at low tide.

Large Scale, Large Detail

Large Scale, Large Detail, that's the easy way to remember the difference between small-scale charts and large-scale charts. A large-scale chart shows a small part of the earth's surface, but in large detail. Conversely, a small-scale chart shows a large part of the earth's surface, but of course in small detail.

Yes, it's counter-intuitive and confusing, but that's how it is.

In the Northwest, large scale harbor charts typically have scales of 1:6,000, 1:12,000, 1:24,000. Medium scale charts have a scale of 1:40,000. Small scale charts have scales of 1:73,000 or 1:80,000.

At a scale of 1:12,000, 1 inch on the chart equals 12,000 inches (1,000 feet) on the earth. At a scale of 1:80,000, 1 inch on the chart equals 80,000 inches (6,667 feet) on the earth. When you are looking for the rock or picking your way through a narrow channel, the larger the scale of your chart, the easier your task will be.

If this book is obsessed with anything, it is with safe navigation and the tools needed to accomplish safe navigation. Nautical charts are the single most important tools a boat can carry. Large scale, large detail. It works.

—Robert Hale

The long dock at Coupeville has a store and deli at the end. Showers are on the back side of the building. Fuel dock is beyond. Mooring floats are on the right.

Northeast Puget Sound—Oak Harbor to Blaine

Oak Harbor • LaConner • Deception Pass • Anacortes • Bellingham
Semiahmoo Bay • Point Roberts

Charts

18421	Strait of Juan de Fuca to Strait of Georgia (1:80,000)
18423SC	FOLIO SMALL-CRAFT Bellingham to Everett including San Juan Islands (1:80,000) Blaine (1:30,000)
18427	Anacortes to Skagit Bay (1:25,000)
18428	Oak and Crescent Harbors (1:10,000)
18441	Puget Sound – Northern Part (1:80,000)
18443	Approaches to Everett (1:40,000)
18445SC	FOLIO SMALL-CRAFT Puget Sound – Possession Sound to Olympia including Hood Canal

OAK HARBOR TO ANACORTES

Oak Harbor. Use chart 18428 *(large-scale, recommended)*; 18441. Oak Harbor is a shallow and well protected port with a major, city-owned marina. We strongly suggest that you use large-scale chart 18428. The entrance channel is marked by red and green markers, beginning with buoy 2, offshore about 1 mile south of Maylor Point. From buoy 2 the entry channel runs northward into Oak Harbor, and makes a 90-degree turn to the east for the final mile that leads to the marina. Shoals line each side of the channel all the way in. At low tide especially, you will go aground if you stray.

Do not pass between buoy 2 and Maylor Point. The water there is very shoal. The bottom is littered with large boulders, and has been known to tear stern drive units out of boats.

The only moorage is at the spacious Oak Harbor Marina (see description below). The marina has complete facilities, and park grounds ashore for dog-walking, games, or strolling. It's a bit of a walk to town and the nearest grocery store is 1¾ miles away. Bus service is free, or you may want to call a cab.

Good anchorage can be found just outside the marina, close to the entry channel. A small float for dinghies is in front of the business district, about a 1-mile walk from the marina. The float goes dry at low tide. Use with caution.

Golf. The 18-hole Gallery Golf Course at the Whidbey Island Naval Air Station is open to the public year-round. You'll need a car or cab. The course overlooks the east end of the Strait of Juan de Fuca. Smith Island is clearly visible. Telephone (360)679-6150.

① **Oak Harbor Marina,** 865 SE Barrington Dr., Oak Harbor, WA 98277, (360)679-2628; fax (360)240-0603; or e-mail OHMARINA @whidbey.net. View their web site at www.whidbey.net/ohmarina. Monitors VHF channel 16, CB channel 35. Open all year, 115 slips of guest moorage, unoccupied slips used when available. The fuel dock has mid-grade gasoline, diesel and propane. Depth at zero tide is 10 feet. Call ahead if your boat length is over 50 feet.

The marina has 20 & 30 amp power, restrooms, showers, laundry and pumpout. One set of restrooms and showers is on the lower level of the administration building, at the head of the docks. Additional restrooms and showers (recently rebuilt and excellent), and the laundromat are in buildings a short distance away. A huge, 100-foot-wide concrete launch ramp, built in 1942 to launch Catalina seaplanes, is located at the south end of the marina. Haulout to 6500 lbs. is available. Extended parking for trailers and tow vehicles is available while the boat is out cruising. Catalina Marine Service has repairs and a chandlery. Free bus service to town. Nearby doctor, post office, liquor store. Entering Oak Harbor, keep red buoys close to starboard (see section above). Guest moorage is not available during Whidbey Island Race Week, July 15-22, 2000.

The Oak Harbor Marina is protected by a floating concrete breakwater. Guest moorage is along the inside of this breakwater and along the long float that leads to shore. Prior to the 1999 boating season, the marina's concrete floating breakwater was moved westward 38 feet and extended northward 250 feet to create more guest moorage. A dredged channel, 100 feet wide with a least depth of 13½ feet at zero tide, leads along the west face of the breakwater and around the new section. *Water outside this channel is shoal.* If you plan to moor along the north side the marina, the safest approach is to head directly for the entrance light at the south end of the breakwater. When you reach the breakwater turn to port and proceed along the outside (west side) of the breakwater to the north moorage.

The Oak Harbor marina is well maintained, easygoing and friendly. With its spacious guest moorage, it's a popular destination for boating clubs. Dave Williams is the harbormaster. *(Marina map this page)*

Crescent Harbor, just east of Oak Harbor, is controlled by the Navy. Use chart 18428 *(large-scale, recommended)* or chart 18441. The Navy facility along the western shore near the head of the bay has large old hangars that once housed Catalina flying boat aircraft. The docks are for Navy use.

Rocky Point. Use chart 18441. Tidal currents meet off Rocky Point. North of the point they flood south out of Deception Pass and Swinomish Channel. South of the point they flood north out of Saratoga Passage.

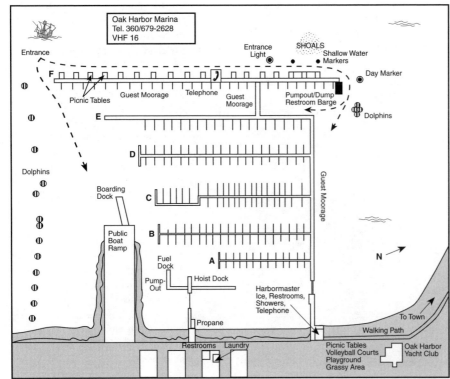

Oak Harbor Marina

Reference only — not for navigation

Skagit Bay. Use chart 18427. Skagit Bay extends from Polnell Point and Rocky Point to Deception Pass. The bay becomes increasingly shoal toward the east. The navigable channel parallels the Whidbey Island shore, and is well marked by buoys. Use caution in this channel, since buoys can be dragged out of position by tugs with tows. The village of Utsalady, with a launch ramp, is on the Camano Island side of the channel. Anchorage at Utsalady is possible, mud bottom, although not protected from northerly winds and waves.

Hope Island. Use chart 18427. Hope Island is a State Marine Park, with mooring buoys on the north side and good anchorage, particularly along the south shore. **Skagit Island** just to the north no longer has mooring buoys. **Similk Bay** is shoal, but navigable over most of its area for shallow draft boats. Anchorage is possible anywhere.

Deception Pass Marine State Park, Skagit Island and Hope Island area. Use charts 18427; 18423sc. Open all year for day use and overnight camping and mooring. The park has 7 mooring buoys, 2 of them located off the north shore of Skagit Island, 5 of them off the north shore of Hope Island. No power, water, restrooms or showers. Boats also can anchor.

Cornet Bay. Cornet Bay, tucked in behind Ben Ure Island, indents the north shore of Whidbey Island just east of Deception Pass. A dredged channel marked by pilings leads to the Deception Pass Marina and a state park, both of which offer visitors' moorage. The passage west of Ben Ure Island should not be attempted except at high tide, and then only by shallow draft boats.

② **Deception Pass Marina,** 200 West Cornet Bay Road, Oak Harbor, WA 98277, (360)675-5411. Monitors VHF channel 16, switch to 68, CB channel 10. Open all year. The marina has several slips reserved for visiting boats, and uses unoccupied slips as available. The docks have 30 amp power, but only limited room for larger boats. Gasoline and diesel at fuel dock, stove alcohol, kerosene and propane available. The store carries groceries, bait, tackle, fishing licenses, charts, books, beer and wine. Restrooms, no showers (showers are available at the state park next door). Call ahead for availability of guest moorage. Laundry, haulout, towing and emergency rescue. Stay in the marked channel. *(Marina map page 76)*

② **Deception Pass Marine State Park, Cornet Bay area**. Open all year for day use and overnight moorage. The park has 1140 feet of dock space, restrooms, showers and pumpout, but no power. Moorage is at a T-dock with slips and floats. There are also floats that are not connected to land. A 4-lane launch ramp has boarding floats. Nearby are hiking trails and picnic areas. Groceries, laundromat and services are at nearby Deception Pass Marina. Park has campsites, but not near this area.

Deception Pass. Use chart 18427; 18421. Deception Pass narrows to 200 yards at Pass Island, which is one of the anchors for a spectacular 144-foot-high bridge that connects Whidbey Island and Fidalgo Island. Currents at maximum can hit 8 knots, with strong eddies and overfalls. Dangerous waves can form when a big ebb tide meets strong westerly winds. It is best to time your approach to enter the pass at or near slack water. Tidal current predictions are shown under "Deception Pass" in the tide and current books. An even narrower pass, Canoe Pass, lies north of Pass Island. Kayaks use Canoe Pass, but lacking local knowledge, we wouldn't run our boat through it.

From the west, the preferred route to Deception Pass lies just to the south of Lighthouse Point and north of Deception Island.

North of Lighthouse Point, **Bowman Bay**, also known as Reservation Bay, is part of Deception Pass State Park. Bowman Bay offers good anchorage, a mooring float and buoys in season, and a launch ramp.

③ **Deception Pass Marine State Park, Bowman Bay (Reservation Bay).** Use chart 18427 (preferred) or 18421. Open all year for day use and overnight camping & mooring. Five mooring buoys. Restrooms, no power, no showers. Bowman Bay has a gravel 1-lane launch ramp. Standard campsites are on the north shore. The park has picnic sites and kitchens. An underwater park for diving is near the mouth of Bowman Bay, near Rosario Head. When entering Bowman Bay take care to avoid Coffin Rocks and Gull Rocks, which cover at high tide. Safe entry can be made by staying fairly close to the Reservation Head side of the entrance. Anchorage is also available in the bay north of Rosario Head, but it is exposed to wave action from Rosario Strait.

③ **Deception Pass Marine State Park, Rosario Bay/Sharpes Cove**. Open all year for day use and overnight camping & mooring. The park has 128 feet of dock space, restrooms, showers, portapotty dump, but no power. Picnic sites, kitchen, standard campsites are located east of Sharpes Cove on the north shore of Bowman Bay.

Reference only — not for navigation

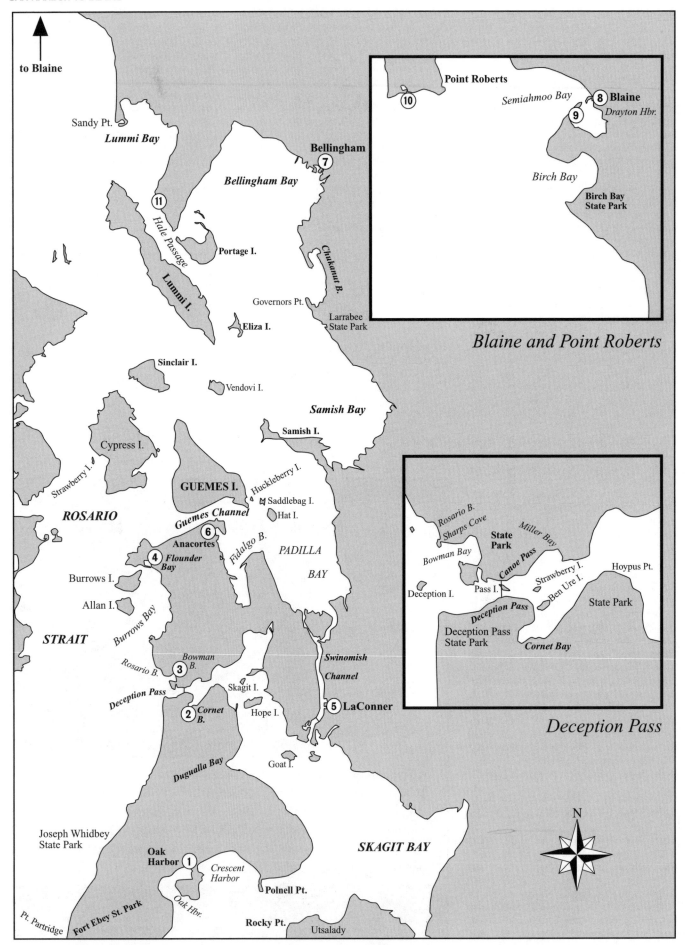

to Blaine

Sandy Pt.

Lummi Bay

Point Roberts

Semiahmoo Bay

⑧ **Blaine**

Drayton Hbr.

⑩

⑨

Birch Bay

Birch Bay State Park

Bellingham Bay

Bellingham ⑦

⑪

Hale Passage

Portage I.

Chukanut B.

Lummi I.

Governors Pt.

Larrabee State Park

Eliza I.

Sinclair I.

Vendovi I.

Samish Bay

Samish I.

Cypress I.

Huckleberry I.

Saddlebag I.

GUEMES I.

Hat I.

Strawberry I.

Guemes Channel

ROSARIO

⑥

Fidalgo B.

Anacortes

④ *Flounder Bay*

PADILLA

BAY

Burrows I.

Allan I.

Burrows Bay

STRAIT

Rosario B.

③

Bowman B.

Skagit I.

Swinomish

Channel

Deception Pass

② *Cornet B.*

Hope I.

⑤ **LaConner**

Dugualla Bay

Goat I.

Joseph Whidbey State Park

Oak Harbor ①

Crescent Harbor

SKAGIT BAY

Polnell Pt.

Pt. Partridge

Fort Ebey St. Park

Oak Hbr.

Rocky Pt.

Utsalady

Blaine and Point Roberts

Rosario B.

Sharps Cove

State Park

Miller Bay

Bowman Bay

Canoe Pass

Strawberry I.

Hoypus Pt.

Deception I.

Pass I.

Ben Ure I.

State Park

Deception Pass

Deception Pass State Park

Cornet Bay

Deception Pass

N

The Good Old Days

Now that I'm getting a little long in the tooth, I've joined that group of oldsters who bore everyone else with stories about the "good old days," when everything—please believe us—was much better than now. Let me tell you a tale about the good old days.

Three of us, my business partner Ole Hansen, our friend Rick Ballinger, and I, had been cruising the San Juan Islands for a several days in my little steel-hulled yawl. With no wifey people to make the meals we were forced to cook for ourselves, which meant we ate to stay alive and to heck with how it tasted. We'd worked out a system under which each of us in turn would cook dinner.

On the way home we were off the Skagit Flats when the dinner hour approached. It was Ole's turn to cook.

"Tell you what," quoth Ole in a transparent effort to get out of cooking, "Let's go into Oak Harbor, go ashore to a restaurant, and I'll spring for dinner." That was the best offer we'd had after too many lousy dinners, and Rick and I jumped at it.

Now understand, this was back in the good old days. There weren't any navigation markers along the channel into Oak Harbor (well, almost none, compared with today), and there wasn't a convenient marina with the world's friendliest staff, as there is today. The Navy was there, with a big concrete ramp for its Catalina seaplanes, and a long piling pier that once served the "mosquito fleet" of steamers stretched into the middle of the bay. But the steamers were long gone and part of the dock had fallen down, although the outer end was still standing.

In the falling darkness we found our way by gosh and good luck into the harbor and anchored in the deepest part of the bay, just off the end of the broken-down pier. Then the fun began.

The three of us eased ourselves into the 8-foot plywood pram that was our dinghy. Consider: Ole is a BIG man, Rick is pretty good sized, and I am rather small. The three of us together sank that little dinghy just about to the oarlocks. I figure we were drawing about a foot, and we rowed, very gently, toward shore.

About 200 feet from "dry" land, the dinghy grounded in very soft mud. After probing the mud with an oar we determined that if we got out to wade, we'd probably sink out of sight in that mud. So we backed off and tried a little farther along. Same result. We tried all along the Oak Harbor shoreline, always grounding long before we could walk to shore. The Navy seaplane apron was inviting, but we assumed it was a no-no for us civilians. It was black night now, and we were getting really hungry. We began to giggle at our silly situation, and before long we were laughing so hard we could barely get back to the boat, where Ole dutifully whomped up some concoction that we ate without complaint.

The good old days. We did have fun.

—*Tom Kincaid*

Fort Ebey State Park, west side Whidbey Island, (360)678-4636. Open all year for day use and overnight camping. The park has restrooms and showers, but no power. Anchoring only, or small boats can be beached. Standard campsites, picnic sites. Interesting bunkers and gun batteries are in the old fort.

Joseph Whidbey State Park, northwest shore of Whidbey Island on Admiralty Inlet, (360)678-4636. Open summers only, April through September, day use only. Toilets, no power, water or showers. Anchor or beach only. One mile of sandy beach on Puget Sound. Picnic sites.

Allan Island. Allan Island is privately owned, but anchorage can be had in the little bight on the east shore.

Burrows Island State Park, open all year, no facilities. Use chart 18427. This is an undeveloped 330-acre state park. Anchor in Alice Bight on the northeast shore, or beach. No camping or fires. Pack out all garbage. Do not disturb wildlife or surroundings. Most of the shoreline is steep cliffs. A lighthouse is on the west tip of the island.

Flounder Bay. Use chart 18427. Flounder Bay has been dredged to provide moorage for the Skyline real estate development. The Skyline Marina and ABC Yacht Charters are inside the spit. There are chandleries, a restaurant, Travelift and other facilities, including a large building that is used for the dry storage of boats. Entry is from Burrows Bay, along a dredged channel marked by pilings.

Caution: We have received reports of silting in the entry. On low tides some deeper draft vessels, such as sailboats, have grounded (softly), especially in the narrow part of the entrance. We are told the deepest water is on the west side of the channel.

④ **Skyline Marina/Penmar Marine,** 2011 Skyline Way/Flounder Bay, Anacortes, WA 98221, (360)293-5134; (888)973-6627

(888-9-PENMAR), web site www.penmar.com. Monitors VHF channel 16, switch to 68. Open all year, gasoline and diesel at two fuel docks. A seaplane float is at the outer fuel dock. Guest moorage has 20 & 30 amp power, restrooms, showers, laundry, pumpout and new vacuum pumpout system. Customs clearance is available 0800-1700.

The marina has a 50-ton Travelift for boat launching, haulout and repairs. Also propane, CNG, marine charts, books, supplies, bait and tackle. Groceries and restaurant nearby. Secure storage for tow vehicles and trailers. Water taxi available to San Juan Islands. The marina is 4 miles from downtown Anacortes. *(Marina map page 78)*

Washington Park, west shore of Fidalgo Island. Open all year for day use and overnight camping. Restrooms, showers, no power. Anchoring or beaching only at this 220-acre city-owned park at Sunset Beach on the Guemes Channel. Launch ramp, picnic tables, picnic shelters, fireplaces, campsites. Playground equipment. The loop road is 3.5 miles in length, and is good for walking or jogging. The park has forested areas and viewpoints along the beaches.

Swinomish Channel. Use chart 18427. The southern entrance to Swinomish Channel lies just north of Goat Island. Do not to turn into the channel until the range markers in Dugualla Bay are in line. Check that range as you go; tidal currents flow across the channel and can sweep a boat off course. The channel is well marked but narrow, particularly if you meet a tug with a tow of logs. The channel bends sharply at **Hole in the Wall**, around a high rock outcropping. Swirling currents in this area can call for close attention.

Watch your wake throughout the Swinomish Channel, particularly when you are passing through LaConner. We recognize that the trip can be slow, especially when the current is flowing against you, but the channel is narrow and it doesn't take much to put out a wake large enough to do a lot of damage. If a longer, faster boat is overtaking, we recommend that you slow down briefly to let it by.

North of Hole in the Wall, the entrance to Shelter Bay, with its numerous private moorages, indents

LaConner, on the east side of Swinomish Channel, is a popular stop in North Puget Sound.

the western shore of Swinomish Channel. The town of LaConner stretches along the eastern shore of the channel. Before arriving at LaConner, you pass under the Rainbow Bridge, a lovely structure with a vertical clearance of 75 feet in the center. The Swinomish Indian Reservation occupies most of the west side of the channel. Across the channel, several privately-owned floats lead to restaurants and other businesses along LaConner's waterfront, as well as a fuel station.

Just north of LaConner is another point where the flood and ebb currents meet, ebbing south past LaConner, and north toward Anacortes. The channel is marked by buoys and ranges, but follows a generally northerly direction until it passes under a swinging railroad bridge and fixed highway bridges to enter Padilla Bay. The railroad bridge is seldom used, and normally is open. The highway bridges are high enough that they don't impede pleasure craft traffic.

LaConner. Use chart 18427. The Port of Skagit County's LaConner Marina, with two large moorage basins, is just north of downtown LaConner. Both moorage basins have guest moorage and full facilities for visitors, including laundry, showers, haulout and repair, and nearby chandleries. Fuel is available adjacent to the marina at LaConner Landing, and propane is available at Boater's Discount, a marine supply store located between the two basins. (Boater's Discount is also the source of the attractive cockpit hardtops seen on various Bayliner models). Currents in Swinomish Channel can be quite strong and difficult to predict. Make allowances for the current before landing anywhere along the channel.

The town of LaConner is completely charming. It has excellent restaurants, many galleries, museums, and shops (including a bookstore with a good nautical selection), and antiques dealers. All are are worth visiting. Public floats line the business district. During the

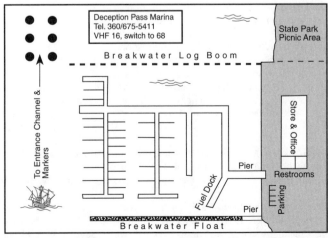

Deception Pass Marina
Tel. 360/675-5411
VHF 16, switch to 68

State Park
Picnic Area

Breakwater Log Boom

To Entrance Channel &
Markers

Store & Office

Fuel Dock

Pier

Restrooms

Pier

Parking

Breakwater Float

Deception Pass Marina   Reference only — not for navigation summer, hordes of visitors arrive by auto and tour bus. Even when crowded, though, the town is enjoyable.

⑤ **LaConner Marina,** 613 N. 2nd St., LaConner, WA 98257, (360)466-3118; fax (360)466-3119. Monitors VHF channel 68. Open all year, 2400 feet of dock space for visiting boats, unoccupied slips used when available. If the moorage appears full, call anyway. They try to fit everybody in. The marina has 30 amp power, restrooms, showers, laundry, pumpout. A fuel dock is adjacent. All shopping and services within walking distance. A monorail launcher can handle boats to 7500 lbs. Trailers must be roller style only, no bunks. A paved, lighted storage yard is available for trailers and tow vehicles while the boat is out cruising. Haulout to 100 tons. *(Marina map page 78)*

⑤ **LaConner Landing Marine Services,** P.O. Box 1020, La-Conner, WA 98257, (360)466-4478. Open all year. Fuel dock with gasoline and diesel. Has a restroom and pumpout, but no power or showers. The store has tackle, bait, ice, beer and wine, marine items and some groceries.

Padilla Bay. Use chart 18427. The well-marked channel through Padilla Bay is about 3 miles long, between drying flats. Don't take any shortcuts until past beacon 2, which marks the edge of Guemes Channel. Deeper draft boats, such as sailboats, should hold to a mid-channel course, especially at low tide. We once put a sailboat gently aground while toward the edge of the marked channel. To the west of the channel are long docks serving tankers calling at the two major oil refineries in Anacortes. Often, one or more tankers lie at anchor awaiting room at the docks.

Tell Them You Read About Them In the Waggoner.

Charts—Anacortes to Blaine	
18421	Strait of Juan de Fuca to Strait of Georgia (1:80,000)
18423sc	FOLIO SMALL-CRAFT Bellingham to Everett including San Juan Islands and Blaine
18424	Bellingham Bay (1:40,000) Bellingham Harbor (1:20,000)
18430	Rosario Strait—Northern Part (1:25,000)
18429	Rosario Strait—Southern Part (1:25:000)

ANACORTES TO BLAINE

Anacortes. Use chart 18427; 18421. Anacortes is a major boating center, with fishing and pleasure craft facilities both in Fidalgo Bay and along Guemes Channel. The city's marine businesses can provide for boaters' every need, from food and fuel to complete overhaul.

Three marinas are located on the Fidalgo Bay side of town. The first, the privately-owned Marine Servicenter has fuel, haulouts, and repairs. The marina is protected by a piling breakwater, and is entered through a dredged channel marked by pilings that extend from deep water near Cap Sante.

The second, the Fidalgo Marina offers permanent covered moorage.

The third, the Cap Sante Marina is owned by the Port of Anacortes, and offers guest moorage, fuel, water, electricity, and haulout facilities. The marina is entered between the arms of a piling breakwater due west of Cap Sante. Guest moorage is along "C" float, the first long float to the north of the entrance. The harbormaster's office is just north of the head of this float.

⑥ **Cap Sante Boat Haven/Port of Anacortes,** P.O. Box 297, 1019 Q Ave., Anacortes, WA 98221, (360)293-0694; fax (360)299-0998, or e-mail at marina@portofanacortes.net. Monitors VHF channel 66A; CB channel 05. Open all year. Visiting boats use the guest dock and unoccupied slips when available. Phone ahead or call by radio for slip assignment. The fuel

dock (Cap Sante Marine, see below) has gasoline, diesel and propane. Docks have 20 & 30 amp power, with some 50 amp power available. The marina has several pumpouts (free), a portapotty dump, and excellent restrooms, showers and laundry. Marilynn Hale likes the laundry because the room is surrounded by windows. She feels more secure there. In the summer, 12 mooring buoys are installed south of the breakwater. Customs clearance is available. This is a clean and popular stop, located in the heart of downtown Anacortes. Complete facilities, including several excellent restaurants, a large Safeway, and marine stores (Cap Sante Marine, West Marine, Marine Supply & Hardware) are nearby. *(Marina map this page)*

⑥ **Cap Sante Marine,** Cap Sante Marina, P.O. Box 607, Anacortes, WA 98221, (360)293-3145; (800)422-5794; fax (360) 293-2804. Monitors VHF channel 16, switch to 09. Open all year. Fuel dock with gasoline, diesel and propane, well-stocked marine supply store with charts, parts, sundries, gifts, repairs, boat launch, haulout to 55 tons and rescue service for boaters. Look for the Shell sign. Fuel dock is open 24 hours.

⑥ **Marine Servicenter,** P.O. Box 1506, 2417 T Avenue, Anacortes, WA 98221, (360)293-8200; fax (360)293-9648. Open all year. Fuel dock with gasoline, diesel and propane. Limited guest moorage may be available. Call ahead. Restrooms, free pumpout, 30 amp power, showers. Complete repair facilities, haulout to 60 tons. Located a short distance south of Cap Sante Marina.

Wyman's Marina. Wyman's Marina, on Guemes Channel, closed in 1998.

Guemes Channel. Use chart 18427; 18421. The Port of Anacortes owns docks along the Guemes Channel side of Anacortes, where fish boats and other large vessels often are moored. Farther west, Lovric's Sea Craft marina has two large marine ways and facilities for repairing any kind of vessel.

Ship Harbor is the landing for ferry boats that serve the San Juan Islands. Remember that commercial vessels have right of way over pleasure vessels. Don't cross close ahead of ferries. Even if you must deviate from your course, pass astern.

GUEMES ISLAND TO POINT ROBERTS

Guemes Island. Use chart 18429; 18424; 18421. Guemes Island has no facilities specifically for boaters, although anchorage can be found along the north shore. Anchorage also can be found on the eastern shore, in a tiny notch called Boat Harbor. A ferry connects Guemes Island to Anacortes.

Saddlebag Island Marine State Park. Open all year for day use and overnight mooring and camping. Use chart 18429 (preferred), or 18421. Boat access only. Anchorage is good off the north or south shore, mud bottom, but there is no float. Water depths are inconveniently deep on the west side, and inconveniently shallow on the east. The better anchorage is on the north side; not much protection on the south side. Vault toilets, primitive campsites. Cascadia Marine Trail campsite. One-mile hiking trail. "Hot spot" for crabbing.

Huckleberry Island State Park, north end of Padilla Bay. Open all year, day use only. No services. This is an undeveloped 10-acre island, with anchoring or beaching only. No fires or camping. Pack out all garbage. Attractive to kayakers and scuba divers. Gravel beach on the southwest side of the island.

Cypress Island. Use chart 18430; 18424; 18421. A park ranger told us he considers

Cap Sante Boat Haven

Reference only — not for navigation

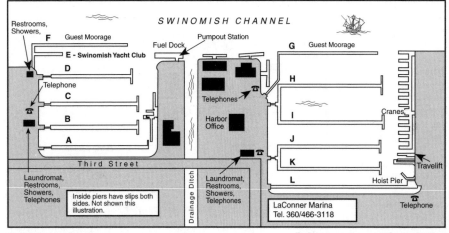

LaConner Marina

Reference only — not for navigation

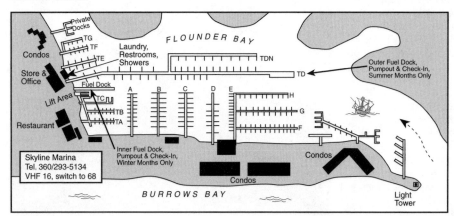

Skyline Marina

Reference only — not for navigation

Cypress Island to be the "crown jewel" of the San Juans. We wouldn't want to argue with him. Cypress Island, now largely in public ownership, is beautiful, and is an excellent place to stretch the legs. Access is hindered by a shortage of good anchorages, though, so you won't be bothered by large crowds. Several trails lead off from Pelican Beach at the northeast corner of the island. They can provide leisurely walks or vigorous hikes.

About a half-mile south of Pelican Beach, just past a small headland, two little coves are quite pretty, and have room for one or two boats each.

Eagle Harbor is shallow, especially at low tide. Watch out for a shoal in the middle. If you have sufficient depth, Eagle Harbor is quite protected. Deepwater Bay, with its fish farms, is unattractive. If you get downwind from the fish farms you're in for a sensory experience.

Pelican Beach Park, a DNR park on the northeast side of Cypress Island. Open all year for day use and overnight camping and mooring. The park has 6 mooring buoys, a gravel beach, 4 campsites, clean vault toilets, picnic shelter, fire pit, information board. Many kinds of wildlife and birds can be observed. Public DNR beaches extend from the park around the north end of Cypress Island for 1.5 miles until just south of Foss Cove, and south of the park for 0.5 mile to Bridge Rock. The moorage is unprotected to the north. If an-

chored or moored to a buoy and the northerly wind comes in, you'll not want to stay.

Cypress Head, east side of Cypress Island. Open all year for day use and overnight camping and mooring. The park has 5 mooring buoys and 5 campsites, picnic sites, vault toilets, no other facilities. Three miles of public tidelands extend from the moorage/recreation area. Many types of birds and wildlife, good fishing. Tide rips at the south end of the island cause high wave action.

Strawberry Island State Park, west of Cypress Island in Rosario Strait. Open all year. Anchoring or beaching only, anchorage in settled weather only. Strong currents and submerged rocks make landing difficult; skiffs or kayaks are best for landing. Park has 3 Cascadia Marine Trail campsites, vault toilet.

Sinclair Island. A piling breakwater protects a loading and unloading dock on the south shore of Sinclair Island, but there are no facilities specifically for pleasure boaters. **Vendovi Island** is privately owned, with no public facilities. **Eliza Island** is also privately owned, with a private dock and float on the north side. Anchorage is possible several places around the island.

Chuckanut Bay. Use chart 18424. Chuckanut Bay is a good anchorage, with protection from

prevailing winds in the north or south arms. Enter close to Governors Point to avoid extensive rocky shoals that partially block the entrance. The land around the bay is privately owned.

Larrabee State Park, 7 miles south of Bellingham on Samish Bay, (360)676-2093. Open all year for day use and overnight camping. The park has restrooms and showers. This was Washington's first official state park, dedicated in 1923. It covers 2000 acres and is heavily used. Facilities include a launch ramp, kitchen shelters, picnic tables, standard, utility and primitive campsites. Fishing, clamming, crabbing, scuba diving. Trails allow access to two freshwater lakes within the park. A 5.5

See area map page 74

mile walking/bicycling trail connects with Bellingham.

Bellingham. Use chart 18424. Bellingham, with its international airport, is the largest city north of Everett, and has complete marine facilities for both commercial and pleasure craft. Moorage, fuel, marine supplies and repairs are available at the Port of Bellingham's Squalicum Harbor. The harbormaster's office is located in the Squalicum Mall, in the older section of the harbor development. Bellingham Yacht Club and Squalicum Yacht Club are nearby. BYC has moorage for members of reciprocal yacht clubs. Taxi and bus service connect the harbor with downtown.

Mooring buoys and a new linear moorage system are now located at Fairhaven, in the south part of Bellingham Bay. Turn-of-the-century Victorian buildings, coffee shops, dining, and interesting shops make Fairhaven a delightful stop. Fairhaven is also the southern terminus of the Alaska Marine Highway Ferry System. As with Squalicum Harbor, you'll take a bus or taxi to downtown Bellingham.

⑦ **SqualicumHarbor/Port of Bellingham,** PO Box 1677, Bellingham, WA 98227, (360)676-2542; fax (360)671-6149. Or view at www.portofbellingham.com. Monitors VHF channel 16. Open all year, guest moorage along 1500 feet of dock in two basins. Unoccupied slips are used when available, and they work hard to fit everybody in. The ma-

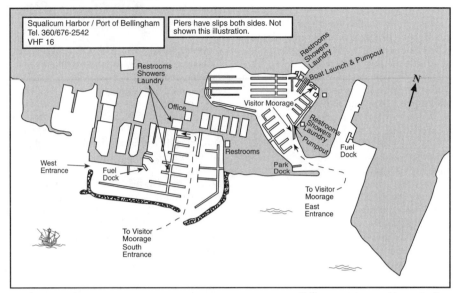

Squalicum Harbor   Reference only — not for navigation

rina has 20, 30 & 50 amp power (mostly 30), restrooms, showers, security, laundry, pumpout, and portapotty dump. The docks in both basins are gated for security. Customs clearance is available. Call ahead for availability of guest moorage. A full service shipyard is in the harbor. They also have a marine life tank. Groceries, restaurant, and a snack bar are nearby. Also chandleries and engine repair shops.

Squalicum Harbor is divided into two moorage basins, each with its own entrance and guest moorage. The northernmost, or older, basin has been rebuilt, with new docks, improved power, and restrooms located about halfway out the main pier. Portable pumpout carts are kept at the restroom station. Side-tie guest moorage is on the south side of the main pier, next to shore. In the southern basin, guest moorage is just inside the breakwater entrance.

A 4-lane launch ramp, with extended-term

See area map page 74

Port of Bellingham's new guest moorage float at Squalicum Harbor.

Reference only — not for navigation

Fairhaven Moorage (Port of Bellingham)
Tel. 360/647-2469 or 360/676-2542

Fairhaven Moorage (Port of Bellingham)

parking for tow vehicles and trailers, is just south of the newer, southernmost, basin. *(Marina map page 80)*

Fairhaven moorage. The Port of Bellingham has installed mooring buoys and a side-tie linear moorage system at Fairhaven. Take one of the moorings or tie to the linear moorage, dinghy in to the dock, drop your fee in the box and walk up to shops and eateries in Fairhaven's lovely Victorian buildings. Just south of the business district you'll find a beautiful old park, with mature plantings and great expanses of lawn. Fairhaven moorage is available April through October only. Water and garbage drop are available at the dock. A portable pumpout cart is available. A launch ramp is nearby. On-site management is by FairhavenBoatworks (360) 647-2469. *(Marina map above)*

⑦ **Hawley's Hilton Harbor,** 1000 Hilton Ave., Bellingham, WA 98225, (360)733-1110. Fuel dock with gasoline only. Located at the south entrance to Squalicum Harbor at the foot of Hilton Avenue. Look for the Texaco sign. Travelift, repairs. Oil disposal available.

⑦ **Harbor Marine Fuel,** 21 Squalicum Fill, Bellingham, WA 98225, (360)734-1710. Open all year. Fuel dock with gasoline and diesel. Store carries motor oils, snacks and ice. Located in northern Squalicum Harbor, behind the breakwater. Look for the big Shell sign.

Lummi Island. Use chart 18424; 18421. Lummi Island is very high (1480 feet), and has no facilities specifically for visiting boaters, although anchorage is good in several places, including Inati Bay and along either shore of Hale Passage. A ferry connects Lummi Island to the mainland, and a mooring float is located alongside the mainland ferry dock. Restaurants and other businesses are near this dock. The Lummi Indians haul their boats, including reef net boats, on the beach south of the ferry dock.

⑪ **Fisherman's Cove Marina,** 2557 Lummi View Dr., Bellingham, WA 98226, (360)758-

7050. Open all year, fuel dock with gasoline only, propane, haulout to 34 feet, repairs. Adjacent to the ferry dock on Gooseberry Point.

Inati Bay. Use chart 18424; 18421. Inati Bay is located on the east side of Lummi Island, approximately 2 miles north of Carter Point. It is the best anchorage on Lummi Island, protected from all but northeasterly winds (rare in the summer), with good holding. Great views, picnic facilities ashore. All are welcome at Bellingham Yacht Club's outstation at Inati Bay.

Lummi Island Recreation Site, southeast shore of Lummi Island. Open all year, 1 buoy, vault toilets, campsites.

Sandy Point. No public facilities are available at Sandy Point, at the north entrance to Lummi Bay. It is a private real-estate development consisting of several canals with homes on them. Long docks serving a refinery and an aluminum plant extend from shore north of Sandy Point.

Birch Bay. Use chart 18421. Birch Bay is very shoal, but could provide anchorage in calm weather. Watch your depths. The Birch Bay State Park ashore has campsites, picnic and playground equipment, but no facilities for boaters. For reservations (800)452-5687.

Blaine. Use chart 18421. Blaine has two moorages in Drayton Harbor. One of them is owned by the Port of Bellingham; the other, Semiahmoo, is privately owned. The approach through Semiahmoo Bay is shoal at all stages but high tide. Pay close attention to the buoys along the drying bank on the south side of the bay, and turn into the entrance channel before getting too close to the eastern shore.

The Port of Bellingham's marina is on the east (port) side as you enter. Entry to that marina is through an opening in the piling breakwater, with a fuel dock on the land side. Once through the breakwater, turn to starboard and follow the signs to the guest moorage, located about in the middle of the harbor.

The Semiahmoo Marina is on the west side

of the entrance channel. Both marinas have fuel, water, electricity, small chandleries, and other facilities ashore. The Port's marina gives access to the town of Blaine and a number of boating-related businesses. The Semiahmoo Marina has a hotel and a fine golf course, but is a considerable distance by road from town. Blaine is a U.S. Customs port.

⑧ **Blaine Harbor/Port of Bellingham,** 275 Marine Drive, Blaine, WA 98230, (360)647-6176; fax (360)332-1043. Or view web site at www. portofbellingham.com. Monitors VHF channel 66A. Guest moorage along 500 feet of dock, unoccupied slips used when available. Services include 30 amp power, restrooms, showers, pumpout, portapotty dump, and laundry. Phone-in customs clearance. Repairs, haulout, supplies available. Two blocks to town. Launch ramp, fishing charters, restaurants nearby.

In 1998 work began on a major rebuilding and expansion of Blaine Harbor. The new construction should be completed by the 2000 season. *(Marina map page 83)*

⑧ **Blaine Marina,** PO Box 1849, Blaine, WA 98231, (360)332-8425. Open all year. This is the fuel dock at the Blaine Harbor Marina. Gasoline and diesel, restrooms. Waste oil disposal is available at Blaine Harbor.

⑨ **Semiahmoo Marina,** 9540 Semiahmoo Parkway, Blaine, WA 98230, (360)371-5700; fax (360)371-2422. Or view at www. semiahmoo.com. Monitors VHF channel 68. Open all year. Gasoline and diesel at fuel dock. Propane available. Guest moorage at 500 feet of dock space, unoccupied slips used when available. Call for availability. Services include 30 amp power, restrooms, showers, laundry, pumpout, portapotty dump, chandlery with marine supplies, haulout. Mechanics on duty. Access to Inn at Semiahmoo Resort health club for additional $5 per person. Resort has an Arnold Palmer 18-hole golf course, restaurant, snack bar. Foot ferry to Blaine May-Sept. Friday-Sunday. *(Marina map this page)*

Golf: Semiahmoo is outstanding. Telephone (360)371-7005.

Blaine Harbor

Over 300 new slips!
Moorage Available

- Port of Entry
- Vessels 26' to 100'
- 700' of guest moorage
- Restaurants
- 30,50,100 amp
- Berthside phone service
- Laundry facilities
- Shipyards
- Chandleries
- Dock box storage
- Two-lane boat launch
- Restrooms/Showers

Take a walk to the parks.
Dinghy to a beautiful resort.

Located on the U.S.- Canada border

The Beginning of Your Boating Adventure

BLAINE HARBOR
Port of Bellingham
Blaine, WA

Call now for moorage information (360) 647-6176

e-mail alanb@portofbellingham.com

White Rock, in Canada, is almost due north of Blaine, in Boundary Bay. White Rock is a Canadian Customs port of entry. Call (888)226-7277. A long pier crosses tide flats, with floats at the outer end. The village has interesting shops and galleries.

Point Roberts. Use chart 18421; 3463 (Cdn.). Point Roberts is a low spit of land extending south from Canada into U.S. waters. Although physically separated from the U.S., Point Roberts is U.S. territory and part of the state of Washington. The Point Roberts Marina is on the south shore. Enter via a dredged channel through drying flats. Ice, groceries, liquor, and doctor are available.

⑩ **Point Roberts Marina,** 713 Simundson Drive, Point Roberts, WA 98281, (360)945-2255; fax (360)945-0927. Open all year, gasoline and diesel at fuel dock. Propane available. Guest moorage at a float near the entrance and in unoccupied slips, call ahead. Services include 30 & 50 amp power, restrooms, showers, laundry, pumpout. Customs clearance is available. The Dockside Pub and The Grotto restaurant are open all year, shorter hours in the winter. Other restaurants and groceries are nearby. Westwind Marine Services, with repairs and a well-stocked chandlery, is in the main building. *(Marina map page 83)*

Lighthouse Marine County Park, Point Roberts, WA. Open for day use and overnight camping in summer, day use only in winter. The park is located on the southwest corner of Point Roberts. Anchor north of the park and row in, or moor at Point Roberts Marina. The park has a launch ramp. Boarding floats are installed in May and removed in October. Facilities include campsites, picnic shelters, fire pits, stoves, restrooms but no showers, sand and gravel beach. Also a whale exhibit. A viewing platform allows you to watch the three local whale pods that follow the salmon.

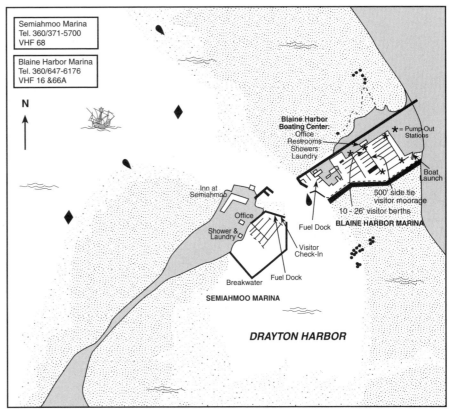

Drayton Harbor

Reference only — not for navigation

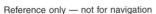
Reference only — not for navigation

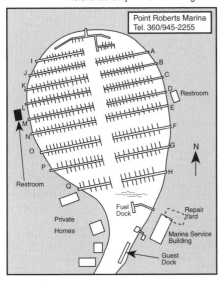

Point Roberts Marina

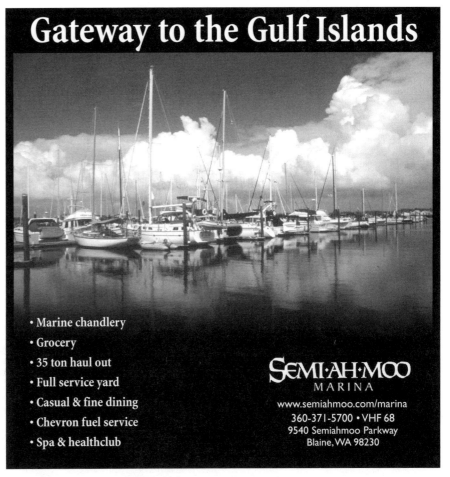

Strait of Juan de Fuca

Sequim • Port Angeles • Clallam Bay • Neah Bay
Port San Juan • Sooke Inlet

Downtown Port Angeles has embarked on an ambitious murals project. This building is near the city pier.

U.S. Charts

18423SC FOLIO SMALL-CRAFT	Bellingham to Everett including San Juan Islands
18460	Strait of Juan de Fuca Entrance (1:100,000)
18465	Strait of Juan de Fuca – Eastern Part (1:80,000)
18468	Port Angeles (1:10,000)
18471	Approaches to Admiralty Inlet – Dungeness to Oak Bay (1:40,000)
18484	Neah Bay (1:10,000)
18485	Cape Flattery (1:40,000)

Canadian Charts

3410	Sooke Inlet to Parry Bay (1:20,000)
3411	Sooke (1:12,000)
3461	Juan de Fuca Strait, eastern part (1:80,000)
3606	Juan de Fuca Strait (1:110,000)
3647	Port San Juan and Nitinat Narrows Port San Juan (1:18,000) Nitinat Narrows (1:12,000) Nitinat Narrows (1:2,000)

THE STRAIT OF JUAN DE FUCA generally is 10 miles wide and 80 miles long. Depending on the weather it can be flat calm or extremely rough. The typical summertime pattern calls for calm mornings, with a westerly sea breeze rising by mid-day, increasing to 30 knots or more late in the afternoon. If this sea breeze opposes an outflowing ebb current, the seas will be unusually high, steep and close together. Often, the "typical" weather pattern does not prevail, and the wind blows around the clock. Or it can be calm, even on a warm summer afternoon. The weather reports must be monitored. If wind is present or predicted, stay off the strait.

Discovery Bay. Use chart 18471. Discovery Bay lies west of Point Wilson on the Washington side. It is somewhat protected from the Strait of Juan de Fuca by Protection Island, a wildlife refuge. Discovery Bay is open and unobstructed, but is seldom used as an overnight anchorage by pleasure craft. Gardiner, halfway down the bay, has a launch ramp.

Sequim Bay. Use chart 18471. Sequim Bay is tucked in behind Dungeness Spit. It is a beautiful, quiet anchorage with a public marina and a state park with floats. Sequim Bay is protected by a spit that extends from the eastern shore. To enter, steer for the middle of this spit, then turn sharply west and run

parallel to the spit. Like many Northwest bays, Sequim Bay has a large shoal in the middle, with passage around the eastern and western sides. The marked channel, which leads to the Port of Port Angeles John Wayne Marina, is around the west side. This route is best when approaching Sequim Bay State Park.

The actor John Wayne, who visited Sequim Bay often aboard his *Wild Goose*, donated 22 waterfront acres to the Port of Port Angeles, on condition that the Port build a marina on the site.

① **John Wayne Marina,** 2577 W. Sequim Bay Road, Sequim, WA 98382, (360)417-3440; fax (360)417-3442. Open all year, gasoline and diesel at the fuel dock, guest moorage at 30 slips and 200 feet of dock. Services include 20 & 30 amp power, restrooms, showers, laundry, pumpout, portapotty dump and launch ramps. A restaurant, and a store with marine supplies, sundries and books, are ashore. Groceries are nearby, also a picnic area and beach access. Use the latest edition of chart 18471. Land at the first float inside the breakwater to check in.

① **Sequim Bay Marine State Park.** Sequim Bay Marine State Park occupies 92 acres along the western shore of Sequim Bay. The park has floats, campsites, a launch ramp with a small parking area, as well as other state park facilities. Open all year, day use and overnight mooring & camping, 424 feet of dock space and 6 buoys. Facilities include restrooms, showers, portapotty dump, but no power. The mooring buoys are in deep water. The water around the dock and mooring float is shallower. Watch your depths at low tide. Boarding floats at the launch ramp are removed in the winter. Beachfront, scuba diving. The park has picnic sites and kitchen shelters.

Dungeness Spit. Use chart 18471. Beautiful Dungeness Spit, 9 miles long, is the world's longest natural sand spit. It provides protec-

tion from westerly weather, and convenient anchoring depths along its inner edge before an attached cross-spit forces the channel south. Shallow draft boats can continue into the inner harbor, where there is a launch ramp and protected anchorage. Dungeness Spit is a wildlife refuge, open to hikers, but has no public facilities. The spit has at least 45 varieties of birds, as well as deer, small animals, and seals.

Port Angeles. Use harbor chart 18468; small-scale chart 18465. Port Angeles is a substantial small city on a bay protected by Ediz Hook. The Port Angeles City Pier, with guest moorage available, is near the south end of the business district. The Port of Port Angeles Boat Haven is a breakwater-protected marina at the southwest corner of the bay.

Port Angeles is a customs port, and is the terminus for a ferry to Victoria. The northern side of the bay is taken up by log storage serving the several mills around the bay. The outer end of Ediz Hook is a Coast Guard station. Just west of the Coast Guard station is the Port Angeles Pilot Station, where ships bound to or from Puget Sound ports board and disembark pilots. Contributing Editor Tom Kincaid recalls that when he was much younger, he spent a couple of enjoyable years skippering the pilot boat at the station.

② **Port Angeles Boat Haven,** Port of Port Angeles, 832 Boat Haven Drive, Port Angeles, WA 98362, (360)457-4505. Open all year, gasoline and diesel at the fuel dock. Guest moorage along 700 feet of dock space, rafting allowed; unoccupied slips used when available. Maximum boat length 120 feet. Services include 15 amp power, restrooms, showers, pumpout, portapotty dump. Customs clearance is available. Kerosene, stove alcohol, marine supplies, charts, snacks are available. The cafe is open 6 days. Marine repairs and haulout: boat lift and marine railway handle up to 200 tons. Groceries, doctor, post office, laundry, liquor store are nearby. *(Marina map page 85)*

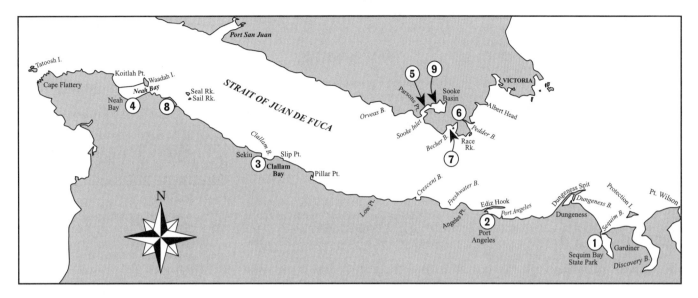

② **Port Angeles City Pier,** 321 E. 5th, Port Angeles, WA 98362, (360)457-0411. Open Memorial Day through Labor Day only, with guest moorage in 1 60-foot slip and 4 40-foot slips. Restrooms, but no showers, no power. These are floats, right downtown. Watch depths at head of floats. Nearby groceries, restaurants, laundry. Showers are available at City pool. Adjacent to City park. Look for the viewing tower in front of the hotel.

② **Thunderbird Boat House & Gift,** 826 Boat Haven Drive, Port Angeles, WA 98362, (360)457-4274. Open summers only, beginning in April. Gasoline only at fuel dock. Guest moorage along 400 feet of dock, 30-foot maximum boat length. Services include restrooms, pumpout, no power, no showers.

Crescent Bay. Use chart 18465. Crescent Bay is a possible anchorage if conditions on the Strait of Juan de Fuca become untenable. Close to the western shore it offers a little protection from westerlies, but swells can still work into the bay and make for an uneasy stay.

Pillar Point. Use chart 18460. Pillar Point

has a fishing resort with launch ramp and float, but is not available for transient moorage. In a westerly, the area close to and a little east of the point is a notorious windless spot—a "hole" in sailboaters' language. A Waggoner reader wrote to tell us the anchorage is good along the eastern shore.

SEKIU/CLALLAM BAY

Clallam Bay. Use chart 18460. Clallam Bay, with Sekiu on its western shore, is somewhat protected from westerlies, and has convenient anchoring depths along the shore. A serious reef, marked by a buoy at its outer end well offshore, extends from the eastern point. *Leave the buoy to port when entering the bay.* Two breakwater-protected marinas, one at the village of Clallam Bay, on the southeast part of the bay, and the second at Sekiu, will take transient boats unless the slips are taken by trailerable boats there for the fishing. Sekiu has several fishing resorts, as well as stores catering to fishermen. Recent salmon fishing cutbacks have hurt the town, however. It's best to call ahead to confirm that your needs can be met.

③ **Van Riper's Resort,** P.O. Box 246, 280 Front Street, Sekiu, WA 98381, (360) 963-2334. Monitors CB channel 14. Open summers, closed winters. Guest moorage along 2800 feet of dock space. Services include restrooms, showers, portapotty dump, no power. Includes campground, concrete launch ramp. Boat and motor rentals, charter service, ice, groceries, charts and books. Nearby post office, restaurant and bar, liquor store, marine supplies.

③ **Olson's Resort,** P.O. Box 216, Sekiu, 444 Front St., WA 98381, (360)963-2311; fax (360)963-2928, e-mail at olsons@olypen.com. Monitors CB channel 21. Open February 1 - October 15. Gasoline and diesel at the fuel dock. Guest moorage in 300 slips behind a breakwater, 40-foot maximum boat length. Services include restrooms, showers, laundry, concrete launch ramp, no power. Motel units available. Busy during salmon season. Charter fishing trips, boat and motor rentals.

③ **Curley's Resort,** P.O. Box 265, Sekiu, WA 98381, (360)963-2281; (800)542-9680. Open April 1 - October 15, guest moorage along 750 feet of dock space, 30-foot maximum boat length. This is a resort with moorage, motel units and cabins for rent.

③ **Coho Resort,** HCR 61, Box 15, Sekiu, WA 98381, (360)963-2333. Open April through Sept., some guest moorage, 25-foot maximum boat length, call ahead. Services include restrooms, showers, laundry. The launch ramp is open all year. No power or water. Carries bait, tackle, licenses.

NEAH BAY

Neah Bay. Use chart 18485; large-scale chart 18484. Neah Bay has several resorts and a brand-new marina, the Makah Marina, with moorage for transient boats. Except for the Coast Guard dock, all boats now moor in the Makah Marina. Fish company and resort floats no longer are in the bay. A long breakwater

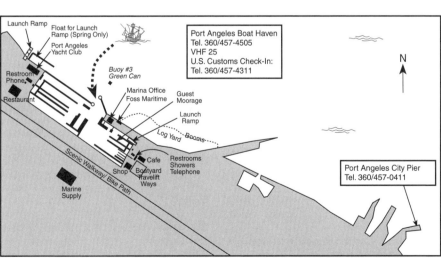

Port Angeles

See area map page 85

connects the mainland and Waadah Island, and blocks ocean waves from getting in. Anchorage is good, sand bottom, throughout the bay. A second breakwater protects the Makah Marina. The Coast Guard station at the entrance to the bay serves the west end of the Strait of Juan de Fuca and the northern Pacific Ocean coast. Neah Bay is a customs port (phone-in only). The general store is well stocked, except for spirits. Neah Bay is dry.

The Makah Culture & Research Center museum, which features artifacts from the Ozette archealogical dig site, a wide array of Curtis photos, and wood sculpture by the remarkable Makah carver Young Doctor, is world-class, and simply must be seen. The Ozette dig was a village buried by a mudslide before contact with whites. It is a time capsule of coastal Indian life. The tools, clothing, furniture, weapons and fishing implements are exquisitely preserved and displayed.

④ **Makah Marina,** P.O. Box 137, Neah Bay, WA 98357, (360)645-3015; fax (360)645-3016; e-mail mtcport@olypen.com. Monitors VHF channel 16 & 66A. Open all year, ample guest moorage for boats to 100+ feet, 30 & 50 amp power, drinking water on the docks, gasoline & diesel at the fuel dock, restrooms, showers and laundry nearby, pumpout station, portapotty dump, 2-lane launch ramp with extended parking available for tow vehicles and trailers. Shopping and lodging (on the rough-and-ready side) are nearby. The extraordinary Makah museum, with its display of artifacts from the Ozette archaeological dig, is an easy walk.

This is one of the best-built marinas we have seen. The concrete docks are extremely stable, and each mooring slip is served by several sturdy mooring cleats. Commercial craft are moored separately from pleasure craft. The slips are spacious and the waterways between docks are wide. For the year 2000 season a new administration building, with its own restrooms and showers, is expected to be open.

④ **Big Salmon Resort,** P.O. Box 204, Front Street, Neah Bay, WA 98357, (360)645-2374. Monitors VHF channel 68; CB channel 16. Open Apr. 1 - Sept. 15. Gasoline and diesel at fuel dock. Guest moorage in the Makah Marina. They have a 2-lane concrete launch ramp with long-term parking. Small store carries tackle, some groceries, local charts. Motels, doctor, post office nearby.

Farwest Resort is closed.

⑧ **Snow Creek Resort,** P.O. Box 248, Neah Bay, WA 98357, (360)645-2284. Monitors VHF channel 16, switch to 17. Open April 15 - Oct. 1. Guest moorage in the Makah

Marina. They have campsites and RV parking, limited groceries, diving air, haulout.

PORT SAN JUAN

Those needing a place to get off the Strait on the Canadian side can consider **Port San Juan**, about halfway between Victoria and Barkley Sound. Port San Juan is a rectangular notch in Vancouver Island, with Port Renfrew on the eastern shore near the head of the bay. A public dock is at Port Renfrew, but if heavy swells are running in the Strait, it becomes an uncomfortable place to lie.

Better protection can be had anchoring close to shore along the west side, or rafting to one of the log rafts boomed in the mouth of the Gordon River, at the northwest corner of the bay.

The old hotel at the head of the public dock has rooms, and just beyond is the Lighthouse Pub, nearly new and very upscale-feeling. Port Renfrew is the end of the road and the pub seems out of place until it's explained that in the summer some 2,000 people per day—hikers, kayakers and sightseers—pour through the town.

SOOKE

Sooke Harbour. Sooke Harbour is entered between Company Point and Parsons Point. The harbor is protected by Whiffen Spit, which nearly blocks the passage. Enter by keeping Whiffen Spit (with its small lighthouse) close to port, and follow the marked channel to town. An area just inside Whiffen Spit has good anchorage. The Sooke Harbour Marina, with guest moorage and other facilities, is south of the Sooke government wharf. The city floats usually are taken by commercial fishboats, but pleasure craft will find room when the fleet is out.

Sooke has a wide variety of services close to the city floats, including a marine railway and machine shop, groceries, fuel, and restaurants. Currents run quite strongly along the city waterfront. Be careful when landing.

The inner harbor at Sooke is seldom visited by pleasure craft. The channel—very shallow—follows the curve of the shoreline on the east side of the bay until the inner harbor opens up, where there is ample water. Contributing Editor Tom Kincaid has anchored in a little, almost landlocked bay behind Pim Head.

Sooke is the only completely protected harbor between Victoria and Barkley Sound. It is 15 miles closer to Barkley Sound than downtown Victoria, and often used as a departure point for boats heading up the west coast of Vancouver Island.

Cruising this coast, you will occasionally see a local fishboat anchored along the shore. With local knowledge, it is possible to anchor in several places, including the mouth of the Jordan River.

No customs clearance is available in Sooke. The nearest Canadian Port of Entry is Victoria.

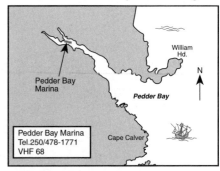

Reference only — not for navigation

Pedder Bay Marina

⑤ **Sooke Harbour Marina,** RR 4, 6971 West Coast Road, Sooke, B.C. V0S 1N0, (250)642-3236. Or view at www.sookenet.com/sookemarina/. Monitors VHF channel 16, switch to 68. Open all year. Guest moorage along 200 feet of dock space, and in unoccupied slips when available. Services include washrooms, showers, 20 amp power, laundry, and 2-lane concrete launch ramp with long term parking. This is the first marina as you come into the harbor.

Sooke Harbour Authority, open all year, guest moorage along 797 feet of dock. No washrooms, showers or power.

⑨ **Sunny Shores Resort & Marina,** 5621 Sooke Rd., Sooke, B.C. V0S 1N0, (250)642-5731; fax (250)642-5737. Monitors VHF channel 16; CB channel 13. Open all year. Gasoline and diesel at fuel dock. Guest moorage for 6-10 average size boats, call ahead for availability. Services include 15 amp power, washrooms, showers, laundry. Motel accommodations and campground. Swimming pool, mini-golf, playground. Convenience store carries ice, fishing tackle, limited groceries, local charts. Boat maintenance, haulout and repairs available. Taxi to town 3 miles away; bus to Victoria, 28 miles away.

Pedder Bay. Pedder Bay is a mile-long inlet, shallow and narrow, just south of William Head. A launch ramp with floats is at the head, and moorage might be available for larger boats.

⑥ **Pedder Bay Marina,** 925 Pedder Bay Drive #12, Victoria, B.C. V9C 4H1, (250)478-1771; fax (250)478-2695. Monitors VHF channel 68. Open all year, gasoline only at fuel dock. Most guest moorage maximum 26-foot boat length. Call ahead for larger boats. Services include 15 amp power, washrooms, showers, laundry, 5-lane concrete launch ramp, snack bar. The Galloping Goose Trail and diverse sea life are attractions. Approaching, use chart 3410; watch the breeze. Located between Pearson College and Dept. of National Defence (you can't stop there; it has a prison facility).

Becher Bay. Becher Bay is a pleasant anchorage. There is a bay on the west side with excellent anchorage, being careful of a drying rock near the south end. Contributing Editor

Tom Kincaid has anchored behind the island in the middle of the bay. The water is a bit deep for convenience, but protection is good and the holding ground is excellent.

⑦ **Pacific Lions Marina Ltd.,** RR 6, 241 Becher Bay Rd., Sooke, B.C. V0S 1N0, (250)642-3816; fax (250)642-3836; or e-mail at pacificlions@ampsc.com. Monitors VHF channel 16, switch to 68. Open May 1 - Sept.

30. Limited guest moorage by reservation only, maximum boat length 30 feet, call ahead. Services include washrooms, showers, launch ramp, 2-lane concrete launch ramp, no power. Full RV parking available.

⑦ **Cheanuh Marina,** Box 1, RR 1, 4901 E. Sooke Rd., Sooke, B.C. V0S 1N0, (250)478-4880; fax (250)478-3585. Monitors VHF channel 16, CB channel 13. Open all year.

Gasoline only at fuel dock. Guest moorage in 310 slips, unoccupied slips used when available, call ahead. Services include 3-lane launch ramp, washrooms, no showers or power. Popular fishing marina. Around 300 boats are launched per day in summer; someone on staff usually stays until all have returned. Owned by the Becher Bay Indians.

The Learning Never Stops

EVERY BOAT OWNER goes through a learning curve that never stops. A person can, of course, start a little farther along the curve by spending time with others aboard their boats, or have the smarts to be born into a boating family, or, at the very least, take a Power Squadron or Coast Guard Auxiliary course. It may also be possible to take a few practical lessons from the person who sold you the boat.

But the curve remains, stretching endlessly into the future. After more than 60 years of boating, I'm still struggling to learn more, and seldom leave the harbor without some new problem presenting itself, calling on me to find a solution resulting in another little inch of travel along that curve.

Stretching out along the learning curve usually means doing something you haven't done before, whether it's adjusting the valves on your diesel engine or crossing the Strait of Juan de Fuca. Once you've done these things, they seem to be pretty simple. But until you try, they appear to be the product of some occult art.

Most people, when they first buy a boat, spend enough time close to the dock to get used to the "feel" of the boat: how quickly it turns, how it steers in reverse, how long it takes to stop, and where the sides of the boat are in relation to the dock. Before long, however, it will be time to head out for larger waters. If those first experiments were in Seattle's Lake Union, as many are, the skipper is going to have to deal with the Ballard Locks before those larger waters can be experienced. Approaching the locks for the very first time takes a leap of courage. You sure don't want to make a fool of yourself in front of all those "expert" skippers and the usual crowd of gawkers lining the lock walls.

But having screwed up the courage to try, you will soon find that running the locks doesn't take the skill of a brain surgeon. A little common sense and patience, and you're free of the confining lakes and out into the broad reaches of Puget Sound, where a boating family can easily spend a cruising lifetime.

On the other hand, you will have heard about the glorious San Juan Islands, invitingly situated only 20 miles or so across the Strait of Juan de Fuca. If you're like most of us, eventually you'll take a deep breath and brave the Strait for a chance to vacation in our own world famous islands. Once again, you'll discover that making that crossing is not beyond your ability, and that trip can become almost routine. Almost, I say, because the Strait can kick up a fuss, and part of your learning curve will will be discovering how to handle rough water, how to pick a time to avoid the rough water, or some combination of both.

In any event, you will have made another major step up the learning curve. You can handle yourself and your boat under another set of conditions. And the steps stretch out as far as you can imagine. There's the Strait of Georgia in order to reach Desolation Sound; a series of rapids and Johnstone Strait in order to reach the Fife Sound cruising area; Queen Charlotte Strait, Dixon Entrance, the West Coast of Vancouver Island. All are milestones on the learning curve. All can be (and have been) negotiated by thousands of people in all sorts of boats.

And they aren't all brain surgeons or old salts either. Most are just ordinary folks, screwing up the courage to take that next step up the learning curve.

—Tom Kincaid

San Juan Islands

Lopez Sound • Lopez Island • San Juan Island • Orcas Island • Sucia Island

Charts
18421 Strait of Juan de Fuca to Strait of Georgia (1:80,000)
18423sc FOLIO SMALL-CRAFT Bellingham to Everett including San Juan Islands
18429 Rosario Strait, Southern Part (1:25,000)
18430 Rosario Strait, Northern Part (1:25,000)
18432 Boundary Pass (1:25,000)
18433 Haro Strait – Middle Bank to Stuart Island (1:25,000)
18434 San Juan Channel (1:25,000)
3462   Juan de Fuca Strait to Strait of Georgia (1:80,000) (Canadian)

The Port of Friday Harbor Marina, with docks reconfigured in 1999, is protected and has room for many visitors. Call on VHF channel 66A when approaching.

Everywhere I turn on Orcas Island, there is something to paint.—Paula Griff McHugh, Fine Artist

THE WORLD-FAMOUS SAN JUAN ISLANDS are the dream destination for thousands of boaters each year. The scenery is stunning, the fishing good, the anchorages plentiful, and the amenities—marine resorts, settlements, villages and towns—are many and varied. The islands contain the U.S.'s largest flocks of bald eagles south of Alaska. Sailing in the company of porpoises and whales is almost commonplace.

The San Juans have a feel about them that is different from most other coastal cruising areas. In the San Juans you don't just head down the coast to another bay, or out to a little clutch of islets for the night. Instead, you are cruising among the peaks of a majestic sunken mountain range, and each island peak is different from the others. You truly have left the city behind, and you've found a corner of paradise.

The San Juans have so much to see and do that a first-time visitor can be overwhelmed.

We have a short list of stops that we recommend to friends, and we'll share it with our readers. We emphasize that these are not the only places to experience, but they are unique. Nothing like them exists anywhere else. Our short list is as follows: Rosario, Roche Harbor, English Camp (Garrison Bay), Stuart Island (Prevost Harbor and Reid Harbor), Sucia Island, and Friday Harbor. You will make many other stops (including at all our advertisers!) as well. But these six are musts.

Rosario is a mansion and estate built by Robert Moran, a turn-of-the-century pioneer ship builder. Rosario is now a luxury resort hotel, with marina and mooring floats. Roche Harbor is another turn-of-the-century monument, this one built around limestone quarrying. It too is now a deluxe resort, and, like Rosario, is a don't-miss experience. English Camp is at Garrison Bay, a short distance from Roche Harbor. This is where the British garrison was stationed during the amazing 1859-1872 Pig War tensions. The blockhouse, formal gardens and several buildings remain, and are now a National Park, with an interpretive center.

Stuart Island is a gem. In both Prevost Harbor and Reid Harbor you can anchor, hook onto a mooring buoy, or tie to a dock. Which-

ever you do, you will be surrounded by beauty. A hike along a well-marked up-and-down trail leads to the dirt road that runs out to the Turn Point Lighthouse. Along the way, the Treasure Chest.

Sucia Island, with its weather- and water-sculpted sandstone, fossils and fascinating shoreline, is the definitive anchorage of the San Juans. The problem will be to choose which of Sucia Island's five bays to stay in. And Friday Harbor is a lovely little town where you will buy groceries and everything else you need.

Although summertime tourism is a major industry in the San Juan Islands, the settlements have retained a small village atmosphere. Minutes out of town, you will be on winding roads in pastoral farm country. Island people are easygoing and friendly, and many of them are highly accomplished. Movie stars and industrialist families have estates there. The late author Ernest Gann lived on San Juan Island. One famous author's book bio says simply that he lives on an island. What it doesn't say is that the island is in the San Juans.

IF YOU ARE APPROACHING from the east, the heart of the San Juans archipelago can be entered through four passes: Lopez Pass, Thatcher Pass, Peavine Pass, and Obstruction Pass.

At times the waters outside these passes can be turbulent, dangerously so, the result of tidal current and wind opposing each other (see sidebar on page 91). Be sure you have a complete tide and current book, and are able to read it. You can't go wrong with the official government publications, but our preferred tide book is *Captn. Jack's Tide & Current Almanac,* available at marine supply stores. In an easy to understand page-a-day format, *Captn. Jack's* gives complete tide and current information for Puget Sound and the San Juan Islands. It's the book we use, and we swear by it.

Drinking water is in short supply in the San Juan Islands. In almost every case you'll find no water for boat washing. Go to the San Juans with full water tanks, and conserve while you are there.

Fossil Bay, Sucia Island, has the best facilities for visiting pleasure craft.

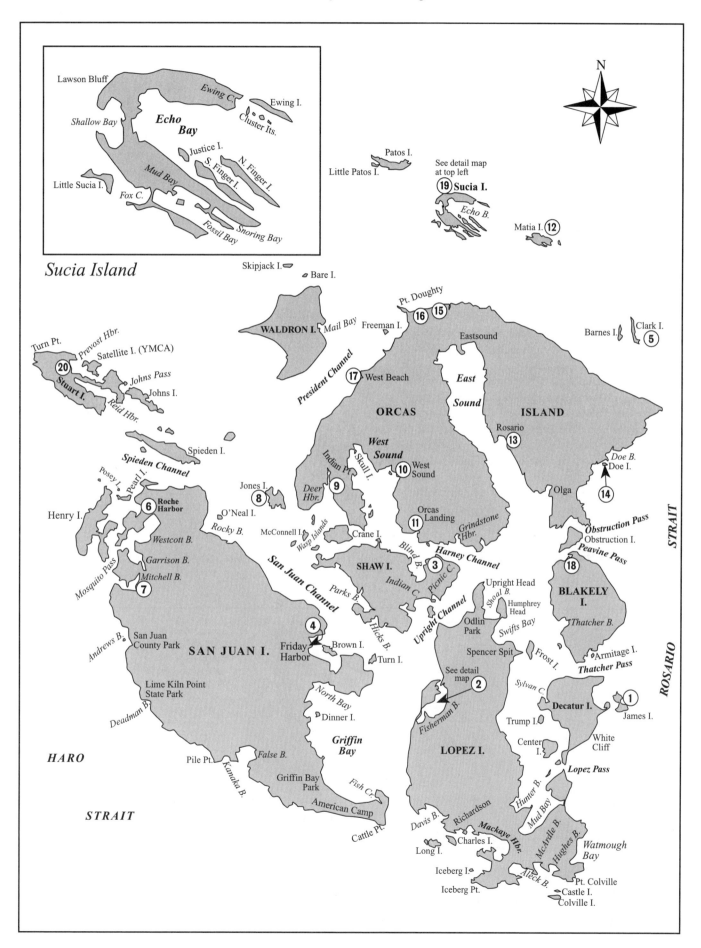

Lawson Bluff

Ewing C.

Ewing I.

Shallow Bay

Echo Bay

Cluster Its.

Justice I.

Mud Bay

Little Sucia I.

Fox C.

S. Finger I.

N. Finger I.

Snoring Bay

Fossil Bay

Sucia Island

Skipjack I.

Bare I.

Patos I.

Little Patos I.

See detail map
at top left

(19) **Sucia I.**

Echo B.

Matia I. (12)

Turn Pt.

Prevost Hbr.

Satellite I. (YMCA)

Pt. Doughty

Freeman I.

(16) (15)

Barnes I.

Clark I.

(5)

(20)

Stuart I.

Johns Pass

Johns I.

Reid Hbr.

WALDRON I.

Mail Bay

President Channel

(17) West Beach

Eastsound

East

Sound

ORCAS

ISLAND

Rosario

(13)

Doe B.

Doe I.

Spieden I.

Spieden Channel

West

Sound

Indian Pt.

Skull I.

West
Sound

(10)

Olga

(14)

Posey I.

Pearl I.

Jones I.

(8)

Deer
Hbr.

(9)

Orcas
Landing

(11)

Grindstone
Hbr.

Obstruction Pass

Obstruction I.

Peavine Pass

Henry I.

(6) **Roche**
Harbor

O'Neal I.

Rocky B.

McConnell I.

Wasp Islands

Crane I.

Blind B.

Harney Channel

(3)

Picnic C.

(18)

BLAKELY
I.

Westcott B.

Garrison B.

Mitchell B.

(7)

Mosquito Pass

SHAW I.

Indian C.

Parks B.

San Juan Channel

Upright Channel

Upright Head

Shoal B.

Humphrey
Head

Thatcher B.

ROSARIO

STRAIT

Andrews B.

San Juan
County Park

SAN JUAN I.

(4)

Friday
Harbor

Hicks B.

Brown I.

Turn I.

Odlin
Park

Swifts Bay

Spencer Spit

Frost I.

Armitage I.

Thatcher Pass

Lime Kiln Point
State Park

Deadman B.

North Bay

Dinner I.

See detail
map

(2)

Fisherman B.

Sylvan C.

Trump I.

Center
I.

Decatur I.

(1)

James I.

White
Cliff

Lopez Pass

HARO

Pile Pt.

False B.

Kanaka B.

Griffin Bay
Park

Griffin
Bay

Fish Cr.

LOPEZ I.

Davis B.

Richardson

Mackaye Hbr.

Hunter B.

Mud Bay

McArdle B.

Hughes B.

Watmough
Bay

STRAIT

American Camp

Cattle Pt.

Long I.

Charles I.

Iceberg I.

Iceberg Pt.

Aleck B.

Pt. Colville

Castle I.

Colville I.

Going Cruising? Pack Your Imagination

THE PRINCESS SERVED WINE in a golden goblet as the pirate sorted through his booty: a silver tray heaped with precious rings, rubies, emeralds and pearls. Then, armed with a magic whip and swords with strange powers, it was off on their ship to explore other lands of mystery and wonder.

Actually, the golden goblet was the bulb end of a piece of kelp. The rings were kelp cut up in small sections, and the whip was the long, leftover part of the kelp. The rubies, emeralds and pearls were the multicolored stones that covered the beach. The ships were logs rolled into the water, and their captains wielded driftwood swords. And the princess and pirate were Sonja and Erik, ages five and 10. Batteries weren't included, nor were they needed. Everything was right on the beach, but the kids had to bring their own imagination.

Imagination is as essential to the sailor as sails are to his ship. Without sails, the hull just sits there. Without imagination, we all just sit there. Kids have no trouble crossing the line between reality and fantasy, but that line seems to thicken as we grow older. As adults, the line becomes difficult to cross, but the effort is worthwhile.

It is imagination that brings history and places to life. On Matia Island, for example, there's a little cove that looks like a hundred other places in the San Juan Islands: rock, driftwood, overhanging vegetation. This particular cove, however, is different. This is where the "hermit" used to come ashore, having rowed his skiff across open water from Orcas Island. If you explore and look closely, you can find evidence of the hermit's homestead and gardens. What must it have been like to have this island all to himself, his own piece of the planet, shared only by seals and puffins?

Or Patos Island. As we explore Patos Island, it's impossible not to think of what life was like in the barracks there, surrounded by tide rips and unhindered winds, as ships groped through the angry waters at night, the beam from a stalwart lighthouse marking their path through a dangerous passage.

Or Sucia Island. Stand back from the fiberglass and the people, and imagine the campsites of the Indians as they harvested their traditional seal-hunting grounds for food and the materials of life. Look at the blocks of stone and picture hundreds of workers in the sandstone quarry, cutting a fledgling Seattle's new buildings.

The Northwest is rich with history. First came the Indians, then the Spanish and English, and finally the Americans. Each place we sail to has its own reason for being and its own tales to tell. Guidebooks and histories reveal at least some of the secrets of most of these places. Read, listen, learn, and imagine, so the place in which we've anchored won't be just a mark on the chart, but our living connection to a vibrant past and our fellow sailors before us.

—Rich Hazelton

Rich Hazelton is editor of 48° North, a popular Northwest sailing magazine. This piece appeared in slightly different form as an editorial in the October 1998 issue of 48° North.

James Island, looking northeast. A rugged but inviting park in the San Juans.

Good charts greatly enhance the pleasure of cruising the San Juans. It's a mistake to carry only U.S. chart 18421 or Canadian chart 3462 and think you will be safe. Those two charts show a large area and are good for planning, but they don't show enough close detail to get you past rocks and around reefs into the bays you have your eye on. As long as you are going to spend the time and resources to be in the San Juans, invest a little more and get a complete chart set. This means small scale chart 18421 or 3462 for the big picture, and large scale charts 18429, 18430, 18431, 18432, 18433, and 18434 for the close-up view.

Do you really need all these charts? We can answer by telling you that we know our way around the San Juans, and we won't leave our anchorage or mooring without the above charts on the table and stacked up in order of use. There are simply too many rocks, reefs and shoals to trust our day's passage to the small scale charts 18421 or 3462.

Caution in Rosario Strait

LOPEZ PASS, THATCHER PASS, Peavine Pass and Obstruction Pass all connect with Rosario Strait. Especially during an ebb, when current in Thatcher Pass and Lopez Pass sets east into Rosario Strait, expect rougher water off their mouths. If a big southflowing ebb in Rosario Strait is opposed by a strong southerly wind, expect severe turbulence. The tide-rips and heavy seas can persist completely across the strait.

We have seen some vicious rips at the south end of Rosario Strait. Walt Woodward (*How to Cruise to Alaska without Rocking the Boat Too Much*) recalls that a rip outside Lopez Pass was the worst he had ever encountered.

The waters between Guemes Channel and Thatcher Pass can be rough or even dangerous in these conditions (southflowing ebb in Rosario Strait opposed by fresh southerly wind). Guemes Channel enters Rosario Strait from the east, and Thatcher Pass enters from the west. Bellingham Channel angles in from the northeast. The conflict of the four currents, combined with the opposing wind, creates confused, high and steep beam seas as you cross. It seems that all experienced local yachting families (ourselves included) have their own horror stories of crossings in such conditions.

We have learned to treat Rosario Strait with great respect. Thus, one year when a 20-knot southerly was blowing, we left the San Juans for Seattle via Peavine Pass, at the north end of Blakely Island. As we suspected, Rosario Strait was rough, especially to the south. We angled northward and eastward across the top of Cypress Island, and looked down Bellingham Channel. It too was a mass of whitecaps.

So we continued eastward, and found calm water on the east side of Guemes Island. Our route plan now went past LaConner and south through Saratoga Passage. It was longer and slower than a fast run across the Strait of Juan de Fuca and down Admiralty Inlet, but it was unruffled.

—*Robert Hale*

① **James Island Marine State Park.** Use chart 18429; 18421. Open all year, day use, overnight mooring & camping. James Island is one of our favorite spots. We enjoy hiking its trails and watching its wildlife. Visiting boats can use both sides of a 65-foot-long float, and mooring buoys. Toilets are ashore, but no power or water. Anchoring can be difficult in the west cove. Use the float (removed in winter).

The east cove is exposed to wakes from passing traffic in Rosario Strait, but has mooring buoys. The park has a picnic shelter and 13 primitive campsites. A Cascadia Marine Trail campsite is at Pocket Cove (high bank gravel beach). Excellent hiking, picnicking, scuba diving. Pack out all garbage. Raccoons will go aboard unattended boats at the dock if food is left in the open. Best to stow food well and close the boat tight.

Unnamed Island #3. This island, an undeveloped state park, is in the little bay at the south tip of Decatur Island, and joins Decatur Island at low tide. Open all year, day use only. Anchor out. No fires or overnight camping. Pack out all garbage. Do not disturb wildlife or alter the surroundings. This is one of Contributing Editor Tom Kincaid's favorite anchorages. When the Kincaid children were small, they would use the concrete structure on the island as a fort.

See area map page 89

Spencer Spit is a popular park, with mooring buoys and good anchoring.

LOPEZ SOUND

Lopez Sound, the body of water between Decatur Island and Lopez Island, has several favorite anchorages. Among them, **Mud Bay** and **Hunter Bay** are good. Use chart 18424 (larger scale, preferred) or 18421.

Mud Bay Tidelands, south end of Lopez Sound. Open all year, day use only. No facilities. Includes all of the southwest end of Mud Bay and the southeast shore of Mud Bay up to Shoal Bight, except some private tidelands on the southeast side of the bay. Anchor out at this undeveloped state park property.

No fires or overnight camping. Pack out all garbage. Do not disturb the wildlife or alter the surroundings.

Hunter Bay, southwest corner of Lopez Sound. Hunter Bay is a good place to anchor, surrounded by forest, protected from all but northeast winds, with good bottom. The small float is for loading and unloading only. No facilities are ashore, and the land is privately owned. Nice spot to put the hook down, though.

Center Island. Good anchorage can be found by simply cruising around Center Island into **Reads**

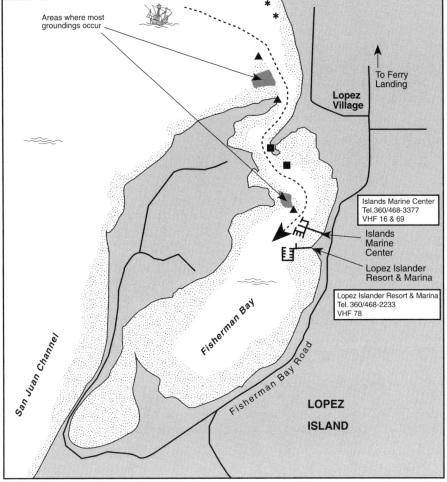

Fisherman Bay, Lopez Island

Reference only — not for navigation

drying shoal. Leave this beacon to starboard, then follow the well-marked channel into the bay. Anchorage can be found in 1-5 fathoms, mud bottom. Resist the temptation to cut inside any navigation marks (remember: Red, Right, Returning). *(See map of Fisherman Bay this page)*

The northernmost marina in Fisherman Bay belongs to Islands Marine Center. The middle marina belongs to the Lopez Islander resort. It was extensively rebuilt and enlarged during 1993, with further improvement under new ownership in 1997, 1998 and 1999. The Galley Restaurant and Lounge has moorage (free to diners), and is the third float from the bay's entrance.

Golf: The Lopez Island Golf Course, 9 flat holes next to the airport, is kept up entirely by volunteers. You'll need a ride to get there. (360)468-2679.

② **Islands Marine Center,** P.O. Box 88, Fisherman Bay Road, Lopez, WA 98261, (360)468-3377; fax (360)468-2283; email: imc@rockisland.com. Monitors VHF channels 16 & 69. Open all year, except closed Sundays during the winter. Guest moorage along 1000 feet of dock space. Call ahead. Services include 20 & 30 amp power, restrooms, showers, pumpout and portapotty dump. This is a large, well-run, full-service marina with haulout, repairs, and complete marine supplies. Good depth at all docks. Ron Meng is the longtime owner. Lopez Village shopping is nearby.

② **Lopez Islander Resort & Marina,** P.O. Box 459, Fisherman Bay Rd., Lopez, WA 98261, (800)736-3434, (360)468-2233; fax (360)468-3382. Monitors VHF channel 78. Open all year. Gasoline & diesel at the fuel dock. Guest moorage for large and small boats at 60 slips. Services include 30 & 50 amp power, restrooms, showers, laundry, swimming pool and Jacuzzi. The dock store has ice and bait. The resort has a restaurant and sports lounge, with lodging and camping by reservation.

Odlin Park, west side of Lopez Island. Use chart 18434; 18421. Open all year. Located between Flat Point and Upright Head. Good bottom for anchoring, but exposed to northwest winds. Small float for dinghies, or they can be beached. Campsites, restrooms. Beach area and sea wall, picnic sites and tables, cooking shelter and fire pits. Baseball diamond, open areas and trees.

Upright Channel State Park, northwest side of Lopez Island. Day moorage only at 3 mooring buoys. Services include restrooms but no other facilities. Day use only, 4 picnic sites.

Bay until you find an area out of the prevailing wind.

Brigantine Bay, between Trump Island and Decatur Island, is pretty, with anchorage in 4-7 fathoms, but the dock and all the land ashore are private.

Sylvan Cove is in the northwest corner of Decatur Island, and offers good holding bottom in convenient depths. The bay is truly beautiful, with New England-style buildings ashore. All the land ashore is private, as are the mooring buoys, the dock, and float that serve homeowners in the area.

Spencer Spit Marine State Park, east shore of Lopez Island, (360)468-2251. Open all year, day use and overnight mooring and camping. The park has 16 buoys. Services include a pay phone and restrooms upland but because of limited water supply, no showers. Spencer Spit is a popular park. Mooring buoys usually fill up quickly, but anchoring is good as long as your anchor is properly set. A saltwater lagoon, fed from the north side, is in the middle of the spit. If you are on the north side, you must walk around the tip of the spit and back down the south side to get to the upland areas of the park. The park has standard and primitive campsites. Bunny rabbits

abound. Interpretive signs help exploration. Spencer Spit is a Cascadia Marine Trail campsite. Close to the ferry dock. Although the pass between Spencer Spit and Frost Island is narrow, it is deep and safe.

Swifts Bay. Use chart 18429; 18421. Swifts Bay, lying behind Flower Island and Leo Reef, is shallow and strewn with several rocks and reefs. An anchored boat is subject to northerly winds and the wakes from passing craft. Not a good choice.

Shoal Bay. Use chart 18430; 18421. Shoal Bay indents the northern tip of Lopez Island between Humphrey Head and Upright Head, and offers good, fairly protected anchorage. We think the best spot is behind the breakwater and off the marina along the east shore. Numerous crab pot buoys must be avoided in picking an anchorage.

Fisherman Bay. Use chart 18434 (strongly recommended); 18421. Fisherman Bay extends southward about 1.5 miles into the western shore of Lopez Island. The entrance is winding and shallow, and should not be attempted by deep draft boats at less than half tide. Use chart 18434, which provides a comfortable, large-scale view of the waters. About 200 yards off the entrance, a beacon marks the tip of a

Tell Them You Read About Them In the Waggoner.

See area map page 89

SOUTH LOPEZ ISLAND

Use charts 18429 and 18434 (larger scale, preferred), or 18421. The southern end of Lopez Island is heavily indented by several bays, and guarded by numerous rocks and reefs. The geography is rugged and windblown, the result of the prevailing westerly winds from the Strait of Juan de Fuca. It is a fascinating shore to explore when the wind is down. The village of **Richardson** used to be famous for its quaint general store (which stocked everything anybody might need, ever), but the store burned to the ground a number of years ago, and has not been rebuilt. The Richardson fuel dock, with gasoline and diesel, is still operating, but you must lie next to a high pier while fueling. Most of its customers are fish boats and larger vessels. Anchorage at Richardson is marginal.

Mackaye Harbor. Use chart 18429 or 18434 (larger scale, preferred), or 18421. Mackaye Harbor and **Barlow Bay** are a favorite overnight for boats planning an early morning crossing of the Strait of Juan de Fuca, before the summer westerly fills in. The harbor has excellent anchorage, although swells from an afternoon westerly in the strait cause a certain amount of motion at anchor. Mackaye Harbor is the site of a fishboat marina, and during the summer months a large fishboat fleet can be found in the harbor.

Iceberg Island, an undeveloped state park in outer Mackaye Harbor. Open all year, day use only. Anchor out. No facilities. No fires or overnight camping. Pack out all garbage. Do not disturb wildlife or alter the surroundings.

Aleck Bay. Use chart 18429 (larger scale, preferred) or 18421. Aleck Bay is not particularly scenic, but it is big and easy to get into. Anchor close to the head of the bay in 5-6 fathoms. The bay is open to the east.

Hughes Bay. Use chart 18429 (larger scale, preferred) or 18421. Hughes Bay is exposed, but Contributing Editor Tom Kincaid has anchored overnight as far into the bay as he could get and still have swinging room.

McArdle Bay. Use chart 18429 (larger scale, preferred) or 18421. McArdle Bay provides good anchorage in 4-5 fathoms, but is completely exposed to southerly winds coming off the Strait of Juan de Fuca. Lovely homes are on the hills above the bay. Just outside, the chart shows a rock in the passage between Blind Island and Lopez Island. The rock is actually a reef.

Castle Island, an undeveloped state park off the southeast end of Lopez Island. Use chart 18429 (larger scale, preferred) or 18421. Anchor out. No facilities, day use only. No fires or overnight camping. Pack out all garbage. Do not disturb wildlife or surroundings.

Blakely Island Marina has excellent docks. It also has a good supply of fresh water.

Watmough Bay. Use chart 18429 (larger scale, preferred) or 18421. Watmough Bay has been one of Contributing Editor Tom Kincaid's favorites for 50 years. While a northerly could be a problem, Watmough Bay is protected from weather on the Strait of Juan de Fuca, and is the first such bay to offer refuge after a stormy crossing from Port Townsend. A beautiful high sheer rock wall is on the north side. The chart shows the bottom as rocky, but we have found excellent holding in blue mud in 2-3 fathoms, about halfway in.

BLAKELY ISLAND

Use chart 18430 (larger scale, preferred) or 18421. Blakely Island lies east of Lopez Island and Shaw Island. It and tiny Armitage Island, off the southeast corner, are privately owned, with no shore access. Anchorage is possible in Thatcher Bay, and, with care, be-

hind Armitage Island. The Blakely Island General Store & Marina, at the north end of Blakely Island, is a popular destination. Since Blakely Island, including the roads, is private, confine your stays to the marina property.

⑱ **Blakely Island General Store & Marina,** #1 Marina Drive, Blakely Island, WA 98222, (360)375-6121; e-mail blakely@rockisland.com. Or view at www.rockisland.com/~blakely/. Monitors VHF channel 68. Open all year, except closed in January. Fuel dock has gasoline and diesel. Facilities include excellent concrete docks with approximately 30 slips, 30 amp power, ample water, restrooms and showers, and laundry. The resort has a large covered picnic area. The general store serves island residents as well as marina guests, and is well stocked with food, clothes, and gifts.

This marina slipped a little in recent years,

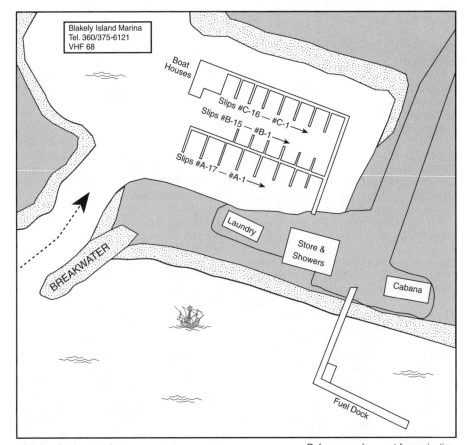

Blakely Island General Store & Marina

Reference only — not for navigation

but in 1999 Rick and Norma Reed came on board as managers and brought the property back to its former self. The restrooms, showers and laundry are fixed up and painted, and are a pleasure to use once again.

The channel leading to the boat basin is shallow, and may keep out a very deep draft vessel at the bottom of a very low tide. Other than those conditions, though, you should have plenty of water. If in doubt, call the marina office for advice. *(Marina map page 94)*

SHAW ISLAND

Blind Bay. Use chart 18434 (larger scale, preferred) or 18421. Blind Bay, on the north side of Shaw Island, has good anchorage throughout the center portion. Blind Island is a minimally developed state park, with several mooring buoys on its south side. A notable collection of rocks obstructs the waters west of Blind Island. *Do not pass west of Blind Island.* East of Blind Island, a white, privately maintained beacon marks a rock that lies midway between Blind Island and the Shaw Island shore. Enter Blind Bay midway between Blind Island and that beacon. The water will shoal abruptly as you pass between Blind Island and the beacon, but there's no danger unless you are close to the island.

Blind Island Marine State Park, Blind Bay. Open all year, overnight mooring. Facilities

include 4 mooring buoys, toilets. Accessible by boat only. Four primitive camping and picnic sites. Cascadia Marine Trail campsite. Pack out all garbage. Must enter bay on east side. Watch channel and rock markers carefully.

③ **Little Portion Store,** P.O. Box 455, at Shaw Island Ferry Terminal, Shaw Island, WA 98268, (360)468-2288. Open all year, shorter hours in winter. Closed Sundays. Limited guest moorage, call ahead. Groceries, ice, gift items, restrooms. The store is run by Franciscan nuns, who greet the ferries wearing their distinctive brown habits. The marina is adjacent to the ferry dock.

Parks Bay. Use chart 18434; 18421. Parks Bay is a fine anchorage. The land ashore is owned by the University of Washington as a biological preserve, and is off limits to visitors. There are stub pilings at the closed end of Parks Bay, but there is plenty of anchoring room, mud bottom, throughout the bay. Parks Bay Island, at the mouth of the bay, no longer is a state park. The island is under UW management as a biological preserve, no visitors allowed.

Hicks Bay. Hicks Bay has good anchorage, although exposed to southerlies. When entering, take care to avoid a reef that extends from the southern shore.

Indian Cove. Use chart 18434; 18421. Indian Cove, a popular anchorage area, is big and open feeling, somewhat protected from southerlies by nearby Lopez Island and Canoe Island. Watch for drying rocks between Canoe Island and Shaw Island, and a shoal 200 yards west of the southern point of Canoe Island. The Shaw Island County Park, with launch ramp, has an excellent beach.

Picnic Cove. Use chart 18434; 18421. Picnic Cove is immediately east of Indian Cove. It's a pretty little nook with room for a couple of boats. A mid-channel entrance is best, to avoid reefs on each side of the cove. The head of the cove shoals to drying flats. Anchor in 3-4 fathoms.

SAN JUAN ISLAND

San Juan Island is the second largest of the San Juan Islands, and the most heavily populated. Friday Harbor, the only incorporated town, is the seat of county government.

Fish Creek. Fish Creek is a tiny indentation near the southern tip of San Juan Island. It is lined with the docks and mooring buoys of the private homes along its shores. Fish Creek has no public facilities, and swinging room is very restricted between the homeowners' floats.

Middle Channel (Cattle Pass). Use chart

See area map page 89

18434 (larger scale, preferred) or 18421. Middle Channel, locally known as Cattle Pass, runs between the south end of San Juan Island and Lopez Island. It is the only southern entrance to the San Juan Islands, and connects with San Juan Channel. Whale Rocks lie just outside the southern entrance to the pass. It's easy to get close to them if you're not careful. When we enter Cattle Pass from the south, we try to leave Buoy 3, the gong buoy marking Salmon Bank, to port, and make a course for the middle of the entrance. This avoids Whale Rocks.

Tidal currents run strongly through Cattle Pass, and the waters can be turbulent with rips and eddies. A big ebb against a westerly wind can be unpleasant. Current predictions are shown under San Juan Channel in the current books.

It's possible to pass behind Goose Island and avoid foul current, but local knowledge is called for.

Griffin Bay. Use chart 18434 (larger scale, preferred) or 18421. You can anchor in several places in Griffin Bay. A stretch of beach inshore from Halftide Rocks is Griffin Bay Park, a public campground. From the campground it is a short walk to American Camp, maintained by the U.S. Park Service as a historical monument to the 1859 "Pig War." The Pig War resulted in setting the boundary between the U.S. and Canada in Haro Strait, and so kept the San Juan Islands in the U.S.

Griffin Bay Park, next to American Camp. Open all year, 2 mooring buoys. Toilets, no other facilities. Four campsites and picnic area. Watch for shallow water and pilings.

Unnamed Island #119, in Griffin Bay, south of Dinner Island. Open all year, day use only, no facilities. Anchor out at this undeveloped state park property. No fires or overnight camping. Pack out all garbage. Do not disturb wildlife or alter the surroundings.

Turn Island Marine State Park, in San Juan Channel, at the southeast entrance to Friday Harbor. Use chart 18434 (larger scale, preferred) or 18421. Turn Island is open all year for day use and overnight mooring and camping. It's a beautiful park, completely wooded, with many trails. Outhouse toilets are coveniently located, as are campsites and firepits. Turn Island is a popular stop for kayaks and beachable boats. Along the south side of the island the trees (madrona, cedar, hemlock, cypress) are bent and twisted, with much evidence of blowdown. The wind must howl here in the winter.

Three mooring buoys are placed along the west side, in the pass that separates Turn Island from San Juan Island. Currents can be quite strong in this pass, but the moorings are located safely out of the current. While anchoring is possible, it will be in the current, seaward of the buoys. We recommend the buoys. Toilets, no other facilities. Boat access only. Camping in designated primitive campsites only. Pack out all garbage. Hiking, fishing, crabbing, birdwatching. Most of this park is a designated wildlife refuge. Do not disturb animals in their natural habitat.

to serve them. A liquor store is convenient to the marina, as are a post office and laundromat. Two well-stocked grocery stores are on the main street. Regular bus service connects Friday Harbor with Roche Harbor and points between. In 1999 the round-trip fare was $7.00, $4.00 1-way.

You can moor at the Port of Friday Harbor marina or anchor out. Anchorage is good in the cove north of the marina, and throughout the area behind Brown (Friday) Island.

Enter Friday Harbor around either end of Brown Island. An unlighted daybeacon marks the end of a drying reef off the southwest corner of the island. Take care to avoid interfering with the ferries and the large number of float planes taking off and landing in the harbor. Brown Island is privately owned, and has its own dock and floats.

A fuel dock is located between the Port marina and the ferry dock. The floats just south of the ferry dock are owned by the condominium apartments ashore. Jensen's Marina, at the south end of the harbor, is a complete boat yard where repairs of any kind can be done.

Golf: San Juan Golf & CC, 9 interesting holes, is a short taxi ride away. Telephone (360)378-2254.

④ **Port of Friday Harbor,** P.O. Box 889, 204 Front Street, Friday Harbor, WA 98250, (360)378-2688; fax (360)378-6114. Web site www.portfridayharbor.org. Monitors VHF channel 66A. Open all year, gasoline and diesel available nearby. Ample side-tie guest moorage along 1500 feet of dock, plus slips in guest docks, and unoccupied slips as available. The slips handle a maximum length of 40 feet. Call ahead for reservations. Services include

A young couple enjoys close conversation outside the Front Street Ale House in Friday Harbor.

Friday Harbor. Use chart 18434 (larger scale, preferred) or 18421. Friday Harbor is the government and commercial center of the San Juan Islands. It is a customs port, and the terminus for ferries from Anacortes that also serve Sidney, B.C. Friday Harbor swells with tourists during the summer months, and has many boutiques, shops, galleries, restaurants and lounges

30 & 50 amp power, restrooms, showers, garbage, pumpout, nearby laundromat. Customs clearance is available.

If you do not have reservations, call on the radio for a slip assignment, but wait until you are within sight of the marina before you call. In the summer, a slip assignment station is staffed at the end of the customs dock. Boats

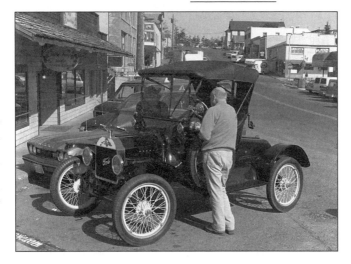

This beautifully restored 1915 Model T stopped at a Friday Harbor cafe. It has a 1921 engine, and is driven regularly. Owned by Wally and Nell Weaver of Friday Harbor.

larger than 40 feet must side-tie to the floating breakwater/guest dock. A dinghy float and day moorage are available. Kerosene, stove alcohol and propane are available. Nearby haulout and repairs. Mobile and stationary pumpouts.

This is one of the busiest marinas in the Northwest, and the pressure on staff and facilities is enormous. To their great credit, they keep the docks, showers and restrooms up quite well. Because they are so busy, when you depart it is courteous to call the marina on channel 66A to tell them your slip is available. *(Marina map this page)*

④ **Port of Friday Harbor Fuel Pier,** 1 Front Street, Port of Friday Harbor, Friday Harbor, WA 98250, (360)378-3114; fax

(360)378-4699. Open all year, 7 days a week. Fuel dock with gasoline and diesel. Carries oil, lubricants, propane, ice, and bait.

Rocky Bay. Use chart 18434 (larger scale, preferred) or 18421. Rocky Bay, close inshore from O'Neal Island, is a good anchorage and fairly well protected. Take care to avoid a drying shoal and a covered rock.

Lonesome Cove Resort, 5810 Lonesome Cove Rd., Friday Harbor, WA 98250, (360)378-4477. Open all year, moorage available only for resort guests. Docks not available in winter. Log cabins with fireplaces. A "hideaway" resort with no TV or phones in the cabins.

Photo / John Dustrude

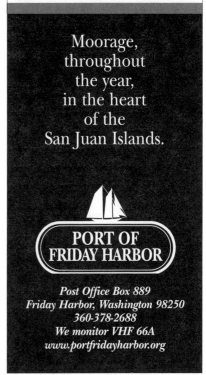
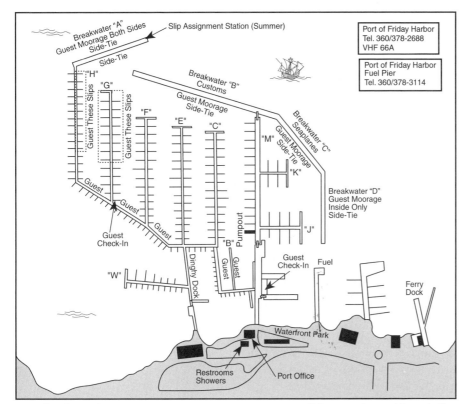

Breakwater "A"
Guest Moorage Both Sides
Side-Tie

Slip Assignment Station (Summer)

Side-Tie

"H"

"G"

Guest These Slips

Guest These Slips

Breakwater "B"
Customs

Guest Moorage
Side-Tie

"F"

"E"

"C"

Breakwater "C"
Seaplanes

Guest Moorage
Side-Tie

"M"

"K"

Breakwater "D"
Guest Moorage
Inside Only
Side-Tie

"J"

Guest

Guest

Guest Check-In

Guest

Guest

"B"

Pumpout

Guest Check-In

Fuel

"W"

Dinghy Dock

Guest

Guest

Ferry Dock

Waterfront Park

Restrooms Showers

Port Office

Port of Friday Harbor
Tel. 360/378-2688
VHF 66A

Port of Friday Harbor
Fuel Pier
Tel. 360/378-3114

Port of Friday Harbor

Reference only — not for navigation

See area map page 89

Roche Harbor. Use chart 18433 (larger scale, preferred) or 18421. Roche Harbor is enormously popular and attractive, and has a number of interesting anchorages and moorages. From the north (Speiden Channel), enter Roche Harbor past Pearl Island. Most boats favor the west side of Pearl Island, although shallow draft boats can use the passage on the east side. From the south (Haro Strait), entry is through **Mosquito Pass**. The flood current sets north in Mosquito Pass. The ebb current sets south, out of Roche Harbor. Currents can be strong at times. The channel is narrow but well-marked. *Stay in the channel.*

The mooring buoys that were in place off the Roche Harbor Resort were removed in 1997 to make way for a major new dock installation. The resort is also is a customs port, and the Customs dock is clearly identified. Many boats anchor in Roche Harbor, but we've heard of anchor dragging in strong winds. Check your set and use ample scope.

⑥ **Roche Harbor Resort and Marina,** P.O. Box 4001, Roche Harbor, WA 98250, (360)378-2155, (800)451-8910. Monitors VHF channel 78A. Open all year, 200 feet of dock space, 110 guest slips, unocccupied slips used when available. New docks have been added and the mooring buoys removed. Call ahead for reservations. Gasoline and diesel at the fuel dock. Services include 30 & 50 amp power, restrooms, showers, laundry. Telephone hookup available, extra charge. Customs clear-

ance is available at the Customs dock. In the summer, a bus circles the island between Roche Harbor and Friday Harbor. (*Marina map this page*)

This is one of the most popular spots in the islands, and in our opinion is a must-see destination (photo presentation page 100). The historic Hotel de Haro, Olympic-size swimming pool, formal gardens, tennis courts, well-stocked grocery store, gift shops, and excellent restaurant and bar are something apart from the usual tourist fare. An informal coffee shop also is available. The moorage fee includes water, power, trash disposal, and use of resort facilities. Excellent management. When we visited at the end of a busy day at the end of summer, we found all the facilities, including the showers, to be in first-rate condition.

Be sure to walk up to the Afterglow Vista Mausoleum. You've never seen anything like it. Another good walk is up the small mountain past the limestone quarries to a lookout. The trail is easy and well-maintained, and the view is excellent. The entire loop took us approximately a half-hour. If we had stopped to smell the flowers, it would have taken an hour. The hotel lobby has complimentary walking tour maps. For $1.00 they also have a pamphlet that details the remarkable history of Roche Harbor. Buy one.

A formal flag ceremony is conducted each evening at sundown during the summer season. The U.S. and Canadian flags are lowered and folded amid all appropriate pomp, respect,

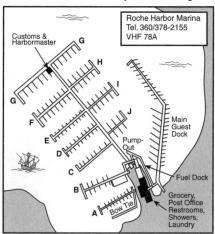

Reference only — not for navigation

Roche Harbor Marina

and salutes. Against a fiery sunset backdrop it's dazzling.

Posey Island Marine State Park, north of Roche Harbor. Use chart 18433 (larger scale, preferred) or 18421. Day use and overnight mooring and camping. Services include pit toilet, no other facilities. Cascadia Marine Trail campsite (primitive). The island is less than 1 acre in size. Water surrounding the island is shallow. Anchor out and row in by dinghy. Great sunset views on the west side.

These formal gardens are part of English Camp National Historic Park, San Juan Island.

Henry Island. Use chart 18433 (larger scale, preferred) or 18421. Anchorage is possible in Open Bay on Henry Island, although it is exposed to southerly winds. Nelson Bay is the site of a Seattle Yacht Club outstation. Nelson Bay is shallow, so use your depth sounder and tide tables before anchoring.

Wescott Bay. Use chart 18433 (larger scale, preferred) or 18421. Wescott Bay has good anchorage, but is partly taken up with a major shellfish culture business. Although the bay is shallow, adequate anchoring depths can be found throughout. The public beach has excellent clamming.

Garrison Bay. Use chart 18433 (larger scale, preferred) or 18421. Garrison Bay, the location of English Camp, is a popular and excellent anchorage, with room for a large number of boats. British troops were garrisoned here during the 1859 Pig War, and the buildings and grounds have been restored as a historical site by the U.S. Park Service. You can tour the grounds and several of the buildings. The grounds include a cemetery where several people from that era are buried. Rangers are on duty to provide information, and an interesting film tells the history. It's a good stop for families with children. A steep trail leads to the top of Young Hill, the highest point

on San Juan Island, for a marvelous view.

English Camp Historical Park, San Juan Island, (360)586-2165. Open all year. Excellent park, described above. Restrooms, no other facilities.

Mitchell Bay. Use chart 18433; 18421. Snug Harbor Marina offers moorage, a launch ramp, a store, and cabins ashore. Past the marina there is shallow anchorage. At the entrance to Mitchell Bay, a shoal extends from the south shore almost to the middle. A rock is at the outer end. Leave this rock to starboard when you enter. Large scale chart 18433 shows the entrance clearly.

⑦ **Snug Harbor Resort,** 2371 Mitchell Bay Road, Friday Harbor, WA 98250, (360)378-4762; fax (360)378-8859, e-mail sneakaway @snugresort.com, or view at www. snugresort.com. Use chart 18433 (larger scale, much preferred) or 18421. Open all year. Guest moorage, maximum boat length 70 feet, depth at zero tide is 6 feet. Gasoline only at the fuel dock. Propane available. Concrete launch ramp and refurbished docks. Long-term parking is available for tow vehicles and trailers. Services include 15, 20 & 30 amp power, restrooms, showers, garbage drop and recycling, pumpout may be installed soon. An on-site convenience store has ice and limited groceries, fishing and boating supplies. New and attractive cabins

Two Unique Destinations in the San Juan Islands

Rosario Resort & Marina

The marvelous mansion at Rosario is surrounded by walkways and lawns, perfectly maintained. In many ways, it is a step back in time.

This pool overlooks East Sound. The hotel, with spa, shops and museum, is behind the camera.

Roche Harbor Resort & Marina

The Afterglow Vista Mausoleum, a 15-minute walk from the marina, was built with Masonic symbolism, and is an astonishing sight in the forest.

The restful promenade in front of the Hotel de Haro is paved with bricks from the lime kilns. Each brick has the name of its maker inscribed in its face.

are available for rent. Reservations are good idea. This longtime resort in Mitchell Bay is under new and energetic ownership. They have rebuilt and upgraded the entire property.

Haro Strait is a favorite hunting ground for orcas, the so-called "killer whales," that often cruise within a few yards of shore. Washington State Parks has acquired a site at Lime Kiln Point, where people can watch and photograph the whales. Anchorage offshore from this park would be very difficult, and is not recommended.

San Juan County Park, 380 West Side Road N., Friday Harbor, WA 98250, (360)378-2992. Use chart 18433 (larger scale, preferred) or 18421. Open all year. Facilities include launch ramp, restrooms, no power, no showers. A popular park for kayak campers who can pull up on the beach.

Unnamed Island #40, on the southwest side of San Juan Island, approximately 1 mile northwest of Pile Point. Use chart 18433 or 18434 (larger scale, preferred), or 18421. Open all year, day use only, no facilities. Anchor out at this undeveloped state park property. No fires or overnight camping. Pack out all garbage. Do not disturb wildlife or alter the surroundings.

Unnamed Island #38, southwest side of San Juan Island, near the center of Kanaka Bay. Use chart 18433 or 18434 (larger scale, preferred), or 18421. Open all year, day use only, no facilities. Anchor out at this undeveloped state park property. No fires or overnight camping. Pack out garbage. Do not disturb wildlife or alter the surroundings.

Wasp Islands. Use chart 18434 (strongly recommended) or 18421. The Wasp Islands are a rock- and reef-strewn area where navigation should be done very carefully. Not all the underwater hazards are marked, and the unwary can come to grief. Wasp Passage, however, is free of dangers, and the skipper who pays attention to stay in the channel will have no problems.

All the Wasp Islands are privately owned except **Yellow Island,** which is owned by The Nature Conservancy.

Northwest McConnell Rock, northwest of McConnell Island. Use chart 18434 (strongly recommended) or 18421. Open all year, day use only, no facilities. Anchor out only at this undeveloped state park property. No fires or overnight camping. Pack out all garbage. Do not disturb wildlife or alter the surroundings. At low tide McConnell Rock is connected to McConnell Island by a sandspit.

Unnamed Island #112, east of McConnell Island. Open all year, day use only, no facilities. Undeveloped state park property; anchoring only. No fires or overnight camping. Pack out garbage. Do not disturb wildlife or alter the surroundings.

The dock at Jones Island Marine Park has room for several boats.

⑧ **Jones Island Marine State Park.** Use chart 18434 (larger scale, preferred) or 18421. Open all year, day use and overnight mooring and camping. The bay at the north end of Jones Island is an excellent anchorage. Boats anchoring near the beach will run stern-ties ashore, leaving swinging room for boats anchored in the middle. Currents can swirl through the bay, so leave ample swinging room when you anchor.

Seven mooring buoys are in the bay. A 264-foot-long mooring float leads to shore. A well ashore provides drinking water. The well often runs dry in late summer, so use the water sparingly.

A few mooring buoys are in the small bay on the south side of the island. In the middle of this bay, watch for a rock that lies awash at zero tide. The rock is shown on the charts, but the symbol is easy to overlook. Jones Island is a Cascadia Marine Trail site, with 19 primitive campsites.

Jones Island suffered a major blow-down of mature trees during a severe storm in 1990. For environmental reasons, most of the downed trees were left to rot on the ground, although campsites and trails were cleared and the logs bucked up for firewood. Evidence of the blow-down can be seen everywhere.

Jones Island is excellent for families with children. Families will enjoy the hikes and probably will meet tame deer. During the summer, mooring buoys and float space can be hard to get. *Caution:* Raccoons will go aboard unattended boats at the dock if food is left in the open. Stow food well, and close the boat tight.

ORCAS ISLAND

Orcas Island is the largest of the San Juans, and is deeply indented by Deer Harbor, West Sound and East Sound. Deer Harbor is the most westerly and the smallest of these inlets. It is the location of the Deer Harbor Marina, at the village of Deer Harbor on the eastern shore. The resort is a popular destination, and anchorage is excellent throughout the bay. One of our favorite anchoring spots is behind little Fawn Island, close to the western shore.

Golf: The San Juan Golf Course, 9 holes, is hilly but easily walked. During dry summer months even well-played shots can roll downhill and into oblivion. Fun course. (360)376-4400.

⑨ **Deer Harbor Marina**, 200 Deer Harbor Road, Deer Harbor, WA 98243, (360)376-3037; fax (360)376-6091. Use chart 18434 (larger scale, recommended) or 18421. Monitors VHF channel 78A. Open all year. Facilities include gasoline and diesel at the fuel dock, ample guest moorage, 30 amp power, new restrooms and showers, pumpout, laundry. The Deer Harbor Marina and fuel dock came under new ownership in 1996, and a major rebuilding, with new docks, took place in 1997 and 1998. The new restrooms and showers are outstanding.

Deer Harbor is a popular spot, with restaurant, pool, gift shop, market, shuttle to Orcas ferry dock and Eastsound, and more. The shoreside services are under separate ownership, but marina guests have full access. During the busy months it's almost essential to call ahead for mooring reservations. Mike Wallace is the manager. Mike

Reference only — not for navigation

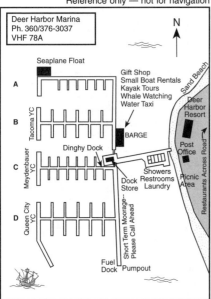

Deer Harbor Marina

told us that the dock help's mission is to "make the skippers look good and the wives proud." *(Marina map above)*

Pole Pass. Use chart 18434 (larger scale, preferred) or 18421. Boats bound between Harney Channel and Deer Harbor will go through Pole Pass, a narrow notch that separates Crane Island from Orcas Island. This pass is *narrow,* and rocks obstruct the edges and approaches. The current can run through the pass. A mid-channel course is safe (we have gone through in a Washington State ferry), but you *do* want to stay in the middle. For most skippers, good sense would dictate slow speeds through the pass. Unfortunately, not all skippers have seen it that way, and wakes have caused considerable damage to docks along the shoreline. So now speeds are limited to 7 knots maximum. The reduced speed zone extends from just west of Pole Pass eastward almost to Bell Island, and is marked by white cylindrical buoys.

West Sound. For all of West Sound, use chart 18434 (larger scale, recommended) or 18421. West Sound is the middle inlet of Orcas Island, where the Wareham family's West Sound Marina offers limited overnight moorage and complete service facilities. Next to the marina is the home of the Orcas Island Yacht Club, with moorage for visiting members of reciprocal clubs. A San Juan County day use only public dock lies next to the Orcas Island Yacht Club dock. Good anchorage is available at the head of the bay (stay well clear of Harbor Rock, marked by a daybeacon). Anchorage is also good off the village of West Sound, and behind Double Island. We have anchored behind Double Island several times over the years, and enjoyed it each time.

⑩ **West Sound Marina,** P.O. Box 119, Orcas Island, WA 98280, (360)376-2314; fax (360)376-4634. Monitors VHF channel 16, switch to 09. Open all year, except closed Sundays in the winter. Facilities include gasoline and diesel at the fuel dock, propane, 6 guest slips, 300 feet of guest dock, 20 & 30 amp power, restrooms, pumpout. Full service haulout to 30 tons and repairs, including enclosed area for major work. The chandlery has most boating supplies. Grocery and deli nearby. When approaching, stay well off Picnic Island. A rock ledge extends into West Sound from the island. Once at the marina, stay very close to the docks. The water shoals toward Picnic Island.

Victim Island, west side of West Sound. Open all year, day use only, no facilities. Anchor out at this undeveloped state park. No fires or overnight camping. Pack out all garbage. Do not disturb wildlife or alter the surroundings.

Unnamed Island #80, west of Indian Point in West Sound. Open all year, day use only, no facilities. Anchor out at this undeveloped state park property. No fires or overnight camping. Pack out all garbage. Do not disturb wildlife or alter the surroundings.

Skull Island, north end of Massacre Bay. Open all year, day use only, no facilities. Anchor out at this undeveloped state park. No fires or overnight camping. Pack out all garbage. Do not disturb wildlife or alter the surroundings.

Unnamed Island #81, near the West Sound Marina. Open all year, day use only, no facilities. Anchor out at this undeveloped state park property. No fires or overnight camping. Pack out all garbage. Do not disturb wildlife or alter the surroundings.

⑪ **Orcas Landing.** Use chart 18434 (larger scale, recommended) or 18421. Orcas Landing has a float next to the ferry dock, but stays are limited to 30 minutes. Dock space near the ramp is for fueling only. The store at the head of the ferry dock is open. Other shops in the village, aimed at serving the summer ferry lineup, are good for browsing. Great sandwiches and ice cream cones, too. Fuel service is available. Be well-fendered and securely tied to the dock at Orcas Landing. Passing boat and ferry traffic in Harney Channel can make for a rough ride.

⑪ **Island Petroleum Services,** Orcas Village, (360)376-3883. Open all year, closed Sat. and Sun. in the winter, fuel dock with gasoline and diesel.

Grindstone Harbor. Use charts 18434 or 18430 (larger scale, recommended), or 18421. Grindstone Harbor is a small, shallow anchorage, with two major rocks in its entrance. One of these rocks became famous a few years ago when the Washington State ferry *Elwha* ran aground on it while doing a little sightseeing. Favor the east shore all the way in. Private

Drift

THROUGHOUT THESE COASTAL WATERS, from Olympia north, skippers must watch for debris in the water. While some of the debris is in the form of cushions, fenders, and other equipment lost from boats, most of it is wood. Lumber, tree branches, entire trees, logs, and chunks of wood of all sizes are floating around out there, ready to bend a propeller or damage a bottom.

Collectively, this debris is called drift, and whoever's on the helm must watch for it constantly. It's a good idea, in fact, to have two pairs of eyes watching ahead whenever the boat is underway — especially if the boat is traveling faster than 10 knots.

Drift can be anywhere, but usually it collects along the shear line where two currents meet. If you see one piece of drift, look sharp for more. Usually it'll be there. On calm days shear lines will seem to meander across an entire waterway. In many areas the currents eddy, forming shear lines that appear, one after another, for what seem like miles. When approaching a shear line, the wise skipper of a faster boat slows from cruise speed to 6-8 knots, and picks a relatively safe way through the rubble. Often a shift to neutral is called for, to protect the propeller.

Much drift is easy to see, but sometimes it is not. I have seen 60-foot-long logs floating barely awash, almost invisible until the boat is right upon them. At sunrise or sunset, while running toward the sun, reflections off the water can hide a lot of drift. Occasionally a log will hang vertically in the water, the upper end hardly visible. These are called deadheads. When such a log buries its lower end in the bottom, a boat hitting the upper end can suffer catastrophic damage.

—Robert Hale

See area map page 89

Pastoral Olga, in East Sound, is served by a float in the summer.

mooring buoys take up much of the inner part of the bay, but there's room to anchor if you need to.

Guthrie Bay. Use charts 18434; 18430 (larger scale, recommended) or 18421. Guthrie Bay indents Orcas Island between Grindstone Harbor and East Sound. It's a pleasant little spot with private mooring buoys around the perimeter and homes on the hillsides. Anchor in 4-7 fathoms.

East Sound. Use chart 18430 (larger scale, recommended) or 18421. East Sound, the largest of Orcas Island's indentations, extends about 6 miles north from Foster Point. The shores on both sides are steep-to, and offer few anchorage possibilities. The Rosario Resort is on the east side, a short distance up the sound. The village of Eastsound is at the head. Fresh winds sometimes will blow in East Sound, while outside the air will be calm.

Eastsound. Use chart 18430 (larger scale, recommended) or 18421. The village of Eastsound, located at the head of East Sound, is the largest settlement on Orcas Island. A small public mooring float is on the eastern shore. A 10-minute walk leads from the float to town. Anchorage, in 5 to 10 fathoms, is possible off the town. Eastsound has several very good restaurants, a large grocery, a liquor store, many interesting shops, and on Saturdays during the summer, an excellent farmers' market.

Anchoring note: A sign on the county mooring dock announces that the bottom inshore, from a line between the dock and the small islet off the town, is sensitive eelgrass habitat, and asks that you anchor to seaward of that line.

⑬ **Rosario Resort,** 1400 Rosario Rd, Eastsound, WA 98245, (360)376-2222;

(800)562-8820; fax (360)376-3038. Or view at www.rosarioresort.com. Monitors VHF channel 78A. Use chart 18430 or 18434 (both of them larger scale, preferred) or 18421. Open all year, gasoline and diesel at the fuel dock (fuel dock closed Nov. 1 - April 1), 32 slips, 30 amp power, 28 mooring buoys, restrooms. Showers & laundry included with moorage. Car rentals, convenience store, pay phones, seaplane service to Seattle. Rosario does *not* have customs clearance. If entering from Canada, the nearest customs are at Roche Harbor or Friday Harbor.

Rosario is a world-renowned, deluxe resort. The more notice the better to assure reservations. Nelson Moulton, an unusually bright and agreeable young man, is the harbormaster.

In our opinion, Rosario is one of the places that simply *must* be seen on a San Juan Islands cruise (photo presentation page 100). The center of the resort is the magnificent Moran Mansion, listed on the National Register of Historic Places. The Mansion houses restaurants, a lounge, a boutique, a gift shop, indoor pool, outdoor pool, spa facilities and exercise equipment, all of them available to

marina guests. The organ concert, beginning at 1900 every day in the summer, Fridays and Saturdays in the winter, is famous. The second floor of the mansion is a fascinating museum—well worth the visit. Golf and tennis are nearby. Moran State Park is 1½ miles away. *(Marina map this page)*

Olga. Use chart 18430 (larger scale, recommended) or 18421. Olga, a pastoral, tiny village, is on the east shore of East Sound, near the entrance. While Olga has a dock and 105-foot-long mooring float, it has no power, no restrooms, no showers. The float is removed in winter. A box for overnight moorage payment is at the bottom of the ramp. A sign above the dock lists local stores and locations. Olga Village has a post office and (summer only) a store. Orcas Island Art Works, about ¼-mile up the road, sells interesting arts and crafts, and has an excellent cafe. Good anchoring offshore, but exposed to southeasterly winds.

Twin Rocks, west of Olga. Open all year, day use only, no facilities. Anchor out at this undeveloped state park property. No fires or overnight camping. Pack out all garbage. Do not disturb wildlife or alter the surroundings.

Lieber Haven Resort, P.O. Box 127, Olga, WA 98279, (360)376-2472. In the middle of Obstruction Pass. Marina open April 1 – October 1, resort open all year. Not your usual place. Day moorage only. Store carries charts, groceries, beer and wine, and some marine supplies. Cabins for rent. Kayaks and Poulsbo boats for rent. Sailboat and fishing charters. See Kitty and Dave Baxter, daughter Sharie and their parrots.

Obstruction Pass Campground, southeast tip of Orcas Island. Open all year, moorage at 2 buoys, toilets, no power or showers. Good anchoring on a gravel bottom. Campground has campsites, fireplaces, picnic tables, hiking trails.

⑭ **Doe Island Marine State Park,** southeast side of Orcas Island. Use chart 18430 (larger scale, recommended) or 18421. Open all year for day use and camping, overnight mooring in summer only. This is a beautiful

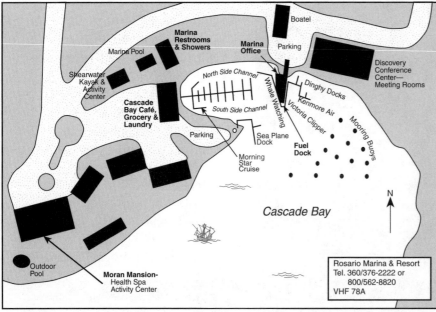

Rosario Resort & Marina

Reference only — not for navigation

tiny island with a rocky shoreline dotted with tidepools. Dense forest, lush undergrowth. A trail leads all around the island. The mooring float is 30 feet long. Tie on either side and raft out if necessary. The park has toilets, but no power, water or showers. Primitive campsites. Pack out all garbage. Adjacent buoys are privately owned. Don't use them. Currents run strongly between Doe Island and Orcas Island. If anchored, be sure of your set and swing.

⑮ **Smuggler's Resort,** P.O. Box 79, Eastsound, WA 98245, (360)376-2297, (800)488-2097; fax (360)376-5597. Or view at www.smuggler. com. Use chart 18430 or 18431(larger scale, preferred), or 18421. Located on the north coast of Orcas Island. Open all year, restrooms, showers, launch ramp and 400-foot dock available to guests of the resort only.

⑯ **Bartwood Lodge,** Rt. 1, Box 1040, Orcas Island, WA 98245, (360)376-2242. North coast of Orcas Island. Open all year, guest moorage available, 12 mooring buoys (summer only). The fuel dock is closed. Launch ramp with long term parking. Lodging and restaurant on site.

Freeman Island, on President Channel. Use chart 18432 (larger scale, preferred) or 18421. Open all year, day use only, no facilities. Anchor out at this undeveloped state park property. No fires or overnight camping. Pack out all garbage. Do not disturb wildlife or alter the surroundings.

⑰ **West Beach Resort,** Rt. 1, Box 510, Orcas Island, WA 98245, (360)376-2240; toll-free (877) 937-8224; fax (360)376-4746; e-mail vacation@westbeachresort. com, or view at www.westview beachresort.com. Use chart 18432 (larger scale, preferred) or 18421. Open all year, gasoline only at the fuel dock, 26-foot maximum boat length in the slips. Keel sailboats tie to mooring buoys. The dock and mooring buoys can take between 35 and 38 boats. The store has a little bit of everything, including groceries, ice, propane, kerosene, stove alcohol, scuba air, beer and wine. West Beach is a popular fishing resort, with cabins for rent, private launch ramp and parking. Be careful if you anchor out. The eelgrass bottom is not good in many places and you can drag.

Barnes Island and **Clark Island.** Use chart 18430 (larger scale, preferred) or 18421. These two beautiful islands lie parallel to each other in Rosario Strait, between Orcas Island and Lummi Island. Barnes Island is privately owned, but Clark Island is a state park, with mooring buoys installed during the summer. Camping and picnicking sites are ashore, and trails along the island.

⑤ **Clark Island Marine State Park.** Open all year, day use and overnight mooring and camping. Clark Island is exposed to Rosario Strait and Georgia Strait, and best for settled weather only. Mooring buoys are deployed between Clark Island and Barnes Island, and in the bay on the east side. Note the nasty rock that lies in the entrance to the bay. Park has 9 mooring buoys. Toilets, no power, no water. Picnic sites, fire rings, primitive campsites. Pack out all garbage.

⑫ **Matia Island Marine State Park.** Use charts 18430 or 18431 (larger scale, preferred), or 18421. Open all year, day use and overnight mooring and camping. Facilities include a float in Rolfe Cove, 2 buoys, toilet, no power, water or showers. The mooring float is removed in winter. The favored anchorage is in Rolfe Cove, which opens from the west. Strong currents can run through Rolfe Cove. The bottom is rocky. Be sure the anchor is well set, and swinging room is adequate. Anchorage also is good in the bay that indents the southeast corner. The remains of an old homestead are located at the head of that bay.

There is some disagreement about the pronunciation of Matia. Bruce Calhoun's book, *Cruising the San Juan Islands,* says it's pronounced "Mah-TEE-ah." We've been informed, however, that a number of genuine old hands have always pronounced it "Mah-CIA," as in "inertia" or "militia." However the name is pronounced, Matia Island is a popular destination, beautiful and interesting. The island is part of the San Juan Island National Wildlife Refuge (run by the U.S. Fish and Wildlife Service). All access is restricted except the loop trail and the designated 5-acre moorage and camping area. The rest of the island is off-limits to protect nesting wildlife.

See area map page 89

⑲ **Sucia Island Marine State Park.** Use chart 18431 (larger scale, *much preferred*) or 18421. Open all year, day use and overnight mooring and camping. For information call (800)233-0321. Facilities include dock space, mooring buoys, toilets, portapotty dump. Water, but no power, no showers. This probably is the most heavily used marine park in the system. As many as 700 boats can visit on one weekend in the high summer season. Like Matia and Patos Islands, Sucia Island is made of sandstone carved by water and wind into dramatic shapes. Many fossils can be found in Sucia Island's sandstone. It is illegal to disturb or remove them.

The park has 55 primitive campsites, and 2 group campsites which can be reserved. Camping is permitted in designated areas only. The day use/picnic area, with picnic shelters, is on the neck of land separating Echo Bay and Shallow Bay, and can be reserved. The park has several miles of hiking trails and service roads. The most developed facilities are at Fossil Bay. Fresh water is available April through September at Fossil Bay and near Shallow Bay.

Sucia Island has several fingers that separate small bays. Facilities in these bays are as follows: Fox Cove: 4 mooring buoys; Fossil Bay: dock, 16 mooring buoys; Snoring Bay: 2 mooring buoys; Echo Bay: 14 mooring buoys; Ewing Cove: 4 mooring buoys; Shallow Bay: 8 mooring buoys;

Navigation note: A considerable reef extends westward from Little Sucia Island. West Bank, with shoal water, lies a short distance beyond that reef. The reef and West Bank are shown clearly on the larger-scale chart 18431 (1:25,000), but not at all clearly on the smaller scale 1:80,000 chart 18421. Nor does the Canadian chart 3462 (1:80,000) show the dangers very well. Sucia Island is surrounded by such hazards. We strongly recommend that vessels in these waters carry and use chart 18431.

Shallow Bay. Shallow Bay is an excellent, popular anchorage. Lots of room. Tie to a mooring buoy or anchor. Easy entry as long as you pass *between* the 2 beacons that mark the entrance. Beautiful sunsets.

Fox Cove. Enter Fox Cove from either side. Waters off the southern entry can be turbulent. At the west entry the foul ground extends west farther than you expect. Tie to mooring buoys or anchor behind Little Sucia Island. A pretty spot with deeply carved sandstone cliffs.

Fossil Bay. Fossil Bay is easy to enter, nicely protected and beautiful. Anchor out, tie to one of the mooring buoys, or moor at the dock. At the head of the dock a plaque commemorates the yacht clubs that were members of the Interclub Boating Association of Washington, when Interclub bought the island and gave it to the state as a state park forever. One of the points of land overlooking Fossil Bay is named for Ev. Henry, the first president of Interclub, who conceived the idea and carried out the project.

Snoring Bay. Snoring Bay is easy to enter, and has 2 mooring buoys. A good spot.

As we understand the story, a park ranger was caught sleeping on duty in this bay, hence the name.

Echo Bay. Echo Bay is the largest of Sucia's bays. While it is the most exposed, it is the most popular. When the wind blows expect some anchor dragging. Mooring buoys line the western shore. Picnic facilities are on the narrow neck of land that separates Echo Bay from Shallow Bay.

The two long islands in Echo Bay (North Finger Island and South Finger Island) are privately owned. The south half of Justice Island (the small island off South Finger Island) is park-owned but closed to the public as a nature preserve.

Ewing Cove. In our opinion, cozy little Ewing Cove, tucked in behind Ewing Island on the north side of Echo Bay, is the most charming of Sucia Island's bays. The cove has 4 mooring buoys and a lovely beach at the northeast end. We've had reports of a rock in Ewing Cove's southern entrance, from Echo Bay. The rock lies east of a white can that marks a fish haven, shown on large scale chart 18431. We're told the rock is black and hard to see, and feeds on propellers at low tide. Be extra cautious. The narrow pass at the northeast end of Ewing Cove is deep and easily run. Danger Reef lies just outside.

Looking out the mouth of Active Cove, Patos Island, on a perfect September late afternoon. The lighthouse is on the point.

Patos Island Marine State Park. Use chart 18432 (larger scale, preferred) or 18421. Open all year, day use and overnight mooring and camping. Facilities include 2 mooring buoys in Active Cove, toilets, primitive campsites. The only possible anchorage is in Active Cove, one of the most scenic spots in the San Juans, on the west tip of the island. The cove, with its sculpted sandstone walls, feels extremely remote. You can find considerable current activity outside the entrances. Inside Active Cove the currents are reduced, but can still make for interesting anchoring. The remains of the dock that served the lighthouse on Alden Point are still there, but the dock is not usable for moorage. Use the mooring buoys when possible. Pack out all garbage. The island is a breeding area for birds.

Waldron Island. Use chart 18432 (larger scale, preferred) or 18421. Waldron Island has no public facilities. In settled weather anchorage is good in Cowlitz Bay and North Bay. Mail Bay, on the east shore, is rocky but usable. The mail boat from Bellingham used to call here, leaving the mail in a barrel hung over the water.

Navigation note: Strong currents and tide-rips occur frequently in President Channel, Speiden Channel, and off the west side of Stuart Island. Especially on spring tides, exercise caution.

Stuart Island. Use chart 18432 (larger scale, preferred) or 18421. The center portion of Stuart Island, including Reid Harbor and Prevost Harbor, is a state park. A trail and dirt road from Reid Harbor and Prevost Harbor lead out to the automated Turn Point lighthouse. It's an excellent walk. Once you get to the road, it's 0.7 mi. to the Treasure Chest, near the schoolhouse. T-shirts, stationery and the like have been enhanced with local scenes. Strictly the honor system. Select the items you like and mail a check for your purchases. We did it, and got a nice thank you note in reply. It's a fund-raiser for the school.

⑳ **Stuart Island Marine State Park, Prevost Harbor.** Use chart 18432 (larger scale, much preferred), or 18421. Open all year, day use and overnight mooring and camping. Facilities include 256 feet of dock space, 7 mooring buoys, 18 primitive campsites, toilets. The favored entrance to Prevost Harbor is around the west end of Satellite Island. *Caution:* Other than at low water, use caution. Two reefs in the entrance are covered at high tide. One is off the Stuart Island shore, and dries 6 feet. The other is off Satellite Island, and dries 4 feet. The reefs are clearly charted, but when they cover, the route to the dock looks wide-open. Well, it's not.

The passage to the east of Satellite Island is foul, and many people recommend against it. Contributing Editor Tom Kincaid, however, reports that with care these waters are passable at half-tide or better, or by shallow draft boats. Use caution. (We don't attempt that passage in our boat.) Prevost Harbor is a popular destination, with good anchoring and miles of trails and roads on Stuart Island. Shoreside facilities are shared with Reid Harbor, on the narrow but steep neck of land that separates them.

Lots of room to tie up at the dock in Prevost Harbor, or hang off a park buoy. Good anchoring, too.

Reid Harbor, from the head of the bay. Floats, mooring buoys and excellent anchoring.

Navigation Tip

Tom and Barbara Wilson, on their boat *Toba,* have a good system to keep them out of trouble. "We agree where we are, or we stop the boat until we do," they told us one day. Mrs. Hale and I have followed that practice somewhat over the years, but since meeting the Wilsons we have tried to follow it religiously.

In the summer of 1996 the Wilson's system paid off handsomely. At high tide, we were entering Montague Harbour from the northwest, off Trincomali Channel. We would leave Wise Island to port and Sphinx Island to starboard. As the chart shows, it's important to favor the Sphinx Island side of the passage, because a reef lies off the south end of Wise Island. A dot islet is on the reef, approximately in the middle of the passage.

At high tide I mistook the dot islet for Sphinx Island, and prepared to pass between the islet and Wise Island. Mrs. Hale, bless her, was not so sure. She didn't like the look of the water where I intended to go, and insisted that we confirm our location. Grudgingly I complied, remembering the Wilson's requirement that they stopped the boat until they agreed where they were.

Careful observation confirmed that Marilynn was correct. Chagrined, I went through the proper passage instead of over the top of the reef.

Thank you Tom and Barbara Wilson.

—Robert Hale

Stuart Island Marine State Park, Reid Harbor. Open all year, day use and overnight mooring and camping. The entrance is straightforward. A mooring float is located on the north shore, mooring buoys dot the bay, and mooring floats are placed within easy dinghy distance of the landing pier. Facilities include toilets, pumpout, portapotty dump. Reid Harbor is long and narrow, and protected by high hills. The bottom is excellent for anchoring, and the harbor holds a great number of boats. The setting is beautiful. It is a popular destination. Shoreside facilities are shared with Prevost Harbor, on the narrow but steep neck of land that separates them. The county dirt road leading to the Turn Point Lighthouse (and the Treasure Chest along the way), begins at the head of Reid Harbor. No dock, but if tides are favorable you could beach your dinghy there without having to carry it back through the mud.

Johns Pass. Use chart 18432 (larger scale, preferred) or 18421. Johns Pass separates Stuart Island and Johns Island, and is used regularly. At the south end of the pass foul ground, marked by kelp, extends about 0.6 miles southeast from Stuart Island. Boats heading southeast through Johns Pass should head for Gull Reef, then turn when well clear of the kelp. Anchorage is possible in Johns Pass and along the south side of Johns Island.

Not one but two treasures in this photo. The first is Marilynn Hale, and the second is the famous Stuart Island Treasure Chest. Marilynn selects T-shirts for the two grandsons, and note cards for casual correspondence.

Honor system only. Take an envelope, add up your purchases and send a check. A gracious thank you is sent promptly by return mail.

Proceeds go to the school.

Southern Gulf Islands

Victoria • Sidney • Saanich Inlet • Ganges • Active Pass
Montague Harbour • Saturna Island

GULF ISLANDS, GENERAL

(For convenience, the Gulf Islands sections of this book include the southern tip and the east side of Vancouver Island as far up-island as Nanaimo.)

THE GULF ISLANDS are British Columbia's answer to Washington's San Juan Islands, only they are different. The San Juan Islands are the peaks of a sunken mountain range. The Gulf Islands, for the most part, are a different geology, made of sandstone that has been uplifted until it sticks out of the sea. The Gulf Islands are beautiful.

Like the San Juan Islands, the Gulf Islands are in the lee of mountains. They receive much summertime sun and little summertime rainfall. Water is in short supply. Boat washing is something that just isn't done, at least in the islands themselves.

The Gulf Islands are blessed with dozens of anchorages, from 1-boat notches to open bays that hold dozens of boats. Provincial marine parks provide anchorage, mooring and docking possibilities, and facilities ashore. Private marinas run the spectrum from rustic to deluxe, many with excellent on-site or nearby dining.

For shopping, the largest town in the Gulf Islands proper is Ganges. If your definition of the islands expands (as ours does) to include southern and eastern Vancouver Island, then Victoria, Sidney, Ladysmith and Nanaimo would be larger than Ganges.

Most boats coming from the U.S. will clear customs somewhere between Victoria and Nanaimo. It could be Bedwell Harbour (sum-mer only), Victoria, Oak Bay, Sidney or Nanaimo. The best provisioning stops are Victoria, Sidney, Ganges and Nanaimo. Fuel is available throughout the islands.

Navigation is straightforward, but pay attention. It's easy to get confused, and the waters are dotted with rocks and reefs. You want to know where you are at all times. Unfortunately, no single chart sheet covers all the waters, so you will be working among the 1:40,000 scale charts 3440, 3441, 3442 and 3443, plus several large scale charts and Plans charts. Plans charts are a collection of large scale charts all on one sheet.

The Canadian Hydrographic Service chart 3313 is an excellent chartbook for the Gulf Islands. At $85 Cdn., this chartbook is not inexpensive, but it has everything.

We carry all the charts on board, including chartbook 3313, and we use them. We plot our general routes on the 1:40,000 charts, then use the larger scale charts and Plans charts to stay off the rocks. The waters northeast of Sidney, for example, are quite rocky, and the 1:40,000 chart 3441 does not inspire confidence. But with large scale (1:10,000) chart 3476, the rocks are much more readily identified. Safe routes are more easily chosen.

Charts are expensive, and we recognize that many boaters, especially new boaters or those making a one-time visit to an area, resist buying complete sets. Our own experience argues strongly against this approach. We use charts and they keep us out of trouble. In the Gulf Islands especially, charts will make your boating holiday more enjoyable.

ABOUT CUSTOMS

Vessels entering Canada are required either to have a CANPASS customs pre-clearance or to clear Canadian Customs at their first stop in Canada. Most boats will clear customs at Bedwell Harbour, Victoria (includes Oak Bay and Cadboro Bay), Sidney or Nanaimo. Bedwell Harbour is on South Pender Island, just 4 miles north of Stuart Island in the San Juan Islands, but its customs station is open only from May 1 through September 30. For more information about clearing customs, see the chapter titled "U.S. & Canadian Customs."

VICTORIA AREA

Esquimalt Harbour. Use chart 3419; 3440. Esquimalt Harbour has some anchorage toward the head of the bay. The Canadian Navy moors some of its ships just inside Duntze Head, and a drydock there handles Navy as well as other large ships. The head of the bay is used to boom logs, but Contributing Editor Tom Kincaid reports that he has always found plenty of room to swing at anchor without interfering with the tugs.

Docks at Victoria, Parliament buildings in the background.

Fleming Beach, west of Victoria Harbour, in Esquimalt. Use chart 3419; 3440. Open all year. Facilities include launch ramp (fee charged), and washrooms. This is a charming little cove, protected by a rock breakwater, overlooked by most boating people. It is the home of Esquimalt Anglers' Association, a private sportfishing and fish enhancement group. The launch ramp boarding floats have room for temporary moorage while shopping nearby, or you can anchor out. Walkways and picnic areas have been built. Fleming Beach is adjacent to old coastal gun emplacements, which are interesting to explore.

Victoria. Use chart 3415; 3440. Victoria is the provincial capital, and the largest city on Vancouver Island. There is regular ferry service from Port Angeles, Vancouver and Seattle. Scheduled float planes also connect with Vancouver and Seattle.

Victoria is absolutely beautiful. The Empress Hotel, for which the word "majestic" could have been created, dominates the Inner Harbour. The Empress is flanked on the south by the B.C. provincial parliament buildings, themselves the embodiment of dignity, thoughtful deliberation and orderly progress—the buildings, that is. Between the Empress and the parliament buildings stands the Royal British Columbia Museum, a must-see, especially for families. A giant mastodon dominates the entry, and the rest of the museum delights with a recreation of Capt. Vancouver's ship, a Victorian town, a west coast seashore, and an Indian bighouse. The Visitor Information Centre is located on top of the causeway at the head of the Inner Harbour, across from the Empress Hotel. It's easy to find.

Caution: All vessels 65 feet LOA and less must enter and depart the Inner Harbour between Shoal Point and Laurel Point along the south shore, as shown in the accompanying harbor map. Inbound vessels favor the favor the docks; outbound vessels a little farther out. The traffic lanes are not marked. The more open water in the middle is used by the large number of seaplanes that land and take off constantly. Because of the volume of boat and seaplane traffic, no sailing is allowed inside the breakwater. Even sailboats under power must have sails lowered.

Reservations. All but the Coast Victoria Harbourside Marina and Victoria Marine Adventures Center moorages in the Inner Harbour are public docks, which take no reservations. The one exception to this policy is for vessels 65 feet LOA and larger. The Port asks that those larger vessels fax a berthage request detailing the vessel's needs to (250)363-6947, so space can be found.

For vessels smaller than 65 feet, it's first-come, first-served—but with a heart. The Port of Victoria has a "meet and greet" program for visiting boats. When you enter the Inner Harbour, hail them on VHF channel 73 and they will direct you to available guest moorage. If you have questions ahead of time you can call the Port at (250)363-3760. Don't give up hope if a machine answers. They re-

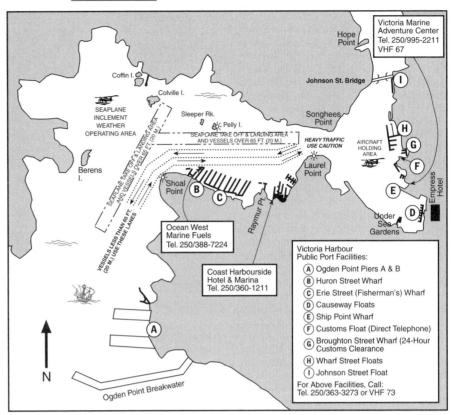

Victoria Harbour

Reference only — not for navigation

See area map page 112

turn their calls.

Inside Ogden Point, the Erie Street Wharf is reserved primarily for commercial fishboats and monthly pleasure craft, but often has room for pleasure craft when the fleet is out. A large chandlery (Trotac Marine) is across the street from this marina. (Boats mooring further inside the Inner Harbour have another well-stocked chandlery—Bosun's Locker—nearby on Johnson Street.) The Coast Victoria Harbourside Hotel docks are adjacent to the Erie Street Wharf, overnight moorage welcome.

The Broughton Street Wharf customs dock, well-marked, is at the head of the Inner Harbour, across the street from the buildings of downtown. A seaplane float and moorage for government fisheries patrol vessels are at the same location. The Wharf Street Wharf and Floats, a public marina with transient moorage, power and water, is to the left of the customs dock. The Ship Point wharf, usually used by larger commercial fishing boats, is to the right of the customs dock. If you tie up at the Ship Point wharf, you'll have to tend your lines as the tide rises and falls.

The City of Victoria Causeway Floats are to the right of Ship Point and in front of the Empress Hotel. These are the docks that fill up first. Another small moorage, the Johnson Street Wharf, is near the Johnson Street Bridge (the Blue Bridge, locally). It sometimes has room for one or two visiting boats.

For an interesting side trip, take the dinghy through Gorge Waters to Portage Inlet. You'll travel first through the industrial

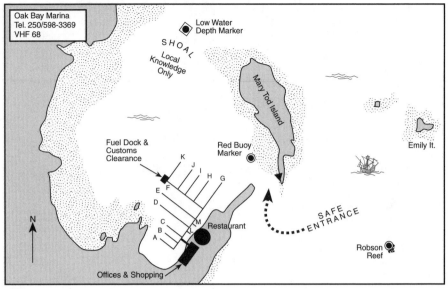

Oak Bay Marina

Reference only — not for navigation

part of the city, then through park and residential areas. It's about a 3-mile trip; currents are a factor if you intend to row.

① **City of Victoria Causeway (James Bay),** (250)363-3273. Monitors VHF channel 73. Open all year. Facilities include 1300+ feet of dock space, washrooms, showers, laundry, limited power. No reservations taken, and a 2-day limit if full. Rafting is mandatory. These are the picturesque and popular floats located directly in front of the Empress Hotel. Downtown Victoria surrounds. Fabulous restaurants, shopping, hotels, museums, sightseeing. Marine supplies are nearby at Bosun's Locker. In the winter the washroom hours are reduced, and the showers and laundry are closed.

① **Victoria (Ogden Point) Public Wharf,** (250)363-3273. This wharf is for larger commerical vessels. No guest moorage for pleasure craft.

① **Coast Victoria Harbourside Hotel,** 146 Kingston Steet, Victoria, BC V8V 1V4, (250)360-1211, fax (250)360-1418. Open all year, 30 & 50 amp power, fresh water on the docks, holding tank pumpout. This is a quality hotel with an excellent dining room and lounge, indoor/outdoor pool, Jacuzzi, sauna and fitness facilities. Marina guests have full access. Located adjacent to the Erie Street Public Wharf, within walking distance of downtown.

① **Victoria (Erie Street) Public Wharf,** (250)363-3273. Monitors VHF channel 73. Open all year, 3180 feet of dock space, 20 amp power, washrooms, showers. Also known as Fishermen's Wharf. When fish boats are out, usually you'll find lots of dock space. Rafting is mandatory. Fuel is next door.

① **Ocean West Marine Fuels,** 327 Maitland St., Victoria, B.C. V9A 7G7, (250)388-7224. Open all year, but with shorter hours in winter. Fuel dock with gasoline and diesel. Carries kerosene and stove alcohol, fishing licenses, snacks, food items. Chart agent. This is the only fuel dock in the Inner Harbour.

① **Victoria (Broughton Street) Public Wharf,** Open all year, 24-hour customs clearance. If you are visiting Canada and have not yet cleared customs, stop here before going to your moorage. Look for the orange dock. No guest moorage.

① **Victoria Marine Adventure Center,** 950 Wharf St., Victoria, B.C. V8W 1T3, (250)995-2211; fax (250)995-1222. Monitors VHF channel 67. Open all year, guest moorage with 30 amp power, washrooms, showers, laundry. Reservations are accepted. Licensed restaurant. Between the James Bay (Empress) floats and the Wharf Street Public Wharf.

① **Victoria (Wharf Street) Public Wharf,** (250)363-3273. Monitors VHF channel 73. Open all year, 1780 feet of visitor dock space, 20, 30 & 50 amp power, washrooms, showers, garbage collection. Right downtown, to the left of the Causeway docks as you come in. Washrooms and showers are a 5-minute walk down the causeway. In the winter, washroom hours are reduced and the showers and laundry are closed. Power availability varies, depending on location.

① **Victoria (Johnson Street) Public Wharf,** (250)363-3760. Monitors VHF channel 73. Open all year, 220 feet of dock space, no power, washrooms or showers. Rafting is mandatory.

Oak Bay. Use chart 3424 (larger scale, much preferred) or 3440. Oak Bay is on the east side of the south tip of Vancouver Island, west of the Chatham Islands. The channels between the various rocks and reefs are well marked. This is the route taken by many tugs with tows, and commercial fishing boats of all sizes. The Oak Bay Marina and a separate small repair yard, with marine railway, are located behind the breakwater.

② **Oak Bay Marina,** 1327 Beach Drive, Victoria, BC V8S 2N4, (250)598-3369, (800)663-7090 ext. 247; fax (250)598-1361. Or view at www.obmg.com. Monitors VHF channel 68. Open all year. Gasoline and diesel at the fuel dock, customs clearance telephone at the fuel dock. Ample guest moorage for boats to 80 feet LOA, call ahead for availability. Facilities include 15 & 30 amp power, washrooms, showers, laundry. The marina has undergone a major upgrade, with new docks, a good restaurant, deli and gift shop added. A small chandlery carries essential marine hardware. Repairs are available at a small boatyard in the next building with haulout to 48 feet. Complete shop-

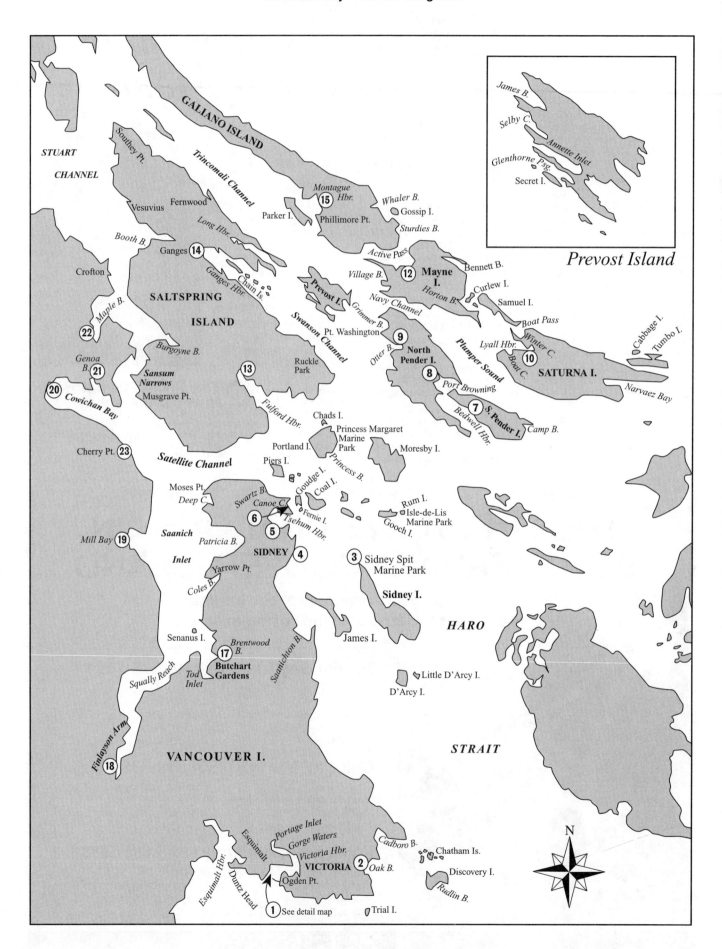

ping at quaint Oak Bay Village, a short distance away. Regular bus service to downtown Victoria, with extra shuttle bus service in the summer.

Discovery Island Marine Park. Open all year. An undeveloped park suitable for beachable boats only. The island was once the home of Capt. E.G. Beaumont, who donated the land as a park. The northern part of Discovery Island, adjacent Chatham Island, and some of the smaller islands nearby are Indian Reserve lands; no landing.

Cadboro Bay. Use chart 3424; 3440. Cadboro Bay is entirely residential except for the Royal Victoria Yacht Club, which has a breakwater-protected marina on the western shore. Anchorage in Cadboro Bay is excellent, mud and sand bottom, beyond the yacht club moorage. Moorage at RVYC is available for members of clubs with reciprocal agreements with Royal Vic. Customs clearance available.

SOUTHERN GULF ISLANDS

D'Arcy Island Marine Park. Use chart 3441. Open all year, 2 mooring buoys. This is an undeveloped island park with no facilities other than some primitive campsites. Numerous reefs and shoals are in the area, so approach with caution. Enter from the west, south of the lighthouse. D'Arcy Island was B.C.'s first leper colony; from 1891 until 1926 it housed Chinese lepers. The colony was closed in 1926 and the island reverted to provincial jurisdiction. Plans for the island as a federal penitentiary were never realized. D'Arcy Island remained undeveloped, and was established as a marine park in 1961. To the east, Little D'Arcy Island is private property.

③ **Sidney Spit Marine Park.** Use chart 3441. Sidney Spit Marine Park is exceptional. It occupies much of Sidney Island and all of the mile-long Sidney Spit that extends northwest from the island. Anchor, or hang off one of 35 mooring buoys, or tie to the well-maintained dock. Picnic and camping areas are ashore. An easily walked 2 km loop trail winds around the island though dense forest of cedar, hemlock, fir, bigleaf maple and vine maple. While we haven't seen them, a herd of fallow deer is supposed to be on

The remarkable red brick beach is part of the 2 km loop trail at Sidney Spit Marine Park.

the island. A large saltwater marsh lagoon is habitat for many animal and plant species. The remains of a brick-making factory are near the marsh, and the beach there is covered with broken red bricks. The dock at that site is signed, "Private Dock, Restricted Moorage." The park is open all year. In the summer a passenger ferry runs to Sidney.

Isle-de-Lis (Rum Island). Use chart 3441. Open all year, anchoring only, no facilities. This is a small, undeveloped and very pretty natural park area with a walking trail and beaches. Rum Island is located at the east end of Gooch Island, where Prevost Passage meets Haro Strait. Anchorage is either to the north or the south of the gravel spit that connects Rum Island to Gooch Island. The northern anchorage is preferred. Rum Island is said to have come by its name honestly during Prohibition. In 1995 the warship HMCS *Mackenzie* was sunk in 17 fathoms close north of Gooch Island to create an artificial reef for divers. It is marked with four cautionary/information buoys and has three mooring buoys.

Princess Margaret Marine Park, Portland Island, (250)387-4363. Use chart 3476; 3441. Open all year, picnic and camp sites, toilets, no other facilities. In honor of her last visit to Victoria, Portland Island was donated to Her Royal Highness Princess Margaret, who later deeded the island to British Columbia. Portland Island is now Princess Margaret Marine Park.

Portland Island is hilly and heavily wooded, with hiking trails that provide excellent exercise. Anchor in Royal Cove (behind Chads Island) on the north side

of the island, or in Princess Bay, behind Tortoise Island on the south side. Royal Cove is often used as an anchorage, but suffers mightily from the wash of passing B.C. ferries. If you can get well inside the cove you can have a quiet night. Princess Bay is more roomy, but somewhat exposed to southerly winds. In summer it usually is fine. Watch your depths as you approach the head of Princess Bay. The bottom shoals rapidly, farther from shore than you might expect.

The *G.B. Church*, a sunken freighter off the southwest shore of the island, provides an artificial reef for divers. The freighter lies in 15 fathoms of water and is marked with bow and stern buoys.

Sidney. Use chart 3476 (larger scale, preferred) or 3441. Sidney and nearby Tsehum Harbour have much to attract boaters, including excellent bakeries just up Beacon Avenue (Sidney's main street). The town also offers good dining, several art galleries, many interesting shops, marine supplies, several bookstores and nautical chart agencies, a liquor store, and and three

well-stocked supermarkets. The Sidney Museum, at the foot of Beacon Avenue, has an outstanding whale exhibit, including photographs of the whaling station at Coal Harbour, at the north end of Vancouver Island. This station operated from 1910 until the 1960s. The museum also has an excellent exhibit of early history in Sidney. Admission by donation. *Highly* recommended, especially for families.

For boats crossing from Roche Harbor or the northern San Juan Islands, Sidney is a natural first stop to clear customs, stroll around, and re-stock with fresh produce, meat, spirits, and other consumables. The Port Sidney Marina is delightful, with efficient staff, large, clean washrooms and showers, and wide concrete docks.

Sidney is the western terminus of the Washington State ferry run from Anacortes and Friday Harbor, and is a Canadian customs port. The customs dock used to be located at the public pier at the end of Beacon Street. Now the customs dock is part of the Port Sidney Marina, just north of the public pier. During summer months customs officers may be stationed at the check-in dock (with its unique canopy) just inside the breakwater entrance. When officers are not present, customs check-in can be accomplished by a telephone at the dock.

For an entirely different feeling, try Tsehum Harbour, a short distance north of downtown Sidney. The pace is much slower, and many of the moored boats funkier. Something about Tsehum Harbour attracts excellent restaurants, too. Tsehum Harbour's only disadvantage is the longish walk to major shopping. You'll probably take a taxi.

Service note: In 1998 we arrived in Sidney with our lower station depth sounder not working. Greg Nutt and Steve Jones of Mar Tech Marine Repair Services, (250)656-5684, arrived at the boat shortly after our call, and traced down the problem. They were efficient, competent, and a pleasure to have aboard. The bill was fair.

Golf: Glen Meadows, 18 holes, (250)656-3921; Ardmore, 9 holes (250)656-4621.

④ **Port Sidney Marina,** 9835 Seaport Place, Sidney, B.C. V8L 4X3, (250)655-3711; fax (250) 655-3771. Monitors VHF channel 68. Open all year, 325 slips plus guest dock. Facilities include 30 & 50 amp power, water, washrooms, showers, laundry, pumpout, customs clearance. Call on VHF channel 68 for slip assignment. The customs dock is located just inside the entrance.

When entering, pass between the two buoys just off the breakwater. The northernmost of these buoys marks a reef. Do not try to enter between the north end breakwater and the shore. If you are directed to the shore side of the long, main pier, do not stray outside the marked channel. The bottom has been dredged alongside the dock, but shoal water lies just a few feet inshore. This is a popular marina, new and well-maintained, adjacent to downtown. In the summer the docks are decorated with hanging flower pots. *(Marina map page 116)*

④ **Sidney Beacon Ave. Public Wharf,** Open all year, 738 feet of dock space, no power, water, washrooms or showers. Garbage collection at dock.

Tsehum Harbour. Use chart 3476 (larger scale, preferred) or 3441. About 1.5 miles north of Sidney is Tsehum Harbour, a shallow but navigable inlet that contains a number of public, private, and yacht club moorages. Enter favoring the Armstrong Point (south) side to

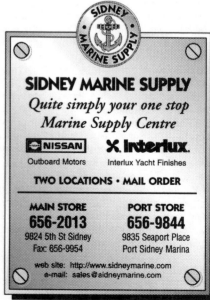

avoid a marked rock. This is the working waterfront of Sidney, with several excellent boat yards. Van Isle Marina, the first marina on the south side, has a customs check-in telephone, fuel, and guest moorage. Philbrooks Shipyard is next door to Van Isle Marina. Other moorages in Tsehum Harbour belong to Capitol City, Royal Victoria and other yacht clubs, and private marinas.

(5) **Tsehum Harbour Public Wharf,** located in Shoal Harbour. Open all year, 1043 feet of dock space, power, washrooms, no showers. Commercial fishing vessels have priority. Launch ramp. Breakwater. Garbage collection. Lights, telephone.

(5) **Van Isle Marina,** 2320 Harbour Road, Sidney, B.C. V8L 2P6, (250)656-1138; fax (250)656-0182. Or view at www.vanisle marina.com. Monitors VHF channel 68. Open all year, 7 days, gasoline and diesel at fuel dock, customs clearance, 15, 30, 50 & 100 amp power, oil pumpout, excellent washrooms, showers and laundry, holding tank pumpout, portapotty dump. Best to call ahead for guest moorage availability. This is a large and busy marina, about a mile from downtown. Much new dock space has been added in recent years. Haulout and repair services are available. Launch ramp. Yacht brokerage. Car rentals and taxi. The restaurant is excellent. The famous Latch Restaurant is a short walk away, and the Blue Peter Pub is next door. We have had an excellent informal supper at the Blue Peter Pub. Van Isle is a good stop. *(Marina map below)*

(5) **Westport Marina,** 2075 Tryon Road, Sidney, B.C. V8L 3X9, (250)656-2832; fax (250)655-1981, e-mail at westport@ horizon.bc.ca. Open all year, 15, 20 & 30 amp power, washrooms, showers. Uses unoccupied slips as available for guest moorage. Call ahead

for availability. Has marine parts, ice, some charts and books, limited groceries. Marine ways and repair facilities. *(Marina map page 116)*

(5) **North Saanich Marina,** P.O. Box 2001, 1949 Marina Way, Sidney, B.C. V8L 3S3, (250)656-5558; fax (250) 656-1574. Open all year, gasoline and diesel at fuel dock. Primarily a fuel dock and permanent moorage marina. Store carries charts, bait, tackle, ice. They might have some transient moorage if you are desperate. Call ahead.

Canoe Bay. Use chart 3476 (larger scale, preferred) or 3441. Canoe Bay, commonly called Canoe Cove, is tucked in behind a group of islands, only some of which have navigable passages between them. The clearest passage is **John Passage**, along the west side of Coal Island. From John Passage turn west into **Iroquois Passage**, and follow Iroquois Passage between Fernie Island and Goudge Island into Canoe Bay. From the south, **Page Passage**, west of Fernie Island, will lead to Canoe Bay, and many boats use Page Passage. *Caution*: Page Passage should be run only with local knowledge or close study of large-scale chart 3476. Tidal currents can run strongly, especially on spring tides. Canoe Bay has moorage with all amenities.

Reference only — not for navigation

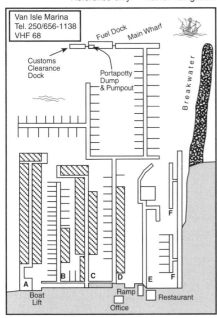

Van Isle Marina

See area map page 112

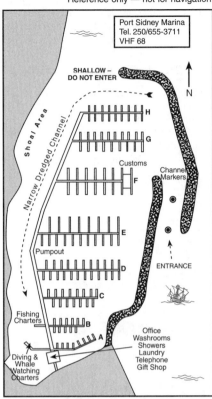

Reference only — not for navigation

Port Sidney Marina

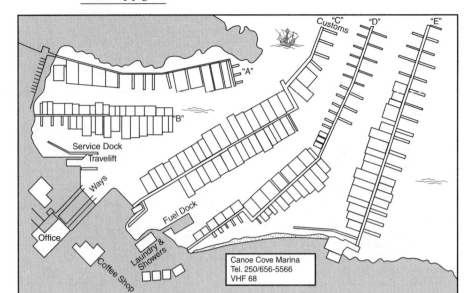

Reference only — not for navigation

Canoe Cove Marina

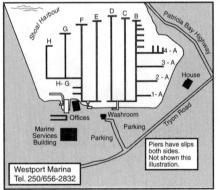

Reference only — not for navigation

Westport Marina

⑥ **Canoe Cove Marina,** P.O. Box 2099, 2300 Canoe Cove Road, Sidney, B.C. V8L 3S6, (250)656-5566; fax (250) 655-7197. Monitors VHF channel 68. Open all year, gasoline, diesel, propane at fuel dock, 30 amp power, washrooms, showers, laundry, 24-hour customs clearance. This is a 460-berth marina with mostly permanent moorage. Visiting boats are assigned unoccupied slips as available. Rarely is anyone turned away. They have a full repair facility with marine railway, haulout to 65 tons, extensive covered work area, and a well-stocked chandlery. They can do anything. A coffee shop is on the premises, and the Stonehouse Pub is nearby. A short trail leads to the Swartz Bay ferry terminal. A harbor taxi connects the marina with Sidney. Watch your navigation as you approach the marina. Rocks are marked, often by sticks, and must be avoided. Easy to do if you pay attention. The staff and management are friendly and competent. *(Marina map above)*

Swartz Bay Public Wharf. Use chart 3476 (larger scale, preferred) or 3441. Open all year, adjacent to the ferry terminal. Has 85 feet of dock space with no facilities.

Piers Island Public Wharf. Use chart 3476 (larger scale, preferred) or 3441. Open all year. Has 200 feet of dock space, no facilities.

Bedwell Harbour. Use chart 3477 (larger scale, preferred) or 3441. Bedwell Harbour has a resort with mooring floats that give access to a pub and restaurant, fuel, and a store. Anchorage is good at Beaumont Provincial Park, north of the resort, and in Peter Cove, on the west side of the harbor. The Pender Canal, a man-made channel between North Pender Island and South Pender Island, connects Bedwell Harbour with Port Browning. The canal is crossed by a bridge with a 27-foot vertical clearance.

Peter Cove. Use chart 3477 (larger scale, preferred) or 3441. Peter Cove is located at the southern tip of South Pender Island. It is a well protected little anchorage, but permanently moored boats make anchoring a bit tight. A significant reef guards the mouth of the cove. Enter and depart north of the reef.

⑦ **Bedwell Harbour Island Resort & Marina,** 9801 Spalding Road, RR #3, South Pender Island, B.C. V0N 2M3, (250)629-3212; (800)663-2899; fax (250)629-6777; e-mail bedwell@islandnet. com. Monitors VHF channel 68. Open March through October, closed all winter. Gasoline, pre-mix, diesel and ice at the fuel dock. Facilities include 100 slips for guest moorage, 15 & 30 amp power, washrooms, showers, laundry. Customs clearance available 0800-2000 May-Sept., extra charge for after-hours clearance. This is a popular resort, with groceries, fresh meat and produce, some marine supplies, swimming pool, restaurant, bar and bistro, live entertainment, and kids' activities. Hotel accommodations are available. Moored guests have access to selected services. Lots to do, and a golf course is 20 minutes away by resort shuttle.

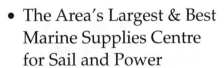

Bedwell Harbour Public Wharf, South Pender Island. Open all year, 312 feet of dock space. No facilities, but customs clearance is available (see above for hours). Lights and telephone at dock. Fishing vessels have priority.

Beaumont Marine Park, west side of South Pender Island, in Bedwell Harbour. Open all year. Facilities include 15 mooring buoys, toilets, no power, no showers. Walk-in campsites, picnicking, walking and hiking trails. A beautiful and popular park. Enter from Swanson Channel from the south, or from Plumper Sound and Port Browning through the Pender Canal.

Port Browning. Use chart 3477 (larger scale, preferred) or 3441. Port Browning has a resort (Port Browning Marina) with moorage and other facilities. Anchorage is good throughout the harbor. The Driftwood Centre shopping area is located about a ½-mile walk from the marina. The center has groceries, a bank, gift shop, bakery, liquor store, pharmacy, post office, hair care, and laundromat.

⑧ **Port Browning Marina,** North Pender Island, B.C., (250)629-3493. Monitors VHF channel 68. Open all year, 100 slips, 15 amp power, washrooms, laundry. Facilities include launch ramp, swimming pool, groceries, beer & wine store, limited marine hardware and charts, tackle, bait. Coffee shop and pub. Shop-

ping center ½-mile away at the Driftwood Centre. Port Browning is a popular marina in the Gulf Islands. The atmosphere is very relaxed, and the pub serves decent meals. In 1998 major improvements were made to the property, including new showers and washrooms, much work around the pool, and general upgrading.

Browning Harbour Public Wharf, Open all year, 89 feet of dock space, no facilities. Commercial fishing vessels have priority.

⑨ **Otter Bay Marina,** RR 1, North Pender

Island, B.C. V0N 2M0, (250)629-3579; fax (250) 629-3589. Monitors VHF channel 68. Use chart 3442. Open all year, 15 & 30 amp power, washrooms, showers, laundry, launch ramp, new docks, gazebo and heated pool. Kayak, bike, and boat rentals. Nearby restaurant. The ferry is nearby. Reservations recommended. We think this is one of the nicest places you'll find. It is maintained in spotless order, the grounds are beautiful, the gift shop well stocked, and the management efficient. The pool has adult hours in the afternoons. The showers, which take $1 coins (loonies) only, are some of the best on the coast. The

Otter Bay Marina's guest moorage on a quiet, sunny morning. Look at that handsome powerboat in the foreground!

See area map page 112

marina is located on the west side of North Pender Island, facing Swanson Channel. Look for the tall flagpoles. Kay and Chuck Spence are the managers.

Caution: A green spar buoy lies off the corner of the marina docks. Red, Right, Returning means that you leave this buoy *to port* as you enter. Especially at low tide, do not pass between the buoy and the dock.

Golf: The Pender Island Golf Course is about a 15-minute walk from the marina. No tee times needed, and the marina has discount golf packages available. They will give you a ride up the hill to the course. You'll walk back.

Port Washington Public Wharf, North Pender Island. Use chart 3442. Open all year, 147 feet of dock space, unoccupied slips used when available. No facilities. Watch for a rock located off the southeast dock. Aircraft float.

Hope Bay Public Wharf, east side of North Pender Island, facing Navy Channel. Use chart 3442. Open all year, 226 feet of dock space, lights and telephone but no other facilities. Commercial fishing vessels have priority. The historic Hope Bay Store burned in 1998.

Irish Bay. Use chart 3477; 3442. Irish Bay, on the west side of Samuel Island, is a good anchorage, but the island is privately owned. If you venture above the foreshore the caretaker will shoo you off.

Winter Cove. Use chart 3477 (larger scale, much preferred) or 3442. Winter Cove, between Samuel Island and Saturna Island, has an attractive park (Winter Cove Provincial Park), on the Saturna Island side, and shallow anchorage between numerous rocks and reefs. We think the best anchorages are behind Winter Point, north of the cable line, or just off the provincial park. The charts show shallow water in the middle of the cove, but you can patrol around—carefully—with the depth sounder and find anchoring sites away from the preferred spots. The mooring buoys in the southwest corner of the cove are private. **Boat Pass** connects Winter Cove with the Strait of Georgia. Currents in Boat Pass can run at 7 knots past several nasty rocks and reefs. Take this pass only at or near high water slack, preferably after seeing it at low water so you know where the rocks are.

Minx Reef partially blocks the Plumper Sound approach to Winter Cove. As we approach, we have found the best way to avoid the reef is to point the bow at the northern shore of Irish Bay, and run well past Winter Point before turning south into the cove.

Winter Cove is exposed to northwest winds.

Winter Cove Marine Park, north tip of Saturna Island. Open all year, toilets, no other facilities. This is a spacious, attractive and popular park looking out on the Strait of Georgia. It has broad sand and mud beaches and for-ested uplands, open fields and picnic areas. Hiking and walking trails. The launch ramp is for small boats only.

Lyall Harbour. Use chart 3477 (larger scale, preferred) or 3442. Lyle Harbour, on Saturna Island, is a large but fairly well protected anchorage, with a ferry landing and store near the entrance. Nearby **Boot Cove** is a beautiful spot with anchorage in 2-3 fathoms, but it can be subject to willawaws blowing over a low swale on Saturna Island. Contributing Editor Tom Kincaid anchored there one afternoon, and before night his anchor line was stretched tight by 40-knot winds, which remained that way the next morning. "I dinghied to the nearest beach that afternoon and walked to the store for a loaf of bread," he reports. "I asked the proprietor if he'd heard when the wind was supposed to die down. 'Oh, you must be in Boot Cove,' he said. 'It always blows in Boot Cove.' So we weighed anchor, set sail, flew out the entrance—and coasted to a stop, windless, just outside."

Lyall Harbour Public Wharf, located next to the ferry dock. Open all year, 200 feet of dock space, gasoline, diesel at nearby fuel dock, no power, no water, no washrooms, no showers. Commercial fishing vessels have priority. Garbage collection at dock.

⑩ **Saturna Point Store & Fuel,** 102 E. Point Rd., Saturna Island, B.C. V0N 2Y0, (250)539-5725. Open all year. Gasoline and diesel at fuel dock. Grocery store, ice, fishing gear and licenses. Nearby restaurant with take-out area, and the Lighthouse Pub. Liquor store is 1½ miles away.

Cabbage Island Marine Park. Use chart 3441 or chartbook 3313. Open all year, 10 mooring buoys, toilets, no water, no showers. This is a pretty anchorage between Cabbage Island and Tumbo Island, out on the edge of the Strait of Georgia. The chart shows the entrance from the north, between two long reefs. A friend told us we could cross the reef on the Tumbo Channel side if we went between two patches of kelp, a short distance from the north tip of Tumbo Island. We followed his suggestion, and showed 5 fathoms under the keel all the way across. Chartbook 3313, p. 24, shows good depths at that loca-

Reference only — not for navigation

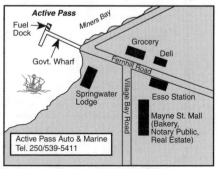

Active Pass Auto and Marine

tion, confirming our experience. We picked up one of several mooring buoys, and enjoyed a quiet lunch. The park has picnic sites, campsites, and a wonderful sandy beach. Crabbing is reported to be excellent.

Georgeson Passage. Use plans chart 3477 (larger scale, *much* recommended) or 3442. Georgeson Passage, between Mayne Island and Samuel Island, is short and pretty. Currents, based on Active Pass, are about one-half as strong as those in Active Pass, both flooding and ebbing. Still, they run vigorously. See the Georgeson Passage secondary station under Active Pass in the Tide & Current Tables, Vol. 5. If entering from the Strait of Georgia through the narrow pass between Campbell Point and Georgeson Island, be aware that a drying reef extends from Campbell Point into the pass. Favor the Georgeson Island side. Watch for rapids in this pass.

Horton Bay. Use Plans chart 3477 (larger scale, *much* recommended) or 3442. Horton Bay is a perfect landlocked bay, with lots of room to anchor, mud bottom. The government wharf has room for 10-12 30-foot boats, plus rafting. Entering the area between Mayne and Samuel Islands requires some care, but is completely navigable. From the Gulf Islands side the best route is through Georgeson Passage, east of Lizard Island. Be careful of a kelp-covered rock in less than 1 fathom of water, fairly close to Mayne Island. If entering *west* of Lizard Island, the rock is in the middle of your path into Horton Bay. A reef extends from Curlew Island into Robson Passage, which separates Curlew Island from Mayne Island. A study of chart 3477 shows a mid-channel course is called for.

ACTIVE PASS AREA

Active Pass. Use chart 3473 (larger scale, recommended) or 3442. Active Pass, which separates Mayne Island and Galiano Island, has long been one of the most popular fishing areas in the Gulf Islands. It also is the route taken by commercial traffic, including ferries that run between Tsawwassen and Swartz Bay. Currents in Active Pass run to 7 knots at springs. They flood eastward toward the Strait of Georgia. See the Tide and Current Tables, Vol. 5. Unless your boat is quite fast, a slack water passage is recommended. If you are in the current, you can minimize turbulence by sagging into Miner Bay.

Dinner Bay. Dinner Bay, between Crane Point and Dinner Point, looks to be a good anchorage, but is exposed to ferry wash and northwest winds.

Oceanwood Country Inn, 630 Dinner Bay Road, Mayne Island, B.C. V0N 2J0, (250)539-5074. Buoy available May-Nov. for guest moorage, cozy rooms, excellent dinners.

Village Bay. Use chart 3473 (larger scale, recommended) or 3442. Village Bay is wide and deep, but with convenient anchoring depths near the head. The bay is open to northwest winds and waves, but well protected from everything else. Village Bay has a ferry terminal.

Miners Bay. Use chart 3473 (larger scale, recommended) or 3442. A government wharf is in Miners Bay on the south side of Active Pass, but it is subject to swirling tidal currents and the wash from passing ferries. Fuel is available at a float alongside the public wharf. Convenient anchoring depths are close to shore—most of the bay is quite deep.

⑫ **Active Pass Auto & Marine,** Mayne Island, B.C., (250)539-5411. Open all year, gasoline and diesel at fuel barge. Mechanic on duty for repairs. Propane, stove alcohol, tackle, bait, fishing licenses, soft ice cream. Affiliated service station 200 yards away has a snack bar. *(Marina map page 118)*

Sturdies Bay. Use chart 3473 (larger scale, recommended) or 3442. Sturdies Bay, on Galiano Island toward the eastern end of Active Pass, is another ferry stop for boats coming to and from Tsawwassen. A public float is alongside the ferry dock. The community of Sturdies Bay, just up the road, has a number of stores and a post office.

Whaler Bay. Use chart 3473 (larger scale, recommended) or 3442. Whaler Bay is on the east side of Galiano Island, just north of Active Pass. It is full of rocks and shoal water. Enter (very carefully) through a rock-strewn pas-sage from the south, or through a more open passage around the north end of Gossip Island. Whaler Bay has a public wharf. There is good protection near the wharf, but very little swinging room for those choosing to anchor.

Whaler Bay Public Wharf. Open all year, 350 feet of dock space, no facilities except garbage collection. Commercial fishing vessels have priority.

MAYNE ISLAND, CAMPELL BAY TO HORTON BAY

Campbell Bay. Use chart 3442. Campbell Bay, on the northwest side of Mayne Island, is entered between Edith Point and Campbell Point, on the northeast corner of Mayne Island. It is open to southeasterly winds, but has anchoring depths near the head, mud bottom.

Bennett Bay. Use chart 3477 (larger scale, preferred) or 3442. Bennett Bay, south of Campbell Point, has good anchorage, but is exposed to southeast winds. Cur-lew Island and Samuel Island are privately owned.

SALTSPRING ISLAND, FULFORD HARBOUR TO LONG HARBOUR

Fulford Harbour. Use chart 3478 (larger scale, preferred) or 3441. Fulford Harbour is wide and open. Fulford Village, a public wharf, and the Fulford Harbour Marina are near the head, all adjacent to the ferry landing. The charming village has a good grocery store (Patterson's), and an assortment of interesting art galleries, crafts, collectibles, and country clothing. Everything feels very "island."

By all means take a 15-minute walk down the road to St. Paul's Catholic church (called the Stone Church), built in 1880. The graveyard, with island history chiseled into its headstones, is adjacent to the church. We found the church's door unlocked, and stepped inside. It was lovely. "This is where God lives," I said—this from a guy God seldom hears from.

⑬ **Fulford Harbour Marina,** #5-2810 Fulford-Ganges Rd.,

SOUTHERN GULF ISLANDS

See area map page 112

Saltspring Island, B.C. V8K 1Z2, (250)653-4467; fax (250)653-4457; e-mail fulford harbourmarina@saltspring.com. Monitors VHF channel 68. Open all year, gasoline and diesel at Roamers Landing fuel dock. Guest moorage is available, 20 & 30 amp power, washrooms, showers. Tennis courts.

The village of Fulford is next door. A pub and the lake are a short walk away. The ferry to Swartz Bay lands at the village. In late 1998 the marina was sold to new owners, and improvements are planned. Part of the improvements are the docks, which were storm-damaged in 1999. Later, the ferry hit the floating breakwater, damaging it. Improved docks and breakwater are coming. Scott and Shannon Wood are staying on as managers. *(Marina map this page)*

⑬ **Roamers Landing,** 2878 Fulford Ganges Road, Saltspring Island, BC V8K 1X6, (250)653-4487. Fuel dock at Fulford Harbour Marina. Gasoline and diesel fuel.

Harbour Authority of Salt Spring Island Fulford Harbour Wharf. Open all year, 52 feet of dock space, no facilities. Exposed to winds, wash. Near ferry terminal.

Isabella Island. Use chart 3441. A smallish anchorage is available behind Isabella Island, a short distance west of the the mouth of

St. Paul's, the "Stone Church," is a popular stop at Fulford Harbour. Photo by Marilynn Hale.

Fulford Harbour. Although exposed to the west, it's a cozy little spot for 1 or 2 boats. Anchor in 4 fathoms.

Ruckle Park, Beaver Point on Saltspring Island. Use chart 3441. Open all year, day use and overnight camping. No mooring facilities, exposed anchorage on each side of Ruckle Point. Probably the best of these anchorages is in the the first cove south of Ruckle Point. There's not much room to swing, and the cove is exposed to ferry wash and southeast winds. It's pretty, though, and in settled weather would be a good day stop. This is an extensive park, with miles of shoreline and rocky headlands. Walk-in campsites. Great views of southern Gulf Islands.

Ganges. Use chart 3478 (larger scale, preferred) or 3442. Ganges, at the head of Ganges Harbour, is a recommended stop. Excellent marinas, good anchorage, and a bustling seaside village with shops, galleries, restaurants (including the exquisite Hastings House), a large Thrifty Foods supermarket, and Mouat's, a huge old hardware and house goods general store, plus separate gift shop, and next to that a quality apparel store (real quality—nice stuff). On Saturdays a farmer's market, very popular, is held in Centenial Park at Grace Point. In 1998 a dinghy dock was built at Rotary Park, below Mouat's and Thrifty Foods.

While boats and tourists are important to summer trade, Ganges is not a summer resort

Reference only — not for navigation

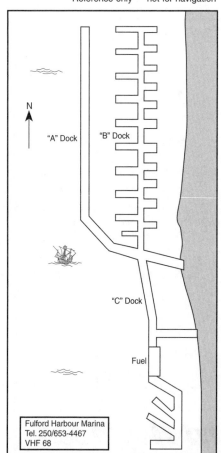

Fulford Harbor Marina

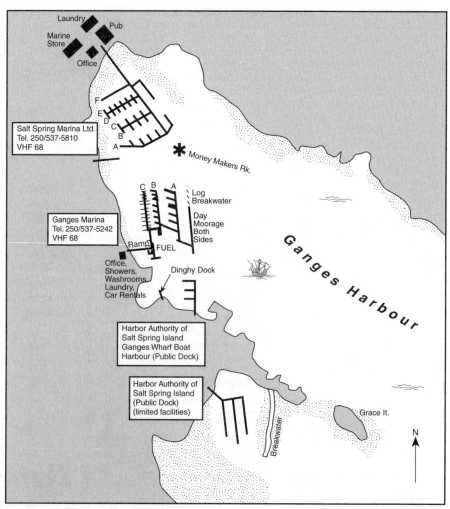

Ganges Harbour

Reference only — not for navigation

town, it's a bustling center of local commerce. The town is filled with excellent galleries, a wide variety of dining choices, and nearly every service.

In 1999, for example, the nosepiece of our glasses frame broke. The village optometrist referred us to Wolf Kranz Jewels Ltd., downstairs from her office. Mr. Kranz interrupted his work to disassemble the glasses, silver-solder the delicate metal nosepiece to the frame, and put the lens back into place. He said he repairs 30-40 sets of glasses every summer. It cost us $23, and took a little more than an hour. Wolf Kranz Jewels is a lovely shop, with many pieces designed and crafted by Mr. Kranz.

We recommend a visit.

Navigation: There's only one safe way to get into Ganges by water, and that is to leave all the Chain Islands to starboard. This will put you in a safe fairway, amply wide and easily run. *Watch out for crab pot buoys.* Do not cut through any of the islands. *No shortcuts.* Money Maker Reef, which extends northwest from Third Sister Island, is well-named, but Money Maker Reef is not the only problem. "It's a minefield out there," as one local boatman put it.

Once you've reached town, you'll probably tie up either at Ganges Marina or Salt Spring Marina, or anchor out. During high summer season they say you can walk to town across the decks of anchored boats. The Saltspring Island Sailing Club's docks, to port

See area map page 112

as you enter, have some space for reciprocal clubs. It's about a 1-mile walk to town. The public dock at Grace Point behind Grace Islet is convenient to town and has some power and water, but usually is packed with resident boats. The Kanaka Public Visitors' dock off Mouat's has no power or water.

Bird sanctuary: While you can anchor a short distance south of the Sailing Club's docks, Walter Bay and the spit that creates it are a sanctuary for black oystercatchers. Please leave the sanctuary area alone.

In the summer an electric-powered launch makes a regular run between town, the Ganges Marina, and the Salt Spring Marina. It certainly makes shopping at Thrifty Foods more convenient. The launch is cute and the service is popular. In the past a small fee has been asked, but they are hoping for merchant payment in the future.

The laundromat at Salt Spring Marina will wash and fold for a reasonable charge. The laundromat shares a building with with a yummy ice creamery. Cars may be rented at Ganges Marina. Both marinas have motor scooter rent-als. Saltspring Island is famous for its artists and craftspeople. You'll need some kind of transportation to see all of them. A map is available.

If you're in Ganges and don't see the Hastings House, you're missing something important. The Hastings House is an elegant historic country inn and restaurant, set on the hill overlooking the bay, with easy access from Salt Spring Marina. On their extensive and manicured grounds they grow their own herbs and flowers, rent extremely private cottages at top-drawer rates, and serve stunning suppers (one sitting only) to a small number of dinner guests. We were not able to have a meal, but we have toured the property and spoken with those who have had dined there. We're believers. Reservations, (250)537-2362.

Golf: Salt Spring Island Golf & Country Club (250)537-2121. Blackburn Meadows (250)537-1707. Both courses are 9 holes. We have played the Country Club course and enjoyed it.

⑭ **Harbour Authority of Salt Spring Island Ganges Wharf**

Spectacular rock tidelands extend from the north shore of Montague Harbour Marine Park. Here, a tide pool is investigated.

Boat Harbour. This is the Grace Point facility. Open all year. Has 1070 feet of breakwater-protected dock space, power, washrooms, showers. Also has a launch ramp, garbage collection, waste-oil disposal. Telephone at dock.

⑭ **Ganges Marina,** P.O. Box 299,161 Lower Ganges Road, Ganges, B.C. V8K 2V9, (250)537-5242; fax (250)537-4322. Monitors VHF channel 68. Open all year, gasoline and diesel at fuel dock. Guest moorage in 125 slips, 5500 feet of dock space. Facilities include 15, 30 & 50 amp power, washrooms, showers, laundry. Propane available a short distance away. Complimentary muffins and coffee on the dock each morning. Groceries, restaurants, all services within walking distance. Car and scooter rentals. This is the closest marina to town. It is clean and well-run. Free shuttle to golf. *(Marina map page 120)*

⑭ **Salt Spring Marina,** 124 Upper Ganges Rd., Saltspring Island, BC V8K 2S2, (250)537-5810; (800)334-6629, www.mobyspub.com. Monitors VHF channel 68. Guest moorage for all sizes of boats, 15 & 30 amp power, washrooms, showers, laundry, concrete launch ramp but no long term parking. Facilities include chandlery, gift shop, scuba shop, fishing tackle and bait, and the popular Moby's Marine Pub, with full dining and takeout. Kayak, boat, and scooter rentals. Budget Rent-a-Car. Harbor shuttle to downtown *(Marina map page 120)*

Caution: Money Makers Rock lies a short distance off the marina entrance, marked by a bright inflatable buoy. Despite the buoy, each year a few boats still find the rock.

Long Harbour. Long Harbour lies parallel to Ganges Harbour, but is much narrower. It is the site of the ferry that serves Saltspring Island from Vancouver. Good anchorage can be found beyond the ferry dock, taking care not to anchor over a posted cable crossing. Royal Vancouver Yacht Club has an outstation in Long Harbour.

PREVOST ISLAND

Prevost Island. Use chart 3442. Prevost Island has been a favorite of ours for many years, particularly the four bays that indent its northwest end. The bays indenting from the southeast also look inviting, but with ferry traffic flying by in Swanson Channel, it might get a little lumpy. We've never spent the night in one of these bays. But the northwest bays are excellent. **Glenthorne Passage** is the westernmost of these bays. The bottom is good, the water quiet, and the surroundings agreeable. In summer months the sun sets in the narrow passage between Glenthorne Point and Secret Island. **Annette Inlet** is a little wider than Glenthorne Passage, with a good sandy beach at the head and a farmhouse ashore, a good anchorage. **Selby Cove** is narrow, with a house and dock on the right side as you enter. **James Bay** is even wider, with room for perhaps 30 boats in a pinch (such as on a beautiful summer weekend). There is no ferry service to Prevost Island, and thus less population than the larger islands.

MONTAGUE HARBOUR

Montague Harbour. Use chart 3473 (larger scale, preferred) or 3442. *Proposed No Discharge Zone. Gray water okay. See p. 15.* Montague Harbour is a popular stopping spot in the central Gulf Islands. It is well protected, and has an excellent marine park. Depending on wind direction, you can find good anchorages around the bay—except in the southwest corner, behind the narrow peninsula that ends at Winstanley Point. Holding can be iffy in that area.

A shuttle bus service called Go Galiano connects the golf course, the marina, the ferry dock at Sturdies Bay, and the interesting restaurants and guest lodgings on Galiano Island. Montague Harbour Marina is a pick-up point. The marina has a fuel dock. A small public float is between the marina and the Montague Harbour ferry dock. Entrance to the harbor is unobstructed, either from the southeast past Phillimore Point, or from the northwest, east of Parker Island.

Dining: Everybody enjoys the Hummingbird Inn Pub. In summer, the Pub Bus ride is memorable.

⑮ **Montague Harbour Marine Park.** Montague Harbour Marine Park, at the north end of Montague Harbour, is beautiful and much used. The park is open all year, has ex-

Montague Harbour Marina has ample room for visitors. This is where the bus to the Hummingbird Inn Pub picks up customers.

cellent white sand beaches on the south side and astonishing rock beaches on the north and west sides. Walk-in campsites and toilets. A dinghy dock and 300-foot-long mooring float extend into Montague Harbour, and 25 mooring buoys lie off the dock. The park has anchorage for many boats on both sides of Gray Peninsula, depending on wind direction.

⑮ **Montague Harbour Marina,** RR 1, Site 21-C17, Galiano, B.C. V0N 1P0, (250)539-5733; fax (250)539-2010. Monitors VHF channel 68. Open Easter to Canadian Thanks-

giving (mid-Oct.). Gasoline and diesel at the fuel dock, also stove alcohol. Facilities include guest moorage, 15 & 30 amp power, washrooms (but no showers because of severe water constraints) store, charts and excellent selection of local interest books.

This is a delightful and extremely well-run facility. Bob Walker and his family bought the marina in late 1994, and have expanded the small store, added an espresso bar, a licensed cafe, and stocked the gift shop with local Galiano Island arts and crafts, along with high-quality souvenir T-shirts and sweatshirts.

See area map page 112

A new building, added in 1997, houses another gift shop and kayak rentals. Motor scooters can be rented from Scoot Galiano. The docks are being rebuilt and extended, and service is outstanding. In season they serve thousands of hand-dipped hard ice cream cones.

⑮ **Montague Harbour Public Wharf.** Open all year, 160 feet of dock space, no facilities. **Walker Hook.** Use chart 3442. Walker Hook, on the west side of Trincomali Channel, has a beautiful beach on its eastern shore where it connects with Saltspring Island. Anchor there in 4 fathoms. An approach between Atkins Reef and Saltspring Island takes the worry out of identifying just where the various rocks are.

Fernwood Public Wharf, Use chart 3442. Walker Hook, Saltspring Island. Open all year, 40 feet of dock space, no facilities.

SAANICH INLET

Use chart 3441. Saanich Inlet extends south into Vancouver Island for about 12 miles. The northern part of the inlet is fairly civilized, especially along the Saanich Peninsula shore to Brentwood Bay, the location of Butchart Gardens. For a beautiful and often-overlooked trip, continue your run south through Squally Reach and Finlayson Arm. Boat traffic usually is minimal, and the high mountains rising from the shorelines make for a remote feeling only a short distance from the more popular spots.

Deep Cove. Use chart 3441. Wain Rock, with good water on both sides, lies about 0.2 miles off Moses Point. The remains of a public wharf are in the south part of the cove. The float was removed in 1978 and only the pier, unused but still robust, remains. The Deep Cove Marina (formerly named Chart House Marina) is adjacent to this pier.

Deep Cove Marina, 10990 Madrona Dr., Deep Cove, B.C. V8L 5R7, (250)656-0060. Open all year, limited guest moorage available, 15 amp power, washrooms, showers.

Patricia Bay. Patricia Bay, locally called Pat Bay, is open, but all the facilities are reserved for the Canadian Government's Institute of Ocean Sciences. It is here that the Canadian Hydrographic Service develops and maintains charts and related publications for western Canada and the Arctic.

Coles Bay. Coles Bay lies east of Yarrow Point. It is good for temporary anchorage, but open to southerly winds. If approaching from the north, the Canadian *Small Craft Guide* recommends that you give Dyer Rocks, off Yarrow Point, a 0.5-mile berth to avoid shoals extending south from the rocks.

Brentwood Bay. Use chart 3441. Brentwood Bay can be entered on either side of Senanus Island. Telephone customs clearance can be made from Angler's Anchorage Marina. The Mill Bay ferry departs from Sluggett Point. A rock, marked by buoy U22, lies close to the ferry dock. Do not pass between the buoy and the daybeacon, or you risk going aground on rocks. The town of Brentwood Bay is worth a visit. In addition to Angler's Anchorage Marina and the Brentwood Inn Resort, there is a public dock and floats. The town has the look of an English seaside resort, complete with afternoon tea.

⑰ **Butchart Gardens.** Brentwood Bay is the back door to the celebrated and astonishing Butchart Gardens. The Gardens are a must-see attraction. At night they are lighted, creating an entirely different effect from the day. On Saturday evenings during the summer a fireworks display is held on a large field in the gardens. Many people arrive early and have a picnic supper while waiting for darkness. Bring blankets, cushions, and folding chairs or camp stools. Even for jaded viewers, it's worth the trip. The most interesting fireworks are done at ground level—you have to be on the scene to see it.

The Gardens' dinghy dock is in a small cove, with 4 mooing buoys for overnighting yachts. Most visitors put the anchor down in adjacent Tod Inlet and go by dinghy to the dinghy dock.

Tod Inlet. Use chart 3441. Tod Inlet reaches back behind the Butchart Gardens, and has ample anchoring room. The inlet is narrow when seen from Brentwood Bay, but opens somewhat after a bend. In the narrow sections you should plan to run a stern-tie ashore. Boats in the more open sections around the bend can swing without a stern-tie.

⑰ **Angler's Anchorage Marina,** 933 Marchant Road, Brentwood Bay, B.C. V8M 1B5, (250)652-3531. Monitors VHF channel 68. Open all year with 1000 feet of guest moorage, 15 & 30 amp power, washrooms, showers, laundry, restaurant, customs clearance. The marina has locked gates for security, and is close to Butchart Gardens.

⑰ **Brentwood Inn Resort,** 7172 Brentwood Drive, Brentwood Bay, B.C. V8M 1B7, (250)652-3151; fax (250)652-2402. Monitors VHF channel 68. Open all year, 15 & 30 amp power, washrooms, showers, laundry. Ample guest moorage, plus a large pub with outside dining in the summer, live music on weekends, two restaurants, motel units. They sell fishing tackle and bait. Close to doctor, post office, liquor store. Close to Butchart Gardens. When entering, keep between the ferry dock and the red spar at the end of the dock.

Brentwood Bay Public Wharf. Open all year, dock is 72 feet, no facilities.

(18) **Goldstream Boathouse.** 3540 Trans-Canada Hwy, Victoria, B.C. V9E 1K3, (250)478-4407; fax (250)478-6882. Use chart 3441. Open all year, gasoline only at fuel dock (a new fuel dock is under construction). Guest moorage available, with new 300-foot dock, best to call ahead. Marina has complete repair facility and haulout, new 2-lane launch ramp, 15, 20, & 30 amp power. Friendly, relaxed atmosphere. Overnight accommodations available. Goldstream Boathouse is located at the head of Finlayson Arm, at the edge of drying flats off the mouth of the Goldstream River. The shoal water seems to be extending farther north, so come in close to the docks. If the approach is made from mid-channel, the unsuspecting skipper could find himself aground.

Mill Bay. Use chart 3441. Mill Bay is a good anchorage. The west shore provides a lee from the usual summer west or northwest winds. The bay is, however, open to southeast winds. In addition to the public dock, the Mill Bay Marina is friendly and equipped with all the amenities.

(19) **Mill Bay Marina,** P.O. Box 231, 740 Handy Road, Mill Bay, B.C. V0R 2P0, (250)743-4112, (800)253-4112. Monitor VHF channel 68, CB channel 10. Gasoline and diesel at fuel dock, guest moorage available, 15 amp power, washrooms, showers, laundry, portapotty dump. They carry marine supplies and charts; tackle and bait. Good launch ramp, some extended-term vehicle parking available. Close to good restaurants, shopping, hospital, liquor store. This is an easygoing and informal marina, owned and cared for by Fred and Marilyn Laba. Nice people.

(19) **Mill Bay Public Wharf.** Open all year, 50 feet of dock space, no facilities, commercial fishing vessels have priority.

(23) **Cherry Point Marina,** RR#3, 1241 Sutherland Road, Cobble Hill, B.C. V0R 1L0, (250)748-0453. Open all year, limited guest moorage, call ahead. Washrooms, 15 & 20 amp power, portapotty dump, haulout, launch ramp, RV and picnic areas.

COWICHAN BAY

Use chart 3478. The town of Cowichan Bay, located near the southwest corner of Cowichan Bay, is picturesque and worth a stroll. The public docks are behind a log and plank breakwater, with the entrance near shore. The privately owned marinas are located west of the public wharf. At low tide the entrance can seem rather narrow, but it is navigable.

Cowichan Bay Fishermen's Wharf. Open all year, 941 feet of dock space, 20 amp power, washrooms, no showers. Breakwater protected, garbage collection, waste oil disposal.

(20) **Masthead Marina,** P.O. Box 8, Cowichan Bay, B.C. V0R 1N0, (250)748-5368. Open all year, 2 guest slips, 20 amp power, washrooms. This is a dinner restaurant and small marina located next to the public dock. Moorage availability varies, so call ahead.

(20) **Howard Johnson Suite Hotel,** 1681 Cowichan Bay Rd., Cowichan Bay, B.C. V0R 1N0, (250)748-6222; fax (250)748-7122. Open all year, 400 foot dock, washrooms, showers, laundry, swimming pool. Beer and wine store. Located behind the breakwater. Call ahead.

(20) **Bluenose Marina,** P.O. Box 38, 1765 Cowichan Bay Road, Cowichan Bay, B.C. V0R 1N0, (250)748-2222 phone/fax. Guest moorage available on outside 100 foot dock, 15 amp power, washrooms, showers, laundry, 5

mooring buoys. Fine dining and coffee shop on site. Nearby launch ramp. Public playground. Groceries within walking distance.

(20) **Coastal Shipyard & Marine Services,** 1759 Cowichan Bay Rd., Duncan, B.C. V9R 1N0, (250)746-4705. Open all year, but full of commercial boats in the winter. Call ahead always. Facilities include 30 amp power, washrooms, no showers. Haulout and repairs available. Five minutes to downtown Duncan, maritime museum next door.

(20) **Pier 66 Marina Ltd.,** 1745 Cowichan Bay Rd., Cowichan Bay, B.C. V0R 1N0, (250)748-8444; fax (250)748-8444; e-mail rufus@islandnet.com. Open all year, gasoline, diesel, pre-mix at fuel dock. Washrooms, no showers, 15 amp power, haulout. Limited moorage for boats to 50 feet. Marine hardware, supplies, charts, kerosene, alcohol, tackle, groceries. Walking distance to services, maritime museum, and marine biology lab open to the public.

Genoa Bay. Use chart 3478 (larger scale, preferred) or 3441. Genoa Bay indents the north shore of Cowichan Bay. You can anchor off the resort docks, or use one of the transient spaces at the dock. The Genoa Bay Marina has moorage.

The Genoa Bay Marina is a popular stop, with store, and excellent restaurant.

(21) **Genoa Bay Marina,** 5100 Genoa Bay Rd., Duncan, B.C. V8L 5Y8, (250)746-7621. Monitors VHF channel 68 approximately mid-May through Labour Day. Open all year, guest moorage in 30 slips and along 1200 feet of dock space, call ahead. Washrooms, showers, laundry, 15 amp power and launch ramp. This is a popular summer stop for pleasure craft. The Grapevine Cafe (formerly Genoa Bay Cafe) is known for its excellent meals. The cafe is closed Dec. 15 through March. Most marina facilities are closed from September through

See area map page 112

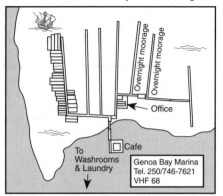

Reference only — not for navigation

Genoa Bay Marina
Tel. 250/746-7621
VHF 68

Genoa Bay Marina

The Musgrave Landing dock is small and often full. Two boats departed moments before this picture was taken.

re-opening sometime in May, but dock space is available with payment on an honor system. Electricity is limited. During the summer season the store carries convenience items. Good fishing. *(Marina map above)*

Musgrave Landing. Use chart 3478 (larger scale, preferred) or 3441. Musgrave Landing is located on the southwest corner of Saltspring Island, at the mouth of Sansum Narrows. Although it has only a small public float, no facilities, and very restricted anchorage nearby, it is a popular stopover. The setting is secluded feeling, and upland you'll find good hiking along miles of logging roads. We took a pleasant

walk, and along the roadside picked a bouquet of thistle, foxglove, dandelion, fern, salal, nicotiana and pearly everlasting for the galley table. A housing development, with private dock, is on Musgrave Point.

SANSUM NARROWS TO DUCK BAY

Use chart 3478 (larger scale, preferred) or 3442. Sansum Narrows connects Satellite Channel to the south with Stuart Channel to the north, and leads between high hills on Saltspring Island and Vancouver Island. The wind fun-

nels down the axis of the narrows, turning at the bends. It also funnels down the valleys leading to the channel, so wind directions can be erratic. Currents seldom exceed 3 knots; usually they are less.

Burgoyne Bay. Use chart 3478 (larger scale, preferred) or 3442. Burgoyne Bay has ample anchorage in 3-5 fathoms at its inner end, but is subject to willawaws that blow across a low swale on Saltspring Island. Most of the bay is too deep for convenient anchoring. A 32-foot public wharf is at the head of the bay, next to the anchorage.

The Shipyard
Restaurant & Pub is
at the head of the dock,
Maple Bay Marina.

Maple Bay. Use chart 3478 (larger scale, preferred) or 3442. Maple Bay is a major pleasure boat center, with public moorages and all needed facilities and services. Birds Eye Cove, off the southwest corner of Maple Bay, is home to the Maple Bay Marina and Birds Eye Cove Marina, both of them with fuel docks, and the Maple Bay Yacht Club, which welcomes visitors from reciprocal clubs. Anchoring is good in Birds Eye Cove, but *avoid anchoring in the area just off the dock located on the east side of the cove, opposite the marina docks.* We spoke with a couple who fouled their anchor on the wreck of a sunken fish boat about 100 feet off the end of that dock, and it took a diver to get the anchor free.

Dining: The Quamichan Inn is renowned, and our suppers at the Shipyard Restaurant & Pub have been good.

㉒ **Maple Bay Marina,** 6145 Genoa Bay Rd., Duncan, B.C. V9L 5T7, (250)746-8482; fax (250)746-8490. Monitors VHF channel 68. Open all year. Gasoline and diesel at the fuel dock, power, washrooms, showers, laundry, propane, CNG. This is a popular stop, scenic and well protected from winds and seas. The grounds are beautiful, and you'll find a lovely rock-walled garden on the hillside overlooking the gazebo. The Maple Bay Marina advertises the "cleanest washrooms on the coast." Our experience confirms that the washrooms are spacious, warm and indeed clean, with good showers. The shopping complex includes a coin-op laundry and a store with convenience groceries, marine supplies, and books and charts. The Shipyard Restaurant & Pub is a lively spot and the food is good. A mechanic and a shipwright are available. A shuttle bus serves Cowichan Bay and Chemainus. Harbour Air provides scheduled float plane service to Vancouver. This is a popular marina for rendezvous and club cruises.

㉒ **Maple Bay Public Wharf.** Open all year. Has 150 feet of dock space, no facilities. Commercial fishing vessels have priority.

㉒ **Birds Eye Cove Marina,** 6271 Genoa Bay Rd., Duncan, B.C. V9L 5T8, (250)748-4255. Monitors VHF channel 68. Open all year, gasoline and diesel at fuel dock, 15 & 30 amp power, washrooms, no showers. Limited guest moorage. Look for the new mural on the side of the building.

Crofton Public Wharf, Box 128 (Infocentre), Crofton, B.C. V0R 1R0. Use chart 3475 (larger scale, preferred) or 3442. Open all year, 518 feet of dock space, 20 & 30 amp power, washrooms, showers, laundry, garbage collection. Breakwater protected. Located next to the terminal for the ferry to Saltspring Island. The adjacent Infocentre houses the washrooms with showers (sunrise to sunset, summer only). The Infocentre has visitors' information for all of B.C. Walking distance to all services, including groceries, restaurants, fishing supplies and licenses. Playground 2 blocks away. Nearby outdoor swimming pool and tennis courts, hiking trails.

Vesuvius. Use chart 3442. North of Sansum Narrows along the Saltspring Island shore, Vesuvius has a public wharf, and is the terminus for the ferry to Crofton. The Vesuvius Inn, an informal pub, is located at the head of the dock.

Duck Bay, just north of Vesuvius Bay, has good anchorage, with steep, wooded cliffs rising on its east side.

Even Electronics Can Fail

First you must understand the boat, a 1976 Glasply 28. The owner is a senior pilot with a major airline. He's smart, he understands equipment and maintenance, and he doesn't cut corners to save a nickel. Although the Glasply was 20 years old when this happened, it looked as if it were brand-new. Everything was shiny, and everything worked.

Except . . . except the electronics. The problem was connected with the trim tabs. On this trip, when the trim tabs were adjusted all the electronics stopped working. Never happened before. Not sure why. No depth sounder, no GPS, no autopilot, no radio . . . no electronics. Hmmm.

Now to the first Waggoner boat, the Tollycraft 26 *Surprise.* That boat had an electronic compass at the lower station, the only way to get the compass away from the magnets in the radar display. For two years the electronic compass worked beautifully, showing the boat direction exactly to the degree.

Then, while proceeding northwest in the Gulf Islands, we saw that the electronic compass showed a course of 380°. There being only 360° in a circle, we figured something was amiss. A call to the compass manufacturer confirmed that indeed something was amiss (a course of 380° needs confirmation?). The compass went back to the manufacturer for repairs.

Lesson: Despite our belief that modern electronics are bullet proof, they can fail. We don't know what backups the Glasply 28 carried. On *Surprise*, we used a hand bearing compass to show our direction. Later, we realized that the autopilot compass was a workable substitute. These two experiences, however, have reaffirmed our policy of carrying non-techie old-fashioned backup methods of doing whatever it is we trust our electronics to do for us.

I sure hope I don't have to use them again, though. The new electronics are fabulous—when they work.

—Robert Hale

We Almost Died from Shellfish Poisoning

M Y HUSBAND AND I manage a beautiful marina on an island in British Columbia. The exact location doesn't matter, because what happened to us could have happened anywhere along the coast.

After a very busy summer, at last the final weekend of the season arrived. It was October 11, 1997, and luckily the weatherman was wrong again. We had a beautiful autumn day—a perfect day for a barbecue. Many of our permanent moorage tenants already had arrived to enjoy a seafood extravaganza.

Two of them were experienced divers, and one had been in the scuba charter business for many years. They would show us their secret spot for harvesting scallops. The seas were calm and in no time we were at our destination. It wasn't long before the divers had harvested enough scallops for all of us.

When we got back to the dock a six-year-old boy questioned the divers about how and where they got the scallops, and begged to try just a couple. How could we look in those big eyes and say no? With two scallops in his tight little fists he ran back to his boat and talked his mother into cooking them right away. One of the divers, knowing that the red tide shellfish ban had been lifted a few weeks earlier, teased the boy's mother that if her son's lips didn't go numb in the next half-hour the scallops would be safe for the rest of us to eat.

Our feast began around nine in the evening, after the children were fed and settled down with a movie. We started off with freshly harvested crab legs, followed by steak, salad, potatoes, and of course the delectable scallops. Somebody suggested that we try a little Tabasco sauce on the scallops. We thought we had died and gone to heaven.

And we almost did.

In a little while my lips began to feel numb. My husband said his lips were numb too, and a few others said their lips were numb. We decided it was the Tabasco sauce, and had the rest of the scallops plain. My husband was eating as if hadn't eaten in days, and loving every mouthful. I was close behind. Cheers for the divers and the cooks! Great food, great wine and great friends. I couldn't think of anyplace I would rather be.

The air was getting cold and my fingers and toes were growing numb. We called it a night, and told our friends we would see them in the morning for coffee. Little did we suspect that our nightmare was about to begin.

When we got home my husband said his feet and hands were so cold that he was going to take a hot bath. I just wanted to snuggle under the covers to get warm and go to sleep. I must have fallen asleep because the next thing I knew my husband was yelling that he could hardly walk and was I all right? I realized my head felt as if it were in a fog, and I couldn't feel my body.

I tried to get up and go to him, but I couldn't feel my feet touch the floor. I tried to tell him this, but the words were so hard to come out. Everything was moving in slow motion. My husband said, "I think we have shellfish poisoning. What do we do now?"

I wasn't sure how serious our situation was, but I knew that I was having trouble breathing and my condition was growing worse. We called the doctor's emergency number, feeling sorry to waken him a 2:00 A.M. The doctor asked if we could make it to the clinic on our own or did we need an ambulance. My stubborn husband said that we could make it on our own.

Getting down the stairs and into the car was easier said than done. We had to concentrate on our feet touching the ground, and it seemed to take forever to get to the car. Luckily it was late and no other cars were on the road. I'm sure the doctor thought we were drunk when we walked into the clinic. It must have been quite a sight to see the two of us holding onto each other, trying to keep our balance.

Once we told the doctor what had happened, all we could think about was the others on the boats. Were they in the same shape or even worse? What if they couldn't get to a phone? What about the little boy? The doctor called the poison control center and then the ambulance and police. We told them the boat names and locations of the 11 other people who had eaten the scallops. Fortunately, only a few of them had symptoms, and they were minor. Other than having been shaken from their sleep at 4:00 A.M., everybody else was all right.

T HERE IS NO ANTIDOTE for this type of toxin. All the doctor could do was start us on I.V.s and monitor our vital signs. And wait. I began to get sick. My heart felt as if it were going to jump right out of my chest. My blood pressure was out of control. I was afraid to close my eyes, because I didn't think I would wake up again.

My husband began to pass out. Somehow, between the doctor and myself, we got him onto a bed. Later, my husband told me that he felt he was floating above us, watching what was happening, everything in slow motion. And he could hear the doctor shouting, "Stay with us!"

Once again the doctor called the poison control center, and they decided that we had to be transported to a hospital in Victoria.

It was our first helicopter ride, and it wasn't supposed to be like this. I was so scared that we were going to die and never see our children again. We were taken to the emergency room, hooked up to heart and blood pressure machines, and monitored very closely. We were given liquid charcoal to drink, to absorb anything left in our stomachs.

By this time it was 7:00 A.M. We were still in the emergency room and I was so tired. But I was afraid to close my eyes. We were seen by a neurologist, who explained that we were suffering from Paralytic Shellfish Poisoning (PSP). He said the reason that we had been affected more than the others could have been that we had eaten more, or that only some of the scallops held the toxin. He told us that death usually occurs within a half-hour of consumption. Since we were still here we should be all right. It would just take time for the toxin to flush out of our systems.

Usually the symptoms last for about 12 hours, but sometimes they last longer. Everyone reacts differently. The doctor tested our reflexes and hand-eye coordination. When I tried to touch my finger to my nose my arm would fly into the air. My legs would not do what I wanted them to do. I was frustrated and frightened. The doctor decided to admit us to the hospital.

While we were in the emergency room a friend arrived with clothes for us (we were still in our pajamas). When he saw us his face went ashen. We just have looked pretty scary, with the charcoal still on our lips and teeth. At least we were alive, and he could take that good news back to the others.

At last we were admitted and taken to our rooms, and I felt safe enough to close my eyes. But nightmares of what could have happened robbed me of my sleep.

By the next afternoon my husband had recovered enough to go home. Unfortunately, I was still in bad shape. I learned the hard way how we take simple things for granted—things such as feeding myself, sitting, walking, even talking. The nurses wanted me to eat something, but the thought of food made me sick. They said that was all right, the soup of the day was clam chowder. It felt good to be able to laugh about it.

The next day I agreed to try to eat. It proved to be quite an ordeal. When the bed was raised to a sitting position I got dizzy, and I had to lie on my side. The next step was to get the fork from the plate to my mouth. My hand and my brain were not communicating, and I had more food on

Northern Gulf Islands

Chemainus • Wallace Island • Pirates Cove • Gabriola Passage
Silva Bay • Dodd Narrows • Nanaimo

the bed than in my mouth. At last I found that if I used two hands I could manage. It took more than an hour to eat just half of what was on the plate.

As each day passed I got stronger. I could feed myself and sit up in a chair. By the fifth day, with the help of physiotherapists and a walker, I was walking. That night I practiced and practiced with the walker. I knew I couldn't go home until I proved to the doctor that I could walk on my own. On the sixth day I showed the doctor that I could walk to the door. He agreed to let me go home.

I'm writing this three weeks since that eventful night, and every day I count my blessings that my husband and I are alive. It could have been very different.

THIS DEADLY PSP TOXIN can remain in bivalve shellfish for as long as a year. (When does the year begin?) Some shellfish might contain the toxin while others might not, even if they have been harvested from the same area. The toxin cannot be killed by cooking or freezing.

Typically, symptoms begin with numbness or tingling of the lips and tongue. The numbness and tingling spread to the fingers and toes. These symptoms can be followed by nausea, a floating feeling, and a loss of muscular coordination. Danger of death occurs when the breathing muscles are affected, which necessitates the use of a respirator.

We, and others, have always believed that in the absence of a red tide alert bivalve shellfish were safe to eat. The lifting of this red tide alert brought a false sense of security. Our experience has proven that there is always a risk.

—*Kay Spence*

For latest information on
Paralytic Shellfish Poison (PSP)
closures, call:

Washington state
800/562-5632

British Columbia
604/666-2828

Charts

3313	SMALL CRAFT CHARTS (chartbook) – Gulf Islands & adjacent waterways
3442	North Pender Island to Thetis Island (1:40,000)
3443	Thetis Island to Nanaimo (1:40,000)
3457	Nanaimo Harbour & Departure Bay (1:8,000)
3458	Approaches to Nanaimo Harbour (1:20,000)
3473	Active Pass, Porlier Pass & Montague Harbour (various)
3475	PLANS – Stuart Channel Chemainus Bay (1:12,000) Ladysmith Harbour (1:12,000) Dodd Narrows to Flat Top Islands (1:18,000) Dodd Narrows (1:9,000) Osborn Bay (1:15,000)

General Information. For general information about the Gulf Islands, see the section at the beginning of Southern Gulf Islands chapter, p. 108.

Chemainus. Use chart 3475 (larger scale, preferred) or 3442. Chemainus, on the Vancouver Island side of Stuart Channel, has a small public wharf and floats for visitors, and that's where you will tie up. Anchorage is possible, we suppose, toward the head of the bay, but much of the available anchorage is taken up by rafted logs. Chemainus is a wonderful

town, filled with shops, galleries, and antique shops. Thirty-two of the building owners have had large murals painted on their buildings, most of them depicting the town's past as an Indian campground and its heritage as a mining, logging and mill town. A well-stocked grocery store is at the head of the public wharf. A ferry crosses to Chemainus from Telegraph Harbour.

Ladysmith. Use chart 3475 (larger scale, preferred) or 3442. Ladysmith Harbour is approximately 6 miles north of Chemainus, on Vancouver Island. The town of Ladysmith is located about ½ mile from the public boat basin, up a long flight of stairs and across the highway. The main street looks as if time passed it by. A number of movie scenes have been shot here. In the town you'll find a large supermarket with liquor store nearby, and all the services you would expect in a town, but little for the boat itself.

The public boat basin is the first major set of docks you come to on the south side of the harbor, behind Slag Point. The Ivy Green Marina, farther into the harbor, has no guest moorage. The Page Point Inn (formerly Mañana Lodge & Marina) is at Page Point, on the north shore. Seattle Yacht Club has an outstation along the north side of the Dunsmuir Islands, in Sibell Bay.

② **Ladysmith Fisherman's Wharf.** Open all year, 700 feet of dock space, power, garbage collection, telephone, but no other facilities. Breakwater and tidal grid. Launch ramp. Commercial fishing vessels have priority. Stairs lead up the hill toward the town of Ladysmith, about ½ mile away.

The delightful town of Chemainus has 32 different murals painted on buildings. Chemainus is a favorite stop for antiques enthusiasts.

See area map page 132

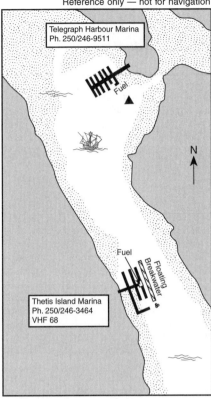

Reference only — not for navigation

Telegraph Harbour Marina
Ph. 250/246-9511

Fuel

N

Fuel

Floating Breakwater

Thetis Island Marina
Ph. 250/246-3464
VHF 68

Telegraph Harbour

② **Page Point Inn (Formerly Mañana Lodge & Marina)**, 4760 Brenton-Page Rd., Ladysmith, B.C. V9G 1L7, (250)245-2312. Open summer 7 days a week for guest moorage and restaurant. Fuel dock has gasoline and diesel. Facilities include power, washrooms, showers, laundry. A popular stop in the summer. The restaurant has an excellent reputation. They have bed & breakfast rooms, gift shop, car rentals. A golf course is 10-15 minutes away. In late 1999 Lawrence and Lexi Lambert bought the facility and changed the name to Page Point Inn. As we went to press they were adding new B&B rooms and upgrading the dining room. They plan a much-needed dock improvement for the 2000 boating season, with dock power upgraded from 15 amp to 30 amp.

② **Ivy Green Marina, Ltd.**, Box 88, 1335 Rocky Creek Rd., Ladysmith, B.C. V0R 2E0, (250)245-4521. Open all year, washrooms, showers, no power. This marina is mostly permanant moorage. Haulout and complete repairs available from Oyster Harbour Marine Services.

Telegraph Harbour. Use chart 3477 (larger scale, preferred) or 3442 or 3443. Telegraph Harbour is one of the Gulf Islands' most popular stops. It is located across Stuart Channel from Ladysmith, between Thetis Island and Kuper Island. Telegraph Harbour has two marinas, the Thetis Island Marina, and the Telegraph

Harbour Marina. Both marinas are served by an inter-island ferry to Chemainus. While you're at Telegraph Harbour, take a short walk up to the Pot of Gold Coffee Roasting Co. It's a fascinating place. We bought a bag of their Colombian coffee, and it was wonderful.

③ **Thetis Island Marina**, Thetis Island, B.C. V0R 2Y0, (250)246-3464, e-mail marina @thetisisland.com, or view at www.thetis island.com. Monitors VHF channel 68. Open all year for full service, gasoline and diesel at the fuel dock, 2800 feet of dock space, 15 & 30 amp power, propane, washrooms, showers, laundry. This is a full-service marina, with good docks, groceries, kerosene, snacks, ice, and post office. It has a fully licensed restaurant and pub with inside and patio dining. The pub has good food, and a satisfying selection of beers, porters and stouts, and single-malt scotches. Mechanic available. Large playground for the kids. It's a 10-minute walk to the ferry to Chemainus.

During the past few years Paul and Dawn Deacon have made substantial improvements to the Thetis Island Marina, including what is perhaps the first commercial water desalination system in the islands. Water is still precious, because the system is expensive to maintain and operate, but they never run out of water.

The marina buildings have received handsome new cedar siding and green metal roofs. A new, covered picnic area has been built. They

See area map page 132

do spectacular pig roasts there for boating groups. A new shower/washroom building was begun in 1999, and should be complete for the 2000 season. One dock at a time, the old docks are being replaced. They plan to expand the dock space during the next few years.

The Deacons are part of the reason we so enjoy researching the Waggoner Cruising Guide each year. They are fine people, dedicated to building a marina/pub/playground worthy of their clientele. *(Marina map page 130)*

③ **Telegraph Harbour Marina**, Box 7-10, Thetis Island, B.C. V0R 2Y0, (250)246-9511; fax (250)246-2668, or view at www. telegraphharbour.com. Open summers 7 days a week; in the winter call for fuel and store hours. Gasoline & diesel at the fuel dock. The marina has 3000 feet of dock space. Because of its popularity with boating groups and large rendezvous (the Canadian Tollycraft rendezvous, for example, completely fills the marina in late September), call ahead for moorage availability and reservations. Facilities include 15 & 30 amp power, washrooms, showers, and laundry.

The general store carries groceries, charts, fishing tackle, bait, licenses, and gifts. The coffee shop serves sandwiches and guilt-laden old-fashioned hard ice cream milk shakes, sundaes and ice cream specialties. For Marilynn Hale, a cruise to the Gulf Islands is not complete without one of Jan Ohman's ice cream

The International Volleyball Championship is hotly contested at the Canadian Tollycraft Rendezvous.

Telegraph Harbour Marina has room for large groups. Here, the Canadian Tollycraft Rendezvous takes all the dock space.

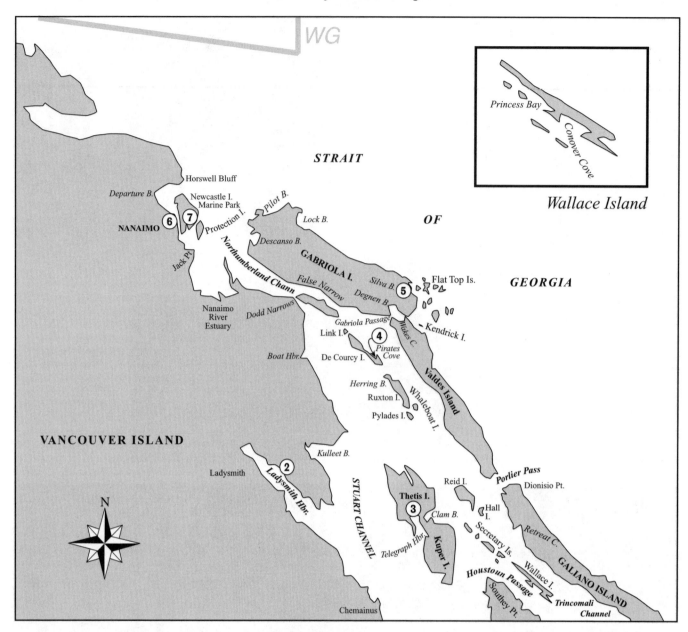

Wallace Island

Princess Bay

Conover Cove

STRAIT

OF

GEORGIA

Horswell Bluff

Departure B.

Newcastle I.
Marine Park

Pilot B.

Lock B.

⑥ ⑦

NANAIMO

Protection I.

Descanso B.

GABRIOLA I.

Silva B.

Flat Top Is.

⑤

Jack Pt.

Northumberland Chann.

False Narrow

Degnen B.

Wakes C.

Kendrick I.

Nanaimo
River
Estuary

Dodd Narrows

Gabriola Passage

Link I.

④

*Pirates
Cove*

Boat Hbr.

De Courcy I.

Valdes Island

Herring B.

Ruxton I.

Whaleboat I.

Pylades I.

VANCOUVER ISLAND

Kulleet B.

Ladysmith

②

Ladysmith Hbr.

Reid I.

Porlier Pass

Dionisio Pt.

Thetis I.

③

Clam B.

Hall
I.

STUART CHANNEL

Secretary Is.

Retreat C.

Kuper I.

Telegraph Hbr.

GALIANO ISLAND

Houstoun Passage

Wallace I.

Southey Pt.

*Trincomali
Channel*

Chemainus

N

---

indulgences for lunch. The marina has a playgound for kids, a large covered area for group functions, and a picnic area with tables and barbecues. It's a 10-minute walk to the Chemainus ferry.

We have learned that after several very successful years, John and Jan Ohman have sold the property. The new owners are Ron and Barbara Williams, and will take over April 1, 2000. *(Marina map page 130)*

North Cove. Use chart 3443 or 3442. North Cove, which indents the north end of Thetis Island, is a good anchorage, although open to the usual summer northwesterly winds.

Clam Bay. Use chart 3442 or 3443. Clam Bay is a large, relatively open bay with good anchoring in convenient depths. The mouth of the bay is partly blocked by Centre Reef, and Rocket Shoal is in the middle of the bay. Lacking familiarity, the safest entry is south of Centre Reef, between buoy U42 and

Penalakut Spit, which extends from Kuper Island. The chart shows everything. Clam Bay is one end of The Cut, a drying channel that separates Thetis Island from Kuper Island. The Cut leads to Telegraph Harbour, but should be tried only in a small boat or with local knowledge, and at half tide or higher.

Southey Bay. Use chart 3442. At the north tip of Saltspring Island, tucked in beside Southey Point, is a little notch that Contributing Editor Tom Kincaid has used as an anchorage in past years. An increasing number of private mooring buoys have restricted swinging room, but it's still a possible anchorage.

Secretary Islands. Use chart 3442. The Secretary Islands have several nice little anchorages, with emphasis on *little*. One of the easiest is in the notch on the Trincomali Channel side between the two Secretary Islands.

Mowgli Island. Use chart 3442. Mowgli

Island, off the NW tip of the Secretary Islands, has good anchorage in a cozy bay between it and the first Secretary island. We suggest a stern-tie across the gravel beach to driftwood ashore. There isn't much room to swing. Mowgli Island is surrounded by reefs. They are easily seen at low tide, but be cautious at high tide.

Wallace Island Marine Park. Use chart 3442. Open all year. Wallace Island, a marine park purchased with the help of the local boating community, is a low and beautiful tree-covered island in Trincomali Channel, and we recommend a visit. Enter from Houstoun Passage. You'll find sheltered anchorage and a dock at Conover Cove, anchorage for many boats in locally-named Princess Cove, and room for a couple of boats just inside Panther Point. The park has toilets, campsites and picnic areas, and trails that cover the entire length of the island. It's a fine place to stretch the legs. Old cabins set in an orchard near Conover

This delightful orchard is near Conover Cove, Wallace Island.

Lots of room to anchor. Princess Cove, Wallace Island.

reach 9 knots. Current predictions are shown in the Tide and Current Tables, Vol. 5. The current floods north, into the Strait of Georgia, and ebbs south, into the Gulf Islands. The best time for transit is at slack water. A study of the chart shows that it is safest to transit Porlier Pass on the south sides of Black Rock and Virago Rock, keeping toward the Galiano Island side of the pass.

Approaching from the Strait of Georgia, begin your entry near lighted bell buoy U41. South of the buoy, pick up the range on Race Point and Virago Point. Follow that range into Porlier Pass, to clear the rocks that extend from the northeast tip of Galiano Island. Once clear of the rocks, you can turn to follow a mid-channel course between Virago Rock and Galiano Island. Charts 3442 and 3443 show the range and the rocks to be avoided on both sides, but the larger scale chart 3473 really helps understanding. Chartbook 3313 (replaces strip charts 3310) also shows the pass in excellent detail. We recommend that you carry either chart 3473 or chartbook 3313.

De Courcy Group. Use chart 3443. The De Courcy Group has several interesting small anchorages. **Whaleboat Island**, just off the southeast shore of Ruxton Island, is a relatively undeveloped provincial park. The preferred anchorage is south of the island, taking care to avoid a drying rock. The north end of **Ruxton Island** has **Herring Bay**, one of the most attractive small anchorages in the northern Gulf Islands, and frequently used when the anchorage at Pirates Cove is overfull (which often it is in the summer).

Whaleboat Island Marine Park, just south of Ruxton Island. No facilities. Whaleboat Island is undeveloped, but provides limited alternate anchorage to Pirates Cove Marine Park. Use chart 3443.

Herring Bay. Use chart 3443, plans 3475. Herring Bay indents the northwest end of Ruxton Island, off Ruxton Passage. The bay is bordered by weather-sculpted sandstone walls, and has a beautiful sand beach on the southeast side. Good anchoring in 4 fathoms, much to explore by dinghy. Recommended.

④ **Pirates Cove Marine Park**. Use chart 3475 (larger scale, preferred) or 3443. Open all year, toilets, no other facilities. Pirates Cove is a lovely little harbor, protected from seas but not all winds, with room for many boats (on short scope). Iron rings for stern-ties are set into the beautiful sandstone cliffs that encircle the bay. There are two dinghy docks. Most of the land surrounding the cove is a provincial park, with walk-in campsites, hiking and walking trails, and picnicking. As you enter, the dock to starboard is private.

The entrance is guarded by a reef that extends parallel to the shoreline to a point a little beyond a concrete beacon. When entering, you *must* leave this beacon to port. A range, consisting of a white-painted arrow of the ground and a white vertical stripe on a tree,

Cove are locked shut, awaiting funds for restoration. A dock with room for several boats is in Conover Cove. Please respect the two private properties on the island.

Conover Cove. A reef lies directly offshore from the entrance to Conover Cove on Wallace Island, but the reef can be avoided by going around either end. Especially from the southeast, give the reef ample room. When you leave, remember the reef is there. We are told that each year boats depart at high tide and drive up on the rocks. A dock, with room for several boats, gives access to the island. Conover Cove is fairly shoal at the dock, and shoals even more toward both ends of the bay. Deeper draft vessels, check the tides. You can anchor and stern-tie to rings set in the rocks on shore. Be sure to check your depths. The entrance to Conover Cove is shallow at low tide.

Princess Cove. Princess Cove lies just northwest of Covover Cove, and has room for quite a few boats to anchor. Mooring eyes, now marked with yellow painted arrows, are installed in the rock along the Princess Cove shoreline for stern-ties. At low tide you have to be part mountain goat to get to several of those eyes. Set the anchor carefully in 3-4 fathoms (deeper toward the mouth of the cove), and maintain an anchor watch if the wind comes up. While the sides of the cove are steep, a beach at the head makes dinghy landing easy.

Panther Point. Panther Point is the southeast tip of Wallace Island. There's room for 1 or perhaps 2 boats in 5-6 fathoms just inside

the mouth of the cove it forms, but if you anchor any farther inside, a rock on the north side will restrict your swing. The anchorage is exposed to southeast winds, but protected from other winds.

Retreat Cove. Use chart 3442. Retreat Cove, a lovely small notch protected by Retreat Island, indents Galiano Island across Trincomali Channel from the Secretaries. Enter only from the south. The approach around the north side of Retreat Island is shallow and foul with rocks and reefs. The head of Retreat Cove shelves sharply. There's room to anchor in 3-4 fathoms, but plan your swing to avoid the shelf. A 75-foot public dock, no facilities, is on the southern shore of the cove. Local boats take much of the space on the dock.

North Galiano. Use chart 3442 or 3443. North Galiano has anchorage and a small public dock, no facilities. A well-stocked store is up the road from the dock.

Dionisio Point Park. Use chart 3473 (larger scale, preferred) or 3442 or 3443. Open all year, day use and overnight camping, toilets, no power, no showers. Anchor only. The park overlooks Porlier Pass. It has sandy beaches, rocky headlands and forested uplands.

Porlier Pass. Use chart 3473 (larger scale, preferred) or 3442 or 3443. Porlier Pass separates Galiano Island and Valdes Island. Several times a year, currents on large tides will

See area map page 132

shows where to make your approach. Align the stripe on the tree above the arrow on the ground, and proceed slowly until just past the concrete beacon to port. Then turn sharply to port and leave the red buoy U38 to starboard. The entry is shallow. At lower tides deep-draft boats should be especially cautious.

Pirates Cove has only a fair holding bottom of sticky mud. If the wind comes up during the night, you can expect a fire drill as boats drag anchor. When departure time arrives, be prepared to spend extra time cleaning the anchor as it comes aboard. The Waggoner boat *Surprise* has an anchor washdown system, and it earns its keep in Pirates Cove.

On Ruxton Passage, the little notch at the south end of De Courcy Island is also part of this park, and has mooring buoys. Additional anchorage is available at Whaleboat Island Marine Park, nearby. Another "Pirates Cove overflow" notch is just north of Pirates Cove off Link Island.

Boat Harbour. Use chart 3443. Boat Harbour, across Stuart Channel from the De Courcy Group, used to be home to a man named Ken Kendall, who looked and dressed like a pirate, and sometimes fired a brass cannon to herald your arrival in his lair. The actor John Wayne was a regular visitor. Alas, Kendall died some years ago. Beth Hill writes engagingly of him in her book *Seven-Knot Summers*.

At **Kenary Cove** in Boat Harbour, Julian Matson runs Boat Harbour Marine Ltd., a boatbuilding and repair shop. Julian Matson worked with Kendall before Kendall's death, and recalls that Kendall was brilliant and creative, an engineer by training, with a fondness for explosives. Kendall made cannons, but also set off some blasts just for the fun of seeing them go. Kenary Cove is a blending of Ken and Mary, Mary being one of Kendall's wives. Kenary is pronounced "Canary," like the bird. The cove is almost fully occupied by mooring buoys, and has little room to anchor. The marina in the cove is private.

Silva Bay Marina has extensive docks, a pub and fine restaurant ashore, and haulout.

GABRIOLA PASSAGE TO NANAIMO

There are three routes north out of the Gulf Islands: Gabriola Passage, Dodd Narrows, and False Narrows. False Narrows is so tricky that for most boats it's not a viable choice.

Gabriola Passage. Use chart 3475 (larger scale, preferred) or 3443. Gabriola Passage (Gabriola is pronounced "Gay-briola") is the northernmost entrance to the Gulf Islands from the Strait of Georgia. From Bowen Island on the east side of the strait, it is 14 miles to Gabriola Passage, the shortest crossing between the lower mainland and the islands. The B.C. *Small Craft Guide* recommends that mariners avoid an afternoon crossing in the summertime, when winds can create rough conditions on the west side of the Strait. Instead, an early morning crossing is recommended, or a crossing in late afternoon or early evening, after the afternoon wind has died.

Tidal currents at springs can run to 8 knots in Gabriola Passage, both flood and ebb. Typical maximum currents are around 4 knots, so transiting is best at slacks. The current in Gabriola Passage sets east on the flood and west on the ebb. Times of slacks and maximum cur-

rents are given in the Tide and Current Tables, Vol. 5.

Degnen Bay. Use chart 3475 (larger scale, preferred) or 3443. If you take Gabriola Passage you will pass Degnen Bay, a good anchorage but a little crowded with boats on moorings. If you go into Degnen Bay, favor the east side, close to Josef Point, to avoid rocks in the middle of the entrance. An Indian petroglyph of a killer whale is on a slab of rock near the head of the bay. A public dock provides access to Gabriola Island.

Degnen Bay Public Wharf. Has 190 feet of dock space, power, garbage collection, telephone, but no other facilities. Commercial fishing vessels have priority.

Wakes Cove. Use chart 3475 (larger scale, preferred) or 3443. Wakes Cove, on Gabriola Passage at the north end of Valdes Island, is a safe anchorage, but open to northwest winds and to the wash of boats in the pass.

Kendrick Island. Use chart 3475 (larger scale, preferred) or 3443. Kendrick Island, on the south side of Gabriola Passage at the east entrance, creates a narrow and shallow bay, known locally as **Dogfish Bay**. Dogfish Bay is well protected and the holding ground is good. West Vancouver Yacht Club has an outstation on Kendrick Island.

Flat Top Islands. Use chart 3475 (larger scale, preferred) or 3443. The Flat Top Islands are appropriately named, and from the north or east they're a little hard to tell apart. If approaching from the Strait of Georgia, pass on the north side of **Thrasher Rock Light**. The light marks the northern end of Gabriola Reefs. All the Flat Top Islands are privately owned.

Silva Bay. Use chart 3475 (larger scale, preferred) or 3443. Silva Bay is a popular destination in the Flat Top Islands, well protected, with good holding bottom. From the north, entry can be made behind Vance Island; from the south, between Gabriola Island and Sear Island. Many boats, however, go through Commodore Passage, between Acorn Island and Tugboat Island. They enter Silva Bay between

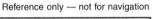

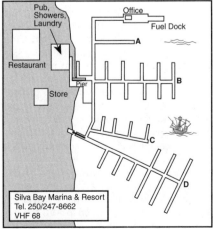

Silva Bay Resort and Marina

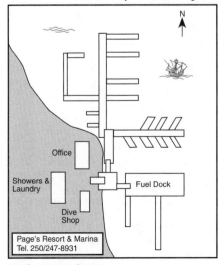

Page's Resort and Marina

Tugboat Island and Vance Island. In this passage lies the notorious *Shipyard Rock*, on the south side of the channel.

When entering, give the beacon that marks Shipyard Rock a wide berth to port, and *do not turn at once for the Silva Bay floats or other facilities*. Shipyard Rock is larger than it appears on the charts. Continue instead until about halfway to Law Point before making your turn. A buoy now marks the inner end of Shipyard Rock, but give the rock plenty of room anyway. Royal Vancouver Yacht Club has an outstation on Tugboat Island.

Silva Bay has gone through rough times in the past, with the boatyard and Silva Bay Resort closed for a couple of years. In 1995, however, Sterling Resorts bought the Silva Bay Marina & Resort and is in the process of making it a good marine destination.

⑤ **Silva Bay Boatel & Store**, RR#2, Site 33-C2, Gabriola, B.C. V0R 1X0, (250)247-9351. Open all year, 600 feet of dock space, 4 feet of depth, no big sailboats. Facilities include 15 amp power, washrooms, laundromat, no showers. More suited to the smaller boats. The store has groceries, fishing tackle and licenses.

⑤ **Silva Bay Marina & Resort (Sterling Resorts)**, RR #2, Site 31, Comp. 2, Gabriola, B.C. V0R 1X0, (250)247-9992; fax (250)247-8663. Monitors VHF channel 68. Open all year with guest moorage. Facilities include 15

& 30 amp power, washrooms, showers, laundry, swimming pool, tennis courts, mountain bikes, marine ways for larger boats and Travelift for boats to approximately 7 tons. Quality dining at Latitudes, their upscale restaurant. Reservations recommended. There is also the Bitter End Pub (good food) and a dive shop with air. In 1997 a large deck was added, and it has been quite popular. Daily flights to Vancouver aboard Pacific Spirit Air. *(Marina map page 134)*

⑤ **Page's Resort & Marina**, RR#2, C-1, Site 30, Gabriola Island, B.C. V0R 1X0, (250)247-8931. Or view at www.island.net/~.tpreeve/index.htm. Open all year, gasoline and diesel, guest moorage in 10 slips and along the dock. Facilities include 15 amp power, washrooms, showers, laundry. Cottages for rent in addition to moorage. The store has interesting books and charts; the dive shop has an air refill station. Short walk to grocery store, cab service available. Ted and Phyllis Reeve are the owners.

For those who love music, the arts and literature, Page's is the most compelling stop on the coast. Concerts and recitals are held in Ted and Phyllis Reeve's home, on the other side of the wall from the office. On one visit, we heard a lovely soprano voice rehearsing for a recital. Quality musicians perform all year long at Page's. Excellent art is on the walls. *(Marina map page 134)*

Drumberg Provincial Park, south end of Gabriola Island. Use chart 3475 (larger scale, preferred) or 3443. Open all year, day use only, toilets, no other facilities. Overlooks Gabriola Passage. Has shelving sandstone rocks and a small sandy beach.

False Narrows. Use chart 3475 (larger scale, preferred) or 3443. False Narrows lies east of Dodd Narrows, and offers an alternate but risky connection between the Gulf Islands and Northumberland Channel. If you choose to go by way of False Narrows, you will be traveling between reefs in a shallow channel that is best used at half tide or better. Maximum currents in False Narrows are about half what they are in Dodd Narrows, which is about

GABRIOLA ISLAND
250) 247-8931
tpreeve@island.net

See area map page 132

the only reason for going this way.

Dodd Narrows. Use chart 3475 (larger scale, preferred) or 3443. Dodd Narrows has tidal currents to 9 knots as the water swirls through the narrow but deep passage between rock cliffs. The narrows are best taken at slack water. For the hour or so before the predicted turn, boats collect at each end waiting for the right time. These boats include commercial craft, even tugboats with tows of logs, so the period around slack water can get pretty exciting. Generally, the boats on the upstream side will go first, as they catch the last of the dying fair current. When they are through, the boats on the other end will go through, picking up the beginnings of the new (for them) fair current. It all works well as long as no one gets pushy.

Northumberland Channel. Use chart 3458 (larger scale, preferred) or 3443. Northumberland Channel is the road from the Gulf Islands to Nanaimo. It starts at False Narrows and runs northwest between Gabriola Island and Vancouver Island. Northumberland Channel exits in the Gulf of Georgia, or, at Jack Point, makes the turn to Nanaimo. Because of considerable log boom towing in the area, watch for floating debris. Trust us, the debris is there. If you are not yet ready for civilization, you might lie over at **Pilot Bay,** on the north end of Gabriola Island. It's a good anchorage in a southeasterly, but appears to be

*From Newcastle Island.
The evening view of Nanaimo is beautiful.*

somewhat open to northwesterlies. *Proposed No Discharge Zone. Gray water okay. See p. 15.* Gabriola Sands Park is at the head of the bay.

Gabriola Sands Park, north end of Gabriola Island. Use chart 3458 (larger scale, preferred) or 3443. Open all year, day use only, toilets, no other facilities. This park fronts on Taylor Bay and Pilot Bay. It has a sandy swimming area and a playfield. Good for kids.

Sandwell Park, northeast side of Gabriola Island. Use chart 3458 (larger scale, preferred) or 3443. Open all year, day use only, toilets but no other facilities. This is a small sea-front park with a sandy beach and forested uplands.

Nanaimo. Use chart 3457 & 3458 (both larger scale, preferred) or 3443. As you pass Jack Point the city of Nanaimo opens up. Head for the prominent highrise condominium building, easily seen from Jack Point. The harbor

Margaret Harvey has been selling fresh fish at the Nanaimo dock for more than a decade.

is wide, and protected from the Strait of Georgia by Protection Island and Newcastle Island. The Nanaimo Port Authority public marina is located at the south end of the business district near Nanaimo's famous bastion (block-house), with access to downtown Nanaimo. A Thrifty Foods supermarket and ATM are in the shopping mall near the public marina.

Canada Customs and moorages for float planes are just north of the public marina. Other moorages, including the Nanaimo Yacht Club and the new Townsite Marina, are in Newcastle Island Passage, the channel that leads behind Newcastle Island to Departure Bay. The Nanaimo Yacht Club has guest moorage for visiting members of reciprocal clubs.

Newcastle Island Passage is posted for "No-Wake" speeds, and the harbor patrol enforces the speed limit. Oregon Rock, marked by a beacon, lies in the channel. Pass between the rock and Newcastle Island. Fuel docks and repair facilities capable of handling any needed job are located along the channel.

Nanaimo is the natural point of departure for boats headed across the Strait of Georgia or north to Campbell River or Desolation Sound and beyond. It is the second largest city (behind Victoria) on Vancouver Island, and filled with surprises. Shops of all kinds line the narrow, winding streets. Just about any needed supplies and repairs are readily available. The small but beautifully-done Centennial Museum features a lifelike reproduction of a coal mine. A winding promenade takes walkers and joggers along the waterfront. A casino, the only one on Vancouver Island, is within an easy walk.

Dining: Katerina's Place has wonderful Mediterranean dinners. And the Wesley Street Restaurant is just plain superb.

⑥ **Nanaimo Port Authority**, P.O. Box 131, 104 Front Street, Nanaimo, B.C. V9R 5K4, (250)754-5053; fax (250)753-4899. Monitors VHF channel 67. Open year-round for visiting pleasure craft. In winter many commercial fishing vessels are in the basin, but pleasure craft moorage is available. Water at selected docks in the winter. Gasoline and diesel at the fuel dock.

A new floating breakwater dock has been installed in the center of the marina entrance, and the Eco Barge for pumpout and portapotty dump is adjacent to this dock. Arriving and departing vessels must pass south of the floating breakwater dock. The northern entrance is reserved for aircraft. *(Marina map this page)*

Marina facilities include 9000 feet of dock space, 15, 30, 50 & 100 amp power, washrooms, showers, laundry, waste oil disposal, 1000 pound hydraulic crane. Customs clearance available. Three hours of moorage no charge; charges assessed thereafter.

The public boat basin has room for most summer crowds, although it is wise to arrive early rather than late. During the summer, all the docks except F dock are open on a non-reserved basis for pleasure craft. Reservations are taken for the 600-foot breakwater pier and the Cameron Island floats, which give good inside protection for larger boats. During July and August call (250)755-1216.

The basin can hold 250-300 boats at a time. Summertime turnover averages about 100 boats a day. Rafting is permitted. In summer, dock assistants can help you tie up. Most days, fresh fish is for sale at the dock. Theaters, walkway, tennis courts, golf nearby. Adjacent seaplane terminal. All of the Nanaimo commercial district is at hand.

⑥ **Petro Canada Marine**, P.O. Box 938, Nanaimo, B.C. V9R 5M2, (250)754-7828. Open all year, gasoline and diesel at the fuel dock. Lubricants, accessories, and snacks. At the end of "E" dock.

⑥ **Nanaimo Yacht Club**, 400 Newcastle Ave, Nanaimo, B.C. V9S 4J1, (250)754-7011. Open all year, 15 amp power, washrooms, showers, laundry, customs clearance available. Moorage is for members of reciprocal yacht clubs only.

⑥ **Townsite Marina,** 20 Townsite Rd., Nanaimo, B.C. V9S 5T7, (250)716-8801; fax (250)716-7288. Monitors VHF channel 73. Docks have 30 & 50 amp power, washrooms, showers, locked gates, nighttime security patrol. Limited guest moorage. This is a new marina, located immediately north of the Nanaimo Yacht Club. The slips are aligned

Reference only — not for navigation

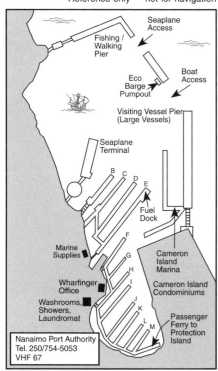

Seaplane Access

Fishing / Walking Pier

Eco Barge Pumpout

Boat Access

Visiting Vessel Pier (Large Vessels)

Seaplane Terminal

B C
D
E
Fuel Dock
F
Marine Supplies
G
Cameron Island Marina
H
I
Cameron Island Condominiums
J
Wharfinger Office
K
Washrooms, Showers, Laundromat
L
M
Passenger Ferry to Protection Island

Nanaimo Port Authority
Tel. 250/754-5053
VHF 67

Nanaimo Port Authority

See area map page 132

parallel with the channel, making landings easier in the prevailing winds. Menno Jongsma is the manager.

⑥ **Moby Dick Boatel**, 1000 Stewart Ave., Nanaimo, B.C. V9S 4C9, (250)753-7111; (800)663-2116. Open all year, 20 amp power, no washrooms, no showers. The marina can hold about 60 boats, but the slips fill up April through October, so there's not much left for transients. Phone ahead for availability.

⑥ **Stone's Marina and RV Park**, 1690 Stewart Ave., Nanaimo, B.C. V9S 4E6, (250)753-4232; e-mail stonesmarine@ home.com. Open all year, 30 amp power, washrooms, showers, laundry, customs clearance available. This is an RV park and campground with a 260-berth marina. Call ahead for availability. The complex has two marine pubs and a coffee shop that serve food, with 500 feet of guest moorage. Extended term tow vehicle and trailer storage is available.

⑥ **Brechin Point Marina**, P.O. Box 178, 2000 Zorkin, Nanaimo, B.C. V9R 5K9, (250)753-6122; fax (250)753-9378; e-mail landahl@island.net. Open all year, gasoline and diesel at fuel dock, washrooms, no power, no showers. They have a 200-foot dock for temporary moorage. Also carry aviation fuel and jet-B fuel, 50:1 mix, kerosene, propane, stove alcohol. Customs clearance point. Located at the north end of Newcastle Channel, close to Departure Bay and ferries to Vancouver and Tsawwassen.

⑥ **Newcastle Marina**, 1300 Stewart Ave., Nanaimo, B.C. V9S 4E1, (250)753-1431; fax (250)753-2974; e-mail nmarina@nanaimo. ark.com. Open all year, guest moorage in un-

Newcastle Island has been a holiday destination since the Indians used it in the summers. Today it is an exceptional provincial park.

Marilynn Hale peers into the hole left by pulpstone quarry work on Newcastle Island.

occupied slips when available, 42-foot maximum boat length. Facilities include 15 amp power, washrooms, showers, laundry, 60 ton Travelift, drydock, repairs. *(Marina map this page)*

⑥ **Anchorage Marina**, 1520 Stewart Ave., Nanaimo, B.C. V9S 4E1, (250)754-5585. Open all year, guest moorage in approximately 10 slips, 20 & 30 amp power, washrooms. The store carries marine hardware, accessories, boats and motors, charts, books, fishing tackle and licenses. Restaurants, pub within walking distance. Located ½ mile from

Nanaimo, halfway along Newcastle Channel.

⑥ **Nanaimo Harbour City Marina**, 1250 Stewart Ave. Nanaimo, B.C. V9S 4C9, (250)754-2732; fax (250)754-7140. Open all year, limited moorage available, 20 amp power, washrooms, showers. Call ahead by phone to check availability. They have a full-service boatyard with a 40-ton Travelift and brokerage. *(Marina map this page)*

⑥ **Nanaimo Shipyard**, 1040 Stewart Ave., Nanaimo, B.C. V9S 4C9, (250)753-1151, 753-

Reference only — not for navigation

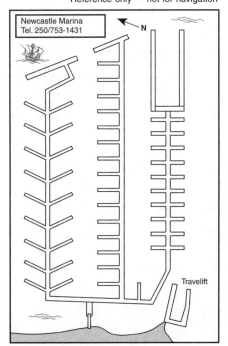

Newcastle Marina
Tel. 250/753-1431

N

Travelift

Newcastle Marina

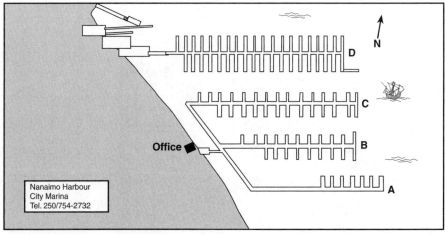

Nanaimo Harbour
City Marina
Tel. 250/754-2732

Office

D

N

C

B

A

Nanaimo Harbour City Marina

Reference only — not for navigation

1244; fax (250)753-2235. Open all year, guest moorage in unoccupied slips, 20 & 30 amp power, washrooms, customs clearance available. Full service shipyard. Moorage usually no problem in summer, but larger boats should call ahead. Right on the channel, look for blue and white striped shed at the end of the dock.

Dinghy Dock Pub, Nanaimo, B.C. V9R 5M2, (250)753-2373. Monitors VHF channel 18. Temporary moorage only, no charge while dining. If you are anchored out nearby, call on VHF channel 18, ask for "Dinghy Dock." A shuttle will pick you up and bring you to the pub. They serve lunch and dinner, and have showers and a laundry facility at the pub. Located across from Nanaimo Harbour, at Protection Island.

⑦ **Newcastle Island Marine Park.** Open all year, visitor moorage at 1500 feet of dock space, washrooms and showers, no power. Several small bays. Beaches and playing fields. Many hiking trails. Walk-in campsites and picnic areas. In summer a passenger ferry connects the island with Nanaimo. The Pavilion houses a dance floor, a restaurant & snack bar, a visitor's center, and interpretive displays on the natural and human history of the area. Perfect for families.

This is an extraordinary park. Before the white men came, Newcastle Island was a summer campsite for Indians. Since the white men came it has supported a shipyard and been mined for coal. In the early 1870s it was quarried for sandstone that built the San Francisco Mint. Between 1923 and 1932 its sandstone was quarried for pulpstones, giant cylinders that ground wood into pulp for paper making. Before WWII, Japanese fishermen ran herring salteries here. And always, Newcastle Island has been a popular holiday spot.

On its 750 acres Newcastle Island has a small lake, miles of trails, play areas, campsites for individual campers, fields for group camping, and relics of its rich history. The 1931 pavilion charms. The pulpstone quarry astonishes. The bays and beaches intrigue. We enjoy this park.

You might see rare albino raccoons, and dozens of bunny rabbits. Arrive early enough to get literature from the visitor center. Try to spend the night. We anchor between Newcastle Island and Protection Island. The lights of Nanaimo are beautiful.

Petroglyph Park, a few miles south of Naniamo on the Island Highway—take a taxi or bus. The park contains rock carvings created hundreds and thousands of years ago. Both original petroglyphs and castings can be seen. You may take rubbings of the castings.

**Tell Them You Read
About Them
In the Waggoner.**

Naming Names

THE EARLY EXPLORERS got to name all the important places after themselves (Vancouver Island), officers on board (Puget Sound), or important friends back home (Mount Rainier). Many other places were given names adopted from the Indians (Stillaguamish River), or perhaps the first homesteader (Ebey Island). But we found we could name the less prominent places ourselves.

We were cruising in Desolation Sound with two youngsters on board, both named Michael. One was our son, Michael George. The other was Michael Edward Lust, the son of our neighbors across the back alley. With two Mikes on board, we quickly adopted the device of calling them by their middle names.

One day we dinghied to a little rock islet in Malaspina Inlet, and later tried to identify the islet on the chart. We found it didn't have a name. It quickly became George's Rock. The next place we discovered without a name became Edward's Point. In rapid succession over the next few days we discovered, named and officially entered on the chart such places as King Edward Bay, Prince George's Islet, Edward George Point, and George Edward's Reef, among many others.

Soon the kids were poring over the chart and discovering other places to name. Of course, we had to land on each rock or beach and officially declare its name, and then ceremoniously enter the name on the chart. Officialdom never recognized our efforts, so our names don't appear on anybody else's charts. But we decided that as explorers we had just as much right to name places as Capt. George Vancouver did. Those names still appear on an old, wrinkled, coffee-stained chart that lives in the bottom of the chart drawer.

—Tom Kincaid

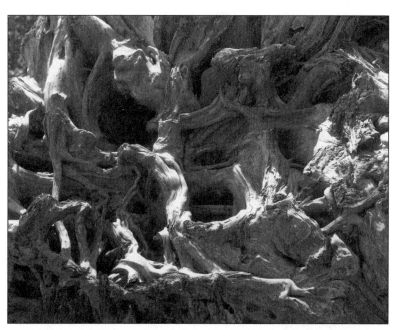

In 1999 we crossed paths several times with Larry and Sue Kopel aboard their Pearson 39 sailboat PICES. *Larry is an accomplished photographer, and we were attracted to this art photo of twisted roots, found in the Gulf Islands. We reproduce it with his permission.*

National Défense
Defence nationale

NOTICE

CANADIAN FORCES MARITIME EXPERIMENTAL AND TEST RANGES

The Canadian Forces Maritime Experimental and Test Ranges tests ship and aircraft systems and torpedoes. Torpedoes may be launched by a surface vessel, submarine, or aircraft. No explosives are used; however, a hazard exists due to the possibility of the torpedo homing on vessels and then the vessel being struck by the torpedo on its way to the surface.

Testing is usually carried out from 0800–1730 Tuesday to Friday and occasionally on Monday or Saturday.

During testing Area "WG" is "Active". Any vessel within the area bounded by the following coordinates:

a. 49°21'00"N 123°48'24"W;
b. 49°14'50"N 123°48'24"W;
c. 49°16'45"N 124°00'54"W;
d. 49°19'21"N 124°07'42"W; and
e. 49°21'21"N 124°07'42"W

will be required to clear or stop on demand from the Canadian Range Officer at "Winchelsea Island Control" or any of the range vessels or range helicopter. The positions of these coordinates are clearly marked on the diagram.

A transit area 1,000 yards north of Winchelsea Island and 1,000 yards east of South Ballenas Island has been established to enable mariners to transit safely around the active area. It also facilitates unimepeded access to marina facilities in Schooner Cove and Nanoose Bay. This area is clearly depicted on charts 3512 and 3459 by means of pecked lines.

Additional information on active hours or for safe transit through the area may be obtained from:

a. Winchelsea Island Control (250)756-5080 or (250)468-5080 (next day's activity only);
b. CFMETR Range Officer (250)756-5002 or (250)468-5002 (long range planning);
c. Winchelsea Island Control VHF CH 10 or 16 (for safe transit area information when approaching area "WG");
d. VHF 21B or Weather 3 (listen only, for active times), or
e. CB channel 9.

Area "WG" constitutes a "Defence Establishment" as defined in the National Defence Act to which the Defence Controlled Access Area Regulations apply. Vessels which do not comply with direction from either Winchelsea Control or Range Patrol Vessels may be charged for trespassing.

Range vessels exhibit a flashing red light in addition to the prescribed lights and shapes. These vessels may operate outside of scheduled hours and should not be approached within 3,000 yards because they may be in a three-point moor with mooring lines extending to buoys 1,500 yards away. Additionally, lit as well as unlit mooring buoys are randomly located within the area and mariners are advised to use caution when transitting this area.

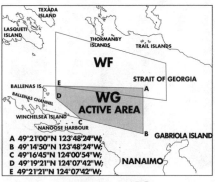

A 49°21'00"N 123°48'24"W;
B 49°14'50"N 123°48'24"W;
C 49°16'45"N 124°00'54"W;
D 49°19'21"N 124°07'42"W;
E 49°21'21"N 124°07'42"W;

Canada

The Strait of Georgia

THE STRAIT OF GEORGIA is not to be trifled with. It's a big body of water, 110 miles long and 15-20 miles wide. Pleasure craft cross the strait all the time, but the locals know better than to go out when the wind is blowing. They are especially careful when wind blows against current.

When conditions are right, the strait need not be intimidating. The "typical" summertime fair weather wind pattern calls for calm mornings followed by a rising northwesterly sea breeze by early afternoon. By mid-afternoon the sea breeze can be 20-25 knots. In the evening the wind dies down. We have crossed early in the morning and in the evening and had no problems.

Frequently, though, the typical pattern doesn't hold. If a weak frontal system passes over the area, the higher pressure behind the front will produce northwesterlies of 20-25 knots. These winds can blow around the clock for three days or even longer, essentially closing the Strait to small craft.

Summer afternoon winds known as Qualicums can blow as hard as 40 knots between Qualicum Beach and False Bay, at the northern tip of Lasqueti Island. When wind opposes current in Sabine Channel, between Lasqueti Island and Texada Island, 8-foot seas can result. Malaspina Strait, off Cape Cockburn and Grief Point, can be rough, especially when wind is against current. Currents from Howe Sound and Burrard Inlet meet off Point Atkinson, and create rough seas. Wind makes them worse.

When the wind is up it produces a difficult 4-5 foot chop—sometimes higher—in the middle of the strait away from land influences. These aren't long, lazy ocean swells. Strait of Georgia seas are steep and close together. A well-handled boat often can run with these seas, but taken on the bow or beam they are no fun at all. As noted above, dangerous 8-foot seas are not unknown, especially off points or in channels where mountains funnel and accelerate the wind.

Even in calm conditions, you will find tide-rips off many of the points, and wherever passes or channels join the strait. When the current flows out of a pass or inlet into the strait, confusion results. Add wind, and big confusion results. While the ebb current flows from inlets into the strait, note that it is the *flood* current that flows out of the Gulf Islands into the strait. At the eastern mouths of Active Pass, Porlier Pass and Gabriola Pass, look for rough seas on the flood, especially when the wind is blowing.

WE LIST THESE CAUTIONS not to frighten the reader but to inform him. Weather patterns do exist and the bad spots are known. The skipper who monitors the VHF Continuous Marine Broadcast will gather a sense of what is happening, where it is happening, and *why* it is happening. Go and no-go decisions get easier.

—*Robert Hale*

Nanoose Harbour to Texada Island
Lasqueti Island

Schooner Cove • French Creek • Denman Island • Hornby Island
Comox • Oyster River • False Bay • Squitty Bay

Charts

3311	SMALL CRAFT CHARTS (strip charts) Sunshine Coast to Desolation Sound
3312	SMALL CRAFT CHART (chartbook) Jervis Inlet & Desolation Sound
3443	Thetis Island to Nanaimo (1:40:000)
3457	Nanaimo Harbour & Departure Bay (1:8,000)
3458	Approaches to Nanaimo Harbour (1:20,000)
3459	Approaches to Nanoose Harbour (1:15,000)
3512	Strait of Georgia, Central Portion (1:80,000)
3513	Strait of Georgia, Northern Portion (1:80,000)
3527	Baynes Sound (1:40,000); Comox Harbour (1:15,000)
3536	PLANS – Strait of Georgia (various)

Whiskey Golf. Use chart 3512. Boats headed north from Nanaimo are at once faced by the notorious "Whiskey Golf" (WG) restricted area. Whiskey Golf is a deepwater range operated by the Canadian and U.S. Navies, and is used to test torpedoes (always unarmed) and various ships' systems. The area consists of a network of underwater sensing devices joined by cables to a control site on Winchelsea Island. Torpedoes are fired from range vessels along a predetermined course; they are tracked from the Winchelsea control center. After the run the torpedoes are recovered, either by a helicopter or range vessels. Unauthorized craft are not permitted in the area while the range is in operation.

When the range operates, normally it will be Mondays through Fridays, sometimes Saturdays, from 0700 to 1730. Winchelsea Range Control monitors VHF channels 16 and 10, and should be contacted before attempting to enter the area. In addition, The Continuous Marine Broadcast, Comox Coast Guard radio, Vancouver traffic, and CB Channel 09 carry notices. These notices are broadcast only when the range is operating or scheduled to be operating. In the absence of any notices, you can cross the range safely.

The Whiskey Golf restricted area lies on the direct course across the Strait of Georgia from Nanaimo to Secret Cove, Smugglers Cove, Pender Harbour, and other destinations along the Sunshine Coast.

The Canadian Navy has established a safe transit route along the edges of the restricted area while the range is in use. After clearing Nanaimo Harbour or Departure Bay (being careful to avoid Hudson Rocks and Five Finger Island), head directly for the Winchelsea Islands, passing to the east of the islands within 1000 yards. Turn to pass east of the Ballenas Islands within 1000 yards. Once well past the Ballenas Islands, steer a course for your destination on the mainland side of the Strait, or northwest along the Vancouver Island side.

If your boat is equipped with Loran-C or GPS, you can use waypoints shown in our Weatherly Press sister publication, *Weatherly Waypoint Guide, Vol. 2: Gulf of Georgia,* to run a safe route past Whiskey Golf. Be aware that the waypoints shown in that book mark the corners of Whiskey Golf. You should steer a course to give those corners a clearance of a few hundred yards.

Nanoose Harbour. Use chart 3459 (larger scale, preferred) or 3512. Anchorage is good just inside the sandy spit on the south side of the entrance. The Snaw-Naw-As Marina, with moorage for visiting boats, is located at Fleet Point on the south shore, just inside the entrance. The 55-acre Arbutus Grove Provincial Park, on the south shore, houses a stand of old arbutus trees that is reputed to be the most spectacular on Vancouver Island. The docks and mooring buoys along the north shore are the base for Royal Canadian Navy and U.S. Navy vessels engaged in activity on the Winchelsea (Whiskey Golf) torpedo range.

① **Snaw-Naw-As Marina Ltd.,** 209 Mallard Way, Lantzville, B.C. V0R 2H0, (250)390-2616. Open all year, gasoline & diesel at fuel dock. Guest moorage is available, best to call ahead. Moorage has 15 & 30 amp power, washrooms, showers. Launch ramp, picnicking, camping. Snack bar open seasonally. Bait available. Shopping mall is 2 miles away.

② **Schooner Cove Resort & Marina,** 3521 Dolphin Dr., Nanoose Bay, B.C. V9P 9J7, (250)468-5364; (800)252-5404; fax (250) 468-5744, or view at www.fairwinds.bc.ca. Monitors VHF channel 73, winters monitors channel 16, switch to 73. Use chart 3459 (larger

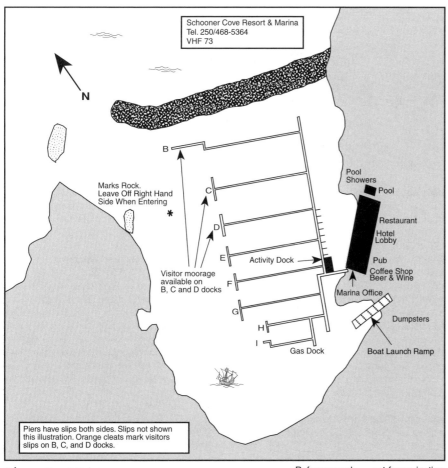

Schooner Cove Resort & Marina
Tel. 250/468-5364
VHF 73

N

B

Marks Rock.
Leave Off Right Hand
Side When Entering

*

C

D

E
Activity Dock

Visitor moorage
available on
B, C and D docks

F

G

H

I
Gas Dock

Pool
Showers
Pool

Restaurant
Hotel
Lobby

Pub
Coffee Shop
Beer & Wine

Marina Office

Dumpsters

Boat Launch Ramp

Piers have slips both sides. Slips not shown
this illustration. Orange cleats mark visitors
slips on B, C, and D docks.

Schooner Cove Marina

Reference only — not for navigation

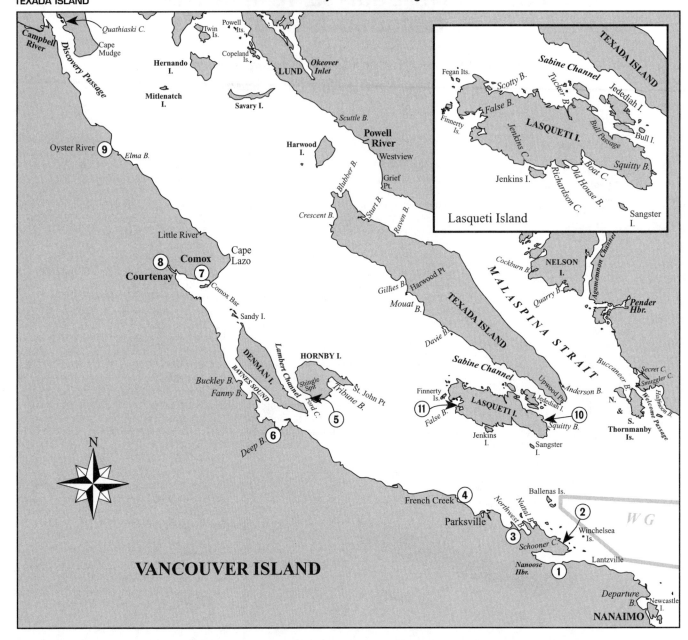

Lasqueti Island

VANCOUVER ISLAND

scale, preferred) or 3512. Schooner Cove is an outstanding marina resort, open all year, with gasoline at the fuel dock. Guest moorage is available, 15, 30 & 50 amp power, washrooms, showers, laundry, floating launch ramp, some repairs. Reservations recommended. Just inside the breakwater entrance, watch for a rock marked by a red buoy. Keep the buoy well to starboard when entering. The moorage fee includes use of the pool, hot tub, and tennis courts. A drop-in fee is charged for the fitness room. The marina has a hotel, a good restaurant and a friendly pub. The outstanding Fairwinds golf course is part of the resort. A courtesy shuttle takes you there. *(Marina map page 141)*

Nuttal Bay. Use chart 3459 (larger scale, preferred) or 3512. Nuttal Bay is exposed to northwesterly winds, but protected from southeasterly winds. Lacking local knowledge, the cautious entry would be to leave the Dorcas Rock

buoy to port. A fishing resort at the head of the bay has some facilities, but no floats or docks.

③ **Beachcomber Marina,** P.O. Box 21, Beachcomber RR 1, Nanoose Bay, B.C. V0R 2R0, (250)468-7222. Monitors VHF channel 16, switch to 68. Open all year in **Northwest Bay,** gasoline & diesel at fuel dock. Guest moorage, 15 & 30 amp power, washrooms, no showers. To enter the marina, pass between the green and red buoys. Do not pass between the green buoy and the end of the breakwater—a reef runs south from the breakwater. Watch for several drying and underwater rocks along the eastern shore.

Mistaken Island. Mistaken Island is privately owned and posted with No Trespassing signs.

Parksville. Use chart 3512. Parksville is an interesting town with a very nice beach, but

shoal water extends out some distance. Except for the marina at French Creek at the north end of Parksville, no facilities are available for boaters.

④ **French Creek Boat Harbour,** 1055 Lee Rd., Parksville, B.C. V9P 2E1, (250)248-5051; fax (250)248-5123. VHF is on scan. Use chart 3512. Open all year, gasoline & diesel at fuel dock. Waste oil disposal available. Marina has washrooms, shower, laundry. Power is 15 amp with 20 amp connectors. Groceries, restaurant, pub, marine supplies, launch ramp and haulout. Fish market sells fresh seafood. Commercial vessels have priority, but much room for pleasure craft is available July-September when the fleet is out.

French Creek is the only breakwater-protected harbor in the 25-mile stretch between Northwest Bay and Deep Bay. Enter through a dredged channel with a least depth of 2 fathoms. French Creek is the western terminus of the passenger ferry to Lasqueti Island. *(Marina map below)*

Hornby Island Use chart 3527 (larger scale, preferred) or 3513. Hornby Island has anchorages in Tribune Bay, at Ford Cove, and south of Shingle Spit (where a little ferry runs to Denman Island). Tribune Bay and Shingle Spit are exposed to southeast winds.

Tribune Bay. Use chart 3527 (larger scale, much preferred) or chart 3513. Tribune Bay is a wonderful place to visit and justifiably

Tribune Bay is large and open. Splendid sand beach; excellent park.

popular. Anchor offshore in 3-5 fathoms and dinghy in to a superb sand beach. Visit Tribune Bay Provincial Park. Take the 3-mile hike to Helliwell Provincial Park, on St. John Point. Tribune Bay has excellent protection from northwesterlies, but is open to the southeast. You'll bounce in a southeasterly. For a more private nook, check out the little cove near St. John Point. Anchor there in 3-5 fathoms. Neat spot.

Ford Cove. Use chart 3527 (larger scale, much preferred) or chart 3513. Some space may be available at the Ford Cove Marina or the public dock, but most boats anchor out. A green spar buoy marks the southern end of Maude Reef. You'll also see a floating breakwater. To enter Ford Cove, leave the green spar buoy and the floating breakwater to port, and the rock breakwater to starboard.

⑤ **Ford Cove Marina, Ltd.,** RR1, Hornby Is., B.C. V0R 1T0, (250)335-2169. Use chart 3527 (larger scale, much preferred) or 3513. Open all year, gasoline, diesel, lubricants. The fuel dock is the northernmost of the three docks. Groceries, fishing tackle and bait. Art gallery, cottages. No fresh water available. Good anchorage on rocky bottom. Most larger boats anchor out.

⑤ **Ford Cove Public Wharf.** Open all year, guest moorage available, 280 feet of dock space. Tidal grid. Waste oil disposal, garbage pickup, telephone.

Baynes Sound. Use chart 3527 (larger scale, much preferred) or 3513. Chart 3527 shows navigation aids not shown on chart 3513. These aids are buoys marking extensive shoals off Gartley Point, Union Point, Denman Point and Base Flat (Buckley Bay); two buoys near Re-

pulse Point; and two buoys marking the shoal off Mapleguard Point. Baynes Sound, a 12-mile-long refuge, is protected from the Strait of Georgia by Denman Island. A ferry to Denman Island crosses from Buckley Bay. Comox lies at the northern end of Baynes Sound, and Deep Bay at the southern end. The northern entry to Baynes Sound is across the Comox Bar, marked by buoys and a lighted range on the Vancouver Island shore. The southern entry is past Chrome Island.

⑥ **Deep Bay.** Use chart 3527 (larger scale, preferred) or 3513. Anchorage is good in Deep Bay, though in deeper water than most boaters like. The public wharf and floats are open all year, with 1130 feet of dock space, guest moorage available. Commercial vessels have priority. Garbage pickup, waste oil disposal, telephone, tidal grid, launch ramp. *Navigation note:* A considerable shoal extends into the mouth of Baynes Sound outside Deep Bay. The shoal, and shoaling along the shoreline of Denman Island, opposite, are marked by buoys that are shown on chart 3527 but not on chart 3513.

Fanny Bay. Use chart 3527 (larger scale, preferred) or 3513. Fanny Bay is primarily a camping area, but does have a small public mooring float. Gasoline is available at the float. A small freighter has been beached at Fanny Bay for many years.

Denman Island. Use chart 3527 (larger scale, preferred) or 3513. A public dock and float once were alongside the landing for the ferry that runs to Buckley Bay, on Vancouver Island, but they are gone. The Denman General Store, with groceries, post office, and liquor store, is a short distance from the ferry dock. The north end of Denman Island peters out into a long spit, dotted with small islands and rocks. One of these islands, Sandy Island, is a recent addition to the provincial park system.

Sandy Island Marine Park. Use chart 3527 (larger scale, preferred) or 3513. This park includes the Seal Islets, and is accessible only by boat. Anchor in Henry Bay, south of Longbeak Point. This beautiful park has pic-

Reference only — not for navigation

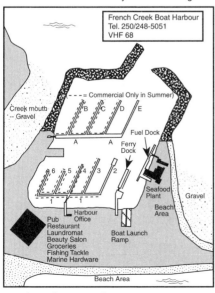

French Creek Boat Harbour
Tel. 250/248-5051
VHF 68

French Creek Boat Harbour

The Chrome Island lighthouse off the south end of Denman Island is a dramatic landmark.

Searching for the Bar

Several years ago my then-teenage daughter and I were coming south along the Vancouver Island side from Desolation Sound. A southeast gale was blowing, with flying haze that obscured the shoreline. I had just about given up trying to find the outer buoy to the channel across Comox Bar and was prepared to jog offshore all night, when a small Canadian troller passed me close aboard, and almost immediately turned west onto the heading (222 degrees true) of the channel. Feeling lucky to have local knowledge so close at hand, I immediately followed him, and eventually wound up in Comox safe and sound, although thoroughly wet.

After getting secured, I walked up the dock where the troller was tied to thank its skipper for leading me in. "Hell," he said, "I bought this boat yesterday and have never been here before. I was totally lost, and just guessing where that damn bar was. But when I saw you turn right behind me, I figured I must be in the right place!"

The halt leading the blind.

—*Tom Kincaid*

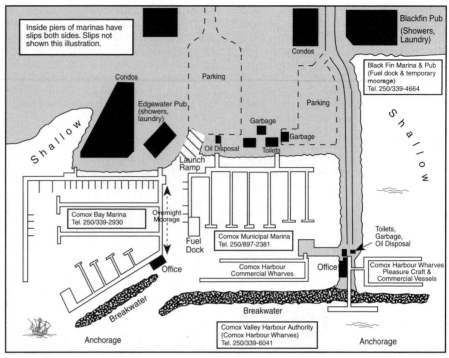

Comox Harbour

Reference only — not for navigation

nic areas, swimming, fishing, hiking trails and wilderness campsites. Sandy Island is a popular campsite for kayakers. At low tide it is possible to walk along the sandy spit all the way to its end—halfway to Comox.

Comox. Use chart 3527 (larger scale, preferred) or 3513. If you plan to go to Comox, we strongly urge that you have Chart 3527 (1:40,000), with its inset (1:15,000) of Comox Harbour and the Courtenay River up to the Lewis Bridge. Chart 3527 shows the various ranges and other navigation aids in excellent detail, and could save you from much uncertainty. Comox is a busy little city, with a population of 8,000 and a breakwater-protected marina. The Coast Guard base that covers the northern Strait of Georgia is located at nearby Goose Point.

From Baynes Sound the entrance to Comox is well marked, but be careful of drying flats off Gartley Point and in the inner half of the bay. The Comox Harbour Authority floats (formerly the government dock) are entered around the east end of the breakwater.

The other marinas are reached by entering in the middle of the breakwater. The Comox Municipal Marina is to starboard as you enter, beyond the fuel dock. To port, the Comox Bay Marina has guest moorage.

You'll find showers and laundry at the

Edgewater Pub, located just above the Comox Bay Marina, and in the lower level of the Black Fin Pub, located on the far side of the beautiful park that borders the marina area. Both the Edgewater and Black Fin facilities are almost new. (We have used the Black Fin facilities and found them excellent.) Comox has good shopping, a delightful bookstore, and a number of restaurants. See the Crow's Nest for marine supplies, books, and charts. A hospital overlooks the bay. The town fathers have plans to make Comox into a first-class destination port, so there's a good chance future facilities will be even better.

Golf: The Comox Golf Club, a well-maintained, flat and fun 9-hole course, is within walking distance of the docks. (250)339-7272

Festival: The Filberg Festival, an arts, crafts, food and entertainment celebration, draws 20-25,000 visitors each year. It's held at Filberg Park, east of the public floats in Comox Harbour. Dates: July 30-August 2.

⑦ **Black Fin Marina & Pub,** 132 Port Augusta St., Comox, B.C. V9M 3N7, (250)339-4664. Monitors VHF channel 68. The marina has the fuel dock, with gasoline & diesel, and a few slips, 15 amp power. Open all year. The pub, located across the park, has washrooms and laundry facilities. As you approach, look for the Esso and Black Fin sign.

⑦ **Comox Municipal Marina,** 1809 Beaufort Avenue, Comox, B.C. V9M 1R9, (250)339-2202 (Town Hall); (250)897-2381 (caretaker). Permanent moorage only. Launch ramp, tidal grid, nearby washrooms.

⑦ **Comox Bay Marina,** 1805 Beaufort, Comox, B.C. V9M 1R9, (250)339-2930, monitors VHF channel 68. Open all year, guest

moorage available, please call ahead. One of their docks can handle the largest yachts, and often hosts 150-footers. Washrooms, showers, laundry, 15 & 30 amp power. A hydrolift at the marina can pull a boat out of the water for repairs. Look for the Edgewater Marine Pub & Grill, above the marina.

⑦ **Comox Valley Harbour Authority,** Box 1258, Comox, B.C. V9N 7Z8, (250)339-6041. Monitors VHF channel 68. Guest moorage available on 1400 feet of docks located around the east end of the Comox breakwater. Half the dock space is reserved for pleasure craft. The docks have 15 amp power, garbage pickup and waste oil disposal. This is a working waterfront dock, busy and interesting. Fresh seafood usually is available "off the boat" at the dock. They are working hard to make visiting pleasure boaters feel welcome and comfortable.

⑧ **Courtenay.** Use chart 3527. For a pleasant diversion, take the dinghy a short distance up the Courtenay River to the town of Courtenay. A dredged channel, marked by ranges, leads through the delta to the river mouth. The river is an interesting break from the saltwater experience out on the Strait of Georgia. Just before you reach the Lewis Bridge, the Courtenay Slough leads off to the right, with an extensive Comox Valley Harbour Authority dock paralleling the shore, and a restaurant near the head. The dock is for vessels with a draft of 4 feet or less, pleasure craft welcome, excellent security. Shopping and several restaurants are located within easy walking distance.

Museum: We highly recommend a visit to the Courtenay & District Museum, where you will see hung from the ceiling the 40-foot-

*Kayakers explore
the slough at
Courtenay.*

*Jump! Swimming at
Courtenay. Jumping from
the bridge no longer
is allowed.*

long skeletal reconstruction of an 80-million-year-old elasmosaur, excavated from the banks of the nearby Puntledge River. This is the most dramatic exhibit in an outstanding paleontological display. Some other things you will see are dinasaur footprints, a marine reptile that resembles a 33-foot-long alligator, and an ancient fish they call a "sabre-toothed salmon." We have toured this museum and were very impressed. Families with inquisitive children will be richly rewarded. There's much more than we can cover here, including fossile digging tours. Call for information, (250)334-3611.

Comox Bar. Use chart 3527 (larger scale, preferred) or 3513. While Chart 3513 (1:80,000) seems to show the passage across the Comox Bar, the larger-scale Chart 3527 (1:40,000) shows the buoys that will guide you across safely. *We urge you to use Chart 3527.* The Comox Bar nearly joins Denman Island and Cape Lazo, with a shallow channel (least depth 15 feet) through the bar. A lighted range, consisting of two white poles with vertical red stripes on them, is on the Vancouver Island shore. The range's lights are clearly visible at night, but during the day the range is hard to see. The lighted red bell buoy P54 marks the Strait of Georgia end of this channel. Red buoys P52 and P50 show the

course across the bar. Stay close to the south of each of these buoys.

Cape Lazo. Use chart 3513. Cape Lazo is marked by a lighthouse on a high cliff. Buoys PJ and PB, offshore, mark the edge of deep water. (In 1998, buoy PK, shown on chart 3513, was moved seaward about 0.25 mi. due east, and renamed PB.)

Somewhere just north of Cape Lazo is the point at which the tidal currents change direction and begin flooding south from the north end of Vancouver Island, rather than north from Victoria.

Little River. Use chart 3513. Little River, located 3 miles up-island from Cape Lazo, is the western terminus for the ferry to Westview/ Powell River. Marginal moorage for a few small craft can be found behind the ferry dock.

Oyster River. Use chart 3513. A channel, dredged annually and marked by piles, leads to the protected Pacific Playgounds Marina next to the mouth of the Oyster River.

⑨ **Pacific Playgrounds Resort,** 9082 Clarkson Drive, Black Creek, B.C. V9J 1B3, (250)337-5600. Open all year, gasoline and diesel at the fuel dock, 15 amp power, tidal grid, washrooms, showers, laundry. Marina is entered via a

dredged channel, least depth 4 feet at zero tide. The resort has a driving range, RV sites, mini-golf, and a 9-hole golf course. The store carries marine supplies and charts, bait and tackle, limited groceries.

LASQUETI ISLAND

Use chart 3312; 3512; 3513; 3536. Chartbook 3312 has an excellent chart (1:40,000) of Lasqueti Island, with harbor charts of Squitty Bay, Scottie Bay and False Bay. Recommended. Lasqueti Island is often overlooked by pleasure craft as they hurry across the strait between Nanaimo and the Sunshine Coast, or run along the Vancouver Island shore between Nanaimo and Campbell River. Lasqueti Island is beautiful. It has a number of good anchorages, and a small resort and grocery store at the village of Lasqueti, in False Bay at the northwest corner.

The south and west shores of Lasqueti Island are indented by a number of bays that invite anchorage. Along the south shore are Boat Cove, Old House Bay, Richardson Cove, and Jenkins Cove, all of which are somewhat open to southerlies, but offer good protection

from northerlies or in settled weather. This part of the Lasqueti shoreline is rugged and beautiful. On the southeast end is Squitty Bay—tiny, but with a public float. Several little dogholes for anchoring can be found in Bull Passage. Little Bull Passage, between Jedediah Island and Bull Island, has a number of good anchorages in both ends. Little Bull Passage is passable for most boats. Other anchorages are available in Boho Bay, Tucker Bay, and Scottie Bay. Spring Bay is only partially protected from the north by a group of small islands offshore.

False Bay. Use chart 3536; chartbook 3312; 3513. False Bay is the major settlement on Lasqueti Island, with a public float with dock space and a float plane tie-up. The Lasqueti Island Hotel & Resort is at the head of the dock. A passenger-only ferry runs from False Bay to French Creek on Vancouver Island. Anchorage is possible off the public float, but the preferred anchorage is the north shore of the bay. On warm summer afternoons, strong winds, called Qualicums, can blow through False Bay and make anchoring unpleasant.

See area map page 142

⑪ **Lasqueti Island Hotel & Resort,** Lasqueti Island, B.C. V0R 2J0, (250)333-8846; fax (250) 333-8897. Open all year, gasoline and diesel at the fuel dock, washrooms, showers, store carries ice, groceries, tackle and bait. The hotel has a restaurant and lounge.

⑩ **Squitty Bay.** Use chartbook 3312 (much preferred) or 3512. Squitty Bay is a tiny, narrow and shallow notch at the southeast corner of Lasqueti Island. It would be harrowing to enter Squitty Bay in a roaring southeasterly, but at other times entry should be easy. Rocks border the north side of the entrance; favor the south side. The public dock, 150 feet long, may be largely occupied by local boats. Rafting is permitted. Ashore, the trees in this area are bent and broken, obviously by strong winds. Tall trees are rare. A walk along the roads is fascinating.

Squitty Bay can be tight, especially at low tide. Rafting may be necessary.

Bull Passage. Use chartbook 3312 (much preferred) or 3512. Bull Passage and the islands that lie off the south end of Jedediah Island are some of the most rugged and scenic on the coast. **Little Bull Passage**, between high rock cliffs, is narrow and beautiful. Watch for the charted rock on the Jedediah Island side. It hides at high tide. Our notes say, "The east end of Little Bull Passage is absolutely fabulous. So much variety and strength in the rock walls and islands. Worth a side trip just to see the sights."

Jedediah Island. Use chartbook 3312; chart 3512. Jedediah Island now is a marine park. We think, however, that it will not be overrun with visitors, because good anchorages are scarce. One of the best anchorages is in the little notch opposite the south end of Paul Island. Stern-ties to shore will be needed. The bay just south of the notch is usable, too. Long Bay goes dry a short distance inside the mouth.

One interesting spot is the steep-sided notch at the southeast end of Jedediah Island. The notch is narrow but protected. Its sheer walls will discourage much on-shore exploration, though.

TEXADA ISLAND

Use chart 3512; 3513; 3536. Texada Island

has three main anchorages: Anderson Bay on Malaspina Strait at the south end; Blubber Bay at the northern tip of the island; and Sturt Bay a couple of miles south along the Malaspina Strait (eastern) side. Although it has a ferry landing and public float, **Blubber Bay** is dominated by an enormous quarry, and is not inviting. Anchorage, if needed, is possible, though.

Anderson Bay. Use chart book 3312; strip chart 3311; chart 3512. Chart 3512 (1:80,000) is not our first choice, due to its small scale. Chart book 3312 or strip chart 3311 (both 1:40,000) are much better. Anderson Bay is located at the south end of Texada Island, on Malaspina Strait. It is a beautiful spot, lined with sheer rock walls. Anchor in 4 fathoms near the head.

The safest approach is from the southeast. In our opinion, the pass between Texada Island and the unnamed 20-meter island is not as open as the charts suggest. We explored this pass at the bottom of a 1.6-foot low tide, and found rock shelves extending from the Texada Island side well into the pass. Be especially careful of the reef that extends from the southwest point of Texada Island. At low tide the reef dries, but at higher stages of tide it could be a nasty surprise.

Sturt Bay, on Malaspina Strait near the north end of Texada Island, has the best anchorage and moorage on Texada Island. The Texada Boating Club has extensive floats, well protected, with visitor moorage welcomed. Pay at the head of the dock. The floats have water, but not much power. Anchorage is available elsewhere in the bay. If Malaspina Strait is kicking up, Sturt Bay could be a delight.

Harwood Point Regional Park, Gillies Bay, Texada Island. Use chart 3513. Anchor out only and dinghy in to a 40-acre park. Grass fields, picnic tables, campsites, pit toilets.

Vananda/Sturt Bay Public Wharf, in Sturt Bay. Use chart 3513. Dock has 98 feet of mooring space. Exposed and not very interesting. Nearby Sturt Bay is preferred.

Lots of dock space at Sturt Bay on Texada Island. Paybox is at head of dock, off photo to right.

The Southeast Coast, White Rock to Vancouver

Boundary Bay • Fraser River

The Sand Heads light marks the entrance to the South Arm of the Fraser River. Especially in springtime, onshore winds can create large seas.

THE COASTLINE BETWEEN Boundary Bay and Vancouver is uninteresting river delta, and the waters often uncomfortable. Sediment from the Fraser River has created shoal depths for some distance offshore. The prevailing winds tend to blow against the river current in the shallow water, and steep seas can build quickly. Usually it's best to stay well off in deeper water, but even there a 20-knot wind can make for a rough ride. It is for good reason that most pleasure craft choose to go north through the Gulf Islands, then pick a patch of good weather to cross the Strait of Georgia to Vancouver or Howe Sound. The shortest distance across the strait, from Gabriola Pass to Howe Sound, is 14 miles. Even slow boats can make the crossing in 2 or 3 hours; faster boats can cross in an hour or less.

① **City of White Rock Pier.** Use chart 18421 (U.S.); chart 3463 (Cdn). White Rock is a Canadian Customs port of entry. Call (888)226-7277. The south side of the eastern float is reserved for transient moorage. The village of White Rock has a number of interesting shops and galleries.

Crescent Beach. Use chart 18421 (U.S.); 3463 (Cdn). North of White Rock, the Nicomekl River empties into Boundary Bay, creating a channel that leads to the village of Crescent Beach. The channel is marked by port and starboard daymarks, and dredged every few years. While Crescent Beach is not visited by many cruising yachts, you'll find there an important luxury motoryacht manufacturing facility, and the Crescent Beach Marina. The marina is located just beyond the Burlington Northern Railway swing bridge that crosses the river to Blackie Spit. Depending on tide, bridge clearance ranges from 9 to 20 feet. The bridge is manned 7 days a week from 0630 until 2230, and will open to 3 whistle blasts. You can call the bridge at (604)538-3233. You can also call the marina at (604)538-9666, and they will contact the bridge tender.

② **Crescent Beach Marina, Ltd.** 12555 Crescent Road, Surrey, B.C. V4A 2V4,

(604)538-9666. Open all year, gasoline & diesel at the fuel dock, telephone for customs clearance. Guest moorage is available for boats to 65 feet. Call first. Haulout to 30 tons, 15 amp power, repairs, chandlery, launch ramp.

Harbour Authority of Crescent Beach Wharf. Just 40 feet of dock, with temporary moorage for 2-3 boats. Customs clearance.

Tsawwassen. Use chart 3492; 3463. For members of reciprocal yacht clubs, moorage

to swinging moorings is available at the Tsawwassen Yacht Club basin, on the south side of the Tsawwassen ferry dock. A dredged, narrow channel leads to the moorage. The 1997 large scale chart 3492 (1:20,000) shows this area in clear detail. We recommend it.

Canoe Passage. Use chart 3492; 3463 (1:80,000). Canoe Passage is the southernmost mouth of the Fraser River. The seaward entrance is marked by a government buoy, but private dolphins mark its winding path through

Reference only — not for navigation

See area map page 147

Roberts Bank. Although mainly used by commercial boats with local knowledge, Canoe Passage can be used by small craft, especially at half tide or better on a rising tide. The swing bridge connecting Westham Island with the mainland is manned 24 hours a day, and opens to 3 whistle blasts. The bridge tender can be contacted on VHF channel 74, or by telephone (604)946-2121. In 1997 the Canadian Hydrographic Service published large scale chart 3492 (1:20,000) which shows Canoe Passage, but we would be skeptical. Locals who use the passage re-mark the channel at least yearly, after major runoff has moved the sand bars.

Sand Heads. Use chart 3490 (1:20,000, recommended); 3463. Sand Heads marks the mouth of the South Arm (also called the Main Arm) of the Fraser River. The South Arm is the Fraser's major entry, and is protected on its north side by the Steveston Jetty. The Sand Heads Light, located at the end of the jetty, is a major lighthouse, constructed on pilings topped by a wooden house. Currents in the Fraser River can run to 5 knots, depending on the volume of water in the river, which in turn depends on rain and snow melt upstream. Large flood tides will at times slow or reverse the current. *Caution:* An on-shore wind meeting an ebb current, combined with heavy outflow from the river, will create dangerously steep and high seas in the river mouth. Friends who keep their boats on the river tell of their entire boat being airborne in such conditions.

The lower part of the Fraser River is delta country, low and flat. The marshlands are havens for wildlife, and you'll see many eagles. The river itself contains much drift. The river is used heavily by fish boats, tugs towing barges or log booms, Coast Guard boats, work boats of all description, and freighters. Water-oriented industrial companies are located along the shores.

Relatively few cruising boats go up the Fraser, in part because no destinations of wide interest are found there, and in part because the entire coast between Point Grey and Point Roberts is uninteresting to view and hostile in any kind of wind. Most of the marinas on the Fraser exist primarily for permanent moorage tenants, with few facilities for visitors.

Steveston. Use chart 3490. The first stop on the Fraser River is Steveston, a long, slender harbor on the north side, protected by a sand island (Steveston Island). Although Steveston is primarily a fishing town with moorage and other services for commercial fishermen, it is becoming a tourist destination as well. Pleasure craft may use the moorage when the fishing fleet is out. Steveston has 3 fuel docks. Chandleries and all the other facilities of a small city are ashore. The streets of Steveston are quaint; the local movie industry sometimes films scenes there.

③ **Steveston Harbour Authority Wharf.** Open all year, power and water on docks. Pleasure craft may use outermost dock only. Com-

mercial vessels have priority. Wash from passing traffic makes outside face of dock a little bumpy. We recommend that you find a spot along the inside face.

③ **Steveston Chevron,** (604)277-4712. Fuel dock with gasoline, diesel, stove oil, washrooms. Limited marine supplies available, also bait, ice, snacks.

③ **Steveston Esso Marine Station,** (604)277-5211. Fuel dock with gasoline, diesel, stove oil. Waste oil disposal available. Limited hours in winter.

③ **Steveston Petro Canada Barge,** (604)277-7744. Open all year, gasoline, diesel, stove oil. Limited marine supplies available, also ice and snacks.

Ladner. Use chart 3490. Ladner is a pretty town and an interesting visit. Leave the main branch of the Fraser River and take Sea Reach and Ladner Reach to the town, which is fronted by float homes. A fish boat moorage is on the port side. Pleasure craft are welcome when the fleet is out. Although Sea Reach and Ladner Reach are shallow, they are passable for most pleasure craft except at extreme low river levels. Beyond Ladner, a low bridge blocks passage for larger boats.

There is moorage behind Gilmour Island on the north shore of the river, used primarily by float homes. The river is lined on both sides by various industries. B.C. ferries are repaired in a basin next to the Deas Tunnel. Several large hotels near the confluence of the south and north arms of the river have mooring floats, mostly in the east end of Annacis Channel. Captain's Cove Marina, the site of another yacht club, is on the Annacis Channel, as are the Bar Port Marina and fuel docks.

⑪ **Captain's Cove Marina,** 6100 Ferry Road, Delta, B.C. V4K 3M9, (604)946-1244. Open all year, guest moorage available for boats

to 60 feet, best to call ahead. The fuel dock has gasoline, diesel and lubricants. Water is available on the guest dock. You'll find washrooms, showers, laundry, waste oil disposal. Power is 30 amp. They have a cafe and pub on site, haulout to 30 tons, and a yard for repairs.

④ **Ladner Yacht Club,** (604)946-4056. Depending on what's available, they may take an overnight visitor. Worth a call.

⑩ **Shelter Island Marina Inc.,** 120-6911 Graybar Rd., Richmond, B.C. V6W 1H3, (604)270-6272; fax (604)273-6282. Monitors VHF channel 68. Open all year, guest moorage, call ahead first. The marina has 20, 30 & 50 amp power, washrooms, showers, laundry, pumpout, Travelift for all sizes to 150 tons, and full service chandlery. Restaurant and pub. Shelter Island is a big, busy facility.

New Westminster. Use chart 3490. New Westminster is located at the confluence of the north and south arms of the Fraser River, and is heavily industrialized along the waterfront.

Contributing Editor Tom Kincaid has run the river past New Westminster to the Pitt River, where he spent the night at the Pitt Meadows Marina. A few friends have continued to the Harrison River, running up the Harrison River to Harrison Hot Springs on Harrison Lake. All suggest having a fast boat and a knowledgeable pilot aboard before attempting to run either of these rivers. The Fraser River beyond Richmond is poorly marked, with sand bars that are constantly changing. The river is navigable as far as Hope during high water stages, but mariners should rely on local knowledge before attempting this run.

Note: In 1995 the Canadian Hydrographic Service published two new strip charts of the Fraser River. Chart 3489 covers Patullo Bridge to Crescent Island; Chart 3488 covers Crescent Island to Harrison Mills.

Keep a sharp watch for deadheads, particularly outside the main commercial channels.

Catherwood Towing, 8069 Coleman St., Mission, B.C. V2V 6R5, (604)462-9221. Monitors VHF channel 69. Fuel dock located on the north side of the river, just under the railroad bridge, in Mission. They have gasoline and diesel. A launch ramp is adjacent to the fuel dock.

North Arm Fraser River. Use chart 3491 (1:20,000); 3463 (1:80,000). The North Arm of the Fraser River is lined with boat building and repair yards and other businesses that serve the marine community. A jetty runs through Sturgeon Bank along the south side of the North Arm, parallel to the Point Grey shoreline. A dredged basin, known locally as "Coward's Cove" or the "Chicken Hole," is on the north side of the channel, just before the North Arm enters Strait of Georgia. The basin gives good protection to skippers while they assess conditions on the strait.

⑤ Delta River Inn Marina, 3500 Cessna Drive, Richmond, B.C. V7B 1C7, (604)278-1241. Open all year, guest facilities are limited, so call ahead. Limited 15 amp power. Haulout to 70 feet (operated by Delta Charters). The marina is part of the Delta Vancouver Airport Hotel. The hotel has several restaurants, a bar, and a pool. They run a bus to the local shopping mall.

⑨ North Arm Marine, 7831 Grauer Rd., Sea Island, Richmond, B.C. V7B 1N4, (604)276-2164. Open all year, Petro Canada fuel dock with gasoline, diesel, kerosene, washrooms, ice, bait, and fishing licenses. They also have waste oil disposal.

⑥ Richmond Chevron, 7891 Grauer Rd., Richmond, B.C. V7B 1N4, (604)278-2181. Open all year, gasoline, diesel, kerosene, lubricants and waste oil disposal.

⑦ Bridgepoint Marina, 8831 River Road, Richmond, B.C. V6X 1Y6, (604)273-8560. Open all year, guest moorage available along 200 foot dock. The docks have 15 & 30 amp power, washrooms, showers, and laundry. Least depth is 6-7 feet. This is a big marina on south side of the river, with a restaurant, pub and coffee shop.

⑧ Vancouver Marina, 8331 River Road, Richmond, B.C. V6X 1Y1, (604)278-9787. Open all year, no guest moorage, gasoline & diesel at the fuel dock. They carry fishing licenses, bait and ice. Repairs and a chandlery are located at the marina. The marina is located on the Middle Arm of the Fraser River.

⑫ Skyline Marina, 8031 River Road, Richmond, B.C. V6X 1X8, (604) 273-3977. Open all year, guest moorage available, call ahead. The maximum boat length is 50-60 feet, power is 15 amp. The marina has haulout and repair facilities, or do your own work. Restaurants and all services are nearby. Located on the Middle Arm of the Fraser River.

Charts	
3311	SMALL CRAFT CHARTS (strip charts) Sunshine Coast to Desolation Sound
3463	Strait of Georgia – Southern Portion (1:80,000)
3481	Approaches to Vancouver Harbour (1:25,000)
3493	Vancouver Harbour, Western Portion (1:10,000)
3494	Vancouver Harbour, Central Portion (1:10,000) Second Narrows (1:6,000)
3495	Vancouver Harbour, Eastern Portion (1:10,000) Indian Arm (1:6,000)
3512	Strait of Georgia, Central Portion (1:80,000)
3526	Howe Sound (1:40,000)
3534	PLANS – Howe Sound: Mannion Bay, Snug Cove, Fishermans Cove, Horseshoe Bay, Shoal Channel, Squamish Harbour

Point Grey. Use chart 3481; 3463. Point Grey marks the southern entrance to Burrard Inlet. When approaching from the south, it is unwise to cut too close to Point Grey, or you risk going aground on Spanish Bank. Leave the buoys to starboard when entering.

Spanish Bank. Use chart 3481; 3463. Spanish Bank is an extensive drying bank off the north shore of Point Grey. The outer edge of the bank is marked with buoys. The daybeacons you see do *not* mark the outer edge of the

Vancouver and Howe Sound

False Creek • Vancouver Harbour • Indian Arm
Horseshoe Bay • Howe Sound • Gibsons

bank. They mark a measured nautical mile, and are set on the bank itself. Royal Vancouver Yacht Club has its main clubhouse and sailboat moorage about 3 miles from Point Grey along the south shore of English Bay. A launch ramp is close to the Kitsilano Coast Guard station near the entrance to False Creek.

HOW TO VISIT VANCOUVER

Vancouver is probably our favorite city in the Northwest. It is the largest city in British Columbia, and the major deepwater port on the west coast of Canada, handling cargo from across Canada and from all maritime nations of the world. The city is clean, safe, and thoroughly cosmopolitan. Its architecture is exciting. Vancouver's parks, museums, hotels, and dining are wonderful. Until 1997, however, guest moorage was not easy to find, and Vancouver was a little difficult to visit by boat. That changed with the opening of the new Coal Harbour Marina, in the lap of downtown.

Then, in late summer 1999, a city effort called Blueways Program got underway. Squatters were moved out of much of False Creek, 13 mooring buoys were installed a short distance east of Granville Island, and a boater information center was established to advise visitors where moorage is available. We took the boat to Vancouver in September, 1999, and tried out the new Blueways program. It had a small number of teething problems, but on the whole it worked well (see False Creek entries, below).

If you are approaching Vancouver from the south, you could go up the North Arm of the Fraser River to a number of marinas in the Richmond area, and take a bus into the city.

Cosmopolitan Vancouver, from Burrard Inlet. The concentration of high-rise apartments makes the population density of Vancouver's West End the highest in North America.

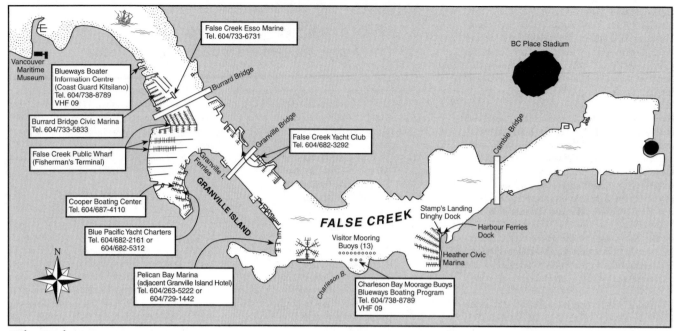

BC Place Stadium

False Creek Esso Marine
Tel. 604/733-6731

Vancouver
Maritime
Museum

Blueways Boater
Information Centre
(Coast Guard Kitsilano)
Tel. 604/738-8789
VHF 09

Burrard Bridge Civic Marina
Tel. 604/733-5833

False Creek Public Wharf
(Fisherman's Terminal)

Burrard Bridge

Granville Bridge

Cambie Bridge

False Creek Yacht Club
Tel. 604/682-3292

Cooper Boating Center
Tel. 604/687-4110

Granville
Ferries

GRANVILLE ISLAND

Blue Pacific Yacht Charters
Tel. 604/682-2161 or
604/682-5312

FALSE CREEK

Stamp's Landing
Dinghy Dock

Harbour Ferries
Dock

Heather Civic
Marina

Visitor Mooring
Buoys (13)

Pelican Bay Marina
(adjacent Granville Island Hotel)
Tel. 604/263-5222 or
604/729-1442

Charleson B.

Charleson Bay Moorage Buoys
Blueways Boating Program
Tel. 604/738-8789
VHF 09

N

False Creek

If you are approaching from the north, you could tie up at Horseshoe Bay or at Snug Cove, on the south side of Bowen Island. You would take the ferry from Snug Cove to Horseshoe Bay, then board a bus for the trip into Vancouver—or as far south as White Rock if that's where you wanted to go. The Vancouver bus system is excellent and affordable. A friend who lives in Vancouver has high praise for it.

For moorage in Vancouver proper, you will choose either the Vancouver Harbour area or the False Creek area. Each has its advantages, and each is good. Use large scale Chart 3493 (1:10,000) to navigate English Bay, Vancouver Harbour, or False Creek. Once you're settled, Vancouver's bus system allows you to get around the entire area with minimum delay.

FALSE CREEK

Chart 3493 shows False Creek in excellent detail. We strongly recommend that you use it.

You might find a slip in the Burrard Bridge Civic Marina, directly behind the fuel dock. On the north shore of False Creek, the False Creek Yacht Club usually has guest slips available. If the fishing fleet is out, a good bet for moorage is the large public marina on the south shore. If you want to be close to great shopping and excellent marine supply outlets, try the docks of Cooper Boating Center or Blue Pacific Charters, adjacent to each other on the west side of **Granville Island**. To reach these docks, you will see the prominent Bridge Restaurant on the south side as you enter False Creek. Turn just before the restaurant and work your way down to the docks. On the east side of Granville Island the Pelican Bay Marina, next to the Granville Island Hotel, has some guest moorage.

Granville Island is an active and vibrant place, full of people. You'll find an interest-

ing and busy food market, many eateries, lots of galleries and shops, and a variety of marine supplies, both on the island and a short walk away. Docks, posted for 3-hour maximum stay, face the waterway. While they will hold larger boats, we think you'll have no problem with longer stays if you moor elsewhere and commute by dinghy. Two harbor ferry fanchises serve False Creek as well. If moored, you could hail a passing ferry for transportation around the creek.

Blueways Program, (604)738-8789, VHF channel 09. The Blueways Program in False creek consists of 13 mooring buoys located in Charleson Bay, a short distance east of Granville Island. The buoys are quite visible, even from near the entrance to False Creek. Fee is $15 per night, 3-night maximum. The buoys are fairly closely spaced, limiting boat size to 40 feet or less. At one point, the swim step of our 37-footer touched the buoy next to us. Holding tanks are required in False Creek. Watch your depths: the outermost buoys have

a least depth of 3 meters (9.8 feet) on a zero tide, but the inner buoys have only 2 meters least depth.

The Blueways Program's office is in the Kitsilano Coast Guard base, just west of the Burrard Bridge. Hours are 1000-2000, May-October. They stay in regular contact with other marinas in Vancouver, and know who has moorage available. Call them on the radio or cell phone as you approach. If you plan to use one of the mooring buoys but get no answer, moor at an available buoy (one boat per buoy). They will come by later to collect moorage and leave you with an information packet.

A dinghy dock has been established at Stamps Landing in the Heather Civic Marina, east of the mooring buoys. A large sign reading "Monk's" on Monk McQueen's restaurant marks the spot. (While we are not aware of any formal connection between the restaurant and the boats, the name obviously was inspired by the famous Monk-designed powerboats built by McQueen's boat works

False Creek is urban and exciting. Here, a harbor ferry chugs along the north side.

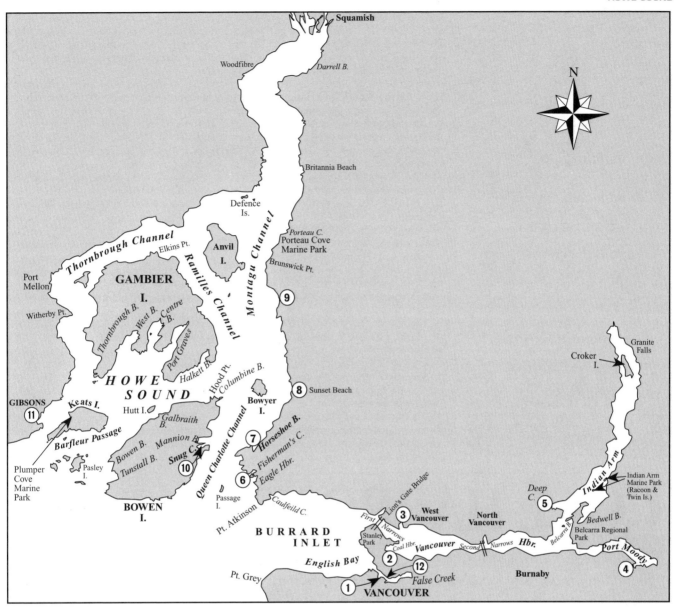

in Vancouver.) The Blueways Program is work-ing to develop other, more convenient, din-ghy dock locations in False Creek, particu-larly on the north shore.

① **Burrard Bridge Civic Marina,** 1655 Whyte Ave., Vancouver, B.C., V6J 1A9, (604)733-5833. Open all year, guest moor-age limited to unoccupied slips when avail-able. This is a permanent moorage marina, with launch facilities, and the office is open dur-ing normal office hours only.

① **False Creek Esso Marine,** P.O. Box 34125, Station D, Vancouver, B.C. V5J 4M1, (604)733-6731. Open all year. They carry gasoline & diesel, kerosene, heating oil, fish-ing tackle and bait, ice and snacks. They have an engine oil pumpout for oil changes, and waste oil disposal. Located at the Burrard Bridge Civic Marina, as you enter False Creek.

⑫ **False Creek Yacht Club,** 1661 Granville St., Vancouver, B.C. V6Z 1N3, (604)682-3292.

Open all year, located on the north side of False Creek, directly under the Granville St. Bridge. Guest moorage in unoccupied slips. Slips usually are available. Call ahead. Facili-ties include 15 & 30 amp power, washrooms, showers, laundry, and pumpout. A passenger ferry runs regularly to Granville Island.

① **False Creek Public Wharf.** Open all year, a large facility located on the south shore of False Creek, west of Granville Island. Fish-ing vessels have priority, but space often is available in the summer.

① **Blue Pacific Yacht Charters,** 1519 Fore-shore Walk, Granville Island, Vancouver, B.C. V6H 3X3, (604)682-2161; (604)682-5312. Open all year, moorage in unoccupied slips as available, haulout, towing, and repairs. Lo-cated on the west side of Granville Island.

① **Cooper Boating Center,** 1620 Duranleau St., Granville Island, Vancouver, B.C. V6H 3S4, (604)687-4110; fax (604)687-3267, (888)

999-6419. Or view at www.cooper-boating.com. Open all year, guest moorage in unoccupied slips as available. Washrooms, showers, 15 amp power. Located on the west side of Granville Island.

① **Pelican Bay Marina,** 2235 W. 32nd, Vancouver, B.C. V6L 2B1, (604)263-5222; fax (604)683-3444. Open all year, adjacent to the Granville Island Hotel on the east end of Granville Island. Unoccupied slips used when available, with 30 & 50 amp power, wash-room, and water. Access to all amenities.

Vancouver Maritime Museum. If you can, spend some time at the Vancouver Maritime Museum. It's located on the south shore of English Bay at the entrance to False Creek. The museum's docks are for display boats only. The vessel *St. Roch,* which explored the North-west Passage across the top of Canada be-tween the Atlantic and Pacific Oceans, is on display in its own building.

Vancouver Harbour. Vancouver Harbour is entered under the Lions Gate Bridge through First Narrows, in the northeast corner of Burrard Inlet. Because of heavy commercial traffic, strong currents and narrow channels, sailing craft must be under power from westward of **First Narrows** until well into Vancouver Harbour. No sailing is permitted through Second Narrows, either. In First Narrows, a strong ebb current meeting a fresh northwesterly can create high, steep seas. A friend in a large Cheoy Lee motorsailer suffered damage while exiting First Narrows in such conditions. Current predictions are shown in Tide and Current Tables, Vol. 5. Monitor VHF channel 12 for Vancouver Vessel Traffic information.

Once into Vancouver Harbour, your best bet for moorage is along the southern shoreline in the Coal Harbour area. Be prepared to spend more than is charged at outlying marinas. The Harbour Ferries docks are the westernmost of the marinas. They are located beside Stanley Park, near the Vancouver Rowing Club docks. The Bayshore West Marina, next to the Harbour Ferries docks, is closed for renovation. The Westin Bayshore Marina, however, often has slips. The Westin Bayshore charges more, but you're a guest of the Bayshore Hotel, with full access to its facilities, even room (boat) service.

The Coal Harbour Marina, just east of the Bayshore Hotel, makes a visit to Vancouver a real pleasure. It is first-class in every way, and is an excellent base for a few days on the town.

The final choice in the Coal Harbour strip is the Barbary Coast Marina, a short distance east of the hotel. Barbary Coast is set up to cater to larger yachts. Its smallest slip is 40 feet.

These marinas are close to downtown Vancouver, a pleasant walk or short cab ride away. Wright Mariner Supply, occupying a floating structure in the Coal Harbour Marina, sells a complete range of marine supplies, clothing, charts, and books. Stanley Park is nearby.

Robson Street's shops, galleries and wide range of restaurants are just a few blocks away.

The north shore of Vancouver Harbour is mostly heavy commercial. The Mosquito Creek Marina, roughly across from the Bayshore Hotel, does not solicit visitor moorage, although a boat needing repairs should try to get in. Complete repairs are available from the various shops at Mosquito Creek. Farther east, you can find guest moorage at the Lynnwood Marina on the north shore, just west of Second Narrows. A number of good repair shops are located at the Lynnwood Marina.

② **Barbary Coast Yacht Basin,** 1601 W. Georgia St., Vancouver, B.C. V6G 2W6, (604)669-0088. Limited guest moorage available, call ahead for reservations. They can take the largest yacht. The smallest slip is 40 feet. Depending on the location, power includes 20, 30 & 50 amp 110-volt; 60 and 100 amp single phase 220-volt; and 100 amp 3-phase

220 volt. They have an adapter for 50 amp single-phase 220 volt. They also have ample water capacity. Showers, laundry, and cable television hookup.

② **Coal Harbour Chevron,** (604)681-7725. Fuel barge in Coal Harbour open 24 hours a day, all year. They carry gasoline, diesel, kerosene, heating oil, convenience items, rain gear. They do oil changes and have waste oil disposal. Washrooms, showers.

② **Coal Harbour Marina,** 1525 Coal Harbour Quay, Vancouver, B.C. V6G 3E7, (604)681-2628; fax (604)681-4666; e-mail coalhbr@seatosky.com. Monitors VHF channel 68. Open all year, guest moorage available for boats to 170 feet, reservations recommended. They have 30, 50, 100 & 150 amp power, concierge services, TV and telephone hookups, vacuum sewage system, washrooms, showers and laundry. This is a first-class marina with wide concrete docks, complete security, a restaurant, marine supply store (Wright Mariner), and easy access to downtown Vancouver. A much-needed and welcome addition to the Vancouver waterfront. *(Marina map this page)*

② **Wampler Marine Services Ltd.,** Box 3888, Vancouver, B.C. V6B 3Z3, (604) 681-3841. Esso fuel barge in Coal Harbour, open 24 hours a day, all year long, with gasoline, diesel, stove oil, washrooms, showers, and waste oil disposal. The convenience store carries snacks, pop, fishing licenses, and some fishing tackle.

② **Harbour Ferries Marina,** No. 1 North, foot of Denman St., Vancouver, B.C. V6G 2W9, (604)687-9558; fax (604)683-0684; or view at www.boatcruises.com. Open all year, 15 & 30 amp power, guest moorage limited to unoccupied slips when regular tenants are away.

No showers or washrooms. Call for availability.

② **Petro Canada Coal Harbour,** (604)681-6020. Open 24 hours a day all year long, with gasoline, diesel, stove oil, oil pumpout, washrooms, and a small convenience store with party ice, frozen bait, and snacks.

② **Westin Bayshore Yacht Charters,** 1601 West Georgia St., Vancouver, B.C. V6G 2V4, (604)691-6936. Monitors VHF channel 68. Open all year, located in Coal Harbour, directly in front of the Westin Bayshore Hotel. Guest moorage available, 30 & 50 amp power, washrooms, showers, pumpout. Health club and pool. All the services of the Westin Bayshore Hotel are available.

③ **Mosquito Creek Marina,** Foot of Forbes Ave., North Vancouver, B.C. V7L 4J5, (604)980-4553; fax (604)987-6852. The marina docks are showing their age and major replacement is in the plans. For now, the marina does not solicit visiting boats. Several repair facilities are located at Mosquito Creek, however, and a boat needing repair should see what can be arranged.

③ **Lynnwood Marina,** 1681 Columbia St., North Vancouver, B.C. V7J 1A5, (604) 985-1533. Open all year, guest moorage available, but call ahead first. The marina has 15 & 30 amp power, complete repairs including sailboat mast repair, and haulout to 60 tons. Shopping is about a 10-minute walk away.

BURNABY, PORT MOODY, INDIAN ARM

Second Narrows. Use chart 3494. To proceed eastward from Vancouver Harbour to Burnaby, Port Moody, and Indian Arm, you

first must go through Second Narrows. On springs, flood currents can reach 6.5 knots and ebb currents 5.5 knots, so these narrows are not to be treated lightly. Wind and current opposing each other can create difficult seas. The best advice is to go through near times of slack, although on small tides the current should present few problems for boats with adequate power. Current predictions are shown in the Tide and Current Tables, Vol. 5. Because of extensive heavy displacement commercial traffic, monitor VHF Channel 12. No sailing is permitted in Second Narrows.

Cates Park. Cates Park is at Roche Point, near the entrance to Indian Arm. The park has a paved launch ramp, a beach, trails, playground, changing room, and picnic shelter. Temporary anchorage only.

Burnaby. Use chart 3494. A park is at Burnaby, at the site of an old sawmill. The park has no public float, but anchorage is good just east of the fishing pier.

Port Moody. Use chart 3495. Port Moody ends in drying flats, but on the south shore a dredged channel through the flats leads to Rocky Point Park. The park has a launch ramp, swimming pool and picnic areas, and is the location of the Port Moody Museum. Further development is underway. The Reed Point Marina, with moorage for about 1,000 boats, has a guest float, fuel, and the usual amenities associated with a large marina.

④ **Reed Point Marina,** 850 Barnet Highway, Port Moody, B.C. V6H 1V6, (604)931-2477; fax (604)931-2132. Open all year, gasoline and diesel, guest moorage available. Facilities include 30 amp power, washrooms, haulout to 38 tons, repairs, marine supplies and service on site. They can handle boats to 70 feet, larger boats with advance notice.

INDIAN ARM

To cruise in beautiful Indian Arm, use chart 3495 or chart 3311, sheet 1. Indian Arm extends 11 miles into mountains that soar to 5000 feet. Indian Arm is largely unpopulated beyond Deep Cove, because Deep Cove is the end of the road from North Vancouver. The waters in Indian Arm generally are calm, but can be ruffled by local downdraft winds off the mountains. Indian Arm is a little secret that Vancouver boaters have. It is remote-feeling, yet close to the city.

Indian Arm Marine Park. In 1996 the Indian Arm Marine Park was expanded from the Twin Islands and Racoon Island to include most of the fjord. Croker Island and Granite Falls are now part of the park.

Belcarra. Belcarra Regional Park is located on the east shore of Indian Arm, near the entrance. The public float is for loading and unloading only. Anchorage is good in Belcarra Bay. The park has 2 lakes, 4 miles of shore-

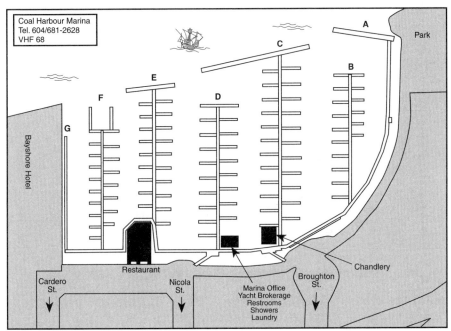

Coal Harbour Marina

Reference only — not for navigation

Union SteamShip Marine Resort

UNION STEAMSHIP CO. MARINA located at the head of Snug Cove, Bowen Island is a first class year-round facility with plenty of space for visiting boats from 20 to 200 feet long. The marina has electrical outlets for 30 & 50 amps, water, laundry and showers.

The resort features DOC MORGAN'S INN a marine pub and fine dining restaurant, located on the boardwalk that winds around a collection of unique shops. On the boardwalk there's a chandlery that offers provisions, gifts, charts, bicycle rentals, fishing licenses and gear for that great nearby fishing. COTTAGES from the original Union Steamship Co. are also available for overnight lodging and group functions.

Phone: (604) 947-0707 Fax: (604) 947-0708 • 49°23'N - 123°19'W • **VHF Channel 68**
P.O. Box 250, SNUG COVE, Bowen Island, British Columbia, V0N 1G0, Canada
A great and secure destination for a crew change.

line, and complete facilities. It's a popular stop.

Strathcona. The small Strathcona municipal float is located at the mouth of Indian Arm across from Belcarra, behind White Rock and the Grey Rocks Islands. The float dries at low tide.

Deep Cove. Deep Cove is a city of about 5,000 people. The public float provides access to shopping in the town of Deep Cove, and overnight moorage is okay. The commercial village, adjacent to the public float, is definitely upscale. Deep Cove is the location of the Deep Cove Yacht Club. The Seycove Marina at the north end of Deep Cove has moorage, fuel, and other amenities.

Deep Cove Public Wharf. The dock is 145 feet long, and is within walking distance of grocery stores, restaurants, live theater and other facilities.

⑤ **Seycove Marina,** 2890 Panorama Drive, North Vancouver, B.C. V7G 1V6, (604)929-1251. Open all year, gasoline and diesel at the fuel dock, limited guest moorage. Call ahead. Facilities include washrooms, showers, laundry, and convenience store. Deep Cove Village, with restaurants and shopping, is nearby.

Bedwell Bay. Bedwell Bay has the best anchorage in Indian arm. It is sheltered from the summer fair weather winds that blow from the south up Indian Arm.

Twin Islands and **Racoon Island.** The larger of the Twin Islands has a dinghy float on its east side, and picnic and sanitary facilities ashore. Anchorage offshore is quite deep (between 13 and 24 fathoms). Both the Twin Islands and Racoon Island are used by kayakers and canoeists who pull their craft ashore.

Granite Falls. Granite Falls, the largest of the falls that enter Indian Arm, tumbles off a cliff along the east bank. Anchorage is fair just offshore, and the climb up the cliff is good exercise for cramped muscles. Because of the questionable anchoring bottom, overnight anchoring is not recommended.

Wigwam Inn. The Wigwam Inn, at the head of Indian Arm, is a luxury resort whose rich history goes back to 1906. Today it is a Royal Vancouver Yacht Club outstation. Royal Vancouver Yacht Club members only.

POINT ATKINSON TO HORSESHOE BAY

Caulfeild Cove. Use chart 3481; 3526. Caulfeild Cove is a tiny bight, protected from nearly all winds and seas, tucked into the shoreline just east of Point Atkinson. A 52-foot public float lies along the east side of the cove, with 6 feet of depth alongside.

Point Atkinson. Use chart 3481; 3526. Point Atkinson is the north entrance to Burrard Inlet. The waters just off Point Atkinson can be very rough, especially on a large ebb flowing against a fresh onshore wind. A course well to seaward often is called for, and even that can be heavy going. Point Atkinson is well known and highly respected by Vancouver boaters.

Eagle Harbour. Use chart 3481; 3526. Eagle Harbour is the site of the Eagle Harbour Yacht Club.

Fishermans Cove. Use chart 3481; 3526. Fishermans Cove, the home of West Vancouver Yacht Club, is filled with the Thunderbird Marina. Be sure to follow the markers into Fishermans Cove. There is a false entrance that could put you in trouble.

⑥ **Thunderbird Marina,** 5776 Marine Drive, West Vancouver, B.C. V7W 2S2, (604)921-7434. Open all year, limited guest moorage (call ahead), 15 amp power, washrooms, showers, waste oil disposal. They have haulout to 25 tons and complete repairs. Our good friend John Zavaglia operates Thunderbird Marine Supplies at the marina, and does an excellent job of it.

⑥ **Fishermans Cove Esso,** 5908 Marine Drive, West Vancouver, B.C. V7W 2S1, (604)921-7333. Fuel dock with gasoline, diesel, stove oil, kerosene, CNG, propane, premix, waste oil system, miscellaneous supplies.

HOWE SOUND

Use charts 3526 and 3534. Howe Sound, located about 12 miles from the city, is the "backyard" for Vancouver area boaters. The sound is largely unpopulated, and provides a wilderness feeling close to home. Considerable drift is floating in Howe Sound, so watch carefully or you may be visiting your propeller repairman. Howe Sound, although beautiful, is a little stingy with its anchorages.

Horseshoe Bay. Use chart 3534; 3526. Horseshoe Bay is the eastern terminus of the ferries that serve the Gulf Islands, Sunshine Coast, and Vancouver Island. Sewell's Marina, a large, breakwater-protected public marina, is located to the west of the ferry docks. Boaters transiting this area are urged to use caution because of the steady procession of large ferryboats.

⑦ **Sewell's Marina Ltd.,** 6695 Nelson Ave., West Vancouver, B.C. V7W 2B2, (604)921-3474; fax (604)921-7027, or view at www.sewellsmarina.com. Open all year, gasoline and diesel fuel, 15 & 20 amp power, 2 concrete launch ramps. Guest moorage for boats 40-45 feet maximum is available. They carry frozen and live bait. Restaurants, groceries, and a post office are nearby.

⑦ **Horseshoe Bay Public Wharf.** Dock is 210 feet in length, commercial vessels have priority.

⑧ **Sunset Marina Ltd.,** 34 Sunset Beach, West Vancouver, B.C. V7W 2T7, (604)921-7476. Open March 1 to October 15. Gasoline, guest moorage available for boats to 30 feet, haulouts to 25 feet, repairs, launch ramp with long term parking. They carry marine supplies, tackle and bait.

⑨ **Lions Bay Marine Ltd.,** 60 Lions Bay Ave., Lions Bay, B.C. V0N 2E0, (604) 921-7510. Open all year, hours vary in winter. Gasoline and propane available. They have 400 feet of dock space, and haulout to 30 feet with repairs on site. Groceries and a post office are nearby.

Bowen Island. Bowen Island, with a number of good stops, is served by ferry from Horseshoe Bay. You can stay at Snug Cove across from Horseshoe Bay; at Columbine Bay and Smugglers Cove on the northeast corner; Galbraith Bay (public float); Bowen Bay; and Tunstall Bay on the west side.

Snug Cove. Use chart 3534; 3526. One of the favorite stops in Howe Sound is Snug Cove on Bowen Island. Snug Cove, with a public dock and two marinas, is served by ferry from Horseshoe Bay. *(Marina map page 156)*

The Union Steamship Marine Resort docks front on the beautiful mountains of Howe Sound.

10 Bowen Island Marina, 19 Cardena Dr. RR 1 A 1, Bowen Island, B.C. V0N 1G0, (604)947-9710; e-mail: norma@bowen-island.com. Monitors VHF channel 16, switch to 69. Open all year, guest moorage available, 15 & 20 amp power, located on right side as you enter Snug Cove. Fishing licenses, tackle, bait, and scuba air. They also serve handmade ice cream. *(Marina map this page)*

10 Snug Cove Public Wharf. This dock, with 350 feet of space, is next to the ferry landing in Snug Cove, and is exposed to ferry wash.

10 Union Steamship Company Marina, P.O. Box 250, Bowen Island, B.C. V0N 1G0, (604)947-0707; fax (604)947-0708. Monitors VHF channel 68. Open all year, ample guest moorage, 30 & 50 amp power, washrooms, showers, laundry. This is one of a small number of excellent places to stop for awhile. Rondy Dike, an old friend and an architect by training, and his wife Dorothy, have restored the Union Steamship Co. landing into a wonderful destination resort. Lots of shops, a good restaurant and pub, boardwalks, a chandlery, a 600-acre park to explore, and more. A small number of cottages are available, reasonable rates. We have stayed in two of the cottages, and

were completely charmed. Take the ferry to Horseshoe Bay and ride the bus to enjoy Vancouver. Reservations recommended. *(Marina map this page)*

Mount Gardner Park Public Dock, Galbraith Bay, northwest side of Bowen Island. Has 110 feet of space.

Gambier Island. Use chart 3526. Gambier Island has three significant inlets, **West Bay**, **Centre Bay**, and **Port Graves**, all opening from the south, and a smaller inlet, **Halkett Bay**, at the southeast corner of the island. **Thornbrough Bay**, on the west side of the island, has a public dock. We are told that boats often tie to log booms on the western (Port Mellon) side of the island. In the summertime the water around Gambier Island warms to swimming temperatures.

West Bay. Favor the west shore when you enter West Bay, to avoid the reef that extends from the eastern shore. Until recently, West Bay was a major log booming site, and the bottom is sure to be foul with old cable and equipment. You can anchor in West Bay, though, in at least two places. The first is on the north side of the reef, close to the reef. The second is in the bight at

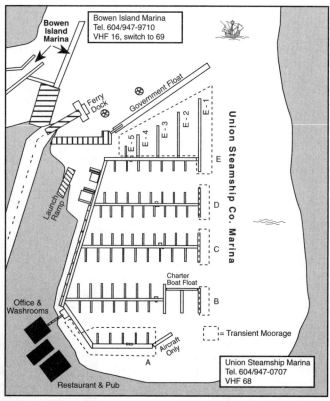

Snug Cove, Bowen Island

Reference only — not for navigation

CONVERSION TABLES

TEMPERATURE

Fahrenheit to Celsius

To convert temperature from
Fahrenheit to Celsius:
(F° - 32) × .555 = C°

Example: Convert 40° F to C:
(40 - 32) = 8; 8 × .555 = 4;
thus 40° F = 4° C

Celsius to Fahrenheit

To convert temperature from
Celsius to Fahrenheit:
(C° × 1.8)+32 = F°

Example: Convert 4° C to F:
(4 × 1.8) = 7.992;
7.992 + 32 = 39.992 (round to 40);
thus 4° C = 40° F

32° Fahrenheit =
0° Celsius

0° Fahrenheit =
-17.8° Celsius

VOLUME

U.S. Gallons to Liters

1 U.S gallon = 3.7854 liters
To convert U.S. gallons to liters, multiply U.S. gallons
× 3.785.
Example: 40 U.S. gallons × 3.785 = 151 liters

To convert liters to U.S. gallons, divide by 3.785.
Example: 151 liters ÷ 3.785 = 39.89 U.S. gallons (round
to 40)

Imperial Gallons to Liters

1 Imperial gallon = 4.546 liters
To convert Imperial gallons to liters, multiply Imperial
gallons × 4.546.
Example: 40 Imperial gallons × 4.546 = 182 liters

To convert liters to Imperial gallons, divide by 4.546.
Example: 182 liters ÷ 4.546 = 40.035 (round to 40)

U.S. Gallons to Imperial Gallons

1 U.S. gallon = .833 Imperial gallons
To convert U.S. gallons to Imperial gallons, multiply U.S.
gallons × .833.
Example: 40 U.S. gallons × .833 = 33.32 Imperial
gallons

To convert Imperial gallons to U.S. gallons, multiply
Imperial gallons × 1.20.
Example: 33 Imperial gallons × 1.20 = 39.6 U.S. gallons

Liters and Quarts

1 liter = 1.0567 quarts, or 33.8 ounces
1 quart = .9467 liters, or 947 ml

WEIGHT

1 kilogram (kg) = 2.2 pounds (lbs.)
1 pound = .4545 kilograms
1 U.S. gallon of fresh water weighs 8.333 lbs.
or 3.787 kg
1 Imperial gallon of fresh water weighs 10 lbs.
or 4.545 kg
1 liter of fresh water weighs 2.2 pounds or 1 kg

1 U. S. gallon of gasoline weighs 6.2 lbs. or 2.82 kg
1 Imperial gallon of gasoline weighs 7.44 lbs. or 3.38 kg
1 liter of gasoline weighs 1.64 lbs. or 0.744 kg
1 U.S. gallon of No. 2 diesel fuel weighs 6.7 pounds
or 3.05 kg
1 Imperial gallon of No. 2 diesel fuel weighs 8.04 pounds
or 3.66 kg
1 liter of No. 2 diesel fuel weighs 1.77 pounds or 0.8 kg

DISTANCE

1 foot = .3048 meter
1 meter = 3.28 feet
1 fathom = 6 feet
1 fathom = 1.83 meters
1 cable = 120 fathoms

1 cable (British) = 0.1 nautical mile
1 statute mile = 5280 feet; 7.4 cables; 1.609 kilometers
1 nautical mile = 6076 feet; 8.5 cables; 1.852 kilometers
1 statute mile = 0.868 nautical mile
1 nautical mile = 1.15 statute mile

SPEED

Convert knots to miles per hour: Knots × 1.15

Convert miles per hour to knots: MPH × .868

CONVERSION TABLES

CURRENCY

Generally, the most favorable exchange rates are on credit card transactions. Banks give slightly less favorable rates, and merchants tend to be the least favorable. Expect to pay more than the official exchange rate when you buy currency, and receive less when you sell.

Examples:

Assume an official exchange rate of $.65 U.S./$1.5385 Cdn. (Exchange rates change constantly.)

To convert $100 Canadian to U.S. $, multiply Canadian $ by 0.65 or divide by 1.5385:
$100 Cdn × 0.65 = $65.00 U.S.
$100 Cdn ÷ 1.5385 = $65.00 U.S.

To convert $65 U.S. to Canadian $, multiply U.S. $ by 1.5385 or divide by 0.65:
$65 U.S. × 1.5385 = $100 Cdn.
$65 U.S. ÷ 0.65 = $100 Cdn.

INTERNATIONAL MORSE CODE & PHONETIC ALPHABET

A ALPHA •—	**N** NOVEMBER —•	**1** ONE •————
B BRAVO —•••	**O** OSCAR ———	**2** TWO ••———
C CHARLIE —•—•	**P** PAPA •——•	**3** THREE •••——
D DELTA —••	**Q** QUEBEC ——•—	**4** FOUR ••••—
E ECHO •	**R** ROMEO •—•	**5** FIVE •••••
F FOXTROT ••—•	**S** SIERRA •••	**6** SIX —••••
G GOLF ——•	**T** TANGO —	**7** SEVEN ——•••
H HOTEL ••••	**U** UNIFORM ••—	**8** EIGHT ———••
I INDIA ••	**V** VICTOR •••—	**9** NINE ————•
J JULIET •———	**W** WHISKEY •——	**0** ZERO —————
K KILO —•—	**X** X-RAY —••—	
L LIMO •—••	**Y** YANKEE —•——	**DISTRESS - SOS**
M MIKE ——	**Z** ZULU ——••	••• ——— •••

BEAUFORT WIND SCALE

Scale Number	Wind Speed		Effects
	Knots	**MPH**	
0	under 1	under 1	Calm
1	1-3	1-3	Ripples
2	4-6	4-7	Small wavelets
3	7-10	8-12	Large wavelets; small crests
4	11-16	13-18	Small waves; some whitecaps
5	17-21	19-24	Moderate waves; some spray; many whitecaps
6	22-27	25-31	Larger waves; whitecaps everywhere
7	28-33	32-38	Sea heaps up; white foam from breaking waves
8	34-40	39-46	Moderately high; waves of greater length; foam blown in well-marked streaks
9	41-47	47-54	High waves; sea begins to roll; dense streaks of foam; spray reduces visibility
10	48-55	55-63	Very high waves with overhanging crests; sea takes on a white appearance; rolling is heavy
11	56-63	64-72	Exceptionally high waves; sea covered with white foam patches; visibility still more reduced
12	64 & over	73 & over	Air filled with foam; sea completely white with driving spray; visibility greatly reduced.

TIME • SPEED • DISTANCE

KNOTS

MINUTES	1	2	3	4	5	6	7	8	9	10	11	12	13	14	15
				DISTANCE		*TRAVELED*	*IN*		*NAUTICAL*		*MILES*				
1	0.0	0.0	0.0	0.1	0.1	0.1	0.1	0.1	0.2	0.2	0.2	0.2	0.2	0.2	0.2
2	0.0	0.1	0.1	0.1	0.2	0.2	0.2	0.3	0.3	0.3	0.4	0.4	0.4	0.5	0.5
3	0.0	0.1	0.2	0.2	0.2	0.3	0.4	0.4	0.4	0.5	0.6	0.6	0.6	0.7	0.8
4	0.1	0.1	0.2	0.3	0.3	0.4	0.5	0.5	0.6	0.7	0.7	0.8	0.9	0.9	1.0
5	0.1	0.2	0.2	0.3	0.4	0.5	0.6	0.7	0.8	0.8	0.9	1.0	1.1	1.2	1.2
6	0.1	0.2	0.3	0.4	0.5	0.6	0.7	0.8	0.9	1.0	1.1	1.2	1.3	1.4	1.5
7	0.1	0.2	0.4	0.5	0.6	0.7	0.8	0.9	1.0	1.2	1.3	1.4	1.5	1.6	1.8
8	0.1	0.3	0.4	0.5	0.7	0.8	0.9	1.1	1.2	1.3	1.5	1.6	1.7	1.9	2.0
9	0.2	0.3	0.4	0.6	0.8	0.9	1.0	1.2	1.4	1.5	1.6	1.8	2.0	2.1	2.2
10	0.2	0.3	0.5	0.7	0.8	1.0	1.2	1.3	1.5	1.7	1.8	2.0	2.2	2.3	2.5
11	0.2	0.4	0.6	0.7	0.9	1.1	1.3	1.5	1.6	1.8	2.0	2.2	2.4	2.6	2.8
12	0.2	0.4	0.6	0.8	1.0	1.2	1.4	1.6	1.8	2.0	2.2	2.4	2.6	2.8	3.0
13	0.2	0.4	0.6	0.9	1.1	1.3	1.5	1.7	2.0	2.2	2.4	2.6	2.8	3.0	3.2
14	0.2	0.5	0.7	0.9	1.2	1.4	1.6	1.9	2.1	2.3	2.6	2.8	3.0	3.3	3.5
15	0.2	0.5	0.8	1.0	1.2	1.5	1.8	2.0	2.2	2.5	2.8	3.0	3.2	3.5	3.8
16	0.3	0.5	0.8	1.1	1.3	1.6	1.9	2.1	2.4	2.7	2.9	3.2	3.5	3.7	4.0
17	0.3	0.6	0.8	1.1	1.4	1.7	2.0	2.3	2.6	2.8	3.1	3.4	3.7	4.0	4.2
18	0.3	0.6	0.9	1.2	1.5	1.8	2.1	2.4	2.7	3.0	3.3	3.6	3.9	4.2	4.5
19	0.3	0.6	1.0	1.3	1.6	1.9	2.2	2.5	2.8	3.2	3.5	3.8	4.1	4.4	4.8
20	0.3	0.7	1.0	1.3	1.7	2.0	2.3	2.7	3.0	3.3	3.7	4.0	4.3	4.7	5.0
21	0.4	0.7	1.0	1.4	1.8	2.1	2.4	2.8	3.2	3.5	3.8	4.2	4.6	4.9	5.2
22	0.4	0.7	1.1	1.5	1.8	2.2	2.6	2.9	3.3	3.7	4.0	4.4	4.8	5.1	5.5
23	0.4	0.8	1.2	1.5	1.9	2.3	2.7	3.1	3.4	3.8	4.2	4.6	5.0	5.4	5.8
24	0.4	0.8	1.2	1.6	2.0	2.4	2.8	3.2	3.6	4.0	4.4	4.8	5.2	5.6	6.0
25	0.4	0.8	1.2	1.7	2.1	2.5	2.9	3.3	3.8	4.2	4.6	5.0	5.4	5.8	6.2
26	0.4	0.9	1.3	1.7	2.2	2.6	3.0	3.5	3.9	4.3	4.8	5.2	5.6	6.1	6.5
27	0.4	0.9	1.4	1.8	2.2	2.7	3.2	3.6	4.0	4.5	5.0	5.4	5.8	6.3	6.8
28	0.5	0.9	1.4	1.9	2.3	2.8	3.3	3.7	4.2	4.7	5.1	5.6	6.1	6.5	7.0
29	0.5	1.0	1.4	1.9	2.4	2.9	3.4	3.9	4.4	4.8	5.3	5.8	6.3	6.8	7.2
30	0.5	1.0	1.5	2.0	2.5	3.0	3.5	4.0	4.5	5.0	5.5	6.0	6.5	7.0	7.5
31	0.5	1.0	1.6	2.1	2.6	3.1	3.6	4.1	4.6	5.2	5.7	6.2	6.7	7.2	7.8
32	0.5	1.1	1.6	2.1	2.7	3.2	3.7	4.2	4.8	5.3	5.9	6.4	6.9	7.5	8.0
33	0.6	1.1	1.6	2.2	2.8	3.3	3.8	4.4	5.0	5.5	6.0	6.6	7.2	7.7	8.2
34	0.6	1.1	1.7	2.3	2.8	3.4	4.0	4.5	5.1	5.7	6.2	6.8	7.4	7.9	8.5
35	0.6	1.2	1.8	2.3	2.9	3.5	4.1	4.7	5.2	5.8	6.4	7.0	7.6	8.2	8.8
36	0.6	1.2	1.8	2.4	3.0	3.6	4.2	4.8	5.4	6.0	6.6	7.2	7.8	8.4	9.0
37	0.6	1.2	1.8	2.5	3.1	3.7	4.3	4.9	5.6	6.2	6.8	7.4	8.0	8.6	9.2
38	0.6	1.3	1.9	2.5	3.2	3.8	4.4	5.1	5.7	6.3	7.0	7.6	8.2	8.9	9.5
39	0.6	1.3	2.0	2.6	3.2	3.9	4.6	5.2	5.8	6.5	7.2	7.8	8.4	9.1	9.8
40	0.7	1.3	2.0	2.7	3.3	4.0	4.7	5.3	6.0	6.7	7.3	8.0	8.7	9.3	10.0
41	0.7	1.4	2.0	2.7	3.4	4.1	4.8	5.5	6.2	6.8	7.5	8.2	8.9	9.6	10.2
42	0.7	1.4	2.1	2.8	3.5	4.2	4.9	5.6	6.3	7.0	7.7	8.4	9.1	9.8	10.5
43	0.7	1.4	2.2	2.9	3.6	4.3	5.0	5.7	6.4	7.2	7.9	8.6	9.3	10.0	10.8
44	0.7	1.5	2.2	2.9	3.7	4.4	5.1	5.9	6.6	7.3	8.1	8.8	9.5	10.3	11.0
45	0.8	1.5	2.2	3.0	3.8	4.5	5.2	6.0	6.8	7.5	8.2	9.0	9.8	10.5	11.2
46	0.8	1.5	2.3	3.1	3.8	4.6	5.4	6.1	6.9	7.7	8.4	9.2	10.0	10.7	11.5
47	0.8	1.6	2.4	3.1	3.9	4.7	5.5	6.3	7.0	7.8	8.6	9.4	10.2	11.0	11.8
48	0.8	1.6	2.4	3.2	4.0	4.8	5.6	6.4	7.2	8.0	8.8	9.6	10.4	11.2	12.0
49	0.8	1.6	2.4	3.3	4.1	4.9	5.7	6.5	7.4	8.2	9.0	9.8	10.6	11.4	12.2
50	0.8	1.7	2.5	3.3	4.2	5.0	5.8	6.7	7.5	8.3	9.2	10.0	10.8	11.7	12.5
51	0.8	1.7	2.6	3.4	4.2	5.1	6.0	6.8	7.6	8.5	9.4	10.2	11.0	11.9	12.8
52	0.9	1.7	2.6	3.5	4.3	5.2	6.1	6.9	7.8	8.7	9.5	10.4	11.3	12.1	13.0
53	0.9	1.8	2.6	3.5	4.4	5.3	6.2	7.1	8.0	8.8	9.7	10.6	11.5	12.4	13.2
54	0.9	1.8	2.7	3.6	4.5	5.4	6.3	7.2	8.1	9.0	9.9	10.8	11.7	12.6	13.5
55	0.9	1.8	2.8	3.7	4.6	5.5	6.4	7.3	8.2	9.2	10.1	11.0	11.9	12.8	13.8
56	0.9	1.9	2.8	3.7	4.7	5.6	6.5	7.5	8.4	9.3	10.3	11.2	12.1	13.1	14.0
57	1.0	1.9	2.8	3.8	4.8	5.7	6.6	7.6	8.6	9.5	10.4	11.4	12.4	13.3	14.2
58	1.0	1.9	2.9	3.9	4.8	5.8	6.8	7.7	8.7	9.7	10.6	11.6	12.6	13.5	14.5
59	1.0	2.0	3.0	3.9	4.9	5.9	6.9	7.9	8.8	9.8	10.8	11.8	12.8	13.8	14.8
60	1.0	2.0	3.0	4.0	5.0	6.0	7.0	8.0	9.0	10.0	11.0	12.0	13.0	14.0	15.0

VHF CHANNELS FOR PLEASURE CRAFT

Washington Waters

05A VESSEL TRAFFIC SYSTEM—NORTHERN PUGET SOUND. Vessels not required to participate are highly encouraged to maintain a listening watch. Contact with VTS is encouraged if essential to navigational safety.

06 INTERSHIP SAFETY. Only for ship-to-ship use for safety communications. For Search and Rescue (SAR) liason with Coast Guard vessels and aircraft.

09 INTERSHIP AND SHIP-SHORE ALL VESSELS and CALLING & REPLY FOR PLEASURE VESSELS (optional, U.S. only). *Working channel.*

13 Vessel BRIDGE to Vessel BRIDGE, large vessels. *Low power only.* May also be used to contact locks and bridges BUT use sound signals in the Seattle area to avoid dangerous interference to collision avoidance communications between large vessels. Call on Channel 13 or by phone at 206/386-4251 for nighttime bridge openings (after 2300) in the Lake Washington Ship Canal, Seattle.

14 VESSEL TRAFFIC SYSTEM—SOUTHERN PUGET SOUND. Vessels not required to participate are highly encouraged to maintain a listening watch. Contact with VTS is encouraged if essential to navigational safety.

16 INTERNATIONAL DISTRESS AND CALLING. *Calling channel.* Used only for distress and urgency traffic, for safety calls and contacting other stations. Listen first to make sure no distress traffic is in progress; do not transmit if a *SEELONCE MAYDAY* is declared. Keep all communications to a minimum. Do not repeat a call to the same station more than once every two minutes. After three attempts, wait 15 minutes before calling the same station. Pleasure vessels may also use Channel 09 for calling.

22A COAST GUARD LIASON. A government channel used for Safety and Liason communications with the Coast Guard. Also known as Channel 22 US. The U.S. Coast Guard does not normally monitor 22A so you must first establish communications on Channel 16.

66A PORT OPERATIONS. All marinas in Puget Sound are being encouraged to use this common frequency for arranging moorage.

67 INTERSHIP ONLY FOR ALL VESSELS (U.S. only, Puget Sound.) *Working channel.*

68 INTERSHIP and SHIP-SHORE FOR PLEASURE VESSELS ONLY. *Working channel.*

69 INTERSHIP and SHIP-SHORE FOR PLEASURE VESSELS ONLY. *Working channel.*

70 DIGITAL SELECTIVE CALLING ONLY (No Voice) FOR DISTRESS AND CALLING.

71 INTERSHIP and SHIP-SHORE FOR PLEASURE VESSELS ONLY (Not available in Canada). *Working channel.*

72 INTERSHIP ONLY FOR ALL VESSELS (U.S. only, Puget Sound.) *Working channel.*

78A INTERSHIP and SHIP-SHORE FOR PLEASURE VESSELS ONLY (Not available in Canada). *Working channel.* All marinas in Puget Sound are being encouraged to use this as a secondary working channel.

British Columbia Waters

05A VESSEL TRAFFIC SERVICE SEATTLE—Strait of Juan de Fuca west of Victoria.

06 INTERSHIP SAFETY. Only for ship-to-ship use for safety communications. For Search & Rescue (SAR) liason with Coast Guard vessels and aircraft.

09 INTERSHIP AND SHIP-SHORE. All vessels. *Working channel.*

11 VESSEL TRAFFIC SERVICE VICTORIA—Strait of Juan de Fuca east of Victoria; Haro Strait; Boundary Passage; Gulf Islands; Strait of Georgia.

VESSEL TRAFFIC SERVICE PRINCE RUPERT—North of Vancouver Island

12 VESSEL TRAFFIC SERVICE VANCOUVER—Vancouver and Howe Sound

16 INTERNATIONAL DISTRESS AND CALLING. *Calling channel.* Used only for distress and urgency traffic, for safety calls and contacting other stations. Listen first to make sure no distress traffic is in progress. Do not transmit if a *SEELONCE MAYDAY* is declared. Keep all communications to a minimum. Do not repeat a call to the same station more than once every two minutes. After three attempts, wait 15 minutes before calling the same station.

22A COAST GUARD LIASON. A government channel used for Safety and Liason communications with the Coast Guard. Also known as Channel 22 US.

To contact the Canadian Coast Guard, use Channel 16 to call the station nearest you: Comox, Prince Rupert, Tofino or Vancouver.

67 INTERSHIP AND SHIP-SHORE. All vessels. *Working channel.*

68 INTERSHIP AND SHIP-SHORE. Pleasure vessels. *Working channel.* Also for MARINAS SOUTH OF COURTENAY. Do not call marinas in Canada on Channel 16—they are not authorized to use 16. All marinas monitor a common frequency, depending on their geographical location.

69 INTERSHIP AND SHIP-SHORE. Pleasure vessels. Also MAREP channel. *Working channel.*

70 DIGITAL SELECTIVE CALLING ONLY (No Voice) FOR DISTRESS AND CALLING.

71 VESSEL TRAFFIC SERVICE COMOX—Northern Strait of Georgia east of Vancouver Island to Cape Caution.

72 INTERSHIP. All vessels. *Working channel.*

73 INTERSHIP AND SHIP-SHORE. All vessels. *Working channel.* Also for MARINAS CAMPBELL RIVER AND NORTH.

74 VESSEL TRAFFIC SERVICE VANCOUVER—Fraser River.

VESSEL TRAFFIC SERVICE TOFINO—West of Vancouver Island.

Even though you may use alternate communication means such as cellular phone, MONITOR VHF 16.
The safety of yourself, your family and your friends is enhanced by a watch on 16 by *all vessels.*

Radiotelephone Procedure Signals:

MAYDAY ------------------- Vessel threatened by grave and imminent danger and requests immediate assistance

PAN PAN ------------------- Urgent message concerning safety of vessel or person on board or in sight.

SECURITÉ --------------- Message concerning safety of navigation or meteorological warning.

SEELONCE MAYDAY -- Mayday in progress, do not transmit normal communications.

SEELONCE FEENE ---- Resume normal communications.

the northeast corner of the bay. Easy anchoring depths are close to shore in this bight, so you'll probably run a stern-tie to shore.

Centre Bay. Most of Centre Bay is deep, but the little bight on the west side, just inside the entrance, has 3-4-fathom anchoring depths, and is delightful. Run a stern-tie to a tree to control your swing and make room for others. The lands around this bight are being developed, but as of late 1999, no construction yet. We anchored in this bight during a roaring westerly out on the Strait of Georgia, and enjoyed flat calm all night long. Royal Vancouver and West Vancouver yacht clubs have outstations in Centre Bay. The docks belonging to the Centre Bay Yacht Station are at the head of the bay.

Port Graves. Port Graves is definitely the most scenic of Gambier Island's inlets, and has good anchoring depths at the head. A public wharf with small float is located at the head of the bay, and a private dock a short distance to the west. Anchor in the area off those docks and between them to avoid logging cable on the bottom.

Halkett Bay. Halkett Bay, at the southeast corner of Gambier Island, has room for 4-5

Gibsons Landing founder George W. Gibson looks perpetually out to sea from his perch on the main street of his town.

boats, and can be somewhat active in southerly winds. Rocks are on the west side of the bay. Approach along the east shoreline. A small float provides access to Halkett Bay Marine Park, pit toilets, primitive campsites, hiking trails.

Brigade Bay. Brigade Bay is on the eastern shore of Gambier Island, and is a good possibility. Anne Vipond, reporting in *Pacific Yachting,* suggests that because of deep water fairly close to shore, a stern anchor be set toward the beach and the main anchor set offshore.

Gambier Harbour Public Wharf has 100 feet of dock space.

New Brighton Public Wharf, Thornbrough Bay, has 390 feet of dock space.

Plumper Cove Marine Park. Use chart 3526. Plumper Cove Marine Park is in a cove formed Keats Island and two small nearby islands. The park has a dinghy float and several mooring buoys. A rock, marked by a buoy, lies a dozen yards off the dinghy float. There is anchorage for quite a few boats, and 78 acres of park land ashore on Keats Island. While the anchorage is protected from many winds, the fresh westerly mentioned in the Centre Bay entry, above, rolled people out of their berths that night.

Porteau Cove Marine Park. Porteau Cove is located on the east shore of Howe Sound, at latitude 49° 33' N. The park is open all year, mooring buoys, toilets, launch ramp, walk-in campsites, hiking trails and a picnic area. Sunken ships and manmade reefs provide excellent scuba diving. Watch your depths; some of the cove dries at low tide.

Squamish Boat Harbour, open all year, 775 feet of dock space. Located at the north end of Howe Sound, on the west bank of the east arm of the Squamish River.

The Gap, a sandy shoal with a least depth of 5 feet is between Keats Island and Steep Bluff. Although waves off the Strait of Georgia tend to break on this shoal, if you know your draft and the state of the tide you can approach Gibsons from the Strait of Georgia via The Gap and have no problems—unless it's rough, and then you should go around Keats Island.

Gibsons. Use chart 3534; 3526. As you approach the marina complex at Gibsons you will see the fuel dock just ahead. Gibsons Marina is to port of the fuel dock, and the Gibsons public dock, which should be much upgraded by the 2000 cruising season (see entry below), is to starboard.

A shoal extends from the shore between the public dock and the Hyak Marine fuel dock. Approach each dock directly from seaward. Avoid the water between them.

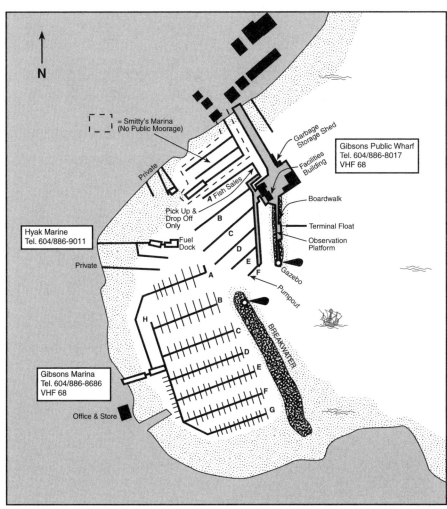

Gibsons

Reference only — not for navigation

The town of Gibsons recently completed a $1.5 million revitalization, with new lights, paving, and other niceties. The restaurant and merchant population is growing. In the town you will find a well-stocked grocery store, book store, and most other supplies you might need. Also an interesting maritime museum. Gibsons is a good place to stretch your legs. The ferry from Horseshoe Bay arrives at Langdale, a couple of miles upsound from Gibsons.

⑪ **Gibsons Marina**, P.O. Box 1520, Gibsons, B.C. V0N 1V0, (604)886-8686. Monitors VHF channel 68. Open all year except Christmas and New Year, guest moorage available, 15

amp power, washrooms, showers, chandlery, laundry, pumpout, concrete launch ramp. This is a nice size marina, friendly folks, close to shopping.

⑪ **Hyak Marine**, P.O. Box 948, Gibsons Harbour, Gibsons, B.C. V0N 1V0, (604)886-9011, fax (604)886-9011. Open all year (closed Mondays October-March), gasoline & diesel fuel, marine supplies, haulout to 60 feet or 100 tons, repairs, towing available.

⑪ **Gibsons Landing Harbour Authority**, (604)886-8017, monitors VHF channel 68. Open all year with guest moorage, 30 amp

power, washrooms, laundry, pumpout station. The Public Wharf has substantial improvements planned for the 2000 cruising season, including expanded guest floats and power upgraded from 15 amp to 30 amp. A television camera security system has been installed. Look for a new promanade on top of the breakwater, with a gazebo at the end. Twelve mooring buoys are scheduled to be installed in spring 2000. Gone from the wharf will be the portable office and toilets, and in their place a new building. An attendant is on duty during the days, every day of the year. Fresh seafood is available "off the boat" on the commercial floats. Complete shopping is nearby.

Stern-Ties, and How to Carry Them

STERN-TIES ARE DESIRABLE and often necessary when a boat anchors in the Northwest. In crowded anchorages, stern-ties keep boats from swinging into one another. Often they are essential if a boat is to remain safely at anchor between two rocks, rather than swing onto them.

We have seen stern-tie tackle of varying lengths and appropriateness, from sailboat spinnaker sheets tied together, to reels of rope cleverly mounted, ready for use.

While rope of any kind will serve in a pinch, we think the best choice is polypropylene. It's strong, it floats, and it's cheap. We also think it's better to have too much rope, not too little. A 600-foot reel of ½-inch polypropylene rope will meet almost any need, yet stow nicely on nearly any size boat. With 600 feet available, a stern-tie can be run around a tree and back to the boat. When it's time to depart the tie can be recovered without rowing ashore.

The trick is to mount the reel of rope so it can pay out and be recovered quickly, easily, and without tangling. The pictures here show some alternatives.

SURPRISE'S *stern-tie setup. It is made from ⅞" stainless steel tubing and off-the-shelf rail fittings. The tubing is stored disassembled until it is needed. The 600' reel of ½" polypropylene rope is stored below deck.*

A carefully built, side-mounted reel.

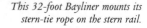

This 32-foot Bayliner mounts its stern-tie rope on the stern rail.

This reel is mounted on its own stanchion.

Gower Point to Sechelt Inlet

Welcome Passage • Buccaneer Bay • Smuggler Cove • Secret Cove
Pender Harbour • Egmont • Sechelt Rapids • Sechelt Inlet

Charts	
3311	SMALL CRAFT CHARTS (strip charts) Sunshine Coast to Desolation Sound
3312	SMALL CRAFT CHART (chartbook) Jervis Inlet & Desolation Sound
3512	Strait of Georgia, Central Portion (1:80,000)
3514	Jervis Inlet (1:50,000); Malibu and Sechelt Rapids
3535	PLANS – Malaspina Strait: Pender Harbour, Secret Cove/Smuggler Cove, Welcome Passage

Beautiful Smuggler Cove is a maze of inlets and anchorages.

FROM HOWE SOUND to Pender Harbour the coast is largely a barren run. The exceptions are the Port Stalashen facility at Wilson Creek, Buccaneer Bay, Secret Cove, Smuggler Cove, and to a lesser extent Halfmoon Bay. When the weather gets up the going can be wet and slow. But with a weather eye, the passages can be easy.

(19) **Port Stalashen**, RR#1, Field Site C26, Sechelt, B.C. V0N 3A0, (604)885-4884; (604)740-0163. Use chart 3311 sheet 3 (larger scale, preferred); 3512. This is a breakwater-protected private marina at the deluxe new condominium development at Wilson Creek, south of Trail Bay. Until condo residents take all the moorage some slips are available for transient boats. Power is 30 amp, washrooms and showers not yet in service. The approach is shallow, only 2-3 feet of water at zero tide.

Trail Bay. Use chart 3512. A rock breakwater protects a small moorage at **Selma Park**, on the south shore of Trail Bay. We once waited out a nasty southeasterly, riding on the hook in this hideout.

Halfmoon Bay. Use chart 3535 (larger scale, preferred) or 3512. A public dock with 170 feet of mooring space is at the head of Halfmoon Bay, with a store (a longtime landmark) a short distance away. Henry Hightower, a resident of Halfmoon Bay and a Grenfell 32 owner, provided us with the following insider's view of the facilities and anchorage possibilities. He writes:

"The store at the Halfmoon Bay government wharf is well stocked, and has the best bacon and free-range eggs, as well as fresh and packaged meat, fruit, vegetables and staples, fishing gear, beer, wine and liquor, convenience store stuff, and a gift shop.

"If a strong wind is blowing or forecast, there will almost certainly be at least one tug and log boom fixed across the open south side of Priestland Cove, between the shore and

the charted rocks. There is quite a bit of room to anchor behind its shelter."

Priestland Cove is southeast of the government dock. It is shown clearly at 1:25,000 on large-scale chart 3535, but not well on the 1:80,00 chart 3512.

Welcome Passage. Use chart 3535 (larger scale, preferred) or 3512. Welcome Passage separates South Thormanby Island and the Sechelt Peninsula, and is used by boats of all types bound up or down the Sunshine Coast. Currents run to 3 knots at the north end of the pass and 2 knots off Merry Island at the south end. When wind and current oppose each other, the waters can be rough and uncomfortable. Watch for drift. The passage west of Merry Island is deep and easily navigated.

Buccaneer Bay. Use chart 3535; 3512. Buccaneer Bay lies between North Thormanby and South Thormanby Islands, and has a beautiful white sand beach at the south end and west side. The beach is a popular picnic and play area for people in boats of all sizes. Be careful to enter Buccaneer Bay by leaving the Tattenham Ledge light buoy Q51 to port. The buoy is well north of South Thormanby Island, but it marks the end of Tattenham Ledge and should be respected. Once in Buccaneer Bay, you can find anchorage in 5-6 fathoms behind the Surrey Islands or in 4-5 fathoms in Water Bay. The Surrey Islets anchorage is particularly cozy and attractive. A private moorage is in Water Bay. During the day small boat traffic to and from the dock will rock you some, but it dies down at night. Watching your depths, you can also snug up to the shoaling waters off Gill Beach, at the south

end of the bay. In a southerly, you'll get some wind but no seas.

Smuggler Cove. Use chart 3535 or 3311. *Proposed No Discharge Zone. Gray water okay. See p. 15.* Smuggler Cove has a tricky entrance, but opens to a beautiful anchorage area that is protected from all weather. Before entering, first-timers should have in hand Chart 3535, or sheet 3 from Chart 3311, Sunshine Coast strip charts. As the charts show, the channel lies very close to the Isle Capri side of the entrance, to avoid rocky shoals extending from the south shore. Inside is **Smuggler Cove Marine Park**, which has no facilities for boaters or campers, but does have trails through the park's 400 acres of woodlands. A favorite diversion is simply paddling the dinghy among all the little islets and coves. Because Smuggler Cove is such a popular area, most boaters will reduce swinging room by taking a stern-tie to rings placed in the rock ashore.

Reference only — not for navigation

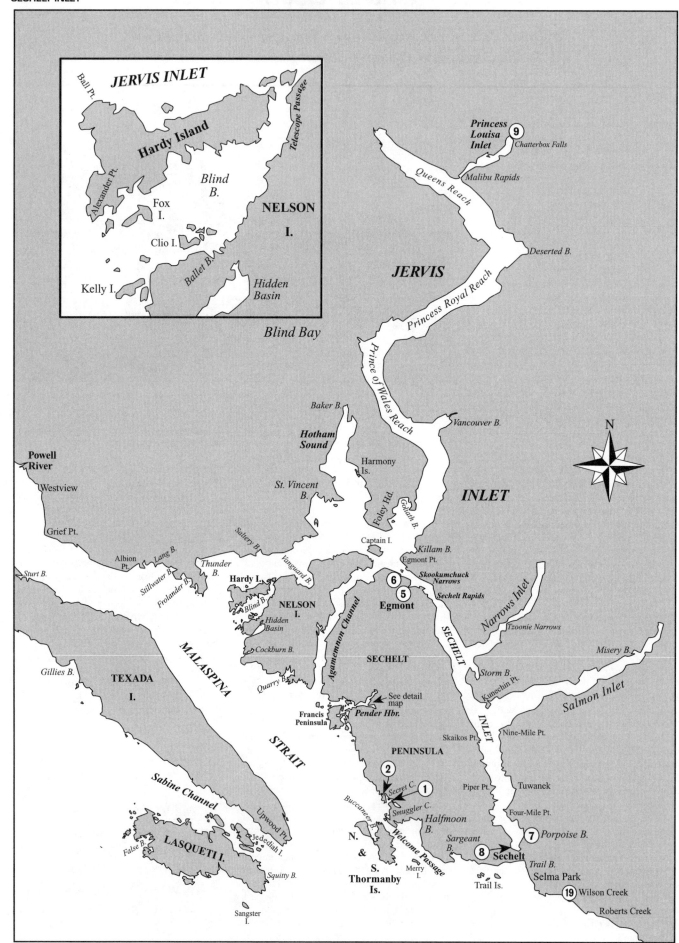

JERVIS INLET

Ball Pt.

Telescope Passage

Hardy Island

Alexander Pt.

Blind
B.

NELSON
I.

Fox
I.

Clio I.

Ballet B.

Kelly I.

Hidden
Basin

Blind Bay

Princess
Louisa
Inlet ⑨ Chatterbox Falls

Malibu Rapids

Queens Reach

Deserted B.

JERVIS

Princess Royal Reach

Prince of Wales Reach

Baker B.

Vancouver B.

Hotham
Sound

Harmony
Is.

St. Vincent
B.

INLET

Foley Hd.

Goliath B.

Powell
River

Westview

Captain I.

Killam B.

Egmont Pt.

Grief Pt.

Saltery B.

Vanguard B.

Skookumchuck
Narrows

Narrows Inlet

Albion
Pt.

Lang B.

Thunder
B.

⑥
⑤ Sechelt Rapids

Sturt B.

Stillwater B.

Frolander B.

Hardy I.

Egmont

Tzoonie Narrows

Blind B.

NELSON
I.

Misery B.

SECHELT

Hidden
Basin

SECHELT

Gillies B.

Cockburn B.

Storm B.

TEXADA
I.

Kunechin Pt.

MALASPINA

Quarry B.

See detail
map

Salmon Inlet

Pender Hbr.

Francis
Peninsula

STRAIT

INLET

Nine-Mile Pt.

PENINSULA

Skaikos Pt.

Sabine Channel

②

Secret C. ①

Piper Pt.

Tuwanek

Upwood Pt.

Buccaneer B.

Smuggler C.

Four-Mile Pt.

Jedediah I.

Halfmoon
B.

⑦ Porpoise B.

False B.

LASQUETI I.

Welcome Passage

N.
&
S.
Thormanby
Is.

Merry
I.

Sargeant
B.

⑧ Sechelt

Squitty B.

Trail Is.

Trail B.

Selma Park

⑲ Wilson Creek

Sangster
I.

Roberts Creek

Secret Cove. Use plans chart 3535 (highly recommended) or chart 3311, or small scale chart 3512. Secret Cove has three branches, each with excellent weather protection and easy anchoring depths. Unfortunately, the Secret Cove bottom is notorious for anchor dragging in strong winds, so be sure you are well and safely set if you do anchor.

Enter Secret Cove north of a light on a small rock in the middle of the entrance. Inside are the three arms. The southern arm has a very narrow entrance but adequate depths inside. This arm is surrounded by private docks that restrict the swinging room in the middle. You can find room, however, off the Royal Vancouver Yacht Club outstation docks about halfway in. The holding ground there is only fair. The center arm has the moorage of the Buccaneer Marina. The north arm is occupied almost entirely by the Secret Cove Marina. There is still plenty of room for anchoring in the north arm, using stern-ties to the shore if need be. A public float is adjacent to Secret Cove Marina.

① **Buccaneer Marina & Resort Ltd.,** Site C2, RR 2, Halfmoon Bay, B.C. V0N 1Y0, (604)885-7888; fax (604)885-7824; e-mail Buccaneer_Marina@sunshine.net. Open all year, limited guest moorage, gasoline & diesel fuel. A full service marina with 15 amp power, chandlery, washrooms, tackle and bait, boat rentals, haulout to 40 feet, paved launch ramp with long term parking, and repairs.

Located in the center arm of Secret Cove. *(See marine page this page)*

Secret Cove Public Wharf, adjacent to the Secret Cove Marina. Dock has 144 feet of moorage, commercial vessels have priority.

② **Secret Cove Marina,** P.O. Box 1118, Sechelt, B.C. V0N 3A0, (604)885-3533; fax (604)885-6037. Open April 1 through Sept. 30. This is a full service marina in the north arm of Secret Cove, with gasoline and diesel fuel, guest moorage, 15 & 30 amp power, washrooms, clean showers, liquor agency, restaurant, store with groceries, block and cube ice, fishing licenses and tackle. Reservations requested. The marina came under new and very competent ownership for the 1999 season, and we heard rave reviews all summer long. We visited by boat in June and again in September. Each time, the premises were clean and in good order. The store has a wide selection of foods and other essentials, including a good wine selection. While we didn't try the restaurant, we heard good reports about it from our readers. This marina had developed a mixed reputation in recent years, but that's all changed now. *(See marine map this page)*

Lord Jim's Resort Hotel, Ole's Cove Road, RR 1, Halfmoon Bay, B.C. V0N 1Y0, (604)885-7038; fax (604)7036. Lord Jim's is a popular resort hotel with an excellent dining room, licensed lounge, rooms, and fishing char-

ters. Courtesy pickup from Secret Cove Marina.

Bargain Bay. Although its entrance is actually off the Strait of Georgia, Bargain Bay is properly a part of the complex of bays that

Reference only — not for navigation

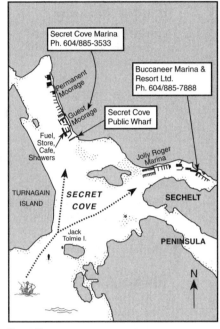

Secret Cove

See area map page 160

John Henry's Marinas Inc.
Pender Harbour

Come in for complimentary coffee. Meet the owners, Wayne & Lucy Archbold.

At John Henry's, you'll find **_complete waterfront shopping._** Extended hours, 7 days a week.

**Fresh Produce, Meat & Groceries
Fuel Dock • Propane • Ice
Bait • Tackle • Charts
Fishing & Hunting Licences
Liquor Agency • Lotto
Post Office • Video Rentals
Fax, Copy & Office Services
Harbour Electronics**

(604)883-2253
P.O. Box 40
Garden Bay, BC V0N 1S0
Fax (604)883-2147

FISHERMAN'S RESORT & MARINA

PENDER HARBOUR
On British Columbia's Sunshine Coast

Moorage—Nightly, Weekly, Monthly
Waterfront Cabins & RV Sites
Charters—Fishing & Cruising
Boat Sitting Service
Secure Parking
Showers & Laundry
Ice & Bait
Tackle—Sales & Rental
Marine Repairs
Launching Ramp
Boat Rentals
Charts, Clothing & Books
Next to General Store
Adjacent Restaurants, Pubs & Fuel
Nearby Hiking Trails & Golf

BOX 68 GARDEN BAY
BRITISH COLUMBIA V0N 1S0
24-HOUR PHONE (604) 883-2336

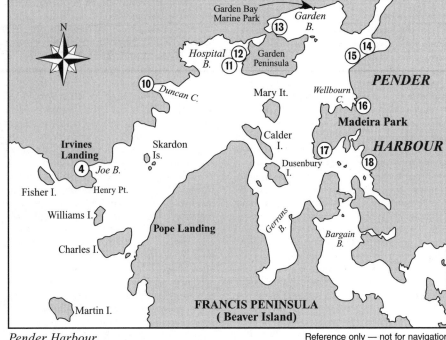

Pender Harbour

Reference only — not for navigation

make up Pender Harbour. The entrance to Bargain Bay is easy and open until well into the bay, where a drying reef and an underwater rock extend out from the west shore. A shallow, high-water-only channel, spanned by a low bridge, runs between Bargain Bay and Gerrans Bay.

Fuel, Moorage and Great Food in a friendly pub atmosphere

the bite's on!
at
**Irvines Landing
Marina & Pub**

Marina 7am-8pm
Pub 11am-11pm
Phone 883-1145

Garden Bay
HOTEL & MARINA
PUB & RESTAURANT

Ocean View Fine Dining
Ocean View Pub & Grill with Patio
Live Entertainment in Pub
Overnight Moorage

(604) 883-2674 PHONE/FAX
PO BOX 90, GARDEN BAY BC V0N 1S0

PENDER HARBOUR

Use chart 3535 (recommended) or 3512. Pender Harbour is a natural stopover for boats heading north or south in Georgia Strait. For northbound boats, it's just the right day's run from Nanaimo or Howe Sound. For boats southbound from Desolation Sound, it's a good place to prepare for the long, exposed legs back to Nanaimo or Howe Sound. Boats bound to or from Princess Louisa Inlet often use Pender Harbour both coming and going.

Pender Harbour has a number of good marinas and anchorages, restaurants to enjoy, stores for shopping, and facilities for repair. A look at the chart will show that Pender Harbour is a complex of coves tucked in behind the Francis Peninsula. The entrance is by way of a marked channel north of Williams Island and the Skardon Islands.

The first marina is Irvines Landing, in Joe Bay, just inside Henny Point. Irvines Landing has moorage and fuel, and a good pub.

The second marina on the north shore is the Duncan Cove resort. Hospital Bay is the third bay along the north shore, with Fisherman's Resort and Marina, John Henry's store and fuel dock, and a public dock. Hospital Bay once was the site of the St. Mary's Columbia Coast Mission Hospital, built in 1929. The hospital, which overlooks the bay, now is the Sundowner Inn & Restaurant.

Garden Bay, at the northeast corner of Pender Harbour, has two marinas, one of them with a restaurant and pub. Seattle Yacht Club and Royal Vancouver Yacht Club have outstations in Garden Bay. The holding ground is good and the protection excellent. Many boats anchor out and dinghy either to the marinas or to Madeira Park. Garden Bay Provincial Park has about 50 feet of frontage on the north shore, but no facilities for boaters.

John Henry's fuel dock and grocery store faces Hospital Bay, on the narrow peninsula that separates Garden Bay and Hospital Bay. John Henry's store is not quite a supermarket, but it is well stocked, carries produce and meats, and has a post office and a liquor agency. Across from Garden Bay, the town of Madeira Park has a substantial public wharf, much upgraded since 1999 to be more appealing to visiting boats. A small shopping center is located about a block from the Madeira Park public wharf. For real provisioning, Madeira Park is where you'll go.

Pender Harbour has several drying and underwater rocks throughout, but most of them are marked. With a detailed chart and a little care, the visitor should have no problems. Just remember to pay attention.

Golf: The Pender Harbour Golf Club 9-hole course is terrific. If you walk the course you'll get a workout, and the scenery is beautiful. Call (604)883-9541.

④ **Irvines Landing Marina & Pub,** RR #1, S10, C9, Garden Bay, B.C. V0N 1S0, (604)883-2296; fax (604)883-2080. Open April to mid-October, gasoline and diesel fuel at the fuel dock, 15 amp power, washrooms, showers. Guest moorage is available, and they have a pub with very good food. This is the first marina to port as you enter Pender Harbour.

⑩ **Duncan Cove Resort,** 4686 Sinclair Bay Rd. RR#1, Garden Bay, B.C. V0N 1S0, (604)883-2424. Or view their web site at www.duncancoveresort.com. Open all year, guest moorage available, 15 & 30 amp power, washrooms, showers, laundry, portapotty dump. They have 2400 feet of dock space, a small store, cottages, motel units, launch ramp, and RV sites. Located on the north side of Pender Harbour, a short distance past Irvines Landing. Judy and Albert Hull are the owners.

Hospital Bay Public Wharf, in Hospital Bay, with 520 feet of dock space.

⑪ **Fisherman's Resort & Marina,** P.O. Box 68, Garden Bay, B.C. V0N 1S0, (604)883-2336. Open all year, guest moorage available along 2300 feet of dock, 15 & 30 amp power, washrooms, showers, laundry. Located in Hospital Bay, adjacent to John Henry's fuel dock and store. Wally and Susan Nowik have created a quiet, well-cared-for marina, with beautiful lawns and flower gardens, cottages and RV sites, and good docks. They handle boats of all sizes, including the large motor yachts. *(Marina map page 164)*

⑫ **John Henry's Marinas, Inc.,** P.O. Box 40, Garden Bay, B.C. V0N 1S0, (604)883-2253. Open all year. John Henry's is located in Hospital Bay. It has a fuel dock and a well-stocked store, including fresh produce and meats, charts, liquor agency, and post office. They also have fishing tackle, bait, ice, and video rentals. Wayne and Lucy Archbold are the owners.

⑬ **Garden Bay Hotel & Marina,** P.O. Box 90, Garden Bay, B.C. V0N 1S0, (604)883-2674; e-mail gardenbay@sunshine.net. Open all year, guest moorage available along 1200 feet of dock, 15 & 30 amp power, washrooms available. This is a large, full-service marina with a gift shop, a popular pub, and good dining. Guest moorage is limited in the winter, but the pub is open 7 days a week all year. Ted Meisinger and Heather Gratland are the owners.

⑬ **Sportsman's Marina & Resort,** P.O. Box 143, Garden Bay, B.C. V0N 1S0, (604)883-2479. Open all year, 150 feet of guest moorage, 15 amp power, water, showers, laundry, 2 rental cabins. This marina is located just east of the Garden Bay Hotel & Marina. It has been there for years, but hasn't promoted guest moorage until recently. Dennis Brown is the manager.

Dining: The Garden Bay Hotel & Marina is good, and the Sundowner Inn, in the restored St. Mary's Columbia Mission Hospital building, is a good spot.

Gunboat Bay. Gunboat Bay is entered through a very narrow channel with a least depth of 4 feet. An underwater rock lies just to the north of the centerline. Currents in this channel are quite strong except at slack water. The bay opens up into a good anchorage before it peters out into drying flats.

⑭ **Headwater Marine,** P.O. Box 71, Madeira Park, B.C. V0N 2H0, (604)883-2406. Monitors VHF channel 68. Open all year, some

off

Come To Pender Harbour BC

Situated at the junction of the Malaspina Strait & the Agamemnon Channel, Pender Harbour offers perhaps the safest & most beautiful anchorage on the Sunshine Coast.

A complete upgrade of the moorage at Madeira Park has just been completed. It includes 500 ft of dedicated pleasure craft moorage c/w 15, 30 and 50 amp power. A new office c/w showers & toilets, holding tank pump out. A small park at the head of the dock has picnic tables etc.

The Village stores are just two blocks away. They include: banks, food stores, hair stylists, pharmacy, craft store, liquor store, real estate, insurance, legal office, post office, canoe, car and kayak rentals.

Excellent fresh water lakes nearby provide the visitor with safe swimming.

Come check us out for amenities and hospitality. Call: 604-883-2234 or VHF channel 68

Welcome to IGA of MADEIRA PARK PENDER HARBOUR

Here at Pender Harbour's largest market, you'll find a wonderful selection of groceries. We offer many choices and fully stocked shelves in every department.

WE OFFER COMPLETE SHOPPING:

ABUNDANCE OF FRESH PRODUCE

FRESH DAIRY, MEATS & SEAFOOD

WIDE SELECTION

"CITY" PRICES

NEW COFFEE, ICE CREAM & LOTTO CENTER

FREE DOCKSIDE DELIVERY ON ORDERS $50 OR MORE

WE'RE TODAY'S IGA

MADEIRA PARK, PENDER HARBOUR TEL. (604)883-9100 FAX (604)883-9145

*Early morning in
Garden Bay,
showing the
anchored boats.*

*John Henry's,
on the Peninsula
between Garden Bay
and Hospital Bay,
has a complete
grocery selection,
and liquor agency.*

guest moorage. Campsites available, washrooms, showers. Marine railway haulout for boats to 42 feet.

⑮ **Sunshine Coast Resort Ltd.,** P.O. Box 213, Madeira Park, B.C. V0N 2H0, (604)883-9177 phone/fax. Monitors VHF channel 16, switch to 69. Open all year, 600 feet of guest moorage, 15 & 30 amp power, washrooms, showers, laundry, live bait, boat rentals, accommodations. Tidy and well-maintained. The docks are at the bottom of a steep mountainside. Offices, showers, laundry, road to town are a considerable climb up the hill. The marina is located in the small bay to the right as you approach Gunboat Bay, about ½ mile north of Madeira Park shopping. Ralph Linnmann is the manager.

Reference only — not for navigation

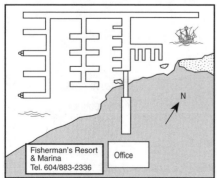

Fisherman's Resort and Marina

⑯ **Pender Harbour Authority Madeira Park Public Wharf,** Box 118, Madeira Park, B.C. V0N 2H0, (604)883-2234; fax (604)883-2152. Open all year, 640 feet of dedicated visitor moorage space, 30 amp power, washrooms, showers, waste oil disposal, pumpout station, aircraft float, BBQ area, close to two supermarkets (one of them the well-stocked IGA), a drugstore, liquor store, other shopping and services. In 1999 considerable upgrading was begun at this public dock, to make Madeira Park not just a dock for the dinghy, but a destination in its own right. A walkway and gazebo, a small park and new offices were built, much of it by volunteer labor. At press time the washrooms, showers and a pumpout station were in the works and should be completed for the 2000 boating season. Watch our web site www.waggonerguide.com for updates.

⑯ **Madeira Marina Ltd.,** P.O. Box 189, Madeira Park, B.C. V0N 2H0, (604)883-2266. Open all year. Guest moorage for their RV and motel guests only. Marine supplies available at chandlery. Complete repairs. A marine railway, with haulout to 35 tons, 45 feet, is planned to be completed by spring 2000.

Gerrans Bay. Anchorage is good in Gerrans Bay.

⑰ **Coho Marina,** P.O. Box 160, Madeira Park, B.C. V0N 2H0, (604)883-2248. Monitors VHF channel 68. Open all year, some guest moorage available, 15 & 30 amp power,

washrooms, showers, tackle, snacks, ice, camping. 5 minute walk to shopping. Just off Gerrans Bay, look for the sign.

⑱ **Lowes Resort Motel,** P.O. Box 153, Madeira Park, B.C. V0N 2H0, (604)883-2456; fax (604)883-2474. Lowes is in the cove on the east side of Gerrans Bay, and is reached via a narrow entrance. They are primarily a fishing resort.

Agamemnon Channel. Agamemnon Channel runs northeastward between Nelson Island and the mainland, and is the shortest route for those heading for Princess Louisa Inlet, Egmont, or the Sechelt Inlet. The only reasonable anchorage is at Green Bay. There is a private marina at Agamemnon Bay. The ferry to Saltery Bay leaves from Agamemnon Bay.

SECHELT INLET

Egmont. Use chart 3514 or chartbook 3312. Egmont, on the Sechelt Peninsula, is near the entrance to Skookumchuck Narrows and the Sechelt Rapids. The Sechelt Inlet lies beyond the rapids. The Egmont Marina and the Bathgate General Store and Marina both have fuel. The Egmont Marina fronts on Skookumchuck Narrows; Bathgate lies in Secret Bay, behind a well-marked reef. The public dock is adjacent.

The reef in Secret Bay can confuse a first-time visitor, especially a visitor with limited familiarity with the navigation aids. Remember: *Red, Right, Returning.* When entering, leave the red daymark well off your right hand and you'll have no problems. If you still aren't sure, just remember to go around the ends, *not between the two beacons. (See map below)*

⑤ **Bathgate General Store & Marina,** 6781 Bathgate Rd., Egmont, B.C. V0N 1N0, (604)883-2222; fax (604)883-2750; or view at www.bathgate.com. Monitors VHF chan-

Reference only — not for navigation

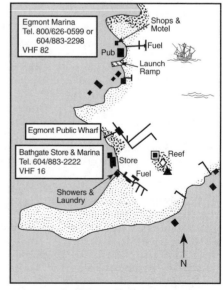

Secret Bay (Bathgate & Egmont Marinas)

This is the reef at the entrance to Secret Bay. Round the beacons at the ends of the reef, don't go between them.

nel 16, switch to 68. Open all year, gasoline and diesel at the fuel dock, limited guest moorage available, 15, 20 & 30 amp power, showers, laundry. The store carries fresh vegetables, marine supplies, and has a full liquor agency. Propane is available. They have haulouts to 40 tons, with repairs available. See Doug and Vicki Martin. *(Marina map page 164)*

⑤ **Egmont Public Wharf,** in Secret Bay, 500 feet of dock space. Commercial vessels have priority. The outer end of the eastern float is reserved for float planes.

⑥ **Egmont Marina Resort,** General Delivery, Egmont, B.C. V0N 1N0, (604)883-2298 phone/fax, (800)626-0599. Or view at www.egmont-marina.com. Monitors VHF channel 16, switch to 82. Open all year, gasoline and diesel fuel available, guest moorage available for boats to 90 feet, 15 & 30 amp power, washrooms, showers, laundry, gravel launch ramp. Located opposite Sutton Island on the south shore. Watch the current as you approach—someone is usually available to help. The Backeddy Pub serves food. We've been told that their Skookumchuck Burger is outstanding. Bring a friend because the burger is *big*. They have a small store with convenience items, ice and kerosene, live bait, kayak rentals, diving air and diving charters. They also have a launch ramp, hotel, RV park, cabins, and emergency service to Princess Louisa Inlet. See John and Margaret Mills. *(Marina map page 164)*

Sechelt Rapids. Use chart 3514 (larger scale, preferred), 3512 or chartbook 3312. The Sechelt Rapids, also known as the Skookumchuck Rapids (skookum means "big" or "strong," and chuck means "body of water"), can be extremely dangerous except at or near slack water. At full flow the rapids are a boiling cauldron, with 8-foot overfalls and 12-16 knot currents. Even an hour before slack, when many other rapids may have calmed down, the Sechelt Rapids can be menacing.

Times of turn and maximum current are shown in the Tide and Current Tables, Vol. 5. On neap tides the maximum current can be as little as 1-2 knots, and quiet. But the next exchange could have a 7.4-knot current and be very dangerous. Check the Tide and Current Tables and plan accordingly.

Lacking prior experience, do not even think about going through without chart 3514 with its 1:20,000 insert of the rapids, or chartbook 3312, with large scale insets not only of the Sechelt Rapids but also of Secret Bay. Sailing Directions says the best route through the rapids is west of Boom Islet (choked with kelp, but safe) and west of the Sechelt Islets Light.

We, however, have run a dogleg course without discomfort through the middle of the channel, between the Sechelt Islets and the unnamed islet directly north of the Sechelt Islets. This area is where dangerous whirlpools can develop on ebb flows, so be careful. Give Roland Point a wide berth, especially on a flood. You may meet tugs with tows in the rapids.

Either direction, the Sechelt Rapids are just fine at slack, and if you time it well (easily done) you'll slide through with no problems at all. But when the rapids are running, their roar can be heard for miles. They aren't the place to show off how brave and hairy-chested you are by going through whenever you happen to get there, without referring to the current tables.

Before making your own entrance it can be instructive to walk to the rapids from Egmont, or from a little notch just outside the rapids, to watch the channel in full boil.

Sechelt Inlet. Use chart 3512 or chartbook 3312. Beautiful Sechelt Inlet with few anchorages and limited facilities for pleasure craft, is often passed by—especially with Princess Louisa Inlet at the end of nearby Jervis Inlet. Sechelt Rapids also serve as a gate to keep out all but the determined.

To explore Sechelt Inlet and its arms, use chart 3512 (1:80:000) or chartbook 3312. The inlet is shown at 1:40,000 in chartbook 3312. Sechelt Inlet extends about 15 miles

The Egmont Marina Resort has guest moorage, fuel dock, and pub.

south of Sechelt Rapids. It ends at Porpoise Bay, the back door to the town of Sechelt, where there is a public float and easy anchorage. Two long arms, Salmon Inlet and Narrows Inlet, run from the eastern side of Sechelt Inlet into the heart of the Earle mountain range. There are a number of small provincial park sites in Sechelt Inlet, most of them best suited to small boats that can be pulled up on the beach.

Inflow winds can blow from south to north in Sechelt Inlet, and up Salmon Inlet and Narrows Inlet. The northern parts of Sechelt Inlet may be near calm, but the southern part increasingly windy. In Salmon Inlet and Narrows Inlet, the inflow winds will grow stronger as the inlets deepen and narrow. Outflow winds can develop at night, but in the summer they often don't unless a strong southeasterly is blowing out on the strait.

The tidal range does not exceed 10 feet in Sechelt Inlet, and the times of high and low tide are 2-3 hours after Point Atkinson. Two secondary ports, Porpoise Bay and Storm Bay, are shown in Tide and Current Tables, Vol. 5. Current predictions for Tzoonie Narrows, in Narrows Inlet, are shown under Secondary Stations in Tide and Current Tables, Vol. 5.

⑦ **Poise Cove Marina,** RR#3, Plumridge Site, Site C-2, Sechelt, B.C. V0N 3A0, (604)885-2895. Monitors VHF channel 16, switch to 68. Open all year, limited guest moorage, limited 15 amp power, concrete launch ramp, no long term parking. Located on the east side of Sechelt Inlet, about 0.3 mile from Sechelt Village, close to Porpoise Bay Marine Park, which has washrooms and showers. They have emergency towing service available and haulout to 25 feet.

⑧ **Royal Reach Marina & Hotel,** 5758 Wharf Rd, Sechelt, B.C. V0N 3A0, (604)885-7844. Open all year, guest moorage available on 1200 feet of dock, 15 amp power. Located at the head of Sechelt Inlet, about 0.25 mile from Sechelt Village. A restaurant and pub are nearby. Watch your depths at low water. *(Marina map page 167)*

⑦ **Midcoast Marine,** 5987 Sechelt Inlet Road, Sechelt, B.C. V0N 3A0, (604)740-8889. Open all year, limited guest moorage to 24 feet only, mid-grade gasoline only at fuel dock. Washrooms, no showers.

Narrows Inlet. Narrows Inlet is mostly 25 to 30 fathoms deep except at the head, where the Tzoonie River makes a delta. **Tzoonie**

Then the engine died . . . .

W HEN WE WERE LEAVING the Sechelt Inlet after a visit, we arrived at the Sechelt Rapids an hour and 20 minutes before low water slack, and eased our way down to the Sechelt Islets to see how the rapids looked. Our Tolly 26 *Surprise* had a large and powerful 454 Crusader engine that gave us the luxury of changing our minds, even in strong current. The current was carrying us faster and faster into the rapids when we decided that we were *too early.* I spun the helm and gave the engine full throttle to get back to safety. Even with the 454 wide open and gulping gasoline at 25 to 30 gallons per hour, we made just enough progress against the current to feel comfortable.

Then the engine died. In a second it caught and speeded up, *but then it died again.* Fortunately, by this time we were free of the worst of the current, and I reduced throttle. The engine had acted as if it were starved for fuel when it died. At less than full throttle it seemed to run well. Later testing showed that we had a restriction in our fuel supply, and the fuel lines were replumbed to deliver full flow.

Lesson: Even when you think you have a situation well in hand, the unexpected can occur and threaten to ruin everything. We had been imprudent in getting too close to the rapids just to save a few minutes if we found them passable. A heretofore unknown mechanical problem revealed itself at a most inopportune time, and scared us half to death. Patience, caution, and conservatism are the way to go.

—Robert Hale

Jervis Inlet

Blind Bay • Ballet Bay • Hotham Sound • Jervis Inlet
Princess Louisa Inlet

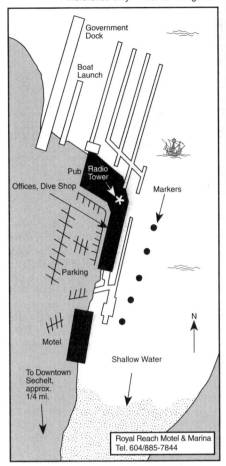

Reference only — not for navigation

Government
Dock

Boat
Launch

Radio
Tower

Pub

Offices, Dive Shop

Markers

Parking

N

Motel

Shallow Water

To Downtown
Sechelt,
approx.
1/4 mi.

Royal Reach Motel & Marina
Tel. 604/885-7844

Royal Reach Marina

Narrows, about a third of the way along, is a spectacular cleft in the high mountains that surround the inlet. Tidal currents run to a maximum of 4 knots through Tzoonie Narrows, but the passage is free of dangers. All but the slowest or lowest powered boats could run them at any time. Arguably the best anchorage in this area is in **Storm Bay,** at the mouth of Narrows Inlet. Storm Bay is very pretty, with a dramatic rock wall on its eastern shore. Anchor behind the little islets at the entrance or near the head of the bay.

Tzoonie Narrows Provincial Park. This park takes in both sides of the narrows, and is good for swimming, fishing, diving, picnicking. It has walk-in campsites. The 1-foot islet shown on the chart is a long, narrow reef, with large extensions under the surface. You can anchor inside the reef, or in the deep bight on the other side of Narrows Inlet.

Salmon Inlet. Salmon Inlet is very deep, although anchorage is possible in **Misery Bay**. A drying shoal almost blocks the inlet at Sechelt Creek, but can be passed safely by staying close to the north shore.

Charts

3311	SMALL CRAFT CHARTS (strip charts) Sunshine Coast to Desolation Sound
3312	SMALL CRAFT CHART (chartbook) Jervis Inlet & Desolation Sound
3512	Strait of Georgia, Central Portion (1:80,000)
3514	Jervis Inlet (1:50,000) Malibu Rapids (1:12,000) Sechelt Rapids (1:20,000)

Quarry Bay. Use chart 3512 or chartbook 3312. Quarry Bay faces the Strait of Georgia, and is too deep and exposed to be a destination of first choice. If you must anchor there, you could work your way in among the rocks in the southeast corner of the bay. It would be a good idea to run a stern-tie to keep you from swinging onto a rock. At the north end of Quarry Bay a little cove, surrounded by homes, is well protected and has good anchoring depths. It would be a good hideout if you needed one. Chart 3512 (1:80,000) and chartbook 3312 (1:40,000) show a stream connecting this cove with Quarry Lake. Three rocks in this cove are shown in chartbook 3312.

Cockburn Bay. Use chart 3512. Cockburn Bay is completely plugged by drying rocks, and is accessible only by small craft at or near high water.

Hidden Basin. Use chartbook 3312; chart 3512. Hidden Basin is blocked by drying shoals and rocks, and currents run strongly through the restricted entrance. At a scale of 1:40,000, chartbook 3312 shows Hidden Basin better than chart 3512 (1:80,000). Entrance to Hidden Basin should be made—carefully—at high water slack. Secure anchorage is available once inside the entrance.

Blind Bay. Use chartbook 3312, strip chart 3311, chart 3514, or chart 3512. Blind Bay has numerous anchorages, including one of the most popular in the area, Ballet Bay. Depending on the weather and your mood, the shores of Nelson Island, and especially Hardy Island, should be checked out for good spots to put the hook down. Chart 3512 (1:80,000) shows Blind Bay fairly well, but chart 3514 (1:50,000) is better, except where Blind Bay joins the Strait of Georgia. Chartbook 3312 (1:40,000) is better yet, as is strip chart 3311 sheet 4 (1:40,000). Nearly all anchorages will require a stern-tie. Use your chart and depth sounder, watch for rocks, and go slowly. Our notes say, "Use your eyes."

The area behind Fox Island has several good anchoring possibilities. One of them is **Musket Island Marine Park.** Another is the narrow, almost landlocked cove that indents Hardy Island at the northwest corner of the marine park.

Near the opposite end of Hardy Island, we anchored one night behind a little thumb of land just where Telescope Passage opens

Beautiful Musket Island Marine Park has room for several boats.

Blind Bay. Hardy Island has many cozy little nooks for anchoring. Watch the depths and watch for rocks.

See area map page 160

Kipling Cove in the Harmony Islands was empty in mid-June, so we had room to swing. In crowded summer months, stern-ties will be needed.

up. The water was deep until close to shore and the bottom looked rocky, but the Bruce anchor bit on the first try. A stern-tie held us in place.

Musket Island Marine Park. Use chartbook 3312; strip chart 3311; chart 3512. Located behind Fox Island. A beautiful spot. Anchor behind the tiny islet, or in the bay that opens up to the north of the islet. In most cases you'll stern-tie to shore.

Ballet Bay. Use chartbook 3312; strip chart 3311; chart 3512. Ballet Bay, on Nelson Island, is a popular anchorage in Blind Bay. It is well protected, very pretty, and definitely worth a stay. While at high tide you could enter Ballet Bay from the north, many rocks obstruct the path and close attention is called for. The easier entry is from the west, between Nelson Island and Clio Island. (Clio Island is marked "Aquaculture" in chartbook 3312.) If you do enter from the west, the rock shown at the point before you turn into Ballet Bay truly is there, and farther offshore than you might expect. Give it a wide berth. While many rocks in the area around Ballet Bay are marked with sticks or small floats, don't count on all of them being marked. Not all the rocks are charted, either. Go slowly and pay attention. The center of Ballet Bay is good-holding mud, but the bottom grows rockier toward shore. A trail connects Ballet Bay and Hidden Basin.

Telescope Passage. Use chartbook 3312; charts 3514, 3512. Telescope Passage connects Blind Bay with Jervis Inlet, but is partly blocked by underwater rocks that extend from the 70-meter island at the north entrance. Strongly favor the Nelson Island side until past the 70-meter island. Then trend toward the middle of the passage to avoid charted and uncharted rocks along the Nelson Island side. When approaching Telescope Passage from Jervis Inlet, you might be confused (we were) by the presence of a tiny islet almost 100 feet high, just outside the entrance. Check the chart closely: the islet is shown as the smallest oval imaginable, with (26), for 26 meters high, directly beside it.

JERVIS INLET

Use chart 3514; chartbook 3312. Jervis Inlet (Jurvis or Jarvis? We've heard good voices pronounce it each way) extends 46 miles into the British Columbia coast range, and is the route to the fabled Princess Louisa Inlet. Jervis Inlet ranges 1–1.5 miles in width, and often is more than 600 feet deep. Steep-to shores, with mountains rising directly above, make for few good anchorages. Currents in Jervis Inlet are light, and often affected by winds. Watch for drift. We heard one old-timer joke(?) that in Jervis Inlet the same tree trunks had been floating back and forth for years. Heading up-inlet, Egmont and Bathgate are the last fuel stops.

Once beyond Foley Head and Egmont

Point, you'll find only indifferent anchorages at Vancouver Bay, Deserted Bay, and Killam Bay. The 30 miles of Princess Royal Reach, Prince of Wales Reach and Queen's Reach do not have useable anchorages. Unlike the other deep fjords that penetrate from the sea, however, Jervis Inlet has a spectacular prize at the end, a prize described at the end of this short chapter: Princess Louisa Inlet.

Thunder Bay. Use chartbook 3312; charts 3514, 3512. Thunder Bay, immediately inside the north entrance to Jervis Inlet, has anchorage along its western shore.

Saltery Bay. Use chartbook 3312; charts 3514, 3512. Saltery Bay has a public float, a boat launch, and picnic sites. It is the ferry landing for road travel along the Sunshine Coast.

Saltery Bay Public Wharf, adjacent to the ferry landing. Visitor moorage is available on the 435 feet of dock space. Garbage pickup. Commercial vessels have priority.

Saltery Bay Provincial Park. Open all year, anchor only, or moor at the government wharf next to the ferry landing, a 1 km walk from the park entrance. Picnic facilities and a dive rinse station are located above the small sandy beach. Most of the shoreline is rock, however, and very impressive. In Mermaid Cove, scuba divers can look for the underwater statue of the mermaid. The dive reef is marked by white buoys. A launch ramp is a short distance west of Mermaid Cove.

St. Vincent Bay. Use chartbook 3312; charts 3514, 3512. Much oyster culture activity. Sykes Island and Junction Island offer possibilities.

Hotham Sound. Use chartbook 3312; charts 3514, 3512. Hotham Sound is a beautiful, 6-mile-long body of water, surrounded by high, rugged mountains. The sound is sheltered from most strong winds, and in the summertime the water is warm for swimming. Friel Lake Falls tumble 1400 feet down sheer mountainside near the Harmony Islands. Unfortunately, good anchorages in Hotham Sound are few indeed.

Wolferstan *(Cruising Guide to British Columbia Vol. 3, Sunshine Coast)* devotes an entire chapter, with superb aerial photos, to Hotham Sound, but for the most part even his advice comes down to finding little niches along the shoreline. In general, if you find a creek mouth you can find anchoring depths. Baker Bay, at the head of Hotham Sound, is an anchorage.

Spectacular scenery surrounds Hotham Sound. This mountain is on the west side.

Harmony Islands Marine Park. Use chartbook 3312; charts 3514, 3512. The Harmony Islands in Hotham Sound are a popular spot. The best anchorage is in Kipling Cove, among the three northernmost islands. The bottom is rocky, so be sure you have the right ground tackle and that it's well set. During high season you'll run a stern-tie to shore.

We have heard that flies can be aggressive. Our visit was in late June, and we were troubled by only a few flies in the evening—but they were indeed determined.

Malibu Rapids. Use chart 3512; chartbook 3312. Malibu Rapids mark the entrance to Princess Louisa Inlet. The rapids are narrow and dogleg-shaped, and boats at one end cannot see the boats at the other end. It is courteous—and wise—to warn other vessels via VHF radio that you are about to enter the rapids, and the direction you are traveling. Most boats use channel 16 because it is the one VHF channel each boat is supposed to monitor. The transmission can be brief: "Sécurité, Sécurité. This is the 37-foot motor vessel SURPRISE, entering Malibu Rapids eastbound." Currents in Malibu Rapids run to 9 knots, and create large overfalls. Run this passage at slack water. High water slack occurs about 24 minutes after high water slack at Point Atkinson, and low water slack about 36 minutes after low water slack at Point Atkinson. High water slack is preferred because it widens the available channel slightly. High slack or low, before entering or leaving Malibu Rapids, local knowledge says to wait until the surf created by the overfall subsides entirely.

Princess Louisa Inlet. Use chart 3512; chartbook 3312. Princess Louisa Inlet, 4 miles long, is the "holy grail" for cruising people from all over the world. Entered through Malibu Rapids, the inlet is surrounded by mile-high mountains that drop almost vertically into the deep water (1,000 feet deep) below. Yachtsmen have said entering Princess Louisa Inlet is like entering a great cathedral. The author Earle Stanley Gardner wrote of Princess Louisa Inlet, "It is more than beautiful. It is sacred." Please observe a 4-knot speed limit. Larger washes bounce off the sides of the inlet.

The Young Life Christian summer camp for teenagers is on the north shore, just inside Mailbu Rapids. The kids are welcoming and polite. They'll show you around. Farther into the inlet, several mooring buoys have been installed behind Macdonald Island. In many places, mooring rings for stern-ties have been driven into the shoreside rocks.

At the head of the inlet, at Princess Louisa Provincial Marine Park, an 895-foot-long dock will hold a large number of boats. If you wish to anchor out, anchor directly below Chatterbox Falls, which drops in a series of cascades from mountains at the head of the inlet. The inlet is deep until quite close to the stream that runs from the falls. Keeping the stream outlet in front of you, take your boat as closed as you dare and put the anchor down in 10 feet of water. Then back down to set the hook. The current will hold your boat facing the falls. It's elegant.

The dock is available at no charge, and stays are limited to 72 hours. Since most people don't stay longer than a day or two, there's ample turnover. A boat at anchor need only wait for the twice-daily departure of boats from the dock. Space then can be found before the next fleet of boats arrives from Malibu Rapids. Water (not potable, unfortunately) is available, but no electricity.

Bailey and Cummings (Gunkholing in Desolation Sound and Princess Louisa, now out of print) mention that life on this dock is more sociable and polite than often found, and our experience mirrors theirs. For those so inclined, a short walk to the pools near the base of Chatterbox Falls will yield a bracing bath/shower. A shampoo followed by a power rinse from the spray will make you tingle.

Trapper's Cabin is about a 2-hour very demanding hike from the dock area. The trail is poorly maintained and we have not made the hike. Bailey and Cummings describe it in excellent if unconventional detail in Gunkholing.

⑨ Princess Louisa Society. The Princess Louisa Society was formed to buy and preserve the area around Chatterbox Falls for perpetuity. The Society gave the property to BC Parks, but maintains an active role in the care of the facilities. Memberships are affordable and encouraged.

Aground Again

I HAVE REMAINED relatively grounding-free most of my boating life, until I got our last Nor'westing, a Romsdal trawler that draws 7½ feet. I recall a conversation with the late John Locke, whose 52-foot sloop Angelica also drew 7½ feet. John said he never had trouble with the first seven feet of draft, but the last half-foot always found the bottom. Me, too, John.

Sometimes it's just a little bump, like when we slid over a shallow spot just east of Goat Island, in Swinomish Channel. Or when we tied to a state park buoy at Hope Island and woke up the next morning thoroughly aground in mud. I hadn't checked the depth the night before. I thought the state would put its buoys where even I could float.

Sometimes it's more embarrassing, such as when I ran too close to the west side of the channel after a Stimson Trophy predicted log contest. One of the other boats passed me a line and pulled me off, but it was in full view of a whole passel of some of the most experienced boaters in the area. Oh, my.

I've been fooled a few times by a peculiarity of many bays and coves in Alaska and northern British Columbia, such as misnamed Safety Cove on Calvert Island. Safety Cove is a nice little bay at the mouth of a river, a river that deposits silt into the deeper waters of the cove, creating a nearly vertical shelf. As I poked around looking for something a little less than 20 fathoms deep I bumped into the edge of that shelf, where the water went directly from 20 fathoms to no fathoms. I backed off okay, and decided I didn't like Safety Cove that much.

Do you suppose that if I had sawn a few inches off my keel I'd have stayed afloat better? After all, it's only that last inch or two that got me into trouble. Or maybe it's time to relearn an important lesson: When the depth of the keel exceeds the depth of the water, I am most surely aground—again.

—Tom Kincaid

Malaspina Strait to Sarah Point

Grief Point • Westview • Lund • Copeland Islands

Charts	
3311	SMALL CRAFT CHARTS (strip charts) Sunshine Coast to Desolation Sound
3512	Strait of Georgia, Central Portion (1:80,000)
3513	Strait of Georgia, Northern Portion (1:80,000)
3536	PLANS – Strait of Georgia (various)
3538	Desolation Sound and Sutil Channel (1:80,000)

Malaspina Strait. Use chart 3512; 3513; strip chart 3311. Malaspina Strait separates Texada Island from the mainland, and is about 36 miles long. While it looks protected from the open water of the gulf, storms can create high seas. In settled weather, Malaspina Strait poses no threat.

These bays on the Texada Island side of Malaspina Strait are covered in an earlier section.

Anderson Bay. See page 146.
Vananda. See page 146.
Sturt Bay. See page 146.
Blubber Bay. See page 146.

Grief Point. Use chart 3513; strip chart 3311. Grief Point marks the northern end of Malaspina Strait on the mainland side. When the wind is getting up, the seas off Grief Point can be very rough.

① **Beach Gardens Resort & Marina,** 7074 Westminster Ave., Powell River, B.C. V8A 1C5, (604)485-7734; (604)485-6267. Monitors VHF channels 16 & 68. Open all year, gasoline and diesel at the fuel dock, guest moorage available, 15, 20 & 30 amp power, washrooms, showers, laundry. This is a good, protected marina, just south of Grief Point, served

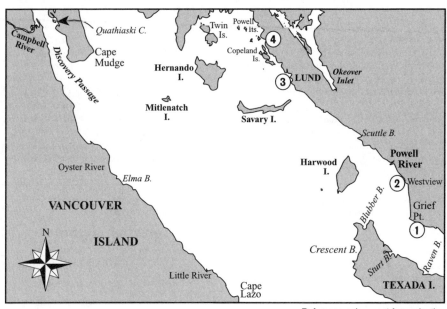

Reference only — not for navigation

by a busy resort. Rooms and cottages are available. The indoor pool, sauna, showers, and fitness center are available at nominal charge. A cold beer and wine store is adjacent. The Myrtle Point Golf Club is nearby. The hotel has a restaurant.

Beach Gardens has undergone financial uncertainty in recent years, but the marina has remained in good condition. An ownership change in late 1999 bodes well for the resort's future. *(Marina map this page)*

② **Westview/Powell River.** Use charts 3536, 3513; strip chart 3311. The public wharf at Westview is the pleasure craft moorage for the town of Powell River. The north section of the breakwater-protected marina is primarily permanent moorage; the south section is reserved for transient boats. Fuel, water and power are available, and nearby stores have supplies. Major shopping centers are a taxi ride (or courtesy bus in season) from the marina.

If the south section of the marina appears full when you pull in, don't give up hope. The dock manager usually can fit one more boat in—and another, and another. The Chevron fuel dock is located at the entrance to the south moorage. Marine and fishing supplies are available at the head of the dock, as are ice, garbage drop, and waste oil disposal. Eateries, including good pizza, are on the main commercial streets, a short walk away. If you prefer to walk to find groceries, wear good shoes. The Town Centre Mall, with Wal-Mart, Overwaitea supermarket, liquor store and many other shops, is located some distance away, up a steep hill (they call it Cardiac Hill), and it's a hike.

The town of Powell River is a couple of miles up the road from Westview. It's a pleasant walk. The promotional literature says many of the houses in Powell River date from the 1940s, as if this were old. We were born in 1940, and we are getting a little tired of see-

Reference only — not for navigation

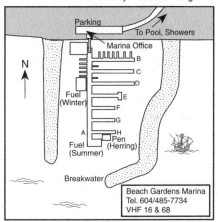

Beach Gardens Resort and Marina

The Beach Gardens Marina is well protected by breakwaters.

ing things we grew up with displayed as artifacts in museums, and houses built in the early 1940s or just before considered historical. Harumph!

Unrelated to the above grouchy commentary, the small historical museum along the main road leading to Powell River is definitely worth a visit.

Golf: The 18-hole Myrtle Point Golf Club is a short distance south of Westview. From mid-May until Sept. 30 they can provide complimentary pickup and return from Saltery Bay, Westview, even Lund if necessary. Call (604)487-4653.

② **Chevron Fuel Dock,** 4391 Marine Ave., Powell River, B.C. V8A 2J9, (604)485-2867. Gasoline, diesel, Delo lubricants, kerosene and ice, at the entrance to the south section of the Westview marina.

Dinner Rock. Use chart 3538, 3513, strip chart 3311. Dinner Rock, exposed at all tides, lies approximately 0.2 mile off the mainland shore, slightly southeast of Savary Island. In 1998, a 1000-lb cross was erected on the rock. It is a memorial to the five people who died there in October 1947, when the vessel *Gulf Stream,* proceeding in darkness with rain falling, struck the rock and sank.

Savary Island. Use chart 3538; 3513; strip chart 3311. Savary Island is a 4-mile-long sandy island that lies approximately east and west, and is served by water taxi from Lund. On the north shore, a small public dock is for loading and unloading only. Anchorage is good, sand bottom, within easy dinghy distance of the shore. Savary Island has no real protected harbor. A number of years ago we anchored off the north shore for the night and got away with it. Contributing Editor Tom Kincaid, however, once anchored overnight in the same area, but by morning the wind had come in from the north and he was on a lee shore.

Nearby **Hernando Island** is surrounded by rocky shallows, and is seldom visited by cruising boats.

Mitlenatch Island. Use chart 3538; 3513. Mitlenatch Island, a barren, uninviting rock,

The Lund harbor, public docks to the left. The boardwalk in the foreground leads to Flo's Starboard Cafe.

is located in the middle of the Strait of Georgia, roughly west of Hernando Island. It is a wildlife refuge, with a small, protected anchorage on its east side. Rangers ask people to stay on the trails to avoid disturbing birds.

Lund. Use chart 3538; chartbook 3312; strip chart 3311. The small village of Lund marks the north end of the road that leads all the way to the tip of South America. "Set your trip meter to zero and start driving,"said one local. Lund is a busy place in the summer, a jumping-off point for Desolation Sound. The town was busier in past years, when commercial fishing and the forests were booming. Today, Lund is trying to redefine itself as a tourist stop. This is not without its ups and downs. The historic Lund Hotel was closed all of 1999, denying the community of its business anchor, and leading some to say the town is dead. But it isn't.

In late 1999 (we stopped the presses to rewrite this section) the Lund Hotel received new ownership, with the vision and resources to rebuild its reputation to earlier glory. The new ownership promises that the hotel, general store, restaurant, pub and fuel dock will be up and running for the 2000 season. They also have purchased the Lund Marine property to the north, and the RV site nearby, all with development plans. For 2000 we would expect a positive but caretaker approach to the facilities. In years to come, we look for-

ward to imaginative development.

Lund is the mainland's closest launch site to Desolation Sound, with long-term trailer and tow vehicle storage at Lund Auto & Outboard and Dave's Parking. In 1999 the cafe on the boardwalk got a new and experienced owner in Flo Turgen, and a new name, the Starboard Cafe (although folks we talk to just call it Flo's). Nancy's Bakery and small coffee shop continues to turn out the tastiest pastries, pizzas and other specialties. Nancy's is famous on the coast. At Dave's Parking, a trailer with a sign reading "Lund-Done" serves superb fish and chips. The neighboring trailer park has a cafe called Lund Lubber's.

Over in Finn Cove, Jack Elsworth, who has the biggest, strongest hands we've seen in a long time, has blasted a boat storage yard

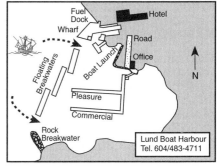

Lund Boat Harbour

Lund prawn fishermen relax after transferring their catch to the fish buyers.

of of solid rock, and welded up the darndest haulout machine imaginable. Think Travelift, then make it completely different. You have to see it.

The town assumed operation of the public docks following divestiture by the federal government. With commercial fishing in decline, these docks and shoreside facilities are being upgraded to make them more inviting to visiting pleasure craft. The docks are protected by two concrete floating breakwater floats. You can tie to the shore side of these floats, no power or water, and you must dinghy ashore. You still have to pay overnight moorage. If you want to anchor, anchor in **Finn Cove,** on the north side of the bay. A public float, with no access to shore, is in the middle of Finn Cove. You're apt to find local boats that haven't moved for awhile taking most of the space.

In 1999 the launch ramp was enlarged, and new public washrooms with excellent showers were built at the public dock. The trailer park also has public washrooms and showers.

③ **Dave's Parking,** PO Box 94, Lund, BC V0N 2G0, (604)483-3667. Long-term tow vehicle and trailer parking. Call ahead for reservations.

③ **Hoeger Yachting Ltd.,** Box 73, Lund, B.C. V0N 2G0, (604)483-9002; fax (604)483-4914. Marine ways for vessels to 75 feet or 80 tons, mechanical and electrical repairs, marine hardware, moorage. This is the facility formerly known as Lund Marine & Diesel, which closed in autumn 1997. Horst Hoeger reopened the business in 1998, and has been building it. Horst is a good man. We've heard several happy comments about his service.

Lund Automotive & Outboard Ltd., General Delivery, Lund, BC V0N 2G0, (604)483-4612. Long-term tow vehicle and trailer parking, call ahead for reservations. Good mechanics are on staff, and they are an authorized service facility for several engine brands. In 1998 we had a series of electrical problems, and

The Lund launch ramp has been widened since June 1998, when this photo was taken.

called them for help. A skilled mechanic was on the job promptly. He diagnosed the problems and solved them efficiently. The bill was fair.

③ **Lund Harbour Authority Wharf.** Call (604)483-4711. Open all year, 670 feet of breakwater-protected dock space, 20 amp power, no garbage or oil disposal. The northern float is reserved for pleasure craft. Don't give up if the docks appear full. Rosie O'Neill, the harbormaster, knows how to fit more boats in, and asks that you give her the chance. The green spar buoy Q29 lies between the docks and the launch ramp. The buoy marks a rock ledge that extends from shore. Pass between the buoy and the docks, not between the buoy and shore.

③ **Lund Hotel,** General Delivery, Lund, B.C. V0N 2G0, (604)483-3187. Unfortunately, the hotel, general store, restaurant, pub and fuel dock were closed during much of 1998 and all of 1999. As reported above, however, new

ownership is committed to getting everything going again. We are optimistic but also realistic. Bringing a property back is a big job. If many things are right but a few things still not done, give them a break. If everything is right, give them applause. And tell them you read about them in the Waggoner. See our web site www.waggonerguide.com for updates.

Jack's Boat Storage, Box 138, Lund, BC, (604)483-3566. In Finn Bay. Haulout to 60 feet or 30 tons, storage available for repairs. Can haul sailboats.

Copeland Islands. Use chart 3538; strip chart 3311. The Copeland Islands (locally known as the Ragged Islands) are a provincial park, with no facilities specifically for boaters. Anchorage is possible in several little nooks and coves among the islands, although most are exposed to wakes of passing boats passing in Thulin Passage. Check your swing when you anchor. A few years ago, at low tide, we saw a Grand Banks 42 high and dry, propped up with driftwood.

④ **Ragged Islands Marine Ltd.,** P.O. Box 22, Lund, B.C. V0N 2G0, (604)483-8184. If you hear people referring to Wendy's, this is Wendy's. Open March 1-October 31. Located on the Malaspina Peninsula, at the north end of the Copeland Islands, a little south of Sarah Point. Primarily a fuel dock with gasoline and diesel, but they do have limited guest moorage along 50 feet of dock space. Washrooms, no showers, no power. Clean, friendly, convenient.

Sarah Point. Use chart 3538; chartbook 3312; strip chart 3311. For boats running north through Thulin Passage, Sarah Point, at the tip of the Malaspina Peninsula, is the dramatic entrance to Desolation Sound. The high hills of the Malaspina Peninsula hide the Coast Mountain Range, but on a clear day, once Sarah Point is cleared the mountains come into magnificent view.

Tell Them You Read About Them In the Waggoner.

Desolation Sound

Cortes Bay • Squirrel Cove • Von Donop Inlet • Gorge Harbour • Drew Harbour
Surge Narrows • Octopus Islands • Hole in the Wall • Discovery Passage • Malaspina Inlet
Prideaux Haven • Roscoe Bay • Refuge Cove • Teakerne Arm

Charts

3312	SMALL CRAFT CHART (chartbook) Jervis Inlet & Desolation Sound
3513	Strait of Georgia – Northern Portion (1:80,000)
3537	Okisollo Channel (1:20,000); Whiterock Passage (1:10,000)
3538	Desolation Sound and Sutil Channel (1:40,000)
3539	Discovery Passage (1:40,000) Seymour Narrows (1:20,000)
3540	Approaches to Campbell River (1:10,000)
3541	Approaches to Toba Inlet (1:40,000)
3542	Bute Inlet (1:40,000)
3555	PLANS – Vicinity of Redonda Islands & Loughborough Inlet
3559	Malaspina Inlet, Okeover Inlet & Lancelot Inlet (1:12,000)

DESOLATION SOUND

Navigation note: New for 2000, tide information for Desolation Sound is shown in Canadian Tide and Current Tables, Vol. 5 (they are shown as secondary ports, based on Point Atkinson Tides). Until this year, Desolation Sound tides were contained in Vol. 6. Currents for Beazley Passage, Hole in the Wall and Discovery Passage, and corrections for Upper and Lower Rapids in Okisollo Channel are still contained in Vol. 6. Owen Bay tides and Okisollo Channel secondary port tide corrections also are in Vol. 6.

WITH ITS NAME OF DESOLATION SOUND, its location beyond the end of the road and its incredible physical beauty, Desolation Sound is one of the Northwest's most dreamed-about and sought-after cruising destinations. We remember clearly the feeling of accomplishment the first time we cleared Sarah Point in our own boat and saw the mountains of Desolation Sound. *"We made it,"* we cried.

Officially, Desolation Sound is that body of water north of Sarah Point and Mary Point, and south of West Redonda Island. When most people think of cruising these waters, however, they consider Desolation Sound to include all the area north of Cape Mudge and Sarah Point, and south of Yuculta Rapids and Chatham Point.

It's not a huge area. Even slow boats can go from one end to another in a day. But Desolation Sound offers a wilderness setting, generally easy waters, hundreds of bays and coves

to explore and anchor in, and marinas where fuel and supplies are available. Campbell River, in Discovery Passage, is a full-fledged small city, with complete supplies and even a shipyard for repairs.

Since it is close to the point where the tidal currents change, the water in Desolation Sound is not regularly exchanged with cold ocean water. During the summer, water temperatures of 70 to 80 degrees Fahrenheit are not unusual in some of the bays, making for excellent swimming.

Navigation is straightforward, with few hazards in the major channels. Closer to shore it's a different story, but the rocks and reefs are charted. You'll need only a few charts to cover all the waters, so get every one. You'll also need Canadian Tide & Current Tables, Volumes 5 & 6.

The most popular time to cruise Desolation Sound is from mid-July through the end of August, when the prospects for sunny, warm weather are best. It's also when the anchorages and facilities are most crowded. Our own cruising schedule takes us north through Desolation Sound in mid-June. June weather can be cool and rainy, but crowds are not a problem at all. It's then that the waterfalls are most awesome and the resorts and businesses, while open and fully-stocked, are least harried. We must confess, though, that a dry cabin with dependable cabin heat are critical for our day-after-day comfort.

If your calendar permits, the *very* best time to cruise Desolation Sound is early- to mid-September. By then the high-season crowds have departed, yet summer hangs on for a last and glorious finale. Stock in the stores may be thin and summertime help back in school, but the low slanting sunlight paints the hills and mountains with new drama, and the first colors of autumn make each day a new experience. Watch the weather closely. Leave while you can get home before the fall storm pattern begins, although usually that's not before October.

Twin Islands. Use chart 3538; chartbook 3312; chart 3513. Twin Islands, located off the southeast side of Cortes Island, are really a single island joined by a drying spit. Anchorage is possible close to the drying spit on either side, but a better anchorage is opposite the islands on Cortes Island.

CORTES ISLAND

Recommended book: Destination Cortez, a wonderful book by author June Cameron, describes the early days on Cortes Island, and we recommend it highly. In our opinion this book joins *The Curve of Time* as essential and enter-

taining background reading about the B.C. coast. After reading *Destination Cortez* you will have an entirely different outlook about your explorations of Cortes Bay, Squirrel Cove, Von Donop Inlet, Whaletown, Gorge Harbour, Mansons Landing, and the entire Desolation Sound area. Published in Canada by Heritage House, with Fine Edge Productions the U.S. co-publisher.

① **Cortes Bay.** *Proposed No Discharge Zone. Gray water okay. See p. 15.* Use chart 3538; chartbook 3312; chart 3513. Cortes Bay is well protected, but in many places the soft mud bottom doesn't hold well. Be sure to use chart 3538 when approaching. Several charted rocks and reefs near the entrance have claimed the inattentive. These include Central Rock, north of Twin Islands; several rocks around Three Islets; and a rock off the headland that lies midway between Mary Point and the entrance to Cortes Bay.

As you approach Cortes Bay, pay close attention to the beacon in the middle of the entrance. This beacon, with its red triangle dayboard, marks the south end of a nasty reef. Leave the beacon to starboard (Red, Right, Returning) as you enter. If you doubt the existence of this reef, one look at low tide will convince you. A small public wharf is at the head of Cortes Bay. It is usually full during the summer. Rafting is required.

Seattle Yacht Club has an outstation along the south shore of Cortes Bay, at the location of a former marina. Royal Vancouver Yacht Club has a new outstation along the north shore. For anchoring, we have found the best holding bottom to be a strip east of the SYC outstation, a couple hundred yards offshore.

Squirrel Cove. *Proposed No Discharge Zone. Gray water okay. See p. 15.* Use chart 3555 (recommended); chartbook 3312; chart 3538. Squirrel Cove is made up of two bays. In the outer bay, a public float gives access to the Squirrel Cove General Store and Suzanne Minogue's Caffe Suzanne. The inner bay has better protection, and during the summer the inner bay is usually full of anchored boats. A saltwater lagoon is at the head of the inner bay, with a connecting stream that acts like a river. The stream runs into the lagoon at high tide, and out of the lagoon at low tide. Contributing Editor Tom Kincaid's kids used to beat up the dinghy running these "rapids."

The bake shop is closed. For a decade a colorful character named Bill Rendall ran a bake shop in his cabin in the inner bay of Squirrel Cove. His baked goods were famous, and Bill, with his chatty manner, made many friends. But at the end of 1997 he decided "at three score and ten" that it was time to rest. We saw

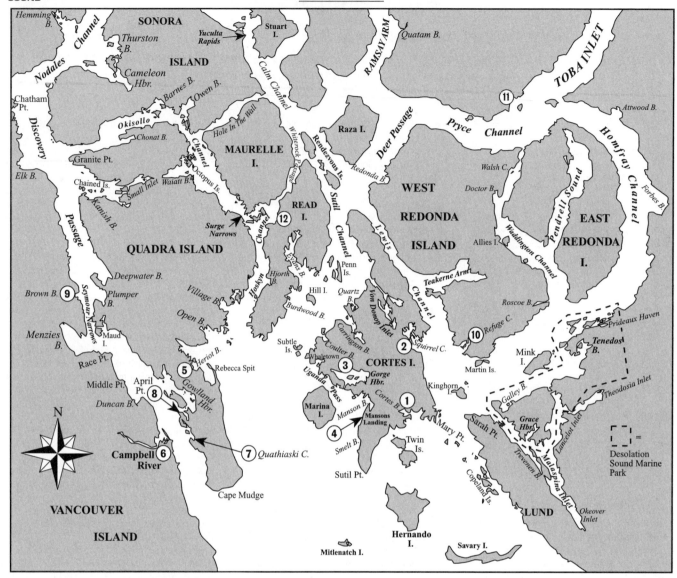

Bill in June, 1998, and he looked great. In November that year, he was dead of cancer.

Although Bill the Baker is gone, two other food outlets have opened. One is Marilyn's, on the west side of the inner bay. The other is Caffe Suzanne, in the outer bay, just west of the public wharf. Marinlyn's has take-out salmon sandwiches, chowder, and so forth, and Caffe Suzanne has regular restaurant fare. A major yacht club's Gourmet Cruise had dinner at Caffe Suzanne and reported it very good. Shoal water and limited dock space make it wise to visit either place by dinghy only.

At one time the inner bay was used for log booming, and author June Cameron even wrote an article in *Pacific Yachting* telling of a tangle of sunken logs on the bottom. When we aksed Bill Rendall about the sunken logs, he said they had rotted away by now. Unfortunately, at least one tough old log is still down there. In 1998 Bob and Delia Spanfelner, sailing shipmates of ours from years ago (Bob joined us for our 1999 trip down the West Coast of Vancouver Island), anchored between the two islands in the inner bay and snagged a large log with their anchor rode. It took three hours

and much effort to work the log to the surface, and then it slipped free and sank back to the bottom. Until we get an accurate report from a diver, we would be cautious about anchoring between the two islands.

② **Squirrel Cove Public Wharf.** Guest moorage available along 200 feet of dock. Close to the Squirrel Cove store. Garbage drop and pay telephone available. Local boats often take much of the space. The best chance for moorage is by dinghy.

② **Squirrel Cove General Store,** Box 1, Squirrel Cove, B.C. V0P 1K0, (250)935-6327. Open all year, washrooms, showers, laundry. Gasoline is available, but it is upland; no fuel dock. Propane is available. This is a good provisioning stop, with groceries, charts, books and videos, marine hardware, liquor and a post office. The lower level of the store is devoted to hardware, just about anything a person might need.

Von Donop Inlet. Use chart 3538; chartbook 3312. Von Donop Inlet, on the northwest

corner of Cortes Island, is entered through a narrow, 2-mile-long channel through the trees. In the narrowest part of the channel, about halfway in, you'll find a rock, often covered by kelp. When entering, we have found it better to keep that rock to port, even if tree branches try to brush the starboard side of the boat or rigging. Once inside, you'll find several coves that provide perfectly protected anchorage. The largest of these coves takes in the entire head of the inlet and has room for many boats. The bottom in this area is sticky mud. It is ideal for holding, but requires extra cleaning time when the anchor is brought aboard. A trail leads from the head of Von Donop Inlet to Squirrel Cove.

Von Donop/Háthayim Provincial Marine Park is a 3155 acre park, established in December, 1993. The park includes Von Donop Inlet, Robertson Lake, and Wiley Lake.

Quartz Bay. Use chart 3538; chartbook 3312. Quartz Bay is unusually pretty, with good holding bottom. The eastern cove of the bay has several homes and two private docks along the shoreline. Near the head, you can anchor in 5-7 fathoms with swinging room, but you're in their front yards. The western cove has some aquaculture, one cabin on the shore, and anchoring depths near the south and west shores. You may have to run a stern-tie to shore. Just as you enter Quartz Bay you'll find a little nook on your starboard side. It is exposed to north winds, but it's a nice spot.

Carrington Bay. *Proposed No Discharge Zone. Gray water okay. See p. 15.* Use chart 3538; chartbook 3312. Carrington Bay is very pretty, and well protected except from the north. The bottom is reported to be rocky, so be sure your anchor is properly set before turning in for the night. Carrington Lagoon, at the head of the bay, is interesting to explore. Drag the dinghy across the logs that choke the entrance to the lagoon. June Cameron, in *Destination Cortez,* says the lagoon entrance was blasted out of rock, with amazingly smooth sides—a tribute to the skills of the man who did the blasting. On a recent visit, a family that just had made the exploration described the lagoon as "untouched." A suggested anchorage is to the right, near the entrance to the lagoon, with a stern-tie to shore. We have seen other boats anchored in the little bight a short distance to the left of the lagoon entrance, and behind the tiny island just off the eastern shore of the bay.

Coulter Bay. Use chart 3538; chartbook 3312. Coulter Bay is quite pretty, but as the chart indicates, most of the bay is too shallow for anchoring. You could anchor in the tiny nook behind Coulter Island, beside a little unnamed islet to the west. Some cabins are nearby, but they are screened from view and you won't feel as if you're in their kitchens.

Subtle Islands. Use chart 3538; chartbook 3312. The two Subtle Islands are separated by a drying shoal. There is good anchorage off this shoal on the east side, particularly in settled weather. The little bay on the north side is very deep except at the head. It has a lovely (and exposed) view to the north. The islands are privately owned, and marked with "stay off" and "keep away" signs.

Hill Island. Hill Island is privately owned. According to Sailing Di-

rections, a private lodge with a floating breakwater is located at Totem Bay. The island is not open to the public.

Whaletown. Use chart 3538; chartbook 3312. Whaletown is the terminus of the ferry between Cortes Island and Quadra Island. A small public float, with garbage drop, is alongside the ferry dock. A store is at the dock. If you anchor north of the ferry dock watch for several marked and unmarked rocks, normally covered by kelp.

Uganda Pass. Use chart 3538; chartbook 3312. Uganda Pass separates Cortes Island from Marina Island. The pass is narrow and winding, but well marked and easy to navigate. Red, Right, Returning assumes that you are returning from the south. Shark Spit is long and low, with superb sand. Swimming is good. You can find anchorage south of the pass on either the Cortes Island or Marina Island side.

④ **Mansons Landing.** *Proposed No Discharge Zone. Gray water okay. See p. 15.* Use chart 3538; chartbook 3312. The historic store at Mansons Landing has been closed and the building moved. The 177-foot public dock is still there. Anchorage is good north of the public dock. The entire area is exposed to the south.

Mansons Landing Marine Park, 117 acres, open all year. The park has no dock of its own, but can be reached from the Mansons Landing public dock or you can anchor out. Hague Lake, with warm water and swimming beaches safe for small children, is a 10-minute walk from the public dock.

Gorge Harbour. *Proposed No Discharge Zone. Gray water okay. See p. 15.* Use chart 3538; chartbook 3312. Gorge Harbour is a large bay with many good spots to put the hook down. The entry is through a narrow cleft in the rock cliff. Orange-colored Indian pictographs, including a stick figure man, a man on what appears to be a turtle or fish, and several vertical lines, are on the rock wall to port as you enter. You have to look closely to identify them. Current runs through the entrance. At maximum flow a slow boat proceeding against the current could have a difficult time, but there are no hazards. Inside you'll find good,

The Gorge Harbour Marina Resort has ample dock space, fuel, restaurant, store and large picnic grounds upland.

protected anchorage in many parts of the bay. The Gorge Harbour Marina Resort, on the northwest shore, has many amenities, including an excellent restaurant. Chart 3538 shows a number of rocks behind islets along the north shore. A few years ago, a chartered 45-foot trawler, running at six knots, reportedly found one of those rocks, holing the hull and almost sinking. Caution advised.

Gorge Harbour Public Dock, located a short distance east of the Gorge Harbour Marina, commercial vessels have priority.

③ **Gorge Harbour Marina Resort,** P.O. Box 89, Whaletown, B.C. V0P 1Z0, (250)935-6433; fax

(250)935-6402. Monitors VHF channel 73. Open all year, gasoline and diesel at the fuel dock, guest moorage available along 1800 feet of dock. Facilities include 15 & 30 amp power, washrooms, showers, laundry, well-stocked convenience store with fresh vegetables, meats, dairy products, ice, video rentals, propane. The resort has an RV park, a campground, lodge accommodations, a very good restaurant (open May-Sept.), scooter, mountain bike and kayak rentals, float plane service, and a launch ramp. Glen and Verlie Carleton are the owners.

Smelt Bay Provincial Park, 1 mile north of Sutil Point, on the west side of the peninsula. Good

temporary anchorage is available close to shore. The park has 23 campsites, picnic tables, and a white sand beach.

READ ISLAND, EAST SIDE

The east side of Read Island is deeply indented from the south by Evans Bay, where several little notches are worth exploring as anchorages. Most have drying flats at their heads. Bird Cove is probably the best protected, although Contributing Editor Tom Kincaid has spent a quiet night behind the little islets in the bay just to the north of Bird Cove. A small public float is near the entrance to Evans Bay, where there is a store and post office.

Burdwood Bay. Use chart 3538; chartbook 3312. Burdwood Bay has a number of possible anchorages, particularly on the lee side of the little islands that extend from the south side of the bay, and in a notch in the north end. Burdwood Bay is not particularly pretty, but could be a good hideout in a storm.

HOSKYN CHANNEL

Hoskyn Channel runs between Read Island and Quadra Island, and connects at the north with Whiterock Passage and Surge Narrows. Although they are just south of Hoskyn Channel, we include Drew Harbour and Heriot Bay in this section.

Drew Harbour/Rebecca Spit Marine Park. Use chart 3538 or 3539; chartbook 3312. Drew Harbour is large and well-protected, especially behind Rebecca Spit, where you'll find ample anchoring room in 4-6 fathom depths. Rebecca Spit Marine Park is very popular. The Drew Harbour side of Rebecca Spit has a lovely sand beach, and the exposed Sutil Channel side has a beach of remarkable small round boulders. Bill Wolferstan's cruising guide to Desolation Sound contains an excellent section that describes silvered tree snags on the spit, the result of subsidence during a 1946 earthquake. It also describes the mounded fortifications, thought to be defenses built 200-400 years ago by the local Salish Indians against Kwakiutl Indian attacks.

Heriot Bay. Use chart 3538 or 3539; chartbook 3312. Heriot Bay is the location of the ferry to Cortes

Island, also of a public dock, grocery store, and the Heriot Bay Inn. During the summer high season the public dock usually is full and rafted several deep. The Heriot Bay Inn Marina lies between the ferry dock and the public dock. Quadra Island Market, a short walk away, is the best-stocked grocery store in Desolation Sound, with complete groceries, including fresh vegetables and meats, a post office, gift shop, and liquor store.

⑤ **Heriot Bay Public Wharf,** open all year, 670 feet of dock space, garbage disposal, telephone, launch ramp. Watch for ferry wash on the outer face.

⑤ **Heriot Bay Inn & Marina,** P.O. Box 100, Heriot Bay, B.C. V0P 1H0, (250) 285-3322; fax (250)285-2708. Monitors VHF channel 73. Open all year, gasoline, diesel, propane, ice. Guest moorage available on 1800 feet of dock, power is mostly 15 amp with a little 30 amp, washrooms, showers, laundry. Reservations recommended June through August. They have an historic hotel and cottages, restaurant and pub, and offer sea kayaking lessons and rentals. The hotel store has charts and souvenirs. The docks have side-tie moorage only. Find an unreserved open spot and take it. *(Marina map page 177)*

Hjorth Bay. Use chart 3538 or 3539; chartbook 3312. Hjorth Bay, on Hoskyn Channel along the west side of Read Island, is a good anchorage except in a strong southerly.

⑫ **Surge Narrows General Store**, Box 31, Surge Narrows, B.C. V0P 1W0, (250)287-6962. Use chart 3539. The Surge Narrows General Store is located just north of Surge Point on Read Island, across Hoskyn Channel from Beazley Passage. The float at the end of the public wharf is only 60 feet long. Often, such a place would be of little interest to visiting boaters, but the revitalizing of the old, high-ceiling store has changed all that. The store will take you back to the 1920s or 1930s: dim lighting, wood floors, the shelves stocked but not merchandised, large woodstove for cold days. It's a gathering place for locals, some of them rough-hewn, some of them sophisticated, all of them independent. In addition to the usual foodstuffs, the store carries bulk herbs

There's no missing the "store" sign at Surge Narrows. A small float (behind camera) provides access.

SURGE NARROWS/ OKISOLLO CHANNEL

Surge Narrows and Beazley Passage. Use chart 3537; chartbook 3312; chart 3539. Surge Narrows should be run at or near slack water. Spring floods set eastward to 12 knots, and ebbs set westward to 10 knots. Current predictions are shown under Surge Narrows in the Canadian Tide and Current Tables, Vol. 6.

Although Beazley Passage, between Peck Island and Sturt Island, has the strongest currents in the Surge Narrows area, it is the preferred route between Hoskyn Channel and Okisollo Channel. Especially on an ebb current in Beazley Passage, watch for Tusko Rock, which dries 5 feet, on the east side of the pass at the north end.

According to Sailing Directions, the duration of slack at Surge Narrows varies between 5 and 11 minutes. We have run Beazley Passage near slack and had no problems. Use large-scale chart 3537 (1:20,000). According to Contributing Editor Tom Kincaid, the passage north of the Settler's Group is useable, but notorious for rocks. Local knowledge is required.

Okisollo Channel. Use chart 3537; chartbook 3312; chart 3539. Owen Bay tides and Okisollo Channel secondary port tide corrections are contained in Canadian Tide and Current Tables, Vol. 6. Okisollo Channel runs along the west and north sides of Quadra Island, from Surge Narrows to Discovery Passage. Use chart 3539 (1:40,000) or large-scale chart 3537 (1:20,000). In the lower part of the channel, the only dangers are Cyrus Rocks on the west side, and Barnsley Shoal, an isolated reef, on the east side. Hole in the Wall, which enters Okisollo Channel about midway, must be run at or near slack. In the upper part of Okisollo Channel, the Upper Rapids and Lower Rapids are dangerous. They too must be run at or near slack. Slack occurs 50 to 55 minutes before slack at Seymour Narrows.

Waiatt Bay. Use chart 3537; chartbook 3312; chart 3539. Waiatt Bay is broad and protected, with convenient anchoring depths behind the Octopus Islands. The bay's entrance is choked with islets and rocks. Sailing Directions (written for large vessels) warns against entering. With the aid of large-scale chart 3537 (1:20,000), however, a small boat can pick its way in along the south shore, or in the middle of the islets, or along the north shore. The chart shows the possibilities. A trail connects the head of Waiatt Bay with Small Inlet. Along the trail you'll come to an ice cold, crystal clear pool.

Octopus Islands Marine Park. Use chart 3537; chartbook 3312; chart 3539. This is a beautiful and popular anchorage and exploration area, wonderfully protected. While you can enter from Waiatt Bay, the usual entry is by a narrow channel from the north. Anchor in any of several coves and run a stern-tie to

Teresa Beyerstein chats with us and has a cup of coffee. This is a pretty relaxed place.

and spices, local crafts, and, in season, fruit from island orchards.

This is not a city store in the country or a country store in the city; this is an old-time country store in the country. The local school, for instance, goes only through grade 6, after which the kids board out. We think it best to

arrive relaxed and with an open heart, with some time to spare. Doug and Teresa Beyerstein are the owners, with their three children, Brandy, Laurel and Nikki. We met Teresa and Brandy. Teresa's picture is to the left.

Whiterock Passage. Use chart 3537; chartbook 3312; chart 3539. Whiterock Passage is sometimes called Propeller Passage in honor of the propellers its rocks have claimed. Whiterock Passage is narrow, and the dredged channel is bounded on both sides by drying shoals studded with angry boulders. Least depth at zero tide is 5 feet. Maximum currents are 2 knots. Running Whiterock Passage at half tide is a good idea—it exposes the shoals on both sides but provides a little extra depth. The unitiated tend to avoid Whiterock Passage, but it's easy to run if you pay attention and know how. Here's how.

First, don't even think about Whiterock Passage without chart 3537 or chartbook 3312, both of which detail Whiterock Passage at a scale of 1:10,000. As the charts show, two ranges are on the Read Island side of the passage. Going either direction, one of these will be a leading range as you enter, and the other a back range as you depart. Approaching, find the leading range and stay exactly on it. Proceed slowly and watch astern as the back range comes into view. When the back range lines up, turn the appropriate direction and let the back range keep you on course as you complete your transit.

Remember that the course lines on the charts are true, not magnetic. You must subtract the magnetic variation from the true heading to get the magnetic course.

I steer when we go through in our little ship *Surprise*. As the back range comes into view, Marilynn turns to stand back-to-back with me. She calls the turn when the back range lines up. If I drift to either side of the back range, Marilynn taps my left shoulder or right shoulder as needed, to indicate the direction toward which I must alter course. The alterations are small because Marilynn watches intently. Touching the shoulders avoids any port/starboard verbal mixups that might occur when each of us is facing a different direction.

Reference only — not for navigation

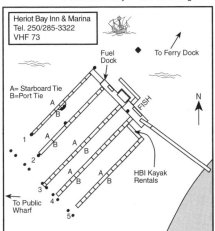

Heriot Bay Inn & Marina
Tel. 250/285-3322
VHF 73

Heriot Bay Inn & Marina

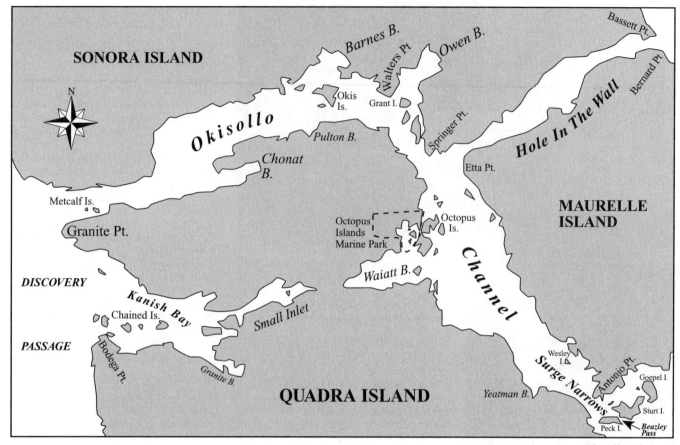

Okisollo Channel

shore. *(See area map this page)*

A rock, clearly shown on chart 3537, obstructs part of the entrance to the first cove on the right, at the end of the channel as you enter from the north. This rock is easily seen as a white smear under the water. You'll be going slowly anyway; watch for it and you'll have no trouble.

Hole in the Wall. Use plans chart 3537; chartbook 3312; chart 3539. Hole in the Wall connects Okisollo Channel with Calm Channel to the east. Boats accumulate on each side of the rapids at the western entrance to Hole in the Wall, waiting for slack water. In general, boats on the upstream side will catch the last of the fair current when the rapids calm down, leaving room for the boats on the other side to pick up the new fair current in the opposite direction. Slacks occur 50-55 minutes before Seymour Narrows, and last about 4 minutes (Seymour Narrows currents are shown in Canadian Tide & Current Tables, Vol. 6). The flood current sets northeast. Maximum currents run to 12 knots on the flood and 10 knots on the ebb.

Upper Rapids. Use chart 3537; chartbook 3312; chart 3539. These are the first rapids in Okisollo Channel north of Hole in the Wall, and are dangerous unless run at or near slack water. Slack occurs 55 minutes before Seymour Narrows (Seymour Narrows currents are shown in Canadian Tide & Current Tables, Vol. 6). At full rush on a spring tide, the rapids, run-

ning at 9 knots, are frightening to watch. Almost until slack, a wall of white water can stretch nearly across the channel. When it's time to go through, trend a little east of midchannel to avoid Bentley Rock. The chart makes the course clear.

Owen Bay. Use chart 3537; chartbook 3312; chart 3539. Owen Bay is large and pretty. The recommended anchorage is in the second little notch on the west side of the bay. This notch is quite protected, and has room for about five boats if the spots are well chosen and shore-ties used. A public float is on the east side of the bay, and a trail leads from near the public float to Hole in the Wall. Correspondent Bruce Evertz informs us that for most of the distance the trail is a road that passes several homes

and homebuilding sites, and then gets overgrown. Shortly before reaching the water in Diamond Bay, it becomes a plank road that turns 90 degrees to the left. Don't turn. Continue ahead, onto a foot path, which leads to a good view of Hole in the Wall rapids, part of Upper Rapids, and the Octopus Islands.

Bill Wolferstan, in his cruising guide to Desolation Sound, says that Owen Bay has an ominous feeling. In person, Bill can tell a few ghost stories about it. We are happy to say that our experience in Owen Bay has been neither ominous nor ghostly.

Enter Owen Bay through a narrow channel between Walters Point and Grant Island. A reef, marked by kelp, extends from Walters Point nearly halfway across this channel. It will inspire you to hug the Grant Island side.

These sailors are anchored in the little bight on the west side of Owen Bay.

Caution: Don't fool around in the islands that separate Owen Bay from the Upper Rapids. The current is reported to run strongly through these islands, and it could suck you into the rapids. Wolferstan writes that in 1967 a dinghy was found floating upturned below the rapids, the occupants lost.

Lower Rapids. Use chart 3537; chartbook 3312; chart 3539. Lower Rapids turns at virtually the same time as Upper Rapids—55 minutes before Seymour Narrows (Seymour Narrows currents are shown in Canadian Tide & Current Tables, Vol. 6). Currents run to 9 knots at springs, and you must steer a course to avoid Gypsy Shoal, which lies nearly in the middle. Go at slack water only. *Recommended:* Avoid Lower Rapids altogether by going through Barnes Bay, north of the Okis Islands. At times other than slack you will still see considerable current, but you will avoid hazards.

Barnes Bay. Use chart 3537; chartbook 3312; chart 3539. Barnes Bay and several small indents in this part of Okisollo Channel could be good anchorages, except for the large amount of log booming and aquaculture. There is possible anchorage in **Chonat Bay** and in the notch behind **Metcalf Island,** before Okisollo Channel enters Discovery Passage.

Granite Point. Use chart 3537; chartbook 3312; chart 3539. If you are going between Discovery Passage and Okisollo Channel, you can safely steer inside Min Rock, north of Granite Point, and run close to Granite Point itself. You will be treated to the sight of some extraordinary rock on Granite Point.

DISCOVERY PASSAGE

Use chart 3539; 3540; chartbook 3312. Use Canadian Tide & Current Tables, Vol. 6. Discovery Passage is approximately 20 miles long, and separates Quadra Island and Sonora Island from Vancouver Island. It is the main route for commercial traffic north and south along the east side of Vancouver Island. Cape Mudge is the south entrance to Discovery Passaage. At the north end, Discovery Passage connects with Johnstone Strait at Chatham Point. An enormous amount of water flows through Discovery Passage, flooding south and ebbing north. Tide-rips are frequent. From south to north, the primary stops for pleasure craft are Campbell River, Quathiaski Cove, April Point, Gowlland Harbour, Seymour Narrows, Brown Bay, and Kanish Bay.

Cape Mudge. Use chart 3539; chartbook 3312. Cape Mudge, at the south end of Quadra Island, has been a graveyard for vessels of all sizes, particularly in the winter months. A strong southeaster blowing against a large, south-flowing flood tide can set up high and dangerous seas. A college classmate of ours, a commercial fisherman, was lost off Cape Mudge in such conditions a few years ago. If a southeaster is blowing, Sailing Directions recommends entering at or after high water slack. Good advice.

On a flood tide, a backeddy often sets up at Cape Mudge, running north along the western edge of Wilby Shoals all the way to the Cape Mudge Lighthouse.

The area around Cape Mudge and Wilby Shoals is a world-famous hot spot for salmon fishing, and often during the summer months it is full of small craft. Several resorts in the area cater to sport fishermen. A large number of guides are available for hire in Campbell River.

Campbell River. Use chart 3539; 3540; chartbook 3312. The city of Campbell River is working to become an important tourist destination, and for sport fishermen especially, it is succeeding. The city calls itself the "Salmon Capital of the World." While dozens of guideboats take sportsfishermen to prime fishing areas in Discovery Passage and off Cape Mudge, each year lunker-size salmon are caught from the marina breakwaters and the public fishing pier.

Campbell River has complete shopping, dining, and marine facilities, all close to the waterfront. An attractive promenade leads from the Small Boat Harbour to the ferry dock. It is scheduled to be extended to the Discovery Harbour Marina.

As you approach Campbell River from the south you will find three marinas, each protected by its own breakwater. The southern-

This Indian cemetery is located a short distance north of the Discovery Harbour Marina.

DISCOVERY HARBOUR
MARINA

CAMPBELL RIVER, BRITISH COLUMBIA

- ▮ MODERN GUEST DOCKS
- ▮ POWER & WATER
- ▮ WASHROOMS & SHOWERS
- ▮ LAUNDRY FACILITIES
- ▮ GARBAGE DISPOSAL
- ▮ TELEPHONES
- ▮ BLOCK & CUBED ICE
- ▮ FISHING GUIDE SERVICES
- ▮ FISH CLEANING FACILITIES
- ▮ FULL NIGHTTIME SECURITY
- ▮ ESSO FUEL DOCK
- ▮ WALK TO SHOPPING, SERVICES & DINING AT THE *NEW* DISCOVERY HARBOUR CENTRE

NOW COMPLETE SHOPPING HERE

A Great Marina Destination In A Great Little City With Great New Shopping Next Door...

The huge new 52-acre, 50-store **Discovery Harbour Centre** is open at last. The Centre joins our marina, and has *everything* you need. Groceries at Superstore. Canadian Tire. Zeller's. Liquor Store. Several restaurants, from fast food to better dining. Starbuck's Coffee. Ocean Pacific marine supplies. Two banks, a spa, even a locksmith and an optometrist. And Wei Wai Kum House of Treasures, Vancouver Island's largest native-owned gallery and gift shop.

So now Discovery Harbour Marina is an even better stop than before. Same breakwater-protected moorage. Same wide concrete docks. Same friendly help. Only now with unmatched shopping, services and dining, right next door. Let us be *your* stop in Campbell River.

TELEPHONE (250) 287-2614 ▮ VHF 73 ▮ E MAIL DHM@OBERON.ARK.COM
FAX (250) 287-8939 ▮ #112 - 1334 ISLAND HWY. ▮ CAMPBELL RIVER, B.C. ▮ V9W 8C9

most marina is the Campbell River Harbour Authority Small Boat Harbour (formerly the Government Dock).

The second breakwater protects the newly rebuilt Coast Marina, which has guest moorage and a fascinating floating waterfront retail village. The ferry to Quathiaski Cove, on Quadra Island, lands adjacent to the Coast Marina. Of the three marinas, this is closest to downtown Campbell River.

The third marina is the Discovery Harbour Marina, with an Esso fuel dock and considerable moorage. The 43-acre Discovery Harbour Centre is immediately adjacent to the marina. Ocean Pacific Marine Supply has a store in this shopping center, in addition to its main store and shipyard on Island Highway, near the Campbell River Harbour Authority Small Boat Harbour.

The Harbour Authority marina does not monitor the radio. The Coast Marina and Discovery Harbour Marina both monitor VHF channel 73. Be sure which marina you intend to call, and use the correct name.

Golf: Story Creek, a little south of town, is excellent. Call (250)923-3673. We haven't yet tried Sequoia Springs (250)287-4970.

⑥ **Campbell River Harbour Authority Small Boat Harbour,** 705 Island Highway, Campbell River, B.C. V9W 2C2, (250)287-7931; fax (250)287-8495. Open all year, water on docks, 20 amp power, ample dock space, washrooms & showers, 2 tidal grids, pay phones. All but one dock are side-tie only, rafting permitted. Ocean Pacific Marine Supplies and shipyard are next door. This was almost entirely a commercial fish boat moor-

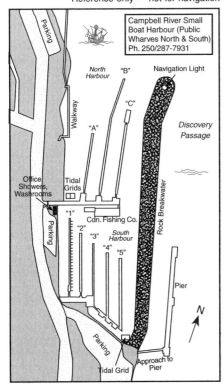

Campbell River Small Boat Harbour

See area map page 174

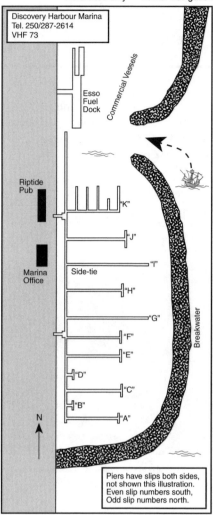

Reference only — not for navigation

Discovery Harbour Marina
Tel. 250/287-2614
VHF 73

Commercial Vessels

Esso Fuel Dock

Riptide Pub

Marina Office

Side-tie

"K"
"J"
"I"
"H"
"G"
"F"
"E"
"D"
"C"
"B"
"A"

Breakwater

N

Piers have slips both sides, not shown this illustration. Even slip numbers south, Odd slip numbers north.

Discovery Harbour Marina

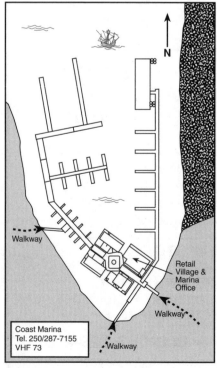

Reference only — not for navigation

N

Walkway

Walkway

Walkway

Retail Village & Marina Office

Coast Marina
Tel. 250/287-7155
VHF 73

Coast Marina

age until operation was taken over locally. They have made several improvements to attract pleasure craft. Office hours are 0730-1530 Mon.-Fri. in the winter; 0730-1530 7 days a week in the summer. If the office is closed when you arrive, take an empty space and register in the morning. Linda Franz is the manager. *(Marina map page 181)*

⑥ **Coast Marina,** 975 Shoppers Row, Campbell River, B.C. V9W 2C4, marina (250)287-7455, hotel (250)287-7155; fax (250) 287-2213. Monitors VHF channel 73. Open all year, guest moorage, 30, 50 & 100 amp power, washrooms, showers and laundry. In 1998 the marina changed its name from Coast Discovery Marina to Coast Marina, to eliminate confusion. It is located behind the middle of Campbell River's three breakwaters, and has facilities for boats to 150 feet in length. This high-quality marina is part of the Coast Discovery Inn hotel; guests have full access to the hotel's facilities. The marina was completely reconfigured and rebuilt for 1998, with wide concrete docks and new power and water to each slip. A unique floating retail village occupies the south end. We found the marina staff friendly, and eager to help with landings and departures—much appreciated when a crosswind is blowing. The marina is just steps away from Foreshore Park and downtown Campbell River shopping. *(Marina map this page)*

⑥ **Campbell River Chevron Marine.** Closed after storm damage in winter 1999, and will not re-open.

⑥ **Discovery Harbour Marina,** #112-1334 Island Hwy., Campbell River, B.C. V9W 5W8, (250)287-2614; fax (250)287-8939. Monitors VHF channel 73. Open all year, Esso fuel dock with gasoline and diesel, washrooms, showers, laundry, garbage drop, ample guest moorage available, 20, 30, 50, 100 amp power. This is the northernmost and largest of Campbell River's three breakwater-protected marinas. The marina has excellent docks, landing assistance and friendly people.

In 1998 the extensive Discovery Harbour Centre shopping plaza was completed adjacent to the marina, with everything you would expect to find in a major center. One of the buildings houses the elegant **Rip Tide Marine Pub & Grill**, which overlooks the docks. The Rip Tide has the north finger pier of the marina and slips 1 & 3 on K dock. The marina's washrooms, showers and coin-operated laundry are in the Rip Tide building.

Guest moorage can fill up at times, especially during high season. Reservations would be a good idea. *(Marina map this page)*

⑥ **Seaway Marine Services Ltd.,** Discovery Harbour Marina, P.O. Box 137, Campbell River, B.C. V9W 5A7, (250)287-3456. Monitors VHF channel 73. Esso fuel dock open all year, gasoline, diesel, washrooms, showers. Located behind the Discovery Harbour Marina breakwater. Also carries ice, small items. Stan Palmer is the owner.

⑥ **Campbell River Public Wharf (north, behind Discovery Harbour breakwater).** Open all year, 4000 feet of dock space behind the same breakwater that protects the Discovery Harbour Marina. This is primarily commercial vessel moorage, although one dock is devoted to pleasure craft. Several are liveaboards, and it's okay to raft off them. If you raft off a fish boat, be prepared to have the fish boat move you if it wants to leave. You'll find washrooms and showers, tidal grid, waste oil disposal, telephone, and a fuel dock adjacent. Contact the Discovery Harbour Marina office.

Yaculta. Use chart 3539; 3540; chartbook 3312. The Indian settlement of Yaculta, located on the east side of Discovery Passage at latitude 50°04'N, is the site of the Cape Mudge Kwakiutl Museum, with its collection of potlatch regalia. Cape Mudge Boatworks, with haulout, is located here. A public dock provides access to the town and repair yard.

Quathiaski Cove. Use chart 3539; 3540; chartbook 3312. Quathiaski Cove is the Quadra Island landing for the ferry to Campbell River. A public dock lies next to the ferry landing, and may be rolly from ferry wash. A small shopping center, with a good grocery store and a tasty informal cafe, is located a few blocks from the ferry landing. Fuel is available. Because of ferry traffic, the best anchorage is farther north, in the cove behind Grouse Island. Fingers of current from Discovery Passage work into Quathiaski Cove at some stages of the tide, so be sure the anchor is well set.

⑦ **Quathiaski Cove Public Wharf,** adjacent to the ferry landing. Dock has considerable mooring space. Waste oil disposal is available.

⑦ **Quathiaski Cove Petro Canada,** (250)285-3212. Gasoline, diesel, and propane, adjacent to the public wharf.

⑧ **April Point Lodge & Fishing Resort,** P.O. Box 248, Campbell River, B.C. V9W 4Z9, (250)285-2222; fax (250)285-2411. Monitors VHF channel 10. Open May 1 - Oct. 1. Ample guest moorage in the marina, 15, 30 & 50 amp power, laundry, cable TV and telephone hookup. This deluxe destination fishing resort is located at the tip of April Point. It has everything for the most demanding guest, including excellent rooms, fishing guides, a renowned dining room, and scheduled air service by three different companies.

In 1998 the Peterson family, longtime owners of April Point, sold the resort and marina to Oak Bay Marine Group, which operates a number of high-quality facilities on the coast. (Painter's, just north of Campbell River on the west side of Discovery Passage, is an Oak Bay property.) The grounds, public areas, rooms and dining room at April Point have been greatly upgraded since the ownership change. The marina has been upgraded

(Continued page 184)

Chart Making

Early July, Joassa Channel. Neil Sutherland, a hydrographer, stood on the foredeck of the survey launch and stuck a pike pole into the water. The tip of the pike pole hit rock. "One-nine!" Neil called, and in the cockpit George Schlagintweit, a second hydrographer, recorded the depth and the time. In the launch's cabin a computer stored the location, as measured by a highly accurate differential GPS. The survey launch moved to a different location around the rock. Neil measured. George recorded. A total of four times the launch approached the rock. When they were finished, the survey crew had measured the rock's depth, described its shape, and, within a margin of error of two meters, fixed its position.

This was hydrographic field work, the raw, on-the-scenes gathering of data that is the foundation of chart making. The exploration of this particular rock took place in little-traveled waters on the central B.C. coast, west of Bella Bella. We (my wife Marilynn and I) had joined the Canadian Hydrographic Service field survey party for two days as observers, to get a better idea of what chart making was all about. I'll have to say we came away impressed— no, overwhelmed is a better word.

Each year, beginning in May and ending in September, the CHS barge *Pender*, with rooms full of electronics, accommodations for at least 12 people, a complete boat repair and machine shop, a water maker and a waste treatment plant, is deployed along the coast. From the barge, the hydrographic surveyors venture out in launches to map the waters and record the depths.

Before the actual surveying can begin, though, preparatory work must be done. Tide gauges, which record the water level at 15-minute intervals, are installed at critical points around the survey area. Once a day a hydrographer goes out to the tide gauges and downloads the previous day's data into a hand-held computer. The data is uploaded into the barge's computers. When soundings are made, the launch's computer makes a record of the depth and the time of the sounding. Back on the barge the soundings are compared with the height of the tide, and actual depths are calculated.

Differential GPS transmitters must be positioned and calibrated. This involves placing differential units at a known locations and monitoring the error in GPS signals through the passage of more than one group of GPS satellites. On the day we were out with the hydrographers, positioning error had been reduced to less than two meters.

Typically, surveys are conducted at twice the scale of the intended new chart. If one inch on the chart would equal 40,000 inches on the earth (1:40,000), the survey is performed as if one inch on the chart would equal 20,000 inches on the earth (1:20,000). This gives the drafters back at headquarters more data than they can use. Better to edit data out than to guess at what might be there.

All this sounds quite electronic, scientific and even dull, but field work is anything but dull. Consider: Equipment must be placed on a rock islet that is exposed to ocean swells. The launch lies just off the face of the islet as the coxswain (helmsman) judges the waves washing up the face of the rock. At the right instant the coxswain pushes the bow of the launch up to the rock. The hydrographer jumps from the foredeck and scrambles to safety while water and launch fall away beneath him.

Getting off the rock involves the same process, only the hydrographer must jump from the rock to the moving deck of the launch. The coxswains are extremely skilled boat handlers. On the morning we were poking at underwater rocks in the calm water of Joassa Channel, the coxswain was Gordon Allison, a 30-year veteran of driving CHS launches. George Schlagintweit, the hydrographer, said, "I have literally trusted my life to the boat handling skills of Gordon Allison."

It is the field survey party's job to find all the places that responsible skippers stay away from. Do we see a reef-strewn area on the chart? It was a coxswain's job to drive the launch into that mess of reefs, and the hydrographers' job to record the reefs' shape, position and depth. They get good at it. "I can smell rocks," Gordon Allison said in Joassa Channel, as he stopped just short of a barely-covered rock.

Whether rocks can be smelled or not, this kind of close-quarters work is hard on equipment. The barge *Pender* carries a full-time mechanic who is qualified in all trades. He has machine tools on board that can cut, wire, bend, flatten, drill, straighten, turn, weld and fasten just about anything. The barge carries complete spares, several layers deep. It carries a spare 325-horsepower turbo-charged Volvo diesel engine, in case one of the launches blows an engine.

Field work develops an astonishing amount of data. After my visit, the CHS gave me a computer generated field sheet of the area we had been in. The field sheet was almost black with data. "This is just one layer," I was told. "If we put all the layers of information on this sheet you wouldn't be able to read it."

When the data gets back to CHS western headquarters in Sidney, it is blended with earlier surveys, land forms, topography, buoyage, commercial fishing boundaries, and scores of other items that get put onto charts. This vast quantity of data is rationalized, so contour lines can be drawn, shallows, rocks and reefs shown, and navigation information displayed. A certain rock, for example, might be a particular hazard to navigation. If placed on the chart at its actual location, the rock might seem insignificant. So the rock is moved into the channel slightly, to call attention to its presence. Judgments are made; decisions reached. At last a new chart is published.

Because of the smoothing, generalizing and interpreting of the myriad discrete bits of data available, the published chart leaves much redundant data out, so important navigation information can be presented. Perhaps 10 percent of what the field surveyors found appears on the finished product.

—Robert Hale

See area map page 174

This unique floating breakwater made of old railroad tank cars protects Brown's Bay Marina.

as well. April Point has recaptured its earlier luster as an outstanding stop.

When you approach, you will see a red spar buoy in the entrance to the bay. The buoy marks a shoal, and must be left to starboard as you enter (Red, Right, Returning). The channel will appear narrow. Especially at low tide, you will be strongly tempted to leave the buoy to port. This might put you aground. *Leave the buoy to starboard.*

The marina, hidden in the cove that extends south of the point, has 3500 feet of dock space, and is set up to handle the larger boats. You can find anchorage in this cove. A passage leads between the cove and adjacent Gowlland Harbour, but the passage is shallow and littered with rocks. If you lack local knowledge, the general advice is to stay out.

Gowlland Harbour. Use chart 3539; 3540; chartbook 3312. Gowlland Harbour is a large, protected bay lying behind Gowlland Island, with considerable log booming activity along the harbor's shoreline. Before entering, study the chart so you can avoid Entrance Rock, which lies north of Gowlland Island.

You'll find good anchoring depths at the north end of the bay, but it's much prettier at the south end, especially behind Stag Island. Good anchoring also lies behind Wren Islet, Crow Islet, and the Mouse Islets, all of them a little to the north of Stag Island. These islets, which are protected as provincial park preserves, make excellent picnic spots.

Seymour Narrows. Use chart 3539; chart book 3312. Use Canadian Tide & Current Tables, Vol. 6. The currents in Seymour Narrows run to 16 knots on the flood and 14 knots on the ebb, flooding south and ebbing north. *This is a passage to be transited at or near slack water.* From the south, you can wait for

slack either in Menzies Bay on the Vancouver Island side, or in the good-size unnamed bay behind Maud Island on the Quadra Island side. South of Maud Island, the flood forms a backeddy along Quadra Island, sweeping northbound boats more easily toward Maud Island. Seymour Narrows is the principal route for north- and south-bound commercial traffic, including cruise ships. Give large vessels ample room to maneuver.

Before going through, we urge you to read the Sailing Directions section on Seymour Narrows. Especially on a flood, Sailing Directions counsels against the west side because of rough water. From the north, Plumper Bay is a good waiting spot on the east side, as is Brown Bay on the west side. Brown Bay has a floating breakwater and a marina.

Both **Deepwater Bay** and **Plumper Bay** are too open and deep to be attractive as anchorages. There may be good anchorage in **Menzies Bay,** being careful to go around either end of a drying shoal which almost blocks the entrance. This area is used as a booming ground for the pulp mill in Campbell River.

In July 1996, the warship HMCS *Columbia* was sunk off Maud Island to create an artificial reef for diving.

⑨ **Brown's Bay Marina & RV Park,** P.O. Box 668, Campbell River, B.C. V9W 6J3, (250)286-3135; fax (250)286-0951; e-mail brownbay@vquest.com. Monitors VHF channel 73. Open all year, gasoline and diesel, guest moorage available along 2000 feet of dock and 50 slips for boats to 26 feet, 15, 20, 30 & 50 amp power, washrooms, showers, laundry, pumpout, and propane. This marina is located on Vancouver Island at the north end of Seymour Narrows. The store carries groceries, ice, fishing gear and bait. The floating restaurant is fully licensed. There is a launch

ramp. Boat rentals and guides are available.

Kanish Bay. Use chart 3539; chartbook 3312. Kanish Bay has several good anchorages. You could sneak behind the **Chained Islands**, and with some thought and planning find a number of delightful spots, especially in settled weather. **Granite Bay** is well protected with a good bottom, but not very cozy feeling. The small bay between Granite Bay and Small Inlet offers protection from westerlies.

Small Inlet. A narrow but easily-run channel with a least depth of 8 feet leads from the northeast corner of Kanish Bay to Small Inlet. Small Inlet, surrounded by steep, wooded mountains, is beautiful. Once through the entrance channel, a number of good anchorages can be found along the north shore. A couple of boats can fit behind a little nob of land near the southeast corner. The chart shows 3 rocks in this anchorage—actually, they're a reef with 3 high points. You can anchor in the cove at the head of Small Inlet, behind two small islands.

Otter Cove. Use chart 3539 or chartbook 3312. Otter Cove lies just inside Chatham Point. It's a useful little anchorage, with convenient depths and protection from seas rolling down Johnstone Strait. If you need a place to hide out until the wind or seas subside, it's a good spot. In 1996 Otter Cove and Chatham Point were preserved as **Rock Bay Marine Park.**

MALASPINA INLET

Use chart 3559; chartbook 3312; chart 3538. Malaspina Inlet, Okeover Inlet, Lancelot Inlet, and Theodosia Inlet all are entered between Zephine Point and Myrmidon Point. Much of the Gifford Peninsula, which lies to the east of Malaspina Inlet, is Desolation Sound Marine Park. You'll find literally dozens of good anchorages throughout this area. You'll also find lots of rocks and reefs, most of which are covered by kelp during the summer and easily spotted. Aquaculture occupies a number of otherwise inviting anchorages. Small-scale Chart 3538 (1:40,000) gives a pretty good picture of the area, but large-scale Chart 3559 (1:12,000) really opens it up. Several pages in the Chartbook 3312 are excellent as well.

Contributing Editor Tom Kincaid has anchored in a little bight behind Beulah Island and a couple of others just to the south, and behind the Cochrane Islands.

Grace Harbour. Grace Harbour has always been one of our favorites. The inner bay is almost completely landlocked, with anchorage for quite a few boats. Many of the anchorages are along the shore, so be prepared to run a stern-tie to shore. A rock, shown on the charts, is in the middle of this innermost bay. The anchor just skids across the rock before finding holding ground on the other side. On a crowded summer weekend, the empty spot

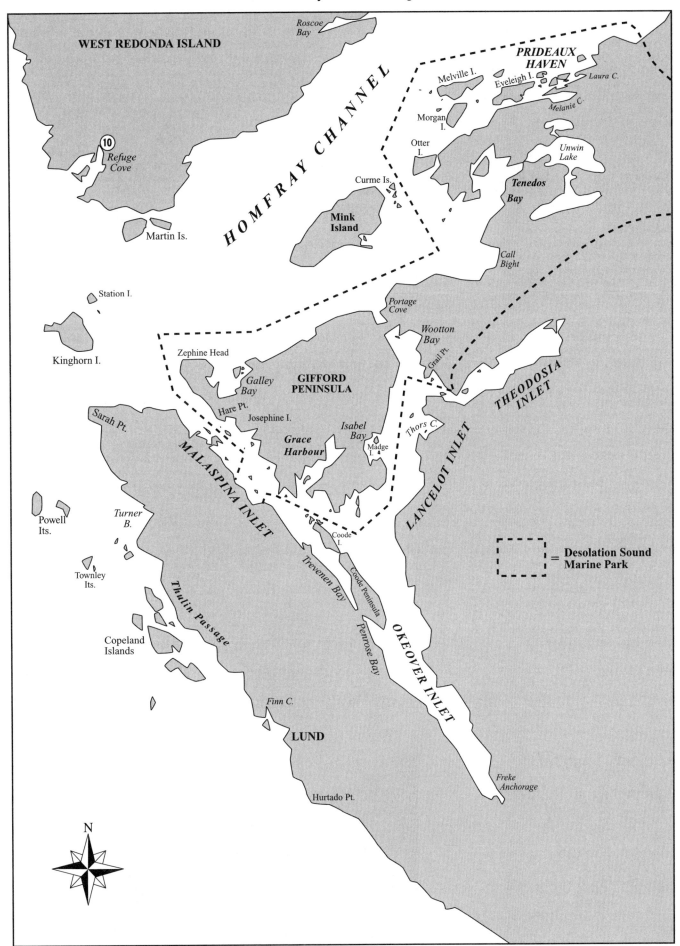

WEST REDONDA ISLAND

Roscoe Bay

PRIDEAUX HAVEN

Melville I.

Eveleigh I. *Laura C.*

HOMFRAY CHANNEL

Morgan I.

Melanie C.

Otter I.

Unwin Lake

10 *Refuge Cove*

Curme Is.

Tenedos Bay

Mink Island

Martin Is.

Call Bight

Station I.

Portage Cove

Wootton Bay

Kinghorn I.

Zephine Head

Grail Pt.

THEODOSIA INLET

Galley Bay

GIFFORD PENINSULA

Sarah Pt.

Hare Pt.

Josephine I.

Isabel Bay

Thors C.

Grace Harbour

Madge I.

LANCELOT INLET

Powell Its.

Turner B.

= **Desolation Sound Marine Park**

Townley Its.

Coode I.

Thulin Passage

Coode Peninsula

Trevenen Bay

Copeland Islands

Penrose Bay

MALASPINA INLET

OKEOVER INLET

Finn C.

LUND

Freke Anchorage

Hurtado Pt.

N

See area map page 174

in the middle is there for a reason.

Trevenen Bay. There appears to be good anchorage at the head of Trevenen Bay, but the bay is largely taken by aquaculture. The head of Trevenen Bay, incidentally, could be considered the real north end of the coast highway that continues through North and South America. At this point it is just a little dirt road, but it is an extension of the road past Lund.

Penrose Bay. You can find anchorage at the head of the bay. The Okeover Marina is on the west shore.

Lancelot Inlet. Isabel Bay in Lancelot Inlet is another of our favorites, with the best anchorage tucked in behind Madge Island. There is also good anchorage in Thors Cove. Contributing Editor Tom Kincaid once anchored right at the head of Lancelot Inlet, rowed ashore, and walked across the narrow isthmus that separates that inlet from Portage Cove on the Desolation Sound side. This little isthmus is private property, however, and should be entered only with prior permission of the owner.

Theodosia Inlet. Theodosia Inlet has a narrow, shallow entrance, but is navigable through kelp by most boats at all stages of the tide. Once inside, the bay opens up. Logging activity takes away from the remote feeling of the bay, but anchorage can be found in a number of gunkholes along the shoreline. Much of the shoreline is taken up with boomed logs.

Okeover Inlet. South of Penrose Bay a public float gives access to the road to Lund, with a natural launching ramp alongside. Oysters and other seafoods are grown in several places along Okeover Inlet, and are on private property where trespassing is forbidden.

In 1998 the restaurant at the public float re-opened as the Laughing Oyster (604)483-9775. We've had lunch and supper there, and recommend it highly. Outstanding menu, lovely surroundings, stunning view.

Galley Bay. Use chart 3559; chartbook 3312; chart 3538. Galley Bay is just east of Zephine Head. It is a good anchorage, particularly in the eastern end. At one time a hippie colony was established on the west shore. By close observation Contributing Editor Kincaid noted that among other idiosyncrasies, they practiced a clothing-optional lifestyle. He reports that some of the ladies would swim out to bargain for cigarettes. Alas, he says, they are now gone.

Mink Island. Use chart 3538; chartbook 3312. Mink Island is private property, but you'll find excellent anchorage in the bay that indents the southeast shore, particularly if you work in behind the little island in the center of the bay. You'll probably run a stern-tie to shore.

Curme Islands. Use chart 3538; chartbook 3312. There is possible fair weather anchorage among the Curme Islands, off Mink Island's eastern shore. Wolferstan describes the waterways as "challenging"; Bailey and Cummings, in their *Gunkholing* guidebook, describe the Curme Islands as being extremely tight, with shallow waterways, but with anchoring possibilities if the boat uses 4-way ties to hold position. For most people, dinghies and kayaks are probably the way to go.

Tenedos Bay. Use chart 3538; chartbook 3312. Tenedos Bay (also called Deep Bay) is a favorite of ours, for a couple of reasons. First, it's a good, protected anchorage, with a landlocked basin behind the island off the northwest shore. This island is joined with the mainland by a drying shoal, shown on the charts. Second, it's a just a short dinghy ride to the mouth of the stream that runs from Unwin Lake, a popular freshwater swimming hole. A path leads beside the stream. Several of the stream's pools, screened by vegetation, make good bathing places.

You'll find anchorages in a number of coves along the shore of Tenedos Bay. We like the little notch at the northernmost corner. Stern-ties to shore are the norm. The center of Tenedos Bay is too deep (50 to 100 fathoms) for anchoring.

Caution: As you enter Tenedos Bay, a nasty rock lies submerged off the south side of Bold Head. Especially if you are headed to or from Refuge Cove, Mink Island, or around Bold Head to Prideaux Haven, this rock is located on your probable course. The rock lies farther offshore than you might expect. Give it an extra wide berth, just to be sure. Remember to study your charts before proceeding in these waters. A number of rocks are shown. All are easy to avoid if you are aware of them.

Otter Island. Use chart 3538; chartbook 3312. A very narrow but navigable channel runs between Otter Island and the mainland. There is room for a small number boats to anchor, taking stern-ties to shore.

PRIDEAUX HAVEN

Proposed No Discharge Zone. Gray water okay. See p. 15. Use chart 3555 (recommended); chartbook 3312; chart 3538. The coves that make up the area generally known as Prideaux Haven are the most popular spots in Desolation Sound, with several anchorages—all of them requiring a stern-tie to increase the number of boats that can be accommodated. This area is just beautiful. It is described in great detail by M. Wylie Blanchet in her classic book *The Curve of Time,* and with different emphasis and stunning aerial photos by Bill Wolferstan in his *Cruising Guide to British Columbia, Vol. 2, Desolation Sound and the Discovery Islands.* Yet another perspective is found in Bailey and Cummings, *Gunkholing in Desolation Sound and Princess Louisa* (now out of print).

You can go ashore and search for the site of the Flea Village, encountered in 1791 by a party of Capt. Vancouver's officers and men in the company of Archibald Menzies, the expedition's botanist. Wolferstan says the Flea Village site can be found, but doesn't say where. Beth Hill, in her book *Seven-Knot Summers,* says she knows the location—Copplestone Point.

At the head of Melanie Cove you can find the remains of Mike's Place, and in Laura Cove the ruins of old Phil Lavine's cabin (both from *The Curve of Time).*

The entire clutch of islands and shallow waterways invites exploration by dinghy or kayak. During high season, the only thing missing is solitude. You'll have lots of company. *(See area map page 185)*

Melanie Cove. A light rain falling in early evening.

Eveleigh Island. Use chart 3555 (recommended); chartbook 3312; chart 3538. You'll find anchorage in Eveleigh Anchorage, the western cove behind Eveleigh Island. A drying reef connects Eveleigh Island with the mainland. Entry to the other Prideaux Haven anchorages is around the east end of Eveleigh Island. A reef almost, but not quite, closes this entrance. The entrance and its reef are shown clearly at a scale of 1:6000 on page 11 of Chartbook 3312. Stay close to the Eveleigh Island side of the passage to pass the reef.

Prideaux Haven. *Proposed No Discharge Zone. Gray water okay. See p. 15.* Use chart 3555 (recommended); chartbook 3312; chart 3538. Inside Eveleigh Island are the main Prideaux Haven anchorage and also Melanie Cove. Except in the very middle of Prideaux Haven and Melanie Cove, stern ties are the rule during the summer. The garbage float that used to be anchored outside Melanie Cove no longer is there, a victim of budget cutbacks.

Melanie Cove. Use chart 3555 (recommended); chartbook 3312; chart 3538. Melanie Cove is perfectly protected, with ample room along both shores for boats to anchor and stern-tie. At the head of the cove you can explore an overgrown apple orchard and the remains of Mike's cabin, described warmly in *The Curve of Time.*

Laura Cove. Use chart 3555 (recommended); chartbook 3312; chart 3538. Laura Cove has a fairly narrow entrance with a least depth of approximately 2 fathoms at zero tide. Rocks extend from both sides. Enter cautiously. The remains of the cabin owned by Old Phil the Frenchman, mentioned in *The Curve of Time,* lie at the head of this bay. Anchorage is to the east of Copplestone Point, since the west end of the bay is a maze of rocks and reefs.

Roffey Island. Use chart 3555 (recommended); chartbook 3312; chart 3538. If you can't find a place at Prideaux Haven, Melanie Cove or Laura Cove, try the little bay behind Roffey Island. There's room for one or more boats, and you're away from the "madding crowd."

Homfray Channel. Use charts 3538 and 3541; chartbook 3312. Homfray Channel curves from the south end of West Redonda Island around East Redonda Island until it merges with Toba Inlet. The only bays of consequence are Forbes Bay and Atwood Bay. Atwood Bay is too deep and exposed for convenient anchoring, but Bob Stephenson of Desolation Sound Charters says Forbes Bay can be good for anchoring.

On p. 100 of his book, Wolferstan tells of two Indian pictographs on the west shore of Homfray Channel, one of a single fish, the other less identifiable. Correspondent Bruce Evertz reports that his GPS showed the location as Lat 124 39.476N Lon 50 11.61W.

Roscoe Bay/Roscoe Bay Marine Park. *Proposed No Discharge Zone. Gray water okay. See p. 15.* Use chart 3538; chartbook 3312. Roscoe Bay, on West Redonda Island where Waddington Channel meets Homfray Channel, is an excellent, protected and popular anchorage. The bay is divided into an inner cove and an outer cove, separated by a drying shoal that is easily crossed by shallow draft boats at half tide or better. At high tide most sailboats can get in.

The inner cove is very pretty, and except for the other boats enjoying the bay with you, is a good example of what cruising in these waters is all about. Dinghy ashore and take the short hike up to the nob that divides the two bays.

At the head of the inner bay a short stream connects with Black Lake. An old logging road leads to the lake. During summer months the water in Black Lake is warm and excellent for swimming or bathing. Trout fishing is said to be good. If you carry your dinghy up the road you can launch it along the lake's shoreline.

Elworthy Island. Use chart 3538; 3539; chartbook 3312. A small bay offers good anchorage behind Elworthy Island, a mile north of Church Point, roughly across Waddington Channel from the entrance to Pendrell Sound.

About Tidal Rapids

MOST TIDAL RAPIDS can be run with safety from 30 minutes before slack water until 30 minutes after slack water. Some can be run as much as an hour before or after. If the difference between high water and low water is small, certain rapids may be safe for an entire tide. But if the difference is large, those same rapids may be dangerous at any time other than a very few minutes on either side of slack water.

In major rapids, it is common for the current to increase until it no longer is a smooth, laminar sweep, and changes into a boiling, crashing, upwelling maelstrom that looks exactly like a fast-falling whitewater mountain stream.

White water is full of air, and less buoyant than green water. Boats float lower. Rudders lose effectiveness and propellers lose bite. When diminished buoyancy and lessened control are combined with strong currents, standing waves, deep whirlpools and boils of upwelling water, very quickly you can have a recipe for disaster. This is why good boats are lost in tidal rapids.

While the time and duration of slack water varies with the individual rapids, each rapids is quite consistent within itself. By long observation, relationships have been established. For example, slack water at Malibu Rapids, at the entrance to Princess Louisa Inlet, occurs 35 minutes after low water at Point Atkinson, and 25 minutes after high water at Point Atkinson. Other rapids, such as Deception Pass, Seymour Narrows, Yuculta Rapids and Dent Rapids, have their own current tables that predict the times of turn and maximum current. Mariners experienced in these waters have those tables and live by them.

We have enormous respect for tidal current rapids, and will not run a major rapids except during the narrow window of time that surrounds slack water. We study the current tables and make our travel plans with any rapids topmost in our minds. This book reflects our cautious approach. We discuss the various rapids frankly and without sugar-coating, and hope our readers will take our cautions seriously.

—*Robert Hale*

See area map page 174

This island is called Alfred Island by Wolferstan, but chart 3538 shows it as Elworthy Island. No name is shown on chart 3541 or in chart book 3312. The latest edition of Sailing Directions makes no mention of Alfred Island. Enter the anchorage from either end, but watch for a drying rock near the north entrance.

Allies Island. Use chart 3541 or chartbook 3312. Allies Island is connected to West Redonda Island by a drying reef. Anchorage is possible behind either end, with the north end preferred. A good spot is behind the small islet that lies between Allies Island and West Redonda Island.

Doctor Bay. Use chart 3541 or chartbook 3312. Doctor Bay would be a good anchorage, but is taken up by aquaculture.

Walsh Cove Marine Park. Use chart 3541 or chartbook 3312. Walsh Cove Marine Park is a beautiful little spot, with room for a few boats to anchor on a rocky bottom. The cove is well protected from most winds. Enter from the south, since Gorges Island is connected to West Redonda Island by a rock-strewn reef. You'll find two sets of Indian pictographs at Butler Point.

Pendrell Sound. Use chart 3541 or chartbook 3312. With summer water temperatures dependably in excess of 68 degrees Fahrenheit, Pendrell Sound has been called the "warmest saltwater north of Mexico." Major oyster culture operations are in the sound, providing seed oysters to growers all over the world.

Strings of cultch material (often they are empty oyster shells) are suspended from floats in the bay until the oyster spat adheres to them, at which point they are shipped. Seed oyster growers ask for a 4-knot speed limit in the vicinity of their operations.

Anchorage can be found at the head of the sound, behind some small islets that are connected to East Redonda Island by a drying reef.

Another good anchorage is located on the western shore, about three-quarters of the way up the sound. This anchorage is tucked in behind a small islet at the outfall from a saltwater lagoon. We tried this anchorage in deteriorating weather a few years ago, but found the best spots, close to the islet, taken.

With nightfall approaching and conditions worsening, we got creative. The charts show the shore on the north edge of this cove as reefs, but we found a nice opening, perhaps 50 feet wide, between two fingers of reef. We were able to set the anchor in front of the opening and back in. A long stern-tie was run to rocks on shore. It took several changes in the stern-tie termination point to align the boat just right, but once done, the anchorage was snug and safe for the night—a windy night filled with rain, thunder and lightning. We were rather proud of ourselves.

Toba Inlet. Use chart 3541 or chartbook 3312. Toba Inlet extends 20 miles into the 8,000-foot-high coast mountain range until it ends in drying flats at the mouth of the Toba River. The water is very deep right up to the rock wall shores. Spectacular waterfalls crash into the sea, especially early in the season when the snow pack is melting rapidly. Toba Inlet reminds us of the inlets north of Cape Caution. Limited anchorage is possible at the head of the inlet, and in Brem Bay off the mouth of the Brem River. Brem Bay, however, is a major log dump. When we visited, the bay was full of debris and not very inviting.

⑪ **Toba Wildernest,** (250)286-8507. This is a new marina, with 400 feet of moorage, 3 cabins, ice, shower with no timer, unlimited power and water, located behind Double Island at the mouth of Toba Inlet. After a visit our notes read: "Amazing place. The smallest cabin is like a doll house. Other cabins well-built, utterly charming." They have their own amazingly-engineered hydroelectric power plant, and leave the lights on all day to keep a load on the generator. The cabins are very German in style and decor. Ed and Mary Schlote are the owners.

LEWIS CHANNEL

Lewis Channel runs between West Redonda Island and Cortes Island, and connects at the north with Calm Channel.

Refuge Cove. Use chart 3555; chartbook 3312; chart 3538. Refuge Cove, with a public marina, fuel dock, shops, and well-stocked store, is the most popular resupply port in the heart of Desolation Sound. Several homes, joined by boardwalks, surround the cove. Most of the moorage is public, although the store does have a small float for its customers. Anchorage is possible toward the head of the bay. During high season traffic is exceptionally heavy. *Approach slowly,* and wait your turn for dock space or fuel. Turnover is rapid; you won't wait long. You may wait longer, though, for the laundromat. The machines seem to run without interruption, and it's not unusual to have several names on the waiting list.

Refuge Cove is a scheduled stop for float plane service. Many boats change crews here, flying new crew in and old crew out.

⑩ **Refuge Cove Public Wharf** serves the general store, gift shop, and hamburger stand at Refuge Cove. Potable water on the dock. While commercial vessels may have priority, during the summer months it is taken entirely by pleasure craft.

⑩ **Refuge Cove General Store,** General Delivery, Refuge Cove, B.C. V0P 1P0, (250)935-6659. The fuel dock and general store are under one ownership; other shops are under different ownerships. For information purposes, we treat the complex as one.

Guest moorage is available along 2000 feet of dock space. The fuel dock has gasoline and

The Refuge Cove Store, with its laundromat and nearby shops, is a major resupply point in Desolation Sound.

Boat traffic is heavy at Refuge Cove, especially around the fuel dock. Approach slowly and be patient.

Church House, at the north end of Calm Channel, is abandoned. The dock is in disrepair.

We know this is Desolation Sound, and we think it's the view out the mouth of Frances Bay, near sunset.

diesel. Propane is available. Washrooms, showers, and laundry are available.

The store carries complete groceries, fresh produce, deli items including cheeses and meats, a complete liquor agency with interesting wine selections, some marine supplies, charts, books and magazines. The store has limited operating hours in the fall.

Other shops sell baked goods, gifts, and hamburgers (although the hamburger stand doesn't open until July 1). On a recent visit, we patronized the fuel dock, the store for supplies, the hamburger stand for lunch, the baked goods shop for breakfast the following morning, and the gift shop for friends back home.

Teakerne Arm. Use chart 3538 or chartbook 3312. Teakerne Arm is a deep inlet extending from Lewis Channel into West Redonda Island. Anchorage in Teakerne Arm is just inside the entrance on the south side, or in front of the waterfall from Cassel Lake at the head of the north arm, or in the south arm. Both arms are deep, except very close to shore.

The area near the waterfall is a provincial park, with a dinghy float connected to shore by an excellent aluminum ramp. Anchorage is in 15-25 fathoms. Stern-tie to cables hanging down the rock wall west of the waterfall. The waterfall is spectacular but short, so scrambling from the dinghy float up to Cassel Lake for a swim is a popular pastime.

Much of the shallow water near shore is taken up with log booms, and often you must tie to the booms if you are to stay in Teakerne Arm.

CALM CHANNEL

Use chart 3541 or chartbook 3312. Calm Channel connects Lewis Channel and Sutil Channel in the south, and with Bute Inlet and the Yuculta Rapids in the north. It is appropriately named, often being wind-free when areas nearby are breezy.

Redonda Bay. Use chart 3541 or chartbook 3312. Redonda Bay, with Church House as a landmark, has the ruins of an old wharf left over from logging days, but otherwise is not a good anchorage. The wharf is no longer usable and the ramp leading from the float to the wharf is gone. Several rocks in the bay are charted.

Rendezvous Islands. Use chart 3541 or chartbook 3312. The Rendezvous Islands have a number of homes along their shores. There is possible anchorage in a bight between the southern and middle islands, but a private float and dolphins restrict the room available.

Rendezvous Lodge, P.O. Box 309, Quathiaski Cove, BC V0P 1N0, (250)287-0318; fax (250) 203-1123; e-mail rbugeaud @online. bc.ca.; web site www.anglingbc.com/rdv/home.html. This is a new lodge and dining spot located on the northerly island of the Rendezvous Islands, recommended by readers. They have a dock for 4 or 5 boats, exposed to wash from passing boats. A sign reads, "Open for Lunches." Owners, Roy and Darlene Bugeaud (pronounced "Bu-jo").

Frances Bay. Use chart 3541. Frances Bay, located on Raza Passage, just off Calm Channel, is a popular anchorage. Its advantage is spectacular views to the southeast; its disadvantage is its exposure to southeast winds. Anchor near the head in 6-8 fathoms, rocky bottom.

Bute Inlet. Use chart 3542 or chartbook 3312. Bute Inlet is very deep. Except in small areas near the mouths of rivers and at the head of the inlet, it is not good for anchorage. Even in the places mentioned, the bottom drops away steeply, making a stern-tie to shore a good idea.

Eastern Johnstone Strait

Yucultas • Big Bay • Cordero Channel • Nodales Channel • Blind Channel
Greene Point Rapids • Whirlpool Rapids • Sunderland Channel • Johnstone Strait

NORTH OF DESOLATION SOUND

THE SOUTHERN TIP OF Stuart Island marks the northern boundary of Desolation Sound cruising waters. North of Desolation Sound you'll find colder water, harsher weather, fewer services, and a greater number of rocks, reefs, and tidal rapids. You should have good ground tackle and know how to use it. The farther north you go, the more remote conditions become, all the way to Alaska.

North of Desolation Sound you find fewer boats. A greater percentage of those boats are 32 feet in length and larger. Many stay out for four to eight weeks or more in the summer, and the larger boats allow more comfortable accommodations. On average the occupants are older, too.

We remember, however, a pair of 22-foot trailerable boats that roared into Sullivan Bay late one afternoon. Each boat held a couple in their 30s and a 12-year-old son. The two families had come from Tacoma in only *three days,* and were bound for a destination beyond Cape Caution. Early the next morning they were gone—a two-week vacation can race by quickly.

Much of the research for this book was done from our first *Surprise,* a very well-equipped Tollycraft 26 powerboat, about the smallest boat that we would rate as a mom-and-pop cruiser. (In late 1997 the Tolly 26 *Surprise* was replaced by a Tollycraft 37, also named *Surprise.*) For the two of us, long-married and used to each other's ways, the Tolly 26 was completely adequate. Nevertheless, when we were north of Desolation Sound the 26 was one of the smallest cruising boats—if not *the* smallest cruising boat—wherever we anchored or docked. Those who are planning extensive cruises north of Desolation Sound should understand the nature of the experience, and look at their equipment accordingly.

Garbage Drops. While occasionally you will find a lack of garbage drops in Desolation Sound and south, garbage becomes a much greater problem until you reach Port McNeill. Garbage must be hauled from marinas and settlements to authorized dumps, usually on Vancouver Island. Since they must pay for hauling and disposal, most marinas charge a fee for garbage, if they accept garbage at all.

It's a good idea to use as little glass as possible, to wash and flatten cans, and pack paper out. We've seen paper burned on the beach, but take care to avoid the spread of fire. All paper must be burned completely.

Fresh Water. Fresh water can be a problem even in Desolation Sound, and northward supplies are fewer. The resorts have access to water for drinking, cooking and cleaning, but few have enough for boat washing. Some stops, such as Blind Channel, have sweet spring water. The water in Shawl Bay is highly regarded. Often you will find water with a brown cast from cedar bark tannin. We don't know of anybody who has had a bad experience from it.

Prices. For each of the facilities in these cruising grounds, the season is short and the costs are high. Nearly everything must be brought in by barge or air. Don't be upset when prices are higher than you see in the city. Remember too that during the season the marina personnel's workday starts early, ends late, and calls for a smile at all times. Smiles come more easily on some days than others.

THE INSIDE ROUTE TO WELLS PASSAGE AND PORT HARDY

Most cruisers heading north choose the sheltered inside route over the possible mayhem of a long passage in Johnstone Strait. The inside route runs from the north end of Calm Channel (the south tip of Stuart Island), through Yuculta Rapids, Gillard Passage, Dent Rapids, Greene Point Rapids, and Whirlpool Rapids. It includes an approximately 14-mile open stretch in Johnstone Strait (which cannot be avoided) between Sunderland Channel and the safety of Havannah Channel, after which the currents of Chatham Channel must be negotiated. Careful planning is paramount. You need to know the times of slack water at each rapids, and you need to know how long it will take to get to each rapids.

Therefore, you *must* have complete and up-

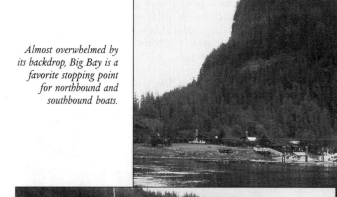

Almost overwhelmed by its backdrop, Big Bay is a favorite stopping point for northbound and southbound boats.

A little rain doesn't deter these kids at Big Bay.

to-date charts on board, and a copy of the Canadian Tide and Current Tables, Vol. 6. Furthermore, using the corrections shown in the Reference and Secondary Current Stations in the front part of the Tide and Current Tables, you must be comfortable calculating the times of slack water at the various rapids. For anchoring and transiting shallow channels, use the corrections in the Reference and Secondary Ports pages to calculate the times and heights of tides.

Those who have not had experience with large tides and reversing tidal rapids may find this research and calculation daunting at first, but an evening spent reading the excellent instructions will clear matters considerably. For clarifications, don't be shy about asking a few old salts on the docks. They (we) love to help.

Since the waters north of Desolation Sound flood southward from the top of Vancouver Island and ebb northward, the northbound boat (if it wishes to clear a number of rapids in one run) has a timing problem. Assuming a start with Yuculta Rapids, all the rapids to the north will have turned before slack water occurs at the Yucultas. The general plan is to approach Yuculta Rapids before the southbound flood current turns to the northbound ebb, and utilize two backeddies (described below) to help your way against the flood for the two or so miles to Gillard Passage and Dent Rapids that lie just beyond. Done correctly, you'll go through Dent Rapids against the last of the then-weak flood current, and let the new ebb current flush you out Cordero Channel.

The ebb will already have been running at Greene Point Rapids, which turned earlier. Depending on your boat's speed, the ebb could be at full force when you arrive. Rather than go through in these conditions, many cruisers choose instead to overnight either at Cordero Lodge or Blind Channel Resort. Both have excellent restaurants. Shoal Bay and the Cordero Islands are other good places to wait for Greene Point Rapids to settle down.

The next day you can depart before high water slack and push through Greene Point Rapids in the dying flood current. Then you'll hurry to Wellbore Channel, to take Whirlpool Rapids early in the favorable ebb current. If this is done early in the morning, it is possible that the wind will not have got

up for the stretch in Johnstone Strait. With luck it can be a pleasant run down Sunderland Channel and into Johnstone Strait, all the way to Havannah Channel. How this works depends on the speed of your boat, the actual conditions that exist, and the tightness of your schedule. *Caution:* A tight schedule is not justification for taking a chance with bad conditions. The dangers are real.

Southbound the options are greater. Take your first rapids against the last of the dying ebb, and let the new flood current flush you south. Each set of rapids in succession turns at a later time. Given the right conditions, even a slow boat can take all the rapids on one tide, with only a few hours' wait if the boat arrives at any given rapids when they are running too hard to risk transit.

We suggest that you carry and use the guidebook *Exploring the South Coast of British Columbia*, by Don Douglass and Réanne Hemingway-Douglass, and *Cruising Beyond Desolation Sound*, by John Chappell. Many cruising boats experienced in these waters use these books. We also urge you to carry and use the Canadian government book Sailing Directions, British Columbia Coast (South Portion), available through Canadian Hydrographic chart agents.

Yuculta Rapids. Use chart 3543; chartbook 3312. The Yuculta (pronounced "YEW-cla-ta") Rapids run between Stuart Island and Sonora Island. Taken at slack they are benign, but at full force on a spring tide, especially against an opposing wind, they can be extremely dangerous. Northbound, Sailing Directions recommends that slow and low-powered boats arrive at the rapids an hour before high slack, and use a back eddy along the Stuart Island shore until off Kellsey Point. Then cross to the Sonora Island shore to use a prevailing northerly current. This should position the boat to go through Gillard Passage and Dent Rapids satisfactorily. If you are late and unsure of Dent Rapids, wait in Big Bay for the next slack.

Big Bay. Use chart 3543; chartbook 3312. Big Bay on Stuart Island is a major fishing resort center. It has both a public dock and a resort and marina. The public floats are 350 feet long, and lie behind a plank and piling breakwater to the south of the Big Bay

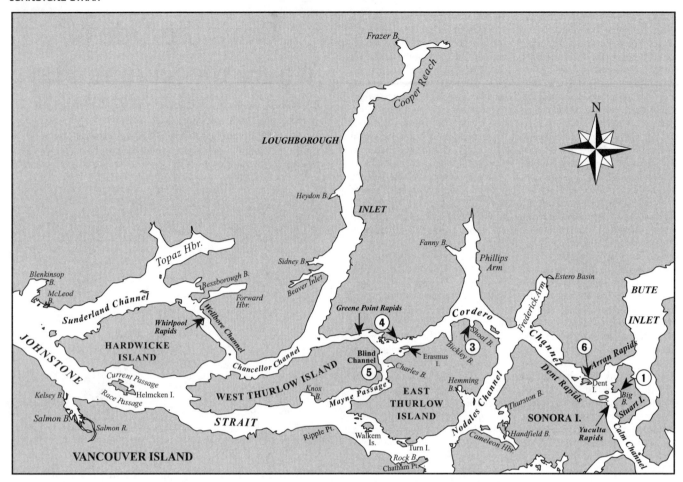

Marina. A pub is near the head of the public dock. The Big Bay Marina offers moorage with power, fuel, supplies, a good restaurant, and scheduled float plane service in season.

① **Big Bay Marina & Fishing Resort,** Stuart Island, B.C. V0P 1V0, (250)286-8107. Open May through September, gasoline and diesel at the fuel dock, 15 amp power, washrooms, showers, laundry. This is a large, friendly, well-run marina with accommodations, a good restaurant, a lounge, a new bakery and pizzeria, and a well-stocked store with liquor agency and galley-to-go items. The lounge is large and very relaxing. A well-equipped game room is adjacent. Big Bay is a principal jumping-off point for waters north. They can handle boats to 130 feet in length, and have guides for salmon fishing in the Yucultas. Bruce and Kay Knierim and their family own and run the resort.

Kill your wake! It's quite likely that you have been running at hull speed or faster in the Yucultas or Gillard Passage, and putting out a sizeable wake. When approaching the marina, stop the boat before you actually get into the bay, and go into reverse to kill the wake. If you don't, the wake will follow you in and create absolute mayhem with the boats at the docks.

⑥ **Dent Island Lodge,** General Delivery, Stuart Island, B.C. V0P 1V0, (250)286-8105;

fax (250)203-1041; e-mail dentisl@oberon.ark.com. Use chart 3543. Open May to October, guest moorage for boats to 140 feet, 30 & 50 amp power, water on the docks, fishing guides available. Sauna, exercise room, hot tub.

Dent Island Lodge is simply outstanding. It is owned by two prominent Northwest families for their own use, but takes guests and corporate groups. The staff is intelligent and highly professional. They treat you as if you were a guest in a small, quiet, private retreat—which you are. At the end of the day, after the guide boats have returned from fishing, an elegant appetizer table is set out in the lounge. The dinner menu is extraordinary. Our notes read, "Seafood chowder unbelievable, Caesar salad unique, on and on I could go."

The lodge is located at the back of a little bay that separates Dent Island from the mainland. It is set next to a canoe pass rapids, where 10-12-knot whitewater tidal currents churn. A spacious deck with hot tub overlooks the pass. It is utterly beautiful. Approach from the southeast. The 1:20,000 inset on chart 3543 shows it well, even the dock. Plan your arrival and departure to coincide with slack water in Gillard Passage. It is considerate to make reservations even in the less busy weeks of the season, and just about essential during high season.

Gillard Passage. Use chart 3543; chartbook

3312. Currents run to 13 knots on the flood and 10 knots on the ebb. Transit near slack water. Times of slack are shown in Canadian Tide and Current Tables, Vol. 6. Pass south of Jimmy Judd Island. Big Bay is a good place to wait if the current is too strong.

Dent Rapids. Use chart 3543; chartbook 3312. Currents run to 9 knots on floods and 8 knots on ebbs. Time corrections are shown under Reference and Secondary Current Stations in Tide and Current Tables, Vol. 6. Per Sailing Directions, "In Devils Hole, violent eddies and whirlpools form between 2 hours after turn to flood and 1 hour before turn to ebb." People who have looked into Devil's Hole vow never to run that risk again. Favor the Sonora Island shore of Dent Rapids.

Tugboat Passage, between Dent Island and Little Dent Island, avoids the potential problems of Devils Hole, and the current is less. Use the large-scale inset on chart 3543, and favor the Little Dent Island side.

Arran Rapids. Use chart 3543; chartbook 3312. *New for 2000:* Current predictions for Arran Rapids now are carried in Canadian Tide and Current Tables, Vol. 6. Arran Rapids lie between the north side of Stuart Island and the mainland, and connect Bute Inlet with Cordero Channel. Arran Rapids are unobstructed, but tidal streams run to 13+ knots. These rapids have a long history of killing the unknowing or foolhardy. *Run them at slack water only.* We have hiked from Big Bay to Arran Rapids, and watched the water during a spring tide. The enormous upwellings, whirlpools and overfalls were sobering.

Frederick Arm. Use chart 3543; chartbook 3312. Frederick Arm is deep, with almost no good places to anchor. You can anchor in several nooks along the eastern shoreline, or near the head, where the bottom shoals rapidly.

Estero Basin. Estero Basin, off the head of Frederick Arm, is uncharted. If the crowds are getting to you, this is where you can avoid them. The narrow passage into Estero Basin, called "The Gut," is passable only at high water slack. A dinghy with outboard motor would be a good way to go. We have not been in Estero Basin, but Wolferstan has. He writes convincingly about the strong currents in The Gut, and the eerie stillness of the 5-mile-long basin behind, with its uncharted rocks. Friends tell us that Estero Basin is absolutely beautiful, usually deserted, with small islands, sheer cliffs, and warm water that grows fresher the farther up you go. "Bring your lunch and shampoo," we're advised.

NODALES CHANNEL

Hemming Bay. Use chart 3543; chartbook 3312. Hemming Bay is pretty, especially at the north end, near the head. Enter the bay leaving the Lee Islands well off your right hand to avoid Menace Rock, in the middle of the bay. Most of the Hemming Bay is deep, but you can find anchoring depths near the head.

Thurston Bay Marine Park. Use chart 3543; chartbook 3312. Thurston Bay Marine Park includes Thurston Bay, Handfield Bay, and Cameleon Harbour. The park is large enough to hold many boats without feeling too crowded, and has good anchorages with exploring ashore. We had a good overnight anchorage in 6 fathoms behind Block Island, and we have overnighted happily in Handfield Bay, described below. The landlocked inlet behind Wilson Point, on the south side of Thurston Bay, is best entered at half tide or higher. Wolferstan calls this inlet Anchorage Lagoon. At the entrance, least depth on a zero tide is 2 feet or

less. We tiptoed in near the bottom of a 2.9-foot low tide with the depth sounder showing 6 feet (*Surprise* draws 3 feet). Inside we found four boats at anchor in a pretty setting, with 9-10 feet of depth. This is a good place to know your vessel's draft and the tidal range during your stay.

Handfield Bay. Use chart 3543; chartbook 3312. Handfield Bay is entered from Binnington Bay, located to port as you enter Cameleon Harbour. Chart 3543 (1:40,000) makes it clear that you should enter Handfield Bay leaving Tully Island to port. Once inside, you'll find excellent protection and good anchoring depths. Good shore access for dog-walking. From the the upper helm station we found the rock north of Tully Island easy to spot at half tide. Handfield Bay is favorite stop for many cruisers. Douglas Rock, in the entrance to Cameleon Harbour, may lie farther off Bruce Point than you expect.

Cameleon Harbour. Cameleon Harbour is one of the nicer anchorages in the area. It is a big, open bay with ample protected anchorage, depending on where you need the shelter. Be aware of Douglas Rock. which may lie farther off Bruce Point than you expect.

Phillips Arm. Use chart 3543; chartbook 3312. Phillips Arm is deep, with little protection along the shores. **Fanny Bay** looks good on the chart, but has considerable log booming activity in it. A northwest wind can blow through a saddle in the mountains at the head of the bay. On one visit we found a stiff breeze in Fanny Bay, while outside in Phillips Arm the air was calm. A friend, much experienced, tells us not to anchor in the area of Dyer Point. The bottom is foul with a tangle of sunken logs.

Shoal Bay. Use chart 3543; chartbook 3312. Shoal Bay has a long public float, with good anchorage off the outboard end of the float. The water shallows dramatically at the head of the bay. Shoal Bay is protected from most winds blowing down Cordero Channnel, but is open to the wash from passing boats. It has a great view up Phillips Arm. This is a good place to wait for slack water at rapids north or south.

③ **Shoal Bay Lodge.** As far as we know, the lodge is still closed. If we learn differently we'll post the information on our web site www.waggonerguide.com.

Bickley Bay. Use chart 3543; chartbook 3312. Bickley Bay on Cordero Channel has anchoring depths toward the head of the bay. Favor the east shore to avoid a shoal area. Friends who have cruised in the area extensively warn of poor holding ground, however, and won't go in anymore. Phil Richter at Blind Channel also warns of poor holding. Caution advised.

④ **Cordero Lodge,** General Delivery, Blind Channel, B.C. V0P 1B0, (250)287-0917; e-mail cordero@island.net, web site www.corderolodge.com. Monitors VHF channel 73. Open April through October. Guest moorage available, restrooms, no power on the dock, 5 guest rooms. Cordero Lodge is on log floats, behind Lorte Island, a short distance east of Greene Point Rapids. The lodge has rooms, a restaurant, and space at its dock for 8-10 medium-size boats, more if they raft out. Currents can be

deceptively strong at the docks. Pay careful attention to your boat handling. The fully licensed restaurant serves excellent food, in the German style (May-mid-Sept.). We're told that a good trail, well marked and not too difficult, leads up the hill through the forest and connects with a logging road. Call ahead on VHF channel 73. Reinhardt and Doris Kuppers and their daughter Kellie are the hosts.

Crawford Anchorage. Use chart 3543; chartbook 3312. Crawford Anchorage, between Erasmus Island and East Thurlow Island, has been deemed chancy at best, with a rocky and poor holding bottom. Friends, however, report that they have anchored in Crawford Anchorage successfully, using a Bruce anchor and a stern-tie to Erasmus Island. We tried anchoring, with indifferent results. A large logging camp, with generators running around the clock, is now in the bay, making it even less appealing. Enter Crawford Anchorage from the west—rocks lie in the eastern entrance. Rocks also lie southeast of Mink Island.

See area map page 192

Mayne Passage (Blind Channel). Use chart 3543; chartbook 3312. Mayne Passage connects Cordero Channel with Johnstone Strait. From Johnstone Strait the entrance can be hard to spot, hence the local name "Blind Channel." The current floods north and ebbs south. Currents reach 5 knots at springs. Chart 3543 (1:40,000) shows rips in the northern part of Mayne Passage, and Sailing Directions warns of whirlpools and overfalls. We can attest that the waters do indeed get up in this area. Passages near slack make life smoother. The Blind Channel Resort, on the west shore of Mayne Passage, is very popular. On the east side of Mayne Passage, Charles Bay has convenient anchoring depths around Eclipse Islet, in the center of the bay. Just east of Eclipse Islet, however, the bay shoals to drying flats.

⑤ **Blind Channel Resort,** Blind Channel, B.C. V0P 1B0, (250)949-1420. Monitors VHF channel 73, e-mail info@blindchannel.com, or view at www.blindchannel.com. Open all year, gasoline, diesel, kerosene, propane. Ample guest moorge on 2400 feet of dock, 15 & 20 amp power, washrooms, showers, laundry, pressurized spring water. This is a complete, well-run and very popular marina and resort, with accommodations, an excellent restaurant, well-stocked store, fresh baked goods, post office, liquor agency, and gift items. It has a sandy beach. The resort is surrounded by excellent hiking trails, developed and maintained by Interfor. One trail leads to an 800-year-old cedar, 16 feet in diameter. It's a good walk

Blind Channel Resort. Room for many boats.

and a splendid old tree. Blind Channel Resort has its own spring for water and they make ice from that water. Edgar and Annemarie Richter bought Blind Channel in the 1970s. Edgar designed and built all the buildings, and continues to build today. Annemarie is an engaging hostess in the dining room. Her distinctive and lovely artwork decorates the dock and the restaurant. Their son Phil Richter is general manager.

Greene Point Rapids. Use chart 3543; chartbook 3312. Currents run to 7 knots at springs in Greene Point Rapids. Sailing Directions warns of "considerable overfalls, whirlpools and eddies," and recommends transiting near slack. On small tides currents are much

less. Slack water occurs about 1 hour and 30 minutes before slack water at Seymour Narrows. Current corrections are shown under Seymour Narrows in the Secondary Stations section in Tide and Current Tables, Vol. 6. When eastbound on flood tides, low-powered boats and boats with tows are cautioned against being set against Erasmus Island.

Loughborough Inlet. Use chart 3543; 3555. Loughborough (pronounced "Loch-brough") Inlet, off Chancellor Channel, is deep, with steep-to sides and few good anchorages. Although the inlet is about 18 miles in length, the best anchorage is just a short distance from the mouth on the western shore, in **Beaver Inlet.** Edith Cove in Beaver Inlet can be anchored in, but it shoals rapidly. Use a stern-tie to shore. It is reported that near the very head of Beaver Inlet the bottom is foul with sunken logging debris. We have had reports that Frazer Bay, at the head of Loughborough Inlet, can be anchored in if you are adventurous and know what you are doing. We have not tried it ourselves.

WELLBORE CHANNEL

Whirlpool Rapids. Use chart 3544. Whirlpool Rapids on Wellbore Channel has currents to 7 knots. The time of turn is based on Seymour Narrows, and the corrections are shown under Secondary Current Stations in the Tide and Current Tables, Vol. 6. The flood sets southeast and the ebb sets northwest. When the current is running, expect strong whirlpools, upwellings, and backeddies. The turbulence occurs south of Carterer Point on the flood, north of Carterer Point on the ebb. It is best to transit within a half-hour of slack, although on small tides boats seem to go through anytime.

Forward Harbour. Use chart 3544. The entrance to Forward Harbour is narrow but unobstructed, with good anchorage throughout. Most of the harbor is 10 to 15 fathoms deep, but a shallower area to port, just inside the entrance, is a good spot for pleasure craft. Farther into the harbor proper, Douglas Bay provides a very pretty anchorage, sheltered from the winds outside. The bottom drops off

quickly, and you may find yourself anchored in 60 feet of water—a good reason to carry at least 300 feet of anchor rode. A trail leads from Douglas Bay to a white sand beach at Bessborough Bay.

Bessborough Bay. Use chart 3544. Although you can find anchoring depths in the southeast corner of the bay, the entire bay is open to strong westerlies blowing up Sunderland Channel.

Topaze Harbour. Use chart 3544. Big and pretty enough, but little shelter for small boats.

Sunderland Channel. Use chart 3544. Sunderland Channel connects Wellbore Channel with Johnstone Strait. If the westerly is blowing and you find whitecaps in Sunderland Channel, local knowledge says that it will be worse in Johnstone Strait. In these conditions many boats wisely choose to wait it out in Forward Harbour.

All of the channels north of Yuculta Rapids—Nodales Channel, Mayne Passage, Chancellor Channel, and Sunderland Channel—lead to Johnstone Strait. Each provides some protection and a chance to observe conditions on Johnstone Strait before venturing out. A strong westerly wind opposed by an ebb current can make Johnstone Strait difficult.

JOHNSTONE STRAIT

Johnstone Strait is a seductive and potentially dangerous body of water. It begins at Chatham Point in the east, and stretches 54 miles along the northeast side of Vancouver Island to Blinkhorn Peninusla. Clearly it is the shortest route up- or down-island. Especially on the Vancouver Island side, Johnstone Strait is bounded by steep, high and beautiful mountains. On a clear day the scenery is awesome.

That is the seductive part. The dangerous part is what the wind and current in Johnstone Strait do to each other. The flood current flows eastward, down-island, toward Discovery Passage and Campbell River. The ebb current flows westward, up-island, toward Queen Charlotte Strait and the North Pacific Ocean. A residual ebb surface current exists in Johnstone Strait, increasing the west-flowing

ebb current's strength and duration. In the summer, the prevailing wind in Johnstone Strait is a westerly, often a gale-force westerly, funneled by the mountains. The result is a classic wind-against-current heaping up of the seas.

Conditions are worst where the meeting of currents creates tide-rips, even in calm conditions. This stretch begins at Ripple Shoal, east of Kelsey Bay. It extends westward past Kelsey Bay, through Race Passage and Current Passage, and across the mouth of Sunderland Channel. Especially on an ebb, when the westerly is blowing you don't want to be there. Period. Leave the heroics to others. Johnstone Strait can take all the pleasure out of a pleasure boat.

Despite the potential problems, we have run the length of Johnstone Strait, both directions, and had an excellent ride each time. But we listened to the weather and went when conditions were calm or near-calm. If the wind had come up, we were prepared to run for cover in a bay or seek out a friendly point to hide behind until conditions improved.

On one trip south in the 26-footer, the westerly filled in behind us as we passed Port Neville. Ahead of us lay Race Passage and Current Passage, and to port lay the entrance to Sunderland Channel. After some discussion, we turned for Sunderland Channel, a little late but still all right. It was an easy run up Sunderland Channel, into Wellbore Passage, through Whirlpool Rapids, and into Chancellor Channel. We arrived at Blind Channel Resort in good shape. A boat we were travelling with, a 45-footer, chose the shorter route through Current Passage and into Chancellor Channel. They got to Blind Channel later than we did, and beaten up quite badly. Current Passage had not been nice to them.

Watch constantly for drift in Johnstone Strait. There's considerable current activity, and many shear lines where scrap wood, tree limbs, logs, and even entire floating trees will accumulate.

Knox Bay. Use chart 3543. Knox Bay is located on the north side of Johnstone Strait, near the mouth of Mayne Passage. It would be a poor choice for an anchorage, but a good hideout to escape a strong westerly in the strait. The northwest corner of the bay is the best

protected. Unfortunately it is deep, and devoted to log booming. We are concerned that sunken logs may foul the bottom, and would tie off a boomstick to wait out the weather. Shallower areas around the bay are increasingly exposed to westerly winds. Normally they are at stream mouths, and shoal abruptly.

Helmcken Island. Use chart 3544. Helmcken Island has a protected anchorage on its north side in **Billygoat Bay**. The island has been clear-cut, but is growing back. Currents in this part of the strait run at 3 to 5 knots. When opposed by wind from the opposite direction, large seas can build rapidly. Billygoat Bay is a good place to hide out. Anchor in approximately 5 fathoms.

Kelsey Bay. Use chart 3544. Kelsey Bay has a breakwater made of five ship hulks—the Union Steamship *Cardena;* three WWII frigates: HMCS *Runnymede,* HMCS *Lasalle,* and HMCS *Longueil;* and one hulk whose name is not known. You can enter alongside this breakwater to a 150-foot-long public float. Quieter moorage can be found farther inside, at a second public wharf with 1160 feet of dock space. Kelsey Bay is about a mile by road from Sayward, where there are stores. An unused ferry dock is located just west of the moorage at Kelsey Bay.

Stay well off the river mouth. The water is quite shoal there.

The waters off Kelsey Bay can be brutal. The current runs strongly, and an opposing wind will build high, steep seas, with no distance between them. Calm conditions only, in our view.

Robson Bight. Use chart 3546. Robson Bight is on the Vancouver Island side of Johnstone Strait, at the mouth of the Tsitika River. This is a gathering place for northern resident killer whales, usually during the summer months. Many of the whales will rub their stomachs on stones in the shallow water near the beach.

Robson Bight has been designated an ecological reserve to protect the whales. Boaters are required to stay at least a half-mile offshore and not approach or chase the whales. Whale watch volunteers make camp at Boat Bay across Johnstone Strait and watch Robson Bight from a high bluff at Swain Point, west of Boat Bay. If they see you within the reserve boundaries they will roar across in a rigid bottom inflatable to *very* politely inform you of the reserve status and accompany you to non-reserve waters. *(See area map page 197)*

Boat Bay. Use chart 3545. Boat Bay lies almost directly across Johnstone Strait from Robson Bight, and is well protected from westerlies. The whale watchers make camp at Boat Bay, so you won't be alone. Be sure to enter from the east. The pass west of the 44 meter high island is choked with rocks. Anchor in 3-4 fathoms northwest of the island.

These friendly chaps came out to answer questions about the restricted area at Robson Bight and escort intruders out.

Western Johnstone Strait

*Port Neville • Havannah Channel • Chatham Channel
Minstrel Island • Clio Channel • Simoom Sound • Echo Bay
Kingcome Inlet • Shawl Bay*

Blenkinsop Bay. Use chart 3564; 3544. Blenkinsop Bay has reasonably protected anchorage along the west shore of Johnstone Strait, but swells from westerly winds work into the bay. The chart shows tide-rips off Blenkinsop Bay, and indeed the rips are there. **McLeod Bay** and an unnamed bay inside Tuna Point are possible temporary anchorages if needed.

Port Neville. Use chart 3564; 3545. Port Neville is an excellent anchorage, with a public float along the eastern shore. This inlet is heavily used by fishing boats in season, but there is plenty of room for everyone. Boomed logs are stored in several places toward the inner end of this 4-mile-long inlet. No other public facilities are in the vicinity.

For years Olaf "Oly" Hansen, at the government dock post office, could be reached by radio for a report on conditions on Johnstone Strait. Oly died in January, 1997 at age 88, another legend gone from the coast. Oly's widow Lilly lives on in the family house, and their daughter Lorna (Hansen) Chesluck lives with her daughter Erica in the house at the head of the dock. Lorna is the postmaster, and she will happily look out on the strait and give a report. Call "Sea Scout III" on VHF channel 06.

Mail is delivered by air three times a week. Boats that plan to be out for extended periods can use Port Neville as a mail drop. Ask that mail be addressed as follows (we use our own name and boat name as examples):

Your name (*Robert Hale*)
Boat name (*M/V Surprise*)
c/o Lorna, Port Neville P.O., B.C.
V0P 1M0
Hold for pickup

Send Lorna a note telling your intentions.

David Thomson and Peggy Sowden live across the bay in a lovely log home they built themslves. Peggy is an artist, doing business as Beehive Mountain Gallery. We bought one of her paintings. Their son James Thomson is an aspiring writer with real promise. He and Erica Chesluk have begun a pair of periodic

We arrived at Port Neville just in time for a birthday party for a neighbor. Lilly Hansen is second from right. Lorna Chesluck is at far right.

Government dock at Port Neville.

The original store at Port Neville. Now locked.

newsletters, $15 for a subscription to both. Erica's newsletter, domestic in content, is called Cocoa and Cookies; James's, which is literary, is called Limbo. We subscribed (as do most visitors), and even bought an ad for the Waggoner.

HAVANNAH CHANNEL

Use chart 3545. Havannah Channel leads northward toward Knight Inlet and other channels to the north and west.

Port Harvey. Use chart 3545. Port Harvey is large, and open to westerlies from Johnstone Strait. You'll find good anchorage, however, mud bottom, at the head of the bay. Do not run the narrow canal that leads between Port Harvey and Cracroft Inlet. The channel dries and is studded with boulders.

Boughey Bay. Use chart 3545. There is anchorage toward the south end of Boughey (pronounced "boogie") Bay. John Chappell *(Cruising Beyond Desolation Sound)* says strong easterly winds can spring up suddenly in the bay.

Bockett Islets. Use chart 3545. Contributing Editor Tom Kincaid has anchored for a few hours among the Bockett Islets awaiting a favorable current in Chatham Channel.

Fishdance Lodge Resort, 15035 73rd Ave., Surrey, B.C. V3S 7H5, (604)591-8536; fax (604)591-8536, web site www.fishdancelodge. com. Monitors VHF channels 06 & 73. Use chart 3545. Located in Soderman Cove in

This floating home at the head of Port Harvey has a sign that reads, "Slow Down."

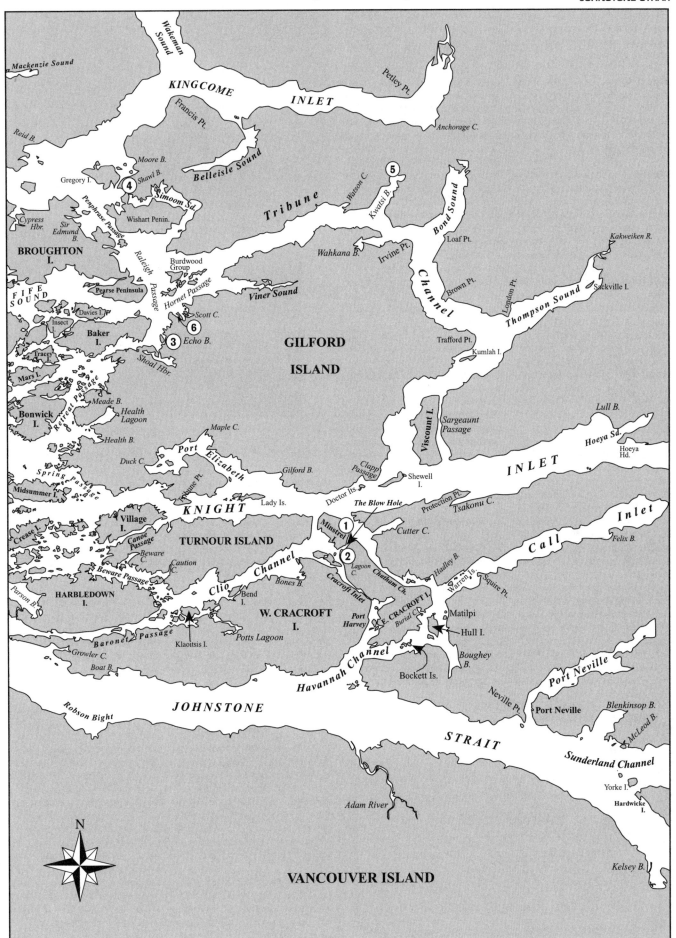

Mackenzie Sound

Wakeman Sound

KINGCOME   INLET

Petley Pt.

Francis Pt.

Reid B.

Anchorage C.

Moore B.

Gregory I.

④ *Shawl B.*

Belleisle Sound

⑤

Watson C.

Kwatsi B.

Simoom Sd.

Cypress Hbr.

Sir Edmund B.

Penphrase Passage

Wishart Penin.

Tribune

Bond Sound

BROUGHTON I.

Raleigh Passage

Wahkana B.

Irvine Pt.

Loaf Pt.

F I F E   S O U N D

Burdwood Group

Hornet Passage

Viner Sound

Channel

Brown Pt.

London Pt.

Thompson Sound

Kakweiken R.

Pearse Peninsula

Davies I.

Insect

⑥ *Scott C.*

Sackville I.

Baker I.

③ *Echo B.*

**GILFORD
ISLAND**

Trafford Pt.

Kumlah I.

Tracey I.

Shoal Hbr.

Mars I.

Retreat Passage

Bonwick I.

Meade B.

Health Lagoon

Viscount I.

Sargeaunt Passage

Lull B.

Health B.

Maple C.

Hoeya Sd.

Hoeya Hd.

Spring Passage

Duck C.

Port Elizabeth

Gilford B.

Clapp Passage

I N L E T

Midsummer I.

Tribune Pt.

Shewell I.

Lady Is.

Doctor Ilts.

The Blow Hole

Protection Pt.

Tsakonu C.

Crease I.

Village I.

Canoe Passage

K N I G H T

TURNOUR ISLAND

Minstrel I.

① *Cutter C.*

C a l l

Felix B.

Beware C.

Caution C.

② *Lagoon C.*

Chatham Ch.

Hadley B.

Warren Is.

Squire Pt.

Parson B.

HARBLEDOWN I.

Beware Passage

Clio

Channel

Bend I.

Bones B.

Cracroft Inlet

W. CRACROFT I.

Port Harvey

E. CRACROFT I.

Burial C.

Matilpi

Hull I.

Growler C.

Baronet Passage

Klaoitsis I.

Potts Lagoon

Boughey B.

Port Neville

Boat B.

Havannah Channel

Bockett Is.

Neville Pt.

Port Neville

Blenkinsop B.

McLeod B.

Robson Bight

J O H N S T O N E

Sunderland Channel

S T R A I T

Yorke I.

Hardwicke I.

N

Adam River

VANCOUVER ISLAND

Kelsey B.

See area map page 197

Havannah Channel. This is a resort with a dock for its room guests' use, or for meal guests. Call ahead for meal reservations.

Burial Cove. Use chart 3545. Burial Cove is pretty, though open to most winds. It is well-protected from seas, however, and has a good bottom in 4 fathoms. A few houses are on the shore.

Matilpi. Use chart 3545. Matilpi is an abandoned Indian village. It is a beautiful spot, with a white shell beach backed up by dense forest. Anchor behind the northern of the two islands, or between the islands. Protection is excellent.

Call Inlet. Use chart 3545. Call Inlet is approximately 10 miles long, and runs back through beautiful, steep-sided mountains. You can find anchoring depths in the Warren Islands, near the mouth of Call Inlet. They would be a pretty spot in which to wait for the current to change in Chatham Channel. A stern-tie to shore would be a good idea for overnight anchorage.

Chatham Channel. Use chart 3564; 3545. Chatham Channel is easier to run than would appear from the chart. The southern section is the narrowest, with the least room in the channel, and requires the greatest attention. The most pleasant approach is to wait for near-slack water, and go on through.

Slacks are based on Seymour Narrows predictions. Correction factors for the times of slack water will be found under Secondary Stations in the Tide and Current Tables, Vol. 6. Chart 3545 (1:40,000) shows the area, including the range locations. Chart 3564

(1:20,000), with its 1:10,000 insert of the southern section, truly helps understanding. We highly recommend chart 3564.

If you are running compass courses through the southern section, remember that the headings shown on the chart are true, and must be corrected to magnetic. We have found that in some lighting conditions the ranges are hard to locate from the far ends of the lower channel. A sharp-eyed crew should sight astern at the near range until it grows difficult to see. By then the range ahead should be visible. Maximum currents run to 5 knots at springs, with no significant swirls or overfalls. Chatham Channel thus can be taken at times other than slack water, but you should know what you are doing, and in the southern section *keep your boat lined up on a range.*

Cutter Cove. Use chart 3564; 3545. Cutter Cove, located across the north end of Chatham Channel from Minstrel Island, is very pretty and an excellent anchorage, although exposed to westerly winds. Convenient depths, mud bottom, are available throughout the western half of the bay, which then shallows to drying flats at its head. Friends tell us that Cutter Cove is "alive with crab."

① **Minstrel Island Resort,** Minstrel Island, B.C. V0P 1L0, (250)949-0215. Monitors VHF channels 73 & 06. Open all year, guest moorage available, gasoline & diesel, 15 amp power, washrooms, showers, laundry, charts. The Minstrel Island Resort has a very rough-and-ready feel. Lodging is available, and the pub is popular with local loggers. A cafe serves meals, and they're reported to be pretty good. During 1996

Top: The Exercise Station #4 at Lagoon Cove Marina is a wood pile with clear instructions—as if they are needed.
Bottom: The marina is inviting and well protected.

the liquor agency was discontinued, although the pub has off-sales of beer. The BEWARE OF DOG sign on the dock is meant for visiting male dogs only. The resort's three large dogs love people, just not other male dogs. A marten, which lives under the docks, can be quite bold about getting aboard boats and leaving his scent behind. Keep transom doors closed. Haulouts to 40 feet. Scheduled float plane service from Seattle and Campbell River. Grant and Sylvia Douglas are the owners.

The Blow Hole. Use chart 3564; 3545. The Blow Hole is a short, shallow, easily-navigated channel between Minstrel Island and East Cracroft Island. The channel gets its name from strong westerly winds that can blow through at times. A short distance inside the west end a reef, shown clearly on chart 3564, extends from East Cracroft Island on the south side of the channel. Favor the north side and you'll have no problems.

Lagoon Cove. Use chart 3545. Lagoon Cove has good anchorage along the shorelines, although the middle of the bay is a little deep for most boats. Locals say the bot-

tom on the west side of the bay is foul with logging cable, and recommend against anchoring there. The Lagoon Cove Marina is on the east side of the bay.

② **Lagoon Cove Marina,** c/o Minstrel Island P.O., Minstrel Island, B.C. V0P 1L0. Monitors VHF channel 73. Open all year, with caretakers in the winter. Lagoon Cove has gasoline, diesel, propane, kerosene, stove oil, washroom, shower. Dock power has been upgraded to 30 amps. The shower is a little primitive, and available only mornings and evenings, when the generator runs to heat the water. The small dock store carries fishing licenses, limited fishing tackle, ice, charts, a few essentials. A separate store up at the house carries an excellent range of souvenirs. In 1998 the fuel dock was extended and a larger generator installed.

The entire property has a whimsical quality about it. The generator house is called a power company, with a horrible collection of burned-out fuses, dangling wires and broken main switches mounted beside the door. Exercise Station #4 is a woodpile. The workshop is an "historic" workshop.

This is one of the friendliest

and most popular stops on the coast. Bill and Jean Barber, the owners, provide personal, attentive service and introductions. Happy hour potlucks are held most days in the "historic" workshop. The marina provides the fresh prawns, guests bring treats from their boats. Marshmallow roasts are organized around sunset (weather permitting). Everybody, by the way, goes up to the marshmallow roasts. While you're standing around the fire, see if you can get Bill to tell about the time a black bear bit though a supply line at the marina, or about the time they taught a bear to water ski.

CLIO CHANNEL

Bones Bay. Use chart 3545. The entire bay is fairly open, although you may find temporary anchorage behind the islets along the south shore. Watch for rocks around the islets. A floating fishing lodge is moored behind these islets. They get going around 0400. Not the best place to anchor.

Bend Island. Use chart 3545. Bend Island is connected to West Cracroft Island by a drying ledge, but good anchorage exists in either end. Friends have anchored in the tiny nook just east of Bend Island, with a stern-tie to shore.

Potts Lagoon. Use chart 3545. Potts Lagoon, very pretty, gets progressively shallower near the drying flats at the head, but convenient anchoring depths can be found. The central portion is only 5 or 6 feet deep at zero tide, so check the tide book before stopping for the night. We have had reports of anchor dragging in the little bay that lies inside the 119 meter headland as you approach the entrance to Potts Lagoon. On a recent visit, we found 2 boats anchored in that bay, 5 boats in Potts Lagoon itself.

Klaoitsis Island. Use chart 3545. There is possible anchorage in the bay northwest of Klaoitsis Island, and in a notch on the south shore of Jamieson Island. Currents can run through these anchorages. For most boats, Potts Lagoon would be a better place to overnight.

Knight Inlet. Use chart 3545; 3515. Knight Inlet extends from its mouth at Midsummer Island to its head, at the mouth of the Klinalini River. The inlet is about 70 miles long and 2 miles wide, the longest of the fjords that indent the B.C. coast. Along most of its length the shores rise steeply to 6,000-foot mountains. Since anchorage is "iffy" at best, the inlet's upper reaches are explored mainly by fast boats able to make the round trip in a single day. Boats with limited fuel capacity should top off at Lagoon Cove or Minstrel Island before making the trip.

In Knight Inlet, **Tsakonu Cove** is a pretty anchorage, protected from westerlies but exposed to the east. We anchored once near the head of Tsakonu Cove for a quiet lunch. Outside, a 20-knot inflow wind blew Knight Inlet into an uncomfortable chop. Logging activity around the cove has ceased and the hills

Family Snapshot at Kwatsi Bay: Doug (Max) and Anca, Marieke with bicycle, Russell at right.

Nothing fancy at the Kwatsi Bay Marina, but the setting is beautiful. Anca and Doug's home now occupies the cleared area on the hill.

are green again. Large driftwood logs on the shore suggest that outflow winds in Knight Inlet probably roar into Tsakonu Cove, accompanied by substantial seas.

Hoeya Sound is pretty, but deep and completely exposed to the westerly winds that are prevalent in the summer. **Glendale Cove,** an abandoned logging camp and cannery, offers minimal protection from strong northeast winds the often blow down the inlet. **Wahshihlas Bay,** at the mouth of the Sim River, looks to be a possible anchorage, although we've never tried it, and anchorage is possible off the drying flats at the head of the inlet.

Port Elizabeth. Use chart 3545. Port Elizabeth is a great big bay bounded on the west by low hills that let westerlies in. Major logging activity is underway on the east side of the bay, near Maple Cove. You can find good anchorage near the western shore, west of the largest of the three islands. The two smaller islands are joined on the west by drying flats.

Sargeaunt Passage. Use chart 3515. Sargeaunt Passage connects Knight Inlet and Tribune Channel, and has anchorage at either end of the narrows. The passage runs between steep-sided mountains, and is beautiful. The shoal in the middle of the passage extends from the east shore across much of the passage. Favor the west shore.

Thompson Sound. Use chart 3515. Thompson Sound has no good anchorages.

Bond Sound. Use chart 3515. Bond Sound has no good anchorages. A reader (Bill Cooke, GB 36 *Pop Pie*) has told us, however, that cutthroat trout fishing is good at the head of the sound.

Kwatsi Bay. Use chart 3515. The inner cove of Kwatsi Bay on Tribune Channel is a stunning anchorage, one of the most impressive on the coast. This cove is surrounded by a high, sheer bowl of rock. Sunsets and sunrises are magnificent. Our log says, "Wow!" The bay is deep, though, 17 fathoms or more in much of the inner cove. We had a peaceful night in 10 fathoms with good holding off the two streams that empty into the western bight of the inner cove. The next morning, a patrol around the shoreline found several other 8-12-fathom possibilities. We suspect, however, that a 3-fathom spot near the north shore is an uncharted rock.

Kwatsi Bay is where grand-parents starved for a grand-child dose go for relief. Marilynn Hale admires the artwork as Marieke and Russell look on.

Bird (vibrantly colored), by Marieke, age 6½.

House with smokestack, by Russell, age 4.

⑤ **Kwatsi Bay Marina,** Simoom Sound P.O., Simoom Sound, B.C. V0P 1S0, cellular (250)949-1384. Monitors VHF channel 73. In 1998 a new marina on floats, owned by Doug (Max) Knierim and his wife Anca Fraser, was established in Kwatsi Bay. They and their daughter Marieke and son Russell are carving out a place to live in the bush, and offering services to passing boaters. This is not a luxury resort; this is the wilderness, at its gentle but hardworking best. The floats may be primitive, but the people are not. In 1998 daughter Marieke drew us a picture, which we reproduced here in the 1999 edition. When we visited last year Marieke had another picture for us, and so did Russell. We recommend a stop.

Watson Cove. Use chart 3515. Watch for a rock in the entrance, and favor the north shore while entering. Watson Cove is surrounded by beautiful rock and a dense forest. The fish farm and large float house located there a few years ago are gone. Anchorage is possible in 10 fathoms halfway down Watson Cove.

Wahkana Bay. Use chart 3515. The inner cove of Wahkana Bay is attractive, but 20 fathoms deep except near shore. The east and south shores have several spots where you can anchor in 8-12 fathoms with swinging room, however. The head of the inner cove shoals rapidly. Watch out. Wind can blow through the saddle that reaches to Viner Sound.

Simoom Sound. Use chart 3515. Simoom Sound is a dogleg inlet, very scenic, but most of it too deep for convenient anchoring. The best anchorages are in O'Brien Bay, at the head of the Sound, and in McIntosh Bay and the bays adjacent to it, along the north shore. You'll be in 8-10+ fathoms in O'Brien Bay, and 3-

6 fathoms in the McIntosh Bay area. We spent a quiet night in McIntosh Bay. In an emergency you could find anchorage off the northeast corner of Louisa Islet, and near the mouth of a creek on the Wishart Peninsula side.

Hayle Bay. Use chart 3515. After a visit to Hayle Bay our log reads, "Too deep, too exposed."

Laura Bay. Use chart 3515. Laura Bay is a very pretty spot, and a popular place to overnight. You'll find anchorage in two sections: one in the long neck that extends westward; the other in the cove between Trivett Island and Broughton Island. The westward-extending neck is marked by rocks at its mouth. Favor the southern shore on entering, leaving the rocks to starboard.

The cove behind Trivett Island is just lovely. A little islet is in the cove, but the chart incorrectly shows good water all around. A rock lies in the narrow passage to the east of the islet. Entering the cove, leave the islet to starboard.

Sir Edmund Bay. Use chart 3515. Sir Edmund Bay should be entered east of Nicholls Island to avoid a rock to the west of the island. This rock lies farther offshore than you might expect. Aquaculture pens are in the bay, but anchorage is possible in a cove at the northwest corner of the bay, and in another cove at the south corner. To use the northwest cove, go in just beyond the rocks that narrow the inlet, and find a suitable spot. The southern cove has anchorage behind a charted rock. When we visited, near the bottom of a 7-foot low tide, we failed to locate the rock. A friend who has anchored there says the cove is a good spot, however.

Viner Sound. Use chart 3515. Viner Sound is pretty, but narrow and shallow. An indent on the north side, a short distance down the narrow channel, will hold one boat near the opening. Just inside that indent the water shoals immediately. The long shoaling area shown on the chart at the head of Viner Sound is real. Watch your depth sounder as you explore.

Burdwood Group. Use chart 3515. The Burdwood Group is a beautiful little clutch of islands, a gunkholer's dream. The group is dotted with rocks and reefs, and Chart 3515 (1:80,000) shows little detail. With a sharp lookout, however, small boats can maneuver among the islands on slow bell. Anchorage is recommended in settled weather only. Given the opportunity, the cruising boat should consider it.

Scott Cove. Use chart 3515. Scott Cove is a busy logging camp. Pierre's Bay Lodge & Marina is on the west shore.

⑥ **Pierre's Bay Lodge & Marina,** Box 257, Gabriola Island, B.C. V0R 1X0, (250)949-2503; (250)247-9704 (Gabriola Island). Monitors VHF channel 73. Use chart 3515. Pierre's Bay is a brand-new facility located just east of Powell Point, on the west shore of Scott Cove. It is clearly visible from outside. At press time construction is continuing, but they plan to be open for the summer boating season with 1000 feet of moorage, a restaurant, shower and laundry facilities, gazebo with

For pure beauty, it's hard to beat this coast. Tribune Channel, 1998.

A concrete breakwater marks the entrance to Echo Bay. Echo Bay Resort has full facilities and is popular.

a store. The store carries a good stock of groceries, including a walk-in cooler for dairy products and fresh produce. They carry charts and fishing licenses, and have a post office. Garbage is burned in an oil-fired incinerator, small charge made. Bob and Nancy Richter are the owners.

③ **Windsong Sea Village,** P.O. Box 388, Alert Bay, B.C. V0N 1A0, phone/fax (250)974-5004; fax (250)974-3009; e-mail wind echo@island.net. Monitors VHF channels 16 & 73, call sign "Windsong Barge." Open May-September, guest moorage available. This is a small resort in Echo Bay, with two float houses for rent, washrooms, showers, and a charming gallery featuring local artists. Bottled spring water is available. James O'Donnell and Christine O'Donnell are the owners. Christine (Muffin) O'Donnell herself is an excellent artist. When we visited in late June, 1999, we found that Corrie and Dave Parker had moved Corkie's Bakery to Windsong Sea Village, and we bought some goodies from Corrie. At press time we were told that Corkie's Bakery will be at Windsong again in 2000.

Shoal Harbour. Use chart 3515. Shoal Harbour has good, protected anchorage, mud bottom. We would anchor just to the right, inside the entrance. Wherever you anchor, check the depth sounder before retiring—parts of the bay are indeed quite shoal.

Billy Proctor's Museum. If you leave Echo Bay and round the peninsula that leads to Shoal Harbour, you can follow the shore around the peninsula and into a small bay with a dock, home and sawmill. This is where the legend-

barbecue, gift shop with local art, and 3 rental suites. No power on the dock, very limited water available. When we saw the partly completed structures last summer, we were impressed with the solid construction and attractive design. Approaching, be sure to give Powell Rock, off Powell Point, a wide berth. Especially if coming out of Cramer Passage, go past Powell Point before turning in. Pierre and Tove Landry are your hosts.

Echo Bay. Use chart 3515. Echo Bay is one of the more popular stops on the coast, with moorage at two marinas, fuel, a hotel, cabins, an art gallery, the most complete store in the area, and a provincial park with float. The Echo Bay Resort has brought in a section of the old Lake Washington Floating Bridge to make a breakwater at the mouth of the bay. The signs requiring 100 yards offing just haven't been removed from the bridge section, and should be disregarded. Fishing is very good in this area. People have caught good-sized salmon and halibut while fishing from the Echo Bay Resort fuel dock.

A thick midden is at the head of the bay, and is easily investigated from the beach. A schoolhouse is on high ground a short distance from the beach. A good hike begins behind this schoolhouse, and leads back into the hills past two dams, across a couple of bridges, and onto a logging road. If you turn left and walk to the end of of the logging road, we're told you'll have a knockout view of Cramer Passage, Penphrase Passage and Tribune Channel.

Echo Bay Marine Park. The dock is old and tired, and limited to boats not more than 24 feet long, no rafting. The holding bottom is poor, so anchoring is not a good idea. The park has walk-in campsites and picnicking.

③ **Echo Bay Resort,** General Delivery, Simoom P.O., Simoom Sound, B.C. V0P 1S0, phone/fax (250)956-2121; e-mail echobay @island.net, or view at www.echobayresort. com. Monitors VHF channel 73. Open all year (limited days in the winter), gasoline, diesel, propane, 15 & 30 amp power, ice and water. The power and water lines have been updated, and each slip's power boxes, designed and built by Bob Richter, are excellent. Ample guest moorage, reservations recommended mid-July through mid-August, washrooms, large, comfortable showers, laundry, haulout. This is a popular full-service marina, with lodging and

Windsong Sea Village is snugged up against a beautiful rock wall. Small structure at the end of ramp is an art gallery.

Here's Corrie Parker, posing in front of her bakery at Windsong Sea Village.

Billy Proctor's place at Shoal Harbour. The fish boat takes only part of the dock. Museum is on left edge of photo.

ary Billy Proctor, who has lived and fished on the coast all his 60-plus years, lives and now has his museum. Over a lifetime Billy has collected a treasure of Chinese opium bottles, Chinese and Japanese beer bottles, engine plates, tools, arrowheads, bone fish hooks, a 1910 mimeograph machine from Minstrel Island, a crank telephone, a scale from the old Simoom Sound post office, and thousands of other artifacts of the coast's past. Finally, in a rectangular structure he built from lumber he milled himself, Billy's remarkable collection is displayed. Tie up at the dock, meet Billy, and go have a look. We think you'll be glad you did.

KINGCOME INLET

Kingcome Inlet winds 17 miles between high and beautiful mountains, terminating at the delta of the Kingcome River. The water is milky from glacier runoff. The surface water can be surprisingly fresh. At the head of the inlet, it is possible to leave the boat and take a powered dinghy up the river to Kingcome Village, occupied by the Tsawataineuk Native Band. Kingcome Inlet's great depths and sheer rock walls allow virtually no suitable anchorages in the upper portions.

Wakeman Sound. Use chart 3515. Wakeman Sound branches off Kingcome Inlet and extends about 7 miles north among mountains. While it has no good anchorages, on a clear day the scenery can rival Princess Louisa Inlet. Wakeman Sound is a center for logging activity. Watch for drift in the water.

Belleisle Sound. Use chart 3515. Belleisle Sound branches off Kingcome Inlet to the south. Entry is between two high green mountains, the kind that make you feel small. Belleisle Sound is beautiful and remote-feeling, but generally too deep for easy anchoring. Only a small area just inside the entrance is useable. Chappell and Sailing Directions warn that strong westerlies can blow through. On the day of our visit it was mirror-calm. The water was warm and people on another visiting boat took a swim, right out in the middle. Some years ago we spent the night in Belleisle Sound without difficulty, anchored and stern-tied to the little islet across from the entrance.

Moore Bay. Use chart 3515. Moore Bay is a short distance inside the entrance to Kingcome Inlet, on the east side. The bay is connected to Shawl Bay by a narrow canal that is reported to be navigable at half tide or better. You can find anchorage behind Thief Island in the south part of Moore Bay (preferred), or near the outlet of the stream that runs from

One of two mooring buoys in Moore Bay. Photo by Ray & Nika Hansen.

Mt. Plumridge at the north end. Two other nooks along the east shore might also serve, depending on the weather. Two mooring buoys now are installed in Moore Bay, with long floating lines that will reach to a cleat on the boat.

Reid Bay. Use chart 3515. Reid Bay, on the western shore just inside the entrance to Kingcome Inlet, is open, deep, and uninteresting. It is no place to anchor. Just south of Reid Bay, however, an unnamed cove has possibilities. It is rather pretty and has good protection from westerlies. The chart indicates depths of approximately 6 fathoms throughout the bay, but our depth sounder showed 10-13 fathoms, except 5-6 fathoms close to the head. If you go into this cove, give a wide berth to the point at the south entrance. We saw one uncharted rock just off the point; Chappell says there are two.

④ **Shawl Bay Marina,** Simoom Sound P.O., Simoom Sound, B.C. V0P 1S0, VHF 73. Use chart 3515. Shawl Bay, connected with Moore Bay by a channel navigable at half tide or better, has a community of float homes along its southern shore. The floating marina in Shawl Bay is a favorite of old-timers, many of whom return yearly to enjoy the extremely relaxed and informal atmosphere. At one time it was possible to buy a "I Survived Happy Hour at Shawl Bay" T-shirt.

The marina went through some uncertain times in recent years, but Lorne Brown and his wife Shawn have taken over and brought it back. The docks have been redecked and extended, a water line brought in, and a second generator. They have 15 & 30 amp power, washroom, showers, and laundry. A "K9 Yacht Club," with lawn, accommodates visiting boats' dogs. The small store has a respectable stock of convenience items. Pancake breakfasts on the dock are regular fare. Jo Didriksen, who for years ran the marina with her sister Edna Brown, is still there, and welcomes her old friends.

Navigation note: Arriving or departing, favor the float home side of the bay. A nasty rock lies off the little islet, and you'll clear it for sure if you stay over on the south side.

Shawl Bay Marina, with visitors again. The docks have been extended and many improvements made.

Eastern Queen Charlotte Strait

Beware Passage • Mamalilaculla • Broughton Archipelago
Retreat Passage • Fife Sound

Baronet Passage. Use chart 3545; 3546. Baronet Passage, very pretty, is partially obstructed by Walden Island, with the preferred passage in the deeper channel to the north of Walden Island. This is a popular passage for boats heading to and from Blackfish Sound. In this area the current floods west and ebbs east, the opposite of the flows in Johnstone Strait a mile to the south, and in Knight Inlet 4 miles to the north.

Beware Passage. Use chart 3545. If you read the place names from chart 3545 (1:40,000), Beware Passage will scare you to death. The first fright is the name itself: Beware Passage. Then Care Rock, Caution Rock, Caution Cove, Beware Rock, Beware Cove, and Dead Point. Beware Passage is aptly named, but you can get through safely.

Sailing Directions recommends that lacking local knowledge, Beware Passage be transited at low water, when the rocks are visible. Assuming a passage from east to west, Chappell *(Cruising Beyond Desolation Sound)* mentions a route across the abandoned Turnour (pronounced "Turner") Island village of Karlukwees, somehow avoiding all rocks, and skirting the shore of Care Island, but he doesn't provide details. Chappell's second, and preferred, alternative is to go through "Towboat Pass."

We offer the Towboat Pass route here, with refinements, courtesy of a couple from Nanaimo with nearly 20 summers' experience cruising these waters. It may be helpful to have Chart 3545 at hand, to identify place names as the instructions proceed. A sketch map illustrating the route is on this page.

Towboat Pass route, east to west: From the east, enter Beware Passage close by Nicholas Point on Turnour Island, and continue until Karlukwees is abeam to starboard. You'll recognize Karlukwees by its abandoned build-

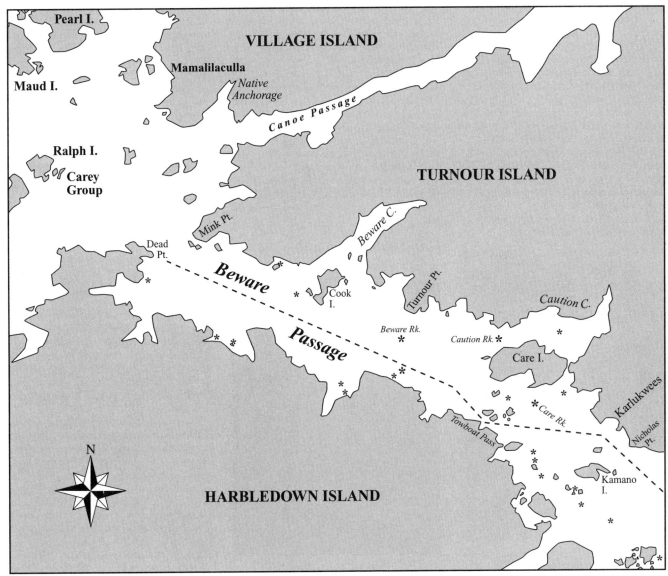

Beware Passage

Karlukwees, with its abandoned buildings, deteriorating pier and shell beach, is unmistakable.

ings, decaying pier, and white shell beach.

When Karlukwees is abeam, turn to a course of 250 degrees magnetic. This course will take you across Beware Passage to the Harbledown Island side, and south of a pair of small islands that lie just offshore from Harbledown Island.

Towboat Pass, marked 3 meters, runs between these small islands and Harbledown Island. The pass has kelp in it, but is reported safe at all tides. Go close to Harbledown Island, turn northward, and proceed through the pass. We went through at dead slow bell, one set of eyes on the water, another set on the depth sounder. Kelp and all, no problems.

Exit Towboat Pass on a course of approximately 292 degrees magnetic. While underway, watch astern to starboard until you see three islands apparently spread across the water behind you. Turn to port, to run on a line that connects the middle island of these three islands with Dead Point, at the far end of Beware Passage. At the time of your turn, the middle island should be a little less than 0.5 mile away. Assuming good visibility, Dead Point, now off your bow, will be easily identifiable on a course of approximately 270 degrees magnetic. This course will put you a little close to a rock that lies off Harbledown Island, but you should clear it easily.

We drew the entire course on the chart before entering Beware Passage, marking all headings and agreeing on our plan. It went so smoothly that when we exited Beware Passage we wondered what all the fuss was about.

Caution Cove. Use chart 3545. Caution Cove is open to prevailing winds, but the bottom is good. Caution Rock, drying 4 feet, is in the center of the entrance. The rock is clearly shown on Chart 3545, as are the rocks just off the drying flats at the head of the cove.

Beware Cove. Use chart 3545. Beware Cove is a good anchorage, very pretty, with protection from westerlies but not southeasterlies. Easiest entry is to the west of Cook Island, leaving Cook Island off your right hand.

Dead Point. The unnamed cove just inside Dead Point offers protection from westerlies.

BLACKFISH ARCHIPELAGO

Use chart 3545; 3546. The name Blackfish Archipelago does not appear on the charts or in Sailing Directions, but generally refers to the myriad islands and their waterways adjacent to Blackfish Sound.

Goat Island. Use chart 3546. You'll find a good anchorage in the cove that lies between Goat Island and the southeast corner of Crease Island. Chart 3546 (1:40,000) shows it clearly. The view to the southeast is very pretty. Weed on the bottom might foul some anchors. This cove is excellent for crabbing. A study of the chart shows the safest entry is to the north of Goat Island, between Goat Island and Crease Island. That is the route we took, and it served well.

Mound Island. Use chart 3546. The Cove

behind Mound Island is a good anchorage, paying mind to the rocks (shown on the chart) that line the shores.

Leone Island. Use chart 3546. A bay lies between Leone Island and Madrona Island. Contributing Editor Tom Kincaid has anchored there and recommends it. Other friends, with extensive experience in these waters, also recommend it. We, however, tried to set our anchor four times over a 2-day period, and failed each time. Twice the anchor did not penetrate large, leafy kelp. Once it refused to set in thin sand and reedy weed. On the last try the anchor seemed to set, but it dragged with only moderate power in reverse.

Farewell Harbour. Use chart 3546. You'll find good anchorage in Farewell Harbour close to the Berry Island side. The **Farewell Harbour Yacht Club,** shown on the chart, is actually a luxury fly-in fishing resort. They welcome all visitors, however, and if they have room in the dining room you can have an elegant dinner there. Pre-planning is advisable, and no guarantees, obviously.

① **Mamalilaculla.** Use chart 3545. In 1921, Mamalilaculla, on the western shore of Village Island, was the site of the "Christmas Potlatch," the last great Indian potlatch on the coast. Potlatches had been banned since 1884, although the law had been largely ignored and unenforced. After the Christmas Potlatch, a number of participants were charged for violation. Their considerable ceremonial regalia was confiscated and distributed among museums and private collections. Today much of it has been recovered, and is on display at the U'Mista Cultural Centre in Alert Bay and the Kwagiulth Museum at Cape Mudge.

Mamalilaculla is the abandoned Indian village and later-day mission and hospital that M. Wylie Blanchet visited in *The Curve of Time.* In her description, Blanchet wove together the old Kwakiutl ways as they came up against the new white man's ways. Then she threw in the likelihood of Polynesian influences on the coast Indians.

With *The Curve of Time* as background, Mamalilaculla is a fascinating place to visit. The last of the totem poles have fallen to the ground and are rotting away. The mission houses and hospital are empty and haunting. Off the established trails, tall grass and expanding blackberry patches make exploring difficult.

When we last visited Mamalilaculla, to our disappointment we found that blackberry vines had overgrown much of the ground and closed off some of the trails. We had to drop down to the beach to get around them. One of two fallen totem poles we had seen earlier was covered by vines, and we couldn't find it. Nature reclaims quickly on the coast. Unless the site is better maintained, it won't be long until little can be seen. If you want to experience Mamalilaculla, our advice is to not delay.

Native Anchorage, near the southwest corner of Village Island, has a good bottom, but

*Mamalilaculla, 1998.
The empty houses do something to visitors.*

These huge timbers are all that remain from a longhouse at Mamalilaculla.

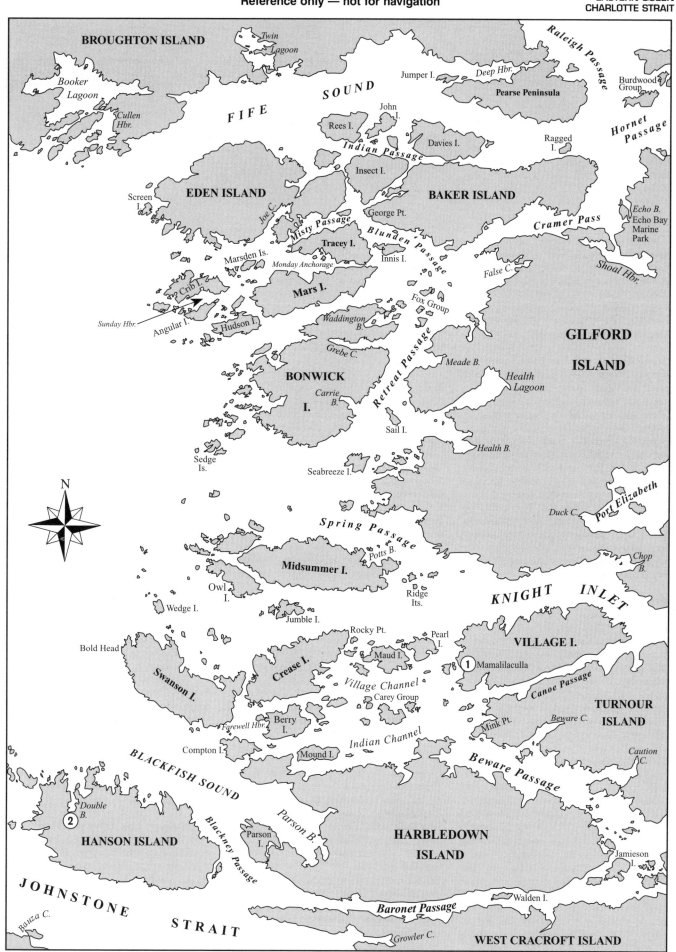

BROUGHTON ISLAND

Twin Lagoon

Booker Lagoon

Cullen Hbr.

F I F E   S O U N D

Jumper I.

Deep Hbr.

Raleigh Passage

Pearse Peninsula

Burdwood Group

Hornet Passage

John I.

Rees I.

Davies I.

Ragged I.

Indian Passage

Insect I.

BAKER ISLAND

Cramer Pass

Echo B.
Echo Bay Marine Park

Screen I.

EDEN ISLAND

Joe C.

Misty Passage

George Pt.

Blunden Passage

Shoal Hbr.

Tracey I.

Innis I.

False C.

Marsden Is.

Monday Anchorage

Fox Group

GILFORD ISLAND

Crib I.

Mars I.

Waddington B.

Retreat Passage

Meade B.

Sunday Hbr.

Angular I.

Hudson I.

Grebe C.

Health Lagoon

BONWICK I.

Carrie B.

Sail I.

Health B.

Sedge Is.

Seabreeze I.

N

Spring Passage

Duck C.

Port Elizabeth

Chop B.

Potts B.

Midsummer I.

Owl I.

Ridge Its.

K N I G H T   I N L E T

Wedge I.

Jumble I.

Rocky Pt.

Pearl I.

VILLAGE I.

Maud I.

Bold Head

Crease I.

Village Channel

① Mamalilaculla

Canoe Passage

TURNOUR ISLAND

Swanson I.

Carey Group

Mink Pt.

Beware C.

Farewell Hbr.

Berry I.

Indian Channel

Caution C.

Compton I.

Mound I.

Beware Passage

B L A C K F I S H   S O U N D

Double B.

②

Parson I.

Parson B.

HARBLEDOWN ISLAND

Jamieson I.

HANSON ISLAND

Blackney Passage

J O H N S T O N E

Bauza C.

S T R A I T

Baronet Passage

Walden I.

Growler C.

WEST CRACROFT ISLAND

See area map page 205

is exposed to westerly winds, and it's a bit of a walk to the village site. If you anchor in the little bay to the north of Mamalilaculla you will have better protection and a short, easy walk to the village. The old wharf is in disrepair and dangerous. We doubt that you will be tempted to use it.

All of Village Island is Indian Reserve, and the band asks that visitors pay fees. Payment is on the honor system, $7.50/person per visit, $5.00/person for groups of 6 or more. Send your fee to the band office at the following address:

Qwe'Qwa'Sot'Enox Band
1400 Weiwaikum Road
Campbell River, B.C. V9W 5W8

While permission to visit and prior payment are appreciated, "Nobody's going to run you off," the nice lady at the band office told us. For more information call the band office, (250)287-2955 or fax (250)287-4655.

Tom Sewid, a band member, will give informative tours if he is on the site. His fee includes the band's visitor fee.

Canoe Passage. Use chart 3545. Canoe Passage runs roughly east-west between Turnour Island and Village Island. The waterway dries at low tide, but can be transited at higher stages of the tide, depending on a vessel's draft.

Hanson Island. Use chart 3546. The rugged and beautiful north shore of Hanson Island is indented by a number of bays and coves that would be a gunkholer's paradise. The most popular anchorage is in Double Bay, also the location of the Double Bay Resort. Double Bay is apt to be crowded with commercial fishing boats during the commercial season. Enter only along the west side of the bay. The bay behind Sprout Islet, to the east of Double Bay, is also good for anchorage.

② **Double Bay Resort,** c/o 371 McCarthy St., Campbell River, B.C. V9W 2R7, (250)949-2500; fax (250)286-1937. Or view at www.doublebayresort.com. Monitors VHF channel 73. Open May through September only, guest moorage along a 700-foot dock, washrooms, showers. This is primarily a fishing resort whose guests fly in. Rooms are available. The cafe serves simple food (hamburgers, pie, etc.), not elaborate, but well prepared and hearty. There is a new restaurant on shore.

Growler Cove. Use chart 3546. Growler Cove, on the west end of West Cracroft Island, is an excellent anchorage, with good protection from both westerlies and easterlies. It is popular with commercial fishermen who work Johnstone Strait and Queen Charlotte Strait. During the prime commercial fishing months of July and August, Growler Cove is apt to be full of commercial boats, with little room for pleasure craft.

If you're approaching from the east, enter along West Cracroft Island, favoring the island as you work your way in. We saw an extensive kelp bed, not shown on the chart, off the point that leads to the entrance. We

Expanding blackberry patches force visitors to Mamalilaculla's beach part of the time.

would keep clear of that kelp. If you're approaching from the west, enter between Sophia Islands and Baron Reef, both of them shown on the chart. Inside, keep a mid-channel course, favoring the north side a little to avoid a charted rock about halfway in. Good anchoring near the head in 3-4 fathoms. Room for lots of boats.

Broughton Archipelago. Use chart 3515; 3546. Much of the Broughton Archipelago is now a marine park. Some of the islands are private, however, so use discretion when going ashore.

Our journal, written while at anchor in Waddington Bay after a day of exploring, reads: "A marvelous group of islands and passages, but few good anchorages. We navigated around Insect Island and through Indian Passage. Very pretty—many white shell beaches. Rocks marked by kelp. A different appearance from Kingcome Inlet or Simoom Sound. The trees are shorter and more windblown. The west wind is noticably colder than farther east. Fog lay at the mouth of Fife Sound; a few wisps blew up toward us. Great kayaking, gunkholing country."

This large group of islands west of Gilford Island does have anchorages, however, including Sunday Harbour, Monday Anchorage, and Joe Cove, all of which either we or Contributing Editor Tom Kincaid have used. The area is strewn with rocks, reefs, and little islands, which in total provide good protection, but also call for very careful navigation.

M. Wylie Blanchet *(The Curve of Time)* was blown out of Sunday Harbour, and we've had mixed reports about Monday Anchorage. Chappell isn't impressed with either one. Joe Cove is considered to be a good anchorage. Chart 3546 (1:40:000) should be studied carefully before going into these waters, and kept close at hand while there. Currents run strongly at times through the various passages.

Sunday Harbour. Use chart 3546; 3515. Sunday Harbour is formed by Crib Island and Angular Island, north of the mouth of Arrow Passage. The bay is very pretty, but exposed to westerly winds. The little cove in the northeast corner looks attractive until you try to enter and realize it is full of rocks. We would

anchor in the middle of Sunday Harbour for a relaxing lunch on a quiet day.

Monday Anchorage. Use chart 3546; 3547; 3515. Monday Anchorage is formed by Tracey Island and Mars Island, north of Arrow Passage. It is large and fairly open. Chapell says you can anchor behind the two small islands off the north shore of the bay. We, however, anchored for lunch fairly deep into the first large cove on the south shore. The anchor bit easily in 7 fathoms, and we had good protection from the westerly that was blowing.

Joe Cove. Use chart 3547. Joe Cove, perfectly protected and private feeling, indents the south side of Eden Island. The best anchorage is near the head. A little thumb of water extends southeast near the head of the cove, but access is partially blocked by several rocks. It is possible, however, to feel your way in. You can tie to the float in the cove.

RETREAT PASSAGE

False Cove. Use chart 3515. Although open to westerly winds, False Cove, on Gilford Island at the north end of Retreat Passage, has anchorage possibilities in two of the three coves at the head of the bay. The middle cove has 8 fathoms nearly to its head, then shoals quickly to 3-5 fathoms. The north cove shoals to 3-5 fathoms about halfway in. The south cove doesn't indent enough to serve. *Anchorage possibility:* South of False Cove, a thumb-like island protrudes northwest from Gilford Island. The cove that lies south of that island has about 5 fathoms at the entrance, shoaling gently toward the head. No name appears on the charts, but according to Chappell it is known locally as **Bootleg Bay.**

Waddington Bay. Use chart 3546; 3515. Waddington Bay indents the northeast corner of Bonwick Island. The bay is well protected, pretty, and popular, with room for several boats. It has good holding ground in 3-5 fathoms. Lacking local knowledge, make your approach from the northeast. The approach is wide enough, but rocks bound it, and careful piloting is called for. Study the chart (chart 3546, 1:40:000), and know your position at

Greenway Sound • Sullivan Bay
Grappler Sound • Mackenzie Sound • Drury Inlet • Sointula
Alert Bay • Port McNeill • Port Hardy

all times. Waddington Bay shoals at the head, but the wind direction and your depth sounder will tell you where to put the hook down.

Grebe Cove. Use chart 3546; 3515. Grebe Cove indents the east side of Bonwick Island off Retreat Passage. The cove shallows to 7-8 fathoms about 200 yards from the head, and 5-7 fathoms near the head. A saddle in the hills at the head might let westerlies in, but the seas would have no fetch. On one visit, a couple in a 20-foot pocket cruiser called out to us, "Great anchorage! The otters will entertain you!"

Carrie Bay. Use chart 3546; 3515. Carrie Bay indents Bonwick Island across Retreat Passage from Health Bay. An aquaculture operation is at the mouth, but the head of the bay is quite pretty, and protected from westerly winds. The bottom shoals rapidly from depths of 7-8 fathoms in much of the bay to around 3 fathoms at the head.

Health Bay. Use chart 3546; 3515. The Health Bay Indian Reserve, with dock, fronts on Retreat Passage. Health Bay itself is strewn with rocks. Anchorage is best fairly close to the head of the bay, short of the first of the rocks.

FIFE SOUND

Cullen Harbour. Use chart 3547. Cullen Harbour is on the south side of Broughton Island, at the entrance to Booker Lagoon. It is an excellent anchorage, with plenty of room for everyone. The bottom is mud, and depths range from 4 to 9 fathoms.

Booker Lagoon. Use chart 3547. The entrance to Booker Lagoon is from Cullen Harbour through Booker Passage, a tricky channel bounded by reefs on both sides. The channel has ample depths, though, and is about 50 feet wide. Aquaculture pens are in each of the four arms of Booker Lagoon, but anchorage can be found between them—the choice of arm depending on the wind.

Deep Harbour. Use chart 3515. The inner part of Deep Harbour is blocked by boomed logs, and the center of the bay is taken over by aquaculture pens, but there are little nooks around the edges with room enough for one boat.

Charts
3546 Broughton Strait (1:40,000); Port McNeill & Alert Bay (1:20,000)
3547 Queen Charlotte Strait, Eastern Portion (1:40,000); Stuart Narrows & Kenneth Passage (1:20,000)
3548 Queen Charlotte Strait, Central Portion (1:40,000); Blunden Harbour & Port Hardy (1:15,000)

SUTLEJ CHANNEL

Cypress Harbour. Use chart 3547. Cypress Harbour is one of the prettiest places in the area, with ample anchorage in Miller Bay or Berry Cove. Behind Roffey Point is a lovely anchorage with room for a few boats. Watch the depth sounder; the bay grows increasingly shoal until it becomes drying flats.

Greenway Sound. Use chart 3547. Greenway Sound has several good anchorages, and one great marina, the Greenway Sound Resort (see entry below). For those who like to anchor, the bay behind Broughton Point, at the east end of Carter Passage, is very pretty. You also can anchor in several little spots behind Cecil Island, near the mouth of Greenway Sound. Broughton Lagoon empties into this area.

Depending on conditions, you can find anchorage in any of a number of little nooks on both sides of Greenway Sound, and behind Simpson Island, near the head of the sound. Leave Simpson Island to starboard as you approach the head. For exercise, Broughton Lakes Park, with access from a dinghy dock on the west shore of the bay due east of Greenway Point, received much work in recent years, and is an excellent hike. The bay itself is a little deep for anchoring, so anchor elsewhere and take the dinghy over. Good trout fishing at the lakes, beautiful views. An aluminum skiff once was kept at one of the lakes, but no longer is there.

① **Greenway Sound Marine Resort,** Box 759, Port McNeill, B.C., V0N 2R0, (250)949-2525, (800)800-2080, winter phone (360)466-4751. Monitors VHF channel 73, switch 72. Washrooms, laundry, 15, 30 & 50 amp power. Reservations required for dinner. Boatsitting available. Open June 1 through September 15, ample guest moorage on 2210 feet of side-tie dock. Greenway Sound is an excellent and popular full-service destination resort. They have an fine restaurant (a tasty dinner is a tradition for us), a well-stocked convenience store with snacks, ice, ice cream and essential food, and a garbage drop.

Excellent fishing and prawning are nearby. A well-maintained trail leads to Broughton Lakes Park in the mountains. The resort has air service from several carriers, including its own Greenway Sounder, with service to Anacortes, Renton and Tacoma, with Sea-Tac International connections. The owners, Tom and Ann Taylor, are extremely knowledgeable and accommodating.

In late 1998 the Taylors announced that the resort would be closed, the result of a serious medical problem with Ann. Risky, delicate surgery followed, and to the relief of boaters throughout the Northwest—not to mention Ann and Tom—the surgery was a complete success. They changed their minds and reopened the resort in 1999, and the boating population flooded in. They're looking forward to seeing their friends and customers once again in 2000.

Broughton Lagoon. Use chart 3547. A friend who explored Broughton Lagoon reported as follows: They entered the lagoon in their Whaler at low slack water, showing a depth of 15 feet going in. Then it dropped off to depths of 300 feet. The lagoon was uncharted, and to all appearances, unvisited. They saw much wildlife, both in the water and on land. Coming out against the flood, they had the Whaler with its 40-horsepower outboard motor on a full plane and barely made headway against the incoming current—this on a neap tide. All went well, though, and our friend was excited about the experience.

Cartwright Bay. Use chart 3547. This bay is open to the wash from passing traffic in Sutlej Channel, but offers easy anchorage at its inner end.

② **Sullivan Bay Marine Resort,** Sullivan Bay Post Office, B.C. V0N 3H0, (250)949-2550. Monitors VHF channel 73. Use chart 3547. Open all year for fuel and post office, seasonally for guest moorage. Services include gasoline, diesel, propane, guest moorage, 15, 30 & 50 amp power, garbage drop, washrooms, showers, laundry. With the exception of the store, however, they have no facilities for sea kayakers.

Sullivan Bay, a fine and popular resort, is legendary among cruising boaters. It has ample moorage for even the largest vessels along 4000

These quaint old float houses are part of the charm of Sullivan Bay.

feet of dock, a well-stocked store with post office and liquor agency, boatsitting service, and daily air service to Seattle and elsewhere. Floating homes provide summer residences for several families, including Pat Finnerty and Lynn Whitehead, the owners.

Pat Finnerty came to Sullivan Bay in 1969, and enjoys recalling the history of Sullivan Bay. The old buildings at the resort date back to the 1940s, although they were brought in from elsewhere after fire destroyed the previous buildings. The whimsical signs, the informal feeling, even the 1-hole golf course, make Sullivan Bay a relaxing place. Alley, the

Alley Cat makes himself at home on this boat visit.

yellow resort cat, visits most boats as if they were his own, but remains a polite guest. We like Sullivan Bay.

Atkinson Island. Use chart 3547. There is anchorage in either end of the passage south of Atkinson Island.

Tracey Harbour. Use chart 3547. Tracey Harbour indents North Broughton Island from Wells Passage. It is pretty and protected. No anchorage is viable, however, until near the head of the bay. There, you can find anchorage on mud bottom in Napier Bay, or on rocky bottom in the bay behind Carter Point. You're apt to find log booms in Napier Bay, and left-over buildings from an old logging operation. In 1997 we anchored near the head of the cove behind Carter Point. The cove was beautiful and cozy-feeling, but the bottom felt like a thin layer of mud on top of rock, and it didn't take much to drag the anchor. The night was calm so we chose to stay, but would not trust the bottom if the wind came in.

Carter Passage. Use chart 3547. Since Carter Passage is blocked in the middle by a boulder-strewn drying shoal, it is actually two harbors, one off Wells Passage and one off Greenway Sound, with good anchorages in either end. The west entrance has tidal currents to 7 knots, and should be taken at or near high water slack. A reef extends from the south shore, so keep to the north of mid-channel. There are two pleasant anchorages in this west end.

The east entrance, off Greenway Sound, is somewhat easier, both as to tidal currents and obstructions. John Chappell's *Cruising Beyond Desolation Sound* describes the explora-

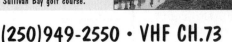

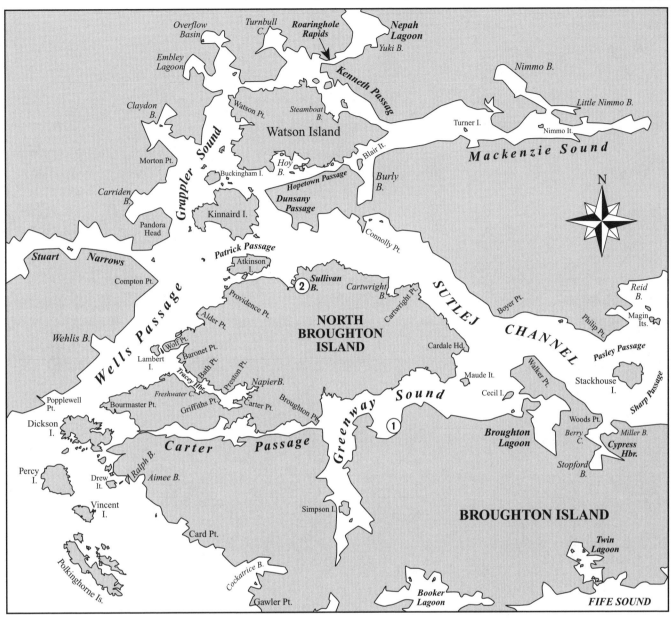

tions needed to safely transit the drying shoal between the two ends of Carter Passage.

Dickson Island. Use chart 3547. Dickson Island is located near the mouth of Wells Passage. The small anchorage on the east end of the island provides good protection from seas, but the low land lets westerly winds blow across the bay. Friends report that a large-diameter blue rope on shore offers a convenient loop to run the stern-tie through and back to the boat. Two other bays along the west side of Broughton Island are considered too exposed to westerly weather to be good anchorages.

Polkinghorne Islands. Use chart 3547. The Polkinghorne Islands are located outside the mouth of Wells Passage. A channel among the islands is fun, particularly on the nice day. The anchoring bottom we've found is not too secure, so an overnight stay is not recommended. *[Kincaid]*

GRAPPLER SOUND

Grappler Sound, north of Sutlej and Wells Passages, has several good anchorages.

Kinnaird Island. Use chart 3547. The bay in the northeast corner of the island is reported to be good in settled weather.

Hoy Bay. Use chart 3547. Some anchorage is possible in Hoy Bay, behind Hopetown Point, west of Hopetown Passage.

Carriden Bay. Use chart 3547. Carriden Bay is located just inside Pandora Head, at the entrance to Grappler Sound. It is a popular anchorage, with a good holding bottom and convenient depths throughout. As you look in, the spectacular nob of Pandora Head rises on the left. If you're in, you see a beautiful vista of mountains out the mouth of the bay. This vista makes Carriden Bay exposed to east winds, however. It would be an uncomfort-

able anchorage in such winds.

Woods Bay. Use chart 3547. Woods Bay is exposed to westerly winds. Friends, however, report it to be a good spot in settled weather.

Embley Lagoon. Use chart 3547. Too shallow for anything but dinghies, but an interesting exploration.

Overflow Basin. Use chart 3547. Dinghies only.

Claydon Bay. Use chart 3547. Entering or leaving, favor the Morton Point side. Foul ground, shown on the chart, extends from the opposite side of the entrance. In Claydon Bay you can pick the north or south arms, depending on which way the wind is blowing. Aggressive flies can be a problem, especially in the north arm. Crabbing is reported to be good.

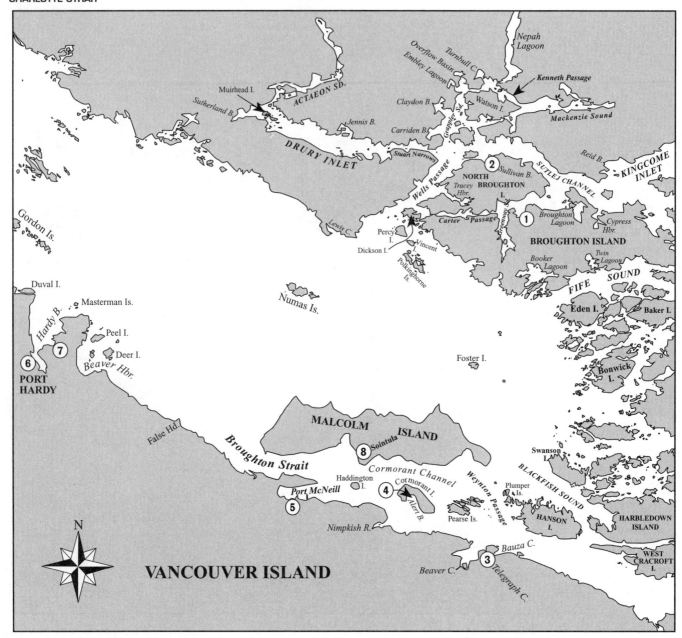

Nepah
Lagoon

Overflow Basin
Turnbull C.
Embley Lagoon

Kenneth Passage

Muirhead I.

ACTAEON SD.

Claydon B.

Watson I.

Mackenzie Sound

Sutherland B.

Jennis B.

Carriden B.

Greaper Sd.

SUTLEJ CHANNEL

Reid B.

KINGCOME
INLET

DRURY INLET

Stuart Narrows

Wells Passage

NORTH
BROUGHTON
I.

Sullivan B.

Tracey
Hbr.

2

Greenway Sd.

Broughton
Lagoon

1

Cypress
Hbr.

Lewis C.

Carter Passage

BROUGHTON ISLAND

Percy
I.

Dickson I.

Vincent
I.

Booker
Lagoon

Twin
Lagoon

Polkinghorne
Is.

FIFE SOUND

Gordon Is.

Eden I.

Baker I.

Duval I.

Masterman Is.

Numas Is.

Bonwick
I.

Hardy B.

Peel I.

Deer I.

Foster I.

7

Beaver Hbr.

6

PORT
HARDY

Swanson
I.

BLACKFISH SOUND

False Hd.

MALCOLM ISLAND

8 Sointula

Broughton Strait

Cormorant Channel

Weynton Passage

HARBLEDOWN
ISLAND

Haddington
I.

Cormorant I.

Plumper
Is.

HANSON
I.

Port McNeill

4

5

Alert B.

Pearse Is.

WEST
CRACROFT
I.

Nimpkish R.

Bauza C.

N

Beaver C.

3

Telegraph C.

VANCOUVER ISLAND

Turnbull Cove. Use chart 3547. Turnbull Cove is a large and beautiful bay with lots of room and good anchoring in 5-8 fathoms anywhere you choose. Chappell warns that an easterly gale can turn the entire bay into a lee shore so beware if such winds are forecast.

Nepah Lagoon. Use chart 3547. The ad-

venturesome might want to try Roaringhole Rapids into Nepah Lagoon, but we haven't done it. Passage, by dinghy with an outboard motor, should be attempted only at high water slack, which lasts 5 minutes and occurs 2 hours after the corresponding high water at Alert Bay. There is just 3 feet of water in this channel at low water. Nepah Lagoon doesn't

appear to have any useable anchorages, except possibly a little notch about a mile from the rapids.

MACKENZIE SOUND

Kenneth Passage. Use chart 3547. Kenneth Passage is navigable at all stages of the tide, being careful of a covered rock off Jessie Point. Currents can be quite strong and whirlpools will sometimes appear. A slack water entry is advised, especially on spring tides. The best advice is to take a look and decide if conditions suit you and your boat.

Steamboat Bay. Use chart 3547. Steamboat Bay is shown on the small insert for Kenneth Passage on chart 3547. It is a good anchorage, with room for a few boats. The bay shoals to drying flats all around. Watch for the drying rocks along the east shore at the entrance.

Four boats from Fidalgo Yacht Club are rafted together in Turnbull Cove.

Monks' Wall

A WEEKEND OF EXPLORING was the plan for David and me during a sunny break in June. There are so many beautiful islands and coves to explore, magic places where Native Indians and early settlers walked a hundred years ago.

After visiting some of the more known historical settlements on our cruise, we were treated to an unexpected surprise. I had heard rumors of a "monks' wall" on an island somewhere southeast of Port McNeill. David and I got some sketchy directions from Bob-the-Hermit, who lives in a cabin on an island, and we set out.

We anchored off a small sandy beach and rowed the dinghy ashore. At first, the island's stand of trees seemed to hide nothing but dense brush within. But as we walked along the edge of the forest, peering into the trees, we spotted what appeared to be a mound of neatly stacked stones. The mound was just inside, yet invisible if we hadn't been close and looking for it. We found an entrance to the woods, and suddenly we were standing in an ethereal landscape of old forest, carpeted with moss, with widely-space trees. Stretching into the distance before us, we saw the wall. It was five feet high in places, built of irregularly-shaped stones. One section culminated in what remained of an arch that reached well above our heads.

The light filtering through the trees and over the moss-covered stones made the scene one of serene and tranquil beauty. In their sanctuary, the stones were so peaceful that even our whispers were more than the stillness could bear. Each stone weighed more than one man could move, much less lift. I can only wonder at the time and effort it took to build such a temple. The wall stretched for more than 500 yards.

Hiltje Binner stands beside a stone wall on a secret island. Chinese monks built this wall around the turn of the century.

When we got back to our boat, I looked up references in the historical atlas we carry, Stephen Hilson's *Exploring Puget Sound & British Columbia: Olympia to Queen Charlotte Sound*. The atlas said that about a hundred years ago, Buddhist monks are reported to have built a temple somewhere in the vicinity. I think the reference is correct. I think we found their temple.

—Hiltje Binner

Hiltje Binner is the manager of the Port McNeill boat harbour.

Editor's Note: The Monks' Wall is a treasure. To keep casual visitors and especially vandals from descending upon it, not even the island on which the wall is located is identified. To the careful and dedicated explorer, however, enough clues are given to find the wall. Please, leave only footprints, take only pictures. Let those who follow discover the adventure the author found.

Burly Bay. Use chart 3547. Burly Bay is a good anchorage, mud bottom, but the muddy shoreline makes going ashore difficult. The little notch just to the west of Blair Island is better. Chappell *(Cruising Beyond Desolation Sound)* was not excited about Burly Bay, but our log reads, "Spectacular scenery, Ansel Adams photograph stuff, with rock wall on eastern shore falling straight into the sea." Guidebooks often are influenced by who visited, and what kind of day was had. Friends tell us of seeing grizzly bears on shore at Burly Bay.

Little Nimmo Bay. Use chart 3547. Little Nimmo Bay is a pretty anchorage, and the rock-strewn entrance is not as difficult as it appears on the chart. A luxury fly-in resort is located there. Anchorage is in 4 fathoms, mud bottom. Several small waterfalls tumble through the forest here. Grizzly bears are reported to be in the area. Make lots of noise if you go ashore. With care it is possible to go through to Nimmo Bay, which also has good anchorage.

Hopetown Passage. Use chart 3547. The eastern entrance into Hopetown Passage is blocked by a drying reef. Explore by dinghy first. If Hopetown Passage is attempted at all, it should be done cautiously, at high water slack in a shallow draft boat.

Stuart Narrows. Use chart 3547. Currents in Stuart Narrows run to a maximum of 7 knots, although on small tides they are reported to be much less. Times of slack are listed under Alert Bay, Secondary Current Stations, in the Tide and Current Tables, Vol. 6. The only hazard is Weld Rock. The current flows faster south of the rock, but passage can be made north of the rock as well. Leche Islet should be passed to the north. A study of the chart shows a rock patch to the south.

Note that Stuart Narrows lies well inside the mouth of Drury Inlet. Do not use the chart inset of the narrows at the mouth of the inlet, as the Waggoner's editor tried to do (blush).

Drury Inlet. Use chart 3547. Drury Inlet is surrounded by logging-scarred low hills that grow lower near the head of the inlet. This inlet is much less visited than other waters in the area. The entrance, off Wells Passage, is clearly marked on the charts, as is Stuart Narrows, 1.5 miles inside the entrance. Anchorage is available in two arms of **Richmond Bay** (choose the one that protects from the prevailing wind); near Stuart Narrows; and in **Sutherland Bay,** at the head of Drury Inlet. Approach Sutherland Bay around the north side of the Muirhead Islands, after which the bay is open and protected from westerlies.

We anchored for the night in the southwestern cove of Richmond Bay, near Stuart Narrows, and found it superb. The cove was protected, tranquil and private. Our notes read,

See area map page 210

"Best if enjoyed without other boats."

Helen Bay. Use chart 3547. Helen Bay lies just east of Stuart Narrows. It is reported to be a good anchorage, and halibut are said to be caught in the area.

Jennis Bay. Use chart 3547. Jennis Bay is the site of a log booming ground and a small settlement, with anchorage very good just offshore and a little to the north of the settlement. A pleasant woman named June Schulz has moorage at the settlement, and some primitive float houses. She had a lodge on the land, but it burned in 1997. Enter Jennis Bay around either end of Hooper Island. Keep to a mid-channel course to avoid rocks along the shores.

Davis Bay. Use chart 3547. Davis Bay looks inviting on the chart, but is not very pretty and is open to westerlies. Enter on the south side Davis Islet strongly favoring the Davis Islet shore.

Muirhead Islands. Use chart 3547. The Muirhead Islands, near the head of Drury Inlet, are rock-strewn but truly beautiful, and invite exporing in a small boat or kayak.

Actress Passage/Actaeon Sound. Use chart 3547. Actress Passage, connecting Drury Inlet with Actaeon Sound, is rock- and reef-strewn, narrow and twisting. It should be taken only at slack water. No time correction is given in the Tide and Current Tables, so you'll have to pick slack for yourself. A few years ago, a good friend, extremely experienced, got sucked into Actress Passage when it was really running, and almost swamped.

We have run Actress Passage near high water slack, when the current was quieter. Using chart 3547, we ran the channel between Dove Island and the mainland to the north, avoiding the charted rock, without problem. Regular traffic, however, uses the shorter channel east of Dove Island, splitting rocks marked with sticks at the entrance to Drury Inlet. Carefully run near slack water, both channels are safe.

Once into Actress Passage, the overriding navigation problem is the area between Skeen Point and Bond Peninsula. At high water, we

'Namgis burial ground, totems.

Looking up from the beach at the dramatic end wall of the U'Mista Cultural Centre building. The entrance is around the corner to the right. The old residental school, now housing government offices, is in the background.

chose to wrap fairly close around Skene Point, but the depths shoaled alarmingly as we went around. We would not want to try it at low water. The better choice is to follow Chappell's suggestion of crossing from Skene Point to Bond Peninsula, and working your way past the charted hazards around the corner.

With slack water in our favor, we did not continue into Actaeon Sound but instead turned back. Earlier, however, we talked with a couple who had spent a day in Actaeon Sound. They told us that Actaeon Sound was uninteresting, and that a huge logging operation occupied the head of the sound. They overnighted in Skene Bay (uninteresting), and said the crabbing was bad.

Queen Charlotte Strait. Use chart 3547 & 3548. Queen Charlotte Strait is about 15 miles wide between the entrance to Wells Passage and either Port Hardy or Port McNeill. The prevailing winds are from the northwest in the summer and and the southeast in the winter. In the summer, morning usually is the best time to cross.

By late morning or early afternoon a sea breeze will begin, and by mid-afternoon it can increase to 30 knots with very rough seas. The sea breeze usually quiets at sundown.

Tom Taylor, from Greenway Sound Marina Resort, has crossed the strait between Wells Passage and Port McNeill hundreds of times, and told us that in good weather he could go (in a fast boat) as late as 1400. Any given day can go against the norm. The prudent skipper will treat Queen Charlotte Strait with great respect.

Bauza Cove. Use chart 3546. Bauza Cove is an attractive but deep bay, with good protection from westerly swells. It is open to the wash of passing traffic in Johnstone Strait.

Telegraph Cove. Use chart 3546. Telegraph Cove, protected from westerly winds and swells, is picturesque, with a number of buildings on pilings, connected by boardwalk. In 1911 the Canadian Government established a telephone station at Telegraph Cove to connect the northern end of Vancouver Island with Campbell River. In World War II a telegraph station was installed and Telegraph Cove became a com-

The boardwalk path leads through the fascinating Gator Gardens at Alert Bay.

The Anglican Church, dating to 1879, is a delight to see.

Looking down Alert Bay's main commercial street from the ferry traffic holding area.

munications relay station. Today, Telegraph Cove is where trailerable boats are launched to fish in Blackfish Sound or explore the waters in this area. The Stubbs Island Charters operation is based in Telegraph Cove. They can take you down to Robson Bight to see the whales.

③ **Telegraph Cove Marina,** Box 2-8, Telegraph Cove, B.C. V0N 3J0, (250)928-3161; fax (250)928-3162; e-mail tcv@island.net. Monitors VHF channel 73. Open all year. This is a new marina, part of one of the most ambitious property developments we have seen in a long time. They have literally blasted from a rock mountain a condominium/hotel/waterfront home/marina complex with views and amenities of the highest order. It's a long way from completed yet. But we have seen the newly-created site for the golf course, and the stunning waterfront building lots. Everything is first-class, no short-cuts. At press time the marina docks are in and usable, but lacking power and water. The 2-lane launch ramp will be in operation by spring 2000. When the work is done, expect excellent showers and laundry facility, everything needed for a pleasant stay. When will the marina be complete? Plans are one thing, reality another. We recommend a call ahead to assure that your needs are addressed. When this development is finished, it will be quite a place.

③ **Telegraph Cove Resorts,** Telegraph Cove, B.C. V0N 3J0, (250)928-3131. Open all year except Tuesdays through Thursdays only during the winter, gasoline, launch ramp. *Moorage is for resort guests only.*

Beaver Cove. Use chart 3546. There is fairly deep anchorage along the shores of Beaver Cove, the site of an old sawmill. Logs may be boomed in the bay, and the bottom of the bay is almost certain to be fouled with sunken logs and debris.

Alert Bay. Use chart 3546. The Indian culture and roots are very much in evidence at Alert Bay on Cormorant Island—one can learn more about it here, in less time, than anywhere on this part of the coast. Chappell *(Cruising Beyond Desolation Sound)* devotes considerable space to Alert Bay's history, so we won't repeat it here.

Be sure to stop at the Visitors' Centre, on the water side of the road, mid-town. There you will get information about the several attractions in Alert Bay—the world's tallest totem pole; the U'Mista Cultural Centre; the "Gator Gardens," where you can see cedar trees stripped of bark; the 'Namgis burial grounds, the Anglican church that dates to 1879, and much more.

You can land at a small public float with room for several boats, or, deeper in the bay, in the breakwater-protected basin adjacent to the Alert Bay ferry landing. The small public float is exposed to all winds, and the current can run swiftly. It is, however, directly across the street from the Isolla Bella Restaurant, which we'll get to in a moment.

Alert Bay has grocery stores, pubs, liquor store, post office, fuel, a shipyard, welding, hydraulics, and the other services you would expect in a fishing port. The protected basin is home to the fishing fleet. If the fleet is out you'll have room. If the fleet is in, you may have to raft off a fishing boat. Call the harbor office, listed below. Often a space can be

See area map page 210

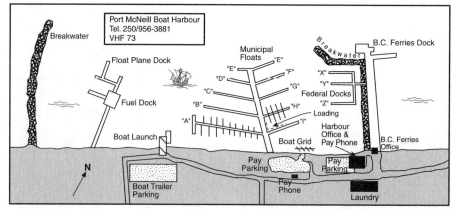

Port McNeill

Reference only — not for navigation

arranged.

Many visitors leave their boat at Port McNeill and take the ferry to Alert Bay for the day, and we recommend the experience. You can catch the 8:40 ferry from Port McNeill and return shortly after 5:00 p.m. The Alert Bay business district has an unplanned, good-enough-for-now feeling, and is very photogenic. The Gator Gardens are a healthy hike up the hill. They're worth the effort.

We've had a good lunch at the Old Customs House restaurant, whose walls are covered with historic photos. The owner, Maxine Williams, told us the delicious Alert Bay drinking water comes from a well more than 300 feet deep. She said the water is absolutely pure—no additives.

In 1999, at the urging of several readers, we had dinner at Isolla Bella Restaurant, owned by Guido and Luisa Morelli. Luisa is an extremely gracious hostess. Guido, who is straight from Italy by way of Vancouver, does all the cooking, and it's superb. Later, when the kitchen is closed, it's not unusual for Guido to come into the dining room and regale the diners with song. He was an entertainer for many years before giving up show biz, and you know you're in the hands of a pro. The setting is elegant and refined. From salad to dessert to entertainment, this is an unexpected and warm memory. Recommended.

If you possibly can, schedule your visit to see the Indian dance performance in the Big

House, newly rebuilt after being destroyed by an arson fire. They explain and perform traditional dances, complete with regalia and masks. Adults, teens and little children share equal roles. At the end, the audience joins in a joyful dance. Even the Waggoner's cautious publisher and his wife took part, and had a terrific time. Afterward, a visit to the U'Mista Cultural Centre takes on greater importance. The masks and other artifacts on display are extraordinary.

Study Chart 3546 before taking your boat to Alert Bay. Note the 3-knot currents shown throughout the area. While summer weather usually is quiet, be aware of the rough water that can make up when wind opposes cur-

rent. Note also the various shallows and other hazards, and plot your courses to stay well clear.

④ **Alert Bay Boat Harbour,** Box 28, Alert Bay, B.C. V0N 1A0, (250)974-5727. Monitors VHF channel 73. This is the breakwater-protected public wharf and floats in Alert Bay, located next to the ferry landing. Primarily commercial fishing boats, but room for a few visiting pleasure craft. It's a good idea to call ahead by radio or telephone to assure a place to tie up. Rafting is mandatory.

④ **Save-On Fuels,** P.O. Box 570, Alert Bay, B.C. V0N 1A0, (250)974-2161. Gasoline,

The Port McNeill Boat Harbour has ample moorage, but call on the radio before you come in.
The office will assign a slip and usually send someone to help you land.

Port McNeill. Use chart 3546. Port McNeill is a modern small city on the Vancouver Island highway, complete with banks, stores, hotels, restaurants, and communication by highway or airplane to the rest of Vancouver Island. With nearly all services located within easy walking distance of the boat harbor, Port McNeill has become a major resupply point for visiting boats.

The Port of Port McNeill marina has ample space except during the July-August high season, when it pays to arrive early in the day. The fuel dock also has moorage available. A laundromat is across the street from the Port marina office. IGA and Super Valu grocery stores are located a short distance away. Both have excellent stocks and free delivery to the docks. Fishing tackle, a post office, a large liquor store, drug stores, doctors, marine supplies and more are within a few minutes' walk. The Shop-Rite store, located only a block from the marina, closed its food market in 1998, although its hardware, sporting goods and furniture stores remain open and fully stocked. Regular float plane service connects downisland and to Seattle. The Port Hardy International Airport is nearby. A fuel float is alongside the marina, as is a launch ramp. Anchorage is possible throughout the bay. The preferred spot is across the bay from the marina.

⑤ **Port McNeill Boat Harbour,** P.O. Box 1389, Port McNeill, B.C. V0N 2R0, (250)956-3881. Monitors VHF channel 73. As you ap-

diesel and lubricants, only fuel in Alert Bay. Close to all services.

Mitchell Bay. Use chart 3546. Mitchell Bay, near the east end of Malcolm Island, is a good summertime anchorage, protected from all but south winds.

⑧ **Sointula.** Use chart 3546. Perhaps because our recent visit was so pleasant, Sointula, on Malcolm Island, is a favorite of ours. The extensive public docks are behind a breakwater at the head of Rough Bay, 1.5 miles beyond the landing for the ferry to Port McNeill. The public moorage can be crowded when the fishing fleet is in port. A shipyard, capable of major work, is located near the boat basin. There is also a small public float in front of the town.

Sointula (meaning "place of harmony" in Finnish) was settled by Finnish immigrants who engaged in logging, fishing, and farming. At the head of the basin the Sointula Coop runs a well-stocked hardware store, including a good selection of marine hardware. The coop also runs an equally well-stocked (but much

larger) grocery store in the village of Sointula. If you need food, you can get it there.

Probably because of the Finnish influence, the architecture in Sointula is a delight, especially when compared to the makeshift and often neglected structures one sometimes finds along the coast. The people are friendly, too. While walking from the boat basin to the village, don't be surprised if you're offered a ride.

proach, call ahead on the VHF for a slip assignment. Open all year, guest moorage available, 20, 30 & 50 amp power, water, washrooms, garbage drop, tidal grid, launch ramp. This is a good, comfortable marina, with friendly management and room for all sizes of boats. While they assign slips to approaching boats, they do not take reservations. No showers at the marina. Showers are available at the Dalewood Inn, about a block away, but only if the rooms aren't full. They do try to hold back a couple of rooms for boaters, and provide soap and towels. At $5 the charge is noticable, but if you want a shower, they have it. *(Marina map page 214)*

⑤ **Port McNeill Marine & Aviation Fuels,** P.O. Box 488, Port McNeill, B.C. V0N 2R0, (250)956-3336. Monitors VHF channel 73. Open all year, gasoline, diesel, stove oil, aviation fuel, propane. Located adjacent to the Port McNeill Boat Harbour. Some overnight moorage available. This dock formerly was called the Shell Marina, but the Shell sign isn't there anymore.

Beaver Harbour. Use chart 3548. The islands in Beaver Harbour are quite picturesque, and offer anchoring possibilities. The west side of the Cattle Islands is protected. You'll anchor on a mud bottom in 5-7 fathoms. Patrician Cove has been recommended to us. Several white shell midden beaches are located throughout the islands.

Port Hardy. Use chart 3548. Port Hardy is the northernmost community on Vancouver Island, and it's a nice town. A public float is attached to a large wharf in front of downtown. Six mooring buoys, reserved for plea-

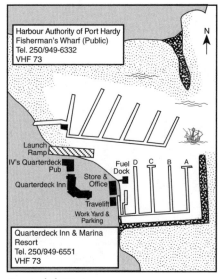

Reference only — not for navigation

Harbour Authority of Port Hardy
Fisherman's Wharf (Public)
Tel. 250/949-6332
VHF 73

Launch Ramp
IV's Quarterdeck Pub
Quarterdeck Inn
Store & Office
Travelift
Work Yard & Parking
Fuel Dock D C B A

Quarterdeck Inn & Marina Resort
Tel. 250/949-6551
VHF 73

Quarterdeck Marina

sure craft only, are adjacent. If the public float is full, you can tie to a buoy and take the dinghy in to the float. For easy access to shopping, this is the place to be.

Port Hardy has a lovely park at shoreside, with a pleasant seaside promonade past tidy waterfront homes. In the park, be sure to read the sign commemorating completion of the Carrot Highway. The Visitor's Centre is in the park. The town is clean and friendly. The library houses a museum and artifacts section.

A mile or so farther into Hardy Bay you'll find the excellent Quarterdeck Marina, which caters to pleasure craft and sport fishermen. A large public moorage for the commercial fleet is next to Quarterdeck Marina. From this inner bay to downtown is a something of a walk, but not bad.

Port Hardy has all city amenities, including hospital and airport, with scheduled flights to and from Vancouver. Being a commercial fish boat center, almost any kind of boat problem can be repaired. Nearby Bear Cove is the terminus for the ferry that runs to Prince Rupert during the summer.

⑥ **Harbour Authority of Port Hardy,** 6655 Hardy Bay Rd., Port Hardy, B.C. V0N 2P0, (250)949-6332; fax (250)949-7433. Monitors VHF channel 73. Has 20 & 30 amp power. This basin is primarily for commercial fishing vessels, but usually has some room in the

summer when the fleet is out. They have a launch ramp, tidal grid, washrooms, waste oil disposal and garbage drop. *(Marina map page 216)*

⑥ **Quarterdeck Inn & Marina Resort,** 6555 Hardy Bay Rd., PO Box 910, Port Hardy, B.C. V0N 2P0. Marina tel. (250)949-6551, fax (250) 949-7777; Inn tel. (250)902-0455; fax (250)902-0454. E-mail quarterdk@ capescott.net. Web site www.capescott.net/ quarterdk/. The marina monitors VHF channel 73. Open all year, gasoline, diesel, propane, guest moorage, 15, 20 & 30 amp power, washrooms, showers, laundry. The fuel dock carries Delo lubricants, for the many U.S. boats that use Delo. This is a busy marina with a well-stocked marine supplies and fishing tackle store, fuel dock, and launch ramp. IV's (pronounced "Ivey's") Pub is on the same property. The RV park has been relocated a couple blocks away. The haulout yard has a 22-foot-wide, 60-ton Travelift, the only Travelift between Nanaimo and Shearwater. Do it yourself, or have the pros do it.

In 1999 a new deluxe 40-room hotel was completed, the best hotel on north island. It is attractive and well-appointed, with full wheelchair and hearing-impaired access, ocean views, hot tub, and a covered walkway to a IV's expanded pub, with a nice area for families.

For some years the docks at this marina were rundown and the service poor, but new owners took over in 1996 and completely renovated the property. They began by installing new docks, with power and lights. Mega-yachts tie up here. Now they've built the hotel. The store is well-supplied and the people friendly, accommodating and efficient. Quality ownership yields quality results. If you're staying away because of a bad experience a few years ago, it's an entirely different story now. *(Marina map 216)*

⑥ **Port Hardy Esso Marine Station** P.O. Box 308, Port Hardy, B.C. V0N 2P0, (250)949-2710. Monitors VHF channel 78, switch to 73. Open all year, gasoline, diesel, stove oil, kerosene, naptha, waste oil disposal, washrooms. Look for the sign, just inside the first marker as you enter Port Hardy. They carry charts, fishing supplies and bait, ice cream and snacks.

⑦ **Petro Canada Bear Cove,** P.O. Box 112, Port Hardy, B.C. V0N 2P0, (250)949-9988. Open all year, gasoline, diesel, kerosene, propane, CNG. Has washrooms and showers. They carry fishing tackle, bait, and ice, have waste oil disposal, and can arrange for towing and repairs.

. . .The face of the water, in time, became a wonderful book — a book that was a dead language to the uneducated passenger, but which told its mind to me without reserve, delivering its most cherished secrets as clearly as if it uttered them with a voice. And it was not a book to be read once and thrown aside, for it had a new story to tell every day. Throughout the long twelve hundred miles there was never a page that was void of interest, never one that you could leave unread without loss, never one that you would want to skip, thinking you could find higher enjoyment in some other thing. . . .

Mark Twain,
Life on the Mississippi

The West Coast of Vancouver Island

WE HAVE BEEN DOWN the West Coast of Vancouver Island twice now, once in 1995 and again in 1999. After the 1999 trip, we concluded that the stretch of water from Port Hardy, at the top of Vancouver Island, down the West Coast to the mouth of the Strait of Juan de Fuca, is the finest cruising ground in the Northwest—save, perhaps, Alaska (we have not yet had the chance to really cruise Alaska). Thus far in our experience, nothing can compare with the variety, beauty, ruggedness, remoteness, and sheer satisfaction of a voyage down the outside of Vancouver Island.

Please allow enough time when you make the trip. Our 1999 trip took three weeks in a fast boat, and left unvisited much country we had seen in 1995. If you take three weeks on the outside of the island, you too will leave much country unvisited. Ah, but the country you do visit! Five inlets and sounds snake their way into the heart of Vancouver Island. Mountains rise around you as you penetrate. Rocks lurk in the waters. Fish and wildlife abound. Only the hardy (and occasionally the foolhardy) are out there with you. This is Northwest cruising writ large.

Except for the rounding of Cape Scott and the long run down the Strait of Juan de Fuca, the distance between inlets and sounds of the West Coast is in the 30-40 mile range. Wait for good weather and dash around. Once inside, let the wind outside blow; you're safe.

The boat. Large or small, a boat for the West Coast should be seaworthy, strong, and well-equipped. The seas encountered on the coastal passages will be a test, especially at Cape Scott, Brooks Peninsula, Tatchu Point, Estevan Point, the entrance to Ucluelet, Cape Beale, and the Strait of Juan de Fuca.

The wind accelerates as it is funneled at the capes and points, and the ocean's currents grow confused. Between wind and current, the seas grow noticeably higher and steeper. Even on moderate days, a boat can be suddenly surrounded by whitecaps. At Cape Scott and off Brooks Peninsula, pyramid-shaped waves can appear, break (or crumble into foam), and sweep past.

Often these "rogue" waves come from a direction different from the prevailing seas. Assuming a summertime westerly wind and a course in following seas, these waves can grab the broad sterns of many powerboats and make broaching a hazard. A double-ender, especially a double-ended sailboat with a large rudder, will not be affected as much. In fact, sailing in these seas with a 25-knot breeze from astern could be high points of the trip. But a planing-hull powerboat skipper will find himself paying close attention to the waves and their effect on his boat.

It is at times such as these that the skipper and crew know they are in serious water, and that their boat and equipment must be dependable. It is no place for old rigging, un-

This boardwalk at Winter Harbour is typical of several West Coast communities. Photo by Bob Spanfelner.

certain engines, sticky steering, intermittent electrical power, broken antennas, small anchors, unswung compasses, or clogged pumps. For a lifelong city-dweller, the West Coast is a wild coast, a wild coast with open seas and rocks a mile offshore. It pays to be prepared.

We think radar is all but essential. The local boats, even the little ones, have radar. GPS or Loran are essential. Even on clear days in mild conditions, GPS or Loran can identify turning points and confirm visual navigation. They take much anxiety out of navigating among ugly black rocks. In thick weather or fog, radar and GPS or Loran will raise the comfort level aboard dramatically.

Weather. Winter on the West Coast is stormy, and not a place for pleasure craft. In early spring the weather begins to improve, and by June or July the pattern of calm early mornings followed by rising westerly winds establishes itself. In the evening the winds subside. Even in summer, storms of considerable force can hit the West Coast. The wise skipper monitors the weather broadcasts, and watches both barometer and sky.

Fog can be a problem, particularly in August and September. We've heard the month of August referred to as "Foggust." The typical fog forms in early morning and burns off in late morning or early afternoon—just as the westerly fills in. If an outside passage is planned but the morning is blanketed in fog, the skipper will appreciate having radar and GPS or Loran. He also will be glad he did his chart navigation the day before, with waypoint coordinates plotted and loaded, distances measured, and compass courses laid.

Plan for rain and cool temperatures as well as sunshine. During the course of two to four weeks or more, most visitors will have a taste of everything.

The Coast Guard broadcasts continuous weather information from several locations along the West Coast. The reports are limited in scope to weather that affects the West Coast only, and include wind and sea state reports from lighthouses and weather-monitoring stations. In surprisingly short time, the attentive visitor learns how to interpret the weather

broadcasts and decide whether the time is right for an outside passage.

Fuel. While the West Coast is a wilderness, it is a wilderness with fuel. Gasoline and diesel are available all along the coast, within workable ranges for virtually any boat capable of safely being out there. The fuel stations exist to serve the large fishing fleet and the pockets of permanent residents, especially Indian communities. The fish boats use diesel; the outboard and IO-powered boats use gasoline. Fuel will be found at Winter Harbour, Coal Harbour, Walters Cove (uncertain at press time), Critter Cove (gasoline only), Zeballos, Esperanza, Tahsis, Ahousat, Tofino, Ucluelet, Bamfield, Port Alberni, Sooke, and Victoria.

Note: The above list of fuel stops is subject to change. Check our web site www.waggonerguide.com for updates.

Ice. Block ice can be a problem. If commercial fishing is allowed, the fish processing plants will have flaked ice for the fish boats, which take it on by the ton. A polite inquiry usually will yield enough ice for the icebox or cooler—sometimes for a charge, often not. Fish ice is "salt ice," and not recommended for the cocktail hour.

Water. Always check with locals before filling the water tank. Esperanza has excellent water.

Fresh vegetables. Scarce, uneven quality. Best to plan ahead and stock accordingly.

Public docks. Every community has a public dock, identified by its red railings, with moorage fees collected by a local resident. At a number of the docks the local resident isn't around, or doesn't bother to come collecting. Accept the no-charge tie-ups where you find them, pay gladly where the charge is collected.

Reference books and guidebooks. The Canadian Tide and Current Tables, Vol. 6 (blue cover) gives tides and currents south to Port San Juan. Vol. 5 (green cover) covers the Strait of Juan de Fuca and inland waters of Georgia

Strait and Puget Sound. Sailing Directions, B.C. Coast, South Portion, is the official government publication, and should be considered essential. The latest edition of Sailing Directions was published in late 1999. Note that Sailing Directions is intended for large vessels. A cove listed as good for anchoring may be too deep or exposed for small craft, but a passage listed as tortuous may be easily run by small craft.

Two good guidebooks exist, and we would buy both. The first is Don Watmough's *Cruising Guide to the West Coast of Vancouver Island.* It was published in 1984, as part of the *Pacific Yachting* series on British Columbia cruising, and republished (unrevised) in 1993 by Evergreen Pacific Publishing Co. Although the unrevised 1993 edition contains now-outdated 1984 information, the rocks are unmoved since 1984, and the excellent aerial photos by George McNutt will help with navigation. The book was written before most boats had GPS, Loran and radar. Its dependence on traditional coastal navigation skills is instructive.

The second guidebook is Don Douglass's almost encyclopedic *Exploring Vancouver Island's West Coast, 2nd ed.,* published in 1999. The book is clear, easy to understand, and describes a large percentage of bays and coves along the West Coast. Not every bay described is a desireable anchorage, but Douglass tells the reader what to expect if he is forced to enter. The first edition of Douglass's book was aboard during our own circumnavigation of Vancouver Island in 1995, and the second edition in 1999. We would not make the trip without it.

Charts. The Canadian Hydrographic Service has more than 30 charts that cover the coast between Port Hardy and Trial Island. Buy them all. Let the few that you don't use be insurance that you will have the chart you need, regardless of where you are. The charts are of excellent quality and easy to read. The West Coast is no place for approximate navigation. If a $20 chart can take even a moment's anxiety out of a passage, the $20 is well spent.

Coast Guard. The Canadian Coast Guard stationed along the West Coast is simply incredible. They watch like mother hens over the fleets of fish boats, pleasure boats and work boats, ready to deploy helicopters and rescue craft instantly. They know what the weather is doing and where the traffic is. They know where help can be found. A call to the Coast Guard brings action.

Local communities often can get help out even faster than the Coast Guard. In the area off Kyuquot Sound, for example, we were told that a call to Walters Cove on VHF channels 06 or 14 would bring help a-running. Be sure to call the Coast Guard on channel 16, too.

Insurance. Insurance policies for most inshore boats do not cover the West Coast of Vancouver Island. Read your policy and check with your agent about extending the coverage for the period of your trip.

(Continued page 220)

Cape Scott

FOR 25 YEARS, Cape Scott, the remote far north tip of Vancouver Island, had been a dream of mine. Cape Scott is exposed to weather and current, and to seas that could have begun thousands of miles away. It is the most significant landmark in a circumnavigation of Vancouver Island—one of the events that marks a *compleat* Northwest boatman. A rounding of Cape Scott implies that such a circumnavigation will become a reality.

Cape Scott can be rough. At their worst, Cape Scott's seas have capsized and sunk substantial vessels. Even quiet days can be uncomfortable, the result of swells that sweep in from the Pacific to meet colliding currents. Rocks lie offshore. If you find yourself in trouble off Cape Scott, you *are* in trouble.

Mrs. Hale, ever stalwart before, refused to face Cape Scott. So long-time friend Tom Hukle came aboard for the first voyage around the north face of Vancouver Island and down the West Coast. Tom is a former sailboat skipper of the year at Seattle Yacht Club, an excellent seaman, knowledgable navigator, and superb shipmate (but lousy cook).

On a breakfast of buns from the bakery and hot coffee, Tom and I departed Port Hardy at first light and ran out Goletas Channel, the early morning sun behind us. *Surprise,* a well-equipped Tollycraft 26 repowered with a "big-block" 454 V-8 Crusader engine, cruises at an easy 15 knots. We made all 15 knots in the flat water of a windless Goletas Channel, and reached Bull Harbour an hour and 15 minutes before the predicted turn at Nahwitti Bar. With time to kill, we inspected and took pictures at Bull Harbour. A few minutes before the turn, we followed two fish boats into the up-and-down rollers of the bar.

We rolled across at slow speed, steering a course for whistle buoy MA, 2½ miles away. A short distance beyond the buoy the the bottom grew deeper and the seas flattened. We powered back up to 15 knots for the run to Cape Scott, confirming major landmarks as we progressed: Cape Sutil, Northwest Nipple, Christensen Point, Nahwitti Cone, Frederickson Point. At last Cape Scott lay ahead, with the uninviting Scott Islands offshore. Cape Scott was uninviting, as well. Rocks extended from the land. Seas broke heavily on the shore. A low salt mist hung over all.

Out where we were, in only 10-15 knots of wind, the seas began to lump up. They were not towering, but for a small boat their closeness and steepness made even modest height significant. It had to be the currents. At first *Surprise* shouldered into the seas well, but after a brief time Tom Hukle, who was on the helm, said, "I'd like to slow down."

Tom and I agreed that if this is what Cape Scott was like in good conditions, it could be unrelenting hell in foul. Speed reduced, we bucked along. Charts slid onto the cabin sole, and a few books rearranged themselves. The wipers cleared spray from the windshield.

At last, at 1015 on 28 June 1995, in erratic writing clearly affected by the motion of the boat, I made the log entry I had waited 25 years to make: "Cape Scott abeam to port 1.5 miles. Light wind. Confused 4-6' seas. We're going home. A major moment."

A major moment indeed. Tom turned chatty, but I stared out the side window at Cape Scott, watching it move past as we began our voyage down the West Coast of Vancouver Island. "Give me a few minutes," I said to Tom. "I know it's corny, but I've waited a long time for this. I want to savor it."

—*Robert Hale*

Hardy Bay to Quatsino Sound

Goletas Channel • Nahwitti Bar • Cape Scott • Sea Otter Cove

Oregon's Secret. Many of the boats cruising the West Coast come from Oregon. For years it's been their playground, their little secret. The reason is obvious. After the trip along the Washington coast, their first stop is the West Coast of Vancouver Island. In good weather it's a long but easy run. Boats from the population centers of Puget Sound or Vancouver/Victoria must fight the Strait of Juan de Fuca or go around the top of Vancouver Island. Often, it is easier for them to enjoy cruising in the protected waters inside Vancouver Island.

Trailer Boats. Trailer boats can be towed to each of the sounds and inlets along the West Coast, where launch ramps are available. Salmon fishing was hot on our 1999 trip, and we saw hundreds of trailer boats. We also saw a great many kayakers, who could see whatever part of the West Coast they chose, without making a summer of it. The West Coast truly is kayak country.

Strait of Juan de Fuca. For boats coming from Puget Sound or Vancouver/Victoria, the Strait of Juan de Fuca can be a difficult body of water. The typical summer weather pattern calls for calm conditions in the early morning, with a thermal wind building by afternoon, often to 30+ knots. When wind and tidal current oppose, large, steep seas result.

On the American side, boats can leave Port Townsend at first light and get to Sequim Bay, Port Angeles, Clallam Bay, or Neah Bay before the wind builds. From Neah Bay, an early morning departure can fetch Barkley Sound while conditions are still calm.

On the Canadian side, boats can depart Victoria or Sooke at first light, and reach Port San Juan or even Barkley Sound, conditions and boat speed permitting.

These thoughts are for typical conditions. Variations often change typical conditions. We have seen the strait windy all day and calm all day. Listen to the weather broadcasts, watch the barometer and sky, and be cautious.

Comments?
Questions?
Corrections?
Let us know.

Contact us
by phone (toll-free),
fax, regular mail
or e-mail.

See our
phone numbers and
address at the
front of the book.

Charts	
3549	Queen Charlotte Strait, Western Portion (1:40,000)
3598	Cape Scott to Cape Calvert (1:74,500)
3624	Cape Cook to Cape Scott (1:90,000)
3679	Quatsino Sound (1:50,000)
3681	PLANS – Quatsino Sound
3686	Approaches to Winter Harbour (1:15,000)

The characters. In 1995 Marilynn Hale did not make the voyage down the West Coast of Vancouver Island. The crew that year was Tom Hukle, old friend, outstanding sailor and navigator, and splendid shipmate. Tom's wife Karen, to her credit but not mine, had spoiled him too long. Tom's approach to cooking was to find somewhere, anywhere, to buy dinner.

For 1999, Marilynn Hale clung steadfastly to her "No West Coast" pledge of 1995. We changed crews at Port McNeill, and Marilynn, by agreement, flew home. In a way it was just as well. Marilynn's aging parents had been weeks without her, and it was time to get back. Bob Spanfelner, another longtime sailing buddy, came aboard for his first trip down the West Coast. It turned out that Spanny was a creative cook, in addition to being a fine seaman and excellent companion.

Actually, we were a pretty good pair. Both of us were 59 (although Bob celebrated his 60th on the trip), both medium height, both fully-fed. Cruisers we met up with began calling us "the two Bobs," or "Bob-Bob a-re-Bob," or "the *Surprise* Bobs." We were out there three weeks, Spanfelner and I. We had a great cruise, but you will understand that when the boat got home, Spanny was was happy to see his wife Delia (as was Hukle to see Karen in 1995), and I to see Marilynn both times.

Please meet Tom Hukle and Bob Spanfelner, two great guys and fine shipmates. The editorial "we" on the West Coast pages that follow includes them.

Goletas Channel. Use chart 3549. Goletas Channel stretches west-northwest 23 miles between Duval Point (entrance to Hardy Bay) and the western tip of Hope Island. At the west entrance of Goletas Channel the notorious Nahwitti Bar blocks westerly swells from entering. Goletas Channel's shorelines are steep-to, so winds can funnel and grow stronger, but in usual summer conditions the channel, while it can get choppy, is not known for dangerous seas. Be alert, however, for turbulence and debris in the water where Christie Passage, Browning Passage and Bate Passage join Goletas Channel. The mouth of Hardy Bay can be slow going as you pick your way through

drift. At the west entrance to Goletas Channel, Bull Harbour, the usual waiting point for slack water on Nahwitti Bar, indents Hope Island

God's Pocket. Use chart 3549. God's Pocket, a favorite layover, is in Christie Passage on the west side of Hurst Island, just off Goletas Channel. Boats bound around Vancouver Island probably will not see God's Pocket, unless to escape a chop in Goletas Channel. But boats planning a direct crossing of Queen Charlotte Sound to the Queen Charlotte Islands, or boats bound past Cape Caution, find God's Pocket to be a good jumping-off spot. God's Pocket is a local name, and not shown on the chart. The harbor is marked on the chart with a marina symbol and the notation, "2 buoys."

God's Pocket Resort, P.O. Box 130, Port Hardy, B.C. V0N 2P0, (250)949-9221. Room for a few boats at the dock, or tie to 2 public mooring buoys. No power or water to the docks. Washrooms and showers. Breakfast, lunch and dinner are available for their diving guests; others can be accommodated on an as-available basis, with reservations. This is primarily a diving resort.

Port Alexander. Use chart 3549. Port Alexander, indenting Nigei Island from Browning Passage, makes a good anchorage for boats bound for Cape Scott or across Queen Charlotte Sound. Anchor near the head in 8-10 fathoms. Good beach for the dog. The westerly wind blows in across the island, but has no fetch for seas to build. The west side of the bay seems more protected than the east. A southerly would be a different matter. The accumulation of large logs on the beach indicates that this is no place to be in a southerly storm. As you enter Port Alexander, a little notch next to Browning Passage looks ideal, but we haven't tried it.

Bull Harbour. Use chart 3549. Bull Harbour is a lovely bay almost landlocked in Hope Island. It is the place to wait both for slack water on Nahwitti Bar and for weather. In 1999, we got to Bull Harbour in late afternoon. Boats that left that morning had been holed up in Bull Harbour for 6 days, waiting for a series of gales to pass.

Enter Bull Harbour around the east side of Norman Island, which blocks the southern entrance. Parts of Bull Harbour grow quite shoal on a low tide. Check the depth sounder and tide tables before anchoring for the night. The bottom is mud and holding is excellent. Sailing Directions says the southern portion of the harbor is reported to be foul with old chain and cable. During the fishing season commercial fish boats often crowd the harbor. A public float, not connected to shore, is in the southern part of the harbor. A public

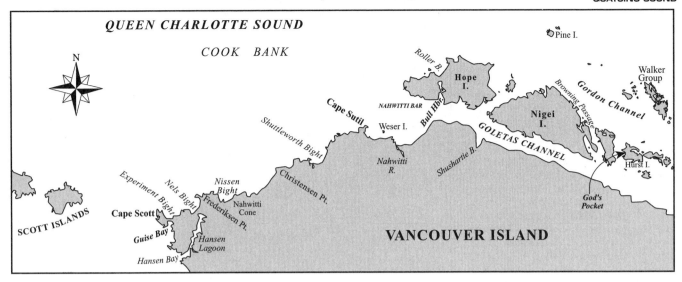

dock is on the east shore, north of Norman Island. If time allows, go ashore and cross the narrow neck of land at the north end of the harbor and watch the seas come into Roller Bay. Westerly winds can enter Bull Harbour, as can southeast gales. Be sure the anchor is well set, with adequate scope. In crowded conditions, achieving adequate scope can be a problem.

Nahwitti Bar. Use chart 3549. Nahwitti Bar should be attempted only at or near slack. Slack water and current predictions are shown in Tide and Current Tables, Vol. 6. Maximum tidal currents over the bar reach 5.5 knots. From seaward, the bar shoals gradually to a least depth of approximately 6 fathoms. When ocean swells from deep water hit the bar, their energy changes them from long and smooth to high and steep. We would be cautious about crossing against a strong westerly wind, even at slack water. If a strong ebb current opposes westerly winds, dangerous and heavy breaking seas will develop.

It is often said that the ideal time to cross Nahwitti bar is at high slack water. At high slack a typical westerly wind blowing with the flood current will tend to keep seas down and permit a crossing a few minutes before the slack. The subsequent ebb current flows as fast as 3 knots along the coast all the way to Cape Scott. Slower boats will appreciate the free ride.

A crossing at high slack is not without its disadvantages, though. The ebb that follows high slack will be in opposition to the prevailing westerly wind. In a fresh westerly, a high, steep chop could develop along the run to Cape Scott. If our choices were between an early morning crossing at low water slack but calm conditions, or an afternoon crossing at high water slack but windy conditions, we would choose morning. Granted, a crossing at low slack water puts a boat into a building flood current. But in smooth water a faster boat will reach Cape Scott in about an hour, and a 6-knot boat will reach the cape in about three hours. Three hours would put the slower boat at the cape about mid tide. The rips off Cape Scott may be too boisterous by then, so the slower boat may choose to wait for slack water again before rounding the cape.

Thus the wise skipper considers all factors before crossing Nahwitti Bar: current, weather, time of day, and the speed and seakeeping qualities of his vessel. At least 30 minutes should be allowed to get through the swells on the bar. Even fast boats usually must go slowly. At slack water in windless conditions, we found impressive swells extending out to whistle buoy MA, a total distance of approximately 2.5 miles, before they began to diminish.

Inner route. In September 1992, an article by June Cameron in *Pacific Yachting* described a quieter inner route that avoids Nahwitti Bar altogether. When we were anchored in Bull

Harbour in 1999 an old and grizzled commercial fisherman told us we were nuts if we didn't take it. He said he hadn't gone across the bar in years. Use chart 3549. Cross to the bay on the south shore of Goletas channel and work in behind Tatnall Reefs. Follow the Vancouver Island shoreline around the bay, passing on either side of Weser Island. If the westerly is blowing, you can hide in the little nook behind Cape Sutil. We did it, it works, and we don't plan to cross Nahwitti Bar again.

Cape Sutil to Cape Scott. Use chart 3598. Sailing Directions says the distance from Cape Sutil to Cape Scott is 15 miles, but this understates the actual running distance after crossing Nahwitti Bar. A more realistic distance would be measured from whistle buoy MA, and would be approximately 16.5 miles. Although the run across the bottom of Queen Charlotte Sound is exposed to westerlies, early morning conditions often are quiet, save for the relentless Pacific swell. Rocks extend as much as a mile offshore all along the way. A good offing is called for.

According to Sailing Directions, temporary anchorage can be found in Shuttleworth Bight, Nissen Bight, Fisherman Bay (southwest corner of Nissen Bight), Nels Bight, and Experiment Bight. Study the chart before entering, and watch the weather.

Cape Scott. Use chart 3598; 3524. Cape Scott is the westernmost point of Vancouver Island. Dangerous rocks extend 0.5 mile offshore, northward and westward. The cape itself is a low piece of land connected by a narrow neck with the main body of Vancouver Island. The Cape Scott Light, on a square tower 13 feet tall, is on higher ground about 0.25 mile inland from Cape Scott.

Currents flowing on both sides of the cape meet at Cape Scott. Especially when opposed by wind, the currents can produce heavy seas and overfalls, dangerous to small craft. It is reported that even in calm conditions, seas can emerge seemingly from nowhere, the collision of currents. Our 1995 rounding of Cape Scott was a little before half tide on a flood,

Waiting for slack water on the bar. Bull Harbour, indenting Hope Island, is a popular place to wait for Nahwitti Bar to calm down.

See area map page 222

with only 10-12 knots of wind. The size and nature of the seas, while not dangerous, definitely were out of proportion to the wind. With its seas, rocks, and shortage of convenient hidey-holes, Cape Scott is not a place to treat lightly. A vessel in trouble at Cape Scott could be in serious trouble, and quickly. (Our 1999 rounding was in virtually calm conditions, completely devoid of drama.)

Despite our easy rounding in 1999, it is with good reason that guidebooks (including this one) and magazine articles emphasize the dangers and cautions at Cape Scott. The waters can be treacherous. Yet in settled summer conditions, a well-managed seaworthy vessel, with a good weather eye, can make a safe and satisfying rounding. The standard advice is to round Cape Scott at slack. Other factors may persuade a skipper round at times other than slack.

In our own case, when in 1995 we sensed that the 10-12-knot westerly was freshening, we decided to get around while we could, even though we were at least two hours past slack. Once around the cape we had wind and current from the same direction (astern), and an easier ride to Quatsino Sound. Each situation, each boat, is different. What worked yesterday may not work today. A careful skipper,

(Continued page 223)

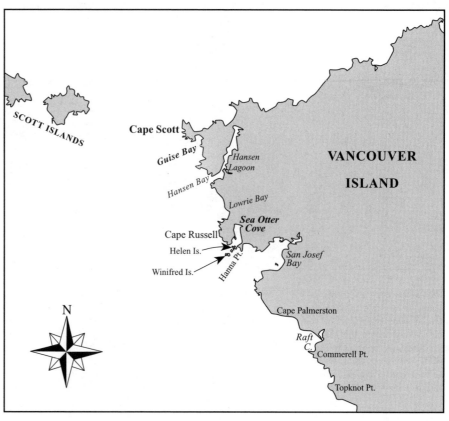

Sea Otter Cove

FOR BOATS rounding Cape Scott heading down the West Coast, the first fully protected harbor is Sea Otter Cove. Kayakers and rowers sometimes stop in Hansen Lagoon, where they can more easily pull their boats up on the beach. But for boats than need to anchor or take a mooring buoy, Sea Otter Cove is a welcome retreat, safe from whatever might be going on out on the ocean.

The entrance to Sea Otter Cove is protected by a group of small islands, each one of which is surrounded by a reef. Entry, using care, can be made on either side of these islands. If you choose the southernmost route, a single red light kept to starboard (Red, Right, Returning) provides a reference point for the very narrow channel between the reefs. The northernmost entry is broader and deeper, but more exposed to the ocean swells until you're well into the bay.

Once inside, you'll note that the entire bay is quite shallow, often less than a fathom. Be very careful during extreme low tides. You'll also note a row of government mooring buoys stretched part-way across the bay, and another row farther into the bay. Depending on how the fishing is going, Canadian trollers often are tied to the buoys.

My business partner Ole Hansen and I once entered Sea Otter Cove from a fairly rough sea, and took a buoy

in the first string. A Canadian troller was on another buoy in our string, and a third troller occupied a buoy in the second string.

Now, you need to understand that Ole Hansen is a very careful seaman, the best I've ever met. Ole has a horror of tying to anyone's buoy if he doesn't know from first-hand knowledge how it's held to the bottom. Never mind that the buoys were put in by the Canadian government to hold fishing boats; never mind that the buoys were big and rugged looking—how were they attached to the bottom?

Ole had his skin diving gear with him, and promptly suited up for a personal inspection of our buoy's anchor. He was down for quite a while, but when he surfaced and peeled back his mask, he said, "If we blow out of here tonight, Vancouver Island is going with us!"

Whoever installed those mooring buoys had begun by using a long length of ship's anchor chain. Each end of the chain was wrapped around a little rocky island, then shackled to a convenient link in the chain. Thus secured, the chain snaked its way across the bottom of the bay, and the mooring pennants were shackled to it. As Ole said, the only way we could drag out of Sea Otter Cove was to take a significant part of Vancouver Island with us. We slept peacefully that night.

—Tom Kincaid

Looking seaward at the mouth of Sea Otter Cove. If this photo looks rugged, wait 'til you see it in person.

One Wave at a Time, One Day at a Time

(or, How to Make Long Cruises into New Waters)

ON PAGE 87, Tom Kincaid's sidebar article, "The Learning Never Stops," tells about facing new waters and new boating challenges. In a brief, personal way, let me add a little to Tom Kincaid's thoughts.

To create this guidebook, we have had to expand our earlier Puget-Sound-to-Desolation-Sound cruising grounds. I have become familiar with the tidal rapids north of Desolation Sound. I have rounded Cape Scott twice. I have crossed Queen Charlotte Sound eight times, and explored the waterways of the Central and Northern B.C. coast.

Cruising in unfamiliar country is a challenge, and I know well the uncertainty of facing a notorious cape or passage for the first time. But I have found that if I take it one wave at a time, one day at a time, and build on lessons already learned, even in unfamiliar waters I can get from here to there with no more effort or distress than in waters close to home. Two of our roughest passages, in fact, were made in local waters, in the month of July.

One wave at a time, one day at a time. The miles melt away, the scenery changes, and place names we've read about become exciting realities. I have learned that I must have a well-equipped and well-maintained boat, with complete charts and navigation tools. I watch the barometer. I listen to the weather broadcasts. I keep in mind the aviators' maxim: There are old pilots and bold pilots, but no old, bold pilots.

One wave at a time, one day at a time. And one evening we are there.

—Robert Hale

fully aware that the safety of his vessel and crew truly are at risk at Cape Scott, must judge conditions and make the right choices.

In 1996 the Cape Scott Marine Park was extended to include nearly all the coastline between Cape Scott and Nahwitti Bar.

Cape Scott to Quatsino Sound. Use chart 3624. The run from Cape Scott to the entrance of Quatsino Sound is approximately 28.5 miles, depending on the courses chosen. This is where the depth sounder becomes an important navigation tool. To stay clear of off-lying rocks and reefs, the general advice is to follow the 20-fathom curve all the way down the coast. Douglass says he prefers the 30-fathom curve for an extra margin of safety. We are inclined toward Douglass's 30-fathom standard. In moderate conditions with excellent visibility we felt comfortable in 25-30 fathoms. Had conditions deteriorated, we would have moved out.

With the summer westerly in place, the run between Cape Scott and Quatsino Sound is a downhill sleighride. Powerboaters, especially those with planing hulls, will have to saw away at the helm and play with the throttle to stay in harmony with the relentless procession of rollers. They will arrive tired. Planing hull powerboats are not happy in powerful following seas. The sailboaters will have all the fun, especially if the boat and crew can handle a spinnaker. They too will arrive tired, but exhilarated.

Given the conditions, many boats make a direct passage between Cape Scott and Quatsino Sound, and leave the bays that lie between for another day. Sailboats, after a long passage at 6 knots, will be apt to put into one of those bays, particularly Sea Otter Cove. Boats heading *toward* Cape Scott might also be more apt to investigate the shoreline, choosing to spend the night in Sea Otter Cove, ready for an early departure and a rounding of Cape Scott before the westerly fills in.

Guise Bay. Use chart 3624. Guise Bay lies just south of Cape Scott. Sailing Directions says the entrance to Guise Bay is encumbered with rocks, and local knowledge is called for. The chart suggests that entrance is possible,

but Douglass says that the rocks are often covered with foam and a strong heart is called for. We haven't even attempted it.

Hansen Bay. Use chart 3624. Hansen Bay was the location of a Danish settlement around 1900. Supply vessels could anchor in good weather only. The settlement failed. Sailing Directions says Hansen Bay "affords no shelter," although commercial fish boats do hole up there.

Sea Otter Cove. Use chart 3624. Sea Otter Cove, south of Cape Scott, is described in Sailing Directions as "indifferent shelter." Nevertheless, Sea Otter Cove is a favorite of fish boats, and well-known to yachtsmen. The rocks and islets outside the entrance are beautiful, if awesome in their ruggedness. Inside, you feel safe but surrounded by hostile ground. Sea Otter Cove is an exciting place to be. We recommend it. Enter from the south, between Hanna Point and the Helen Islands. Watmough shows swells breaking almost across the entrance, but careful attention to the chart will bring you in. The channel is narrow, and grows more shallow as you go in. Contributing Editor Tom Kincaid says he stopped watching the depth sounder because it scared him so. Once inside, 8 mooring buoys have been placed with strong anchors (see sidebar p. 222). We recommend tying to one of these buoys. We heard of a fish boat that anchored in Sea Otter Cove and found itself perched on a rock when the tide went out.

San Josef Bay. Use Chart 3624. San Josef Bay is protected from northerly winds, but open to westerly and southerly winds. Anchor in settled weather.

The Waggoner Web Site
carries changes and updates to this edition throughout the year.
www.waggonerguide.com

Quatsino Sound

Winter Harbour • Koskimo Bay • Pamphlet Cove • Quatsino Narrows • Coal Harbour

Charts	
3624	Cape Cook to Cape Scott (1:90,000)
3679	Quatsino Sound (1:50,000)
3681	PLANS – Quatsino Sound
3686	Approaches to Winter Harbour (1:15,000)

QUATSINO SOUND is the northernmost of the five sounds that indent the West Coast. With the exception of Forward Harbour and Winter Harbour on the north side near the entrance, Quatsino Sound probably is the sound least explored by cruising yachts.

Quatsino Sound is, however, the first quiet anchorage after the 50-mile run from Bull Harbour, and a welcome sight it is after hours of rolling seas and anxiety at Cape Scott. The entrance is straightforward. Using large-scale chart 3686, identify South Danger Rock and Robson Rock (both of them well away from land), stay close to Kains Island, and proceed into Forward Harbour. North Harbour and Browning Inlet both are good anchorages, or you can continue to Winter Harbour.

VHF: We are told the fishermen work on channels 73, 84, and 86.

① **Winter Harbour.** Use chart 3686; 3624. Winter Harbour once was a commercial fishing outpost. B.C. Packers owned the first major set of docks as you enter, including the fuel dock. With the closing of fishing, their docks and fuel facility have been taken over by Grant Sales, the company that owns and runs the store. The Winter Harbour Authority public dock is a short distance beyond, and has moorage for a number of boats, and water. A pay phone is at the head of the wharf.

The high structure at the end of the pier made flaked ice for the fish boats. It's closed now.

A delightful boardwalk and trail connects the public docks with the Grant Sales extremely well stocked general store. The store has what you need: meat, produce, canned goods, packaged foods and fixings, liquor, clothing, sport and commercial fishing equipment, charts.

We were told that good anchorage is available at the head of Winter Harbour, but have not inspected it ourselves. Given the excellent anchorage in North Harbour, we suspect the head of Winter Harbour is not much visited.

① **Grant Sales, Grant Bay Marina,** General Delivery, Winter Harbour, B.C. V0N 3L0, (250)659-4333; fax (250)969-4334. Open all year, moorage, gasoline & diesel, showers, laundry, general store. Excellent water at the fuel dock. Dennis and Bonnie Grant have taken over the BC Packers moorage and fuel dock, and added it to their store offerings. The showers, which once were at the public dock, now are at Grant's dock. The store is a real general store, with just about anything you might need. The liquor agency has a decent wine selection.

North Harbour. Use chart 3686; 3624. North Harbour, north of Matthews Island in Forward Inlet, is an excellent anchorage, popular with boats planning a morning departure from Quatsino Sound. Three mooring buoys are located close to Matthews Island, with good anchoring depths beyond. North Harbour is sheltered and quiet, yet close to the mouth of Quatsino Sound.

Browning Inlet. Use chart 3686; 3624. Browning Inlet is narrow and sheltered, with good holding in 3-5 fathoms. Crabbing is reported to be good.

Koskimo Bay. Use chart 3679. Koskimo Bay has a couple of anchorages, one behind Mabbot Island and one at Mahatta Creek. The Koskimo Islands are at the east end of Koskimo Bay.

Mabbott Island. Use chart 3679. The little area behind Mabbott Island would be a cozy spot to drop the hook if the large fish farm weren't there and a float house didn't take part of the anchorage. If you must anchor behind Mabbott Island it can be done. Given the choice, we would move on—and did.

Mahatta Creek. Use chart 3679. In Koskimo Bay, this is the place to be. Work your way east of the mouth of the creek, anchor in 5-7 fathoms. Put the dinghy out. At high tide explore the creek. Nice.

Koskimo Islands. Use chart 3679. Explore by dinghy. The narrow passage between the largest of the islands and Vancouver Island can be run (carefully), but with safe water just outside the islands, we see no need to.

Koprino Harbour. Use chart 3579. Most of Koprino Harbour is too deep for pleasure craft, but the area of East Cove, near the northeast corner of Koprino Harbour, is excellent. In 1996 a new marine park was created in Koprino Harbour.

East Cove. Use chart 3679. If East Cove were in Desolation Sound instead of Koprino Harbour, it would be filled with 25 boats every night. East Cove is tranquil, snug and tree-lined, with good dinghy access to shore—cruising as it should be. You'll probably run a stern-tie to shore. If East Cove is occupied, anchorage almost as delightful can be had just to the north, behind a group of little islets. The largest of these islets is identified on the chart as Linthlop Islet.

Pamphlet Cove. Use chart 3679. Pamphlet Cove, part of a provincial recreation reserve, is located on the north side of Drake Island, about 3.5 miles west of Quatsino Narrows. Pamphlet Cove is scenic and protected, an ideal anchorage. A tidal grid and remains of old docks are along the shore. You can go ashore and enjoy the reserve. Watmough reports a trail leading from Pamphlet Cove to the south side of Drake Island.

Neroutsos Inlet. Use chart 3679; 3681. "The wind blows hard every afternoon in Neroutsos Inlet," one knowledgable local told us. Neroutsos Inlet is long and straight-sided, with little diversion along the way. An important pulp mill is at Port Alice, near the south end.

Port Alice. Use chart 3679, plans chart 3681. Port Alice is a friendly, prosperous-feeling mill town, and Western Pulp is the mill. Tie up at the public dock. Excellent water. Showers at the swimming pool. Restaurants, liquor store, Super Valu grocery market, other shops and services. The 9-hole golf course is located at

Winter Harbour as we approached in 1999. The boat is tied to the fuel dock.

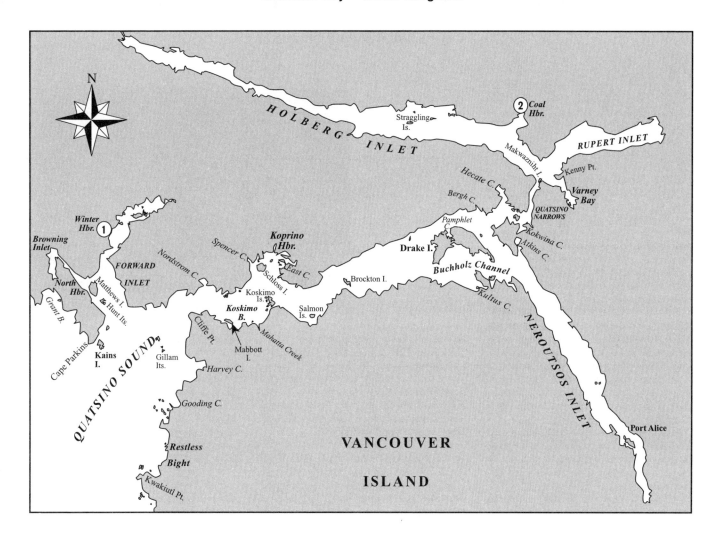

the mill, about a mile south of the town. It's the westernmost golf course in Canada. Visitors warmly welcomed.

Quatsino Narrows. Use chart 3681 *(strongly recommended)* or chart 3679. Quatsino Narrows connects with Rupert Inlet and Holberg Inlet, and the village of Coal Harbour. With tidal streams near Makwazniht Island running to 9 knots on the flood and 8 knots on the ebb, it is best to take the narrows near slack. Predictions for Quatsino Narrows are shown in Tide and Current Tables, Vol. 6. You'll find considerable turbulence near Makwazniht Island. A range on the eastern shore of the narrows will help you stay on course through the turbulence. Turbulence, though less than that found near Makwazniht Island, is present near the south entrance to Quatsino Narrows. At slack water watch for tugs with log boom tows.

Varney Bay. Use chart 3679. We did not visit Varney Bay, east of the north entrance to Quatsino Narrows. Douglass and Watmough, however, both recommend Varney Bay as scenic, tranquil and protected. Watmough calls it a "delight." Anchor behind Kenny Point. Watch for rocks and deadheads as you enter. Varney Bay is a fish preserve. No fishing.

Rupert Inlet. Use chart 3679. Rupert Inlet is the site of the giant Utah Mines open pit copper mine, now closed. Not much reason for the cruising yachtsman to go there.

② **Coal Harbour.** Use chart 3679; 3681. Coal Harbour has a small village with store, haulout and fuel, and is only 8 miles by road from all the facilities of Port Hardy. The fuel dock is operated by Anchor Petroleum Distributors for the benefit of their own fishing fleet stationed at the same location. They are friendly, helpful people and welcome pleasure craft (not that many visit), and their pump can deliver fuel at a great rate. But they do not have the customary attendants waiting to serve you as you arrive. "Be patient with us," they ask. You can call ahead on VHF channel 10. Call "Coal Harbour."

The Coal Harbour Whaling Station was the last whale-processing site on the West Coast, the station ceasing operations in 1967. Photos of the station are shown at the museum in Sidney. A whale's jawbone, several times a person's height, used to stand on display in Coal Harbour, but the weather was destroying it. The jawbone is in storage until a better means of displaying it can be devised.

Holberg Inlet. Use chart 3679. Holberg Inlet is 18 miles long, narrow and deep, a classic fjord. It has few places to anchor, and not much for the cruising yachtsman. With its 36-mile round trip and no facilities or attractions, it is seldom traveled by cruising yachts.

We Are Amazed
at the hundreds of changes, updates and additions we make to each new Waggoner Cruising Guide.

Stay Up to Date.
Make a current edition of the Waggoner Cruising Guide part of your boat's standard equipment.

Quatsino Sound to Kyuquot Sound

Cape Cook • Brooks Peninsula

Canoeists Don Munro and Joy Newham from Victoria were exploring Klaskino Inlet where we met them. This is the way to see the shoreline.

Brooks Bay. Use charts 3680 & 3651. It is approximately 19 miles from a departure point south of Kains Island, at the entrance to Quatsino Sound, to a point about 2 miles due west of Solander Island. From Solander Island to Walters Cove it is another 22-25 miles, depending on the course chosen—a total of at least 40 miles in the open sea. Those heading around Brooks Peninsula during a window of moderate conditions can be excused for not exploring Brooks Bay. Especially so because Brooks Bay is dotted with unmarked (but charted) rocks and reefs, and Brooks Peninsula looks so hostile.

As a result, boats exploring Klaskino Inlet and Klaskish Inlet on the north side of Brooks Bay should not be bothered by overcrowding. If you have the time, however, we recommend it.

Be sure to plot your courses, reciprocals and distances, and enter your waypoints before going into Brooks Bay. The rocks are more intimate than the chart suggests; you won't want to be making things up as you go. Two inlets, Klaskino Inlet and Klaskish Inlet, are beautiful to explore and have good anchorage. Of the two, we think Klaskish Inlet is the more interesting.

① **Klaskino Inlet.** Use charts 3680 & 3651. Assuming an approach from the north, leave Lawn Point approximately 2 miles to port. Continue, to leave Scarf Reef to port. Then turn to leave Rugged Islets to starboard. Turn to pass midway between buoys M17 and M18, then turn to enter Klaskino Inlet.

Now you'll be glad you have large scale chart 3651. If it's just a mooring buoy you're looking for, skirt around Anchorage Island and pick up one of the 4 buoys in Klaskino Anchorage. We shared Klaskino Anchorage with *Pacific Voyager*, a handsome cruiser that is out all summer, exploring the coast. If you prefer to anchor, the small bight north of the buoys will hold you.

If you'd like to explore further, go through Schouler Pass. We recommend that you use the more open northern channel, leaving buoy M23 to port. The kelp will be close enough to hold your attention. Anchor in the bight between the 67- and 53-meter islands, in the area shown as 7 meters at zero tide. The drying flats of the river mouth come up sharply.

Be sure you don't swing onto them.

Leaving Klaskino Inlet, the safest route is back between buoys M17 and M18. The day was quiet when we left, so we went westward, through Steele Reefs, running directly over the word "Steele" on the chart. The surf crashing on rocks seemed closer than we expected. We're not sure we'd go that way again.

② **Klaskish Inlet.** Use chart 3680. If you run from Quatsino Sound directly to Klaskish Inlet, your probable course will take you very near to Hughes Rock, which dries 5 feet. Hughes Rock is clearly shown on the chart. Don't run over it.

The outer anchorage didn't impress us. A low swell came in, even on a calm day. The chart shows 3 mooring buoys. Sailing Directions says there are 2. We counted 1. That's not where you want to be, anyway. You want to be in the magnificent Klaskish Basin, reached through a knockout, must-see, narrow gorge with vertical rock sides, overhung with dense forest. Once through, you are separated from the rest of the world. You'll find 8 big mooring buoys, or you can anchor.

Brooks Peninsula. Brooks Peninsula and the

waters off Cape Cook are, together with Cape Scott, the most hostile on the West Coast. The peninsula itself is a mountainous, rectangular promontory that extends 6 miles out from Vancouver Island, like a growth on the side of an otherwise handsome face. Rocks and reefs guard much of the Brooks Peninsula shoreline. Tangles of driftwood make beaches impassable. Cliffs rise from the beaches. At the tops of the cliffs, wilderness.

Cap on the Cape: When a cloud forms on top of Brooks Peninsula over Cape Cook, it often means that strong northwesterly winds will follow.

Cape Cook. Use chart 3680. Cape Cook is the northwestern tip of Brooks Peninsula. Rocks and shoals extend offshore from Cape Cook nearly to Solander Island. On all but the quietest days, the safe route past Cape Cook is well offshore from Solander Island.

Solander Island. Use chart 3680. Cape Cook (Solander Island) can be an exceedingly difficult patch of water. When conflicting currents meet accelerating winds, conditions become dangerous. The marine weather broadcasts often talk of "local winds off the

Solander Island off Cape Cook, the Cape of Storms, on a rare calm summer afternoon. That rock is ugly.

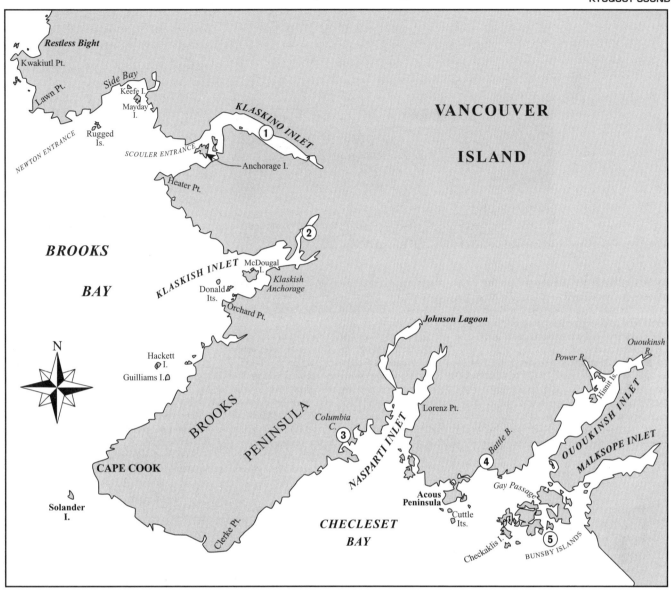

headlands" of 35 knots. The headland they have in mind is Cape Cook. While no headland on the West Coast should be taken lightly, Cape Cook (and Cape Scott) should be given the greatest respect. Listen to the weather broadcasts. If the weather sounds questionable, wait. When your opportunity comes, seize it.

Solander Island is an ugly treeless black rock 300 feet high, with a light on it. In 1995, with only a 10-12-knot morning westerly breeze, we found the Pacific swells shortened and steepened, mixed with pyramid-shaped seas that ran at an angle 30 degrees different from the swells. Local advice was to keep 1.5-2 miles off Solander Island and Brooks Peninsula. We found this advice easy to follow.

We had to pay close attention to keep our broad-sterned cruiser square with the following seas, particularly when a cross-sea would grab the stern and try to twist us into a broach. In Walters Cove later, we spoke with a couple in their 70s who had followed us in a slower but perhaps better boat for the conditions. They appeared relaxed and reported a "pleasant run."

In 1999 we hit Solander Island at 1720 in the afternoon, with only 4-6 knots of wind and a long, easy 3-4-foot swell. We were able to get up quite close and take pictures. So you never know.

Clerke Point. Clerke Point marks the southeast corner of Brooks Peninsula. Shoals extend at least 0.5 mile offshore, but a course following the 20-fathom curve will leave ample room for safety. The pyramid-shaped seas we battled at Solander Island disappeared completely by Clerke Point.

Once past Brooks Peninsula the weather warms and conditions improve. The remaining capes can throw some ugly stuff at you, but the hostility of Cape Scott and Brooks Peninsula are behind.

Checleset Bay. Use chart 3683. Checleset Bay has a number of anchorages, including Columbia Cove and the Bunsby Islands. If you have just rounded Brooks Peninsula, we urge you to make for Columbia Cove.

③**Columbia Cove.** Use chart 3683. Columbia Cove, whose name is not on the chart, lies immediately north of Jackobson Point, snugged up against the base of Brooks Peninsula. Be sure to enter between Jackobson Point and the 215-foot island. Two mooring buoys are in the cove proper, or anchor nearby. Columbia Cove is beautiful. Highly recommended.

Shelter Sheds. The Shelter Sheds are lines of reef extending from Brooks Peninsula into Checleset Bay. Fishermen have found shelter in their lee, hence the name. We have not tried them ourselves.

④ **Battle Bay.** Use chart 3683. Battle Bay, lying north of the Bunsby Islands, has acceptable anchorages roughly off the Indian Reserve, and in the nook that makes up the northeast shore. Approach the Longback Islands before making your turn into Battle Bay. The beach near the Indian Reserve is beautiful. The beach in the northeast cove has considerable drift wood on it, so southerly winds

SOLITUDE *hanging off a buoy in Columbia Cove. We crossed paths with her twice, then she was gone.*

do get in. We think a more interesting anchorage is immediately west of Battle Bay, against the west shore of Acus Peninsula. To reach that anchorage, leave the Skirmish Islands to starboard as you approach.

⑤ **Bunsby Islands.** Use chart 3683. "Did you get to the Bunsbys?" That's what people ask when they learn you've been down the West Coast of Vancouver Island. Don't disappoint them by saying no. The Bunsby Islands are rocky, rugged and beautiful. They have only two anchorages, but those two are large enough to hold all the boats that are likely to be there at one time.

Study the chart and know your location at all times. Enter the Bunsby Islands only through Gay Passage. The two anchorages lie off this passage: either the nook in the southern island or the slightly larger bay in the northern island. Enter the northern island's bay favoring the north shore, to avoid a shoal extending from the south side. In this larger bay, note the rock directly beneath the 6 fathom sounding. A sailboat we were crossing paths with anchored there, and almost swung onto

the rock as the tide dropped. The lagoon adjacent to this bay would be fine for an adventuresome trailerable boat, but we wouldn't want to take our 37-footer in there. We explored the lagoon by dinghy, and found that the rocks were not marked by kelp.

The cove on the west side of Gay Passage is guarded by two rocks that dry 4 feet. They are easy to identify and avoid if you're paying attention, but you must pay attention. The cove has room for several boats. We anchored with two others; all of us had plenty of swinging room.

The Bunsby Islands are reported to have a large population of sea otters, the successful result of an effort to re-establish these delightful creatures. The otters weren't home when we were there. We saw them elsewhere in Checleset Bay, but not in the Bunsbys.

If weather allows, take the dinghy or kayak around the islands. We took the Avon RIB, with its 15-hp outboard, out the south end of Gay Passage and through the rock garden to what Douglass calls False Gay Passage. The rugged, windswept rocks and islets are too stunning to try to describe. It's easy to get disoriented. Carry your chart, compass, handheld GPS and handheld VHF radio. You'll need the chart and compass for sure. Later, we were told that an Indian fish weir in excellent condition is at the head of the long inlet that indents the island on the south side of Gay Passage.

Our final note reads, "Recommended, recommended, recommended."

Bunsby Islands

PEOPLE CRUISING the West Coast really should make a stop in the Bunsby Islands, just offshore from Malksope Inlet. Several delightful, fully protected anchorages are available, but more importantly, the Bunsby Islands are home to a large number of sea otters that were re-introduced to the area several years ago.

We enjoyed one of these otters, called Hollywood, because he's a real ham. If we dropped a spoon over the side he'd dive for it, bring it back, "hand" it to us, and then clap his "hands" with delight.

Hollywood climbed into our dinghy, tied astern, stood on his hind flippers, and clapped loudly. Then he'd dive in and put on a water ballet for us, surfacing from time to time to lead the applause for his act. We knew if we threw him something to eat, he'd perform for us until bedtime.

—Tom Kincaid

These rugged rock islets lie at the east end of the Bunsby Islands, perfect for dinghy or kayak exploration.

CAPRIEAUX *shared the anchorage at the Bunsby Islands, and crossed paths with us for several days later. One evening they rowed over with fresh-baked dessert. Yum!*

Kyuquot Sound

Walters Cove • Dixie Cove • Rugged Point

Charts	
3651	Scouler Entrance and Kyuquot Sound
3682	Kyuquot Sound (1:36,700)
3683	Checleset Bay (1:36,500)

The Walters Cove dock has long floats on each side, with room for several boats

WITH THE EXCEPTION of the outer islands and Rugged Point, Kyuquot (pronounced "Ki-YU-kit") Sound is protected and pretty, surrounded by high mountains, with easy waters. On the inside, only Dixie Cove and Don Douglass's "Petroglyph Cove" are excellent anchorages, but several others are attractive. The settlement of Walters Cove is a favorite.

From the south, enter Kyuquot Sound past whistle buoy M38. Leave the buoy to starboard, and proceed through Kyuquot Channel. Most visiting pleasure craft, however, will approach from the north, and stop at Walters Cove before entering Kyuquot Sound proper.

① **Walters Cove.** Use chart 3651; 3682; 3683. For communication, call on VHF channels 06 or 14. We are completely taken by the little settlement of Walters Cove. It has almost everything you might need after a week or two of working your way along the coast: Red Cross outpost hospital, fuel (maybe), ice, charts, a store, cafe, land line pay phone, relaxed and friendly people, happy kids, lazy dogs, and Miss Charlie, a 36-year-old who's in love with Esko Kayra.

One thing Walters Cove does not have is liquor. Walters Cove is dry, by vote of the Kyuquot Native community, and there's not a drop to be bought. Nor is liquor in evidence, even on the dock.

From seaward, the safest approach to Walters Cove in all weathers (and the approach we took) is from whistle buoy MC, at the entrance to Brown Channel. Use chart 3683. Go through Brown Channel and turn to starboard on a course to pass Gayward Rock to starboard. At Gayward Rock go to large-scale chart 3651 to work your way past the east side of Walters Island and into Walters Cove.

Boats coming down from the Bunsby Islands probably will follow chart 3683's rather obvious passage along the Vancouver Island shoreline, leaving Cole Rock to starboard, and McLean Island and Chief Rock buoy M29 to port. At Gayward Rock they would move to large-scale chart 3651.

Without chart 3651, entry to Walters Cove would be a tricky matter. Although it is marked by buoys and a daybeacon, the channel past

Walters Cove

IT HAD BEEN BLOWING half a gale out of the southeast all day as *Nor'westing* punched her way south through visibility that was frequently only a few hundred yards. We were wet, tired, and trying to find the sea buoy off Kyuquot Inlet—our destination for the day was Walters Cove.

There is an inshore route through miles of rocks and reefs along this coast, but without good visibility we were afraid to get too close, which means we had to stay about five miles offshore to be clear of the hundreds of rocks and reefs, and yet stay as close as we could so as not to miss that sea buoy.

Eventually the buoy showed up through the murk, enabling us to follow a buoyed route into Walters Cove. As we entered the shallow, narrow entrance to the cove, what appeared to be a huge ship was approaching that entrance from the south. We assumed the ship was headed up Crowther Channel into the main part of Kyuquot Sound, so paid it no mind until we arrived inside the cove and anchored off the government float.

Alongside the government pier was a rickety looking cedar log float that gave access to the town's general store and fuel depot. As we watched in amazement, that huge ship (which wasn't really that huge as ships go, perhaps 150 feet) poked its nose through the same entrance we'd just negotiated with our four foor draft, and tied his first few feet to that rickety float, and started discharging fuel.

We got to talk to the crew later that day, because they had to wait for another high tide in order to get back out of Walters Cove. This tanker, because that's what it was, services all the fuel docks and logging camps up and down the coast, from Vancouver to Prince Rupert. It was equipped with Cort nozzles, twin screw, and had a bow thruster, but even so it has to work its way into some of the darndest places you've ever seen.

I've seen that ship many times since then, have had the crew aboard for coffee or a beer, and been given a tour of their ship, but I'll never forget that murky, windy day when a "big" ship followed us into Walters Cove.

—*Tom Kincaid*

the east side of Walters Island is easy to mis-read, and the unwary skipper could find him-self on a rock. With chart 3651 the channel is apparent, and following the rule of Red, Right, Returning, entry is safe. The one daybeacon along the way marks the narrow passage that leads directly into Walters Cove. Remember that beacons are attached to the earth: rock extends into the passage from the beacon. Don't cut it close. Use a mid-channel course favoring the north side between the beacon and the 51-meter island opposite. The chart makes the route clear.

Several locals insisted, "Don't anchor in Walters Cove!" The bottom, they said, is foul with debris. Furthermore, the BC Tel phone line and the water lines serving the white community run across the bottom of the bay where a boat would be apt to anchor. Instead of anchoring, tie up at the public wharf to the left as you enter.

Long mooring floats are on each side of the the public wharf. The general store and post office, owned by Susan (Kayra) Bostrom, is at the head of the wharf. Summer hours are 1930-2130 every evening; 1300-1700 Mon., Wed., Fri.; 1500-1700 Sat. & Sun. Win-ter hours are 1300-1730 Mon., Wed., Fri.; 1500-1730 Sat. Stock arrives every Thurs-day afternoon aboard the supply ship *Uchuck III.* The fish packing plant is closed. The fuel dock may be closed, too. It was open in 1999, but questionable for 2000. We will post in-formation on the Updates page of www. waggonerguide.com.

The Kyuquot Band Native community of 250-300 is across the bay, served by its own public dock.

All transport is by boat in Walters Cove, and from an early age the Kyuquot children (and Indian children all along the coast) are accomplished boatmen. Their outboard-pow-ered craft seem to have but two directions: forward and reverse; and two throttle settings: full-power—and off.

Walters Cove has been a popular gather-ing place for decades. Years ago it was home to five fish camps in the summer. When people were stuck in port waiting for the weather to break, the talk flowed. Long ago Walters Cove got its local name of Bull---t Bay, *BS* Bay in polite company. A cafe at the head of the fuel dock was called the BS Cafe. Sam Kayra's bed and breakfast is named the BS B&B. (The BS Cafe, with its memorabilia-laden walls, burned in 1998.)

In 1995 Sam Kayra opened her new eat-ery, which she calls Miss Charlie's. It's in the old Fishermen's Co-op building (1934), a few steps from the store. Miss Charlie's is bright and airy, and the food is good. In 1995 we happened to be there on opening night. The whole community turned out to get Miss Charlie's off to a good start. Sam, an attrac-tive, charming woman in her 30s, was a little frazzled. Even so, Miss Charlie's got launched good and proper.

In Walters Cove we were struck by the apparent willingness of the Indian and white cultures not only to tolerate each other but work together and get along. For visitors such as ourselves, it made the experience much more enjoyable. At Walters Cove the Indian chil-dren and the white children played together.

Sam Kayra poses for us at a table in Miss Charlie's.

Here's Miss Charlie herself, taking up the whole dock.

And all of them played with Miss Charlie.

Miss Charlie, you might have heard from elsewhere, is a seal. She is age 36 now, the adopted pet of the Kayra family. Miss Charlie's mother was killed before Miss Charlie was born, and Miss Charlie was brought into the world by Caesarean section. The Kayra fam-ily adopted her. The man at the Stanley Park aquarium suggested that she be bottle-fed a mixture of 60 percent cod liver oil and 40 percent milk, but he held little hope of sur-vival. Miss Charlie proved the man at the aquarium wrong. She thrived on the diet, and grew. She had the run of the house, and played in the bathtub.

After a while, in a wrenching but neces-sary move, the Kayra family returned Miss Charlie to the wild. Miss Charlie came back, lumbering up the path from the dock, and climbed the stairs to the house. She has been a pet at BS Bay ever since. She lounges on the docks, swims with the children, and serves as mascot for the community. She used to hang out at the fish packing plant when it was open. When a boat landed, Miss Charlie got a salmon. If the salmon wasn't volunteered, she climbed onto the boat and stole it. With the plant closed, people bring her fish, and she gets some on her own. We were told she has never been fatter.

Although a pet, Miss Charlie had her urges, especially in springtime. Early on, she decided that Esko Kayra, the father of the Kayra fam-ily, was the apple (or herring, or salmon) of her eye, and for a number of years Miss Charlie made Esko uncomfortable with her longings. While we feel it indelicate to ask Esko if Miss Charlie is as forward as ever, we suspect that time has taken its toll and Miss Charlie is more relaxed now.

Barter Cove. Use chart 3682. Barter Cove, in the Mission Group islands outside Walters Cove, is open, unprotected and not nearly as interesting as anchorages inside Kyuquot Sound. Leave Ahmacinnit Island and the tiny islet east of Ahmacinnit Island to starboard, and feel your way in.

Kamils Anchorage. Use chart 3682. This anchorage is more exposed than Barter Cove. Enter, very carefully, through Favourite En-trance.

Amos Island. Use chart 3651; 3682. From Walters Cove, the easiest entrance to Kyuquot Sound is around the east side of Amos Island into Crowther Channel. Use chart 3651 to identify the channel between Walters Cove and Nicolaye Channel, then chart 3682 to find the route past Amos Island. The passage east of Amos Island is deep but narrow, and bounded by rocks. The first time through can be unsettling, but after you've done it once it's easy.

Surprise Island. Use chart 3682. Surprise Island, steep, round, and logged off to stumps, is located in Crowther Channel. On the south side of Surprise Island Crowther Channel is

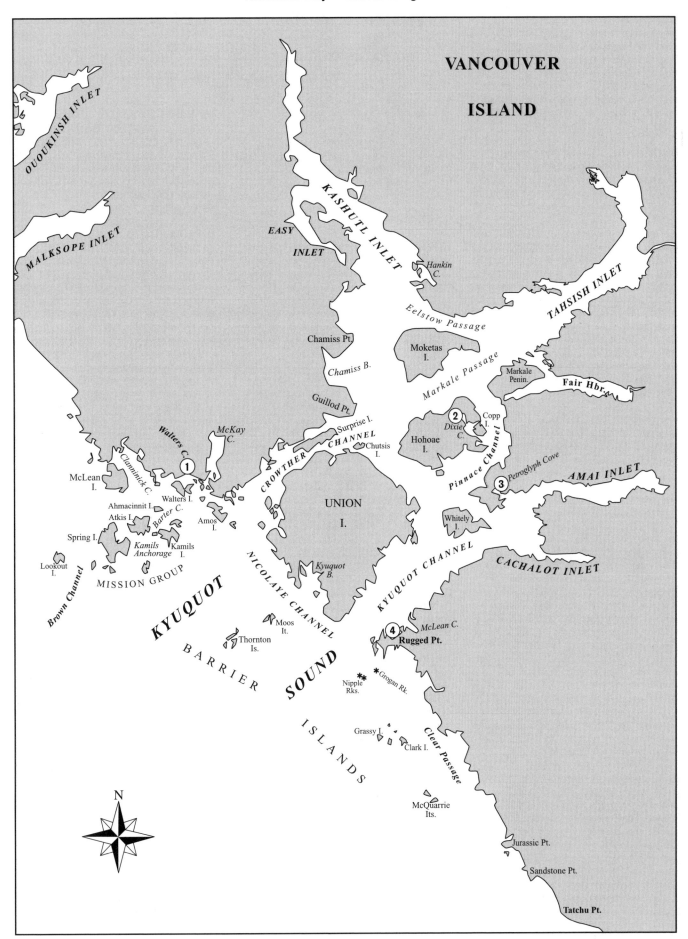

VANCOUVER

ISLAND

OUOUKINSH INLET

MALKSOPE INLET

KASHUTL INLET

EASY
INLET

Hankin C.

Eelstow Passage

TAHSISH INLET

Chamiss Pt.

Moketas I.

Chamiss B.

Markale Penin.

Markale Passage

Fair Hbr.

Guillod Pt.

Walters C.

McKay C.

Surprise I.

CROWTHER CHANNEL

②

Dixie C.

Copp I.

McLean I.

Clanninick C.

①

Chutsis I.

Hohoae I.

Pinnace Channel

③ *Petroglyph Cove*

AMAI INLET

Walters I.

Ahmacinnit I.

Barter C.

Amos I.

Atkis I.

Whitely I.

Spring I.

Kamils Anchorage

Kamils I.

UNION I.

KYUQUOT CHANNEL

CACHALOT INLET

Lookout I.

MISSION GROUP

Brown Channel

KYUQUOT

NICOLAYE CHANNEL

Kyuquot B.

McLean C.

④ **Rugged Pt.**

Moos It.

B A R R I E R

Thornton Is.

S O U N D

* **Grogan Rk.*

Nipple Rks.

Grassy I.

Clear Passage

Clark I.

I S L A N D S

McQuarrie Its.

Jurassic Pt.

N

Sandstone Pt.

Tatchu Pt.

deep and open, but on the north side a narrow passage is interesting. At zero tide least depths in this passage are approximately 3 fathoms. A ledge of rock, shown on the chart, extends from the north shore. Favor the Surprise Island side all the way through. Since our boat is named *Surprise* we felt we had to run this passage. We enjoyed it and we'd do it again.

Hankin Cove. Use chart 3682. Hankin Cove is located near the mouth of Kashutl Inlet, on the east side. It is a beautiful little cove with good holding, completely protected, but the hillsides are marred by evidence of logging.

② **Dixie Cove.** Use chart 3682. Dixie Cove indents the east side Hohoae Island, and is a *wonderful* anchorage. Enter south of Copp Island, through a narrow but deep passage to the first of two anchorages. This outer anchorage is approximately 5 fathoms deep, with good holding. Another narrow passage leads to the inner cove, completely secluded, with rock cliffs on one side. Depths here are approximately 3 fathoms, mud bottom. Getting to shore is a problem, so you're restricted to the boat. As a place to put the hook down, though, Dixie Cove is highly recommended.

Fair Harbour. Use chart 3682. Fair Harbour has a wide dirt launch ramp at the head, with ample parking. The road comes from Zeballos. You'll find a good-sized public wharf, with a long float. Enter Fair Harbour south of Karouk Island, leaving the two lighted beacons to port. The passage north of the island has two newly-reported rocks, not shown on the chart.

③ **Petroglyph Cove.** Use chart 3682. In his excellent book, *Exploring Vancouver Island's West Coast, 2nd ed.* Don Douglass describes this previously-unnamed anchorage and calls it "Petroglyph Cove." Petroglyph Cove is located near the mouth of Amai Inlet, roughly due west of Amai Point. The cove's entrance is hidden until you're right on it. The entrance is narrow, and the channel shallows to a least depth of 2-3 fathoms, but has no dangers. Once inside you are protected. While in our opinion Petroglyph Cove is not as pretty as Dixie Cove, it is an excellent spot.

Volcanic Cove. Use chart 3682. Exposed to the north, small, no room to swing. Temporary only for small boats, in our view.

④ **Rugged Point Marine Park.** Use chart 3682. Rugged Point marks the southern entrance to Kyuquot Sound. Our notes read, "Wow!" The beaches on the ocean side are spectacular, and deserve a visit. Anchor along the inside beaches in 3 fathoms on a kelp-covered hard sand bottom, and dinghy ashore. A trail leads through the park to the ocean beaches. The Pacific swell, though diminished, can get into the anchorage. While people have anchored overnight successfully, we weren't keen about the set of our anchor, and think it best for day use in fair weather.

Kyuquot Sound to Esperanza Inlet

*Clear Passage • Rolling Roadstead • Queen Cove • Zeballos
Nootka Mission • Tahsis Narrows*

Charts		
3682	Kyuquot Sound	(1:36,700)
3675	Nootka Sound	(1:40,000)
	Gold River	(1:10,000)
	Princesa Channel	(1:10,000)
3676	Esperanza Inlet	(1:40,000)
	Tahsis	(1:12,000)

DEPENDING ON THE COURSE CHOSEN, it is approximately 13.5 miles between Rugged Point and the entrance to Gillam Channel, which leads into Esperanza Inlet. In good visibility, the route through Clear Passage is smooth and interesting. In poor visibility, we would head seaward from Rugged Point to entrance buoy M38, then turn southeastward toward Esperanza Inlet.

Clear Passage. Use chart 3682. Clear Passage takes you about 4 miles along the coast in waters protected by the Barrier Islands, past a steady display of rugged rocks and rock islets. The channel is free of dangers. To enter Clear Passage, leave Grogan Rock to starboard, watching carefully for the rock to port, marked by kelp, that dries 4 feet. We got a little close to Grogan Rock, and the depths came up sharply. We moved off and they went back down. You will have no trouble identifying Grogan Rock. It is an awful 23-foot black pinnacle, and it commands attention. Lay a course to take you north of McQuarrie Islets, and exit Clear Passage leaving McQuarrie Islets to starboard. The rocks and islets along Clear Passage all look alike. It helps to plot a GPS or Loran waypoint at the point where you intend to turn to exit past McQuarrie Islets.

Tatchu Point. Use chart 3682; 3676. Several local fishermen told us the waters from Jurassic Point past Tatchu Point could be an "ugly patch of water." In 1995 we ran those waters in only a light breeze, but even then the seas had authority. In stronger conditions we could easily imagine the seas to be difficult. In 1999 we didn't have to imagine. We went out there in a 20-25-knot westerly. Once outside, we were in steep 6-foot seas, many of their crests crumbling into foam. The passage was without incident, but Spanfelner and I agreed we would have been smarter to wait until the next morning. Oh, well.

ESPERANZA INLET

Esperanza Inlet is on the west side of Nootka Island, and ultimately connects with Nootka Sound. Esperanza Inlet is part of the "inside route" through this portion of the coast. This route is served by three communities—Zeballos,

Tahsis, and Gold River—and by the Nootka Mission at Esperanza, with its fuel dock, hospitality, and excellent water. The waterways are beautiful, and contain several good stopping places. Tahsis Narrows connects Esperanza Inlet with Tahsis Inlet on the Nootka Sound side, and is not difficult to run. We like this inside route, and recommend it.

④ **Nuchatlitz.** Use chart 3676. Chart 3476 was introduced in 1999, and replaces chart 3662. The new chart reflects hydrographic survey work performed between 1992 and 1996, including the rocky area off Nuchatlitz. This chart came at the cost of many bent survey launch propellers. The entry to Nuchatlitz (*not* Nuchatlitz Inlet, which we have not visited) is marked by rocks and wildness to seaward, rocks and rock islets to landward. It's beautiful and it's interesting. Inside, a large bay has 3-4-fathom anchoring depths, but you'll sail around when the westerly is blowing. The abandoned Indian village of Nuchatlitz is on the shore, above a marvelous beach. We saw several sea otters. A resort is at the head of the bay; private buoys mark the route past submerged rocks to its docks. The buoys mean something to those who know. The rest of us should follow one of their boats if we want to go there.

The safe entry to Nuchatlitz is from the northeast, passing east of Rosa Island. From there the chart makes the course clear: follow the winding channel east of the 37-meter and 39-meter islands, and east of the two red spar buoys M46 and M48 (Red, Right, Returning). At buoy M48 the bay opens up.

③ **Rolling Roadstead.** Use chart 3676. Rolling Roadstead offers acceptable anchorage in fair weather, but from the west the approach can be tricky. While we have not made this approach, Douglass, Watmough, and Kincaid have, and Douglass and Watmough describe the approach in their books. Kincaid writes about it in a series of articles published in *Nor'westing* magazine in 1975-76. All agree that careful navigation is called for, including the finding and identifying of the various rocks and reefs in the entrance. The hazards are easily identified, either by the breaking surf or kelp growing in the shallows. With the hazards accounted for, the entry is reported to be safe. All agree that it should be run in fair weather only, with good visibility.

If you're coming down from Tatchu Point, especially in a fresh westerly, it's easier to enter Gillam Channel between buoys M41 and M42 and approach Rolling Roadstead from the southwest. Anchor in the lee of the point of juts abruptly from Catala Island. The beach on Catala Island is beautiful.

In 1996 Catala Island, which protects Roll-

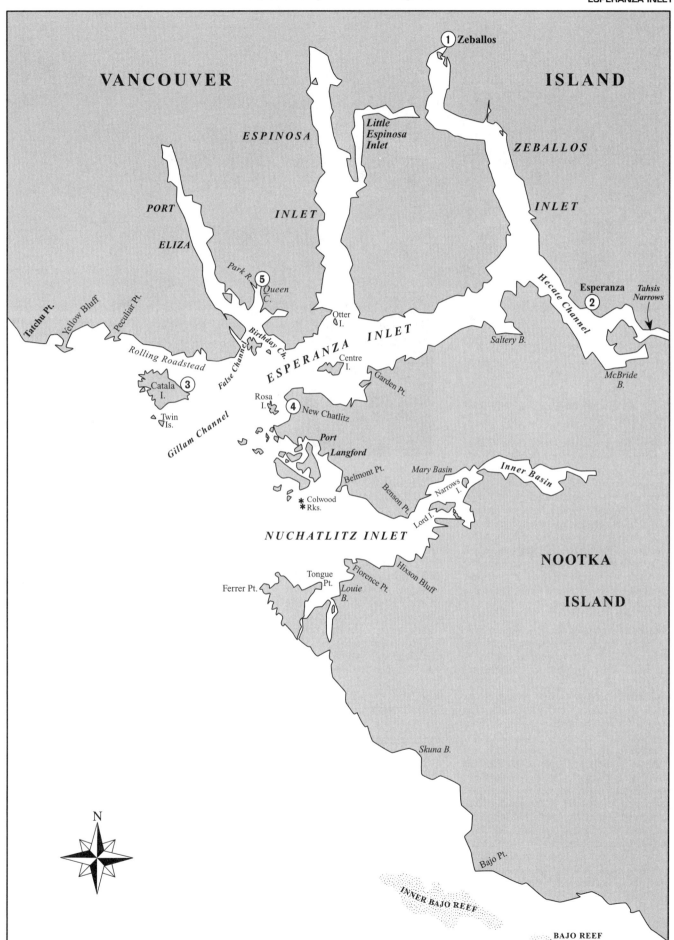

Zeballos. Nick Nekolov built a portable sawmill, and proudly shows off some of his work.

Parking in Zeballos is at a premium as traffic and pedestrians crowd the wide, paved boulevards lined with imposing false-front buildings. (Apologies to Roland Shanks)

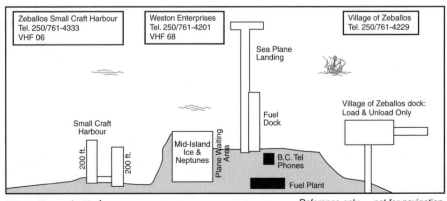

Salmon fishing can be good here. Part of the 1999 harvest.

ing Roadstead, was preserved as a provincial marine park.

Gillam Channel. Use chart 3676. Gillam Channel, more than 0.5 mile wide and well-buoyed, is the safe entrance to Esperanza Inlet. Approaching from a course past Tatchu Point, you can raise entrance buoy MD, then turn into Gillam Channel. Since we were in clear weather, we took a course inside of buoy MD but slightly to seaward of buoy M42, which marks the west end of Blind Reef. When we were close to buoy M42, we turned northward to leave buoy M41 off our port side, and continued into Esperanza Inlet. The course was easy and anxiety-free.

⑤**Queen Cove.** Use chart 3676. Queen Cove lies a short distance inside the entrance to Port Eliza, the first inlet to port as you enter Esperanza Inlet. Queen Cove is a safe and delightful spot to put the hook down and go exploring. The cove is well-protected, has excellent holding in 3-6 fathoms, and is large enough for several boats to swing. A cabin with dock is at the north end. The Park River enters at the north end of Queen Cove, and makes a good dinghy exploration. The most protected anchorage is the nook at the south end of Queen Cove, between the little island and the rock that dries 3.4 meters (11 feet). Swinging room is a little restricted, but workable. In 1999 we overnighted in Queen Cove, anchored in the exposed northern area. At 1700 the wind came in and built to about 25 knots before dying at sundown. We sailed back and forth some, but we didn't budge. Excellent mud bottom.

Espinosa Inlet. Espinosa Inlet is deep and high-walled. No place to anchor.

①**Zeballos.** Use chart 3676. To us, Zeballos ("Ze-BALL-os") is the most interesting and unexpected town on the West Coast. While other settlements range from fishing camp (Winter Harbour) to bustling town (Tofino), Zeballos is singular. It is a mining town that looks like Cicily, Alaska, the fictional town made famous by the television show *Northern Exposure*, with wandering streets and false-fronted buildings. The town is built at the mouth of the Zeballos River, next to mountains that go *straight up.*

Zeballos can provide most of what a cruising boat needs—food, fuel, water, liquor, ice, several eateries, good showers for a reasonable charge at the Zeballos Mini-Motel, laundromat, museum, and post office. The store, located at the head of the public dock, is run by a delightful woman named Anne-Marie Staats. A

1-hole golf course is just outside the store. The store has golf balls and clubs. You shoot across the river mouth. Long drivers try to break the windows in the cabin on the other side.

The mountains around Zeballos are highly mineralized, and much gold has been taken out of them. Over dinner at the hotel in 1995, we talked with a wildcat prospector whose eyes burned bright as he told of pockets of gold still waiting to be taken—*he knew where they were.* We met Nick Nekolov, who spoke English with a thick Bulgarian accent and operated a portable sawmill. The sawmill was next to Nick's trailer, directly across the street from the hotel.

Tie up at the public dock, to the right of the fuel dock as you approach. A pay tele-

Zeballos Small Craft Harbour
Tel. 250/761-4333
VHF 06

Weston Enterprises
Tel. 250/761-4201
VHF 68

Village of Zeballos
Tel. 250/761-4229

Sea Plane Landing

Small Craft Harbour

200 ft.

200 ft.

Mid-Island Ice & Neptunes

Plane Waiting Area

Fuel Dock

B.C. Tel Phones

Fuel Plant

Village of Zeballos dock:
Load & Unload Only

Weston Enterprises Ltd.

Reference only — not for navigation

Anne-Marie Staats, owner of
Zeballos General Store.

The public dock
at Zeballos
has room for
a large number
of boats, and is
close to store, fuel
and laundry.

phone is at the head of the public dock. The Village of Zeballos has built a new float to the left of the fuel dock, but we are told it is for large vessels, loading and unloading only. We don't know how rigid this policy will be. The general store, with pay phone, is nearby, as are a dumpster and waste oil drop. Washrooms are planned to be built near the public dock in time for the year 2000 boating/fishing season. The fuel dock has everything petroleum you might need. An engaging man named Roland Shanks conducts hikes to the old gold mines. Be sure to see the museum. It's small but fascinating.

Dana Pakalnis, the nice lady at the This-N-That Shoppe (and Zeballos Mini-Motel) (250)761-4340, washed and folded our laundry for a reasonable charge.

Zeballos is a good place to spend the night. The inlet leading to the town is long and beautiful. There's no point going both ways in one day. (Marina map 234)

① **Weston Enterprises Ltd.,** P.O. Box 100, Zeballos, B.C. V0P 2A0, (250)761-4201; fax (250)761-4618. Monitors VHF channel 68. Open all year. Gasoline, diesel, and propane are available. Fish ice available in season. Owners: Tom and Alice Weston.

① **Village of Zeballos Dock,** Zeballos, B.C. V0P 2A0, (250)761-4229. Open all year. For commercial vessels, load and unload only.

① **Zeballos Small Craft Harbour,** P.O. Box 42, Zeballos, B.C. V0P 2A0, (250)761-4333. Monitors VHF channel 06. Open all year with 400 feet of moorage, 15 amp power, no washroom, no showers, concrete launch ramp, long

term parking (launch ramp is run by the Village of Zeballos).

② **Esperanza,** Box 398, Tahsis, B.C. V0P 1X0. Use chart 3675. Monitors VHF channel 06, switch to 10. Fuel dock with gasoline, diesel, lube oil. Showers and laundry available. Excellent water. A small store on the pier has a few items. The telephone is available for emergencies.

Located on the north side of Hecate Channel, Esperanza is the home of the Nootka Mission. Its history goes back to 1937, when the Shantyman Mission began a hospital at Esperanza. This was in the tradition of the Shantyman Mission, which was founded in northern Ontario in 1907 to serve shanty dwellers in outlying areas. The Esperanza hospital no longer operates, and the property is now a Shantyman Mission camp for children and families, immaculately kept and welcoming

of all visitors. The fuel dock is an important source of revenue. Meals of wholesome camp food are sometimes available in the dining hall, donation encouraged. The coffee pot is usually on. We had some delicious homemade cookies with our coffee. The recipe for the cookies is contained in the *Esperanza Cookbook*, available at the store.

Overnight boats can tie to "Hospital Wharf," a public dock in the cove just west of the fuel dock. Haulout is available on the marine railway in the cove.

Tahsis Narrows. Use chart 3676. Tahsis Narrows connects the Esperanza Inlet side of Nootka Island with the Nootka Sound side. From the chart, one would think reversing tidal currents rage through the narrows 4 times a day, but they do not. The narrows are deep and free of dangers, with little tidal current activity. Passage can be made at any time.

Rafting Dogs

Sooner or later, rafting dogs come in handy. As the photo shows, a rafting dog is a crude iron casting with an eye at one end and a point at the other. It is designed to be pounded into a log so a line can be passed through the eye. Rafting dogs (sometimes called log dogs) are just the thing for tying mid-way along a log boom, where nothing can be found to pass a line through.

If you use rafting dogs, be sure to pound them into the perimeter boomsticks (the logs that are chained to one another to hold the boom together). Do not put rafting dogs into logs that are bound for the sawblade.

We found rafting dogs at Wood's Logging Supply in Sedro Woolley, Washington, telephone (360)855-0331.

—Robert Hale

Nootka Sound

Tahsis • Princesa Channel • Critter Cove • Santa Gertrudis Cove
Ewin Inlet • Friendly Cove

<table>
<tr><td colspan="2">Charts</td></tr>
<tr><td>3675</td><td>Nootka Sound (1:40,000)
Gold River (1:10,000)
Princesa Channel (1:10,000)</td></tr>
<tr><td>3676</td><td>Esperanza Inlet (1:40,000)
Tahsis (1:12,000)</td></tr>
</table>

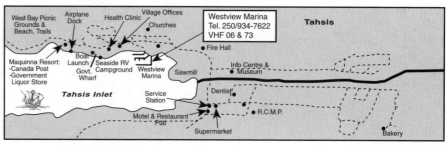

Tahsis and Westview Marina

Reference only — not for navigation

Tahsis Inlet. Use chart 3676. Tahsis Inlet (Tahsis is pronounced with a short-a, as in cat) is long and narrow, and bounded by mountains. The wind funnels and blows up-inlet or down, depending on conditions. We found a 2-foot chop that sent spray flying. The sawmill town of Tahsis, at the head of the inlet, once had full facilities, but times have not been good and several stores have closed. An exception is the Westview Marina, which is very well run, and has a courtesy car to get around town.

The major navigation danger in Tahsis Inlet is **Tsowwin Narrows**, created by the outfall from the Tsowwin River. A beacon marks the edge of the shoal. Pass between that beacon and another beacon on the west shore of the inlet. Remember that beacons are attached to the earth, and shoal water can extend into a channel from a beacon. Give each beacon a good berth. While we did not see much debris, Tahsis Inlet is reported to have considerable drift and dead-heads, depending on logging and sawmill activity. Keep a close watch on the water ahead.

① **Westview Marina,** P.O. Box 481, Tahsis, B.C. V0P 1X0, (250)934-7622. Monitors VHF channels 06 & 73. The fuel dock has gasoline and diesel, washroom, shower, laundry, and a small store with ice and a good gift selection. Moorage is served by 15 & 30 amp power. Propane is available in town. Courtesy car available. This marina, at the head of Tahsis Inlet, is set up to serve the summer flotilla of small sportfishing boats. The docks have been expanded and the welcome mat is out for cruising boats. Call ahead for availability. Readers tell us the Westview Marina treats them very well. The marina is neat and attractive, the people helpful, and the fuel dock easy to approach.

Princesa Channel. Use chart 3675. Princesa Channel runs between Bodega Island and Strange Island, and connects Tahsis and Kendrick Inlets. A route through Princesa Channel gets a boat out of the Tahsis Inlet chop and cuts some distance off a passage for southbound boats making for Friendly Cove. Unfortunately, the Tahsis Inlet entrance to Princesa Channel is narrow and bounded by an underwater rock.

From Tahsis Inlet to Kendrick Inlet (east to west) the problem is the flood tide. The flood current sets northward into Tahsis Inlet, and a boat entering Princesa Channel will find a definite northward set to its course. This northward set will tend to put the boat onto a submerged rock charted about 200 feet north of the Princesa Channel light, at the east entrance to Princesa Channel. Douglass believes the rock is closer to 100 feet from the light. One hundred feet or 200 feet, the rock is not far away. The goal is to wrap around the Princesa Channel light but avoid yet another charted rock south of the light, while not being set onto the rock 100-200 feet north of the light. Chart 3675 shows the rocks clearly. Study the chart and you will understand not only the challenge but the decisions required to meet the challenge.

We ran Princesa Channel in a stout flood current and had no problems. In our case, we ran south in Tahsis Inlet until the Princesa Channel light bore 235 degrees magnetic, then turned toward the light. We kept the light on our nose (we had to crab to make good our course) until the light was close aboard, then laid off to starboard to give the light 50 feet of clearance, and entered the channel. The key was to be aware of the rock 100-200 feet north of the light and keep our course *south of that rock*. Once past the light we held a mid-channel course and waltzed on through.

Bodega Cove. Use chart 3675. Douglass calls this previously unnamed anchorage "Bodega Cove," and we see no reason to argue. Bodega Cove lies at the head of Kendrick Inlet, between Nootka Island and Bodega Island. The area has been logged, so the scenery is not that of primeval forest. Protection is excellent, however, and the shores accessible. Since a reef extends from the Nootka Island side of the entrance, favor the eastern, Bodega Island, side. As we approached we divided the entry channel in half, then split the east-

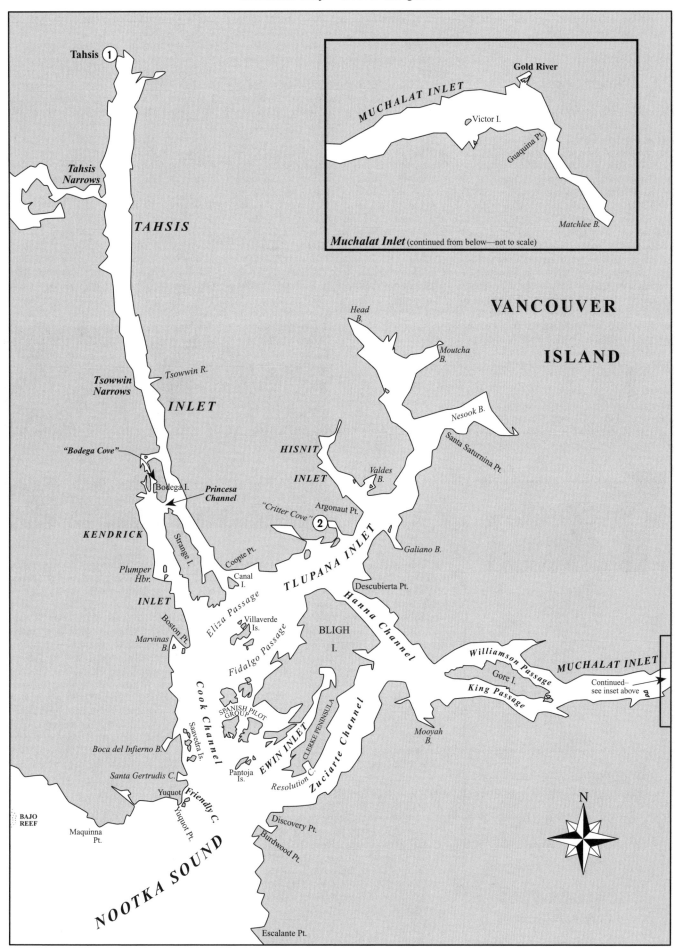

Tahsis (1)

Tahsis Narrows

TAHSIS

MUCHALAT INLET

Gold River

Victor I.

Guaquina Pt.

Matchlee B.

Muchalat Inlet (continued from below—not to scale)

VANCOUVER

ISLAND

Head B.

Moutcha B.

Tsowwin R.

Tsowwin Narrows

INLET

Nesook B.

Santa Saturnina Pt.

HISNIT

"Bodega Cove"

INLET

Valdes B.

Bodega I.

Princesa Channel

"Critter Cove"

Argonaut Pt.

(2)

KENDRICK

Strange I.

Coopte Pt.

TLUPANA INLET

Galiano B.

Plumper Hbr.

Canal I.

Descubierta Pt.

INLET

Eliza Passage

Hanna Channel

Boston Pt.

Villaverde Is.

BLIGH I.

Williamson Passage

MUCHALAT INLET

Marvinas B.

Fidalgo Passage

Gore I.

Continued– see inset above

King Passage

Cook Channel

SPANISH PILOT GROUP

EWIN INLET

CLERKE PENINSULA

Zuciarte Channel

Mooyah B.

Saavedra Is.

Boca del Infierno B.

Pantoja Is.

Resolution C.

Santa Gertrudis C.

Yuquot

Friendly C.

Discovery Pt.

Yuquot Pt.

Burdwood Pt.

BAJO REEF

Maquinna Pt.

N

NOOTKA SOUND

Escalante Pt.

ern, Bodega Island, portion in half again (in other words, we were three-quarters of the way toward the eastern shore), and ran down that line. It was easy.

NOOTKA SOUND

Use chart 3675. Nootka Sound is where European influence in the Northwest began. It was at Friendly Cove in Nootka Sound that Captain James Cook first landed in 1788. In 1790 Captains Vancouver and Quadra negotiated the transfer of control of these waters and lands from Spain to England. At Friendly Cove Captain Meares built the *Northwest America*, 48 feet on deck, the first ship ever built on the West Coast, and launched it in 1788.

The long arms (Muchalat Inlet and Tlupana Inlet) that reach out from Nootka Sound have few anchorages, and they tend to be deep. The Port of Gold River is at the head of Muchalat Inlet. The town is 9 miles from the dock, and the waters are too deep for anchoring. Trailerable boats, most of them come for salmon fishing in Nootka Sound, are launched here.

Hisnit Inlet. Use chart 3675. Hisnit Inlet extends north from Tlupana Inlet, and anchorage is possible at the head. Two submerged rocks lie almost mid-channel a short distance into Hisnit Inlet. Do not be deceived (as we were) by the open and safe appearance of the

inlet as you arrive or depart. We forgot about the rocks on leaving, and remembered them when they must have been very close. A sharp course change followed (gulp). Favor the south shore.

Anchorage at the head of the inlet is in 7-10 fathoms. It is open and not cozy feeling at all, but it is protected. Extensive clear cutting mars the hills. The shoreline is accessible.

Critter Cove. Use chart 3675. Critter Cove is the name given by Cameron Forbes to this previously unnamed spot about 1 mile south of Argonaut Point on Tlupana Inlet. Cameron has established a sportfishing resort in the cove and named it after his nickname of "Critter," when he played hockey. The resort is in the outer bay; the cozy inner cove is ideal for anchoring. A narrow channel with two charted rocks leads to the inner cove. We inspected the channel pretty carefully at a little less than

Quiet time at Critter Cove. Salmon were running and the boats were out fishing. We saw some big ones at the end of the day.

half-tide, and believe the rocks to be underwater outcroppings from the south shore. A mid-channel course will clear them. In 1999, readers Sara and Chuck Cooney anchored their beautiful Pacific Seacraft 31 sailboat *Kansei* with us in this back bay, and next morning sounded the channel with a lead line from their dinghy. They found a least depth of 6 feet near the bottom of a 1.6-foot low tide, which would translate to approximately 4.5 feet at zero tide.

② **Critter Cove Marina,** P.O. Box 1118, Gold River, B.C. V0P 1G0, (604)886-7667. Gasoline only at the fuel dock, moorage, cabins, suites, restaurant, showers. Cameron Forbes, one of the nicest guys you'll meet, has quite a sportfishing camp here. If the docks are full (as they often are from late June through August), you can anchor in the back bay (see above) and take the dinghy over to the resort. The entire facility is on floats. The restaurant is small and rustic, but the food is excellent. Most of the boats at Critter Cove are trailered into Gold River, where they are launched. They do have room for visiting cruisers, though.

Santa Gertrudis Cove. Use chart 3675. The western cove in Santa Gertrudis Cove is an excellent anchorage, cozy, good holding, protected. As you enter you will see an island in the northern cove. A submerged rock extends from that island a considerable distance toward the south shore, farther than we expected. Be sure to identify this rock and give it room as you favor the south shore. We found sufficient room to pass between this rock and the drying rock shown off the south shore on the chart. The north cove of Santa Gertrudis Cove, around the island, is foul and tight.

Resolution Cove. Use chart 3675. Resolution Cove is near the south end of Clerke Peninsula, on Bligh Island. Cook put his ship *Resolution* into the cove to find and fit a new foremast. A flagpole and plaques commemorating Cook have been placed on a knoll above the cove. Anchor in 7-8 fathoms, either with

a stern-tie to shore or enough room to swing. You'll probably make your visit a short one: this is not the best place for small craft.

Ewin Inlet. Use chart 3675. Ewin Inlet indents the south side of Bligh Island some 3 miles, with no anchorages until the head is reached. The cove to the west at the head of the inlet is quite protected and has depths of 5-7 fathoms. We rounded the little islet in the cove at low tide, about 100 feet off, and the depth sounder abruptly but briefly showed a depth of 15 feet. We suspect it found an uncharted rock. This is a nice cove, but the run up Ewin Inlet seems a little long. In 1996 Bligh Island was made into a provincial marine park.

Friendly Cove, at the mouth of Nootka Sound. The Nootka Light Station is in the background, mooring float in the foreground.

This totem lay on the ground a short distance from the mooring float at Friendly Cove. Photo by Bob Spanfelner.

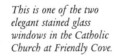

This is one of the two elegant stained glass windows in the Catholic Church at Friendly Cove.

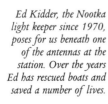

Ed Kidder, the Nootka light keeper since 1970, poses for us beneath one of the antennas at the station. Over the years Ed has rescued boats and saved a number of lives.

Friendly Cove. Use chart 3675. Friendly Cove is big and shallow and fairly protected, with good anchoring on a sand bottom. Nearly all the land ashore belongs to the Mowachat Band, and a fee ($10 in 1999, no credit cards) must be paid to the caretakers for landing or using the primitive log float that extends into the bay. The wharf with its float on the west side of the bay also is subject to the fee. In 1999 the wharf's float and its ramp had been damaged by storms and not yet repaired. We anchored out and took the dinghy to the log float.

Ray and Terry Williams, the caretakers, will tell you where you may and may not go, since much of the land is sacred to the band. A trail runs through camp grounds and above the ocean beach. It passes the Indian graveyard and leads to a lake that's good for swimming. Six rental cabins, small and rustic, are just beyond the lake. The spired Catholic church has two marvelous stained glass windows. They depict the transfer of authority over the area from Spain to England in 1790, and were a gift from the government of Spain.

This is an important stop. We recommend it.

Nootka Light Station. You can walk from the Friendly Cove beach to the Nootka Light Station on San Rafael Island. In a couple places the trail is not marked, but press on, knowing you can get there. Once up at the station, be sure to sign the guest book. In 1995 we were able to climb the tower to the light itself, but liability concerns have closed the tower to visitors.

Ed Kidder and his wife Pat have been the lightkeepers since 1970. Ed is friendly and outgoing, and if he has some time he'll show you around.

Nootka is a repeater station for Tofino Coast Guard radio, and has considerable radio equipment. Every 3 hours, from early morning until nightfall, the Nootka station reports weather conditions for the marine weather broadcast, including estimated wind strength and sea conditions offshore. The light station also is responsible for 5 aviation weather reports each day.

Thanks to the miracle of the Fresnel lens, the light uses only a 500-watt projector bulb to cast a beam that can be seen for 16 miles.

The Nootka Light Station and light keepers such as Ed Kidder are powerful arguments for retaining manned light stations along the coast. We urge anybody who would want to replace these resources with automatic equipment to skipper a small boat down this wild and hostile coast, relying on the light stations for accurate weather information. It is not enough to be a passenger or observer on such a voyage. The critic must *skipper* the small boat, and be responsible for the safety of the vessel and the people on board. *Then* he will understand why manned lighthouses are important.

Nootka Sound to Hot Springs Cove

Estevan Point • Hesquiat Harbour • Hot Springs Cove

HOT SPRINGS COVE is adjacent to Sydney Inlet, the northern entrance to the waters of Clayoquot Sound. Depending on the points of departure and arrival and the exact course chosen, the distance from Nootka Sound around Estevan Point, past Hesquiat Peninsula, and east to Hot Springs Cove, is approximately 30-31 miles. Hesquiat Bay can be a good spot to hole up if the westerly wind makes progress difficult after rounding Hesquiat Peninsula. In good weather, however, most cruising boats will proceed with single-minded determination to the delights of Hot Springs Cove.

Estevan Point. Use charts 3603 (1:150,000) and 3674. Estevan Point is the southwest corner of Hesquiat Peninsula, another of the headlands where winds and seas build and become confused. While Estevan Point can be ugly in a storm, in more settled conditions it does not present the degree of challenge found at Cape Cook or Cape Scott. In fog, the problem with Estevan Point is its low, flat terrain, which makes its shoreline a poor target for radar. The presence of rocks more than a mile offshore makes Estevan Point unforgiving for the navigator who is off-course. We recommend GPS or Loran.

From Nootka Sound, a rounding of Estevan Point first must clear Escalante Rocks and Perez Rocks, both of them on the west side of Hesquiat Peninsula. Unfortunately for the navigator, no single chart shows all of Estevan Point from Nootka Sound to Hesquiat Bay in large scale. You will be forced to plot your course on small scale chart 3603, which doesn't give much close-in detail. Once at Estevan Point, you can use chart 3674 to continue to Hot Springs Cove.

Especially with the lack of a single good large scale chart for the west side of Hesquiat Peninsula, the general advice, heard from several experienced Estevan Point navigators, is to give Estevan Point "lots of room." Give Escalante Rocks and Perez Rocks lots of room, too.

Hesquiat Harbour. Use chart 3674. Hesquiat Harbour is protected from westerly winds, and Hesquiat Bar, with 4 fathoms over it, knocks down the Pacific swell. Beware the bar in a southeasterly; storm seas can break over it. Rae Basin is a cozy nook in the northeast corner of Hesquiat Harbour.

Hot Springs Cove. Use chart 3674. Hot Springs Cove is one of the reasons cruising boats do the West Coast. The challenge of getting to Hot Springs is sufficient to make the reward—a soothing bath in comforting water (no soap, please)—worth the entire trip. In earlier times most visitors came the hard way, up from Barkley Sound or down the West Coast from Cape Scott. Now the springs are visited several times a day by tour boats and even float planes, carrying visitors who have arrived without effort at Tofino, and up they go to Hot Springs. An hour by high-speed boat and they are there.

We got to Hot Springs the old-fashioned way. We came around Cape Scott, and for us Hot Springs was a magnet. The cove is easy to enter. A study of chart 3674 shows that the mouth is open and the channel free of dangers. The marine park dock is approximately 1.7 miles farther into the cove from the springs themselves. Several mooring buoys lie a short distance from the park dock. You can anchor out in 4 fathoms, tie to a buoy, or lie along the dock. A charge is made if you use the public dock.

From the park, a 2-mile walk along a well-maintained boardwalk and path leads to the springs. In the past, visiting craft had a tradition of bringing a 2x6 plank about 4 feet long to add to the boardwalk. On the plank would be carved the name of the boat and the year

A beautiful sunset at the Hot Springs Cove Park dock. Boats offshore lie off mooring buoys or are anchored.

The hot springs provide a welcome soak. The temperature is just right, and several pools are available.

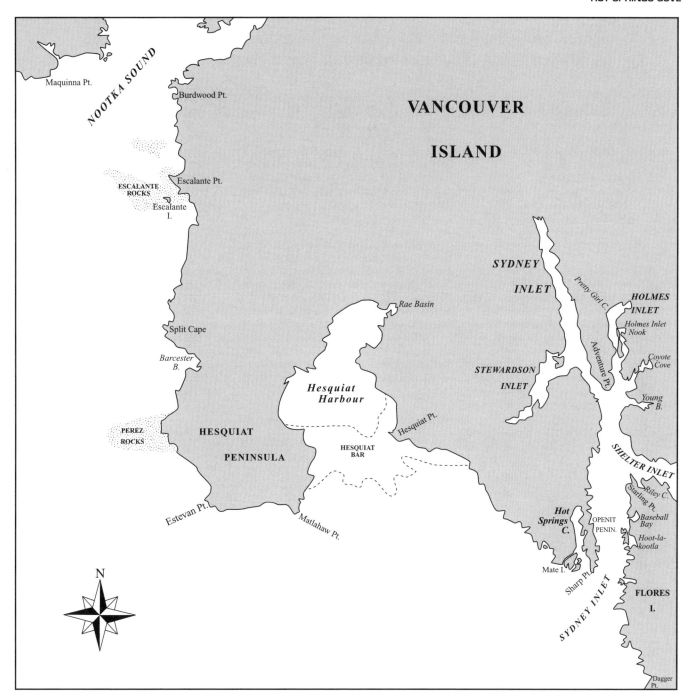

of the visit, plus other information (crew list, etc.) as deemed appropriate. Many of the planks showed remarkable artistic talent. A hike along the boardwalk was a hike down memory lane, a revisiting of earlier calls by boats one often knew.

Well, they rebuilt the boardwalk and replaced the old planks with pressure-treated wood that will resist rot forever. Gone are the planks of before. But the tradition lives on. Determined cruisers have brought woodcarving tools and carved their boats' names in the new planks. As before, some of the work is quite artistic, though not the same as what can be done over the winter in a workshop.

This hike to Hot Springs, through rain forest, is easy and beautiful. Toilets are avail-able at the end. The modest will find a pleas-ant changing room in which clothes may be doffed and a bathing suit put on. Tradition-alists will choose to enjoy the hot springs in the old way, without encumberance of bath-ing suit. That's a little awkward when 25 visitors have arrived by airplane or tour boat, all with bathing suits, and you, who have *earned* the right to a *traditional* hot springs soak (as op-posed to merely paying the fare), suddenly feel uncomfortable.

The kids from the village across the cove play at Hot Springs, in part (as Kincaid sug-gests) to further their study of anatomy, and in part to show off for the *touristas*. The braver young lads dive off the rocks into the surf. It's not Acapulco, but it's not bad. Watch your belongings. We lost a towel.

Dave Letson is the wharfinger at the park dock. Dave ties his handsome, 34-foot Farrell *Die Flyn* to the float, exchanges information with all who care to chat, and collects the fees. Dave used to run the bed & breakfast moored at Hot Springs Cove marine park, but in 1995 the structure burned to the water and was not rebuilt.

Hot Springs has campsites, often used by kayakers. During our 1995 visit, a kayak-borne fisherman brought several catches to the dock and gave them away. They included rock fish, sea bass, and coho salmon. He went out to the rocks just outside the cove, made a pass, and came back with his catch. Each time his line went in the water it came up heavy.

Clayoquot Sound

Sydney Inlet • Young Bay • Bottleneck Bay • Bacchante Bay • Sulphur Passage
Ahousat • Calmus Passage • Heynen Channel • Lemmens Inlet • Tofino

CLAYOQUOT SOUND is a series of inlets and passages that circle islands and indent Vancouver Island for approximately 20 miles along the coast. A boat could spend considerable time poking around in Clayoquot Sound without being exposed to ocean swells. The only town is Tofino.

Sydney Inlet. Use chart 3674. Sydney Inlet is the northern entrance to Clayoquot Sound. It lies adjacent to Hot Springs Cove, and leads approximately 11 miles back into mountains. The fairway is unencumbered by dangers. Sydney Inlet has several good anchorages. Rounding Sharp Point after leaving Hot Springs Cove, beware of two charted but unmarked offlying rocks. The first is fairly close to Sharp Point and easy to avoid. The second lies about 0.2 miles off. Most boats will choose to pass between the two rocks. Be sure you know where you are.

Hoot-la-Kootla. Use chart 3674. We're using Douglass's name for this otherwise unnamed cove, which lies on the west side of Flores Island, approximately 1.4 miles from Sharp Point. The cove is protected by a 190-foot island offshore. You'll see a beautiful white beach as you enter. Although the water is a little shallow near the beach, it's the prettiest spot in the cove. You could also anchor at the north end of the cove, behind the island. Do not attempt to enter the cove at the north end. It is foul.

Baseball Bay. Use chart 3674. Once again we'll use Douglass's name for a bay with no name on the chart. Baseball Bay is located about 0.25 mile north of the 190-foot island in Sydney Inlet. The entrance is shallow, and a charted rock lies in the entrance, just south of mid-channel. We divided the channel north of the rock in half, and entered "mid-channel." Least depth on our sounder was 12.5 feet near the bottom of a 3.6-foot low tide at Tofino.

Norma Bailey's marvelous store (no longer a store) once was moored in Baseball Bay. Now it is up on dry land in Ucluelet, at The Wreckage. See Ucluelet entry.

You can anchor in Baseball Bay.

Riley Cove. Use chart 3674. Riley Cove lies just east of Starling Point, on the northwest tip of Flores Island. It would not be our first choice for an anchorage. The cove is open and uninteresting, and a little deep for anchoring until close to the head. At the the head, Riley Cove is divided into two smaller coves, the

Reference only — not for navigation

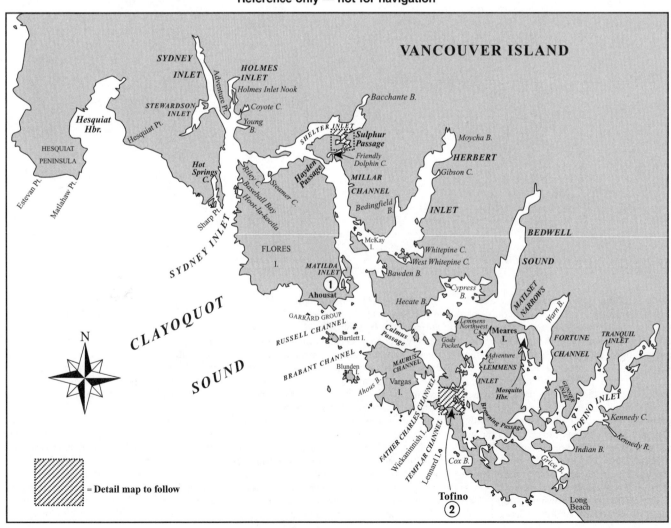

cove to the west having a sandy beach. A rock, not shown on the chart, lies just off the point that separates the two coves. A shoal extends from the east shore near the entrance of Riley Cove. Favor the west shore.

Young Bay. Use chart 3674. Young Bay, on the east side of Sydney Inlet, is a lovely place to anchor, although a little deep unless you get close to shore. The middle is 8-10 fathoms deep, but along the shore it's easy to find 6-7 fathom depths. You may want to run a stern-tie to a tree. On the south shore a stream connects with Cecilia Lake, ½ mile away. Dave Letson, the wharfinger at Hot Springs Cove, told us a trail leads to the lake, and that trout fishing there is good.

Enter Young Bay right down the middle, to avoid shoals that extend from either side. Once inside you will see a small islet with trees on it. Pass to the south side of that islet.

Bottleneck Bay (Coyote Cove). Use chart 3674. This is an otherwise unnamed lagoon that Watmough fell in love with. We think he had a particularly satisfying time there. Bottleneck Bay is located just north of Young Bay, east of Adventure Point. The entrance is narrow but deep, and inside the wonderful treed hills make the feeling of seclusion complete. Easy anchoring in 5 fathoms.

Holmes Inlet Nook. Use chart 3674. This is the little nook that lies behind the 66-meter island in Holmes Inlet. Like Watmough's Coyote Cove, the nook is completely private and surrounded by lush forest, only it is much smaller and very cozy. We'd predict that romance would be almost assured for any couple lucky enough to anchor for the night. A stern-tie would be comforting, but the shore is rock right up to the tree line. At low tide it would be difficult to secure the tie.

To enter, go behind the 225-foot island, past the oyster farm (wave to the farmer), and through the narrow channel to the nook. Watmough says the extremely narrow channel north of the nook can be run at high water. Dave Letson, the wharfinger at Hot Springs Cove, told us he's run that channel in a 33-foot sailboat at nearly all stages of the tide. We didn't try.

Shelter Inlet. Use chart 3674. Shelter Inlet, surrounded by high, beautiful mountains, lies east-west, and connects with Hayden Passage and Sulphur Passage, the quiet inside route through Clayoquot Sound. Shelter Inlet has only two good anchorages, Steamer Cove and Bacchante Bay. Of the two, Bacchante Bay is the more interesting.

Steamer Cove. Use chart 3674. Steamer Cove is on the north side of Flores Island, behind George Island. The small cove at the southwest corner of Steamer Cove is well protected and has easy anchoring depths. Unfortunately, the hillsides around the anchorage have been logged clean right down to the water, so the outlook is uninteresting. If you're looking for

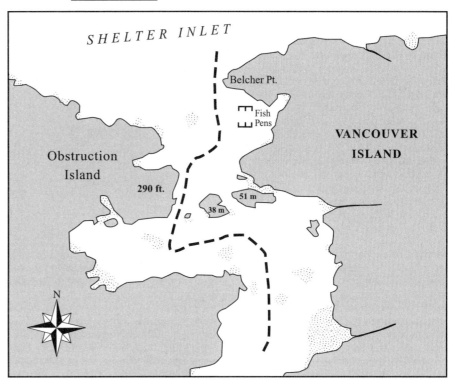

Surprise's route through Sulphur Passage

Reference only — not for navigation

shelter in a storm, the outlook would be irrelevant. Steamer Cove would serve excellently.

Bacchante Bay. Use chart 3674. Bacchante Bay, at the east end of Shelter Inlet, is a lovely spot, with high mountains to the west and an inviting grassy meadow at the head. The narrow, shallow entrance is hidden until you are close.

In 1995 we entered Bacchante Bay slowly, favoring the west shore, looking for a rock shown clearly on then-current chart 3648. We did not find the rock. In 1996, chart 3648 was replaced by chart 3674. The new chart 3674 does not show the rock, but it does show another rock more distinctly on the opposite shore. We saw *that* rock. *Lesson:* Sometimes, even the rocks move. It pays to buy new charts when they come out.

Bacchante Bay has ample room for several boats to anchor in 7-8 fathoms. Holding is excellent. If you run to the head of the bay, watch for abrupt shoaling off the meadow.

Hayden Passage. Use chart 3674, including inset. Hayden Passage is on the west side of Obstruction Island, and connects Shelter Inlet with Millar Channel. Tidal current predictions are shown with Hayden Passage as a secondary station in the Tide and Current Tables, Vol. 6. The flood sets southeast, the ebb northwest. Be sure to pass *west* of the red daymarked beacons (Red, Right, Returning).

Because the flood currents meet at Hayden Passage, you may find that the currents don't behave as predicted. The cautious passage would be at slack water. If transiting at other than slack, maintain a constant watch for current set, and crab as needed to stay in the channel.

Sulphur Passage. Use chart 3674. Sulphur Passage connects Shelter Inlet and Millar Channel on the east side of Obstruction Island, and is far more tortuous than Hayden Passage. The northern portion of Sulphur Passage is the tricky part. There, the channels twist and turn, and are bounded by submerged rocks. Douglass ran Sulphur Passage along the east side of the 38 meter island in the northern portion, and reported it to be a period of "high anxiety." *(See map above)*

With Douglass's experience in mind, we ran a dogleg course from north to south on the *west* side of the 38-meter island. We found it to be straightforward—albeit with careful planning and close cooperation between navigator and helmsman. For reference, we describe our course here, and show it in the accompanying sketch map. (Following this course on chart 3674 will help understanding. The directions North, South, East and West in this description are true, not magnetic.)

Our course left Belcher Point close to port and continued to the south corner of the charted fish farm. Then we crossed to a point of land northeast of a 290-foot hill on the west shore. (This hill was shown on the earlier chart 3648, but is not shown on the new chart 3674. The sketch map makes clear the course followed, however.) We turned south again and favored the west shore until we were past the 38-meter island and the tiny islet that lies south of it. Then we turned east, pointing the bow at the mouth of a creek that enters on the eastern shore. Once in the middle and approximately due south of the 38-meter island's western tip, we turned south once more and motored through. While other courses probably would have been safe, this course had the advantage

See area map page 242

of using easily-identified landmarks (the fish farm, the point under the high hill, the stream outlet, the tip of an islet) either as turning points or as points to aim at.

Friendly Dolphin Cove. Use chart 3674. Friendly Dolphin is Douglass's name for the cove that indents Obstruction Island, just inside the south entrance to Sulphur Passage. The cove is pretty, private and appealing. Anchor near the head in 7-8 fathoms, probably with a stern-tie ashore to control swinging. Dave Letson, the wharfinger at Hot Springs Cove, told us he thought this cove was "too deep and too buggy." We didn't see any bugs, but we weren't there in the early evening, either.

Matilda Inlet. Use chart 3674. Matilda Inlet indents the southeast corner of Flores Island, and is bounded on the east by McNeil Peninsula. Anchorage is possible near the head of Matilda Inlet. From the anchorage, a warm springs in Gibson Marine Park can be visited (best at high tide; at low tide it's a muddy hike) or a trek made to the beach. We have not visited the anchorage or the park, but Watmough did, and describes the area in fond detail. Recently, some friends made their way to the warm springs across the tidelands at low water, hence the advice above about visiting at high water. The Indian community of Marktosis is on McNeil Peninsula. Across the inlet and a short distance north are the store and fuel dock of Ahousat.

① **Ahousat,** General Delivery, Ahousat, B.C. V0R 1A0, (250)670-9575; fax 250-670-9697. Use chart 3674. Ahousat, with its general store, fuel dock, cafe and marine ways, is on the west shore of Matilda Inlet, at the southeast corner of Flores Island. Hugh Clarke is the owner. The store is a rough-and-ready place, but it has what you need: groceries, miscellaneous hardware, and marine supplies. No charts or liquor. Hugh's sister Pat Moseley has the cafe next door. Pat, sturdily built, has an air about her that sees the humor in life, but brooks no nonsense. We enjoyed lunch in the cafe in 1999, after buying bananas and other supplies in the store. In the cafe we noted a humorous sign, seen other places along the West Coast: "This isn't Burger King. You get it my

| If this is tourist season, why can't we shoot them? |

Sign in Miss Charlie's, *Walters Cove (see Kyuquot Sound chapter)*

| No Shoes, No Shirt, No Service Women Topless Okay |

Sign in window of (Ms.) Pat Mosley's Café, Ahousat

way or you don't get the son-of-a-bitch at all." Hugh's and Pat's father gave the Hot Springs Cove property (35 acres) to the Province so it could be a park.

West Whitepine Cove. Use chart 3674. Although unnamed, this delightful anchorage is called West Whitepine Cove by both Watmough and Douglass, and we shall do the same. West Whitepine Cove lies west of Whitepine Cove, near the mouth of Herbert Inlet. Entry is along the south side of the 67-meter island. We entered slowly, strongly favoring this island. Rocks were visible underwater and easily skirted. Once inside, the cove is lovely and protected. Bears are reported to frequent the south shore. We saw only one, briefly, some distance away.

A charted rock is in the cove, off the tip of the little peninsula that extends southwest from the 94-meter island. Although we anchored in the cove overnight, we did not see the rock, so before leaving in the morning we went to find it. We approached the approximate location slowly, but a cats paw of breeze ruffled the water, obscuring vision. As the cats paw passed we saw the rock, close to the surface and menacing. We put the helm over and the boat swung away. As we swung, the calm water behind the retreating cats paw revealed more of the submerged rock, growing closer. *It was as if the rock were swimming toward us.* Find the rock on the chart. When anchoring, stay away from it.

Gibson Cove. Use chart 3674. Gibson Cove indents the west side of Herbert Inlet, about 5 miles north of Whitepine Cove. Since Gibson Cove is not on the way to anyplace else, we suspect it sees few visitors. Those who do visit are in for a treat. The run up Herbert Inlet is even more spectacular than many other inlets along the coast. High, interesting mountains and rock walls line the shores. Deep alpine river valleys lead away into the mountains. Snowcapped peaks can be seen in the distance.

Gibson Cove is beautiful and protected, but a little deep for anchoring. We did find 6-7 fathom depths close to the south shore, and tested the anchor on 3:1 scope in 8 fathoms. The Bruce bit solidly, but if we had stayed we would have run a stern-tie to shore.

Quait Bay. Use chart 3673. Quait Bay is located on the east shore of Cypress Bay. Anchoring would be good just about anywhere in this bay, with its 6-fathom depths. The best spot, though, is in the little cove in the east corner, 1.5 fathoms. An uncharted rock may lie in the mouth of the two nooks at the back of this cove. We saw a red float there, and it looked yellow under the surface. The water was green and murky, and visibility was poor. Enter Quait Bay on the northwest side of the 45-meter island, favoring the northwest shore. The chart makes the course clear. A luxury resort is tied to the western shore of Quait Bay. You can't miss it once you're in.

Matlset Narrows. Use chart 3673. Matlset Narrows run to a maximum of 4 knots on spring tides, the flood setting east. Sailing Directions warns of strong tide-rips in the vicinity of the Maltby Islets at the east end of the narrows. We ran the narrows against an ebb, saw definite current activity, but had no problem. We suspect any tide-rips would be on a flood.

Calmus Passage to Heynen Channel. Use chart 3685; 3673. The route from Millar Channel to Heynen Channel via Calmus Passage and Maurus Channel is the beginning of shallower water. The channels are well marked by buoys and beacons. The depth sounder becomes an important navigation tool, and the navigator must stay alert and know

Eden, *Portland, Oregon, takes a break at Ahousat. From here, with full tanks and a good weather forecast,* Eden *departed for the run down the Washington coast and home.*

the vessel's position at all times. In tight navigation among rocks, it's easy to stay alert. But in these wider, more open-feeling areas, concentration is more difficult. It's no trick at all to go aground in these waters. Large-scale chart 3685 is extremely helpful.

Lemmens Inlet. Use chart 3685; 3673. Lemmens Inlet indents Meares Island, just a few miles from the town of Tofino. Be sure to use large-scale chart 3685 while navigating around Tofino and into Lemmens Inlet. The entry channel to the inlet is amply deep, but bounded by drying flats. Once inside, you have your choice of one superb anchorage (Adventure Cove), and two other possible anchorages.

Adventure Cove. Use chart 3673. Adventure Cove, where Capt. Robert Gray built the small schooner *Adventure* in 1792, is a delightful anchorage, filled with history. The beach is easy to land on. While walking in the woods one can almost feel the presence of Gray's Fort Defiance and the shipbuilding activity. Strips of survey tape mark remnants of the fort. Though now overgrown with large trees, we distinctly felt that in the past *something went on here*. Watmough and Douglass describe the history well. Anchor in 2-3 fathoms. A floathouse is in the north part of the cove.

Lemmens Northwest Cove. Use chart 3673. Lemmens Northwest Cove is Douglass's name for this anchorage in the northwest corner of Lemmens Inlet. It is identified on the chart by the 38-meter island and the fish pens in the mouth. Some drying rocks obstruct the entrance. Locate them and then run in midway between the rocks and the 38-meter island. Once inside, you'll find find good anchoring depths and adequate protection. We were not charmed by the cove, however. We found it somewhat open and uninteresting.

Gods Pocket. Use chart 3673. Gods Pocket is the cove that lies northwest of Lagoon Island, on the west side of Lemmens Inlet. Protection is good, with anchorage in 4-5 fathoms. Two very nice float homes occupy the cove, however. You'll be anchoring in their front yards.

Browning Passage and Tsapee Narrows. Use chart 3685 (larger scale, *much* preferred); chart 3673. Please, please, buy and use chart 3685 for this run. Rocks abound and shoals threaten. The larger scale chart 3685 will show you the way. If you are coming from Heynen Channel or Lemmens Inlet, the course will be clear: pass west of Morpheus Island and east of buoy Y35, and continue down Browning Passage and through Tsapee Narrows. Note that currents on springs can run to 5 knots near Morpheus Island and 4 knots at the narrows. Go slowly. Look ahead and identify all buoys, islands and visibile rocks well in advance. Done this way, the passage should not be difficult.

If you are leaving Tofino, you could run out Deadman Channel and follow the course described above. Or, you could leave buoy Y29, opposite the 4th St. public dock, to starboard, and run toward Arnet Island until you can safely turn to run south, along the west side of Riley Island. Favor Riley Island to pass clear of the rocks shown on the chart. Once south of Riley Island you are in Browning Passage.

FORTUNE CHANNEL

Fortune Channel connects Tofino Channel with Matlset Narrows, which in turn connect with the waters of upper and western Clayoquot Sound. You can choose from three good anchorages in Fortune Channel: Windy Bay, Heelboom Bay and Mosquito Harbour. Chances are, you won't see much boat traffic in this area. We anchored in Heelboom Bay at the end of July, and from late afternoon until we departed the following morning we saw just two boats. One was an aluminum crew boat that went down the far side of the channel. The other was a sailboat that had anchored in Mosquito Harbour.

Windy Bay. Use chart 3685 or 3673. Windy Bay is really beautiful. The south shore is heavily forested, and the north shore is sheer rock wall. The saddle at the head of the bay probably lets westerly winds in, but they would have no fetch to build up seas. Anchor in 5-6 fathoms.

Heelboom Bay. Use chart 3685 (larger scale, preferred) or 3673. Heelboom Bay, located near the south end of Fortune Channel, is a good anchorage. Lush evergreen forest surrounds the bay. We found outstanding holding in 6 fathoms. Approaching, favor the east shore and stay well clear of rocks off the western shore. One of these rocks is considerably detached from the shoreline. Chart 3685 helps understanding.

Mosquito Harbour. Use chart 3673. While not as scenic and cozy as Heelboom Bay, Mosquito Harbour is big and open and easily entered. Anchor in 3 fathoms behind the Blackberry Islets. Approach on either side of the Wood Islets, but from Fortune Channel you'll probably approach by way of Plover Point or Dark Island. Kelp marks rocks off the north end of Dark Island. Note the location of Hankin Rock. We would trend toward Plover Point before turning to enter Mosquito Harbour.

TOFINO INLET

Not much boat traffic here, and in our view only a few attractive anchorages, as follow.

Island Cove. Use chart 3673. Island Cove is easy to enter around either side of Ocayu Island. Study the chart to avoid the rocks that lie off the southwest shore of the approach. Unfortunately, the hillsides surrounding Island Cove have been logged down to the water's edge, and the cove isn't very pretty. Anchor in 7-8 fathoms, close to the west shore.

Gunner Inlet. Use chart 3673. It's tricky to get into Gunner Inlet, and not very scenic when you make it. Approach favoring the east shore, and use a small low islet with a distinctive white top as your leading mark. Make an S turn around the islet, and follow the chart in. The low hills around the bay have been clear-

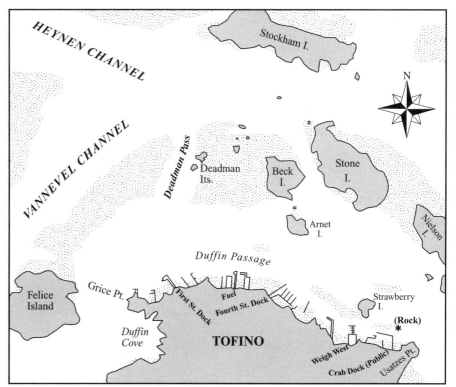

Tofino

Reference only — not for navigation

See area map page 242

cut, but are growing back.

Tranquillo Cove. Use chart 3673. Tranquillo Cove is the name Douglass gave this otherwise unnamed cove on the east side of Tranquil Inlet, near the head. This cove is secluded and beautiful. The rock wall on the north side has been strikingly sculpted by glaciers. Favor the northern side of the entry to avoid a shoal that extends from the point of land on the south side. Anchor in 3 fathoms.

Cannery Bay. Use chart 3673. Cannery Bay, at the mouth of the Kennedy River, is easy to get into and despite it flat terrain, rather pretty. We like the nook just to port as you enter. Anchor in 2.5-3 fathoms.

Kennedy Cove. Use chart 3673. Kennedy Cove is easy to enter by favoring the 68-meter island. A float house is in the east part of the cove. Anchor wherever you like in 3-5 fathoms. It's a pretty spot.

② **Tofino.** Use chart 3685 (larger scale, preferred);3673. If you come from up-island, Tofino will be your first major town since Port McNeill or Port Hardy, and it's busier than either of them. During the summer season Tofino's bustle and busy-ness may surprise you. We found that pedestrians hurried past but didn't look us in the eye. The dogs seemed nervous. It's quite a contrast to the pace up-island, where strangers say hello to each other, and the dogs, when they move at all, do so only to accept a morsel of food or a scratch behind the ears. After growing accustomed to the charms of life up-island, Tofino, with its commerce, fast traffic and and loud engines, can cause culture shock. Welcome to the city.

As long as you're in the city you might as well spend some money. You can choose from several good restaurants, the kind that serve meals without french fries. Waggoner reader Linda Hill tells us that lunch at the Rain Coast Cafe was the most outstanding meal of their 1997 trip. Gift shops—at last!—are available for mementos and presents. The Co-op store, close to the waterfront, is a complete supermarket. It also carries clothes. Showers are available at the Paddler's Inn. The laundromat has enough machines to do all the ship's laundry in one cycle.

From seaward, enter Tofino via Templar Channel. While chart 3673 gives a good overall view, for the close navigation needed we

A drying rock, shown here, blocks the eastern end of the Tofino waterfront. Don't go beyond the last public dock.

Tofino's 4th Street Public Dock can be crowded and intimidating. But it's close to shopping, and rafting is common.

strongly recommend large-scale chart 3685. Note how the buoyed fairway twists and turns to avoid shallows. Be sure to identify each buoy as you proceed, and leave the buoys off the proper hand.

From the north, enter Tofino via Deadman Pass. Deadman Pass is narrow and bounded on both sides by drying flats. Be sure to use large-scale chart 3685. Note that while *you* may be returning to Tofino, the buoyage system in Deadman Pass is not. As you head south in Deadman Pass you will leave the red buoys to starboard. *(See map page 245)*

Stay close to the docks once at Tofino. A serious drying reef lies a short distance off. Currents can run strongly along the docks, so watch carefully as you land.

You can tie up at one of several docks. The public dock near Grice Point is closest to the Co-op and the liquor store, but is busy day and night with water taxis and locals restocking their dwindling stores. Not for nothing is this dock called the Whiskey Dock. Moorage *may* be available at the fuel dock. It tends to be full during the busy season, but you can check.

② **4th Street Public Dock.** Use chart 3685. The best moorage prospect in Tofino is the 4th Street Public Dock, well-signed, and convenient to the commercial district. Watch the current. This moorage is kind of rough, and is off-putting to many cruisers. It can be full of fish boats rafted three deep in places. In all likelihood, you will be forced to raft off of somebody, fish boat or yachtie.

In 1995 we found a good spot with ease. In 1999, though, the docks were packed and we were not so lucky. But we decided we were

in Tofino, and darn it, we were going to make this thing work. We took temporary moorage at the dock adjacent to the launch ramp (don't even consider tying up there for the night, at least on the side that faces the launch ramp), and walked around the docks until we found a neatly-kept fish boat with a crewmember on board. Could we raft for the night? Absolutely. We could raft off his boat or a boat behind him that wasn't going anywhere. We took his boat. When when we worked our way in, he took our lines and helped make us fast. That's how you have to do it.

Farther east, Weigh West may have space, but the docks often are taken by their sport fishing guests. The easternmost public dock is called the Crab Dock. In 1995 the Crab Dock was a little funky for our tastes, but in 1999 most of the derelict boats were gone, and it looked better. It's a longer walk to the commercial district, however.

Do not proceed eastward past the Crab Dock. A major rock blocks the channel at that point.

② **Method Marine Supply,** Box 219, 380 Main Street, Tofino, B.C. V0R 2Z0, (250)725-3251, fax (250)725-2111. Open all year. Gasoline, diesel, lube oils, stove oil, propane, water, ice, divers' air, vacuum waste oil disposal. Moorage has electrical hookup, but moorage often is fully reserved in busy season. This is a modern, well-run facility, with a good chandlery that carries a wide range of equipment and supplies, including sport fishing gear, bait, some groceries, foul weather wear, and charts.

Barkley Sound

Amphitrite Point • Ucluelet • Broken Group • Effingham Bay
Turtle Bay • Wouwer Island • Pinkerton Islands • Port Alberni
Robbers Passage • Bamfield • Cape Beale • Nitinat Narrows

Charts	
3602	Approaches to Juan de Fuca Strait (1:150,000)
3603	Ucluelet Inlet to Nootka Sound (1:150,000)
3646	PLANS – Barkley Sound
3647	Port San Juan and Nitinat Narrows
3668	Alberni Inlet (1:40,000) Robbers Passage (1:10,000)
3670	Broken Group (1:20,000)
3671	Barkley Sound (1:40,000)
3673	Clayoquot Sound, Tofino Inlet to Millar Channel(1:40,000)
3674	Clayoquot Sound, Millar Channel to Estevan Point (1:40,000) Hayden Passage (1:20,000) Hot Springs Cove(1:20,000) Marktosis (1:10,000)

This is the Wreckage, in Ucluelet. It wasn't open when we were there, but it looks fascinating.

The CANADIAN PRINCESS, with charter boats alongside, is a permanent fixture in the Ucluelet Small Craft Harbour.

Clayoquot Sound to Ucluelet. Use chart 3673; 3603; 3671. It is approximately 19 miles from Lennard Island, at the southern entrance to Clayoquot Sound, to whistle buoy Y42 offshore from Ucluelet Inlet. This 19 miles crosses the ocean face of the Pacific Rim National Park, but since you'll probably be about 3 miles out you won't see much of the park. Sailing Directions says to stay 2 miles off the coast; Watmough likes 3 miles. So do we. Plot a waypoint for whistle buoy Y42, go 3 miles offshore from Lennard Island, turn left, and make for the buoy. In fog, radar is a big help in avoiding all the fish boats that work these waters. Absent Loran/GPS and radar, in fog we would go out to at least 30 fathoms and follow the 30-40 fathom curve to buoy Y42.

Amphitrite Point. *Use chart 3646. We italicize this instruction.* Amphitrite Point, at the end of the Ucluth Peninsula, can present a challenge. The essential navigation problem is to get around Amphitrite Point while staying well clear of Jenny Reef, shown on the chart, yet staying off the Amphitrite Point shoreline. The problem is made more difficult in fog, when the radar may lose buoy Y43 against the shoreline.

Carolina Passage is the entry suggested by Sailing Directions, except in thick weather, when Carolina Channel can be too rough for safe navigation. The outer entrance to Carolina Channel is marked by whistle buoy Y42, about 0.5 mile offshore. The channel leads past bell buoy Y43, which lies but 300 meters off the rocky shore. In reduced visibility, life can get interesting when you're trying to raise buoy Y43. If you have trouble seeing buoy Y43 against the rocky shoreline, the light struc-

ture on the east side of Francis Island could serve as a leading mark.

As you approach Carolina Passage, leave whistle buoy Y42 close to starboard, and turn to a course of 030° magnetic to raise buoy Y43. After passing close south of buoy Y43, Sailing Directions suggests using the summit of South Beg Island as a leading mark. It should bear approximately 075° magnetic. Run approximately 0.2 mile until the eastern extremity of Francis Island is abeam, then turn to round Francis Island and enter Ucluelet Inlet.

In 1995, we noticed a steady parade of commercial fish boats that ignored whistle buoy Y42 and instead entered along the Amphitrite Point shoreline, leaving the 1.6-meter-deep shoal to starboard and buoy Y43 to port. We would like to try that route sometime, especially if the weather were good. We would wait to follow a parade of local boats, though, just to be safe.

Ucluelet. Use chart 3646; 3671. (Pronounced "you-CLOO-let.") The channel leading into the village of Ucluelet (pop. approximately 1800) is well buoyed. Following the rule of Red, Right, Returning, you will have no problems. Spring Cove, to port a short distance inside the channel, is where fish boats used to discharge their catches. The plant deep in

Fish boats line the dock at Ucluelet.

the cove is closed and the docks posted with No Trespassing signs.

In 1995 three fuel docks were located in the channel, all vying for fish boat business. With the closing of commercial salmon fishing, only the Petro Canada fuel dock remains. Small public docks are on the town side of the inlet. They are used by large commercial fish boats, and none of them appeals to us. The Ucluelet Indian Band has developed a marina on the east side of the inlet, across from town.

The Ucluelet Small Craft Harbour is the principal marina, and is the one we recommend. It lies west of the north tip of Lyche Island. The Oak Bay Marine Group's *Cana dian Princess,* a large white ship made into a floating hotel and restaurant, is moored in this marina permanently. The ship is part of a major sportfishing resort that has several charter boats. The boats depart early in the morning, filled with eager (if bravely overhung) fishermen, and return in the afternoon. At night the entertainment areas on the *Canadian Princess* are lively.

Another marina to consider is Island West Fishing Resort, on the west side of the inlet just before the turn to the small craft harbor. The docks are built almost entirely for trailerable boats. They have no designated guest dock, so call ahead by telephone or radio.

Showers are available at the West Coast Motel, adjacent to the small craft harbor. Several nice gift shops are in the area, including an excellent Indian gallery and gift shop. (Who cares if it's "tourist art?" We bought a beautiful bead basket to present to Marilynn Hale on our return home.) As you walk toward town you'll pass The Wreckage, one of the most interesting-looking exhibits we've seen. The floating store Norma Bailey used to run in Clayoquot Sound is there. No one was around so we can't tell you much more than that.

In town, halfway up Ucluelet Inlet, Pio-neer Boat Works has a marine railway for haulout and repairs. Their chandlery, next to the ways, has a good selection of marine supplies, commercial and sportfishing tackle, and charts. Around the winding streets of Ucluelet you will find gift shops, art galleries, eateries, a large Co-op grocery and general merchandise store, and other essential services. It's a pleasant hike out the road to the Coast Guard station at Amphitrite Point. We've walked it and we recommend it.

In Ucluelet Inlet, Lyche Island can be passed on either side. If passing on the west side (the town side), check chart 3646 and leave the buoys and beacons off the proper hands.

④ **Petro Canada (Eagle Marine, Ltd.),** Box 430, Ucluelet, B.C. V0R 3A0, (250)726-4262; eves. (250)726-7166. Open 7 days a week all year, summer 0600-2100, winter 0800-1700. Gasoline, diesel, stove oil, lubricants.

① **Ucluelet Small Craft Harbour,** Box 910, Hemlock St., Ucluelet, B.C. V0R 3A0, (250)726-4241; fax (250)726-7335. The floats have 15 amp power, water and washrooms. The outside basin, before entering the large main basin, has two floats marked for recreational and commercial boats. While they are inviting, we continue inside. Docks A & B are marked for commercial boats only; docks C, D & E are for recreational and commercial boats. The facility is completely protected, well maintained, and quiet. It's where we tie up.

④ **Island West Fishing Resort,** Box 32, Ucluelet, B.C. V0R 3A0, (250)726-7515; fax (250)726-4414. Monitors VHF channel 69. Call ahead. A busy and well-run sport fishing resort, often fully reserved a year ahead for August. They have limited 15 amp power, washrooms, showers, laundry, pumpout, portapotty dump, launch ramp, marine supplies, charts, ice, and deli take-out. Also an excellent pub.

BARKLEY SOUND

Use chart 3671, 3670, 3646. Barkley Sound is named after English Captain Charles William Barkley, who in 1787 sailed into the sound on his ship *Loudoun,* which he had illegally renamed *Imperial Eagle* (Austrian registry) to avoid paying a license fee to the East India Company. With Capt. Barkley was his 17-year-old bride Frances. Capt. Barkley came to trade with the Indians for furs. Other than naming, he left no structures, no trace of his presence.

Barkley Sound is roughly square in shape, measuring 15 miles across its mouth and approximately 12 miles deep, not counting the 20-mile-long canal to Port Alberni. The sound is dotted with rocks and islands, and the waters are famous for their excellent fishing. A cruising boat could spend weeks in Barkley Sound, fishing, exploring, and moving from one nook to another.

During the summer months fog often lies just offshore. It can sweep in to penetrate the sound in minutes, even with no wind evident. It is essential, therefore, that the navigator know the vessel's position at all times. GPS or Loran will prove useful in foggy conditions, but be aware that their circles of accuracy (approximately 100 meters) are insufficient for close navigation through narrow passes bounded by barely-submerged rocks. Radar is a big help. Most boats cruising Barkley Sound, large and small, now have radar. Even with electronic help, the navigator simply must remain alert and aware.

If approaching from the south, such as from the Washington coast or the Strait of Juan de Fuca, you'll probably touch first at Bamfield, where customs can be cleared.

If approaching from up-island, you will probably enter Barkley Sound from Ucluelet. If you pick a course to run across Sargison Bank from Ucluelet to the Broken Group, beware of a rock that lies approximately 0.7 miles east of Chrow Island. The rock is shown on the chart not with a rock symbol, but by a depth of 0.5 meters. It is easy to overlook while scanning the chart for hazards.

In Barkley Sound you will find superb exploring everywhere: Pipestem Inlet, the Pinkerton Islands, Julia Passage, the Chain Group, the Deer Group, and the famous Broken Group. Settled summer weather makes it possible to anchor in any of hundreds of coves or nooks and explore by dinghy. (We do not cover all the areas mentioned above, an unfortunate consequence of limited exploration time. Other references—especially Douglass, 2nd ed.—are excellent resources. In the end,

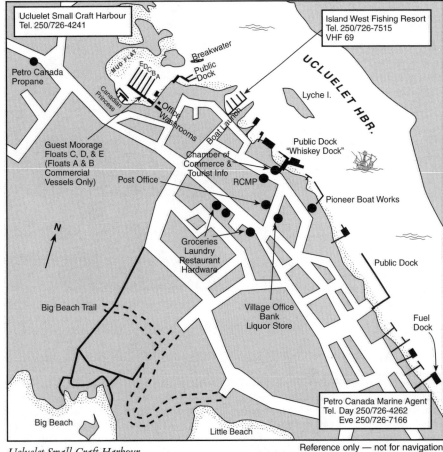

Ucluelet Small Craft Harbour

Reference only — not for navigation

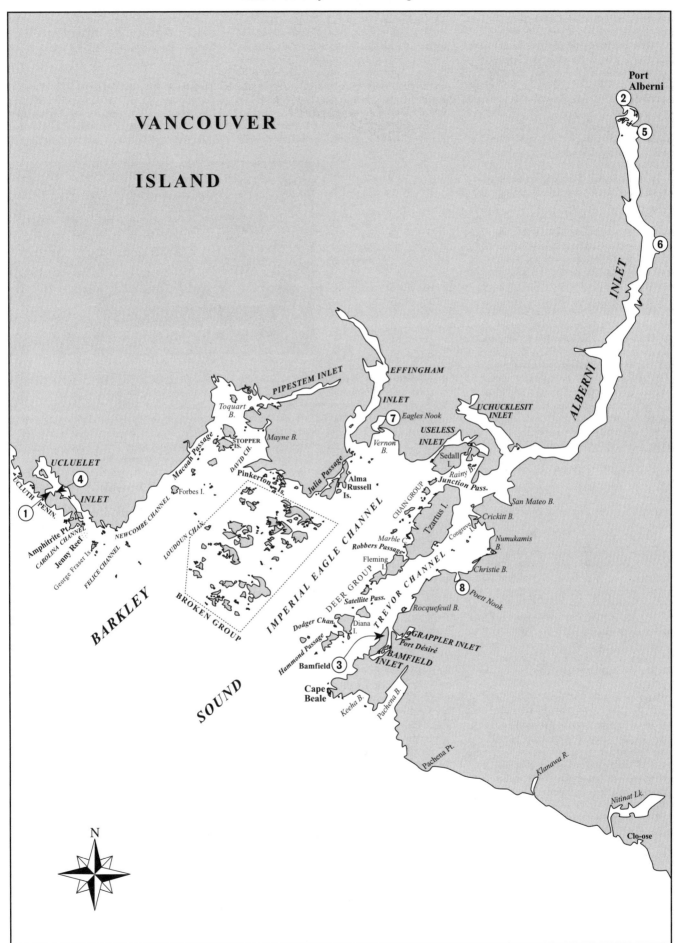

VANCOUVER

ISLAND

Port
Alberni

ALBERNI

INLET

PIPESTEM INLET

EFFINGHAM

INLET

UCHUCKLESIT
INLET

Toquart
B.

Eagles Nook

USELESS
INLET

Mayne B.

Vernon
B.

Sedall
L.

STOPPER
IS.

Macoah Passage

DAVID CH.

Rainy B.

Junction Pass.

San Mateo B.

UCLUELET

Pinkerton Is.

Julia Passage

Alma
Russell
Is.

CHAIN GROUP

Crickitt B.

Forbes I.

INLET

Tzartus I.

Congreve I.

Numukamis
B.

Amphitrite Pt.

NEWCOMBE CHANNEL

LOUDOUN CHAIN

Marble C.

Robbers Passage

Christie B.

CAROLINA CHANNEL

Jenny Reef

George Fraser Is.

FELICE CHANNEL

BROKEN GROUP

IMPERIAL EAGLE CHANNEL

DEER GROUP

Fleming
I.

Satellite Pass.

TREVOR CHANNEL

Poett Nook

Rocquefeuil B.

BARKLEY

Dodger Chan.

Diana
I.

GRAPPLER INLET

Port Désiré

BAMFIELD
INLET

Hammond Passage

Bamfield

SOUND

Cape
Beale

Keeha B.

Pachena B.

Pachena Pt.

Klanawa R.

Nitinat Lk.

Clo-ose

N

your own inquisitiveness and derring-do will determine the range of your exploring.)

While off in the dinghy, we would carry charts in a plastic sleeve, pencil, dividers, a handheld VHF radio with spare battery pack, and a handheld GPS, just to be safe in the event of fog. If the dinghy were not equipped with a compass, we would carry a handheld compass. Everything but the charts could be placed in a small fabric bag. In even the smallest dinghy, an out-of-the-way spot could be found to tie the bag.

In all likelihood this navigation emergency kit would never see use. But if we were suddenly overtaken and disoriented by fog (easy to do), the GPS could tell our position, the dividers and pencil could help find the position on the chart, and the compass could point us in the right direction. The radio would make life less stressful for us and those back at the anchorage.

WESTERN BARKLEY SOUND

Use chart 3671. The western part of Barkley Sound, from Ucluelet to the Pipestem Inlet and over to the Pinkerton Islands, is relatively open and easily run. As long as you stay in the middle, Newcombe Channel and Macoah Passage present no problems. They lead to the Stopper Islands, and beyond them to Pipestem Inlet. Pipestem Inlet is where there await the magical falls at Lucky Creek.

Stopper Islands. Use chart 3671. The Stopper Islands are quite pretty, and beg exploration by dinghy or kayak. Anchor (temporary only, we think) between Larkins Island and the large island.

Pipestem Inlet. Use chart 3670. Pipestem Inlet is beautiful and deep, bordered by high mountains and lined with lovely forest. With one possible exception, though, the only anchoring possibilities are near the mouth. That exception is the little cove near the head, behind the 32-meter island. We saw a 20-foot trailerable boat anchored in there and stern-tied to shore, but didn't have the courage to take the 37 in. Maybe this cove is okay—we don't know.

Near the mouth of Pipestem Inlet, the good anchorages are behind **Bazett Island**, either southwest or southeast, or behind **Refuge Island**. If you choose the Bazett Island, the southwest anchorage is deep in the southwest cove, off the mouth of the drying inlet colored green on the chart. The southeast anchorage is in the little thumb-shaped inlet, or along the adjacent shore, stern-tied.

The Refuge Island anchorage is directly north of Refuge Island, a bit east of the 16-meter island. Our anchor didn't hold solidly on our first attempt, but it bit very hard on the second. At night we could hear the chain dragging across rock on the bottom. This anchorage and the Bazett Island anchorages are within easy dinghy commute to Lucky Creek.

Lucky Creek. Use chart 3670. John Schlagel, fearless longtime explorer, did not *suggest* that we see Lucky Creek, he *instructed* us to see Lucky Creek, and he was right. This is a window-of-opportunity trip, and the window corresponds with high tide. We suggest taking the outboard-powered dinghy up to the falls an hour before high water, and coming out an hour after. The entrance is directly across Pipestem Inlet from Bazett Island. After crossing

These are the falls at Lucky Creek. Warm pools are above. Recommended.

the shallow entry (thoughtfully bordered by meadow grass and wildflowers), the channel winds through marvelous mature forest, with overhanging cedars. The deeper part of the channel tends to follow the outside of the bends, river-style. The water is clear. We kept our eye on the bottom. Close to the falls the bottom shoaled, and we sought out the narrow, U-shaped channel to follow.

Suddenly, before our eyes was a storybook waterfall, directly out of Walt Disney's imagination. Seeing that waterfall, we knew Tinker Bell was about; she was just too quick for us to see. When you go, tie the dinghy off to the side and climb up to a series of warm bathing pools. Enjoy. But remember that just as Cinderella had to run when the clock chimed 12, you cannot stay. If you tarry too long the falling tide will close you in.

You probably won't be alone at Lucky Creek. The lodges and resorts in the area are fully familiar with Lucky Creek's charms, and the boat drivers know the channel well. We got to Lucky Creek a half-hour after high tide, and the guests were all leaving—at top speed in the narrow waterway that was unfamiliar to us. They came right at us and swooped past, all smiles and happiness as we splashed through their wakes. No matter, the trip was worth it.

Entrance Inlet. Use chart 3670 (larger scale, preferred) or chart 3671. Entrance Inlet indents Vancouver Island at the northeast corner of Mayne Bay. Anchor in the outer basin in 7 fathoms. During the day you will have boat traffic from the fishing resort in **Cigarette Cove.** You can anchor in Cigarette Cove, but the resort takes up much of the space. The entry is narrow and bounded by rocks. If you pay attention, you will have no problems.

Mayne Bay, Southeast Cove. Use chart 3670 (larger scale, preferred) or chart 3671. This

cove is open to the west, but is good in settled weather. Anchor in 6-7 fathoms. At low tide we saw two people digging for clams on the beach.

Pinkerton Islands. Use chart 3670. Far from the wildness of the outer islands, the Pinkerton Islands lie north of the Broken Group, next to Vancouver Island. The Pinkertons are small and protected, with narrow channels, and are ideal for gunkholing. Watch for rocks. The easiest anchorage is in the cove northwest of Williams Island. Unless several boats want to share it, no stern-tie should be required. A study of the chart will suggest a number of other possibilities, most of which will require a stern-tie to shore.

UPPER BARKLEY SOUND

Jane Bay/Franks Bay. Use chart 3671. This bay, known locally both as Jane Bay and Franks Bay, is not named on the chart. It is located at the back of Barkley Sound, connected by a narrow but safe passage with Vernon Bay at Lat 48° 59.80'N Lon 125°08.80'W. Anchor, carefully, near the head before the flats shoal too much. Or tie up at the small dock at **Eagle Nook Lodge**, (tel: (250)723-1000; VHF 06) immediately to starboard as you enter the bay. The lodge's exterior is of Spanish-style archicture, but the interior is traditional lodge, English-style. Cruisers welcome. Bob Spanfelner, our crew in 1999, marked his 60th birthday when we were there. We treated him to an excellent lunch in the dining room.

Useless Inlet. Use chart 3668 (1:10,000 insert). The entrance to Useless Inlet is made interesting by a series of large rocks that are covered except at lower stages of the tide. The rocks were covered when we were there, and the wind rippled the water, making the rocks difficult to see. The obvious safe entry is along the north shore, to avoid the rocks in the middle. We tried that route twice but didn't feel comfortable, so for us Useless Inlet will have to wait for another day. *Something* is going on in there, though. We saw several trailerable sport fishing boats roar in and out of Useless Inlet, running between the rocks in the middle. They knew where the channel was; we didn't.

Alberni Inlet. Use chart 3668. Alberni Inlet begins between Chup Point and Mutine Point, where it meets with Trevor Channel and Junction Passage. The inlet continues some 21 miles into the heart of Vancouver Island to Port Alberni. Alberni Inlet is narrow and high-sided, with little to interest the cruiser along the way. Tidal current flows are less than 1 knot both directions, but the surface current can flow as fast as 3 knots when wind and current direction are the same. Boats without a reason to go to Port Alberni seldom make the trip, preferring instead to experience the manifold pleasures of Barkley Sound.

In the summer, an up-inlet thermal wind develops at 1300 ("You can set your clock by it," says a friend in Port Alberni), and will increase to 25-30 knots by mid-afternoon. The wind produces a short, uncomfortable chop. We would run Alberni Inlet in the morning.

Port Alberni. Use chart 3668. Port Alberni is a bustling paper mill and sawmill town, with full services including a hospital. The first place visiting boats can find moorage is the breakwater protected public dock at China Creek, about 6 miles south of Port Alberni. China Creek Provincial Park, next to the marina, has picnic sites and a launch ramp. Close to downtown, Port Alberni Fisherman's Harbour public dock has moorage. Haulout to 100 feet is available at Alberni Engineering and Shipyard. Three major fuel docks are located near Fisherman's Harbour, downtown. At the mouth of the Somass River the Clutesi Haven Marina has moorage. The Port Alberni Harbour Commission, which operates the China Creek and Clutesi Haven marinas, is developing another marina, with pleasure craft in mind, downtown. Development is in early stages, and completion is not expected for a couple years.

A good selection of marine supplies is available in Port Alberni.

In Port Alberni you can visit a nice little museum with changing West Coast history exhibits; take rides on an old steam logging train (summertime only); enjoy free logging shows sponsored by McMillan Bloedel (summertime only); and take tours of the paper mill and sawmill.

⑥ **China Creek,** (250)723-9812. Monitors VHF channels 16 & 18A. Open all year. Gasoline & diesel, propane, 15 amp power, washrooms, showers, laundry, garbage drop. Has 2460 feet of moorage, 4-lane launch ramp.

⑤ **Fisherman's Harbour, Port Alberni,** 2750 Harbour Rd., Port Alberni, B.C. V9Y 7X2, (250)723-2533. Monitors VHF channels 18A & 68. Telephone customs clearance 24 hours (250)723-6612. Open all year, 2700 feet of moorage, power, water, washrooms, garbage drop. Fisherman's Harbour is adjacent to downtown Port Alberni, with all the services of downtown close by.

② **Clutesi Haven,** (250)724-6837. Monitors VHF channels 16, 18A & 68. Open all year, gasoline at the fuel dock, 2460 feet of

In Effingham Bay we had delicious hor d'oeuvres with these three boats. They were going up-island, we were going down-island. Lots of anchoring room, fabulous sunset.

moorage, power, water, garbage drop, 4-lane launch ramp. Clutesi Haven is located behind a breakwater near the mouth of the Somass River, and is best suited to boats 25 feet or less. Transient space is on a first-come, first-served basis. This marina is a popular launching spot for trailerable boats. Facilities, including hotels, pubs, and liquor store are within walking distance. Groceries are 1-2 miles away.

BROKEN GROUP

Use large scale chart 3670; chart 3671. The Broken Group islands extend from the wind-and-wave-lashed outer islands to peaceful islands deep inside Barkley Sound. The Broken Group is part of the Pacific Rim National Park, to be preserved in its natural state in perpetuity. For many Northwest boaters, a holiday spent in the Broken Group is the fulfillment of a lifelong dream.

Boats visiting the Broken Group for several days will find dozens of little nooks and bights to put the hook down, depending on weather and the mood on board. Both Watmough and Douglass describe a number of them in their books. The major anchorages are Effingham Bay, Turtle Bay, and Nettle Island. Of these, Effingham Bay probably is the most popular.

Effingham Bay. Use chart 3670. Effingham Bay is large, pretty, and protected. On the nights of our visits we have shared the bay with 10-20 other boats, yet we didn't feel crowded and everyone had room to swing. The chart shows the entrance. Anchor in 5-8 fathoms, good holding. Sunsets, seen out the mouth of the bay, can be spectacular.

Take the time to dinghy ashore and cross to the ancient Indian village site on the east side of Effingham (Village) Island. The trail begins at the head of the little thumb of water at the head of Effingham Bay. This tiny inlet dries at low tide. The trail leads through lush and mature forest. It is generally easy, but a little primitive in places. A person with walking difficulties probably shouldn't try it. The village site, on the eastern shore, is mystical. Widely spaced trees suggest the location of the main village, and the large midden, with shells poking out of it, proves a long and populous habitation. The place feels ee-

rie—not threatening, but eerie. A sea cave is located there, but inaccessible at high tide, and we were there at high tide. Late in the day the view eastward from the beach—the sea, with the mountains of Vancouver Island beyond painted in low reddish light—is inspiring. Bob Spanfelner, our crew in 1999, walked out onto the beach and stood, feet apart, facing this scene. He raised his arms wide and brought them together above his head, clapping loudly. "*Author! Author!*" he cheered.

Effingham Island

An ancient Indian village site is on the east shore of Effingham Island, reached by a short trail that leads from the bight in the southeast corner of Effingham Bay. There are perhaps a hundred such village sites in Barkley Sound; together they supported as many as 10,000 people.

A terrace at the village site is actually a 100-yard-long midden, 10 feet deep, where for centuries Indians ate shellfish beside their fires. Nurselogs have hemlocks growing out of them. On closer examination, the nurselogs are not round like trees, but squared, identifying them as longhouse beams.

Climbing around the big rocks and drift toward the ocean here isn't easy, but the seascape is worth it. Farther on, at lower tides, sea caves are accessible. One of the caves is 100 feet deep. Be careful to explore this area at low tide only. A rising tide can trap you.

—Norm Culver

Reference only — not for navigation

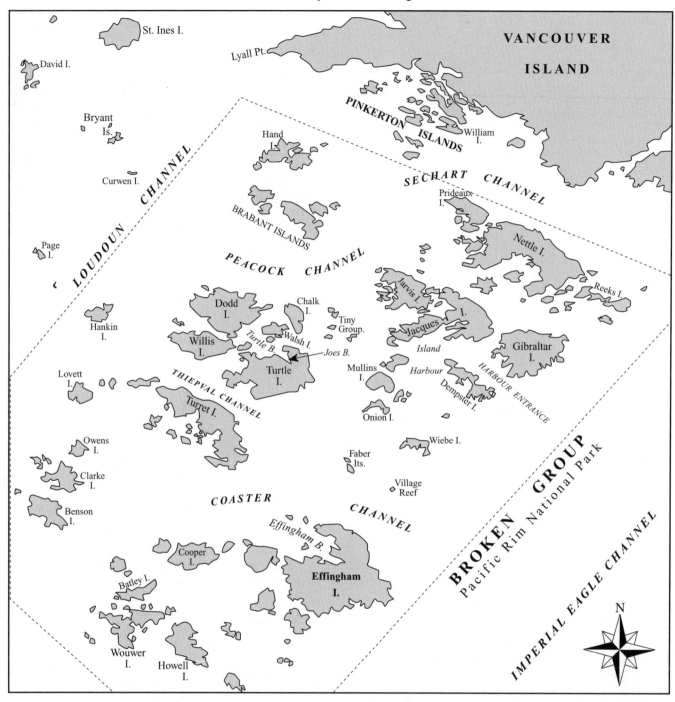

Benson Island. Use chart 3670. In settled weather you can take anchorage off the east shore of Benson Island, in the cove opposite the water faucet icon on the chart.

Clarke Island. Use chart 3670. Temporary or settled weather anchorage can be taken off the east side of Clarke Island, opposite the water faucet icon on the chart.

Turret Island. Use chart 3670. The cove formed by the 36-meter island on the southwest side of Turret Island is okay for anchoring, but in two separate motorings-through, we have found it not very inviting.

Turtle Bay. Use chart 3670. Turtle Bay is a local name for the bay formed by Turtle Island, Willis Island, and Dodd Island. Joes Bay, an appendage of Turtle Bay, indents Turtle Island. It is the little nook where Salal Joe, the Hermit of Barkley Sound, made his home.

The best entrance to Turtle Bay is from the north, off Peacock Channel, between Dodd Island and Chalk Island. A study of the chart shows the entrance channel bounded by rocks and drying rock outcroppings along the way. A careful entry, proceeding slowly and identifying the hazards, will bring you in safely. Those who have been in a few times know where the rocks are and understand that the rocks don't move. They roar right in.

Anchor in 4-5 fathoms on a mud bottom, good holding.

Nettle Island. Use chart 3670. Nettle Island has three good anchorages, one in the large bay that indents the southern shore, and the other two in the channel between Nettle Island and Reeks Island to the east. In Nettle Island's large bay we prefer the eastern portion, off the park ranger's float cabin. The center of the bay is a little deep (8-10 fathoms, depending on state of tide), but you can find 3-5 fathom depths near the shore north of the ranger's cabin.

Watmough describes two other anchorages along the east side of Nettle Island, opposite Reeks Island. These nooks will hold a couple of boats each, and Watmough says they are delightful. The charted rocks are easy to identify and avoid.

2000 Waggoner Cruising Guide

The Ranger floathouse at Nettle Island is a clearing house for Barkley Sound information.

boat by dinghy, you may find the water literally aglow with the phosphorescence of scurrying fish. *[Culver]*

EASTERN BARKLEY SOUND

Limestone Bay. Use chart 3668. Limestone Bay, located at the mouth of Uchucklesit Inlet, has satisfactory anchorage in 2 fathoms, with some protection. A nice float house is tied to shore immediately to port as you enter. A float that once was in the bay is gone. Use the southwest entrance only.

Poett Nook. Use chart 3671. Poett Nook is on the eastern shore, at Lat 49° 53'N. It doesn't look like a nook when you see it. Poett Nook is a spacious, rather pretty bay, with good anchoring in 4 fathoms. The entry is narrow but deep. The Poett Nook Marina, a large sport fishing resort, is on the eastern side of the bay.

⑧ **Poett Nook Marina,** 2178 Cameron Dr., Port Alberni, B.C. V9Y 1B2, (250)724-8525. Gasoline at fuel dock, washrooms, showers. No power at the dock. This is a busy smallboat sportfishing resort, with 160 RV/camping sites and berths for 177 boats. Maximum length 26 feet. Most boats launch at Port Alberni or China Creek. Owners: Flo and Stan Salmon.

Robbers Passage. Use chart 3671 and large-scale chart 3668. Robbers Passage leads between Fleming Island and Tzartus Island in the Deer Group, and is a likely route for boats bound between points near the head of Barkley Sound and Bamfield. A rock that dries 1 meter lies in the western approach to Robbers Passage. Although it is clearly charted, people we met at the Port Alberni Yacht Club told us that this is one rock that moves. They were serious. They warned us to give that rock a wide berth, so we're warning you. The S-shaped channel leading into Robbers Passage requires close attention, but with close attention it is safe. A study of large-scale chart 3668 will make the route clear. Inside the passage, the Port Alberni Yacht Club has its floating clubhouse and docks, and the welcome mat is out for visiting boats.

Across the bay from the yacht club lies an awful black ship. It is a former Greenpeace vessel that once patrolled the seas to protest whaling. If you take the dinghy around to the inshore side, you'll see on the superstructure a collection of badges (like "kills" on the sides of WWII fighter planes) of vessels of various countries rammed, damaged, and sunk. Were the Greenpeacers do-gooders or pirates? For several years this ship lay abandoned at Ucluelet, inhabited by squatters who burned interior woodwork to keep warm and generally made a mess of everything (according to what several people told us). The vessel was purchased at auction and moved to Robbers Passage, where it used for mussel farming.

Port Alberni Yacht Club. We urge our readers to spend at least one night at the Port Alberni

Outer Islands. Use chart 3670. The outer islands of the Broken Group are marked by twisted trees, the result of relentless onshore winds, especially in the winter. If your needs include the desire to navigate "at the edge," the outer islands can satisfy that need. Here, you'll have your opportunity to run in wind and fog, with the Pacific Ocean swells beating against the rocks. Navigate carefully. The low islands are easy to get mixed up. Rocks and reefs are charted, but they're everywhere. This is beautiful, raw country. The kayakers have it best. The favored anchorage is at Wouwer Island. We have not tried it, but old friend Norm Culver has.

Wouwer Island. Use chart 3670. Wouwer Island is breathtaking, both in its scenery and gunkholing. At mid-tide or higher, most boats can make it through the slit between Batley Island and Wouwer Island. A bow watch only will scare you. Once through, and when you're

breathing again, anchor in the middle of either of the next two little bays on Wouwer Island.

Nearly exposed to the ocean like this, the principles of anchoring are important. Use a heavy anchor and plenty of scope. Check throughout the entire 360-degree swing to be sure you have enough water at low tide.

From the deepest indent in Wouwer Island, a short trail (a salal tunnel, actually) leads to a beach that faces the Pacific Ocean. The beach is choked with drift logs tangled like a mass of Tinker Toys. At the south end of the island, the shorelines around the headlands offer teeming tidepools, carpets of mussels, roaring sea lions, and storm-torn trees with eagles perched in them.

Allow a few hours for this apparently short exploration, and carry a flashlight. The return trip is easy to get mixed up, and the salal tunnel is so black that once I almost spent a night in it. If it's dark as you return to your

The former Greenpeace ship in Robbers Passage still carries badges of sinkings and rammings in its zealous career.

Welcome to the delightful Port Alberni Yacht Club facility in Robbers Passage. A recommended stop.

Yacht Club. The facility is clean and well-maintained, and the folks are friendly and helpful. They have a wealth of local knowledge to share. Be sure to walk the beautiful trail around the peninsula behind the yacht club. The moorage charge is modest, and goes back into the facility. All are welcome; no yacht club membership needed.

At several PAYC members' insistance, we took the dinghy across Robbers Passage to the Shahowis Canadian King Lodge, where we met the owners, Wayne and Jennifer Wenstob and their daughters. Wayne is an architect, a very creative architect. The lodge is built largely from timbers salvaged from a wrecked barge, and from wood taken from their own property. It reflects ingenuity, good taste and playfulness. Wayne and Jennifer are enormous good fun, so don't be a sourpuss. Dinners are family-style: you eat what's on the table, and we're told it's terrific. Unfortunately, they couldn't fit us in.

Fleming Island. Use chart 3671. The day was sunny with only a gentle breeze, so we left the boat at the yacht club and motored the dinghy around Fleming Island. The impossibly rugged shoreline is dotted with sea caves. Wayne Wenstob told us some of the caves extend far into the rock. For thousands of years the Indians in Barkley Sound put at least some of their dead in bentwood boxes and hid them in sea caves. Wayne told of crawling on his belly, flashlight in hand, and coming on centuries-old boxes, secreted away. The floors of the sea caves are made of gravel or small round boulders. Kick aside some rock and uncover a skull. We were fascinated by the stories, but didn't follow them up.

We did, however, ease the dinghy through a narrow cleft in the rock and up to the mouth of one cave. The opening loomed above us, and we could see the floor of small boulders rise and disappear in darkness. The rock walls of the cleft were covered with orange and purple sea stars. Other neon-hued sea life (sorry, we don't know our marine biology and won't try to fake it) waved in the surge. The word *impressed* does not begin to describe the effect on us.

On its northwestern side Fleming Island is indented by a large cove, with a much smaller cove, almost blocked by reefs, in the western corner. This smaller cove is blessed with a perfect white beach, the kind you see in movies. Bob Spanfelner, our crew on that trip, said his wife Delia would enjoy that beach, and one day he meant to bring her back to see it. In her honor, we named the spot Delia's Beach.

Temporary or fair weather anchorage can be taken at the western end of Fleming Island, between it and Sandford Island. The trees in this area are twisted and windblown. The rocks are jagged and unworn. On a nice day this is beautiful country.

A cove protected by a small islet is on the east side of Fleming Island, and a trailer is perched haphazardly on the hillside overlooking the cove. A hermit named Stinky lives in the trailer—Stinky and his collection of dogs

that run to the shore, barking angrily. Discretion overruled exploration. Our dinghy departed Stinky's cove.

Fleming Island could be one of many islands in Barkley Sound. It just takes some exploration to see what each island has. Our log records the Fleming Island circumnavigation as a "life-altering experience." The log doesn't exaggerate.

Marble Cove. Use chart 3671. Marble Cove is on the west side of Tzartus Island, and often is mentioned as a good anchorage (we would choose instead the cove 0.5 miles north). A float house is on the north side of the Marble Cove. Anchor in 4-5 fathoms off the gravel beach on the island opposite the float house.

Tzartus Cove. Use chart 3671. Tzartus Cove is the name Douglass gives to this excellent anchorage, about 0.5 mile north of Marble Cove. Rocks extend from both shores, so go right down the middle when you enter. Anchor near the head in 4-5 fathoms. Sea caves are nearby.

Bamfield Inlet. Use chart 3671; large-scale chart 3646. Bamfield Inlet is open and easy to enter. The village of Bamfield is along the shores of the inlet. Several public docks are located on each side. Commercial fish boats have priority, but space usually can be found for pleasure craft. At the head of the inlet, past Rance Island, is a quiet basin where you can anchor. *Sailboaters note:* a cable with 17 meters (55 feet) of clearance crosses the channel between Rance Island and Burlo Island.

③ **Bamfield.** Use chart 3671; large-scale chart 3646. If you arriving from outside Canada, stop at the Customs dock and clear by telephone 1-888-CANPASS (226-7277). The Bamfield General Store, with liquor agency, is in the same area. Gunn's Gallery, Babe Gunn, sculptor, is next door to the General Store. Her work in stone is extraordinary.

The village of Bamfield covers both sides of the inlet. They call the inlet "Main Street." The west side of the inlet is not connected by road with the east side. You cross by boat or you don't cross. A boardwalk runs along the homes and businesses on the west side, and

folks get around by walking.

A small Red Cross Outpost Hospital is located on the west side. It is set up to treat illness or injury, deliver babies, and dispense medication. The hospital is operated by registered nurses, and a visiting physician calls on a regular schedule. They work closely with the Coast Guard for emergency helicopter transport when needed. A fee schedule accommodates non-Canadians who need medical attention.

The east side of Bamfield Inlet has roads that tie its businesses and homes together. They connect with the 60-mile-long dirt logging road that leads to Port Alberni. We like the west side better, but the east side has a good pub, two small convenience stores, motels, a deli and cafe, the fuel docks, and, on Port Désiré, a launch ramp. The trail to Cape Beale begins on the east side of the inlet.

For fuel, see the Bamfield Kingfisher Marina, about halfway down the inlet, or Hawkeye Industries (formerly, Ostrom's), just north of Rance Island .

The large building near the entrance on the east side of the inlet houses the Bamfield Marine Research Station. The station is owned by five universities in British Columbia and Alberta, and began operation in 1971. Visitors are welcomed, and tours are offered Saturdays and Sundays during the summer, no charge. This facility once was the eastern terminus of the transpacific cable that connected North America with Australia. Its first message was sent on November 1, 1902; its last message was sent in 1959.

③ **Bamfield Kingfisher Marina,** Box 38, Bamfield, B.C. V0R 1B0, (250)728-3228. Fuel dock, open all year, with gasoline, diesel, tackle, bait, ice, scuba air.

③ **Hawkeye Industries Fuel & Chandlery,** P.O. Box 7, Bamfield, B.C. V0R 1B0, (250)728-3231. The fuel dock closed in July, 1999, but is scheduled to be re-opened for the 2000 boating season. Gasoline, diesel, lubricants. They also plan to have a small store and coffee shop open. This is the site of the famous but now closed Ostrom's machine shop, which had just about everything mechanical and could make what it didn't have. They hope to turn

We took the dinghy through this narrow cleft to the mouth of the sea cave. Inside, the cave floor of small boulders rose into blackness. Photo by Bob Spanfelner.

The Northern B.C. Coast

the machine shop, with its old tools and machines, into a museum.

Hawkeye also has the Bamfield Trail Motel, with dock, on the north side of the government wharf and floats, a short distance north of fuel dock. Call for reservations at the number above.

Grappler Inlet. Use chart 3671; large-scale chart 3646. Grappler Inlet joins near the mouth of Bamfield Inlet, and leads to **Port Désiré**, a protected anchorage with a launch ramp and a public dock. Although beautiful, Grappler Inlet is surrounded by homes. If it's solitude you seek, you will not have found it yet.

Cape Beale. Use charts 3602; 3671. Cape Beale, surrounded by offlying rocks, marks the eastern entrance to Barkley Sound. Trevor Channel exits at Cape Beale, and is the safest entry to Barkley Sound in thick weather or poor visibility. Seas can be difficult off Cape Beale when an outflowing current from Barkley Sound meets the longshore current outside. The collision of currents, combined with wind and shallow depths around the cape, can make for heavy going.

The usual advice is to round Cape Beale in early morning, before the summertime westerly wind gets up. During our 1995 visit, however, the weather reports indicated calm conditions in the afternoon. We departed Barkley Sound and rounded Cape Beale at approximately 1330, and enjoyed absolutely flat conditions in clear weather all the way to Sooke.

In 1999 we departed Bamfield at 0600, and had light air conditions all the way to Port Townsend. We carried on, and at 1810 reached Winslow, where Bob Spanfelner's wife Delia was waiting aboard their boat—12 hours and 10 minutes for the 150-mile run from Barkley Sound to central Puget Sound. The experiences affirm the importance of listening to the weather reports and making plans not only to fit typical conditions, but conditions as they exist on a given day. (A fast boat can be helpful, too.)

Nitinat Narrows. Use chart 3647. Nitinat Narrows connects Nitinat Lake with the the Pacific Ocean. Entrance to the narrows is obstructed by rocks and a shallow bar. An onshore wind can cause breaking seas over the bar. A crossing of this bar and negotiation of the narrows to Nitinat Lake is considered a supreme Northwest navigation challenge by a small number of adventurers.

Each year during quiet weather a few boats do make it through. We admit that we are far too cautious to risk our boat or peace of mind on such an adventure, so we cannot report our experiences at Nitinat Narrows—there are none.

Douglass, however, took his Nordic 32 tug across the bar, through the narrows, and into Nitinat Lake. His guidebook *Exploring Vancouver Island's West Coast, 2nd ed.* describes the experience, including the comment that his crew on that trip refused ever to try it again.

Northern B.C. Coast, General. The northern limit of most cruisers' explorations seldom exceeds a line that runs from Wells Passage on the mainland to Port Hardy on Vancouver Island. North of this line, Queen Charlotte Sound is a natural barrier. It takes time, a strong boat, and good navigation skills to proceed further up the coast. To be fair, a lifetime of cruising could be spent south of that line, with complete satisfaction.

But, to those with the time and inclination, the coast north of Wells Passage is a treasure. The scenery is magnificent, the population small and self-sufficient, and the fishing exceptional. You can anchor in bays with no

Two fish boats at anchor on a misty morning in Rescue Bay.

other boats, and the boats you do meet along the way often become instant friends. This is the part of the coast where you'll find the famous names: Nakwakto Rapids, Rivers Inlet, Fish Egg Inlet, Hakai, Bella Bella, Ocean Falls, Butedale, Fiordland, Ivory Island, Grenville Channel, Prince Rupert. It's a coast filled with history and opportunity. And if it's wilderness you seek, you can find it there.

Be prepared to be self-reliant. Between Port Hardy and Prince Rupert, only one marina or public dock (Ocean Falls) sees yachties as its primary market. All the others are set up for work boats, and if it weren't for the work boats we yachties would have few places to tie up. Be glad the facilities are there, and don't complain if they're a little rough. Don't expect marina help to come down to take your lines as you land. And don't expect work boat skippers to rush over to help. They figure if you have a boat you should be able to handle it. If a crowd of helpers were to gather, yachtie style, as a work boat were landing, the skipper probably would be insulted. We have found, however, that when asked, work boat crews are happy to help. But they won't question your boat handling abilities by rushing to help when not invited.

Bring cash. Americans, bring Canadian cash. Most facilities and business are set up to take Visa or Master Card, but not all. Forget about ATM services. There aren't any. You'll still have telephones, but not as often. BC Tel (Air Touch shares with BC Tel) has the best cellular phone

coverage, although it is gone shortly after Port Hardy is left behind, and doesn't re-emerge until Chatham Sound. Land line pay phones are in Bella Coola, Shearwater, New Bella Bella, Ocean Falls, and Klemtu.

Insurance. Most vessel insurance policies don't cover these waters without a special rider. Contact your insurance company to extend coverage.

The boat. You won't find many little boats cruising the northern coast. Our first *Surprise*, a Tollycraft 26 powerboat, is definitely at the small end of the scale. It's common to see jerry cans filled with extra fuel or water lashed to the rails or in the cockpits. Radar and GPS are affordable and should be considered standard equipment. (We found that Loran's longitude calculations were off by about 1 minute in the Prince Rupert area. The error grew less as we moved south. Latitude was close enough for safe navigation.) This is remote country. The boat should be in top mechanical condition. Complete spares should be carried.

You'll commonly be anchoring in 10-15 fathoms, sometimes deeper, so you'll need ample anchor rode. For its trips in 1996 and 1997, our first *Surprise* carried an additional 250 feet of rope rode tied to its usual 300 feet, a total of 550 feet. While we never got into the second 250 feet, there were times when we were happy to know we had a good reserve. The present *Surprise* carries 300 feet of chain. Many anchorages along this coast are deep, with shallower water too close to shore to swing in comfort.

Bottoms often are rocky. Because of its resistance to bending and its ability to set and hold in nearly any bottom, including rock, Bruce has become the anchor most often seen. CQR plow anchors also are popular. You don't see as many Danforth style anchors. While Danforth style anchors are good in sand, they can have trouble setting in rock, and once wedged, are easily bent.

Be sure to carry at least two anchors. We carry three. The bow and stern anchors are Bruce, and the backup is a big Danforth that

A traveling peddler from an earlier era. The LILLIAN D, with Barry Mark and Jane Stewart and their two small sons, travels the coast supplying it with everything from flashlight batteries to souvenir sweatshirts to microwave ovens. They take orders one trip, bring merchandise back on the next.

Dogs and hiking. Shorelines often are steep and rocky along this part of the coast, with fewer good places to walk the dog or take a walk yourself. While we have seen pets on board, many cruisers feel it's just too difficult to get a dog ashore. People who enjoy regular walks and hikes will find their options limited, as well. All agree that the coast is beautiful, but some would welcome more opportunity for exercise.

Repairs. While it's best to carry complete spares and know how to fix whatever goes wrong, nobody can be ready for everything. Parts and mechanics can be flown in anyplace along the coast. Between Port Hardy and Prince Rupert the only full-service shipyard is at Shearwater.

came with the boat. The intrepid explorer and author Don Douglass used a CQR primary anchor and Danforth lunch hook, and author Hugo Anderson used a Bruce primary anchor on his several trips. Bill Kelly and Anne Vipond, who have cruised and written extensively on the coast, use a CQR primary anchor. Many commercial fishermen use Northill anchors, but Northills tend to be hard to store on cruising boats. Whatever the anchors chosen, be sure they are big, strong, and ready to deploy.

Fuel and water. Up to Klemtu, fuel is plentiful, both diesel and gasoline. Rivers Inlet has fuel at Duncanby Landing and Dawson's Landing, and you can get fuel at Namu, Shearwater, New Bella Bella and Klemtu. Fuel is available at Hartley Bay, halfway between Klemtu and Prince Rupert. Until 1998, the 140-mile run between Klemtu and Prince Rupert was without fuel stops, and this kept many gasoline-powered boats from making that run. Now that it is roughly 70 miles between fuel stops, more gasoline-powered boats can explore the northern B.C. coast.

Water is available all along the way. Some if it may be tinged brown from cedar bark tannin, but people have been drinking cedar water for decades with no ill effects. Ocean Falls has sparkling clear water, although in 1998 it failed purity tests and boiling was recommended. Until you hear differently, assume that Ocean Falls water is for boat washing only. New Bella Bella, Klemtu and Hartley Bay have installed multi-million-dollar water treatment plants that deliver unlimited amounts of clear, pure water.

Weather. Bring clothes for all conditions, from cold and rainy to hot and sunny. Expect wet weather at least part of the time. The residents of Ocean Falls call themselves "The Rainpeople" for good reason. June 1999 was so wet that a few boats quit their cruise.

Plan for clouds down on the deck, fog, rain (both vertical and horizontal), and storms. Leave enough slack in your schedule to anchor through serious foul weather before moving on. Be sure the boat is well-provisioned, and equipped with generator or battery power to spend several days at anchor in one location.

Plan on sunshine, too, maybe a lot of sunshine. It can get *hot.* Bring bug spray, and equip the boat with screens on hatches, opening ports, and windows.

Cabin heat will make the trip much more enjoyable. Many boats use a Red Dot-style truck heater to warm the boat while powering, and a second heat source while at anchor. Depending on the boat, secondary heat can be electric (generator required), diesel furnace, diesel heater, oil galley stove, wood stove, or propane catalytic heater. The Waggoner boat *Surprise* has a diesel furnace and two electric heaters. We use them.

Sailboaters will need some sort of cockpit protection, from a companionway dodger to full cockpit enclosure. A way *must* be found to keep the cabin warm and dry, or you'll be miserable.

Marinas. There aren't many marinas on this coast. In Rivers Inlet, Duncanby Landing and Dawson's Landing have guest moorage, fuel and supplies. Depending on deliveries, New Bella Bella and Klemtu have a good grocery selection. Shearwater, near New Bella Bella, has moorage, a restaurant, and repairs. Ocean Falls has ample moorage. Hartley Bay has a small amount of moorage. New Bella Bella and Klemtu have public docks, but they are busy and exposed to the wash of passing boat traffic, and would not be our first choice.

If you're in a jam, you could get help at one of the sportfishing lodges along the coast, but remember that their business is serving their fly-in guests, not visiting yachties. Some of the lodges, however, do welcome visitors. Big Spring resort in Home Bay, Rivers Inlet, is friendly. The Hakai Beach Resort in Pruth Bay usually can take drop-ins in its dining room, and often can arrange 1-day fishing charters. They are even advertising for such trade in this guidebook.

Charts and reference books. The Canadian Hydrographic Service has more than 65 charts that cover the coast from Wells Passage to Prince Rupert. Most boats will make the passage with fewer than 65 charts, but the number of charts on board a well-found boat likely will be closer to 65 than 35. Despite their cost ($20 Cdn.), buy every chart, both small-scale and large-scale, in the area you plan to cruise. Include a few extra charts for unplanned side trips, unless your schedule calls for a straight passage up the main route (Interstate 5, as it is sometimes called). It takes a capital investment to cruise this coast safely and enjoyably. Several times on our explorations Marilynn Hale has said—sincerely—"Thank you, Bob, for having the correct chart." That's the sort of appreciation every skipper needs from the crew.

Tides and currents are shown in newly published Canadian Tides and Currents, Vol. 7, (the purple book). North of Cape Caution you'll want Sailing Directions, British Columbia Coast (North Portion).

Most boats carry a copy of *Marine Atlas, Vol. 2.* The charts in the atlas are out of date, and many of the place names have changed, but the course lines are helpful. The book is a good quick reference.

The most complete guidebooks are *Exploring the Inside Passage to Alaska* (now out of print), and *Exploring the North Coast of British Columbia,* both titles by Don Douglass and Réanne Hemingway-Douglass. Other useful books include *Secrets of Cruising – North to Alaska,* by Hugo Anderson; and *How to Cruise to Alaska Without Rocking the Boat Too Much,* by Walt Woodward. Woodward's book is now out of print, but many copies are around. You probably can borrow one. Another interesting book is Iain Lawrence's *Far-Away Places,* an introspective and romantic description of 50 anchorages on the northwest coast.

We also recommend a subscription to *Pacific Yachting,* published in Vancouver, B.C. It is a well-done monthly magazine with special emphasis on boating on the B.C. coast.

Get them all, books and magazine. No single publication can capture the range of conditions, approaches, intricacies and history of this amazing coast.

How to Cross Queen Charlotte Sound

Use charts 3547, 3548, 3549, 3550, 3598, 3921, 3934. Not all charts listed may be needed, depending on the route chosen.

NORTH OF VANCOUVER ISLAND, Queen Charlotte Sound is an imposing challenge to boats that wish to explore the waters of the central and northern B.C. coast. Queen Charlotte Sound seas can be high and steep, the result of shoaling from 100+ fathoms off the continental shelf, to 20-70 fathoms in Queen Charlotte Sound itself. The problem is made worse when outflowing currents from Queen Charlotte Strait, Smith Sound, Rivers Inlet and Fitz Hugh Sound meet the incoming ocean swells.

The "typical" summer weather pattern calls for calm early mornings followed by a westerly sea breeze rising in late morning or early afternoon. By late afternoon gale force winds are not uncommon. When wind and swell meet outflowing current, Queen Charlotte Sound can be ugly. Windstorms do come up. Often they last three days. Caution dictates that when the wind is blowing, you wait.

Usually, one of three routes is chosen to cross Queen Charlotte Sound, depending on whether departure is from Vancouver Island or from the mainland side. We will describe each route as if a northbound passage is contemplated.

PINE ISLAND ROUTE

This is one of two routes taken from Vancouver Island (the other is the middle route). Most boats will provision and fuel at Port McNeill or Port Hardy, then overnight at God's Pocket in Christie Passage, Port Alexander in Browning Passage, or in the cove between Staples Island and Kent Island in the Walker Group. Assuming calm conditions in the morning, an early departure will leave enough time to cross before the sea breeze comes up.

The route leads westward in Gordon Channel to Pine Island, then northward past the tip of the Storm Islands, past Egg Island, to Cape Calvert, Rivers Inlet or Smith Sound. This route will give Cape Caution an offing

of 1.5-2.5 miles.

Gordon Channel is a principal passage for commercial vessels. Be sure to display a radar reflector. In thick weather or fog, radar and GPS are extremely useful. Especially in reduced visibility or fog, most commercial traffic can be avoided by crossing Gordon Channel to the Redfern Island/Buckle Group side, and favoring that side to Pine Island.

Harry Kerr, the friendly and knowledgeable proprietor of God's Pocket Resort, advises that early morning fog should not hold you back. GPS will tell you where you are, and radar will let you see other vessels. When the fog lifts the wind will fill in. If you wait you will miss your chance.

Walker Group. Use chart 3549. A wonderful cove between Kent Island and Staples Island in the Walker Group makes an excellent jumping-off point for a crossing of Queen Charlotte Sound via the Pine Island route or the middle route. Approach from either side. Anchor in 3-4 fathoms. Perfect protection. Ample room for you and all your friends.

MIDDLE ROUTE

A commercial fisherman at Duncanby Landing suggested a middle route across Queen Charlotte Sound. This route passes north of the Storm Islands, rather than going out to Pine Island. The Storm Islands knock down the swell, and reduce the time spent with an uncomfortable motion. We tried this route and it worked well. But it was on a quiet day, when anything would work well. Assuming a northbound passage, here is the route:

From the east end of Goletas Channel (such as off the mouth of Hardy Bay), run northwest to leave the Gordon Islands to starboard and Heard Island to port. Our route took us between the 57-meter island and the two 56-meter islands at the western end of the Gordon Islands.(chart 3549).

Proceed across Gordon Channel and out Bolivar Passage. Davey Rock buoy N32, with its quick flashing red light, makes a good turning mark. Continue northwest past Farquhar

Bank to the vicinity of Lama Shoal (charts 3549 & 3550).

Turn westward to a course that leaves Dominus Rocks and Naiad Islets to port and Middle Rocks to starboard. This course will take you north of the Storm Islands, to a point approximately 1.75 miles west of Cape Caution, at the intersection of Lat 51° 10' and Lon 127° 50' (chart 3550). From Cape Caution north, turn to a course that leads past Egg Island and on to Fitz Hugh Sound.

MAINLAND ROUTE

The mainland route offers more shelter in case of a blow, and lets you visit Blunden Harbour, Allison Harbour, and Miles Inlet. You even could go through the famed Nakwakto Rapids (at slack) and spend time in Seymour Inlet, all prior to rounding Cape Caution. Many boats prefer this mainland route for its greater interest and possibility of shelter.

From the Miles Inlet vicinity it is approximately 10 miles to a point 1.5-2.5 miles west of Cape Caution, from which a course can be laid northward past Egg Island.

Note that both the Pine Island route and the mainland route lead past Egg Island, with Table Island a short distance northeast of Egg Island, in the mouth of Smith Sound. If conditions are deteriorating, the cove between Table Island and Ann Island can be a good place to hide out until things get better.

SUMMARY

The key to a comfortable crossing of Queen Charlotte Sound is being patient enough to wait for calm conditions, and bold enough to move out when the window opens. In the summer of 1996 we went northbound from Christie Passage and southbound along the mainland. Both crossings were without incident, although in both cases the previous days were stormy. In 1997 our southbound departure from Rivers Inlet was delayed until the end of the ebb, which reduced the large ground swell that had been running in the early morning. Then it was a race to get to the safety of Browning Passage before the sea breeze began, a race we won but not by much. In 1998 we had an easy crossing both ways, though on the northbound leg the motion made Marilynn Hale uncomfortable around Pine Island. The southbound leg was sunny and calm, almost flat. In 1999 Marilynn once again was uncomfortable north of Pine Island—no wind, but 6-8-foot swells causing a corkscrewing motion of the boat. Southbound we tried the middle route described above, and found it good.

Pine Island lighthouse. A familiar sight for those who cross Queen Charlotte Sound.

Blunden Harbour to Slingsby Channel

Charts

3547	Queen Charlotte Strait, Eastern Portion (1:40,000)
3548	Queen Charlotte Strait, Central Portion (1:40,000)
3549	Queen Charlotte Strait, Western Portion (1:40,000)
3550	Approaches to Seymour Inlet & Belize Inlet (1:40,000)
3552	Seymour Inlet & Belize Inlet (1:50,000)
3598	Cape Scott to Cape Calvert (1:74,500)
3921	Fish Egg Inlet & Allison Harbour (1:20,000)
3934	Approaches to Smith Sound & Rivers Inlet (1:40,000)

Wells Passage to Blunden Harbour. Use charts 3547 and 3548. The entrance to Blunden Harbour is approximately 11 miles northwest from the mouth of Wells Passage. Use chart 3547 to identify rocks that lie northwest of Wells Passage. Chart 3548 has an excellent 1:15,000 insert that shows the entry to Blunden Harbour. Our sister publication, *Weatherly Waypoint Guide, Vol. 3*, published in 1998, has excellent waypoints for this passage, including the mouth of Blunden Harbour.

Blunden Harbour. Use chart 3548. Blunden Harbour is a lovely, well-protected bay, with excellent holding ground and the remains of an abandoned Indian village on the north shore. As you approach the entrance, it is very important to identify **Siwiti Rock**, which we leave to starboard while entering. Study the Blunden Harbour inset on chart 3548. Note the several rocks that lie along both sides of the passage into Blunden Harbour. These rocks make a somewhat serpentine route necessary as you go in.

Once inside, anchor anywhere in the large basin, or between Moore Rock and Byrnes Island. We feel that Moore Rock lies closer to Byrnes Island than the chart suggests. At least that's the way it looks on the water. Along the north shore of Blunden Harbour the abandoned Indian village with its extensive midden makes an fascinating exploration. The beach

is littered with relics, but they may not be removed.

We have not explored **Bradley Lagoon** at the northeast corner of Blunden Harbour, but those who have say it's interesting. Take the dinghy through the rapids at high water slack.

Southgate Group. Use charts 3548, 3550, 3921. The Southgate Group is a cluster of islands that lie at the corner of the route between Blunden Harbour and Allison Harbour. A passage between Southgate Island and Knight Island makes for a scenic, sheltered shortcut. Basins on either side of the narrows appear to be just right for anchoring. Chart 3921 shows the passage in large detail.

Allison Harbour. Use chart 3921 (preferred), 3550. Allison Harbour is long and nicely protected, but not as pretty as some other anchorages. You're apt to encounter log booms tied to the shore. We're told that crabbing is

good in Allison Harbour. The best holding ground is toward the head, in 3-4 fathoms. Favor the western shore as you enter and leave, to avoid a rock that lies almost mid-channel, about halfway in.

Skull Cove. Use chart 3921 (preferred), 3550. Skull Cove is on Bramham Island, roughly

Skull Cove is a scenic little anchorage.

opposite Murray Labyrinth, and is one of the prettier anchorages you will find. If approaching from the south, we would pass behind Southgate Island and follow the eastern mainland shore almost to City Point. Then we would turn northwest, leaving Town Rock to port, and go through the passage between the Deloraine Islands and Murray Labyrinth, thus avoiding all the rocks and reefs that lie offshore. If approaching from the north, we would follow the Bramham Island shore.

Enter Skull Cove on the east side of the unnamed island, and take anchorage in the cove immediately to port, 3-4 fathoms. The view on the west side of the island is superb.

Miles Inlet. Use chart 3550. Miles Inlet indents the west shore of Bramham Island, and is just beautiful. The narrow passage is lined with silver snags. None of the trees is very tall. Winter storms here must be awful. Once inside, anchor with excellent protection in the T intersection. The two arms of the T shoal rapidly. Explore by dinghy at high tide.

The entrance to Miles Inlet is narrow, but using McEwan Rock as a reference the entrance is easy to locate. Be sure you know exactly where you are at all times. Off lying rocks bound each side of the entrance, and you want to go directly down the middle.

Schooner Channel. Use chart 3921 (preferred), or chart 3550. Schooner Channel, along the east side of Bramham Island, is narrow, and requires constant attention to avoid rocks and reefs. With constant attention, however, the channel need not be difficult to run. Watch tidal currents closely. The flood can run to 5 knots, and the ebb to 6 knots. Schooner Channel currents are shown in Tide and Current Tables, Vol. 6 as a secondary station, based on Nakwakto Rapids.

These log beams are all that remain from an earlier structure. East shore, Blunden Harbour.

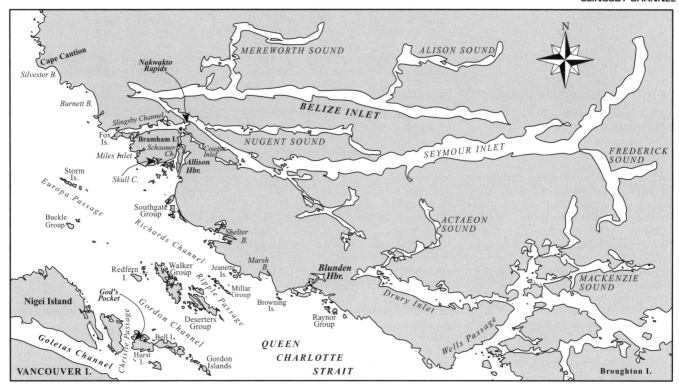

An unnamed bay opposite Goose Point at the north end of Schooner Channel is mentioned in Sailing Directions as a good anchorage for small craft.

Slingsby Channel. Use chart 3550. Slingsby Channel runs between the mainland and the north side of Bramham Island. Currents in Outer Narrows, between the Fox Islands and Vigilance Point, are shown as a secondary station based on Nakwakto Rapids in Tide and Current Tables, Vol. 6. Currents can run to 7 knots on the flood and 9 knots on the ebb. Sailing Directions warns that a westerly wind opposing an ebb current can set up dangerous seas at the entrance to Outer Narrows. Mike Guns, a commercial fisherman with much experience in these waters, reports that when an ebb current opposes a westerly wind, the entrance to Outer Narrows is on a par with the worst conditions that Nahwitti Bar or Cape Mudge can produce. He has seen "noticable

turbulence" as long as 3 hours after maximum ebb at Nakwakto Rapids. Take this water seriously.

We have entered Slingsby Channel via a narrow, scenic channel that runs between the Fox Islands and Bramham Island, thus avoiding Outer Narrows entirely. Sailing Directions mentions the channel but does not encourage it. We found the channel easy to run, and deeper than the chart shows.

Treadwell Bay. Use chart 3921 (preferred) or chart 3550. Treadwell Bay lies at the east end of Slingsby Channel, and is a good, protected anchorage. It is often used by boats awaiting slack water at Nakwakto Rapids. A small resort is located at the northwest corner of the bay. Favor the east shore as you enter, to avoid rocks off the Anchor Islands. The rocks are shown clearly on the charts. Inside, beware of rocks, shown on the chart, off the south shore of the bay.

Nakwakto Rapids. Use chart 3921 (preferred), or chart 3550. Nakwakto Rapids are among the world's fastest. Especially at springs, they *must* be transited at slack water only. At neap tides the window of safety opens a little wider. Turret Rock sits in the middle of the narrows, with the favored passage on the west side. Turret Rock is known locally as Tremble Island because, we are told, it actually trembles during the full rush of a maximum tidal current. Brave mariners have nailed boards with their boat names on Tremble Island's trees.

Behind Nakwakto Rapids lie the extensive waterways of Seymour Inlet, Belize Sound, Nugent Sound and Alison Sound, which until recently have been almost unvisited by pleasure craft. Chart 3552, published in 1993, has opened these waters for the first time.

Turret Rock (Tremble Island) looks tranquil enough when Nakwakto Rapids are slack.

Comments? Questions? Corrections? Let us know.

Contact us by phone (toll-free), fax, regular mail or e-mail.

See our phone numbers and address at the front of the book.

Smith Sound

Charts

3931	Smith Inlet, Boswell Inlet & Draney Inlet (1:40,000)
3932	Rivers Inlet (1:40,000)
3934	Approaches to Smith Sound & Rivers Inlet (1:40,000)

SMITH SOUND doesn't see many pleasure boats, but it's reputed to be full of fish. We visited Smith Sound during an opening for gillnet commercial salmon fishing, and the boats turned out in force. Picking our way among the nets called for close attention, but all went well.

Smith Sound has no resorts or settlements, so you're on your own. Several bays are good for anchoring, although only one, Millbrook Cove, really appealed to us.

Smith Inlet, Boswell Inlet, and Draney Inlet all beg for exploration, now that chart 3931, published in 1992, opens them to cruising.

From the south, enter Smith Sound through Alexandra Passage, passing between North Iron Rock and Egg Rocks. We considered a course between North Iron Rock and South Iron Rock, but Jim Capadouca, a Greek fisherman from Vancouver with more than 70 years' experience on this coast, made it clear that the course between North Iron Rock and Egg Rocks was the one to take.

From the west, enter Smith Sound through Radar Passage. From the north, enter through Irving Passage. If you have GPS or Loran, we suggest that you plot waypoints to keep you clear of rocks. This would be especially true in reduced visibility.

We entered Smith Sound from the north,

through Irving Passage. A westerly was blowing, and we found ourselves in 6-foot beam seas from Paddle Rock to False Egg Island, and on our quarter after we turned into Irving Passage. Low clouds hung overhead, then dropped to the deck. With few visual reference points and an awkward sea, course-holding was difficult. Radar and waypoints brought us in. Our notes, written later, say, "Bless the electronics!"

Table Island. Use chart 3934. Table Island lies in the mouth of Smith Sound, and the casual visitor would not think of it as an anchorage. But Jim Capadouca, the Greek fisherman from Vancouver, said that fish boats anchor along the east side, between Table Island and Ann Island, and have no problems. We have not tried this anchorage, but we have seen several fish boats anchored there. A boat waiting to make a southerly dash around Cape Caution could find this anchorage useful, as could a boat seeking shelter from a westerly in Queen Charlotte Sound.

Millbrook Cove. Use chart 3934. Millbrook Cove is the outermost anchorage on the north side of Smith Sound. To us it is the favored anchorage in the sound. The cove is completely landlocked, with 4-6 fathom depths, good holding ground, and ample room for a large number of boats. Unfortunately, logging has laid bare the hillsides, and much debris is around the shore.

Getting into Millbrook Cove will hold your attention, at least the first time. Begin by finding the red spar buoy E6 marking Millbrook Rocks. The buoy has a small radar reflector on top. Leave buoy E6 to starboard (Red, Right, Re-

turning), and aim the boat toward the 30 meter island. Keep a sharp lookout for rocks on either side, especially the west side, as shown on the chart. The 30 meter island can be passed on either side, although the east side is a little deeper.

Once inside, watch for a drying rock a short distance off the northeast corner of the island. Watching your depths, anchor anywhere you like. The net-drying float that was in the bay for years is gone now.

Dsulish Bay. Use chart 3934. Dsulish Bay is on the north shore of Smith Sound, and has beautiful white sand beaches. A trail is reported to lead to Goose Bay to the north. The best anchorage in Dsulish Bay is behind the 46-meter island deep inside the bay. The anchorage is a little open but certainly workable. We also saw fish boats anchored along the west side of Dsulish Bay. In the right conditions it would be a good lunch stop, though we're not so sure about overnight.

Margaret Bay. Use chart 3931. Margaret Bay is located at the head of Smith Sound, on the point of land that separates Boswell Inlet and Smith Inlet. Chambers Island, rather small, is in the middle of the bay, about halfway in. West of Chambers Island depths are too great for anchoring. East of the island they shallow to 8-9 fathoms. The head shoals sharply, and old pilings take up much of the room at the head. Protection is excellent. A net drying float is moored just east of Chambers Island. Assuming the float is still there and not in use, we would tie to it.

McBride Bay. McBride Bay is on the north

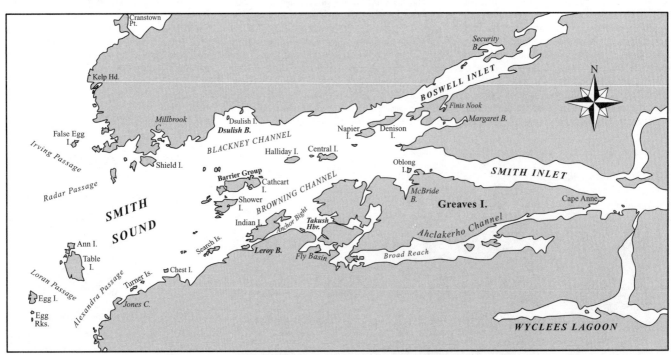

Reference only — not for navigation

Rivers Inlet and Fish Egg Inlet

side of Greaves Island, at the east end of Browning Channel. It is very deep until near the head, where 5-7 fathom anchoring depths can be found. Protection is excellent, but swinging room is a little limited.

Jones Cove. Use chart 3934. Jones Cove is located on the south shore of Smith Sound, near the mouth. The cove is cozy and well protected, and often used by commercial fishing boats. A single piling is in the mouth of the cove, and fish boats tie to it rather than anchor. Anchor in 3 fathoms, with limited swinging room. Depending on the rise and fall of the tide and the presence of other boats, you may choose to run a stern-tie to shore.

RIVERS INLET

Use charts 3934 and 3932. *For tides and currents, use the new for 2000 Canadian Tide and Current Tables, Vol. 7.* Rivers Inlet is a famed salmon fishing area, and at one time contained 17 salmon canneries. All the canneries are closed now, and most are sinking into ruin. Absent its commerce of former years, Rivers Inlet is prime cruising ground. The scenery is beautiful, and the anchorages excellent. The area is served by two well-stocked marinas, Duncanby Landing and Dawsons Landing.

	Charts
3727	Cape Caution to Goose Island (1:73,584)
3784	Kwakshua Channel to Spider Island (1:36,800)
3785	Namu Harbour to Dryad Point (1:40,533)
3921	Fish Egg Inlet & Allison Harbour (1:20,000)
3932	Rivers Inlet (1:40,000)
3934	Approaches to Smith Sound & Rivers Inlet (1:40,000)

Open Bight. Use chart 3934. Open Bight, well named, lies just inside Cranstown Point at the entrance to Rivers Inlet. Anchorage, with protection from westerlies but not northerlies or easterlies, is along the south and west shores. The west shore is preferred. We would put the hook down outside the kelp line in 4-5 fathoms, within view of a stunning white shell midden. Gentle swells will rock the boat.

Home Bay. Use chart 3934. Home Bay, on the south shore a short distance inside the mouth of Rivers Inlet, is a pretty spot, but taken up almost entirely by the Big Spring

Rare photo of Editor/Publisher Hale actually working. Here, he helps move incoming supplies at Duncanby Landing. Photo by Marilynn Hale.

fishing resort. The traffic of guided sportfishing boats makes Home Bay unsuitable for anchoring. The Big Spring resort is friendly to visiting yachties.

Just west of Home Bay is another nook, which Don Douglass calls **West Home Bay** in his books *Exploring the Inside Passage to Alaska* (now out of print) and *Exploring the North Coast of British Columbia* (replaces the earlier book). This bay has no traffic, and offers anchorage behind the first of two islets inside the bay. Contrary to Douglass's illustration, however, low tide reveals rocks that foul the western side of that first islet. We would pass the islet only to the east.

Other anchoring possibilities lie in the unnamed group of islands just west of Duncanby Landing. Larger boats will find good anchoring in deep water in the unnamed cove marked with 29 meter and 35 meter soundings. The large island with the 105-meter hill is at the north end of this cove. Smaller boats can creep into the unnamed cove east of the deep water cove. This cove is marked with a 9 meter sounding in the mouth and a 16 meter sounding inside. A King Salmon fishing resort outpost is moored on the eastern shore. The little nook at the northeast end of the cove offers quiet anchorage in 2-3 fathoms, but be careful when you enter this nook. A reef extends northward nearly halfway across the entrance, much farther than the chart suggests. Favor the north side.

① **Duncanby Landing Store & Marine,** Rivers Inlet, B.C. V0N 1M0, (250)949-3583, www.duncanbylanding.com. Monitors VHF channel 06. Open all year, 7 days a week. Gasoline and diesel, propane, water, 30 amp

Mail time on the North Coast. Nola Bachen at Dawsons Landing receives mail from the 3-times-a-week flight.

Just like the old days at Duncanby Landing. A group of commercial fishermen idles away the early evening before an opening the following day.

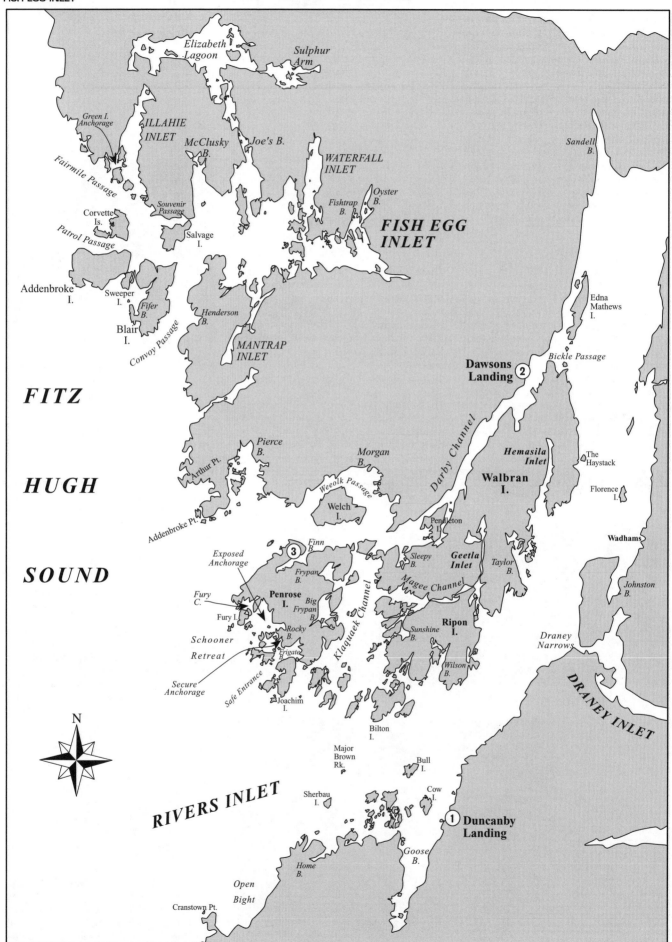

FITZ

HUGH

SOUND

Fairmile Passage

Green I. Anchorage

ILLAHIE INLET

McClusky B.

Joe's B.

Elizabeth Lagoon

Sulphur Arm

WATERFALL INLET

Fishtrap B.

Oyster B.

FISH EGG INLET

Sandell B.

Corvette Is.

Patrol Passage

Souvenir Passage

Salvage I.

Addenbroke I.

Sweeper I.

Fifer B.

Blair I.

Convoy Passage

Henderson B.

MANTRAP INLET

Edna Mathews I.

Bickle Passage

Dawsons Landing ②

Pierce B.

Morgan B.

Weeolk Passage

Welch I.

Darby Channel

Hemasila Inlet

Walbran I.

The Haystack

Florence I.

Arthur Pt.

Addenbroke Pt.

Finn B.

③

Frypan B.

Exposed Anchorage

Fury C.

Penrose I.

Big Frypan B.

Fury I.

Rocky B.

Schooner Retreat

Frigate B.

Secure Anchorage

Safe Entrance

Joachim I.

Pendleton I.

Sleepy B.

Geetla Inlet

Taylor B.

Magee Channel

Klaquaek Channel

Ripon I.

Sunshine B.

Wilson B.

Wadhams

Johnston B.

Draney Narrows

DRANEY INLET

N

RIVERS INLET

Bilton I.

Major Brown Rk.

Bull I.

Cow I.

Sherbau I.

① **Duncanby Landing**

Goose B.

Home B.

Open Bight

Cranstown Pt.

power on the docks, groceries, cube ice, fishing tackle and licenses, souvenirs, liquor. Ample guest moorage, showers, laundry. Good food with daily specials, and a rustic but cozy pub atmosphere at Jessie's Place. For 2000, accommodations are available, six rooms, 12 beds.

Ken Gillis bought Duncanby Landing in 1993, and has upgraded it considerably, now with food and beverage service, and the accommodations mentioned above. Being the only eating place and watering hole for miles around, the locals like to gather and tell stories ("Remember the night old Joe fell in the water? He tried to walk when he should have kept crawling!"). A guitar stands in the corner of the pub, and we are told that Ken will sometimes break into song as the evening gets along. They say he's not too bad.

Duncanby Landing had been a commercial fishing camp since the 1930s, and in later years discouraged pleasure craft from calling. While the commercial boats still gather at Duncanby, Ken eagerly welcomes pleasure craft, and is most helpful. The fishermen are helpful, too. In our several calls at Duncanby, we have found them unfailingly polite and full of local knowledge. Be advised, though, that while Duncanby Landing is old and full of charm, the docks are a little rough. This is hard country.

Goose Bay. Use chart 3934. Goose Bay, beyond Duncanby Landing, is empty now. The Goose Bay cannery is virtually abandoned,

Dawsons Landing, Rivers Inlet. The store is wonderfully stocked. Room for a few boats to tie up.

after an effort to develop a sport fishing operation there was discontinued. The cannery buildings are interesting, though, and very photogenic.

Taylor Bay. Use chart 3934 or 3932. Taylor Bay indents the east shore of Walbran Island, and is a tranquil, lovely, 6-8 fathom anchorage, although swinging room is limited. Anchor all the way in, or try the nook behind the north end of the inner island, between the inner island and Walbran Island. We are told that the net-drying float in the back bay is gone now.

Johnston Bay. Use chart 3932. Johnston Bay is on the east shore of Rivers Inlet just south of Wadhams, an abandoned cannery site. The bay is quiet and beautiful, but deep until very near the head, where for years an old and deteriorating float offered moorage. In 1997 the float was moved to the western shore and looked very rough. We have heard that development is coming to Johnston Bay, and the float will be removed. As the chart shows, a reef lies in the center of the outer part of Johnston Bay, and at the entrance a rock is close to the eastern shore. Favor the western shore all the way in and you'll have ample depths and no hazards.

Draney Narrows/Draney Inlet. Use chart 3931. The current runs hard in Draney Narrows. We looked in 1½ hours before the predicted turn and decided no. Fifteen minutes before the turn the narrows were flat. Predictions are shown in Tide & Current Tables, Vol. 7, and are shown as a secondary station based on Prince Rupert Tides. Draney Inlet, approximately 24 miles long, is bounded by high steep mountains, and is beautiful. Because it is not on the way to anyplace else, it sees little pleasure craft traffic. Good anchorage in 5-6 fathoms is available in Fish Hook Bay, a short distance inside the narrows. A float home with two floating outbuildings is on the south shore of Fish Hook Bay, near the entrance. A large sign reads, "Warning, Private Property, No Trespassing." A very convincing watch dog greeted our boat with don't-mess-with-me barks and growls. We didn't argue.

② **Dawsons Landing General Store Ltd.,** Rivers Inlet, B.C. V0N 1M0, (250)949-3533; fax (250)949-2111. Monitors VHF channel 06. Open all year, gasoline and diesel fuel. Guest moorage, hardware, groceries, ice, wa-

ter, fishing and hunting gear and licenses, liquor, washroom, showers, laundry, post office, some accommodations. A heli-pad takes up part of the dock. In 1999, one visitor suffered a kidney stone attack and was taken by helicopter to the hospital in Port Hardy. They have scheduled air service from Pacific Coastal Airlines. Dawsons Landing is owned by Rob and Nola Bachen, and has been in the family since 1954. This is a real general store, with an excellent stock of standard grocery items, and an astonishing accumulation of tools and hardware. The facility goes back a long way. It's a capturing of coastal history, right be-

We were the second yachtie to tie up at the new Finn Bay Retreat. The pavilion with barbecue is at the end of the dock.

fore your eyes. Rob and Nola are friendly and helpful. The docks, it must be admitted, are a little rough, but that's not unusual on the coast.

Darby Channel. Use chart 3934. Darby Channel, locally called Schooner Pass, bounds the west side of Walbran Island, and is easily run. Southbound boats should favor the west shore of the channel to avoid being lured into foul ground behind Pendleton Island. The rock off the southwest corner of Pendleton Island is clearly marked by a beacon and easily avoided.

Frypan Bay. Use chart 3934. Frypan Bay is at the northeast corner of Penrose Island, and was suggested to us by Rob Bachen at Dawsons Landing. We found the bay to be spacious and well protected, although lacking in scenic quality. Anchoring depths along the south shore are 4-7 fathoms, and in the middle are 8-14 fathoms.

Finn Bay. Use chart 3934. Finn Bay, on the north side of Penrose Island, is well protected. A sport fishing camp is at the head of the

bay, logging activity is on one side, and commercial fishing equipment is on the other. In 1999, a new facility, Finn Bay Retreat, was built on the west shore, a short distance inside the entrance.

③ **Finn Bay Retreat,** General Delivery, Dawsons Landing, B.C. V0N 1M0. Monitors VHF channel 06. No phone, no fax, no e-mail. Pete and Rene (pronounced "Reenie") Darwin have lived at Finn Bay for some time, and decided to build a marina. The result is a massively-constructed float 270 feet long and 14 feet wide, with a covered pavilion and large barbecue at the inshore end.

Finn Bay Retreat is more than just a marina, however. It's an example of the self-reliant life of those who choose to live in remote places. Pete is middle-age, medium-height, and rock-hard. He collects logs. He told us the logs under the floats are spruce, 80 feet long, bought off a logging camp that was closing down. Pete milled the timbers for the cross-pieces that hold the logs together. He milled the framework for the deck, milled the decking, milled the walers around the perimeter, and put it all together. The barbecue in the

pavilion is made from an old steel mooring buoy he salvaged and cut in half with an acetylene torch. The bottom half of the buoy holds the coals and the grate; the top half is the hood, with a smokestack welded into it. Pete is a good welder and a good carpenter. Everything looks strong and proper.

Pete and Rene and their large, exuberant dog Buddy (half malamute, half wolf) live in a float house surrounded by flowers, next to the pavilion. Rene works at the fishing lodge at the head of Finn Bay, and commutes in their outboard-powered skiff. On shore, we saw a large Hitachi UH121 excavator at the bottom of a rough road that led up the rock hillside. The excavator had seen a lot of work picking up logs and moving them around, and knocking the road out of the rock. At the top of the road it had dug a lake. Pete and Rene built a 20×20-foot greenhouse up there, with an innovative self-regulating automatic watering system. Even on a cool, overcast day, the air inside the greenhouse was moist and warm. Lush vegetables grew in trays on tabletops. Pete and Rene plan to move from the float house to the top of the hill, and build two 50×100-foot greenhouses so they can raise more of their food.

We were only the second yachtie to tie up for the night (the first had been there some days earlier), and after supper we were invited in to visit and to sample homemade beer. The beer was very mild and had no effect. (As the evening wore on, though, we noticed how the float house seemed to move under us, especially when we were standing.) A wall was covered with snapshots and newspaper clippings. One clipping was of a beached humpback whale. It dwarfed Pete, who was standing in front, holding a fishing pole. The caption read, "Eighty-nine hours—and on 15-pound-test line!"

They told us about living out on Goose Island, and running tugboats, and life up the coast. "One thing we decided," said Rene, filling our surprisingly empty glass, "we decided we would never live south of Cape Caution."

Fury Island. Use chart 3934. The cove behind Fury Island, on the west side of Penrose Island, is a beautiful and popular anchorage with a perfect white sand beach, although open to southwest winds. Fury Cove, as it is commonly called, is entered by leaving Cleve Island to port, then turning to port to raise the narrow entrance. Cleve Island is mentioned in Sailing Directions, but shown on the chart only as a 61 meter island—no name. In a strong southwesterly, we would expect large swells in the vicinity of Cleve Island. *Breaker Pass:* Breaker Pass separates Fury Island from Cleve Island. Although we left Fury Cove in calm weather via Breaker Pass without difficulty (just to say we'd done it), we could tell that it wouldn't take much of a southwesterly for Breaker Pass live up to its name.

FISH EGG INLET

Use chart 3921 for all the Fish Egg Inlet entries. Fish Egg Inlet indents the east side of Fitz Hugh Sound, behind Addenbroke Island. This is beautiful cruising country, and is rapidly becoming one of the more popular spots on the coast. Those who say you'll be all alone are wrong. The gunkholing possibilities are vast, but here are notes on some of the better-known anchorages.

Green Island Anchorage. Green Island Anchorage, just off Fitz Hugh Sound at the mouth of Illahie Inlet, is about as cozy and pleasing as an anchorage needs to be. Excellent holding in 6-7 fathoms. From seaward, wrap around the 70-meter island and follow the shoreline in. This would be a good spot to rest up after a crossing of Queen Charlotte Sound.

Illahie Inlet. The head of Illahie Inlet would be a delightful anchorage in 5-7 fathoms, mud bottom, good protection, except that logging has scarred the surrounding hillsides. An eagle's nest is in a tree just north of the narrows.

Souvenir Passage. Sailing Directions says that Souvenir Passage is very narrow at its eastern end, and the chart shows a rock on the north shore. We have found that if we favor the south side of the passage we have good water all the way.

Joe's Bay. Joe's Bay has suddenly become quite popular. When we visited one early July, five other boats were already anchored. It was as if we were back in Desolation Sound. Joe's Bay is worth the crowds, though. It's tranquil, tree-lined and snug. Anchoring is straightforward in the southern basin, but rocks and reefs make the northern portion somewhat trickier. A stern-tie to shore might be called for, to keep the boat from swinging onto a rock. Once anchored, the tidal rapids leading to Elizabeth Lagoon and Sulphur Arm are a big attraction.

Waterfall Inlet. Pretty spot, but we couldn't find any comfortable anchorages. We felt that the west entry, leaving the 99-meter island to starboard, was safest. Go slowly and watch for rock ledges that extend from each side of the narrow pass.

Fish Trap Bay. Awfully tight.

Oyster Bay. Oyster Bay, next to Fish Trap Bay at the head of Fish Egg Inlet, is a very nice anchorage, with a remote, end-of-the-line feel to it. We had a late and relaxed lunch there, anchored in 3 fathoms near the head of the bay. Recommended.

Mantrap Inlet. Once you're inside, Mantrap Inlet offers good anchorage. The entrance, however, is narrow, made more narrow by an uncharted ledge of rock that extends from the west shore. We would go in at half tide or higher, dead slow, with lookouts. Our Tolly 26 had no problems, but a 40-footer would want to be very careful.

Bloody Good, Mate!

IT HAPPENED AT PORT MCNEILL. Stacia Green, the Waggoner Cruising Guide's managing editor, was relaxing on the bow of *Surprise* when she saw a sailboat about to land, and jumped down to take a line. The husband was steering and the wife jumped to the stern to fend the boat off and handle the sternline. While the wife was fending off, she somehow caught a finger between the dock and the propeller of their rail-mounted outboard motor. The propeller blade cut right to the bone.

Panicked activity ensued. The wife screamed as blood streamed down her arm. The husband left the helm to help his wife. With Stacia's and others' help the blood-spattered boat was brought alongside the dock and tied off.

A woman from another boat was a nurse, and moved in to help. She sat the victim down, held the arm in the air, and directed first aid. In the midst of the confusion the poor victim, her bloody arm raised, noticed Stacia's Waggoner baseball cap. "Are *you* with the Waggoner?" she exclaimed. "We LOVE that book!"

Such is the passion that our readers feel for the Waggoner Cruising Guide.

(Hint: To avoid pain while cruising, buy the Waggoner.)

P. S. The woman was taken to the hospital and treated. When last we saw her, finger heavily bandaged, she was doing fine.

Fitz Hugh Sound to Finlayson Channel

Hakai • Namu • Ocean Falls • Bella Bella • Fiordland • Finlayson Channel

FITZ HUGH SOUND

FITZ HUGH SOUND begins at Cape Calvert, and continues north to Fisher Channel. Boats crossing Queen Charlotte Sound from the south will find the ocean swells vanishing once Cape Calvert is behind them, although a southwesterly can still make things nasty, especially in a southflowing ebb current. Even in settled conditions, expect to find rougher water where Hakai Passage joins Fitz Hugh Sound.

Chart 3727 shows Fitz Hugh Sound in its entirety, but at 1:73,584, the chart's small scale does not allow much detail. The larger-scale charts 3727, 3784 and 3785 make navigation easier. Northbound boats that don't stop at Rivers Inlet probably will stop either in Safety Cove or Pruth Bay. Now that chart 3921 opens Fish Egg Inlet, Green Island Anchorage would be a good choice for passing traffic.

Philip Inlet. Use chart 3934. Philip Inlet indents the mainland side of Fitz Hugh Sound approximately 3 miles south of Addenbroke Island. On a sunny afternoon we found the entrance hard to identify. Be cautious when you enter: the chart does not show the ledges of rock that extend from each side of the inlet near the mouth.

About halfway in, a small island creates a rock-strewn, tight and tricky narrows. We would not want to go through this narrows without a bow watch or good visibility from a flying bridge.

Once past the narrows the inlet becomes rather open feeling and uninteresting. Depths near the head are approximately 5 fathoms. We went in planning to anchor for the night, but elected instead to anchor in Green Island Anchorage at the mouth of Fish Egg Inlet, a much better choice.

Fifer Bay. Use chart 3921 (larger scale, preferred), or chart 3934. At the larger scale of 1:20,000, chart 3921 provides a much clearer picture of Fifer Bay than the smaller scale 1:40,000 chart 3934. Fifer Bay indents the western side of Blair Island, with lovely 1-2 fathom anchorage for small craft in the head of its southermost cove. There's room for one boat if it swings, or several if all of them stern-tie to shore. When entering the Fifer Bay, favor Sweeper Island to avoid the rocks lying off the southern side of the entrance. When clear of the rocks turn south and work your way into the anchorage. Correspondent Bill Hales, from Victoria, reports the anchorage to be peaceful.

Safety Cove. Use chart 3934 (preferred) or 3727. Safety Cove is a steep-walled, uninteresting bay that indents Calvert Island approximately 7 miles north of Cape Calvert. The bottom shoals sharply a fair distance from the head of the bay, and Sailing Directions recommends anchoring immediately when the depth reaches 17 fathoms. If you press in to find shallower water, watch your swing or you could find yourself aground on the shelf at low tide. Despite its name and regular use, Safety Cove would not be our first choice unless necessary.

Pruth Bay. Use chart 3784 (preferred) or 3727. Pruth Bay is at the head of **Kwakshua Channel**, some 7 miles north of Safety Cove. Pruth Bay has long been a favorite stopover point. It offers ample room, excellent protection, 7-8 fathom anchoring depths, and a flat bottom with good holding. This entire area is part of the Hakai Recreation Area, a huge provincial park. A float house ranger station is moored on the north side of the bay. During the summer it houses two rangers and their wives. We found them to be friendly and helpful.

The Hakai Beach Resort, a *very* deluxe fly-in fishing resort, occupies the head of Pruth Bay. A trail (now a dirt road) leads from the

resort across a narrow neck of land to West Beach, a spectacular fine-sand ocean beach on the west side of Calvert Island. It's a perfect spot to play in the sand, build a beach fire, or admire the wonderful rock walls surrounding the beach. A moderately difficult trail leads from West Beach to North Beach.

Anchor just off the Hakai Beach Resort, or in one of the several bays that indent Calvert Island, or in the bay north of the thumb of land marked by Whittaker Point.

⑩ **Hakai Beach Resort,** P.O. Box 3819, Smithers, B.C. V0J 2N0, (800)688-3474; e-mail fishon@hakai.com or view their web site at www.hakai.com. This is a deluxe fishing resort, with lodge, gift shop, and superb dining room. The dock under the ramp is reserved for dinghies, and pleasure boaters are encouraged to stop for supper. Fishing guides are available. They know where the big ones are. Good anchorage just off the resort docks. It's quite a place.

Hakai Passage. Use chart 3784 (preferred) or 3727. Hakai Passage is one of the great fishing spots, yielding 50-60-pound salmon and large bottom fish. Since Hakai Passage opens to the Pacific Ocean, it can get rough. Treat it with respect. On an otherwise pleasant afternoon we overheard two well-managed boats discussing on the radio whether the swells they were facing in Hakai Passage began in Japan or just Hawaii.

Spider Island. Use chart 3784. For several years we have been urged to cruise the Spider Island area, northwest of Hakai Passage. We were told it was little visited, beautiful, raw, and remote-feeling. In 1999 our schedule and the weather meshed, and we went out. Everything we had been told was true. This area indeed is beautiful, raw, remote feeling and little visited. The waters also are full of rocks. You must pay attention *always,* and you must be able to read a chart.

This is perfect gunkholing country, a para-

This is the view across Spider Anchorage from Hurricane Anchorage, described in this chapter.

See area map page 268

dise for kayakers. You have a choice of two ways to get there, outside or inside. The outside route would go out the mouth of Hakai Passage into Queens Sound, and bend northwest toward the west side of Spider Island. Breadner Point, on the west side of Spider Island, is a famous hot spot for spring salmon. You would enter the archipelago south of Spider Island through Fulton Passage, or north of Spider Island through Spider Channel.

We took the inside route. This route goes through Nalau Passage, across Kildidt Sound, and through rock-choked Brydon Channel into Spider Anchorage. An alternate to the Brydon Channel portion would be Spitfire Channel along the north side of Hurricane Island. Spitfire Channel has one spot so tight, however, that we recommend you explore by dinghy before commiting the mother ship to the risk.

Chart 3784 covers these waters. At 1:36,760 it is not a small-scale chart, but the tightness of the channels makes the navigator wish for a much larger-scale presentation. The waypoints shown assume that the chart was drawn on the NAD 27 horizontal datum. They were adjusted to NAD 83 by adding 0.10' to longitude. We do not warrant these waypoints, but they did work for us.

Last, the information that follows is by no means complete. It would take several days to poke around all the delights of this area, and we had only an overnight. But we do describe the inside route and some of the anchorages, and from there you can expand your explorations.

Ward Channel. Use chart 3784. Ward Channel connects Hakai Passage with Nalau Passage, and is a straightforward run as long as you follow the chart to keep track of the rocks.

Nalau Passage. Use chart 3784. Nalau Passage, scenic and open, separates Hunter Island and Stirling Island, and connects Fitz Hugh Sound with Kildidt Sound. A conservative, mid-channel course has no hazards. The western entrance, however, is made interesting by drying rocks offshore from the north side of the passage. Eastbound boats crossing Kildidt Sound may have anxious moments finding the exact entrance. We used the following waypoint for the western entrance successfully: Lat 51° 57.10'N Lon 128° 07.20'W (adjusted to NAD 83).

Kildidt Sound. Use chart 3784. Except to cross between Nalau Passage and Brydon Channel, we have not explored Kildidt Sound. Our waypoint south of Lancaster Reef is Lat 51° 48.95'N Lon128° 10.10'W.

Brydon Channel. Use chart 3784. Brydon Channel connects Kildidt Sound and Spider Anchorage. Westbound across Kildidt Sound, lay a course well south of Lancaster Reef, then turn north toward the Brydon Channel entrance. When you study the chart, you will see that the easternmost dogleg in Brydon Channel is foul with rocks. Mike Guns, a commercial fisherman with much experience in these waters, told us the safe route through is to *hug the northwest end of the 195-foot island at the eastern end of the channel.* This keeps you clear of the rocks farther out. See the reference map p. 269.

Hurricane Anchorage. Use chart 3784. Hurricane Anchorage is the name given by Douglass to this otherwise-unnamed cove in the hook formed by the south end of Hurricane Island. As shown on the reference map p. 269, enter north of the group of islets that make up the hook. A 45-foot sailboat was anchored there when we investigated.

Passage between Spider Anchorage and Spitfire Channel. Use chart 3784. This passage separates Spitfire Island and Hurricane Island. The route shown was recommended to us by Mike Guns. The passage is clear until the north end, where a shoal or rocks (we're not sure which) extends from Spitfire Island. This area is fairly well covered with bull kelp floating on the surface, and thick leaf kelp below. We went in near the top of a high tide without difficulty. Next morning we departed 1½ hours after a 3.3-foot low tide and gathered a heavy glop of leaf kelp on our props and rudders. A low-powered fin keel sailboat

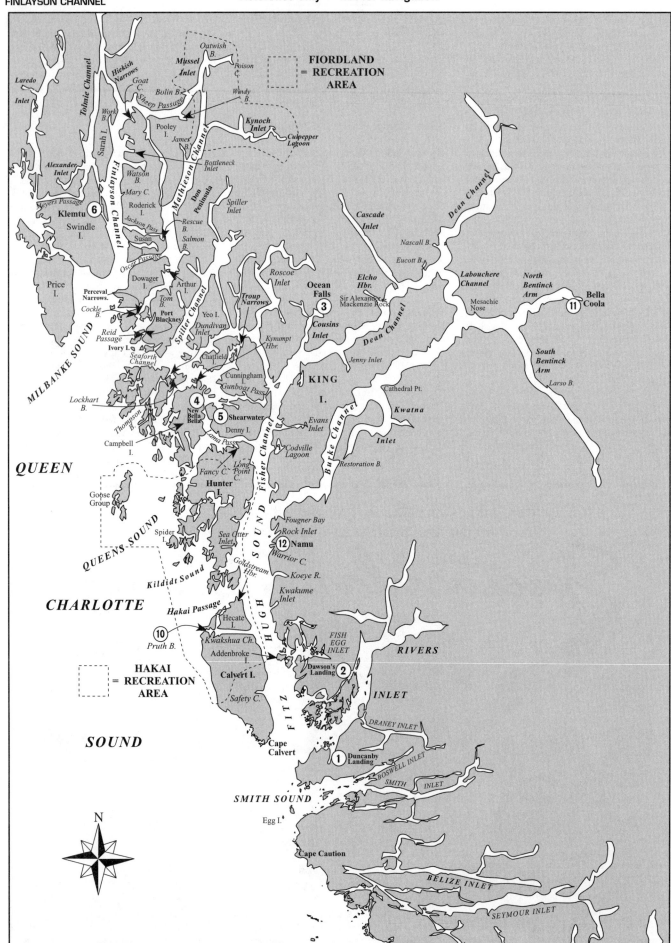

FIORDLAND
= RECREATION
AREA

Laredo Inlet

Tolmie Channel

Hickish Narrows

Oatwish B.

Mussel Inlet

Poison C.

Goat C.

Bolin B.

Sheep Passage

Windy B.

Work B.

Pooley I.

James B.

Kynoch Inlet

Culpepper Lagoon

Sarah I.

Finlayson Channel

Alexander Inlet

Watson B.

Bottleneck Inlet

Mary C.

Roderick I.

Spiller Inlet

Meyers Passage

(6) Klemtu

Swindle I.

Jackson Pass

Susan

Don Peninsula

Mathieson Channel

Rescue B.

Salmon B.

Roscoe Inlet

Ocean Falls

(3)

Cascade Inlet

Nascall B.

Eucott B.

Elcho Hbr.

Dean Channel

Labouchere Channel

North Bentinck Arm

Bella Coola

(11)

Oscar Passage

Dowager I.

Arthur I.

Price I.

Perceval Narrows.

Cockle B.

Tom B.

Port Blackney

Yeo I.

Dundivan Inlet

Troup Narrows

Cunningham

Cousins Inlet

Sir Alexander Mackenzie Rock

KING I.

Mesachie Nose

South Bentinck Arm

Larso B.

Reid Passage

Ivory I.

Seaforth Channel

Chatfield I.

Gunboat Pass.

Jenny Inlet

Cathedral Pt.

Kynumpt Hbr.

Kwatna Inlet

MILBANKE SOUND

Lockhart B.

Thompson B.

New Bella Bella

(4)

(5) Shearwater

Denny I.

Lama Pass

Evans Inlet

Burke Channel

Campbell I.

Codville Lagoon

Restoration B.

QUEEN

Fancy C.

Long Point C.

Hunter I.

Goose Group

FITZ HUGH SOUND

Fisher Channel

Spider I.

Sea Otter Inlet

Kildidt Sound

Fougner Bay

Rock Inlet

(12) Namu

Warrior C.

Goldstream Hbr.

Koeye R.

RIVERS

QUEENS SOUND

CHARLOTTE

Hakai Passage

Hecate I.

Kwakshua Ch.

(10)

Pruth B.

Addenbroke I.

Kwakume Inlet

FISH EGG INLET

Dawson's Landing

(2)

INLET

HAKAI
= RECREATION
AREA

Calvert I.

Safety C.

FITZ

Cape Calvert

DRANEY INLET

(1) Duncanby Landing

BOSWELL INLET

SMITH INLET

SOUND

SMITH SOUND

Egg I.

Cape Caution

BELIZE INLET

SEYMOUR INLET

N

could have been stopped dead. In our opinion this passage is best run around high water.

Spitfire North Anchorage. Use chart 3784. This is our name for the otherwise unnamed cove that indents Hunter Island, west of the Spitfire Channel narrows. Mike Guns recommended it to us. We would anchor in the outer part only. At low water the mouth leading to the inner lagoon appeared to be impassable or nearly so. The east side of this outer cove had a bottom that felt like a thin layer of mud on top of rock, and we dragged easily. The west side of the cove yielded good holding in 8-9 fathoms.

Spitfire West Anchorage. Use chart 3784. This is Douglass's name for the otherwise unnamed cove that indents Hurricane Island, immediately west of the Spitfire Channel narrows. Several people have recommended it to us. Douglass says the bottom offers only fair to poor holding, however.

The view eastward through Spitfire Narrows. It's a lot tighter than the photo suggests.

Spitfire Channel. Use chart 3784. Spitfire Channel separates Hurricane Island and Hunter Island, and except for the narrows at the west end, is easily run. The narrows are another matter. An avid sport fisherman we know says that for years he has run a medium-size cruiser through the narrows without difficulty. Others advise great caution. We explored the narrows in the dinghy at the bottom of a 3.3-foot low tide, and agree they can be run successfully, all right, but with caution and a sharp lookout. Underwater rocks extend into the narrows, especially from the north side. We would go at high water slack—high water, to get the greatest width possible; and slack because we wouldn't want current pushing us where we didn't want to go. The chart and Sailing Directions both say least depth is 9 feet. But it's tight.

Kwakume Inlet. Use chart 3784. Our notes say, "This is the place." Kwakume Inlet is a beautiful and roomy anchorage. If you can get into the inner basin it's unusually secluded and snug feeling. The short fairway into the inner basin is narrow and bounded by rocks, especially on the south side. Favor the north side of the passage. Half tide or higher this little pass, dead slow bell, with alert lookouts.

The outer anchorage will hold the whole yacht club. Anchor north of the islet in the south cove, or east of the islet near the head of the main basin.

Study the chart closely before entering Kwakume Inlet. A rock awash at low tide is shown next to the 6 fathom mark outside the entrance, and you'll want to steer a course to avoid it. Mike Guns, a commercial fisherman with 35 years' experience in these waters, says the preferred approach is from the north. He recommends that you favor the mainland shore, to pass between the rock and the shore.

To enter the inlet, pass *between* the larger islet in the entrance and the little dot islet south of it. Once inside, two rocks are shown a short distance along the north shore, one of them drying 5 feet. Near the head of the main basin and south of its islet, another rock is shown, this one drying 6 feet. The mark-

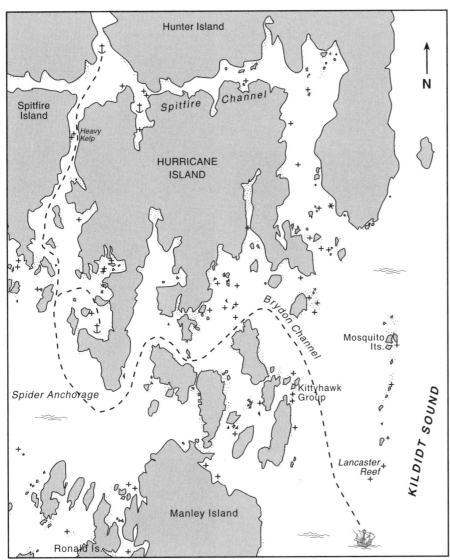

Kildidt Sound and Brydon Channel

Reference only — not for navigation

A beautiful, quiet morning in Kwakume Inlet, Fitz Hugh Sound. We were in the Inner Basin. The entrance channel is more narrow than the photo suggests.

ings for these rocks are inconspicuous on the chart. They would be easy to overlook without careful attention.

Having a high tide when we arrived in early evening, we felt our way into the inner basin for the night. We were treated to glass-smooth water and the most plaintive loon's call we have ever heard. Next morning we were stopped cold by a wolf's cry—a long lonesome troubled howl, repeated just once.

Goldstream Harbour. Use chart 3784. Goldstream Harbour is a lovely little anchorage at the north end of Hecate Island. Enter from the east, favoring Hat Island, which extends from the south shore about 0.2 miles inside. Don't favor Hat Island too closely, though; rocks extend out from it. Once past Hat Island, pass Dinner Rock, leaving it to starboard. Dinner Rock lies about 300 feet

off the northwest corner of Hat Island (It helps to refer to the chart as you read these instructions.). Inside, the middle of Goldstream Harbour is about 10 fathoms deep. Rocks extend out from the shore, so you'll pick your anchoring spot carefully to swing safely. We had lunch in Goldstream Harbour, and cleaned a rockfish we had caught earlier that day. We didn't want to leave, but had to move on. Nice spot.

Koeye River. Use chart 3784. Koeye River is not a good spot for overnight anchoring, but commercial fisherman Mike Guns tells us a dinghy trip up the river to the mine ruins is beautiful. A charted rock lies north of Koeye Point. Enter north of that rock and wrap around into the cove behind the point. A logging show is on the south shore, and a lodge is near the point.

Sea Otter Inlet. Use chart 3784. Sea Otter Inlet, Hunter Island, has two arms that form a T at the entrance. Crab Cove, the northern arm, was recommended to us by Andy Macdonald, when he was the park ranger at Pruth Bay. Anchor near the head in 5-6 fathoms. The south arm is prettier than Crab Cove, and more private feeling. Anchor near the head of the south cove in 6-7 fathoms.

Warrior Cove. Use chart 3784. Warrior Cove is on the east side of Fitz Hugh Sound, approximately 1.5 miles south of Namu. With a typical westerly wind a following sea will chase you into the cove, but the seas subside when you pass the 270-foot island. Inside the inner cove the water is calm. The inner cove is pretty and protected. Scout around for just the right spot, and put the hook down in 3-4 fathoms, good holding.

⑫ **Namu.** Use chart 3785. For latest information, call (604)857-5455 or toll-free (877)870-6677. Namu is crawling back to life. Gasoline and diesel are available, and dock space for approximately 10 boats to overnight. The fuel dock is on the south side of the main Namu pier, and the moorage is in front of the

The docks at Namu are open and in use. Ball floating off wharf marks a rock. Fuel dock is to the right, not shown in this photo.

What will you have? A look through the window at the lunch counter.

Look quick. These buildings at Namu are coming down soon. The walkway leads to Namu Lake.

Namu when it was in full song. We think this photo is from the 1970s.

The docks at Ocean Falls fill up quickly these days. They have ample water for boat washing.

Ocean Falls. A substantial pulp mill city, now a ghost town. Much of the mill now has been torn down.

Greg Ingram and daughters Yarrow and Robin collect daily moorage fees at Ocean Falls. It's pretty relaxed.

low tide the next morning. Another float is in the south cove, with room to anchor nearby. The south cove float is near drying rocks, shown on the chart. Favor the west shore.

FISHER CHANNEL

The north end of Fitz Hugh Sound divides into Burke Channel and Fisher Channel. Burke Channel leads eastward to Bella Coola, which is connected by road to Williams Lake and the highways inland. Bella Coola has facilities and is mentioned often by the few residents on this part of the coast, but is seldom visited by pleasure craft.

Fisher Channel is a continuation of the Inside Passage route, although the Inside Passage soon leads west and north, via Lama Passage or Gunboat Passage, to Bella Bella and Shearwater. Instead of turning west to Bella Bella and Shearwater, if you remain in Fisher Channel you will reach Cousins Inlet and the city of Ocean Falls, the most complete and interesting ghost town on the coast.

③ **Ocean Falls.** Use chart 3781 with large scale inset, or chart 3720. Harbour Manager: Herb Carpenter, General Delivery, Ocean Falls, B.C. V0T 1P0, (250)289-3859. Monitors VHF channels 06 & 09. Open all year, public dock with water and 20 amp power. Rafting required. Although a ghost town (see sidebar), Ocean Falls and its neighboring community of Martin Valley have a population of approximately 160, a lodge with showers and laundry, two eating spots, a saloon, a post office, part-time medical clinic, some groceries and fishing tackle, haulout to 20 tons, ice, garbage drop, portapotty dump, and excellent docks.

The docks have power and all the Link Lake water you need for boat washing. In 1998 the health department found some problems with the water for drinking, and boil signs have been posted. Moorage is collected every evening around 1900. A rustic breakfast and lunch stop called The Shack, with excellent offerings, has been operating on the docks for several years, though lately it has been open only erratically. Phyllis Hooker's cafe is in the old hospital building, which has rooms for rent, with showers and laundry on the main floor. The dam, which dominates the head of the inlet, supplies power for Ocean Falls, Shearwater and New Bella Bella.

Most of the area's residents live in the 85-house community of Martin Valley, about a mile's walk down the road toward the mouth of Cousins Inlet. It's an easy, scenic stroll, past plantings gone wild from what must have been homes years ago. The first house you come to is Saggo's Saloon, which opened to a lively trade in 1998. Saggo's isn't fancy but it's the only place in town. A little farther along, the concrete ramp leading into the inlet at Martin Valley is for float planes. A store is at the head of the seaplane ramp.

The houses in Martin Valley were taken over by the province when Ocean Falls was abandoned, and one at a time they have been

cafe. The cafe appears ready to reopen, but it has been vandalized and we don't hold out much hope. The store has opened, but only to sell souvenirs to the tourists when the B.C. ferry calls.

In 1999 Bob and Tammy Gardiner were caretakers, with their children Katrina and Mitch, ages 12 and 11. Katrina became the self-appointed tour guide, and delighted us with her historical knowledge and enthusiasm. Mitch was more reserved—until the subject of hockey came up. The Gardiners had made much progress with the property. We hope they continue.

The boardwalk to Namu Lake has been extensively rebuilt, and we recommend it. Along the way, you can take a short side trip to see the archaeological dig site, where human habitation has been traced back 10,000 years.

Namu began as a cannery in 1893. During the peak years, the winter population of 600 swelled to 2000 in the summer. Closed now, many of the old buildings cannot last much longer. The old gymnasium, with its small bowling alley hidden in the darkness, is slated

for destruction, as are the hotel, dormitory, and several of the houses. The generator room, its rows of EMD engines now silent, will be gone one day. If you want to see the famous old fish packing operation of Namu, don't wait.

Navigation note: The beacon is gone from Loo Rock, between the Namu floats and the entrance to Rock Inlet, but the Loo Rock still exists. The Namu Harbour inset on chart 3785 shows the rock's location. In 1999 Loo Rock was market by a pink-colored round fender. Off the docks, another rock was marked with a ball.

Rock Inlet. Rock Inlet extends northeast from Whirlwind Bay (Namu), and it's a good, protected spot. Entering or departing, be sure to identify Verdant Island, near the mouth, and pass east of it. Keep a mid-channel course, and watch for rocks. The chart shows the way. Inside, anchor in 4-7 fathoms. We put the hook down in two spots and found the holding only fair to good (maybe). On a subsequent visit we overnighted tied to a run-down float in the west cove, but had to watch our depths at sold to people who enjoyed the solitude of the area. With the now-regular calls by the ferry and its tourists, a small crafts industry has begun.

When we visited Ocean Falls in 1996, Gunter Hogrefe was Chairman and Administrator of the Ocean Falls Improvement District (see adjoining sidebar), and Nearly Normal Norman Brown had only begun his restoration of what was to become the Historical Society Museum. Gunter retired in 1998, and his son Gerald Hogrefe holds the job now. Norman Brown's restoration work had made much progress. The museum is coming along splendidly.

Ocean Falls is a regular stop for the Discovery Coast ferry. Just before the ferry arrives, a trailer is pulled into place near the landing and sells local crafts to the ferry passengers. A few hours later the ferry departs and the trailer is closed up and pulled away.

You can walk up the road to the dam behind Ocean Falls and back along Link Lake. Make noise: you might meet a bear. Trout fishing in Link Lake is said to be excellent. Part of the pulp and paper mill complex has been torn down, and a new bridge built across the river between the town and the mill. Crabbing is good at the docks, and excellent off the mill. Halibut and salmon can be caught in the inlet. We think Ocean Falls is a "don't miss" stopping point.

Codville Lagoon. Use chart 3785. Codville Lagoon, a provincial park on the east side of Fisher Channel, is a popular anchorage, protected and pretty, with ample room for several boats. From out in the channel the narrow entrance is hard to locate, but Codville Hill, with its moonscape of barren rock slopes and three peaks, is a good landmark. Favor the south side of the entrance to avoid a rock off the north shore. Anchor in 6-8 fathoms along the east shore, opposite Codville Island. An unimproved trail runs from the head of the anchorage to Sagar Lake. Several readers have told us that while the trail is rough and difficult, the lake is beautiful.

Long Point Cove. Use chart 3785. Long Point Cove is located on the west side of Fisher Channel, approximately 1 mile south of Lama Passage. Although Sailing Directions mentions Long Point Cove as a good anchorage for small craft, it isn't as scenic or interesting as other anchorages in the area. On entering, favor the west shore to avoid a 3-foot drying rock some 250-300 yards north of Long Point. The rock is shown on the chart.

Lama Passage. Use chart 3785. Lama Passage leads westward and northward from Fisher Channel to New Bella Bella. Cruise ships and B.C. ferries use this passage regularly. Keep a sharp lookout ahead and astern.

Fancy Cove. Use chart 3785. Fancy Cove lies on the south shore of Lama Passage, and is a delightful little anchorage. Don Douglass writes about the cove in his books, and he

deserves thanks from the entire cruising community for telling about it. Anchor in 2-4 fathoms wherever it looks good.

Fannie Cove. Use chart 3785. Fannie Cove, on the south shore of Lama Passage in Cooper Inlet, is a beautiful little spot, with an obvious anchoring nook on its eastern shore just inside the entrance. Unfortunately, the holding ground is only fair. We tried twice to get a good set in the little nook and once farther out, but each time we dragged without much effort. We would overnight in settled weather only. Study the chart before entering. Leave Gus Island and the little dot islet west of Gus Island to port as you approach.

Jane Cove. Use chart 3785. Jane Cove, on the south shore of Lama Passage in Cooper Inlet, offers shelter, but lacks scenic quality. Study the chart carefully before entering, to avoid shoals and rocks. We prefer Fannie Cove, despite its marginal holding, or Fancy Cove, which is spectacular by comparison.

Bella Bella. Use chart 3785. Bella Bella lies on the northeastern shore of Lama Passage, and is largely abandoned. A dock is located there, but if you're looking for a dock we suggest Shearwater instead.

④ **New Bella Bella.** Use chart 3785. New Bella Bella (Waglisla) is a major Indian village, with gasoline and diesel fuel, good water, garbage drop, a well-stocked band store with pay phone, liquor store, post office, bank (limited hours), and hospital. *No laundromat.* The closest laundromat is at Shearwater. Each year, the townspeople seem increasingly friendly toward visitors. Last year many offered warm hellos, and took the time to chat us up. The New Bella Bella fuel dock, which was rebuilt in 1998, is busy. (Good thing it was rebuilt. The old dock was dangerous.) We have found the fuel dock attendants to be courteous, but jealous of their lunch hour. You may have to be patient. The fuel pumps, with meters, are on the wharf above the fuel float.

New Bella Bella's recently-installed water treatment plant provides a steady stream of clear water at the fuel dock. The band store at the head of the dock has a good stock of meats, produce, frozen foods and baked goods. Selection is best shortly after the ferry brings stock. The help is friendly. A stairway leads to the lower level, where you'll find soft goods and souvenirs. The post office entrance is adjacent to the band store's main entry. The liquor store is the lower level of the band store building, in the back. You'll see the entry as you walk up the wharf. A water taxi runs between Shearwater and New Bella Bella.

Cultural note: The white culture, with its nautical etiquette rooted in centuries of British and American naval tradition, does not board or touch another person's boat—emergencies excepted—without first being invited ("Permission to come aboard, sir?"). The Indian

Ocean Falls

This sidebar has appeared each year since 1997, and inspired many boaters to see Ocean Falls for themselves. As noted elsewhere, Gunter Hogrefe is now retired, and the museum has become a reality. But the feeling of the town is unchanged.

OCEAN FALLS, at the head of Cousins Inlet, is a ghost town, lost on the B.C. coast. When you round Coolidge Point in Cousins Inlet you see the "falls," the spillway from the dam. Below the dam are extensive docks, and on top of the docks a huge mill. To the left of the mill are tall, modern buildings. It is only after you land and walk uptown that you realize the buildings are empty, and the north coast wind is whistling through their open windows.

Until it closed in 1973, the Crown Zellerbach mill was the second largest on the coast, and Ocean Falls was a busy community of more than 5,000. We are told that championship swimmers came from its Olympic-size swimming pool. The pool is filled in now. Machinery sits on the dirt. When Crown Zellerbach gave up the mill, the province, unwilling to lose the jobs, tried to run it. In 1980 it too gave up. The mill's machinery was removed, and in 1986 bulldozers came to level the town. The town's residents stood in front of the bulldozers and backed them down, though not until after many of the houses and other buildings had been destroyed.

Downtown, fortunately, was largely spared. The Ocean Falls Hotel, tall and imposing, is empty. Its doors are chained shut and signs warn off trespassers. A dormitory where mill workers lived looks almost ready to accept a new crop of college students. Its doors too are chained shut. A 2-story garden-court apartment complex, 1970s style, is overgrown with weeds. The windows are broken and the plumbing fixtures torn out. We watched as a lonesome wind fluttered the few ragged and water-

(Continued on page 274)

The dam at Ocean Falls supplies power for Shearwater and New Bella Bella.

Norman Brown, President of the Ocean Falls Historical Society Museum. Some restoration work still needed.

stained curtains that remained. We thought, a story longs to be written. A film waits to be made.

The best-maintained building is the Courthouse, occupied by the government. It houses the post office, the clinic, and the office of Gunter H. Hogrefe, the Chairman and Administrator of the Ocean Falls Improvement District. We found Gunter Hogrefe dressed neatly in slacks, necktie and sport jacket, surrounded by papers in his office. He worked in the mill for 30 years, starting in a rotten job called "the salt mine," and finishing as project coordinator. He told us he was one of the small band that defied the bulldozers in 1986.

Now he is looking for new business to revitalize Ocean Falls. A company tried to sell bottled water from the pure offerings of Link Lake, behind the dam. Stock was sold and publicity sent out. The venture failed. Hogrefe points out that Ocean Falls has a perfect deep water harbor, and an infrastructure ready to go to work. Applicants welcome.

We also happened upon another citizen, Norman Brown ("Nearly Normal Norman, they call me"), the proud President of the Ocean Falls Historical Society Museum. The museum consists of what once was the company's large and comfortable guest house.

Vandalism, frozen and burst water pipes, and a leaky roof reduced the guest house to unlivability, and Norman is the one-man construction gang working on the slow restoration. The roof has been replaced, the water pipes

repaired, electricity restored, and several of the rooms brought somewhat back. In the kitchen Norman showed where vinyl floor covering had been removed to reveal a wonderful late 1920s floor. In other rooms the removal of wall coverings brought forth elegant paneling. Norman showed us toilets that flushed—a major achievement. Then he took me (Mrs. Hale said she'd wait) into the attic to see the bats.

Up the stairs we climbed, and through a door into the attic. The space was clean but musty-smelling. Small piles of loose material lay here and there—bat guano, excellent fertilizer.

The light was dim in the attic, and I couldn't see any bats. Norman walked to a corner, reached into the shadows, and produced two handsful of small furry creatures with doglike faces and skin-covered wings. He offered them to me, but I was not used to such animals and

thought my strong grip might harm them. So he set them free. They flew sqeaking around the attic, and settled back in their corner. I urged Mrs. Hale to come see the bats, but she said no.

A short distance from the guest house/museum, a failing boardwalk fronts on what once were pleasant homes with a view of the inlet. The boardwalk is rotting and sagging and the houses are empty. Ocean Falls searches for industry and Nearly Normal Norman Brown makes slow progress on the guest house. Meanwhile, around the edges, Nature reclaims the land.

—*Robert Hale*

Gunter Hogrefe, the now-retired Administrator for the Ocean Falls Improvement District, in his Courthouse Building office.

See area map page 268

SURPRISE *in the slings of Shearwater's
70-ton Travelift.*

*A little outboard
motor repair on
the docks at
Shearwater.*

*Wide concrete docks
fill up in high season
at Shearwater.
This photo was taken
early in the season.*

culture is not rooted in these traditions. Don't
be surprised if they sit on your rail while they
await their turn for fuel, or if the children simply
hop aboard and start looking around.

Kliktsoatli Harbour. Use chart 3785.
Kliktsoatli Harbour is 2 miles east of New
Bella Bella, and is the location of Shearwater.
Those preferring to anchor out can find and
mooring buoys and good anchoring on the
eastern shore, as shown on the 1:12,000 inset on chart 3785.

⑤ **Shearwater Marine Resort,** Denny Island, B.C. V0T 1B0, (250)957-2305;
(250)957-2366 (after hours); fax (250)957-
2422; www.shearwater.ca, e-mail general@
shearwater.ca. Monitors VHF channel 06. Use
chart 3785. Open all year, guest moorage, limited 15 & 30 amp power, propane, washrooms,
showers, laundry, ice, restaurant, pub, telephones, haulout, garbage drop, recycling, store,
boating supplies, charts, lodging, post office.
A fuel dock, with diesel and gasoline, is now
up and running.

Shearwater, 2 miles east of New Bella Bella
in Kliktsoatli Harbour, is the most complete
marine facility between Port Hardy and Prince
Rupert. The docks are wide and comfortable,
although electrical power extends only a short
distance out the dock. They can haul out boats
to 70 tons and repair almost anything, including electronics. The pub is popular, and
the restaurant serves good food. The store carries licenses, charts, ice, boating supplies and
limited groceries. An air field is a short distance away. A water taxi makes regular runs
to New Bella Bella and return. The marina is
the site of a WWII military seaplane base. The
large hangar now serves as the shop.

Several readers have told us the above description, although factually accurate, led them
to think Shearwater was a more elegant than

it is, and so were disappointed. You must understand that while Shearwater is attentively
managed, it is located in the middle of the
wilderness, and is the center for the work boat
and commercial fish boat fleets in that area.
Even in the summer the weather is hard, and
the facilities get hard use. When the fish boats
are in, their crews will include energetic young
men. If these fellows are joined by residents
of New Bella Bella for an evening of relaxing
in the pub, things can get a little high-spir-
ited around closing time. You might find the
night air filled with loud voices and naughty
words, and the boats heading back to New
Bella Bella will not exactly *putt-putt* away. We
enjoy Shearwater, especially the camaraderie
and sense of community we find among fellow cruisers on the docks. But we recognize
that we are a long way from the city, and ad-
just accordingly.

Service note: In 1998 our port propeller hit
a piece of wood—decisively—and we limped
into Shearwater for haulout, inspection, and
any needed repairs. Luckily, *Surprise's* Nibral
propellers were tougher than the wood, and
no repairs were needed. The Shearwater crew,
headed by yard manager Al Tite, was efficient
and helpful. The bill was what one would expect
for haulout and two hours of careful inspection time, no more and no less. We were pleased.
(Marina map this page)

Gunboat Passage. Use chart 3720, with its
1:12,100 inset of Gunboat Passage. Gunboat
Passage connects Seaforth Channel with Fisher
Channel, and provides a scenic route for a run

between Bella Bella/Shearwater and Ocean
Falls. The passage is littered with reefs and
rocks, but well marked with aids to navigation. The trickiest spot is the narrow fairway
between Denny Point and Maria Island. We're
not sure exactly where the rocks are, so we
go through dead slow, with one eye on the
depth sounder. A second tricky spot is the
reef that extends from the southern shore toward Dingle Island. Watch the currents in this
area. Once, we almost swept onto the reef while
motoring slowly and carefully, but with a following current.

A red nun buoy marks the outer end of
the reef. Red, Right, Returning assumes you
are returning eastbound, from the sea. In 1997

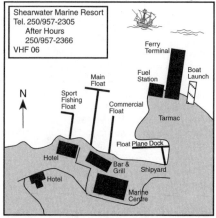

Reference only — not for navigation

Shearwater Marine Resort

we watched helplessly as a small powerboat got it backwards and drove up on the reef at 20 knots. No injuries, fortunately, but their outdrive was badly damaged and we towed the family to Shearwater for repairs. They had brought their boat all the way from the interior, launched at Bella Coola, and were just beginning their holiday. Being hauled out for expensive repairs was not what they had intended.

We find **Gosse Bay**, west of Maria Island, to be a good anchorage along the west side of the westernmost cove. Another good anchorage is the pretty cove lying west of **Dunn Point**, at the west end of Gunboat Passage. The entrance looks tricky on the chart, but if you leave the small islet to port as you enter you'll have good water. Anchor inside in 5-7 fathoms. Excellent protection.

Forit Bay. Use chart 3720. Forit Bay, on the eastern approach to Gunboat Passage, is an excellent, protected anchorage in 3-4 fathoms. The entrance, however, is encumbered by a large rock that lies between Flirt Island and the point of land that marks the inner part of the bay. We could not see the rock at high tide, but it was visible through the water at a little less than half tide.

To enter Forit Bay, leave Flirt Island well to port, and head toward the drying cove inside Wakash Point. A study of chart 3720 will make this clear. When fairly close to the wooded point off your bow, turn south into the an-

This was the view from our anchorage in Discovery Cove.

chorage. Rocks off this wooded point dry 11 feet. As we entered the anchorage our depth sounder showed a least depth of 9 feet. At low tide deeper draft vessels should approach cautiously.

Kynumpt Harbour. Use chart 3720. Kynumpt Harbour indents the north tip of Campbell Island, at the eastern end of Seaforth Channel. Sailing Directions says the local name is Strom Bay. The entrance is open and easy, but study the chart carefully to identify and avoid rocks on the western and southern shores. The northernmost indent on the eastern shore is reported to be a good anchorage, as is Strom Cove, the arm that extends to the southeast. We poked around Strom Cove to find a good

lunch stop, but saw mostly 9-13 fathoms on the sounder. At those depths, even a 3:1 scope would swing us too close to rocks near shore, so we anchored in the outer bay, 7 fathoms, west of Spratt Point.

Troup Passage. Use chart 3720. Troup Passage runs between Chatfield Island and Cunningham Island, and leads to Roscoe Inlet. Troup Narrows is at the northern end. Near the southern end of Troup Passage an unnamed bay sometimes called Discovery Cove is an excellent anchorage.

Discovery Cove. Use chart 3720. Discovery Cove (we're using Douglass's name, which other cruisers seem to be adopting) at Lat 52°

13.50'N is the only major indent of Cunningham Island from Troup Passage. It was first recommended to us by John and Evonne McPherson, who spend the summers cruising the coast in their perfectly-maintained 45-foot Grenfell, *Malacandra*. The chart shows rocks on the southwest shore of the entry, but if you go in along the northeast shore and you'll have no problems. The cove is beautiful, one of the most beautiful on the coast. It is surrounded by high mountains and seemingly immune to any storm winds that might be about. Anchor with excellent holding in either of the two coves along the north shore.

Troup Narrows. Use the 1:6000 inset on chart 3720. Troup Narrows, with maximum tidal currents of only about 2 knots, is easy to run. Assuming a passage from south to north, identify the reef that dries 15 feet near the south entrance to the narrows. As the chart shows, this reef is marked with a beacon. Leave the reef to port, and when past the beacon, slide west to the beautiful rock cliffs of Chatfield Island. Stay on that side until the point of land on Cunningham Island is abeam, then trend east to the far shore of Cunningham Island to avoid the reef that extends from the 140-foot island. Study the chart and find the rocks you must avoid.

Wigham Cove. Use chart 3940 (Wigham Cove is shown on chart 3720 as well, but the depiction on chart 3940 is much more clear.) Wigham Cove, indenting the south shore of Yeo Island, is a popular anchorage and an excellent place to overnight before going out Seaforth Channel. Favor the west shore as you enter, until abeam the islets in the middle of the bay. Then turn to pass north of the islets to the favored anchorage in the northeast nook of the cove. This nook has room for several boats. In 1999 we shared this anchorage with a 60-footer and a 43-footer, with no crowding at all. An 80-footer was anchored in the southeast cove.

Uncharted rock: Be careful if you enter the southernmost nook of Wigham Cove. Notices to Shipping 30 Aug. 1999 reports an uncharted dangerous underwater rock with a depth of 0.5 meters at Lat 52°16.775'N Lon 128° 10.366'W (we converted seconds to tenths of a minute). This rock is close to and due east of the northernmost of the three drying rocks that extend from the eastern shore of the entrance to Wigham Cove. When entering this nook, favor the islets to the east.

Seaforth Channel. Use charts 3720 & 3728. Seaforth Channel connects the New Bella Bella/Shearwater area with Milbanke Sound to the west, and is part of the Inside Passage route. Ivory Island is at the western entrance.

Dundivan Inlet. Use chart 3720. Dundivan Inlet indents Dufferin Island near the eastern entrance to Seaforth Channel. It's a pretty spot, with several islets to break up the scenery, but the water is deep except near hazards. Two arms make up Lockhart Bay near the head.

The western arm is the more attractive anchorage. For overnight we would run a stern-tie to a tree. The eastern arm was deep (10 fathoms) until very near the head, and would require a shore-tie. Dundivan Inlet would not be a first choice unless weather was ugly and we were looking for a place to hole up.

Raymond Passage. Use chart 3787. Raymond Passage connects Seaforth Channel with Queens Sound, and sees few pleasure craft. The passage is open and free of hazards, and connects with Codfish Passage at the south end. If you're looking for a raw and exposed wilderness experience, and have the boat and navigation skills to manage it, Raymond Passage will lead you to it.

Thompson Bay. Use chart 3787. Thompson Bay lies on the west side of Stryker Island. Do not navigate these waters without a close study of chart 3787. At the northeast corner of Thompson Bay an excellent, protected cove indents Potts Island. The Canadian Hydrographic barge *Pender* was moored in this cove in 1997, when we spent two days with their hydrographers as they surveyed the area for a new chart. Enter the cove from the north, at Lat 52° 09.75'N Lon 128° 20.65'W (NAD 27). This entire area is beautiful and of course seldom visited. To get from Raymond Passage to Thompson Bay, run a course from the southern tip of Alleyne Island approximately 239° magnetic to the 140-foot island, then turn to a course of approximately 292° magnetic to Agnew Islet. You will leave Seen Island approximately 0.25 miles to the south. Rocks will be all around you, but as long as you stay in the pass you will have water.

Reid Passage/Port Blackney. Use chart 3710. In most cases, pleasure craft bound north or south will choose to avoid Milbanke Sound, and use the Reid Passage route east of Ivory Island. Chart 3710 makes the navigation straightforward. At the south end, be sure to identify all the rocks and islets, and buoy E50. In the middle of Reid Passage, pass to the east of Carne Rock. Port Blackney, at the north end of Reid Passage, has two anchorages, Boat Inlet and Oliver Cove.

Boat Inlet. Use chart 3710. Boat Inlet, at the southwest corner of Port Blackney, has a delightful basin for anchorage, very untouched feeling. The passage that leads to the basin is shallow, however, and rocks encumber the south shore and middle of the passage. Favor the north shore all the way in, with an alert lookout for the underwater rocks. The little bay on the north shore at the east end of the passage is shallow and rocky. Stay out. Depending on your vessel's draft, wait for half tide or higher. We went in and out near high tide.

Oliver Cove. Use chart 3710. Oliver Cove provincial park, on the east side of Port Blackney, is a safe and pretty anchorage. Enter carefully to avoid a charted rock in the middle of the fairway, and put the hook down

in 6 fathoms.

Perceval Narrows. Use chart 3710. The Inside Passage route leads across Mathieson Channel between Port Blackney and Perceval Narrows. Chart 3710 shows all the rocks and islets clearly. Tidal current predictions are found as a secondary station under Prince Rupert in Tide and Current Tables, Vol. 7. From south to north, lay a course that gives Cod Reefs a good offing to port as you leave Port Blackney. Then turn to approximately 270° magnetic and cross Mathieson Channel toward Martha Island, leaving Lizzie Rocks to starboard. We found noticeable turbulence in Mathieson Channel off Lizzie Rocks on an ebb tide. If you're southbound, once clear of Perceval Narrows steer a course of approximately 090° magnetic to give Walter Island and Cod Reefs a good offing.

Cockle Bay. Use chart 3710 or 3728. Cockle Bay, a short distance north of Perceval Narrows, has a beautiful beach and good protection from westerlies. For anchoring you can find 5-6 fathom depths along the south shore, and 10-15 fathoms in the middle, as shown on the chart.

Tom Bay. Use chart 3728. Tom Bay is on the east side of Mathieson Channel at Lat 52° 24.20'N. It's a good anchorage, though scarred by recent logging activity. As with most bays on this coast Tom Bay shoals at the head. Anchor in 10-12 fathoms.

Arthur Island. Use chart 3734. The coves north of Arthur Island, approximately 1.5 miles south of Oscar Passage on the west side of Mathieson Channel, are mentioned in Sailing Directions as a small boat anchorage, but we're not convinced. Neither cove is very scenic, and driftwood clogs the eastern cove. We would choose Rescue Bay, Salmon Bay or Tom Bay.

Salmon Bay. Use chart 3734. Salmon Bay is on the east side of Mathieson Channel, opposite the mouth of Oscar Passage. It is *deep* until the very head, where the bottom comes up to 8-10 fathoms. The bay is cozy, and we heard a loon—always a refreshing sound.

Oscar Passage. Use chart 3734. Oscar Passage is the wide open Inside Passage route between Mathieson Channel and Finlayson Channel. The seas, however, heap up where Oscar Passage joins Finlayson Channel, the result of swells from Milbanke Sound meeting current exiting Oscar Passage. In relatively quiet conditions we found these seas uncomfortable, and don't plan to repeat the experience. Jackson Passage, a short distance north, is our choice now, even if we must wait for slack water at Jackson Narrows.

Rescue Bay. Use large scale chart 3711 (much preferred) or chart 3734. Rescue Bay is the most popular anchorage in this area. It is well protected, with good holding, and has room for many boats. Study chart 3711 carefully

Marilynn Hale, chart
in hand, steers the boat
toward and through
Jackson Narrows.

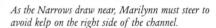

As the Narrows draw near, Marilynn must steer to
avoid kelp on the right side of the channel.

This rock, surrounded
by kelp, is in the squeaky
part of the Narrows.

before entering, and steer a determined mid-channel course between the two islands and their reefs that mark the entrance. We noted that departing fish boats not only steered such a course on their way out, but got well clear of both islands before turning. Once inside Rescue Bay, scout around with the depth sounder and pick your spot carefully. We saw one boat on the western side find the bottom at low tide, after being too eager to get the anchor down. Note the rock that dries 3 feet in the southeast corner of the bay.

Jackson Passage. Use chart 3734 (with inset) and chart 3711. Jackson Passage is the scenic route between Mathieson Channel and Finlayson Channel. The Passage is easily navigated, except for a tight spot at Jackson Narrows at the eastern end. The fairway through Jackson Narrows is quite narrow; kelp marks the rocks. While neither the chart nor Sailing Directions show the current directions, our observations (no guarantee) indicate that the flood current sets east and the ebb current west.

Jackson Narrows is blind. Before entering, either direction, it's a good idea to call ahead on VHF channel 16 to announce your intentions. We did that in 1998 (*Securité, securité, this is the 37-foot motor vessel Surprise, about to enter Jackson Narrows eastbound. Any westbound traffic please advise.*). To our astonishment a boat approaching the other end called back. Since we were about to enter, the other boat waited until we got through. Strongly favor the *south shore* all the way through the narrows, and keep a sharp lookout. A transit near high water slack would be the least anxious, although in 1998 we went through at low water slack with no difficulty.

Nowish Cove. Use charts 3734 and 3711. Nowish Cove lies a short distance south of the mouth of Jackson Passage on the east side

Finlayson Channel. Chart 3734 shows an anchorage symbol in the cove, but we weren't charmed. The bottom is 14 fathoms deep and currents from Nowish Narrows swirl through the bay. If we needed immediate protection from a southerly storm undoubtedly we would revise our somewhat negative opinion of this cove. Otherwise, if we were looking for a place to hide and had the time, Bottleneck Inlet, 11 miles farther north, would be a much better choice.

James Bay. Use chart 3962. James Bay, on the west side of Mathieson Channel, is open to southerly winds, but gets you out of the chop in the channel. It is a pretty spot, but the bottom shoals *abruptly* in the northwest corner. Anchor in 13 fathoms, where the little anchor symbol is on the chart.

FIORDLAND

Use chart 3962. The Fiordland Recreation Area was established in 1987, and is some of the most beautiful country on the coast. The mountains are sheer and beautiful and the wildlife abundant, but the anchorages are just about nonexistent. Fortunately, good anchorage can be found in Windy Bay, only a short distance away.

Fiordland begins just east of Bolin Bay at the north end of Sheep Passage, and includes Mussel Inlet and Kynoch Inlet. We include Bolin Bay in this section because it is so beautiful, and Windy Bay because it is the best anchorage near Fiordland.

Windy Bay. Windy Bay is on the south shore of Sheep Passage, near the eastern end. The chart shows anchorage in the middle, but you can find more protected anchorage in what we call **Cookie Cove**, just east of the little island at the northeast corner of the bay in 10 fathoms. Excellent holding.

Bolin Bay. Bolin Bay is set in a bowl of sheer rock mountains, with a beautiful drying flat at the head and a magnificent rock slide on the south shore. We did not anchor, but did find a few spots with depths of 6-10 fathoms near the head of the bay. With care you might get a safe amount of scope out and stay off the flats. Windy Bay is a better choice.

Oatwish Bay. Oatwish Bay is at the north end of Mussel Inlet, and is shown in "Continuation A" on chart 3962. The bay is too deep for anchoring, but amazing Lizette Falls will have you reaching for the camera. We enjoyed lunch here.

Poison Cove. The run across the top of Mussel Inlet to Poison Cove left us awestruck. Our notes say, "Poison Cove dwarfed us. I run out of superlatives."

Kynoch Inlet. Kynoch Inlet, 8.5 miles long, leads off Mathieson Channel. With its rock walls and waterfalls it is stunning. If you go ashore watch out for grizzly bear. We are sorry we cannot speak from any more experience with Kynoch Inlet, however. When we visited, the hour was growing late and the barometer was falling rapidly. The cloud line was at 200 feet. Mist was gathering. We made for a safe anchorage.

Correpondent Bill Hales, however, reports, "I found Kynoch Inlet to be the highlight of this year's trip. The weather was not the best but the mountains dropping 4000 feet to the sea were spectacular. Waterfalls were everywhere, but the best one was near the entrance. There was even SNOW at sea level, in a narrow valley opposite Culpepper Lagoon."

Culpepper Lagoon. "In the entrance the current turns 15-30 minutes before Bella Bella. The entrance is straightforward as per the chart, with a minimum of 2 fathoms at low tide. Good anchorage in 3 fathoms just east of an old cabin, probably built in the 60s by hippies or religious fanatics and now dilapidated, near Riot Creek." *[Bill Hales]*

Burke Channel, Dean Channel, Bella Coola

North Bentinck Arm • South Bentinck Arm
Labouchere Channel • Elcho Harbour • Eucott Bay

BURKE CHANNEL AND DEAN CHANNEL lie on the south and north sides of King Island, and plunge deep into the coast range of mountains. We had been told that this is some of the most beautiful and awe-inspiring country imaginable, but after seeing so much beautiful country all along the B.C. coast, we expected it to be just more of the same. We were wrong. A circumnavigation of King Island will astonish you. Gone is the raw coast with its low, wave-pounded islands. A short distance up either channel puts you inland, bounded on each side by high mountains. If you're going to spend some time on this coast, see these waters.

Burke Channel. Use chart 3729. Burke Channel leads 38 miles inland, beginning at Edmund Point, just north of Namu. The lower reaches of Burke Channel, from Edmund Point to Restoration Bay, are subject to strong tidal currents and heavy tide-rips, but in the upper reaches the tidal streams are weak. Quite often the surface water is in an almost constant ebb, the result of fresh water flowing toward the sea. When this surface ebb meets a spring flood, the result is tide-rips, whirlpools, and general confusion.

On warm summer days the heating of the air inland produces an up-channel sea breeze that can begin as early as 1000 and blow strongly until sundown. During such conditions, make your runs early and find shelter before the wind starts to blow. Burke Channel has a reputation for being nasty when the wind is up.

The north end of Burke Channel divides into South Bentinck Arm and North Bentinck Arm (Bella Coola is at the head of North Bentinck Arm), and Labouchere Passage, which leads to Dean Channel. When the ebb current is flowing and the up-channel sea breeze is blowing, expect very rough seas at the confluence of these channels—another reason for early morning runs before the B.C. interior heats up.

All these cautions make Burke Channel sound impenetrable, which is not the case at all. The prudent skipper simply will avoid being out there when the conditions exist to make

for a rough ride.

The best anchorage along Burke Channel is at the head of Kwatna Inlet, with a second-best choice in the small cove just north of Cathedral Point.

Approximately 8 miles up the channel from Edmund Point a large logging camp is located near the outlet of Doc Creek. We have been told that while the logging camp definitely is not in the marina business, they will not shoo-away a boat that really needs a place to tie up for the night. We are not encouraging such visits, but it's nice to know the option exists if it is needed.

Fougner Bay. Use chart 3729. Fougner Bay lies on the south side of Burke Channel near the entrance, just east of Edmund Point. The outer part of the bay is somewhat protected, with anchorage in 7-9 fathoms. To us it feels uninviting. An inner cove, however, is a perfect spot. It was recommended to us by our friend John Schlagel, who with his wife Helen has explored this coast for years and years on their 8-meter sloop *Aurora*. Douglass, in his North Coast book, also recommends this cove. Find the 2_2 sounding back in the bay. That's the cove. To get in, pass between the + symbol on the chart (indicating a dangerous underwater rock) and the little clutch of islets southwest of the + symbol. Once clear of the rock, loop into the cove. (Note the tiny dot just off the southernmost of those islets. It's another rock.) Study the chart carefully before entering Fougner Bay. The rocks off the entry are easy to avoid, but you want to know where *they* are and where *you* are.

Kwatna Inlet. Use chart 3729. Kwatna Inlet extends some 12 miles into the mainland, and is too deep for anchoring until near the head. Watch carefully for the drying flats at the head. We have been told by several people that it is an excellent place to put the hook down.

Cathedral Point. Use chart 3729. Cathedral Point, a weather reporting station, marks the north entrance to Kwatna Inlet, and is easily identified by its white building and tower. Just north of the point, a tiny cove with dramatic granite walls makes a good anchorage in 4 fathoms. The cove has excellent protection from up-channel winds, but the mass of large logs on the south beach suggests that down-channel winds and seas blow right in. We patrolled the cove but did not stay. Correspondent Bill Hales, from Victoria, has anchored for the night and reports a pleasant experience.

South Bentinck Arm. Use chart 3730. South Bentinck Arm, 25 miles long, lies between high mountains. The relatively few cruisers who have gone all the way up the arm say it is beautiful. We have gone as far as Larso Bay, which has good anchorage in 6-8 fathoms. A float with a ramp to shore is at the north end of the bay. You could tie to the float or anchor off it. The mountains across from Larso Bay are beautiful.

Talheo Hot Springs. Talheo Hot Springs is located near the mouth of Hotsprings Creek on the west shore of South Bentinck Arm, a short distance south of Bensins Island. Anchorage is exposed.

North Bentinck Arm. Use chart 3730. The water in North Bentinck Arm is green and milky, the result of the Bella Coola River emptying into the head of the arm. We found no good anchorages, so you have to hope for room at the Bella Coola docks. An eatery is in the prominent red buildings on the north side of the arm. A woman we met said it is excellent. Log booming activity is going on, so watch for drift. We saw a large number of floating propeller-benders.

Bella Coola. Use chart 3730 with inset of Bella Coola public floats. Bella Coola is an

Abandoned buildings on the fish packing dock, Bella Coola.

A beautiful bowl sits at the head of Elcho Harbour.

interesting place to visit. The government floats now are run by the Bella Coola Harbour Authority, and they are making improvements. Water is available all the way out the docks, and the 15 amp dock power has been replaced with 20 amp. They are trying to arrange for more guest moorage.

The Shell fuel dock is adjacent to the public floats.

The fish packing facility next to the public floats is closed. We did peer in the office window when we visited Bella Coola in 1997. Desks were inside. Old calendars were on the walls. The room looked as if one afternoon the staff had boxed up their files but little else, and shipped them out. That evening they locked the door and left town. The story of the coast: Ventures come, run, and leave. The docks rot, the buildings sag and eventually fall down. (Since our visit, this property was purchased by Craig Widsten of Shearwater Marine Group, with plans for development.)

The town of Bella Coola is located 3 kilometers (about 2 miles) from the dock. While you can take a cab, try to walk at least one way. The lush vegetation, the waterfalls beside the road, and the Bella Coola River Estuary are wonderful. When walking, stay on the water side of the road. There's more room and it's safer. Be sure to wave to passing vehicle traffic.

Darren Edgar is the Bella Coola goodwill ambassador. An Indian, he knows local lore and legend, and for a reasonable fee will show you things you couldn't find for yourself.

The town has provincial and federal government offices, a post office, hospital, motel, liquor store, laundromat, showers, and a well-stocked co-op store. The co-op delivers to the dock free with purchases of $70 or more. The museum is worth a visit.

Bella Coola is the B.C. interior's window on the coast. A remarkable number of boats are trailered each year from the interior to Bella Coola, where they stay the summer, either tied to the dock or on trailer. Residents of the interior are some of the most enthusiastic saltwater sport fishermen we have met. They come a long way to get to Bella Coola, and when they get there they *fish*. We've met them at Shearwater, Ocean Falls, Namu, and Hakai. Their ice chests and freezers are full of halibut, crab, rockfish and salmon. And they all launch at Bella Coola.

⑪ **Bella Coola Harbour Authority,** Box 751, Bella Coola V0T 2C0, (250)799-5633. They try to monitor VHF channel 06. Open all year with guest moorage. Facilities include 20 amp power, water, portable toilets, tidal grid, garbage drop, waste oil drop, pay phones. Fuel dock adjacent. The Harbormaster's office is at head of pier. The marine ways adjacent to the public dock is in operation. If no one happens to be there, ask around.

The floats are located behind a rock breakwater, and are home port to a large number of commercial fish boats. All of A dock and the south side of B dock are reserved for pleasure craft. The water on the land side of A

dock is shallow, especially at low tide. Feel your way in and find a spot. If the wind is blowing, getting into the docks can be tricky. Quite likely you will have to raft off another boat. If necessary, take temporary moorage at one of the commercial floats, but fender well on your outboard side. Fish boats can land roughly.

Town is 3 km away. Taxis are available. Now that the local Harbour Authority is running the facility more interest is spent on visiting yachties. Even so, Bella Coola is not a "destination marina." Self-reliance is the key.

⑪ **Shell Canada Fuel Dock,** Saugstad Contracting, Ltd., (250)799-5580, home (250) 799-5554 or (250)982-2304. Open Mon.-Fri. 0900-1630 all year, closed at lunch. Call for off-hours service. Gasoline, diesel, lubricants. Gerrald Saugstad is the owner. He told us his great-grandfather led the original band of Norwegian settlers to Bella Coola. Gerrald's grandfather remained, as did Gerrald's father, now Gerrald, Gerrald's son, and Gerrald's son's two children. All have called or presently call Bella Coola their home. Six generations.

Labouchere Channel. Use chart 3730. Labouchere Channel connects the north end of Burke Channel with Dean Channel. **Mesachie Nose**, at the confluence of the two channels, is a magnificent glacier-smoothed rock prominence on the north shore. Tidal currents combined with winds and surface water runoff can create very difficult seas in this area. If the water is flat, see Mesachie Nose up close.

The waters of Labouchere Channel itself are generally smooth and wind-free. The scenery, with waterfalls spilling from high mountains, is fabulous. Our notes say, "So *many* waterfalls!"

Dean Channel. Use charts 3729 & 3730. Dean Channel connects with Fisher Channel at the mouth of Cousins Inlet (Ocean Falls) and continues northward and inland 53 miles. It is bounded on both sides by high, spectacular mountains, and, with Burke Channel, offers some of the finest scenery along the coast. When we were in Dean Channel we felt as if we were high up in the mountains, on a huge lake. We felt as if we should be chewing gum to clear our ears. The concept

of being at sea level in these surroundings was hard to grasp.

Unlike Burke Channel, Dean Channel is not subject to tide-rips. But like Burke Channel, a strong up-channel sea breeze can develop when warm temperatures in the interior heat the air and suck cold ocean air up the various inlets. This sea breeze can begin as early as 1000 and last until sundown. Because summertime freshets often create a nearly permanent ebb surface current, when the wind blows against the current an ugly chop can develop.

The principal points of interest on Dean Channel are Elcho Harbour, Sir Alexander Mackenzie Rock, Eucott Bay and hot springs, and Nascall Bay. Cascade Inlet is reported to be stunning, but not a good place to anchor.

Jenny Inlet. Use chart 3781; 3729. If Jenny Inlet were someplace else it might be interesting. But we found it ordinary, too deep for anchoring, with a logging camp near the head. Elcho Harbour, 8 miles farther up Dean Channel, or Cousins Inlet (Ocean Falls), 5 miles down-channel, are far better choices.

Sir Alexander Mackenzie Rock. Use chart 3781; 3729. Sir Alexander Mackenzie Rock is marked by a cairn at the mouth to Elcho Harbour. On 22 July 1793 Mackenzie completed his overland journey across Canada to the Pacific Ocean, and marked his accomplishment with ochre paint on the rock. Later the inscription was carved into the stone. You can bring the boat right up to the monument, watching for underwater rocks close to shore, and take your own picture of it. Or you can anchor out and dinghy ashore, leaving somebody aboard in case the wind makes up.

Elcho Harbour. Use chart 3781; 3729. If you are looking for a pretty spot, Elcho Harbour will not disappoint. It's stunning. The inlet extends a little more than 2 miles back between steep high mountains, and appears perfectly protected from all winds. Waterfalls plummet from the sides. A lovely bowl captures the head of the inlet, with the obligatory stream that creates an estuary and mudflat. Anchor in 15-18 fathoms off a delightful waterfall on the west side, about one-third of the way in. Or anchor at the head in 15 fath-

Finlayson Channel to Prince Rupert

Klemtu • Butedale • Hartley Bay • Grenville Channel
Prince Rupert

oms before it shelves up to mudflat. Take the dinghy back out to Sir Alexander Mackenzie Rock for a little history.

Eucott Hot Springs, Eucott Bay.

Eucott Bay. Use chart 3729. Eucott Bay is a gorgeous spot, about as pretty as any we have anchored in. The mountains along the eastern and northeastern sides remind us of Ansel Adams' Yosemite photos. Photographers, bring your view camera. Half-dome exists in Eucott Bay. **Eucott Hot Springs** is located near the head of the bay, inshore of a line of pilings. The hot springs have been improved with concrete to make an excellent soaking basin. Unfortunately, the water is too hot for soaking. Perhaps it was cooler in earlier times, or perhaps our present constitution just can't take the heat. The Waggoner's publisher felt that he would go in a baritone and come out a soprano. In our view and in the view of others we've met, you won't get your bath at Eucott Hot Springs.

Craig Widsten, owner of Shearwater Marine Resort, told us that in 1948 his father and he journeyed to Eucott Bay to pack mud and hotspring water for sale to health and beauty fanatics in Europe. We're sure it was elegant—hotspring water and mud from the remote Canadian coast, to smooth away the wrinkles and cure what ails you.

Enter Eucott Bay along the east (starboard) side. Once inside, a large basin unfolds. Find a good spot in the middle and put the hook down. Take the dinghy up to the hot springs. At low tide wear boots. The beach is muddy.

Nascall Bay. Use chart 3729. Nascall Hot Springs is near the mouth of Nascall Bay, but it's been turned into a private resort, developed by a pleasant man named Frank Tracey and his wife Elaine. You'll recognize the buildings by their blue roofs. The Traceys welcome visitors, and when all the building is finished this could be quite a spot. They plan for a total of 800 feet of docks, and possibly fuel. We'd appreciate our readers keeping us informed about this development.

Charts	
3711	PLANS – Vicinity of Princess Royal Island
3734	Jorkins Point to Sarah Island (1:36,000)
3738	Sarah Island to Swanson Bay (1:1,35,800)
3739	Swanson Bay to Work Island (1:35,600)
3740	Work Island to Point Cumming (1:35,500)
3742	Otter Passage to McKay Reach (1:70,900)
3772	Grenville Channel, Sainty Point to Baker Inlet (1:32,200)
3773	Grenville Channel, Baker Inlet to Ogden Channel (1:36,500)
3927	Bonilla Island to Edye Passage (1:77,800)
3957	Approaches to Prince Rupert Harbour (1:40,000)
3958	Prince Rupert Harbour (1:20,000)

⑥ **Klemtu.** Use chart 3734 and large scale chart 3711. Klemtu is a major Indian village, located behind Cone Island on the west side of Finlayson Channel. The fuel dock, open Monday-Saturday, and the band store are at the north end of town. Both are closed for lunch 1200-1300. You'll find gasoline, diesel, propane, and stove oil, and ample clear water from a new water treatment system. The fuel dock faces the channel, and wash from passing boat traffic is apt to bounce you around. Be sure you are well-tied and well-fendered. If the attendant is not in the office shack on the pier, call Steve Robinson on VHF channel 06. The entire village monitors channel 06. If Steve isn't available, somebody else will answer.

Klemtu is the last fuel stop until Hartley Bay, approximately 65 miles north. Until 1997, when Hartley Bay's fuel system became operational, it was necessary to carry fuel for the entire 140 mile run between Klemtu and Prince Rupert.

The band store at the head of the fuel dock pier carries a wide selection of groceries and other essentials (no liquor), but the stock gets thin a few days after the ferry has delivered it. A pay telephone is just outside the store. The post office is some distance away in the village proper. On one visit, Stella Alexander, the store manager, offered to carry our outgoing mail over for us, and we accepted. The village has a public dock, but it is exposed to

wash from passing boats. We would look for a quieter anchorage.

Alexander Inlet. Use chart 3734. Alexander Inlet extends 5 miles into Princess Royal Island, beginning where Meyers Passage and Tolmie Channel meet. If you're fed up with the throngs of yachties and crowded anchorages on this part of the coast (we're joking), here is where you can escape them. The early sections of Alexander Inlet are bounded by steep mountains, and are beautiful. The head, however, is surrounded by low, treed hills, and is rather ordinary. But, being 5 miles off the beaten path, chances are you'll be the only boat.

The chart shows the inlet well. The only tricky part is near Bingham Narrows. After clearing the reef that dries 17 feet before you reach Bingham Narrows, sag to the west shore to avoid the rocks, marked by kelp, that dry 4 feet just before you reach the narrows themselves.

The head of the inlet is wide open, with ample room to avoid the rock that dries 8 feet lying off the west shore. Anchor in 5-6 fathoms with outstanding holding.

One of the hilltops looks like the profile of a woman lying on her side, and we named it Sleeping Woman. See if you agree. We saw a pair of birds that our field guide identified as red-throated loons, not seen as often as common loons. A lagoon pours into the very head of the inlet, making fluffs of white foam on the water's surface. We rowed over and took pictures, but didn't take the time to explore further. It's very pretty.

The next morning our final note, written after the previous day's notes called the head of Alexander Inlet rather ordinary, reads, "This is a neat spot."

Mary Cove. Use chart 3734. Mary Cove is on the east side of Finlayson Channel, across from Klemtu. It is a pleasant little cove, but we found it open to southwest winds. Anchor in 8-9 fathoms inside. A salmon stream empties into Mary Cove. We saw a nice-size salmon jump. Just outside, a gillnetter had his net stretched halfway across the mouth of the cove.

Bottleneck Inlet. Use chart 3734. Bottleneck Inlet, at Lat 52°42.8'N on the east side of Finlayson Arm, is an outstanding anchorage. It is protected and beautiful, and big enough for several boats. The north side of the inlet has superb rock walls. The chart shows a least depth of just over a fathom in the narrow entry. Deeper draft vessels should enter cautiously at low tide. The chart fails to show a 13-15 fathom hole a short distance inside the entry sill. The bottom then comes up to

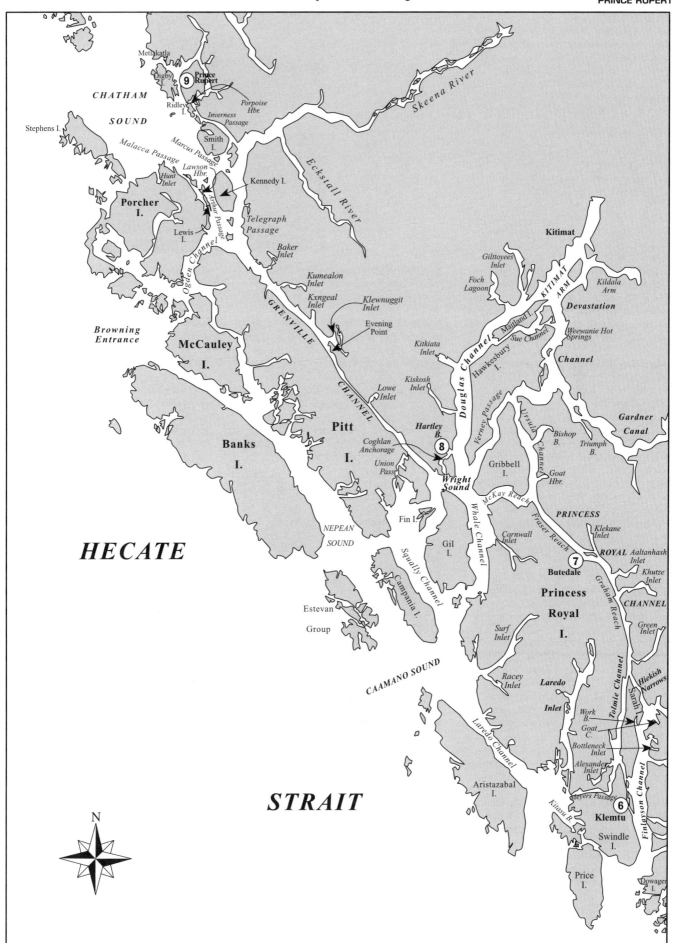

Metlakatla

Digby I.

⑨ Prince Rupert

CHATHAM

Ridley I.

Porpoise Hbr.

SOUND

Stephens I.

Inverness Passage

Smith I.

Marcus Passage

Malacca Passage

Lawson Hbr.

Kennedy I.

Skeena River

Eckstall River

Hunt Inlet

Arthur Passage

PORCHER I.

Telegraph Passage

Lewis I.

Baker Inlet

Ogden Channel

Kumealon Inlet

GRENVILLE

Kxngeal Inlet

Klewnuggit Inlet

Evening Point

Kitimat

Gilttoyees Inlet

Foch Lagoon

Kildala Arm

KITIMAT ARM

Devastation

Maitland I.

Sue Channel

Weewanie Hot Springs

Browning Entrance

McCAULEY I.

CHANNEL

Kitkiata Inlet

Hawkesbury I.

Channel

Douglas Channel

Verney Passage

Kiskosh Inlet

Gardner Canal

Lowe Inlet

Pitt I.

Banks I.

Hartley B.

Ursula Channel

Bishop B.

Triumph B.

Coghlan Anchorage

⑧

Gribbell I.

Goat Hbr.

Union Pass

Wright Sound

HECATE

Fin I.

NEPEAN SOUND

Gil I.

Whale Channel

McKay Reach

PRINCESS

Klekane Inlet

Squally Channel

Cornwall Inlet

Fraser Reach

ROYAL

Aaltanhash Inlet

Campania I.

Khutze Inlet

⑦

Butedale

CHANNEL

Estevan Group

Princess

Graham Reach

Green Inlet

CAAMANO SOUND

Royal

Surf Inlet

I.

Laredo Channel

Racey Inlet

Laredo

Tolmie Channel

Sarah

Hiekish Narrows

Inlet

Work B.

Goat C.

HECATE

Bottleneck Inlet

Alexander Inlet

STRAIT

Aristazabal I.

Klemtu

Finlayson Channel

Kitasu B.

Meyers Passage

⑥

Klemtu

Swindle I.

N

Price I.

Dowager

4-6 fathoms.

We anchored in Bottleneck Inlet prior to the arrival of a forewarned on-shore gale (four people died in that storm). The storm hit at 0130. We could see the clouds racing overhead and hear the wind roaring in the trees above us, but except for four tongues of strong wind that slammed into our boat between 0130 and 0400, the air around us was almost calm.

Goat Cove. Use chart 3738. Goat Cove indents the eastern shore near the north end of Finlayson Channel. An inner basin is reached by running through a narrow neck. Inside, Sailing Directions says good anchorage can be had in 17 fathoms, which is pretty deep. Douglass likes this inner basin, too, and would anchor near the head of the basin in 6 fathoms. We, however, don't like it at all. We went in during a gathering storm, and wind gusts found their way to us with nothing to stop them. The bottom shoaled too quickly for us to anchor in 6 fathoms and pay out scope to stand up to the wind. "Oversold!" we decided, and left.

Work Bay. Use chart 3738. Work Bay is located on the west side of Finlayson Channel, near the north end. The bay appears to be open to southerly winds, but we anchored there in the southerly storm that chased us out of Goat Cove, and found no wind and only remnants of a few rollers from Finlayson Channel. In our opinion Work Bay has room for just one boat at anchor unless all boats stern-tie to trees. The bay is 7-8 fathoms deep. With only a 3:1 scope (150 feet) of anchor rode out, you must be in the center or you will swing onto shore or onto the drying shelf at the head of the bay. Work Bay is pretty and snug-feeling. We like it.

Hiekish Narrows. Use chart 3738 (large scale inset). Hiekish Narrows connects with Sheep Passage and Finlayson Channel at the south end, and Graham Reach, the continuation of the Inside Passage, at the north end. Current predictions are given under Hiekish Narrows in the Tide and Current Tables, Vol. 7. Maximum currents run to 4.5 knots on the flood, 4 knots on the ebb. The flood sets north. The water behind Hewitt Island appears to be a possible anchorage, but the current runs strongly through it. We would choose it only for a short stop or a last resort. On one trip we found an incredible accumulation of drift at the south end of the narrows—trees, logs, rubbish, kelp and weed—a real mess.

Fraser Reach and Graham Reach. Use charts 3738, 3740 and 3742. Fraser Reach and Graham Reach are wide, straight and deep, and marked all along the way with beautiful waterfalls. Cruise ships make this their highway. The principal stopping point for pleasure craft is Butedale.

Horsefly Cove. Use chart 3738. Horsefly Cove is a short distance inside the mouth of Green Inlet, on the east side of Graham Reach.

Butedale continues its slow slide into the sea. This photo was taken in 1999.

The cove is cozy and protected, but 13-15 fathoms deep. You may have to stern-tie to shore to restrict your swing.

Swanson Bay. Use chart 3738 or 3739. Swanson Bay is on the east side of Graham Reach. This bay is exposed, but interesting. Ruins of an old cannery are on the beach; a 3-story building and a tall red chimney are hidden in the trees. Anchor in 8 fathoms off the creek mouth or in 10 fathoms to the left of the pilings.

In 1998, we saw a black-colored wolf on the south shore beach. The wolf watched as our boat slowly approached, then with a dismissive air, ambled into the forest. The beaches at Swanson Bay would be good for dog-walking—keeping in mind, of course, the wolf.

⑦ **Butedale.** Use chart 3739. Oh, how sad. The buildings are collapsing and falling into the sea. The end is drawing near for the ghost town of Butedale, at the south end of Fraser Reach. A group called the Butedale Founders, from Oregon, leased the property a few years ago and poured a lot of work into it. They restored some of the houses to livability, and created a passable, rough-and-ready camping style dormitory. But when we called in 1998, the hard winters had undone much of what had been accomplished. The great warehouse's roof was partly collapsed, and a section of the high pier was gone. In 1999 the warehouse had collapsed completely, and another building was listing terribly over the water.

Shore access is poor. The float is low, and the iron ladder leading up to the pier lacks

The new float at Bishop Bay Hot Springs. Rafting is required.

This bathhouse is where you'll soak. The water is just right, and odor-free.

about 4 feet of length at low tide. We advise good fendering in case a B.C. ferry or a cruise ship goes by, which it will. You also can anchor in 10-12 fathoms out in the bay, sterntied to the pilings, and take the dinghy to the float. Don't anchor off the main pier; the bottom there is reported to be foul with cable. In 1998 and 1999 a friendly, bearded man named Russ Tinkiss, probably in his 40s, was the caretaker.

When we called at Butedale in 1996, the now-collapsed warehouse building was made of timber that would make a builder's mouth water. In the power house the generators turned over lazily, as if awaiting reconnection to the rest of the property. Something about Butedale made us want to walk softly and talk quietly; as if loudness would disturb the memories. But it's going fast. If you want to see what's left, don't put if off.

Bishop Bay Hot Springs. Use charts 3742 or 3743. Bishop Bay Hot Springs are located at the head of Bishop Bay, on the east side of Ursula Channel. This is one of the don't-miss stops along the northern B.C. coast. Kitimat Yacht Club has done an outstanding job building and maintaining the dock, ramp, bathhouse, and boardwalk. In the bathhouse, the hot springs water is an agreeable temperature, and odor-free. The well-executed boardwalk parallels the shoreline through fabulous, moss-covered and moss-hung forest.

It pays to arrive early. Tie to the dock (rafting required), tie to one of two mooring buoys, or anchor in 15 fathoms. The large, metal mooring buoy has a built-in boat magnet; you'll bump against it all night long. If you plan to anchor, note that the bottom is said to be only okay. A short distance south of the dock a shoal, not shown on the charts, extends into the bay from the shoreline. Be aware of that shoal, and plan your swing to stay well off it.

Verney Passage. Use charts 3742 & 3743. Verney Passage, along the west side of Gribbell Island, must be one of the most beautiful places on earth. It is lined, both sides, with raw, polished rock mountains, 3500 feet high. Great bowls are hollowed into the mountains. From the water you can see their forested floors and sheer rock walls. A visit to Bishop Bay Hot Springs should include a circumnavigation of Gribbell Island, just to see Verney Passage.

Wright Sound. Use chart 3742. Wright Sound lies at the junction of Grenville Channel, Douglas Channel, Verney Passage, and McKay Reach. All these passages pour their currents into Wright Sound, where the waters collide and mix. Especially on an ebb, not much wind is needed to make conditions dowright ugly. A local told us that in an outflow wind from Douglas Channel, it is better to lay a course off Juan Point, at the north end of Gil Island. We tried this route in an outflow wind, and found it much smoother than our previous crossing, in which we tried a direct (and wet) route between Point Cumming and Cape Farewell.

Coghlan Anchorage. Use chart 3742 and large scale chart 3711. Coghlan Anchorage lies behind Promise Island, and is connected by Stewart Narrows with Hartley Bay. The anchorage is open to the south, but still decently protected. The mooring buoys in Stewart Narrows are private. We anchored briefly in 6-7 fathoms near a mooring buoy just north of Brodie Point, and found the protection and holding ground excellent, if not very scenic. Anchorage also is possible on the shore opposite Brodie Point, off Otter Shoal.

⑧ **Hartley Bay.** Band office 445 Hayimiisaaxa Way, Hartley Bay, B.C. V0V 1A0, (250)841-2500. Use chart 3742 and large scale chart 3711. Gasoline and diesel, pure water (from the water treatment plant) on the moorage floats, 15 amp power on the floats. Garbage drop on the wharf. Hartley Bay, near the south end of Douglas Channel, is a friendly and modern-looking Indian village, population 140-160, with a government dock behind a rock breakwater. The village has a store, but the hours are erratic and the stock uncertain. No liquor. No pay phone. A medical clinic has two nurses and a visiting doctor.

Ed Robinson is in charge of the fuel dock. His usual hours are 9-5, longer in the spring and summer. In an emergency he's available 24 hours a day. Call "Miss Jaimie" or "Hartley Bay Fuels" on VHF channel 06 or CB channel 14. Cash only, no checks or credit cards. *(Marina map this page)*

Curlew Bay. Use chart 3742. Curlew Bay indents the northeast corner of Fin Island, located immediately west of Gil Island. We anchored there one evening when darkness was nearly upon us, and we wanted a place we hadn't tried before. Curlew Bay isn't a destination anchorage by any means, but it will do in settled weather or a southerly. It appears to be open to a northerly and to outflow winds from Douglas Channel. The chart shows shoaling a very short distance inside the narrows. We anchored in 3 fathoms at the east end of the narrows. The anchor bumped twice on what felt like rock, then set solidly.

Hawk Bay. Use chart 3742. Hawk Bay is on the west side of Fin Island. It is more scenic than Curlew Bay, and has more room. While Hawk Bay appears somewhat open to westerly winds, we saw no accumulation of driftwood on the shores. Anchor in the middle in 10 fathoms, or near the head in 4-6 fathoms.

Grenville Channel. Use charts 3742, 3772 & 3773. Though sometimes called "The Ditch," Grenville Channel is a straight, beautiful and unobstructed channel 45 miles long, running between Wright Sound in the south and Arthur Passage in the north. Tidal currents flow in and out of each end. Flood currents meet in the area of Evening Point, about 25 miles from the south entrance. Ebb currents divide about 1.5 miles north of Evening Point. The waters can be turbulent in these areas, and drift tends to accumulate there.

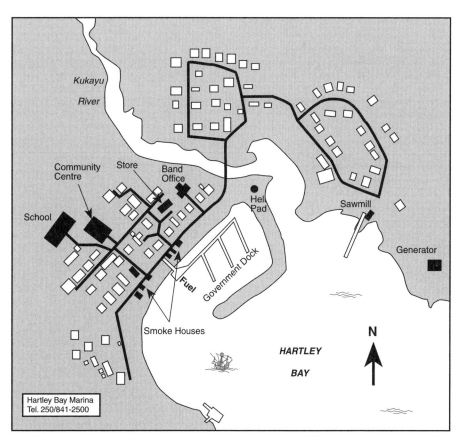

Hartley Bay Marina

Reference only — not for navigation

Tidal currents run to a maximum of 2 knots. The tide and current tables show no current predictions for Grenville Channel, but corrections for high and low tides are shown for Lowe Inlet as a secondary port under Bella Bella in the Tide and Current Tables, Vol. 7 (Index No. 9195). Tidal current flows also are shown in our sister publication, *Southeast Alaska Current Atlas*, by Randel Washburne. The annual *Washburne's Tables, Southeast Alaska*, should be used with the Atlas.

Considerable time and fuel can be saved by timing a passage to carry the flood current into Grenville Channel and the ebb current out. Often pleasure craft will ride an afternoon or early evening flood part way in. They overnight in one of Grenville Channel's excellent anchorages, and ride a morning ebb out.

Be sure to give Morning Reef, north of Evening Point, a wide berth.

Hawkins Narrows (Union Passage). Use chart 3722 (1:18,257, much preferred), or chart 3772 (1:36,225). Union Passage, on the west side of Grenville Channel, is served by Hawkins Narrows from Grenville Channel and Peters Narrows from the south. It is one of those places people talk about but not many visit. The problem is the two sets of narrows. The chart shows 8-knot currents in Hawkins Narrows and 7-knot currents in Peters Narrows. Hawkins Narrows slack is shown as 5 minutes in duration; neither the chart nor Sailing Directions say much about Peters Narrows. Once inside, the scenery is not memorable.

Local knowledge says the currents often are much less than shown, and the window of least current much wider than 5 minutes. We entered Union Passage through Hawkins Narrows at low water slack, poked around for a few minutes, then departed the way we came. The day was windy, rainy and cold. Our spirit was with the great explorers, but our resolve that day was weak.

The entrance to Hawkins Narrows is at Lat 53°22'N. The channel is open until the inner end is approached. There, a rock awash at zero tide lies off the eastern shore. Favor the western shore to avoid it.

Lowe Inlet. Use chart 3772. Lowe Inlet, a provincial park, is 14.5 miles from the southern entrance to Grenville Channel, and long has been a favorite spot to overnight. You can anchor either in the outer basin or in Nettle Basin, the cozier inner cove. Walt Woodward, in his book *How to Cruise to Alaska Without Rocking the Boat Too Much*, recommends anchoring directly in front of Verney Falls where they tumble into Nettle Basin. Current from the falls holds the boat in place, and you are treated to a wonderful view of the falls. Holding ground is reported to be only fair, so be sure the anchor is well set and you have ample scope for high tide. An alternative is to anchor far enough from the falls that the current, while still enough to hold the boat steady, is not very strong.

Don Douglass, in his books, likes the Verney

Falls anchorage, but also suggests an anchorage along the south shore of Nettle Basin, off the shelf formed by a creek that empties into that area. We tried to put the hook down in 10 fathoms off that shore, but found that we would swing too close to the shelf. After two tries in wind squalls and heavy rain showers, we moved out to the middle and anchored in 17 fathoms with 300 feet of rode out. Shortly after we were settled another boat came in, tried to anchor as we earlier tried, then moved out to the middle as we had. Our holding ground was excellent. We had trouble tripping the anchor the next morning.

Lowe Inlet is beautiful. Our notes read, "If you're looking for a scenic spot, this is it."

Klewnuggit Inlet. Use chart 3772. At approximately 20 fathoms, Klewnuggit Inlet is too deep for most boats to anchor. We talked with some folks, however, who found crabbing to be excellent near the head of Klewnuggit Inlet.

East Inlet. Use chart 3772. East Inlet is adjacent to Klewnuggit Inlet. The inner cove of East Inlet is a superb anchorage, surrounded by high mountains and protected from seas. In a storm, however, winds might swirl through. If possible, anchor near the head of the inner basin in 8-9 fathoms. You can also find anchorage in the little cove on the south shore, just inside the entrance to the inner basin. We call this nook Fiddler's Cove, after the GB32 *Fiddler*, which spent a sleepless stormy night there.

Kxngeal Inlet. Use chart 3772. Kxngeal Inlet, on the north side of Grenville Channel approximately 4 miles northwest of Klewnuggit Inlet, is a beautiful bowl in the mountains. Favor either shore as you enter, to avoid a nasty rock that dries 16 feet in the entrance. The inlet is at least 17 fathoms deep until it shelves at the head, and when it shelves, it shelves *right now*. Trees are at the head of the inlet, with logged areas on each side. The shelf is on a line with the points where the trees begin. Anchor in 15 fathoms.

Watts Narrows. Use chart 3772. Watts Narrows is a short passage that connects Baker Inlet with Grenville Channel. A dogleg turn near the inner entrance makes the passage blind. Before entering, either direction, announce your intentions on VHF channel 16. Sound your horn as you approach the turn. The current runs swiftly through the narrows, but people tell us they have gone through even in the presence of current. We have waited for slack water, which occurs about the times of high and low water at Prince Rupert. As the chart shows, the narrows are *narrow*, but they are deep. A mid-channel course will get you through safely.

We once passed Watts Narrows as a 100-foot megayacht, blinding white with black windows, began its entry. According to our tide tables, an outflowing current was running fairly hard. Even in flat water, we thought

yacht of that size would have to be hinged in the middle to negotiate the dogleg turn, so we worried about his running the narrows in a strong current. He proved us wrong, and apparently got in without a hitch.

Baker Inlet. Use chart 3772. Baker Inlet, entered through Watts Narrows, is wonderful. While anchorage is possible all along the shores, the best overnights are at a float just inside Watts Narrows, or at the head of the inlet. A sailboat had the float, so we went to the head, where we anchored in 10 fathoms, good bottom, mountains all around.

Shortly before sunset a commercial crabber came through, and laid crab pots generally around our boat. When we told him his string of crab pots might foul our anchor rode, he said we could cut his line if it fouled us. Fortunately, his crab pots had not fouled our anchor rode. (We put our own crab pot down after he left, but it came up empty. We didn't have good bait.)

In the morning, we began recovering the anchor in a golden early sunrise. By the time the anchor was aboard, however, we were enveloped by fog so thick that we could see the bow of the boat but nothing else. Radar and GPS helped us navigate our way back to Watts Narrows. It was slow and careful going. We worried that we would miss our anticipated slack water arrival at the narrows. If we missed by too much, we would have to fight a strong incoming current or wait 6 hours for a change. We are cautious folk, and don't appreciate great challenges. We did not want problems.

We got to Watts Narrows a few minutes late, but the current did not seem very strong. We went in. The fog was so dense that the shores, only a few yards away, were dim. Fortunately, the narrows are short—tense in the fog, but short. We popped out only moments later, and were in Grenville Channel.

Kumealon Island/Kumealon Inlet. Use chart 3773. The cove behind Kumealon Island and Kumealon Inlet both are good anchorages. Behind Kumealon Island, anchor in 5-7 fathoms near the head.

Kumealon Inlet is well protected and has beautiful scenery, despite logging activity on the north shore of the outer bay. We would anchor in the inner basin. Dave Ellsworth (*De Yata*) reports that they had an excellent overnight in the inner basin, and that two uncharted rocks lie close to shore near the southeast corner.

Grenville Channel to Prince Rupert. The run from the north end of Grenville Channel to Prince Rupert requires three and preferably four separate charts. Chart 3773 shows the northern entrance to Grenville Channel. Chart 3927 covers the run from Grenville Channel, north through Arthur Passage, and continuing through the passage west of Genn Island. Chart 3957 takes you across Chatham Sound from Genn Island to Prince Rupert, though in small scale. Large scale chart 3958 makes the approach to Prince Rupert much less confusing.

Chatham Sound weather tip: Chatham Sound can be downright ugly when the wind blows. Especially on an ebb, when the onshore wind opposes an outflowing current combined with runoff from the Skeena River, the seas can get high, steep and close together. In 1999, seas such as these turned us back to Prince Rupert. So we learned a lesson: on the weather channel, listen to the hourly updates for Holland Rock. If it's blowing at Holland Rock, you'll be in for it if you try to cross.

Oona River. Use chart 3927. Oona River indents Porcher Island at the mouth of Ogden Channel. A public dock lies behind a stone breakwater, and is served by a narrow channel through drying mudflats. Lacking local knowledge, we would not go in without instructions. Call "Oona River" on VHF 06.

Captain Cove. Use chart 3927. Captain Cove is a cozy, protected anchorage at the northwest corner of Pitt Island, near the south entrance to Ogden Channel. The favored spot is along the south shore, either behind the little dot islet or in the 5-fathom basin adjacent.

Lawson Harbour/Kelp Passage. Use chart 3927. Lawson Harbour indents the top of Lewis Island. Kelp Passage lies on the east side of Lewis Island, across Arthur Passage from Kennedy Island. Neither would be our first choice for scenery, but each would serve as an anchorage if needed. A reef extends from the western shore inside Lawson Harbour. Anchor near the south end of the reef in 6-7 fathoms.

In Kelp Passage, anchor in the area marked 4₅ fathoms, mud bottom.

Arthur Passage to Prince Rupert. Assuming a northbound route, on chart 3927 begin your run from a waypoint west of Watson Rock, at the northern entrance to Grenville Channel. Continue north to a waypoint off the flashing light on the southwest shore of Kennedy Island. Then turn westward slightly to run past the southwest corner of Hanmer Island, and leave bell buoy D9, marking Cecil Patch, to port. Continue to a waypoint in the passage west of Genn Island.

At Genn Island, change to chart 3957. Run to a waypoint east of the Holland Rock light. Then run to a waypoint west of Barrett Rock, at the entrance to Prince Rupert Harbour. As you approach Holland Rock it would be a good idea to change to large scale chart 3958. The entire area is well-buoyed, but it is easy to get the buoys confused. We would plot all courses and their reciprocals carefully and double-check our work. So too with waypoint coordinates.

Do not trust Loran in this area. We found that our Loran would take us approximately 0.5 mile east of our desired destination. Our GPS, by contrast, was much more accurate. When we reached Prince Rupert and asked around,

Prince Rupert Rowing & Yacht Club Moorage. 1998.

The Seafarers Memorial at Pacific Mariners Memorial Park points everlastingly ahead. The beaches honor individual mariners who have crossed the bar to Fiddlers Green.

we were told that Loran was not reliable in this area. Loran's latitude is good, but longitude is off. The effect extends some distance southward.

⑨ Prince Rupert. Use chart 3958 (preferred) or chart 3957. From Barrett Rock at the entrance to Prince Rupert Harbour, it is another 5.5 miles of slow speed travel to town. Three marinas serve Prince Rupert: Fairview at the south end, Prince Rupert Rowing and Yacht Club in the middle, and Rushbrook at the north end.

Fairview is primarily a commercial boat moorage, although some pleasure boats do tie up there. Rushbrook has better facilities for pleasure boats, but during the commercial fishing months many commercial boats occupy the slips. Most pleasure boats go directly to the Prince Rupert Rowing and Yacht Club, located at Cow Bay.

Prince Rupert ("Rainy Rupert"), population 17,000, is a bustling city. With a large fishing fleet to support, you can find just about anything you need for your boat. What isn't there can be flown in. Fuel is available from four fuel docks, and waste oil disposal is available.

A shopping mall is a pleasant walk uptown, or you can take a cab. Groceries are available at three supermarkets. The liquor store is between the yacht club and the mall. The Museum of Northern British Columbia is excellent, and sponsors a variety of informative

day and evening programs during the summer. Highly recommended. Several restaurants are in town, some of them pretty good.

Two laundromats (King Koin and Maytag) in the center of town will do your laundry for a very reasonable charge. For two years running, we have left all the ship's sheets, towels and dirty clothes at King Koin, then gone for an excellent supper at the Crest Hotel's dining room. Two hours later we picked up the laundry, clean, dry, and neatly folded. A bargain by any measure.

Up on 3rd Avenue, just beyond the mall, we found a shop with memorabilia in the window—wonderful toys from the 30s and 40s, Canadian Pacific Railroad conductors' caps, old photos and more—and a stuffed and mounted *fur-bearing trout*, very rare. It was caught in Lake Superior, from depths so great trout grow fur to keep warm. This trout's fur is white. Everything is explained on the sign next to the specimen. You have to see it.

If you have time, take the bus to Port Edward for a tour of the North Pacific Cannery, now a museum. You'll see how the workers lived, and how they canned salmon. You'll even see a now politically incorrect Iron Chink.

We like Prince Rupert, and recommend it as a stop. In 1998 we suffered some minor but irritating mechanical problems prior to arriving, and called By Town Diesel for repairs. A skilled mechanic was on the boat shortly and did an excellent job for us. Later, another boat came in with problems, and he too called

By Town Diesel. His experience was similar
to ours.

Golf: The Prince Rupert Centenial Golf
Course has a good 18-hole course. Call
(250)624-2000. You'll probably take a cab.
In early evening the no-see-ums are thick and
ravenous. Cover up.

⑨ **Petro Canada, Fairview,** (250)624-6666.
Monitors VHF channel 78. Open every day,
extended hours in summer. Gasoline, diesel,
stove oil. Washrooms, showers. Garbage drop.
Small convenience store.

⑨ **Prince Rupert Chevron,** (250)624-3316.
Open every day, extended hours in summer.
Gasoline, diesel, stove oil, kerosene, lubricants.
Washrooms, showers, laundry. Block, cube, and
salt ice. Dry ice. Small convenience store on
pier. Garbage disposal, waste oil disposal.
Located in Cow Bay, next to the Yacht Club.

⑨ **Petro Canada, Cow Bay,** (250) 624-
4106. Monitors VHF channel 78. Open every day, extended hours in summer. Gasoline,
diesel, stove oil. Garbage disposal, pumpout.

⑨ **Esso Marine Station,** (250)624-5000.
Open every day 0800-1800, except 0800-
2200 in summer. Gasoline, diesel & stove oil.
There is a new store on the dock that carries
a little bit of everything: hardware, groceries,
snacks. Showers and laundry. Closest fuel to
Rushbrook.

⑨ **Fairview Small Craft Harbour,**
(250)627-3127. This is the first set of docks
as you approach Prince Rupert. Commercial
vessels primarily, but sometimes room for a
few pleasure boats. Electricity, water, garbage.

⑨ **Prince Rupert Rowing and Yacht Club,**
P.O. Box 981, Prince Rupert, B.C. V8J 4B7,
(250)624-4317. Monitors VHF channel 72.
Open all year, 15 & 30 amp power, washroom and shower, block ice, garbage drop, fish-
cleaning station. Located at Cow Bay, a delightful area of shops, eateries and galleries.
This is the preferred pleasure craft moorage
in Prince Rupert. As you approach, call on
channel 72 so they can figure out where to
put you. The outermost docks can be a little
bouncy (a lot bouncy), especially if the commercial fish boats are in the midst of an opening,
and come and go all night. The dock staff
can be busy. Be patient. A pay phone is at the
head of the dock. Close to good dining, walk
or take a cab uptown. Open to all, no yacht
club recripocals needed.

⑨ **Rushbrook Floats Small Craft Harbour,**
(250)624-9400. Open all year, water, 15 amp
power. Mostly commercial vessels in the summer, but room for pleasure craft too. Located
about a mile north of town. Rushbrook has
the only launch ramp in Prince Rupert.

2000 CALENDAR

JANUARY

SUN	MON	TUE	WED	THU	FRI	SAT
					1 New Year's Day	
2	3	4	5	6	7	8
9	10	11	12	13	14	15
16	17 Martin Luther King Jr. Day	18	19	20	21	22
23 30	24 31	25	26	27	28	29

FEBRUARY

SUN	MON	TUE	WED	THU	FRI	SAT
		1	2	3	4	5
6	7	8	9	10	11	12 Lincoln's Birthday
13	14 Valentine's Day	15	16	17	18	19
20	21 Presidents Day	22 Washington's Birthday	23	24	25	26
27	28	29				

MARCH

SUN	MON	TUE	WED	THU	FRI	SAT
			1	2	3	4
5	6	7	8	9	10	11
12	13	14	15	16	17 St. Patrick's Day	18
19	20	21	22	23	24	25
26	27	28	29	30	31	

APRIL

SUN	MON	TUE	WED	THU	FRI	SAT
						1
2 Daylight Saving begins	3	4	5	6	7	8
9	10	11	12	13	14	15
16 Palm Sunday	17	18	19	20 Passover begins	21 Good Friday	22
23 Easter Sunday 30	24	25	26	27	28	29

MAY

SUN	MON	TUE	WED	THU	FRI	SAT
	1	2	3	4	5	6
7	8	9	10	11	12	13
14 Mother's Day	15	16	17	18	19	20
21	22 Victoria Day (Canada)	23	24	25	26	27
28	29 Memorial Day (Observed)	30	31			

JUNE

SUN	MON	TUE	WED	THU	FRI	SAT
				1	2	3
4	5	6	7	8	9	10
11	12	13	14	15	16	17
18 Father's Day	19	20	21	22	23	24
25	26	27	28	29	30	

JULY

SUN	MON	TUE	WED	THU	FRI	SAT
						1 Canada Day (Canada)
2	3	4 Independence Day	5	6	7	8
9	10	11	12	13	14	15
16	17	18	19	20	21	22
23 30	24 31	25	26	27	28	29

AUGUST

SUN	MON	TUE	WED	THU	FRI	SAT
		1	2	3	4	5
6	7 Civic Holiday (Canada)	8	9	10	11	12
13	14	15	16	17	18	19
20	21	22	23	24	25	26
27	28	29	30	31		

SEPTEMBER

SUN	MON	TUE	WED	THU	FRI	SAT
					1	2
3	4 Labor Day (U.S. & Canada)	5	6	7	8	9
10	11	12	13	14	15	16
17	18	19	20	21	22	23
24	25	26	27	28	29	30

OCTOBER

SUN	MON	TUE	WED	THU	FRI	SAT
1	2	3	4	5	6	7
8	9 Columbus Day (Observed) Thanksgiving (Canada)	10	11	12	13	14
15	16	17	18	19	20	21
22	23	24	25	26	27	28
29 Daylight Saving ends	30	31 Halloween				

NOVEMBER

SUN	MON	TUE	WED	THU	FRI	SAT
		1	2	3	4	
5	6	7	8	9	10	11 Veteran's Day Remembrance Day (Canada)
12	13	14	15	16	17	18
19	20	21	22	23 Thanksgiving Day (U.S.)	24	25
26	27	28	29	30		

DECEMBER

SUN	MON	TUE	WED	THU	FRI	SAT
					1	2
3	4	5	6	7	8	9
10	11	12	13	14	15	16
17	18	19	20	21	22	23
24 31	25 Christmas Day	26 Boxing Day (Canada)	27	28	29	30

U.S. Marina and Fuel Dock Numbers

Alderbrook Inn Resort	Hood Canal	(360) 898-2200
Arabella's Marina	Gig Harbor	(253) 851-1793
Ballard Mill Marina	Seattle	(206) 789-4777
Ballard Oil Inc. (fuel dock)	Seattle	(206) 783-0241
Bartwood Lodge	Orcas Is.	(360) 376-2242
Bay Marine	Suquamish	(360) 598-4900
Bell Harbor Marina	Seattle	(206) 615-3952
Big Salmon Resort (fuel dock)	Neah Bay	(360) 645-2374
Blaine Harbor		(360) 647-6176
Blaine Marina (fuel dock)		(360) 332-8425
Blakely Island General Store & Marina (marina & fuel dock)		(360) 375-6121
Boston Harbor Marina (marina & fuel dock)	Olympia	(360) 357-5670
Breakwater Marina (marina & fuel dock)	Tacoma	(253) 752-6663
Bremerton Marina		(360) 373-1035
Camano Island State Park		(360) 387-3031
Cap Sante Boat Haven	Anacortes	(360) 293-0694
Cap Sante Marine (fuel dock & chandlery)	Anacortes	(360) 293-3145
Cap Sante Lake Washington (fuel dock)	Seattle	(206) 482-9465
Captain Coupe Park	Whidbey Is.	(360) 678-4461
Carillon Point	Kirkland	(425) 822-1700
Chandler's Cove	Seattle	(206) 628-0838
Chinook Landing Marina	Tacoma	(253) 627-7676
Coho Resort	Sekiu	(360) 963-2333
Covich-Williams Co. (fuel dock)	Seattle	(206) 784-0171
Curley's Resort	Sekiu	(800) 542-9680
Dash Point State Park	Tacoma	(206) 593-2206
Deception Pass Marina		(360) 675-5411
Deer Harbor Marina (marina & fuel dock)	Orcas Is.	(360) 376-3037
Delta Western Fuel Dock	Seattle	(206) 282-1567
Des Moines Marina, City of (marina & fuel dock)		(206) 824-5700
Dockton Park	Maury Is.	(206) 296-4287
Eagle Harbor Marina	Winslow	(206) 842-4003
Elliott Bay Marina	Seattle	(206) 285-4817
Ewing Street Moorings	Seattle	(206) 283-1075
Fair Harbor Marina (marina & fuel dock)	Grapeview	(360) 426-4028
Fish'n' Hole, The (fuel dock)	Port Townsend	(360) 385-7031
Fisherman's Cove Marina	Lummi Island	(360) 758-7050
Fort Ebey State Park	Whidbey Is.	(360) 385-4730
Fort Worden Marine State Park	Port Townsend	(360) 385-4730
Frye Cove County Park	Olympia	(360) 786-5595
Gene Coulon Memorial Beach Park	Renton	(425) 235-2560
Harbor Marine Fuel (fuel dock)	Bellingham	(360) 734-1710
Harbor Village Marina	Seattle	(425) 485-7557
Harbour Marina	Winslow	(206) 842-6502
Hawley's Hilton Harbor (fuel dock)	Bellingham	(360) 733-1110
Hood Canal Marina (marina & fuel dock)	Hood Canal	(360) 898-2252
Hoodsport Marina & Cafe	Hood Canal	(360) 877-9657
Illahee Marine State Park	Bremerton	(360) 478-6460
Island Petroleum Service (fuel dock)	Orcas Is.	(360) 376-3883
Islands Marine Center	Lopez Is.	(360) 468-3377
Jarrell's Cove Marina (marina & fuel dock)	Harstine Is.	(800) 362-8823
Jarrell Cove Marine State Park	Harstine Is.	(360) 426-9266
Jerisich Park	Gig Harbor	(253) 851-8136
Jetty Island	Everett	(425) 259-6001
John Wayne Marina (marina & fuel dock)	Sequim	(360) 417-3440
Joseph Whidbey State Park	Whidbey Is.	(360) 678-4636
Kitsap Memorial State Park	Hood Canal	(360) 779-3205
Kopachuck Marine State Park	Carr Inlet	(253) 265-3606
LaConner Landing Marine Service (fuel dock)	LaConner	(360) 466-4478
LaConner Marina	LaConner	(360) 466-3118
Lakebay Marina (marina & fuel dock)	Grapeview	(253) 884-3350
Lakewood Moorage	Seattle	(206) 722-3887
Langley Small Boat Harbor	Langley	(360) 221-4246
Larrabee State Park	S. of Bellingham	(360) 676-2093
Leschi Yacht Basin (fuel dock)	Seattle	(206) 328-4456
Lighthouse Marine County Park	Pt. Roberts	(360) 733-2900
Little Portion Store	Shaw Is.	(360) 468-2288
Lonesome Cove Resort	San Juan Is.	(360) 378-4477
Longbranch Improvement Club Marina	Longbranch	(253) 884-5137
Lopez Islander Marina Resort	Lopez Is.	(360) 468-2233
Luther Burbank Park	Mercer Is.	(206) 296-2976
Makah Marina	Neah Bay	(360) 645-3012
Marina Mart	Seattle	(206) 682-7733
Marina Park	Kirkland	(425) 828-1218
Marine Servicecenter (fuel dock)	Anacortes	(360) 293-2600
McMicken Island Marine State Park	Case Inlet	(360) 426-9226
Mercer Marine (fuel dock)	Bellevue	(425) 641-2090
Morrison's North Star Marina (fuel dock)	Seattle	(206) 284-6600
Mutiny Bay Resort	Whidbey Is.	(360) 331-4500
Narrows Marina Tackle (fuel dock)	Tacoma	(253) 564-4222
Oak Harbor Marina (marina & fuel dock)	Oak Harbor	(360) 679-2628
Old Fort Townsend Marine State Park	Port Townsend	(360) 385-3595
Olson's Resort (marina & fuel dock)	Sekiu	(360) 963-2311
Peninsula Yacht Basin	Gig Harbor	(253) 858-2250
Penrose Point State Marine Park	Carr Inlet	(253) 884-2514
Percival Landing Park	Olympia	(360) 753-8379
Pleasant Harbor Marina (marina & fuel dock)	Hood Canal	(360) 796-4611
Pleasant Harbor Marine State Park	Hood Canal	(360) 796-4415
Point Defiance Boathouse Marina (marina & fuel dock)	Tacoma	(253) 591-5325
Point Hudson Resort	Port Townsend	(360) 385-2828
Point Roberts Marina (marina & fuel dock)		(360) 945-2255
Port Angeles Boat Haven (marina & fuel dock)		(360) 457-4505
Port Angeles City Pier		(360) 457-0411
Port Hadlock Bay Marina	Port Hadlock	(360) 385-6368
Port Ludlow Marina (marina & fuel dock)		(360) 437-0513
Port of Allyn & Allyn Dock		(360) 275-2192
Port of Brownsville (marina & fuel dock)		(360) 692-5498
Port of Coupeville (marina & fuel dock)		(360) 678-5020
Port of Edmonds (marina & fuel dock)		(425) 774-0549
Port of Everett Marina (marina & fuel dock)		(425) 259-6001
Port of Friday Harbor		(360) 378-2688
Port of Friday Harbor Dock (fuel dock)		(360) 378-3114
Port of Kingston (marina & fuel dock)		(360) 297-3545
Port of Olympia-East Bay Marina		(360) 786-1400
Port of Port Townsend		(360) 385-2355
Port of Shelton		(360) 426-1151
Port Orchard Marina		(360) 876-5535
Port Washington Marina	Bremerton	(360) 479-3037
Poseidon's (marina & fuel dock)	Gig Harbor	(253) 853-7100
Potlatch Marine State Park	Hood Canal	(360) 877-5361
Poulsbo Marina-Port of Poulsbo (marina & fuel dock) Mon-Fri		(360)779-9905
Weekends		(360) 779-3505
Quartermaster Marina	Burton	(206) 463-3624
Quilcene Boathaven (marina & fuel dock)	Hood Canal	(360) 765-3131
Richardson Fuel (fuel dock)	Lopez Is.	(360) 468-2275
Roche Harbor Resort & Marina (marina & fuel dock) San Juan Is.		(360) 378-2155
Rosario Resort (marina & fuel dock)	Orcas Is.	(800) 562-8820
Saltwater Marine State Park	Des Moines	(206) 764-4128
San Juan County Park	San Juan Is.	(360) 378-2992
Scenic Beach State Park	Hood Canal	(360) 830-5079
Seabeck Marina (marina & fuel dock)	Hood Canal	(360) 830-5179
Seacrest Boathouse	Seattle	(206) 932-1050
Semiahmoo Marina (marina & fuel dock)	Pt. Roberts	(360) 371-5700
Shilshole Bay Marina	Seattle	(206) 728-3006
Shilshole Texaco Marine (fuel dock)	Seattle	(206) 783-7555
Silverdale Marina		(360) 698-4918
Skyline Marina (marina & fuel dock)	Flounder Bay	(360) 293-5134
Smuggler's Villa Resort	Orcas Is.	(360) 376-2297
Snow Creek Resort	Neah Bay	(360) 645-2284
Snug Harbor Resort (marina & fuel dock)	San Juan Is.	(360) 378-4762
South Whidbey State Park	Whidbey Is.	(360) 321-4559
Spencer Spit Marine State Park	Lopez Is.	(360) 468-2251
Squalicum Harbor	Bellingham	(360) 676-2542
Steilacoom Marina		(253) 582-2600
Stutz Fuel Oil Service	Gig Harbor	(253) 858-9131
Sucia Island Marine State Park		(360) 753-5755
Summertide Resort & Marina	Hood Canal	(253) 925-9277
		(360) 275-9313
Sunrise Motel & Resort	Hood Canal	(360) 877-5301
Swantown Marina	Olympia	(360) 786-1400
Thunderbird Boat House & Gifts (marina & fuel dock)	Pt. Angeles	(360) 457-4274
Totem Marina	Tacoma	(253) 272-4404
Twanoh Marine State Park	Hood Canal	(360) 275-2222
Van Riper's Resort	Sekiu	(360) 963-2334
West Bay Marina (haulout & pumpout)	Olympia	(360) 943-2022
West Beach Resort (marina & fuel dock)	Orcas Is.	(360) 376-2240
West Sound Marina (marina & fuel dock)	Orcas Is.	(360) 376-2314
Wilcox's Yarrow Bay Marina (fuel dock)	Kirkland	(425) 822-6066
Winslow Wharf Marina		(206) 842-4202
Wyman's Marina (marina & fuel dock)	Anacortes	(360) 293-4606
Yacht Care (fuel dock)	Seattle	(206) 285-2600
Zittel's Marina Inc. (marina & fuel dock)	Olympia	(360) 459-1950

B.C. Marina and Fuel Dock Numbers

Active Pass Auto & Marine (fuel dock)	Mayne Is.	(250) 539-5411
Ahousat (marina & fuel dock)		(250) 670-9575
Alert Bay Public Wharf		(250) 974-5727
Anchor Petroleum (fuel dock)	Coal Harbour	(604) 949-6358
Anchorage Marina	Nanaimo	(250) 754-5585
Angler's Anchorage Marina		
(marina & fuel dock)	Brentwood Bay	(250) 652-3531
April Point Lodge & Fishing Resort	Quadra Island	(250) 285-2222
Barbary Coast Yacht Basin	Vancouver	(604) 669-0088
Bathgate General Store & Marina		
(marina & fuel dock)	Egmont	(604) 883-2222
Beach Garden Resort & Marina		
(marina & fuel dock)	Powell River	(604) 485-7734
Beachcomber Marina		
(fuel dock with limited moorage)		(250) 468-7222
Bedwell Harbour Resort		
(marina & fuel dock)	S. Pender Is.	(250) 629-3212
Big Bay Marina & Fishing Resort	Stuart Is.	
(marina & fuel dock)		(250) 286-8107
Birds Eye Cove Marina (marina & fuel dock)	Duncan	(250) 748-4255
Black Fin Marina & Pub		
(marina & fuel dock)	Comox	(250) 339-4664
Blind Channel Resort (marina & fuel dock)		(250) 949-1420
Bluenose Marina	Cowichan Bay	(250) 748-2222
Bowen Island Marina	Howe Sound	(604) 947-9710
Brechin Point Marina (fuel dock)	Nanaimo	(250) 753-6122
Brentwood Inn Resort	Brentwood Bay	(250) 652-3151
Bridgepoint Marina	Richmond	(604) 273-8560
Brown's Bay Marina (marina & fuel dock)		(250) 286-3135
Buccaneer Marina & Resort Ltd.		
(marina & fuel dock)	Secret Cove	(604) 885-7888
Burrard Bridge Civic Marina	Vancouver	(604) 733-5833
Canoe Cove Marina Ltd.(marina & fuel dock)	Sidney	(250) 656-5566
Cape Mudge Boatworks (repairs & haulout)	Quadra Island	(250) 285-2155
Captain's Cove Marina (marina & fuel dock)	Delta	(604) 946-1244
Catherwood Towing (fuel dock)	Mission	(604) 462-9221
Chamberlain's	Sechelt	(604) 885-7533
Cheanuh Marina (marina & fuel dock)	Sooke	(250) 478-4880
Cherry Point Marina	Cobble Hill	(250) 748-0453
Chevron Canada Ltd. (fuel dock)	Powell River	(604) 485-2867
China Creek Marina	Pt. Alberni	(250) 723-9812
City of Victoria Causeway		(250) 363-3273
Clutesi Haven Marina	Port Alberni	(250) 724-6837
Coal Harbour Chevron (fuel barge)	Vancouver	(604) 681-7725
Coal Harbour Marina	Vancouver	(604) 681-2628
Coast Marina	Campbell River	(250) 287-7155
Coast Victoria Harbourside	Victoria	(250) 360-1211
Coastal Shipyard & Marine Svcs.	Duncan	(250) 746-4705
Coho Marina	Pender Hrbr.	(250) 883-2248
Comox Bay Marina		(250) 339-2930
Comox Municipal Marina		(250) 339-2202
Comox Valley Harbour Authority		(250) 339-6047
Cordero Lodge	Blind Channel	(250) 286-8404
Crescent Beach Marina Ltd. (marina & fuel dock)		(604) 538-9666
Critter Cove Marina	Nootka Sound	(604) 886-7667
Crofton Public Wharf		(250) 246-2456
Dawson's Landing (marina & fuel dock)	Rivers Inlet	(250) 949-2111
		(250) 949-3533
Deep Cove Marina	Saanich Inlet	(250) 656-0060
Delta Charters (haulout & charters)	Vancouver area	(604) 273-4211
Delta Vancouver Airport Hotel	Vancouver area	(604) 278-1241
Denman General Store (fuel at store)	Denman Island	(250) 335-2293
Dent Island Lodge	Dent Island	(250) 286-8105
Dinghy Dock Pub	Nanaimo	(250) 753-2373
Discovery Harbour Marina	Campbell River	(250) 287-2614
Double Bay Resort	Hanson Is.	(250) 949-2500
Duncan Cove Resort	Pender Hrbr.	(250) 883-2424
Duncanby Landing (marina & fuel dock)	Rivers Inlet	(250) 949-3583
Echo Bay Resort (marina & fuel dock)		(250) 949-2501
Egmont Marina Resort (marina & fuel dock)		(604) 883-2298
Esperanza Marine Svc. (fuel dock)		(250) 859-9622
Esso Marine False Creek (fuel dock)	Vancouver	(604) 733-6731
Esso Marine Prince Rupert		(250) 624-5000
False Creek Yacht Club	Vancouver	(604) 682-3292
Fisherman's Cove Esso (fuel dock)	Vancouver	(604) 921-7333
Fisherman's Harbour	Port Alberni	(250) 723-2533
Fisherman's Resort & Marina	Pender Harbour	(604) 883-2336
Fisherman's Wharf Small Craft Harbour	Port Hardy	(250) 949-6332
Ford's Cove Marina Ltd. (fuel dock)	Hornby Island	(250) 335-2169
Forward Harbour Fishing Lodge		(250) 338-6689
French Creek Harbour (marina & fuel dock)	Parksville	(250) 248-5051
Freshwater Marina	Vancouver area	(604) 286-0701
Fulford Harbour Marina	Salt Spring Island	(250) 653-4467
Ganges Marina	Salt Spring Island	(250) 537-5242
Garden Bay Hotel & Marina	Pender Hrbr.	(604) 883-2674
Genoa Bay Marina	Duncan	(250) 746-7621
Gibsons Landing Harbour Authority		(604) 886-8017
Gibsons Marina		(604) 886-8686
God's Pocket Resort		(250) 949-9221
Gold River Petro Canada (fuel dock)		(250) 283-5214
Goldstream Boathouse (marina & fuel dock)	Finlayson Arm	(250) 478-4407

Gorge Harbour Marina & Resort		
(marina & fuel dock)	Cortes Island	(250) 935-6433
Grant Bay Marina (marina & fuel dock)	Winter Harbour	(250) 659-4333
Greenway Sound Marine Resort	Broughton Island	(250) 949-2525
Hakai Beach Resort	Pruth Bay	(250) 847-9300
Harbour Ferries Marina	Vancouver	(604) 687-9558
Hartley Bay Band Office (marina & fuel dock)		(250) 841-2500
Headwater Marina (repairs & haulout)	Pender Harbour	(604) 883-2406
Heriot Bay Inn & Marina (marina & fuel dock)	Quadra Island	(250) 285-3322
Hawkeye Industries Fuel Dock	Bamfield	(250) 728-3231
Highwater Marina	Vancouver area	(604) 525-0612
Howard Johnson Suite Motel	Cowichan Bay	(250) 748-6222
Hyak Marine (fuel dock)	Gibsons	(604) 886-9011
Irvine's Landing Marina & Pub		
(marina & fuel dock)	Pender Hrbr.	(604) 883-2296
Island West Fishing Resort	Ucluelet	(250) 726-7515
Ivy Green Marina Ltd.	Ladysmith	(250) 245-4521
John Henry's Marina Inc. (fuel dock)	Pender Harbour	(604) 883-2253
Kwatsi Bay Marina		(250) 949-1384
Kyoquot Sound Salmon (fuel dock)	Walters Cove	(250) 332-5219
Lasqueti Island Store & Marine (marina & fuel dock)		(250) 333-8846
Len's Shell & Grocery (fuel dock)	Fanny Bay	(250) 335-0920
Lion's Bay Marina Ltd. (marina & fuel dock)	Howe Sound	(604) 921-7510
Lowes Resort Motel	Pender Hrbr.	(604) 883-2456
Lund Harbour Authority Wharf		(604) 483-4711
Lynnwood Marina	Vancouver area	(604) 985-1533
Madeira Marina Ltd.	Pender Hrbr.	(604) 883-2266
Madeira Park (Pender Harbour Authority)		(604) 883-2234
Maple Bay Resorts	Duncan	(250) 746-8482
Masthead Marina	Cowichan Bay	(250) 748-5368
Method Marine Supply (marina & fuel dock)	Tofino	(250) 725-3251
Midcoast Marine Fuels (marina & fuel dock)	Sechelt	(604) 740-8889
Mill Bay Marina (marina & fuel dock)	Brentwood Bay	(250) 743-4112
Minstrel Island Resort (marina & fuel dock)		(250) 949-0215
Moby Dick Boatel	Nanaimo	(250) 753-7111
Montague Harbour Marina Ltd.		
(marina & fuel dock)	Galiano Is.	(250) 539-5733
Mosquito Creek Marina	N. Vancouver	(604) 980-4533
Nanaimo Harbour City Marina		(250) 754-2732
Nanaimo Port Authority (marina & fuel dock)		(250) 754-5053
Nanaimo Shipyard		(250) 753-1151
Nanaimo Yacht Club		(250) 754-7011
Newcastle Marina	Nanaimo	(250) 753-1431
North Arm Marine (fuel dock)	Vancouver area	(604) 276-2161
North Saanich Marina (marina & fuel dock)	Sidney	(250) 656-5558
Oak Bay Marina (marina & fuel dock)	Victoria	(250) 598-3369
Ocean Falls Public Dock		(250) 289-3859
Ocean West Marine Fuels (fuel dock)	Victoria	(250) 388-7224
Oceanwood Country Inn	Mayne Is.	(250) 539-5074
Okeover Marina	Okeover Arm	(604) 483-2243
Otter Bay Marina	N. Pender Is.	(250) 629-3579
Pacific Lions Marina Ltd.	Sooke	(250) 642-3816
Pacific Playground (marina & fuel dock)	Oyster River	(250) 337-5600
Page Point Inn (marina & fuel dock)	Ladysmith	(250) 245-2312
Page's Resort & Marina		
(marina & fuel dock)	Gabriola Is.	(250) 247-8931
Pedder Bay Marina (marina & fuel dock)		(250) 478-1771
Pelican Bay Marina	Vancouver	(604) 263-5222
Pender Harbour Authority	Madeira Park	(604) 883-2234
Petro Canada Bear Cove (fuel dock)	Port Hardy	(250) 949-9988
Petro Canada Cow Bay (fuel dock)	Prince Rupert	(250) 624-4106
Petro Canada Fairview (fuel dock)	Prince Rupert	(250) 624-6666
Petro Canada Steveston Barge (fuel barge)		(604) 277-7744
Petro Canada Ucluelet (Eagle Marine Ltd.) (fuel dock)		(250) 726-4262
Pier 66 Marina Ltd. (fuel dock)	Cowichan Bay	(250) 748-8444
Pierre's Bay Lodge & Marina	Scott Cove	(250) 949-2503
Pioneer Boat Works (haulout & repairs)	Ucluelet	(250) 726-4382
Poett Nook Marina		(250) 724-8525
Poise Cove Marina	Sechelt	(604) 885-2895
Port Browning Marina		(250) 629-3493
Port Hardy Esso Marine Station (fuel dock)		(250) 949-2710
Port McNeill Boat Harbour		(250) 956-3881
Port McNeill Marine & Aviation Fuels (fuel dock)		(250) 956-3336
Port Sidney Marina		(250) 655-3711
Prince Rupert Chevron (fuel dock)		(250) 624-3316
Quarterdeck Marina & RV Park		
(marina & fuel dock)	Port Hardy	(250) 949-6551
Quathiaski Cove Petro Canada (fuel dock)	Quadra Island	(250) 285-3212
Ragged Island Marine (fuel dock)	N. of Lund	(604) 438-8184
Reed Point Marina (marina & fuel dock)	Vancouver area	(604) 931-2477
Refuge Cove Store	Desolation Sound	(250) 935-6659
Richmond Chevron (fuel dock)		(604) 278-2181
Royal Reach Marina & Hotel	Sechelt	(604) 885-7844
Salt Spring Marina		(250) 537-5810
Saturna Point Store (fuel dock)		(250) 539-5725
Save-On Fuels (fuel dock)	Alert Bay	(250) 974-2161
Schooner Cove Resort & Marina		(250) 468-5364
Seaway Marine Services (fuel dock)	Campbell River	(250) 287-3456
Secret Cove Marina (marina & fuel dock)		(604) 885-3533

(Continued next page)

B.C. Marina and Fuel Dock Numbers (continued)

Sewell's Marina Ltd. (marina & fuel dock)	Howe Sound/Horseshoe Bay		
		(604) 921-3474	
Shearwater Marina (marina & fuel dock)		(250) 957-2305	
Shell Canada (fuel dock)	Bella Coola	(250) 799-5580	
Shelter Island Marina Inc.	Vancouver area	(604) 270-6272	
Sidney (Beacon Ave) Govt. Wharf		(250) 656-1184	
Silva Bay Boatel & Store	Gabriola Island	(250) 247-9351	
Silva Bay Resort & Marina	Gabriola Island	(250) 247-8662	
Skyline Marina	Richmond	(604) 273-3977	
Snaw-Naw-As Marina (marina & fuel dock)	Nanoose Bay	(250) 390-2616	
Sooke Harbour Marina		(250) 642-3236	
Sportsman's Marina & Resort	Garden Bay	(604) 883-2479	
Squirrel Cove Store (fuel dock)	Cortes Island	(250) 935-6327	
Steveston Chevron (fuel dock)		(604) 277-4712	
Steveston Esso Marine Station (fuel dock)		(604) 277-5211	
Stones Marine Centre Inc.	Nanaimo	(250) 753-4232	
Sullivan Bay Marine Resort			
(marina & fuel dock)	Broughton Island	(250) 949-2550	
Sunny Shores Resort & Marina			
(marina & fuel dock)	Sooke	(250) 642-5731	
Sunset Marina (marina & fuel dock)	Howe Sound	(604) 921-7476	
Sunshine Coast Resort Ltd.	Pender Harbour	(604) 883-9177	
Telegraph Cove Marina		(250) 928-3161	

Telegraph Harbor Marina	Thetis Island	(250) 246-9511
Thetis Island Marina		(250) 246-3464
Thunderbird Marina	W. Vancouver	(604) 921-7434
Toba Wildernest	Toba Inlet	(250) 286-8507
Townsite Marina Ltd.	Nanaimo	(250) 716-8801
Tsehum Harbor Public Wharf	Sidney	(250) 363-6466
Ucluelet Small Craft Harbour		(250) 726-4266
Union Steamship Company Marina	Bowen Island	(604) 947-0707
Van Isle Marina Co. Ltd. (marina & fuel dock)	Sidney	(250) 656-1138
Vancouver Marina (fuel dock)		(604) 278-9787
Victoria (Erie St) Public Wharf		(250) 363-3273
Victoria (Huron St) Public Wharf		(250) 363-3273
Victoria (Johnson St) Public Wharf		(250) 363-3273
Victoria (Ships Pt) Public Wharf		(250) 363-3273
Victoria (Broughton St) Public Wharf		(250) 363-3273
Victoria Marine Adventure Center		(250) 995-2211
Wampler Marine Services Ltd. (fuel dock)	Vancouver	(604) 681-3841
Westin Bayshore Yacht Charters	Vancouver	(604) 691-6936
Weston Enterprises (fuel dock)	Zeballos	(250) 761-4201
Westport Marina	Sidney	(250) 656-2832
Westview Marina (marina & fuel dock)	Tahsis	(250) 934-7622
Windsong Sea Village	Echo Bay	(250) 974-5004
Zeballos Small Craft Harbour		(250) 761-4333

TOWING & MARINE SERVICES

U.S. Towing and Emergency Numbers

Block and Tackle Boatyard		(206) 878-4414
CATeam		(360) 378-9636
Fremont Tugboat Co. (TowBOAT/US)		(206) 632-0151
Marine Services & Assist (VHF 16, CB 10)	(360) 675-7900 or	(360) 679-0222
Shiveley Tugboat Co.	(VHF 16)	(206) 842-7595
Tim's Marine (TowBOAT/US)		(360) 376-2332
TowBOAT/US *24 hour dispatch*		(800) 391-4869
Vessel Assist *ALL LOCATIONS 24 hours*		(800) 367-8222
Vessel Assist Anacortes	cellular (360) 929-2661	(360) 336-4402
Vessel Assist Everett	cellular (425) 355-6856	(425) 317-2897
Vessel Assist Lake Washington	cellular (206) 793-7375	(206) 648-2025
Vessel Assist Port Townsend		(360) 301-2000
Vessel Assist San Juans	cellular (360) 317-6273	(360) 336-4108
Vessel Assist Seattle	cellular	(206) 660-6901
Vessel Assist Tacoma	cellular (253) 312-2927	(253) 280-5777
Wilson Marine (24 hour parts service, with air service from Kenmore Air)	(206) 284-3630 or	(800) 875-9111

U.S. Coast Guard Emergencies	*VHF Channel 16 or call 911*
	(206) 217-6000
Cellular Phones Only	*911*
U.S. Coast Guard District Office: Seattle	(206) 220-7000

U.S. Customs Clearance Numbers

The office numbers below are for <u>weekdays only.</u>

Aberdeen	(360) 532-2030
Anacortes	(360) 293-2331
Bellingham	(360) 734-5463
Blaine	(360) 332-6318
Everett	(425) 259-0246
Friday Harbor/Roche Harbor	(360) 378-2080
Neah Bay/Port Angeles	(360) 457-4311
Port Townsend	(360) 385-3777
Seattle	(206) 553-4678
Tacoma/Olympia	(253) 593-6338
For customs entry call:	**(800) 562-5943**

Parks Information Numbers

Wash. State Parks Launch & Moorage Permit Program	(360) 902-8608
B. C. Parks General Information	(250) 387-5002

Paralytic Shellfish Poison (PSP) Numbers

Washington state Paralytic Shellfish Poison closures	(800) 562-5632
B. C. Paralytic Shellfish Poison closures	(604) 666-2828

B.C. Towing and Emergency Numbers

Classic Yacht Services (towing)	pager (604) 361-8001	(250) 361-7528
Vessel Assist (VHF "Bullet")		(604) 731-4595

Canadian Coast Guard Numbers:

Search and Rescue: Vancouver	*VHF Chan. 16 or*	(800) 567-5111
Search and Rescue: Victoria	(800) 567-5111 or	(250) 363-2333
Search and Rescue: Other areas		(800) 567-5111
Canadian Coast Guard District Office: Victoria		(250) 480-2600
Search & Rescue *Cellular Phones Only*		*311

B.C. Customs Clearance Numbers

All locations contact Canada Customs toll-free:	**(888) 226-7277**
CANPASS	(888) 226-7277
Communications Canada: Vancouver	(604) 666-5468
Communications Canada: Victoria	(250) 363-3803

Index

Advertisers' Index

THE SINKING OF THE AMITY, CONTINUED...

Point on the bow. The wind grew stronger and the seas larger. It was a rough, rough ride.

They rounded Point No Point around 1300. Larry was back on the helm. The wind, now unobstructed from the south, increased to what seemed like 40 knots. The waves built in height to six feet. Some appeared to be eight feet high, and close together. These are the worst tide-rip conditions, where currents accelerate and collide, and are met with strong winds from the opposite direction. The bow drove into a wave and green water shot across the foredeck, tearing open the foredeck hatch. Judy looked forward and below. "There's water down there!" she screamed at Larry, and ran below to pull the hatch shut.

The movement of the boat and the force of the wind and water were more than Judy could manage. The hatch remained open. Green water hit the windshield. "I can't see!" Larry shouted. "I'm going to the upper station!" "Get the Whaler ready!" Judy answered.

Larry left the helm, went out the back door and climbed the ladder to the upper station. Their 11-foot Boston Whaler dinghy was lashed in its cradle there, filled with crab traps and other cruising paraphernalia. As Larry reached the upper station a powerful wave swept across the foredeck and crashed into the front window, shattering it and blowing glass across the lower helm station that he had abandoned only seconds earlier.

Judy snatched up their cocker spaniel and ran to the back door. By then the boat had turned its stern to the waves, and seas were coming into the cockpit. With the dog in her arms Judy pushed the door open. A wave pushed it shut. She pushed again, and again a wave pushed it shut, trapping her inside the cabin. A third try, and this time Judy got her body into the opening before the water pressed the door against her. "That's probably where I got my cracked rib," she said later.

At last Judy was in the cockpit. She looked out and to her horror saw Larry in the 11-foot Whaler, floating away from the boat. He had emptied the Whaler of its cruising cargo and removed the tie-downs. When the boat rolled, he had shoved the Whaler straight sideways onto a wavetop and somehow climbed in—no oars, no motor, and no line attached to the boat. Judy picked up a mop and reached the handle across the water. Larry grabbed it. The Whaler came up to the boat and

Judy and the dog crawled in. *Amity* settled in the water. Waves washed across the Whaler and filled it, but the Whaler floated on its bottom. Judy recalls a sense of happiness at their situation. Despite the 50-degree water temperature, it felt warm around her. They were not wearing life jackets. They hadn't even thought of life jackets.

Judy remember calling a Mayday, but says she didn't do very well. To the questions of what size vessel is this, how many persons are on board and so forth, she remembers crying, "We're off Point No Point and we're sinking. Send some help!" The Coast Guard log of the incident, typed in abbreviations and acronyms, records the only Mayday as coming at 1315, when Gary Lange, on a nearby vessel, notified Group Seattle of a vessel sinking in the vicinity of Point No Point. Two minutes later Coast Guard Group Seattle issued an emergency broadcast and ordered a helicopter launched from its Ediz Hook station at Port Angeles. At 1325 the report reads, "CG41387 U/W." The helicopter was underway. The 82-foot Coast Guard Cutter Pt. Doran was diverted and ordered to Point No Point

Gary Lange, who had called in the Mayday, was skipper of a 49-foot Grand Banks. Maneuvering through the dangerous seas, he brought the stern of his boat close to the Whaler. Larry was first off, somehow scrambling across the Grand Banks' swim step, where he was dragged into the cockpit. The Grand Banks swung back toward the Whaler. It rose high on a wave above the Whaler, then settled in a trough as the Whaler rose above the Grand Banks. At one point, the Grand Banks swim step was level with the Whaler and Judy handed the dog to safety.

Again the rising and falling, the huge seas, the enormity of the Grand Banks above the Whaler. At the right moment, miraculously, Judy was able to roll onto the swim step. She lay there, face down, feeling warm water—50-degree water is not warm—splash through the slats of the swim step onto her face and body. She remembers not caring if she moved from the swim step to the cockpit. Somehow, though, she wound up in the cockpit. The adrenaline that had carried them through the ordeal had vanished. Judy and Larry were exhausted. The Whaler drifted away and has not been recovered. At 1335 the high speed catamaran passenger ferry *Victoria Clipper*, which had diverted from its run and was

standing by, reported to Coast Guard Seattle Group that "LANGE HAS RECOVERED 02 POB AND 01 DOG FM VSL'S DINGHY." At 1340 all communications were stood down. Helicopter CG41387 returned to Ediz Hook and Coast Guard Cutter *Pt. Doran* resumed its previous duty.

At approximately 1500 the Grand Banks landed Judy and Larry at the Shilshole Marina in Seattle, where friends were waiting with a car. Larry was almost too weak to walk up the dock. A doctor's examination confirmed that Larry had been having a heart attack since Friday afternoon.

Amity didn't sink completely. Around 1400, vessels in the area reported that she was awash in the southbound Vessel Traffic Lane, her nose barely above water. The Vessel Assist towboat *Negotiator*, already under emergency speed from Port Townsend, got to *Amity* at 1500. The Vessel Assist report is one of bravery, determination and professionalism. Despite high winds and large seas, a diver was able to secure a line to *Amity's* bow and *Negotiator* began a long tow to Port Townsend. They found and plugged a five-foot-long section of missing bottom plank, probably from the pounding *Amity* had endured as she crossed from Port Townsend Canal to Point No Point. That hole is what started the sinking.

The tow didn't end until 0425 the next morning, with *Amity* in the slings at Fleet Marine in Port Townsend. They had fought gale-force winds and heavy seas. They had installed lift bags to raise *Amity* and stabilize her. At 0200 off Kala Point, in high winds and heavy seas head-on, they lost one of the lift bags and were unable, because of the seas, to recover it or lie alongside *Amity*. At 0240 the main pump was drowned in salt water and quit. Ultimately they made it. At 0445 *Negotiator* was back in its slip and stood down. *Amity* was a total loss. The insurance company sold her for $500.

Recalling the event, Judy Wade emphasizes the need for an evacuation plan for every boat and crew. She and Larry had no such plan and were forced to create one—an imperfect one—on the spot. She stresses the need for life jackets easily available. The new inflatable vests would be a good idea, she says. They are comfortable and attractive, and easy to wear more of the time.

And, she says, in a little while they will be looking for another boat.

—*Robert Hale*

The Sinking of the *Amity*

On Sunday, September 5, 1999 a middle age couple in Bellevue rose at dawn for an early morning tee-time at the golf course. The husband looked out the bedroom window at the eastern sky, crimson in color over the top of the Cascade Mountains. "Red sky in the morning, sailor take warning," he said. "Good thing we aren't taking the boat out until tomorrow."

THAT SAME SUNDAY MORNING, aboard the 40-foot Monk-McQueen powerboat *Amity* at Fisherman Bay in the San Juan Islands, another middle age couple, Larry and Judy Wade, got out of bed, greeted their cocker spaniel, and prepared to cut short their cruise and return home to Seattle. Larry hadn't been feeling well for a day and a half. First his arms hurt, then his neck and jaw. Later, he felt nauseated. In jest, Judy asked if he was having a heart attack. "No," said Larry, "It's just a touch of the flu." The weather forecast predicted a calm morning in the Strait of Juan de Fuca, with winds rising to 20 knots in the afternoon. It was a typical weather pattern that called for a morning crossing of the strait. Larry and Judy

were long-experienced Northwest boaters. They had done it many times before.

Cruising at 12 knots, they got to Point Wilson around 1130, in a freshening southerly wind and building seas. The wood-hulled Monk-McQueen took them well, but good sense dictated that they shouldn't continue in those seas if an alternative were available. Admiralty Inlet, ahead of them, is rough when the wind is up. Also, a big southflowing flood tide had begun at 0743; maximum current was at 1151. Wind against current builds high, steep seas. Big wind against big current builds very high, very steep seas.

The Wades' alternative was to turn west and run through Port Townsend Bay, skirting the west side of Indian Island and running through Port Townsend Canal. From there they would run across the mouth of Hood Canal, past Foulweather Bluff, and north of the Skunk Bay shoreline to Point No Point. The course would avoid the rough conditions in Admiralty Inlet and get them to the relatively easier waters of central Puget Sound with as little fuss as possible.

All went well until they emerged from Port Townsend Canal and headed across Oak Bay toward Point No Point. Larry had felt the need for a rest. He was forward and below, lying down, and Judy was helming. The wind continued to build. It was now more than 30 knots from the south. Gray rollers capped with white foam were spread across the water. Off the mouth of Hood Canal the rollers grew larger and steeper, the result of the strong southflowing current meeting the now-shrieking south wind. This was not what the forecast had predicted.

The Wades had confidence in their boat and their abilities. Judy had grown up on boats. Her father was Ed Monk. Ed Jr. is her brother. Her father and her brother, both of them legendary naval architects, had designed the boat. George McQueen, the builder, was famous for good construction.

Amity bucked into the waves. She rose to the crests but came down hard in the troughs. Larry could feel the boat pounding, and called for Judy to slow down. They proceeded across the mouth of Hood Canal, with Point No

(Continued page 299)